From Megaliths to Metal

From Megaliths to Metal
Essays in Honour of George Eogan

Edited by
Helen Roche, Eoin Grogan, John Bradley,
John Coles and Barry Raftery

Oxbow Books

Published by
Oxbow Books, Park End Place, Oxford OX1 1HN

ISBN 1 84217 151 8

A CIP record for this book is available from the British Library

Cover: The decorated flint, Maesmore type, macehead
from the eastern tomb chamber at Knowth, Co. Meath.
Photo: Albert Glaholm, University College, Dublin.

This book is available direct from
Oxbow Books, Park End Place, Oxford, OX1 1HN
(Phone: 01865-241249; Fax: 01865-794449)

and

The David Brown Book Company
PO Box 511, Oakville, CT 06779, USA
(Phone: 860-945-9329; Fax: 860-945-9468)

and

via our website
www.oxbowbooks.com

Printed in Great Britain by
Short Run Press
Exeter

Contents

The Published Works of George Eogan

1957

A hoard of gold objects from Drissoge, *Journal of the Royal Society of Antiquaries of Ireland* **87**, 125–134.

Recent crannóg discoveries in Meath, *Ríocht na Midhe* **1**, No. 3, 50–54.

1958

The gallery graves of Meath, *Journal of the Royal Society of Antiquaries of Ireland* **88**, 179–84.

1960

Two Bronze Age chisels, *Ríocht na Midhe* **2**, No. 2, 35–37.

1961

Excavations at Townleyhall: preliminary report, *Journal of the Louth Archaeological Society* **15**, 11–12.

1962

Some observations on the Middle Bronze Age in Ireland, *Journal of the Royal Society of Antiquaries of Ireland* **92**, 45–60.

1963

A Neolithic habitation-site and megalithic tomb in Townleyhall Townland, Co. Louth, *Journal of the Royal Society of Antiquaries of Ireland* **92**, 37–81.

A new passage grave in Co. Meath, *Antiquity* **37**, 226–28.

1964

Feltrim Hill: a Neolithic and Early Christian site, *Journal of the Royal Society of Antiquaries of Ireland* **94**, 1–38. With P.J. Hartnett.

The excavation of the stone alignment and circle at Cholwichtown, Lee Moor, Devonshire, *Proceedings of the Prehistoric Society* **30**, 25–38.

The Later Bronze Age in Ireland in the light of recent research, *Proceedings of the Prehistoric Society* **30**, 268–351.

1965

Catalogue of Irish bronze swords. Stationery Office. Dublin.

1966

Some notes on the origin and diffusion of the bronze socketed gouge. *Ulster Journal of Archaeology* **29**, 97–102.

A bronze double-edged knife-dagger with openwork handle and ring-terminal from Lagore and its affinities, *Journal of the Royal Society of Antiquaries of Ireland* **96**, 147–56.

A hoard of bronze objects from Booltiaghadine, Co. Clare, *North Munster Antiquarian Journal* **10**, 67–69.

1967

The Knowth (Co. Meath) excavations, *Antiquity* **41**, 302–304.

The Mull ('South of Ireland') hoard, *Antiquity* **41**, 56–58.

The associated finds of gold bar torcs, *Journal of the Royal Society of Antiquaries of Ireland* **97**, 129–75.

1968

Excavations at Knowth, Co. Meath, 1962–65, with historical note by F.J. Byrne, *Proceedings of the Royal Irish Academy* **67**C, 299–400.

1969

Excavations at Knowth, Co. Meath, *Antiquity* **43**, 8–14.

The lock-rings of the Late Bronze Age, *Proceedings of the Royal Irish Academy* **67**C, 93–148.

1971

The excavations of two tumuli at Fourknocks (sites II and III), Co. Meath, *Proceedings of the Royal Irish Academy* **71**C, 35–89, by P.J. Hartnett. Prepared for publication by George Eogan.

1972

The sleeve-fasteners of the Late Bronze Age. In C.B. Burgess and F. Lynch (eds) *Prehistoric Man in Wales and the West*, 189–209. Adams and Dart, Bath.

1973

A decade of excavations at Knowth, Co. Meath, *Irish University Review* **3**, 66–78.

1974

Report on the excavations of some passage graves, unprotected inhumation burials and a settlement site at Knowth, Co. Meath, *Proceedings of the Royal Irish Academy* **74**C, 11–112.

Ireland, Scotland and Wales. In J. Hawkes (ed.), *Atlas of Ancient Archaeology*, 35–46. London.

Regionale Gruppierungen in der Spätbronzezeit Irlands, *Archäologisches Korrespondenzblatt* **4**, 319–27.

Pins of the Irish Late Bronze Age, *Journal of the Royal Society of Antiquaries of Ireland* **104**, 74–119.

A probable passage grave site near Broadboyne Bridge, Co. Meath, *Journal of the Royal Society of Antiquaries of Ireland* **104**, 146–50.

1975

Eighteenth-century find of Late Bronze Age gold disc-mounts near Enniscorthy, Co. Wexford, *Journal of the Metropolitan Museum, New York* **10**, 12–34.

1976

Beaker material from Knowth. In C. Burgess and R. Miket (eds) *Settlement and economy in the third and second Millennia BC*, 251–66. British Archaeological Reports **33**.

1977

Ireland in prehistory. Routledge and Kegan Paul, London. With Michael Herity.

The Iron Age-Early Christian settlement at Knowth. In V. Markotic (ed.) *Ancient Europe and the Mediterranean*, 69–76. Aris and Phillips, Warminster.

Two decorated stones at Knowth, *Antiquity* **51**, 48–49.

A souterrain at Balrenny, near Slane, *Journal of the Royal Society of Antiquaries of Ireland* **107**, 96–103. With John Bradley.

1978

The entrance stones at Knowth, *Antiquity* **52**, 134–135.

The excavation of a round barrow at Long Bredy, Dorset, *Proceedings of the Dorset Natural History and Archaeological Society* **100**, 43–53.

1979

Objects with Iberian affinities from Knowth, Ireland, *Revista de Guimarães* **89**, 275–79.

A find of gold torcs from Coolmanagh, Co. Carlow, *Journal of the Royal Society of Antiquaries of Ireland* **109**, 20–27. With Conleth Manning.

1981

Gold discs of the Irish Late Bronze Age. In D. Ó Corráin (ed.), *Irish Antiquity: Essays and Studies Presented to Professor M.J. O'Kelly*, 147–62. Tower Books, Cork.

Gold vessels of the Bronze Age in Ireland and beyond, *Proceedings of the Royal Irish Academy* **81**C, 345–82.

Ireland's passage tombs, *Archaeology* **34** No. 3, 47–54.

1982

Two maceheads from Knowth, Co. Meath, *Journal of the Royal Society of Antiquaries of Ireland* **112**, 123–38. With Hilary Richardson.

The prehistoric foundations of the Celtic west: passage tombs and early settled life in Western Europe. In R. O'Driscoll (ed.) *The Celtic Consciousness*, 94–117. George Braziller, New York.

1983

The hoards of the Irish Later Bronze Age. University College. Dublin.

Ribbon torcs in Britain and Ireland. In A. O'Connor and D.V. Clarke (eds) *From the Stone Age to the 'Forty Five': studies presented to R. B. K. Stevenson*, 87–126. John Donald, Edinburgh.

A flint macehead at Knowth, Co. Meath, Ireland, *Antiquity* **57**, 45–6.

Bryn Celli Ddu, *Antiquity* **57**, 135–6.

1984

Excavations at Knowth 1: smaller passage tombs, Neolithic occupation and Beaker activity, Royal Irish Academy, Dublin.

Internal features in Irish passage tomb mounds. In Göran Burenhult *The Archaeology of Carrowmore*, 357–59. Institute of Archaeology, Stockholm.

1986

Knowth and the passage tombs of Ireland. Thames and Hudson, London.

Lough Gur excavations by Seán P. Ó Ríordáin: further Neolithic and Beaker habitations on Knockadoon, *Proceedings of the Royal Irish Academy* **86**, 299–506. With Eoin Grogan.

1988

Echange, troc ou influences entre les régions côtières du Nord et de l'Ouest de l'Europe pendant l'Age du Bronze. In *Avant les Celts: L'Europe à l'Age du Bronze*, 64–67. Association Abbaye de Daoulas.

1990

Diffuse picking in Megalithic Art, *Revue Archéologique de L'Ouest, Supplément No. 2.* Mémoire en hommage à Pierre-Roland Giot. La Bretagne et L'Europe Préhistoriques, 121–140. With John Aboud.

Irish megalithic tombs and Iberia: comparisons and contrasts. In *Probleme der Megalith-gräberforschung*, 113–138. Madrider

Forschungen, Band 16. Deutsches archäologisches Institut, Madrid.

The archaeology of Brugh na Bóinne during the early centuries A.D, *Seanchas Ard Mhacha: Journal of the Armagh Diocesan Historical Society* **14**, No. 1, 20–34.

Possible connections between Britain and Ireland and the east Mediterranean region during the Bronze Age. In *Orientalisch-Ägäische Einflüsse in der europäischen Bronzezeit,* 155–163. Bonn. Forschunginstitut für Vor-und Fruhgeschichte, Monographien 15. Romisch-Germanisches Zentralmuseum, Mainz.

Ballynee souterrains, Co. Meath, *Journal of the Royal Society of Antiquaries of Ireland* **120**, 41–64.

1991

Prehistoric and Early Historic culture change at Brugh na Bóinne, *Proceedings of the Royal Irish Academy* **91**C, 105–32.

Irish antiquities of the Bronze Age, Iron Age and Early Christian Period in the National Museum of Denmark, *Proceedings of the Royal Irish Academy* **91**C, 133–176.

Daily life in the Later Bronze Age. In M. Ryan (ed.) *The Illustrated Archaeology of Ireland*, 96–102. Town House and Country House, Dublin.

1992

Scottish and Irish passage tombs: some comparisons and contrasts. In N. Sharples and A. Sheridan (eds) *Vessels for the Ancestors, essays on the Neolithic of Britain and Ireland in honour of Audrey Henshall*, 120–7. Edinburgh University Press, Edinburgh.

1993

The earliest architecture in north Leinster. In C. Casey and A. Rowan, *The buildings of Ireland: north Leinster*, 91–101. Penguin Books, London.

The Late Bronze Age: customs, crafts and cults. In E. Shee Twohig and M. Ronayne (eds) *Past perceptions: the prehistoric archaeology of south-west Ireland*, 121–33. Cork University Press, Cork.

Aspects of metal production and manufacturing systems during the Irish Bronze Age, *Acta Praehistorica et Archaeologica* **25**, 87–110.

1994

The accomplished art: gold and gold-working in Britain and Ireland during the Bronze Age. Oxbow Books, Oxford.

A Grooved Ware wooden structure at Knowth, Boyne Valley, Ireland, *Antiquity* **68**, 322–30. With Helen Roche.

1995

Ideas, people and things: Ireland and the external world during the Later Bronze Age. In J. Waddell and E. Shee Twohig (eds) *Ireland in the Bronze Age*, 128–35. Stationery Office, Dublin.

1996

Aspects of society and settlement in their regional setting in Britain and Ireland during the Bronze Age. In C. Belardelli and R. Peroni (eds) *The Bronze Age in Europe and the Mediterranean*, 173–189. Forlì: A.B.A.C.O, Edizoni.

Symbolism, ritual and deposition in Later Bronze Age Ireland. In P. Schauer (ed.) *Archäologische Forschungen zum Kultgeschehen in der jüngeren Bronzezeit und frühen Eisenzeit Alteuropas*, 81–5. Regensburger Beiträge zur prähistorischen Archäologie, Band 2.

1997

Excavations at Knowth 2: settlements and ritual sites of the fourth and third millennia BC. Royal Irish Academy/Department of Arts, Culture and the Gaeltacht, Dublin. With Helen Roche.

Pattern and place: a preliminary study of the decorated kerbstones at Site 1, Knowth, Co. Meath, and their comparative setting. In

J. L'Helgouach, C.-T. Le Roux and J. Lecornec (eds) *Art et Symboles du Megalithisme European*, 97–104. Revue Archéologique de l'Ouest, Supplément No. 8.

Stonehenge and its wider context. In B. Cunliffe and C. Renfrew (eds) *Science and Stonehenge*, 319–34. The British Academy, London.

Cohesion and diversity: passage tombs of north-western Europe and their social and ritual fabric. In A.A. Rodríguez Casal (ed.) *O Neolitico Atlántico e as oriexes do Megalitismo*, 43–64. Santiago de Compostela.

Overlays and underlays: aspects of Megalithic Art succession at Brugh na Bóinne, Ireland. In J.M. Bello and B. Bas López (eds) *Proceedings of III Colloquio Internacional de Arte Megalitico*, 217–234. Brigantium **10**, La Coruña.

The Discovery Programme: Initiation, consolidation and development. Nederlands Museum Voor Anthropologie en Praehistorie, Amsterdam.

Hair-rings and European Late Bronze Age society, *Antiquity* **71**, 308–20.

Earlier Bronze Age grave-group from Rahinashurock, Co. Westmeath reviewed, *Ríocht na Midhe* **9**, No.3, 28–45.

1998

Heart-shaped bullae of the Irish Late Bronze Age. In M. Ryan (ed.) *Irish Antiquities: Essays in memory of Joseph Raftery*, 17–26. Wordell, Bray.

Further evidence for Neolithic habitation at Knowth, Co. Meath, *Ríocht na Midhe* **9**, No. 4, 1–9. With Helen Roche.

Homes and homesteads in Bronze Age Ireland. In B. Hänsel (ed.) *Mensch und Umwelt in der Bronzezeit Europas*, 307–326. Oetker-Voges Verlag, Kiel.

A decorated stone at Mullagharoy, Co. Meath, *Ríocht na Midhe* **9**, No. 4, 10–15. With Niamh O'Broin.

Knowth before Knowth, *Antiquity* **72**, 162–172.

1999

Megalithic art & society, *Proceedings of the Prehistoric Society* **65**, 415–46.

Grooved Ware from Brugh na Bóinne and its wider context. In R. Cleal and A. Mac Sween (eds) *Grooved Ware in Britain and Ireland*, 98–111. Oxbow Books, Oxford. With Helen Roche.

From Skåne to Scotstown: Some notes on amber in Bronze Age Ireland. In A. Harding (ed.) *From Somerset to Simiris*, 75–86. Oxbow, Oxford.

2000

The Socketed Bronze Axes in Ireland. Prähistorische Bronzefunde. Abteilung IX, Band 22, Stuttgart.

Aspects of passage tomb settlement in Ireland. In K.W. Beinhauer, G. Cooney, C.F. Guksch, and S. Kus (eds) *Studien zur Megalithik-Forschungstand und ethnoarchäologische Perspektiven*, 347–360. Weissbach/Mannheim.

Life and living at Lagore. In A.P. Smith (ed.) *Seanchas: studies in early and medieval Irish archaeology, history and literature in honour of Francis J. Byrne*, 64–82. Four Courts Press, Dublin.

A group of megalithic monuments at Kingsmountain-Clonasillagh, Co. Meath, *Ríocht na Midhe* **11**, 1–16.

2001

Archaeology in Meath: past, present and future, *Ríocht na Midhe* **12**, 1–16.

High Crosses in Brega, *Ríocht na Midhe* **12**, 17–24.

Late Neolithic activity in the Boyne Valley, Co. Meath. In C.-T. Le Roux (ed.) *Revue Archéologique de L'Ouest*, 125–140. Supplément no. **9**. With Helen Roche.

A composite Late Bronze Age chain object from Co. Roscommon, Ireland. In J. Steegstra (ed.) *Essays and Studies in Honour of J. J. Butler*, 195–204. Groningen.

2002

The M1 Motorway and its archaeology: introduction, *Ríocht na Midhe* **13**, 1–7.

Archaeology in Ireland during the last 50 years: an outline, *Antiquity* **76**, 475–484.

2004

Knowth, 40 years on, *Ríocht na Midhe* **15**, 1–11.

List of Contributors

MARTÍN ALMAGRO-GORBEA
El Anticuario Perpetuo de la Real Academia De La Historia, León, 21, 28014 Madrid, Spain.

JAN BOUZEK
Institute of Classical Archaeology, Charles University, Celetná 20, CZ-110 00 Praha 1, Czech Republic.

JOHN BRADLEY
Department of History, National University of Ireland, Maynooth, Ireland.

RICHARD BRADLEY
Department of Archaeology, University of Reading, Whiteknights House, Reading RG6 6AA, England.

COLIN BURGESS
24 Kielder Close, Linden Park, Killingworth, Newcastle, NE12 OTE, England.

MARY CAHILL
Irish Antiquities Division, National Museum of Ireland, Kildare Street, Dublin 2, Ireland.

TIMOTHY CHAMPION
Department of Archaeology, University of Southampton SO 17 1BJ, England.

JOHN COLES
Fursdon Mill Cottage, Thorverton, Devon EX5 5JS, England.

GABRIEL COONEY
Department of Archaeology, University College, Dublin 4, Ireland.

BARRY CUNLIFFE
Institute of Archaeology, 36 Beaumont Street, Oxford OX1 2PG, England.

MAIRE DELANEY†

JAMES EOGAN
National Roads Authority, Tramore House, Pond Road, Tramore, Co. Waterford, Ireland.

DEBORAH FORD
Potteries Museum, Stoke-on-Trent, Staffordshire, England.

SABINE GERLOFF
Institut für Ur- und Frühgeschichte, Kochstr 4/18, D-91054 Erlangen, Germany.

EOIN GROGAN
62 Rockville Drive, Blackrock, Co. Dublin, Ireland.

PETER HARBISON
Royal Irish Academy, Dawson Street, Dublin 2, Ireland.

ALBRECHT JOCKENHÖVEL
Westfälische Wilhelms-Universität Münster, Seminar für Ur- und Frühgeschichte, Domplatz 20–22, D-48143 Münster, Germany.

HEATHER A. KING
The National Monuments Section. Department of the Environment, Heritage and Local Government. Dun Sceine, Harcourt Lane, Dublin 2, Ireland.

CHARLES-TANGUY LE ROUX
22 rue Saint Vincent, 49260 Brézé, France.

FRANCES LYNCH
Halfway House, Halfway Bridge, Bangor, Wales.

FINBAR MCCORMICK
Department of Archaeology, School of Palaeolecological Sciences, The Queen's University, Belfast, Northern Ireland.

CONLETH MANNING
The National Monuments Section. Department of the Environment, Heritage and Local Government. Dun Sceine, Harcourt Lane, Dublin 2, Ireland.

CHARLES MOUNT
Irish Concrete Federation, 8 Newlands Business Park, Naas Road, Clondalkin, Dublin 22, Ireland.

BRENDAN O'CONNOR
48 Rodney Street, Edinburgh, EH7 4DX, Scotland.

MUIRIS O' SULLIVAN
Department of Archaeology, University College, Dublin 4, Ireland.

BARRY RAFTERY
Department of Archaeology, University College, Dublin 4, Ireland.

HELEN ROCHE
Department of Archaeology, University College, Dublin 4, Ireland.

PETER SCHAUER
Lehrstuhl für Vor- und Frühgeschichte, Universität Regensburg, D 93040 Regensburg, Germany.

ELIZABETH SHEE TWOHIG
Department of Archaeology, University College, Cork, Ireland.

ALISON SHERIDAN
Department of Archaeology, National Museums of Scotland, Chambers Street, Edinburgh EHI IJF, Scotland.

HENRIK THRANE
Department of Archaeology, University of Aarhus, Denmark.

PATRICK F. WALLACE
National Museum of Ireland, Kildare Street, Dublin 2, Ireland.

RICHARD WARNER
Ulster Museum, Belfast, BT5 5AB, Northern Ireland.

PETER WOODMAN
Department of Archaeology, University College, Cork, Ireland.

Preface

George Eogan was born at Nobber in county Meath, and has always been extremely proud of his association with the county. He studied archaeology at University College, Dublin, and gained a PhD at Trinity College Dublin. George's interest in archaeology was encouraged by Paddy Hartnett, with whom he worked at Fourknocks in Co Meath. He spent time in the British School of Archaeology in Jerusalem, Oxford University, and Queen's University Belfast, before his appointment as University Lecturer at University College Dublin in 1965, where he was Professor and Head of Department 1979 to 1995, and was a Senator in Seanad Eireann from 1987 to 89.

One of us (JC) met George in the late 1950s in the National Museum of Ireland, during our joint interest in, but separately pursued, PhD researches on the Bronze Age. Then we met regularly, at the British Museum, Oxford, Edinburgh, Cambridge and Dublin, as we each continued to work on archaeological materials in the various museums. During these and later years, George accumulated a host of contacts and awards, in and from the Royal Irish Academy, the Society of Antiquaries of London (Fellow), the German Archaeological Institute, the Academia Europea and many other institutions. He has been the recipient of a number of Fellowships, which allowed him to pursue his two main archaeological interests – metalwork of the European Bronze Age, and megalithic monuments of western Europe. His list of publications attests to the achievements in both these fields.

In his early career George held a series of research positions in Oxford University (where he is closely associated with All Souls College to the present day), Queen's University Belfast and Trinity College Dublin. In Oxford he worked with Christopher Hawkes, Professor of European Archaeology, who had a profound influence on his approach to archaeological research. During his time as lecturer and subsequently as Professor and Head of Department George was a rigorous teacher who shared his extensive scholarship in an accessible and sometimes light-hearted fashion; many of his students will remember

fondly his jokes which were a surprising feature of his intense delivery! In addition to his mammoth courses on the Bronze Age in Ireland, Britain and Europe he taught widely on other topics including intensive modules on the origins of agriculture, and on the Etruscans. Throughout this period he maintained a constant flow of research on his Bronze Age studies, through which he transformed our knowledge of the Late Bronze Age in Ireland, in particular, and established a foundation of scholarship that will contribute to research for many years to come. George also laboured on the post excavation work and publication of the Knowth project. This enabled many of his students and post graduates (including three of us – JB, HR and EG) to serve important apprenticeships in a wide variety of archaeological research, and helped to disseminate George's rigorous scholarship.

In 1979 George was appointed Professor of Archaeology (as successor to Rúaidhrí de Valera), a position that he held until 1995. He brought a renewed vigour to the Department and established higher standards, especially at post-graduate level. He widened graduate training to include teaching and invited specialists from other institutions to give post-graduate seminars. At a wider level George's extensive scholarly network brought many distinguished guest lecturers to the Department.

George has always been active in developing the science of archaeology in its widest perspective, through promotion of field studies, excavations, analyses, education and publication. He has held office on a variety of European bodies, such as the European Science Foundation and the Higher Education Committee of the Council of Europe, and both the Council and Executive of the International Union of Pre- and Protohistoric Sciences. He has also served on the Irish Folklore Commission, the Heritage Council, Councils of the Royal Irish Academy (Vice-President 1979–85), the Royal Society of Antiquaries of Ireland, the Historic Monuments Council of Northern Ireland, the National Monuments Advisory Council of Ireland, and was a Vice President of the Prehistoric Society (1985–88) who awarded him their Europa Prize in 1998. Closer to home he is currently a

Patron of the Meath Archaeological Society. George received a D. Litt from the National University of Ireland, and was awarded an Honorary Doctorate by Trinity College Dublin in 2002. Being proclaimed as Meath Man of the Year' in 2002 was another honour that gave him particular pleasure.

Among these many distinctions we single out his pivotal role in the establishment of the Discovery Programme in 1991, and his Chairmanship of that organisation for its first ten years. The Discovery Programme has allowed Irish archaeologists to pursue research themes that would otherwise have lapsed, and has encouraged a number of local initiatives to promote the survival and the investigation of the heritage of Ireland.

The other major aspect of George's career has been his excavation record. He began under the guidance of Paddy Hartnett at Fourknocks 1 in Co. Meath; he also worked with Hartnett at Fourknocks 2 and 3, and Feltrim Hill, all of which he completed for publication after Hartnett's untimely death. He also excavated with Seán P. Ó Ríordáin at Lough Gur and Tara, and with David Liversage at Dalkey Island. On a more international front George worked on several excavations in Britain, in the Middle East, where he had a scholarship to the British School of Archaeology in Jerusalem (and where, amongst other sites, he worked with Kathleen Kenyon at Jericho), and, more recently, in Japan.

His first excavation as Director was at Cholwichtown in Devon (the pronunciation of which he used to tease his Irish students). George's interest in megaliths had begun with Fourknocks and his own survey of tombs in county Meath. It was to flourish under his great friend and mentor G. F. (Frank) Mitchell who encouraged him to his doctorate on Irish Late Bronze Age swords from Trinity College, Dublin; Frank called George his "son in archaeology". Together they devised a research strategy to investigate the comparative chronology of cruciform and undifferentiated passage tombs which was initiated with George's excavations at Townleyhall. The focus then moved to nearby Knowth which was then believed to be a possible passage tomb cemetery although only one site was identifiable at the time of commencement in 1962. His Herculean work at Knowth, which continues to this day, has uncovered an astonishing array of new information much of which has received world-wide coverage. It has also attracted the admiring visits of numerous

archaeologists and scholars. At Knowth George has carried on the tradition of Hartnett, Ó Ríordáin and M. J. (Brian) O'Kelly, amongst others, of training a new generation of excavators. Amongst the hundreds of Irish, European and American students who worked under his guidance can be numbered no fewer than nine of the contributors to this volume. Amongst his most significant discoveries we might especially mention the cemetery of nineteen tombs, including the two major sites under the main mound, one cruciform and the other undifferentiated. These tombs also produced the largest corpus of megalithic art in Europe. Another major component at Knowth was the extensive early historic settlement associated with the kings of North Brega the study of which has led to an important collaboration with the historian Francis John Byrne. Working at Knowth was also for George a family occasion with Fiona and the children joining him each summer. Fiona, herself an archaeologist, was a very able lieutenant providing much organisational support as well as providing the home-from-home for family, archaeologists and students at Townley Hall. Few will forget George and Fiona's convivial hosting of the famous 'Knowth parties' held towards the end of every season.

George has been active for many years in the dissemination of knowledge about such matters in many areas of the world, particularly throughout Europe but also in North America and the Middle East, and in Japan. His name, when mentioned in many foreign institutions, is always recognised at once, and with a smile – we could not say as much for some widely-travelled archaeologists.

As a proponent of the traditional values of archaeological research, George has few peers and the evidence that he has set out in his many papers and books stands as monuments of objectivity in the presentation of data, of persistence in the acquisition of that data, and of care in the analyses that follow and the interpretations that can therefore be advanced.

In presenting George with this book of essays, we hope to have reflected his wide interests in the development of Irish archaeology, and the Neolithic and Bronze Age periods in particular, and in wider matters as well. His own contributions have spanned more fields than we could assemble here, and these essays come with the wish and the expectation that in future years more insights will emerge from the pen, and the computer, of one of Ireland's great prehistorians.

John Coles, Eoin Grogan, Barry Raftery, Helen Roche and John Bradley

Acknowledgements

The editors would like to express their great appreciation of the contributors whose gracious, enthusiastic and prompt responses to all requests greatly eased the task of compiling this volume.

We are pleased to acknowledge the generous contributions from The Heritage Council towards publication costs, and from University College, Dublin, for a grant towards the costs associated with this volume. Our sincere thanks also to the National Museum of Ireland for its contribution towards the colour plates, and for providing the venue for the launch. A special expression of thanks to Mary Cahill and Anne Holliday for their help at various levels.

Our thanks to David Brown and the enthusiasm and professionalism of Oxbow Books; in particular we are grateful to Julie Blackmore without whose Trojan work, patience, skill and attention to detail, this volume could not have been completed.

In the course of organising and assembling the volume we received much assistance from Suzanne Manning, a co-conspirator who discreetly provided much needed 'intelligence', and from Ines Hagen who kindly read over some of the German texts.

A special word of thanks to Fiona Eogan for her help in sourcing information, and for her enormous generosity in creating a special atmosphere for the occasion of the launch.

1. Hunting wild pig in the Late Mesolithic

Finbar McCormick

Introduction

Moynagh Lough lies in a valley about a quarter of a mile south west of the village of Nobber, Co. Meath. The lake today is no more than a large pond being all that remains of an extensive lake that was drained during the early nineteenth century. The edges of the lake are for the most part inaccessible, comprising a deep and dangerous floating bed of reeds. Only to the west can one gain access to the lake on a low solid knoll. For generations the young boys of Nobber have come here to fish, trying to catch the elusive tench that are said to inhabit its depths. The young George Eogan no doubt spent many hours on this spot blissfully unaware that he was standing on a location that was used for hunting during the Later Mesolithic. George gave me my first job as an aspiring animal bone specialist and it is my pleasure to be able to provide some information on some early hunting activities that occurred at that special place.

Prior to its use as an Early Medieval crannóg, the site had been used during both the Later Mesolithic and the Late Bronze Age (Bradley 1984). Most of the Mesolithic activity was confined to two sub-rectangular knolls which were 2m apart at their nearest point (Bradley 2001, 299). A gravelly layer with scatters of brushwood joined the two platforms (F1604), and the animal bone was almost exclusively from this context. The bone represents discarded food refuse from the platform occupations. The sample was dominated by wild pig, with small numbers of hare, otter and bear also being present. Red deer were absent. This overwhelming dependence on wild pig confirms a pattern that has been noticed in a series of recently excavated Mesolithic sites (McCarthy 1999; van Wijngaarden-Bakker 1989).

Pig

The small sample of bone represented at least four individuals based on the age of the animals present. Most parts of the skeleton were represented (Table 1.1). Both burnt and unburnt remains were identified, the majority

	Wild pig	Otter	Hare	Bear
Skull	13			
Mandible	3	2		
Teeth	1			
Cervical vert.	1			
Thoracic vert.	1			
Lumbar vert.	2			
Scapula	4			
Humerus	1	1		
Ulna	2			
Metacarpal	1			1
Pelvis	1			
Femur	2		2	
Patella	1			
Tibia	7		3	
Fibula	1			
Astragalus	1			
Calcaneus	4			
Carpal/Tarsal	4			
Phalanx 1	1			
Total	51	3	5	1
Total %	85	5	8.3	1.7
MNI	3	1	1	1

Table 1.1: Distribution of fragments by skeletal part.

being unburnt. Calcified bone for the most part consisted of small fragments representing material that had been thrown into a fire after the meat/marrow had been removed and was not representative of the cooking process.

Pigs of different ages were present. The epiphyseal fusion data is presented in Table 1.2. In most cases the long bones present were fused, the unfused cases are all of late fusing elements. In the case of domestic pig, the proximal humerus and distal femur do not fuse until the age of about three and a half years while the calcaneus does not fuse until the animal is two to two and a half

Bone part	Fused	Unfused
Humerus		1
Pelvis	1	
Tibia proximal	1	
Tibia distal	2	
Femur distal		1
Calcaneus proximal	3	1
Phalanx 1	1	

Table 1.2: Pig fusion data.

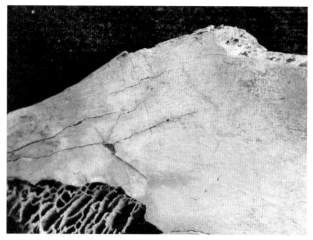

Fig 1.2: Cut marks on ischium area of wild pig pelvis.

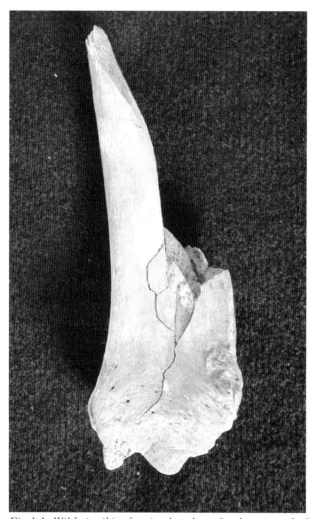

Fig 1.1: Wild pig tibia showing breakage for the removal of marrow.

years of age (Silver 1969, 285–6). The skull and mandibular evidence, however, shows a more varied range. Mature animals are indicated by two large male canines, one of which is still embedded in a mandible. In addition to this, a mandible fragment has an unworn PM4 present. In domesticated pigs this would indicate an individual of approximately one to two months of age (Higham 1967, 10). Finally, a neo-natal skull, which cannot have been from an animal more than a few weeks old, was present. Considering the data in total, it seems to represent a

minimum (MNI) of four individuals. Two of these are mature animals while two are very young individuals, evidenced by the neo-natal skull and the immature mandible. The unfused long bone elements may belong to the immature individual.

The skulls, mandibles and longbones were extremely fragmented indicating deliberate smashing, presumably to remove the brain in the case of the skull, and marrow in the case of the longbones. Cut marks were present on several fragments including the tibiae, the pelvis, a calcaneus and an astragalus. These are generally represented by a series of slight, parallel marks. There is no evidence of chop marks. Where bones are broken it is likely that this was carried out by a blunt and probably unspecialised implement, *i.e.* struck with a stone (Fig 1.1: Pig tibia). The vertical splitting of a metacarpal must have necessitated a more precise approach but as no butchery marks survive on the bone it is not known how this was achieved. The acute fragmentation of the assemblage indicates that a considerable effort was made to remove all edible parts from the carcass.

The cut marks represent two processes. In the first instance there are marks representing the removal of flesh from the bone. These were noted on some tibia shafts and on the ischium area of the pelvis (Fig 1.2: Pig pelvis). Their position suggests that the meat was removed from the bones prior to cooking, as it would have naturally separated from these bone surfaces during the cooking process. Additionally, there was no definite evidence for the roasting of the joints on the bone, *i.e.* burning of the edge of the bones. Such burning was, for instance, noted on domesticated pig bones at the Neolithic English site of Durrington Walls (Albarella and Serjeantson 2002, 41–42).

Other cut marks cannot be related to meat removal but seem to be related either to the separation of joints or the removal of tendons. Cuts near the acetabular lip on a pelvis must be related primarily to the disjointing of a carcass, while some cut marks on the tuber of a calcaneus

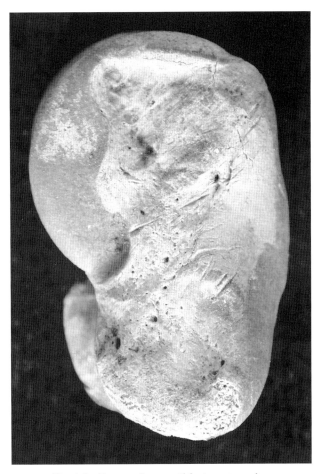

Fig 1.3: Cut marks on wild pig astragalus.

Bone	Measurement	Dimensions	Newgrange range
Calcaneus	GL	93.9	72.9 – 87.8
		96.0	
		93.9	
Tibia	Bp	60.2	48.5 – 54.7
	Bd	38.0	27.8 – 36.5
		37.1	
Astragalus	GLl	44.3	39.6 – 44.9
	Bd	29.3	
Pelvis	LAR	36.8	29.1 – 37.7

Table 1.3: Pig measurements after von den Driesch (1976) (in mm) from Moynagh compared with measurement range of domesticated pigs from the Beaker levels at Newgrange (van Wijngaarden-Bakker 1986, 70).

Fig 1.4: Cut marks on hare tibia (upper) and femur (lower).

and astragalus (Fig 1.3) probably relate to the retrieval of tendons. Pigs do not have hides as such so it is unlikely that skinning accounts for these cut marks, whereas tendons would have been a valuable resource for a wide range of purposes.

The sex of pig can easily be determined by the canine teeth. Two right lower male canines were present, one still attached to a fragment of mandible. While there was no indication of female presence, it is extremely unlikely that the very young individuals could have been available for hunting without their sow also being in the vicinity. Young wild pigs remain with their sow for a considerable period of time and two litters of different ages commonly accompany her (Corbet 1966, 161). Although the sample is small the evidence would tend to suggest the hunting of mature males and immature pigs, with perhaps the deliberate exclusion of mature females.

Most of the wild pig remains retrieved on Irish Mesolithic sites have been calcified so there is little comparative metrical material available. The data from Britain is also extremely limited. A single tibia from Starr Carr has a distal breadth (Bd) of 35.1mm (Legge and Rowley-Conwy 1988, 139), which is slightly smaller than the Moynagh examples. Table 1.3 shows that there was a slight overlap in size between the Moynagh wild pig and the domesticated pigs at Newgrange. The Newgrange pigs were at the upper limits of domesticated pig size, Louise van Wijngaarden-Bakker (1986, 71) speculating that "the largest Neolithic domestic pigs would ... approach in height the smallest wild boars living in the same parts". When van Wijngaarden-Bakker made this suggestion no measurable wild pig remains had been recovered from an Irish Mesolithic site, the Lough Boora and Mount Sandel samples being exclusively calcified. The Moynagh material, however, has shown her suggestion to be correct.

Hare

The few hare bones present were exclusively femur and tibia shaft fragments. One of the tibia fragments was small and from an immature individual. Cut marks were present on two of the femurs, and on one of the tibiae near the breakage points. It seems likely that these were incurred during the removal of tendons (Fig 1.4: Hare). It is unlikely that these vertical cut marks would be associated with boning and some of the cuts were in places that could not be associated with skinning.

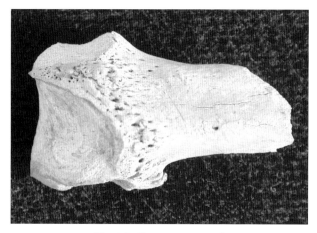

Fig 1.5: Bear metacarpal.

	Left	Right
Total length	71.2	-
Length of cheektooth row	33.4	33.5
Length of carnassial alveolus (M1)	11.9	12.0
Length of carnassial (M1)	12.3	12.3
Height of Mandible behind M1	12.4	12.4

Table 1.4: Otter mandible measurements (in mm) after von den Driesch (1976).

Bear

The single bear bone from Moynagh consisted of a broken first metacarpal. Bear were absent at Lough Boora and Mount Sandel. The only stratified bear bone from excavations at Dalkey Island comprised a phalanx from the basal Mesolithic-Early Neolithic transitional midden (Hatting 1968, 173). Is it possible that these represent the use of skins, with the paws, or part of the paws attached, rather than the actual hunting of animals at these particular sites? A single faint cut mark (Fig 1.5: Bear) above the breakage point could be associated with skinning, but the breaking of the bone suggests marrow removal. The edge of the proximal articular surface of the metacarpal displayed exostosis that is a degenerative disorder caused by wear and tear of the joint (E. Murphy pers. comm.). One can therefore assume that the bear was of an advanced age when killed.

Otter

Two mandibulae and a humerus were noted, none of which displayed cut marks. These are the earliest known otter in Ireland, the previous instance being from a Bronze Age coastal context in Co. Galway (McCormick 1999, 363). Grigson and Mellars (1987, 276) have shown that there is a clear size difference in the sex of otter mandibulae, the smaller being male. The Moynagh examples fall within the lower end of the modern male range. While the bear and hare bones were found mixed with pig remains, the otter bones were present in two separate contexts unconnected with such material. The mandibulae were found in an otherwise barren spread of gravel but stratigraphically of Mesolithic date (F1720). The humerus comprised a very weathered shaft fragment and was found in association with chert from flint tools but in a context (1621) that was otherwise devoid of faunal material.

Discussion

The small sample of animal bone for the most part survived in very good condition owing to the waterlogged nature of the contexts. The associated layers contained a large quantity of implements, predominately of chert (Bradley 2001, 301–2). Charcoal from one of the platforms produced a date of 5270±60 BP (GrN-1 1443). This produced a cal BC range of 4229–4000 at one Sigma and 4313–3980 at two Sigma, which dates to the very end of the Mesolithic. Radiocarbon dates of before 5000 BP have recently been obtained from megaliths at Polnabrone, Co. Clare, and Primrose Grange, Co. Sligo (Irish Radiocarbon Data Base), and it is likely that farming was already being established in Ireland at the time of the Moynagh occupation. Indeed, the problematic cattle tooth dated to 5510 (±70) BP from Ferriter's Cove, Co. Kerry, might imply that the Moynagh material could be more correctly considered an Early Neolithic rather than a Late Mesolithic assemblage (Schulting 1999, 219).

It is unfortunate that the faunal assemblage is so small that any interpretation of the material is tentative to say the least. In the absence of red deer, wild pig were the only large mammal species hunted at Moynagh. This dependence on the species has already been shown to be the norm at Early Mesolithic Mount Sandel and Lough Boora (van Wijngaarden Bakker 1989). They were also the dominant terrestrial species at Ferriter's Cove (McCarthy 1999, 90). In Britain, where the species range was much wider, wild pig were considered the least attractive of the wild mammals as a source of food. At Starr Carr wild pig comprised only 2% of the large mammal bone total, with red and roe deer, elk and aurochs being preferred sources of meat (Legge and Rowley-Conwy 1988, 9). A similar situation was noted in the very small sample from Morton in Scotland (Coles 1971, 349).

The assemblage at Moynagh differs significantly from the other Irish Mesolithic sites mentioned above. Despite the site's lakeside location there was no evidence for the exploitation of fish or wetland birds. This contrasts greatly with Mount Sandel and Lough Boora where salmon, trout and eels were readily exploited and birds were also hunted (van Wijngaarden-Bakker 1989). It is unlikely that differential preservation accounts for this as the bones, being from waterlogged contexts, survived in good condition. In addition to this, calcification helps to preserve fish bones, a factor that accounts for the large quantities present at Mount Sandel and Lough Boora. No fish were present among the Moynagh calcified remains.

Moynagh is essentially a site that specialised in the hunting of wild pig.

Zvelebil (1995) has indicated that there is an increased dependence on wild pig in Late Mesolithic Scandinavia and suggests that there is also evidence for increased management of pigs at this time. He states that there is selectivity in the killing of young pigs and that "restrictions imposed on animal movements" led to a decline in pig size during the Late Mesolithic perhaps due to some form of 'taming' (Zvelebil 1995, 97). The absence of comparative metrical data in Ireland precludes any discussion on size decline but the Moynagh evidence may indicate a managed culling of the wild pig. Is it mere coincidence, or a product of the small sample size, that only adult males and young pigs are present? There is no evidence for the killing of adult females. The fact that the young pigs present must have been accompanied by sows suggests that there was a deliberate policy of not killing the females. It would have been preferable that adult females were kept alive for reproduction and the suckling of young litters.

The absence of evidence for fowling and fishing may reflect a specialisation in food procurement at the Mesolithic/Neolithic transition. The excavator interprets the site as a 'home base' (Bradley 2001, 304). Due to the small sample size, the faunal evidence can neither support nor contradict this interpretation. It should be noted, however, that the pig ageing data only provides evidence for occupation during the late spring and early summer. Only a small part of the Mesolithic horizons at Moynagh have been investigated and further work on the site should provide vital information on the Mesolithic/Neolithic transitional period in Ireland. In the meantime the present faunal sample leaves us with a tantalising glimpse of a changing economic basis at that time.

Bibliography

Albarella, U. and Serjeantson, D. 2002 A passion for pork: Meat consumption at the British Late Neolithic Site of Durrington Walls. In P. Miracle and N. Milner (eds) *Consuming Passions and patterns of consumption*, 33–49. McDonald Institute Monographs, Cambridge.

Bradley, J. 1984 Excavations at Moynagh Crannóg: interim report, *Ríocht na Midhe* **7**, 86–93.

Bradley, J. 2001 A late Mesolithic settlement in eastern Ireland. In B. Raftery and J. Hicky (eds) *Recent developments in wetland research*. 299–306. Department of Archaeology, University College Dublin, Monograph **2**.

Coles, J.M. 1971 The early settlement of Scotland, Excavations at Morton, Fife, *Proceedings of the Prehistoric Society* **37**, 284–366.

Corbet, G.B. 1966 *The terrestrial mammals of western Europe*. G.T. Foulis and Co., London.

Driesch, A. von den 1976 A guide to the measurement of animal bones from archaeological sites. *Peabody Museum Bulletin*, Harvard.

Grigson, G. and Mellars, P. 1987 The mammalian remains from the middens. In P. Mellars *Excavations on Oronsay: Prehistoric human Ecology of a small island*, 243–289. Edinburgh University Press, Edinburgh.

Hatting, T. 1968 Animal bones from the basal middens. In G.D. Liversage, Excavations at Dalkey Island, Co. Dublin, 1956–1959, *Proceedings of the Royal Irish Academy* **66**C, 172–174.

Higham, C.F.W. 1967 Stock rearing as a cultural factor in prehistoric Europe, *Proceedings of the Prehistoric Society* **33**, 84–106.

Legge, A.J. and Rowley-Conwy, P.A. 1988 *Starr Carr revisited: A re-analysis of the large mammals*. University of London, London.

McCarthy, M. 1999 Faunal remains, in P.C. Woodman, E. Anderson and N. Finley *Excavations at Ferrriter's Cove 1983–95*, 85–92. Wordwell, Dublin.

McCormick, F. 1999 Early evidence for wild animals in Ireland. In N. Benecke (ed.) *The Holocene History of European Vertebrate Fauna*, 355–371. Archäologie in Eurasien **6**, Berlin.

Mellars, P. 1987 *Excavations on Oronsay: Prehistoric human Ecology of a small island*. Edinburgh University Press, Edinburgh.

Schulting, R. 1999 Radiocarbon dates. In P.C. Woodman, E. Anderson and N. Finley *Excavations at Ferrriter's Cove 1983–95*, 219. Wordwell, Dublin.

Silver, I.A. 1969 The ageing of domesticated animals. In D. Brothwell and E. Higgs (eds) *Science in Archaeology*, 283–302. Thames and Hudson, London.

Van Wijngaarden-Bakker, L.H. 1986 The animal bones from the Beaker settlement at Newgrange, Co. Meath: Final report, *Proceedings of the Royal Irish Academy* **86**C, 2–111.

Van Wijngaarden-Bakker, L.H. 1989 Faunal remains and the Irish Mesolithic. In C. Bonsall *The Mesolithic in Europe*, 125–133. John Donald, Edinburgh.

Woodman, P.C., Anderson, E. and Finlay, N. 1999 *Excavations at Ferrriter's Cove 1983–95*. Wordwell, Dublin.

Zvelebil, M. 1995 Hunting, gathering, or husbandry. Management of food resources by the late Mesolithic communities of temperate Europe, *Masca Research Papers in Science and Archaeology* **12**, 79–104.

2. Searching the Irish Mesolithic for the Humans behind the Hatchets

Maire Delaney† and Peter C. Woodman

"No burials or ritual sites have been found" (Waddell 1998)

This has been received wisdom for the Irish Mesolithic, but we should always remember "Absence of evidence is not evidence of absence". How often has this maxim been used but so often its meaning has been ignored. Perfectly logical reasons are given for the lack of a particular class of object, faunal elements or even human settlement at a given date. Similarly, with the perfect 20/20 vision of hindsight we later find equally good reasons why we have overlooked the obvious.

Like most experimental disciplines, Archaeology would seem to work best in reactive mode. In spite of the 'scientific' perspective of processual Archaeology questions about absence of evidence were rarely asked and we have rarely worked in a pro-active or predictive mode.

The study of human remains from the Mesolithic provided a perfect example of the re-active approach. In Petersen's seminal review of the Mesolithic of Denmark (Petersen 1973) little attention was given to human skeletal remains. Fragments of human bone and very occasional skeletons had turned up at several Mesolithic settlement sites, but they were not regarded as central to the ongoing discourse of the Mesolithic period. Yet within one year the accidental discovery of Bogebakken cemetery at Vedbaek changed Mesolithic studies (Albrethsen and Petersen 1976). This was to have the knock on effect of encouraging research in Skane, leading to Larsson's discovery of the Skateholm cemeteries (Larsson 1984) and the recognition in the west that the cemetery on Oleni Ostrov in Lake Onega (Gurina 1956) was essentially Mesolithic in date. Similarly interest in the Latvian cemetery of Zvenieki (Zagorskis 1973) was increased. However, to the west in Ireland and Britain, things did not change other than the recognition that nearly 200 years ago, a large cemetery had been found in Aveline's Hole in Somerset (Zvelebil and Rowley-Conwy 1986).

In general, the known Mesolithic human remains on these islands are quite sparse. In England the main concentration of surviving human remains is in the three caves in the Mendips, *i.e.* Aveline's Hole, Gough Cove Cheddar, and Totty Pot (Gardiner 2000), all of which interestingly belong to the earlier half of the English Mesolithic. Schulting and Richards (2002) have also documented the presence of a selection of human bones from the Mesolithic period in South Wales. In Scotland, Mesolithic human remains are concentrated on the three Orkney middens (Mellars 1987). None of Mesolithic date were found in mainland middens at Oban nor were any recovered from Morton (Coles 1971).

In Ireland, the evidence is equally rare with the best known being the scatter of bones and teeth from Ferriter's Cove, Co. Kerry (Woodman *et al.* 1999), and the femur from Rockmarshall, Co. Louth (Woodman *et al.* 1997). O'Sullivan (2002) has drawn attention to the association of human remains and shell middens. However, it should be remembered that only one bone, that from Rock-marshall Site 3 is associated with a midden. It should also be remembered, therefore, that no known Mesolithic remains have been noted at the middens on Dalkey Island and Sutton, Co. Dublin, and Rough Island, Co. Down. No real substantial concentration of shells was found at Ferriter's Cove, where the largest shell heap was just over one metre across and less that 20cm thick. Most were 30cm across. The leg portions were also found stratified at a slightly higher level than the main phases of occupation. Another selection of human remains, which includes some from the Mesolithic period, was recovered from Killuragh Cave in Co. Limerick (Woodman 1997; Woodman and O'Shaughnessy forthcoming). These bones were recovered from deposits that had been disturbed and also included material from the Neolithic and Bronze Age. It should, however, be noted that several microliths were also recovered during investigations of this site.

If we commence with a working, though rather simplistic, assumption that human remains older than 5,200 BP or about 4,000 Cal. BC may be considered to predate the appearance of a full farming economy and could in some sense be regarded as Mesolithic in age then human remains are quite scarce particularly if we exclude the chronological borderline Stoney Island, Co. Galway, skeleton (Brindley and Lanting 1995).

The human remains are as follows (Fig 2.1):

Ferriter's Cove OxA – 4918   Femur   5545±65 BP
    4225–3950 Cal. BC

Ferriter's Cove OxA – 5570   Tooth   5590±60 BP
    4250–3980 Cal. BC

Killuragh Cave OxA – 6749   Mandible   5455±50 BP
    4450–4160 Cal. BC

Killuragh Cave OxA – 6752   Tooth   5725±35 BP
    4690–4460 Cal. BC

Killuragh Cave GrA – 2433   Metatarsal   7880±60 BP
    7040–6590 Cal. BC

Killuragh Cave GrA – 2434   Metatarsal   8030±60 BP
    7140–6690 Cal. BC

Rockmarshall 3 OxA – 4604   Femur   5705±75 BP
    4720–4360 Cal. BC

The numbers could best be regarded as sparse and the remains as very fragmentary. Another explanation for the

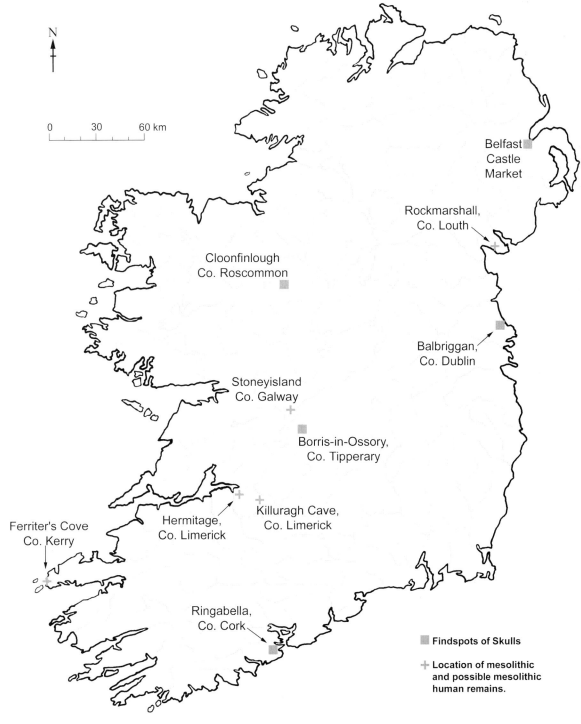

Fig 2.1: Location of Mesolithic and possible Mesolithic human remains in Ireland.

rarity of human remains is demonstrated through excavations by Collins (2001, Collins and Coyne 2003) at Hermitage Townland, Co. Limerick. Here several cremations were uncovered in an area overlooking the River Shannon. The excavations took place along a strip of land that extended for several hundred metres in length. The most significant cremation was within Area A, where a scatter of Early Mesolithic artefacts was recovered. It was associated with a very large stone axe, a burnt microlith and a microblade fragment and appears to have been placed round a post. Charcoal from this grave has been dated to 7550–7290 Cal. BC. A burial pit some distance away in area B has produced a date of 7030–6630 Cal. BC while charcoal from a cremation in area C has produced a date of 6610–6370 Cal. BC. The final date could be associated with the beginning of the Later Mesolithic and it is of interest that a thin scatter of Later Mesolithic material was recovered from across the pipeline area. The implication of the Hermitage material is that cremation may have been used as a burial rite in the Mesolithic period in Ireland. It is of interest that during the initial exploration of Killuragh Cave some traces of burning were noted and some of the bones were charred but, at this stage, it is uncertain as to whether this charring was caused by fires which were lit at a much later date

The study of Mesolithic human remains is hampered by the fact that they are rarely associated with a lasting memorial such as a visible monument. Therefore we end up relying on chance finds whose reasons for survival is not always clear. Obviously these absences raise various questions:

Are we looking at the right types of sites?
Perhaps the main lesson that we can learn from the excavations at Hermitage, Co. Limerick, is that we are usually looking for the wrong things, *i.e.* inhumation skeletons with diagnostic grave goods. In the case of the Hermitage site, the lesson is that we may have been too ready to presume that the rite of cremation was confined to later prehistory and that especially if it was a simple pit grave filled with cremated bones then it could be assumed to be Bronze or Early Iron Age. While significant emphasis is often given to inhumation burials within the Mesolithic period even in Denmark several cremations have also been recorded, most notably two at Gongehusvej 7, Vedbaek (Petersen 1990), while another has been found at Dammen on the northern coast of Bohuslän in Sweden. This cremation may date to earlier than 7,000 Cal. BC. (Eva Schaller – Åhrberg Final Coast to Coast conference Falköping, October 2002).

Have we ever found areas of settlement activity where persistent re-occupation over generations might lead to concentrations of burials in the vicinity?
As in Britain we still lack large numbers of settlement sites where consistent re-occupation might lead to an increased chance of finding an area where there is an increased concentration of burials. This, of course, assumes that burials will take place near areas of settlement rather than at a special locality.

Should we expect burials to occur in certain liminal environments?
One could argue that occurrence in caves or, as O'Sullivan (2002) has suggested, in shell middens, represents the use of such special environments. Similarly if we found a human bone in a hilltop cleft we might be thinking of a sky god cult! In these cases it is difficult to balance the potential special nature of the localities with the equally important fact that these are, in Ireland, the environments that will best preserve human remains. Are these bones there simply because they are amongst the only places where bones will survive?

Should we assume that the dead were always buried?
There are, of course, numerous suggestions for absence and we should not dismiss the possibility that the dead were venerated or incorporated into the world of the living through means other than internment. While it is less fashionable these days to quote ethnographic analogies, the rituals after death in the Murray River area in Australia (Pretty 1977) are a salutary lesson. After death:
i)   The bodies of young children are carried by their mothers until the bodies disintegrate.
ii) The bodies of elderly women are placed in trees.
iii) The bodies of elderly men are placed on platforms.

Pretty also noted that tribes in the Lower Murray River area often mummified bodies through smoking and that peripheral bones such as phalanges were lost. This type of ritual might explain the strange array of bones on Oronsay that perplexed Meiklejohn and Denston (1987)

While excarnation may be followed by deposition as at Goughs Cave (Cook 1991) where Late Glacial fragments of skulls and jaws showed evidence of deliberate dismemberment. It is also possible that ritual after death may not have included deposition.

Any of these hypotheses are still acceptable explanations for the Irish Mesolithic, *i.e.* deliberate deposition in a midden as may have happened at Rockmarshall, or even just exposure of a body as at Ferriter's Cove. In the case of Killuragh cave a case could be made for excarnation outside the cave as some material was recovered from within a narrow fissure leading down into the main part of the cave. It should, however, be noted that unlike parts of Britain there is so far no general trend of finding Mesolithic human remains or other material of a similar age within Irish cave systems.

However, as human bodies are the providers of so many insights into human life ways it seemed a pity to be content to wait until new evidence emerged by chance. It was thought that a more pro-active approach was needed. Perhaps human remains of Mesolithic age had been recovered but, particularly if they had not been associated with formal burial, perhaps they would have remained unrecognised. One potential avenue was suggested through a perusal of C. P. Martin's *Prehistoric Man in Ireland*. Published in 1935, it represents a different view of the past, when objects and monument types were more explicitly associated with people, thus the people of 'the Bronze Age Short cists, the 'People of the Crannogs' *etc*. In 1935, for example, it was still presumed that skeletons A and B from Kilgreany, Co. Waterford, were of Late Glacial, *i.e.* Upper Palaeolithic Age. It is of course now known that both these skeletons are of Neolithic Age (see Woodman *et al.* 1997)

Many of the perspectives, terminology, chronological context *etc*. used in his study are very dated, but Martin did bring together an extensive collection of human remains, many of which had never been discussed by Antiquaries and Archaeologists. Even the idea of morpho-metrical studies based on skull shapes is regarded as extremely questionable:

"Craniometry, the study and measurement of human skulls have in recent years enjoyed about as much prestige as phrenology." (Renfrew 1987)

Though see also Brodie (1994) for a balanced reappraisal.

Quite a number of these remains have long since vanished from studies of the second half of the 20th century. Primarily, it would appear because, on the one hand they were not associated with archaeological artifacts and almost undateable, while on the other the science of Anatomy developed other priorities

From *Prehistoric Man in Ireland* five possible skulls were selected. Four of these came from his "People of the Raised Beach" category. This category included an indivi-dual of known age, through 14C dating, *i.e.* Stoney Island 5210±50 BP (average of 3 dates) (Brindley and Lanting 1995). The skull from White Park Bay Sandhills, Co. Antrim, from its position in the sand dunes could also be presumed to post-date the Mesolithic. This left four skulls: Balbriggan (Co. Dublin), Castle market (Belfast), Clonfin-lough (Co. Roscommon) and Ringabella (Co. Cork).

Looked at objectively, these skulls were, of course, of uncertain age, but there was as good a case for them being Mesolithic as for any other period. Two of the skulls, Belfast and Clonfinlough, were reputed to be from geological contexts that suggested an early Holocene date. The Ringabella skull came from a location on the outer shores of Cork Harbour, which suggested an association with the sea, and was similar in location to Ferriter's Cove. The Balbriggan skull was thought to have been found at a considerable depth close to the sea. Besides their contexts they were all robust skulls and, unlike those listed as from for the Megaliths and Bronze Age short cists, they were quite long or doliocephalic. A fifth skull, that from a riverine context at Borris in Ossory, Co. Laois, was added. Although Martin noted a significant number of long skulls in recent populations, it is felt that the same strategy as that used in the Irish Quaternary Faunas project (Woodman *et al.* 1997) should be adopted. In that case

examination of the age of poorly contexted stoat and hare bones was undertaken with the premise that if a number of potentially, though not certainly, early examples were dated it might be possible to show that these two species existed in the Later Glacial Period. Only one early date in each case would be necessary. In this case even one of the five skulls providing an early date would be a major addition to Mesolithic studies in Ireland and perhaps suggest that other similar even poorer contexted material was worth dating.

The Belfast Skull

This specimen is in the collection of the Anatomy Department, Queens University Belfast. Catalogue No. w3. The accompanying label states:

"Human Skull found 6 feet 6 inches below street level and 3 feet below bed of marine shells in Estuarine Clay at Castle Market, Belfast, 1922."

It was noted by Movius (1942) as the one reasonably certain example of Mesolithic human remains in Ireland. The actual location of Castle Market is uncertain, but it is likely to have been in the area of Castle Place and Cornmarket and is where the original Belfast Castle was situated. This is an area where estuarine clay was known to have existed and Martin noted that Young had re-covered finds of various periods from the same clays in Castle Place. It is unlikely that the location for the discovery of this skull was in the 'Markets' area that is some distance to the east.

Description
Date: OxA – 9793   441±32 BP   13C-20.3 9, 15N 11.7
Cal. AD 95.4%   1410–1620 AD
In this case it was also considered possible that the skull might also be associated with the initial building of Belfast Castle but there is a 93% probability that it dates between 1410 and 1500 AD

The Balbriggan skull, Co. Dublin

This specimen is in the Anatomy Dept. of Trinity College Dublin NO. 330. It is recorded in the register as "a human skull found in a deep railway cutting and apparently of remote antiquity." A note on the skull records that: the well-known railway engineer, Sir Robert Mallet, donated it in 1840. Although it was obviously quite a spectacular find, Du Noyer (1847) makes no reference to it in a paper on the Geology of the Dublin-Belfast Railway line.

Description:
Date: OxA 9795   256+/-34 BP 13C -16.1, 15N 11.6
Cal. AD 95.4%   1510–1950 AD
This skull is of remarkably recent origin. There is an approximately 50% probability that it dates to between 1620 and 1680 AD

Cloonfinlough, Co. Roscommon

This specimen is in the collection of the Royal College of Surgeons, now lodged at the Natural History Museum, London. Catalogue No. 4.9818. It was catalogued as coming from the shell marl on the bottom of Cloonfinlough. Information recorded with it stated that it "lay in the wash of a small channel that had been cut a century earlier as an outlet for the lake". "Other parts of the shell marl was covered by a 9ft bed of peat." This small channel still exists today. The skull is known to have been donated by a local landowner in 1926.

The argument that the skull came from the marl was based on the fact that much of its surface was encrusted with white marl except for the top of the skull that was stained brown as if it had protruded from the marl and was in contact with the peat. These marls are usually assumed to be of Late Glacial or Early Holocene age.

Description
Date: OxA 9792   2820±40 BP 13C-20.2% 15N 12.4
Cal. BC 95.4%   1130–830 BC

In spite of the assumption that it was associated with early Holocene deposits, it would appear to belong to the Bronze Age. Whether it was a ritual offering as with the human skull remains in the Kings' Stables, Co. Armagh (Lynn 1975), or an accidental inclusion is open to debate.

Borris in Ossory, Co. Laois

This skull is in the collection of the Anatomy Dept. of Trinity College Dublin Catalogue No. 339. Martin felt that this might have been a skull that was recorded as being found during dredging operations in the river Nore (Harper 1849).

Description
Date: OxA 10046   2189±34 BP 13c –20.7% 15N 10.7
Cal. BC 95.4%   380–160 BC

Ringabella, Co. Cork

This specimen is in the collection of the National Museum of Ireland. Seán P. Ó Ríordáin (1934) retrieved the skull in 1930. Its recovery was during a rapid rescue excavation after Ó Ríordáin had noted the skull exposed at the top of a section of a sea cliff.

Excavations revealed that the remainder of the skeleton had already vanished; that the skull appeared to lie well below the topsoil and that there was evidence of burning in its vicinity. This was on the edge of a flat field looking out to sea and might just have been a location that would have been occupied in the Stone Age. Martin himself, in an appendix to Ó Ríordáin's report felt that the closest analogy to the Ringabella skull was that from Kilgreany.

Description
Date: OxA 9794   373±32   13C-18.8‰   15N 10.5
Cal. AD 95.4%   1440–1640 AD

Again this skull, which had been compared to Kilgreany, was of recent date. Evidence of reddening can still be seen in the cliff face but its relationship to the burial still remains to be ascertained.

Conclusion

Aside from the obvious disappointment that there are no additional specimens of Mesolithic human skeletal remains, this small project provides us with several important lessons, or rather reinforces them:

a)	These radiocarbon dates take out of the realm of speculation five specimens that might have been considered of Mesolithic age. The most notable is the Belfast skull that had been accepted as Mesolithic.

b)	Particularly in the case of the Cloonfinlough and Belfast examples it re-enforces the dangers of over-reliance on anecdotal locational information as the primary source of evidence for dating. This was very evident in the Irish Quaternary Faunas Project, where, for example, there were suggestions of horse maximum pre-dating the Last Glacial Maximum at Dungiven. This was based on horse teeth that were claimed to be from below glacial deposits. In a second case horse teeth were assumed to be early Holocene due to being associated with the raised beach at Larne. Both turned out to be only a few hundred years old (Woodman *et al.* 1997).

c)	This project reinforces the view that apparently robust and primitive looking skulls are not necessarily of considerable age. Indeed it supports the experience from elsewhere. A very primitive looking skull which had been found in the mid 19th century near Dammen in Sweden (see above) was considered initially by Nilsson to be Neanderthal (!) but in more recent times was suspected to be of Mesolithic age. A recent radiocarbon date of a newly discovered fragment of the skull has shown it to be Iron Age in date (Schaller-Ährberg as above)

In summary all new information is useful, but its relevance may not always be immediately apparent. For example, the robust characteristics of the Balbriggan skull could be due to the life of a fisherman and it is of interest that on the basis of the 13C results, seafood played an important part in that individual's diet. Similarly, although they are not technically Bog Bodies, the Cloonfinlough and Borris in Ossory skulls could be regarded as a useful addition to the data collected on Irish Bog bodies (Brindley and Lanting 1995) and the ongoing Discovery Programme study on human skulls associated with crannogs (C. Fredengren pers comm.). Martin identified numerous other human skulls, which would be worthy of investigation.

Acknowledgements

It is with great sadness that I have found myself finishing the paper without Maire. She was not only a fun person to work with but provided important insights into the research on the skulls. She was also determined to track down material in locations where archaeologists were not normally working and due to her persistence and courtesy we were able to get access to material that was not normally easily available.

We would also wish to thank Robert Kruszinski of the Natural History Museum, Alan Haylings of the Anatomy Department Queens University, The National Museum of Ireland and the Anatomy Department of Trinity College Dublin for giving us access to their materials. Our thanks are also due to the Radiocarbon Laboratory in Oxford and to Paul Pettitt for sampling the material. Hugh Kavanagh provided the map while the text was prepared by Marian Cotter. The project was funded by The National Committee of Archaeology of the Royal Irish Academy, the Department of Archaeology UCC and by the Dean of Arts UCC.

Bibliography

Albrethsen, S.E. and Petersen, E.B. 1976 Excavation of a Mesolithic Cemetery at Vedbaek, Denmark, *Acta Archaeologia* **47**, 1–28.

Brindley, A. and Lanting, J. 1995 Irish Bog Bodies: The Radiocarbon Dates. In R.C. Turner and R.G. Scaife (eds) *Bog Bodies: New Discoveries and Perspectives*, 133–36. British Museum Press, London.

Brodie, N. 1994 *The Neolithic-Bronze Age Transition in Britain: A Critical Review of some Archaeological and Craniological Concepts*. Tempus Reparatum, British Archaeological Reports British Series **238**, Tempus Reparatum, Oxford.

Coles, J. 1971 The Early Settlement of Scotland: Excavations at Morton, Fife, *Proceedings of the Prehistoric Society* **38**, 284–366.

Collins, T. 2001 Additions to the Axe Files, *Archaeology Ireland* **58**, 7.

Collins, T and Coyne, F. 2003 Fire and Water: Early Mesolithic cremations at Castleconnell, County Limerick, *Archaeology Ireland* **64**, 24–27.

Cook, J. 1991 Preliminary Report on Marked Human Bones From the 1986–87 Excavations at Goughs Cave. In N. Barton, A.J. Roberts and D.A. Roe (eds) *The Late Glacial in North West Europe: Human Adaptation and Environmental Change at the end of the Pleistocene*, 160–68. Council for British Archaeology Research Report, Council for the British Archaeology, London.

Du Noyer, G.V. 1847 Remarks on the Geological Sections exposed in the cutting of the Dublin and Drogheda Railway, *Journal of the Geological Society of Dublin* **3**, 255–260.

Gardiner, P. 2000 Excavations at Birdcombe, Somerset: Mesolithic Settlement, Subsistence and Landscape use in the south west of England. In R. Young (ed.) *Mesolithic Life ways: Current Research from Britain and Ireland*, 199–207. Leicester Archaeology Monographs **7**, Leicester University Press, Leicester.

Gurina, N.N. 1956 *Oleneostrovski Mogilnik*. Materialy I Issledovaniya po Arkelogii SSSR **47**.

Harpur, S.C. 1849 Finding of a skull in the River Nore, Borris in Ossory, *Journal of the Royal Society of Antiquaries of Ireland* **1**, 30.

Larsson, L.L. 1984 The Skateholm Project: A Late Mesolithic Settlement and Cemetery Complex at a Southern Swedish Bay, *Meddellanden Från Lunds. Universitets Historiska Museum* **5**, 5–38.

Lynn, C.L. 1975 Trial Excavations at the King's Stables, Tray Townland, Co. Armagh, *Ulster Journal of Archaeology* **40**, 42–62.

Martin, C.P. 1935 *Prehistoric Man in Ireland*. Macmillan and Co. Ltd., London.

Mellars, P. 1987 *Excavations on Oronsay: Prehistoric Human Ecology on a small island*. Edinburgh University Press, Edinburgh.

Meiklejohn, C. and Denston, C.B. 1987 The Human Skeletal Remains. In P. Mellars *Excavations on Oronsay: Prehistoric Human Ecology on a Small Island*, 290–300. Edinburgh University Press, Edinburgh.

Movius, H.L. 1942 *The Irish Stone Age*. Cambridge University Press, Cambridge.

Ó Ríordáin, S.P. 1934 A Prehistoric Burial at Ringabella, Co. Cork. *Journal of the Royal Society of Antiquaries of Ireland* **64**, 86–87.

O'Sullivan, A. 2002 Living with the dead amongst Hunter Gatherers, *Archaeology Ireland* **60**, 10–12.

Petersen, E.B. 1973 A Survey of the Late Palaeolithic and the Mesolithic of Denmark. In S. Kozlowski (ed.) *The Mesolithic in Europe*. 77–127. Warsaw University Press, Warsaw.

Petersen, E.B. 1990 Nye grave fra Jaegerstenalderen: Stroby Egede og Vedbaek, *Nationalmuseets Arbejdsmark* 1990, 19–33.

Pretty, G.H. 1977 The Cultural Chronology of the Roonka Flat. In R.V.S. Wright (ed.) *Stone Tools as Cultural Markers*, 288–331. Australian Institute of Aboriginal Studies, Canberra.

Renfrew, C. 1987 *Archaeology and Language*, Jonathon Cape, London.

Schulting, R.J. and Richards, M.P. 2002 Finding the coastal Mesolithic in South West Britain: Ams dates and stable isotope results on human remains, *Antiquity* **76**, 1011–1025.

Waddell, J. 1998 *The Prehistoric Archaeology of Ireland*. Galway University Press, Galway.

Woodman, P.C. 1997 Killuragh Cave, Co. Limerick. In I. Bennett (ed.) *Excavations 1996*, 00. Wordwell, Bray.

Woodman, P.C., McCarthy, M. and Monaghan, N. 1997 The Irish Quaternary Faunas Project. *Quaternary Science Reviews* **16**, 129–59.

Woodman, P.C., Anderson, E. and Finlay, N. 1999 *Excavations at Ferriter's Cove 1983–95*. Wordwell, Bray.

Woodman, P.C. and O'Shaughnessy, J. forthcoming Excavations at Killuragh Cave, The Heritage Council.

Zvelebil, M. and Rowley-Conwy, P. 1986 Foragers and Farmers in Atlantic Europe. In M. Zvelebil (ed.) *Hunters in Transition: Mesolithic Societies of Temperate Eurasia and their transition to Farming*, 67–94. Cambridge University Press, Cambridge.

Zagorskis, F. 1973 Das *Spätmesolithikum* in Lettland. In S. Kozlowski (ed.) *The Mesolithic in Europe*, 652–69. Warsaw University Press, Warsaw.

3. Stèles en Chambres

Charles-Tanguy Le Roux
(à la mémoire de Pierre-Roland Giot, Jean L'Helgouac'h et Jacques Briard)

Résumé

La perception du phénomène des réemplois en matière de mégalithisme armoricain et la prise de conscience de son ampleur ont connu un véritable tournant avec la publication de l'article "Les idoles qu'on abat..." par J. L'Helgouac'h en 1983. On propose ici un "état de la question" pour les menhirs et les stèles ornées qui ont été reprises d'une manière ou d'une autre dans la construction de tombes mégalithiques armoricaines. L'essentiel du phénomène semble lié aux dolmens à couloir du Néolithique moyen mais il concerne aussi des caveaux clos sous tumulus de la même époque voire plus anciens, ainsi que des galeries funéraires du Néolithique final et même quelques tombes du Bronze ancien.

Summary

The clear perception of "megalithic recycling" and of its importance in Armorican megalithism widely dates from the publication of the paper "Les idoles qu'on abat..." by J. L'Helgouac'h in 1983. A "state of the question" is proposed here for crude menhirs and decorated stelae which have been reused in the architecture of armorican megalithic tombs. Most examples deal with passage tombs of the Middle Neolithic but other cases concern sealed vaults under barrows of the same period (or even earlier) and gallery graves of the Late Neolithic or even tombs of Early Bronze Age.

Mots-clés: Néolithique, Armorique, menhir, stèle, tombe méga-lithique, réemploi.

Key-words: Neolithic, Armorica, menhir, stela, megalithic tomb, re-use.

En Armorique comme ailleurs, des liens ont été perçus très tôt entre les deux grandes familles de monuments mégalithiques que sont les pierres dressées et les sépultures. On ne reviendra pas ici sur la question des "menhirs indicateurs" pour laquelle l'engouement de naguère est - à tort ou à raison - quelque peu retombé; c'est un autre aspect que nous voudrions aborder, celui des stèles incorporées à des constructions sépulcrales. A. Devoir (1911) notait déjà que certains décors de sépultures n'avaient pu être exécutés à l'emplacement où on les observait de nos jours et J. L'Helgouac'h (1965) avait relevé de nombreuses anomalies architecturales dans les monuments qu'il avait étudiés et il envisageait à leur propos la possibilité de signification(s) symbolique(s) tout en restant conscient des limites de cette "manière commode de draper notre ignorance", pour reprendre une boutade de P.-R. Giot. Mais c'est à la suite de son article "Les idoles qu'on abat…" (L'Helgouac'h 1983) que la communauté archéologique prit réellement conscience de l'ampleur et de l'importance des destructions, réemplois et recyclages affectant les mégalithes armoricains. Dans une publication ultérieure (L'Helgouac'h 1997), il devait faire un état des stèles réemployées dans des architectures funéraires. Il n'est évidemment pas question de refaire ici ce travail exemplaire; sept ans après, nous voudrions simplement jeter un regard quelque peu différent sur cette passionnante (et déroutante) question.

I – Identifier un réemploi

La signification particulière d'une pierre donnée au sein d'une architecture mégalithique peut s'apprécier à l'aune de plusieurs critères, d'ailleurs susceptibles de se combiner pour renforcer l'argumentaire. Cependant, ceux-ci ne sont en général que "nécessaires mais non suffisants"; certaines réutilisations peuvent nous échapper et, à l'inverse, toute anomalie architecturale ne signe pas obligatoirement un réemploi.

I A – Les décors anormaux

L'Armorique est bien connue pour représenter l'un des grands foyers européens d'art mégalithique;[1] qu'un monument y soit décoré est donc, spécialement sur le littoral morbihannais, insuffisant pour attirer en soi la suspicion. L'anomalie significative peut être de plusieurs ordres:

– signes disposés de façon aberrante (par exemple tête-bêche) par rapport à leur orientation habituelle, installés sur une surface rarement décorée et mal-

Fig 3.1: Carnac (Morbihan), dolmen de Kermario: stèle à sommet arrondie formant dalle de chevêt dans la chambre; noter sa hauteur clairement supérieure à celle des orthostates voisins (vue prise de l'extérieur; au premier plan, restes du cairn arasé).

commode à observer (comme par exemple un linteau de couloir ou un plafond de chambre), ou plus ou moins occultés dans la construction (et donc d'exécution *in situ* impossible dans le monument en l'état);

– style et/ou exécution différents des autres décors du même monument : répertoire spécifique (c'est ainsi que les signes en "hache-charrue" et en "hache engainée" semblent largement caractéristiques des stèles ornées) ; dimensions de certains signes – même ubiquistes comme l'"écusson" – qui les rendent plus aptes à être observés en pleine lumière avec un certain recul que dans l'espace obscur et confiné d'une crypte funéraire (Le Roux 1997; 1999).

I B – Des morphologies significatives

– La forme naturelle d'une pierre peut avoir été mise à profit, qu'elle soit en prisme étroit plus ou moins styliforme (comme J1 à Barnenez H, L11 à Gavrinis ou C1 à Pen-Hap sur l'Ile-aux-Moines), ou qu'elle se présente comme une dalle évoquant la silhouette du fameux "signe en écusson" de l'art pariétal mégalithique régional (la dalle de chevet C4 de la Table-des-Marchands à Locmariaquer).

– La pierre peut aussi avoir été façonnée par éclatement ou piquetage. Le résultat peut être clairement anthropomorphe, avec "épaulements" dégageant une partie "céphalique" (les stèles de Guennoc III à Landéda, l'orthostate C8 de Kercado à Carnac), ou dessiner un

sommet simplement arrondi comme à Kermario, également à Carnac.

– Ses dimensions peuvent être discordantes par rapport aux autres éléments de la construction, soit que la pierre ait conditionné la taille du monument où elle a été incorporée (c'est notamment le cas à la Table-des-Marchands), soit que sa taille anormalement grande par rapport aux autres éléments conservés implique que des structures complémentaires (par exemple en pierre sèche) aient disparu. Plusieurs cas sont connus, le plus significatif étant peut-être celui – resté curieusement inédit – du petit dolmen situé à la tête des alignements de Kermario à Carnac: la dalle médiane du chevet en est soigneusement taillée en arrondi à la manière de certaines statues-menhirs du haut-pays héraultais, or cette pierre dépasse très largement tous les autres orthostates (Fig 3.1). Parfois enfin, une troncature plus ou moins mutilante a ramené le bloc à un gabarit "normal" par rapport au reste du monument (Gavrinis C5; Mané-Rutual J1).

II – Pierres exposées et pierres cachées dans les tombes à couloir

Faire une stèle en réemploi de tout élément de monument mégalithique répondant peu ou prou à l'un ou l'autre des critères ainsi énumérés serait à coup sûr déraisonnable; déjà la liste des blocs qui montrent au moins deux d'entre eux (dont la concordance peut déjà difficilement passer

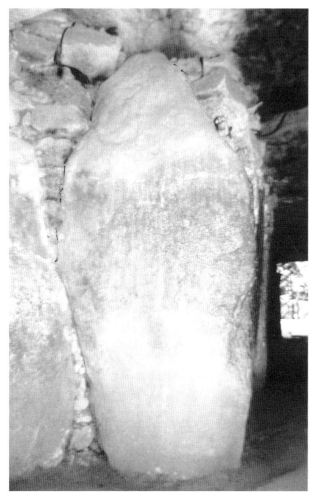

Fig 3.2: Carnac (Morbihan), dolmen de Kercado: grande stèle anthropomorphe incorporée à la paroi de la chambre au débouché du couloir.

pour fortuite) est loin d'être négligeable. Deux grands types de situation doivent être distingués au sein des "architectures-hôtes."

II A – Les situations ostentatoires

La pierre en cause peut être valorisée par sa position dans une perspective privilégiée, soit comme élément structurant de l'architecture, soit qu'elle apparaisse comme un complément à celle-ci.

A 1 – Orthostates engagés dans la paroi

La position face à l'entrée, est celle qui, dans une tombe à couloir, attire le plus notre attention (et sans doute déjà celle des Néolithiques). C'est dans une telle situation que se dresse la grande stèle ogivale (C4) de la Table-des-Marchands dont la surface en grès blanc entièrement travaillée se détache encore aujourd'hui dans la pénombre de la crypte, sitôt que l'on risque un oeil à l'intérieur. Mais ce cas n'est pas unique : pensons à l'étrange motif

en "palmier" qui occupe la grande dalle de chevet (C4) du Mané-Lud, à la pierre sans décor visible mais soigneusement taillée que nous avons déjà évoquée, face à l'entrée du petit dolmen de Kermario à Carnac et à son homologue B1 – décoré cette fois – de Mané-Kerioned B, toujours à Carnac.

Le débouché du couloir dans la chambre constitue une autre position-clé et les cas ne sont pas rares de piliers saillants marquant ce passage, sans doute hautement symbolique pour celui qui entre dans la sépulture comme pour ceux qui y reposent déjà. Rien d'étonnant donc à ce que l'on rencontre des pierres particulières en un tel endroit ; trois exemples nous semblent particulièrement significatifs.

– A Carnac, il est désormais bien connu depuis une observation de P.-R. Giot (1971, 354) que le grand orthostate C8, de presque 2,5m de haut, situé à gauche du couloir de Kercado quand on regarde vers la sortie, présente une silhouette clairement anthropomorphe (déjà dessinée par W. C. Lukis dès 1867 – dessin inédit, archives du laboratoire d'Anthropologie du l'université de Rennes 1), même si celle-ci est quelque peu "enveloppée" et n'est assortie d'aucun décor actuellement décelable (Fig 3.2).

– A Pen-Hap, sur l'Île-aux-Moines, le montant de droite (C1) affecte la forme d'une colonne à base presque carrée. La hauteur hors du sol actuel est cette fois modeste (1,5m), comparable à celle des principaux orthostates de la chambre, mais la présence de deux signes quasi-spécifiques des stèles (une "hache-engainée" côté chambre et une "hache-charrue" sur la face opposée, originellement engagée dans le cairn) montre à l'évidence que l'on a bien là une stèle en position secondaire (Minot 1964).

– A Gavrinis, exactement dans la même situation qu'à Pen-Hap, une étroite colonne (L11) marque le passage de la chambre au couloir ; elle aussi montre, sur sa face cachée, une "hache engainée" indépendante du décor typiquement gavrinien qui occupe toute la surface visible de la pierre (Le Roux 1985); on se trouve donc ici à la limite de la situation ostentatoire claire des cas précédents et de la situation occultée sur laquelle nous reviendrons plus loin).

Cette situation au débouché du couloir peut aussi concerner des pierres sans façonnage ni décor visible bien qu'elles tranchent – par leur grande taille notamment – sur le reste de l'architecture, ce qui amène à soulever la question de leur équivalence avec les exemples précités; c'est notamment le cas du dolmen à chambre circulaire de Kermaric à Languidic (Martin 1911) et de celui de Port-blanc à Saint-Pierre-Quiberon (Gaillard 1883).

A 2 – Colonnes dégagées des parois

Elles sont connues dans divers monuments; la description la plus impressionnante reste sans doute celle de la tombe – hélas détruite – de la Haye à Saint-Gravé (Fouquet

Fig 3.3: Landeda (Finistère), île Guennoc: stèle anthropomorphe dressée dans la chambre A du cairn III.

1874), avec deux grandes pierres dressées au beau milieu d'une chambre vraisemblablement couverte en pierre sèche, mais d'autres cas fort intéressants sont encore visibles de nos jours.

– A Barnenez H (Giot 1987), deux étroits piliers de près de 2m de haut, indépendants de la paroi (bien que contribuant à soutenir la couverture), marquent le passage entre l'antichambre encorbellée et l'arrière-chambre mégalithique. Celui de droite, un peu en retrait, est un simple bloc brut mais son vis-à-vis (J1), situé presque dans l'axe du couloir, est un étroit bloc sub-prismatique à la silhouette naturelle quasi-phallique. Il est orné sur trois faces d'un arc, de trois lames de haches et d'une hache emmanchée, cette dernière au moins étant dans une position difficilement compatible avec son exécution sur place; au surplus, le profond piquetage de tout ce décor se distingue clairement, beaucoup plus léger, de celui qui figure sur les autres dalles.

– Le Mané-Rutual de Locmariaquer montre un plan quasi-identique à celui de Barnenez H, même si la structure y est entièrement mégalithique et nettement plus surbaissée. Cette fois, c'est la colonne de droite (J1) qui est la mieux exposée (et des impacts de balles, tirées dans le monument durant la guerre confirment douloureusement cette situation). Il s'agit d'un fût presque tronconique de près de 1m de grand diamètre à la base pour 1,6m de hauteur visible. Une grande figuration de "hache-charrue" s'y enroule à mi-hauteur et sa "lame" vient se perdre contre la

paroi, dans une situation incompatible avec son exécution sur place. Comme nous l'avons vu plus haut, le sommet du monolithe, qui contribue à soutenir la couverture, a été manifestement retaillé pour s'ajuster à la hauteur des orthostates voisins.

Il est tentant de rapprocher de cette série les colonnes – certes inornées – présentes à l'intérieur de la chambre du Mané-er-Hloc'h de Locoal-Mendon (L'Helgouac'h 1965, fig. 26) et sans doute faut-il aussi s'interroger aussi sur la signification du "menhir" qui encombrait la chambre de Butten-er-Hah D à l'Ile de Groix et de cet autre monolithe gisant dans le couloir de Parc-Guren I à Crac'h (L'Helgouac'h 1965, 63–65). Il faut enfin rappeler la série déjà évoquée des trois stèles anthropomorphes conservées au débouché du couloir dans trois des chambres encorbellées du cairn de Guennoc III (Giot 1987; Le Roux 1999; Fig 3.3). Or ce monument, qui occupe le sommet topographique de l'île et domine ainsi les autres éléments de la nécropole, pourrait bien compter parmi les toutes premières manifestations du mégalithisme dolménique armoricain (même si la date radiocarbone particulièrement haute qu'il a pu fournir doit être maniée avec circonspection, ne serait-ce qu'en raison de sa très large fourchette d'incertitude).

II B – *Situations discrètes ou occultées*

Dans tous les exemples précédents, la visibilité de la pierre – qu'elle montre ou non un décor ou un façonnage – semble être hautement significative même si l'utile se joint à l'agréable pour lui faire jouer un rôle dans la structure architecturale du monument. Dans d'autres cas au contraire, cette préoccupation parait absente et certaines situations semblent même témoigner d'une volonté d'occulter un décor préexistant (donc aussi le message symbolique qui lui était certainement lié). La situation est d'autant plus complexe que, dans certains monuments, on peut trouver à la fois des réemplois ostentatoires et des occultations mais, là encore, plusieurs situations-types sont à considérer.

B 1 – *Orthostates engagés dans les parois*

Parmi les stèles ornées ainsi utilisées, on se limitera à quelques exemples parmi les plus significatifs.

– A Gavrinis, le pilier C5 déjà évoqué, à droite dans la chambre, tranche sur ses voisins par un décor plus sévère, mieux ordonné et moins profondément tracé. Un double registre de crosses emboîtées s'y organise symétriquement par rapport à un axe vertical médian, disposition qui rappelle en plus simple celle de la grande stèle de la Table-des-Marchands. La dalle, aux bords naturellement subverticaux, semble avoir eu un sommet arrondi voire une légère protubérance "céphalique" à en juger par les parties manquantes du décor et le galbe des deux épaulements conservés (Fig 3.4). Toute la partie médiane apparaît décapitée comme pour en ajuster la hauteur à celle des orthostates voisins (alors qu'il eût été possible de jouer sur la profondeur du calage, la fouille ayant montré que celui-ci comportait un lit de sable déposé dans une rigole de fondation (Le Roux 1985; 1992; 1997).

– Toujours à Gavrinis mais dans le couloir, le pilier L5 est bien connu pour son décor archaïsant visible "en palimpseste" sous l'exubérante ornementation de style gavrinien (Le Roux 1992). A la partie supérieure, un grand arceau dessine évoque un large collier ou pectoral qui semble comme accroché aux épaules d'une stèle anthropomorphe, elle aussi décapitée (le sommet de la dalle a été retaillé à grands éclats pour s'aligner sur celui de ses voisines).

– Le Mané-Kerioned B est sans doute la tombe à couloir la plus décorée de Carnac. A droite de la dalle de chevet B1 déjà citée, la paroi latérale de la chambre comporte deux orthostates ornés; le plus remarquable (R11) montre une forme naturelle en écusson, soulignée par un trait piqueté à l'intérieur duquel se développe un décor complexe, l'ensemble évoquant à nouveau une stèle de type "Table-des-Marchands" assez fruste. A la différence de Gavrinis, l'intégrité de la dalle a été respectée mais le moins que l'on puisse dire est que sa position dans le monument est loin d'être privilégiée.

– Au Petit-Mont d'Arzon, la chambre du dolmen II est très largement construite à l'aide de dalles décorées en réemploi. L'orthostate le plus significatif à cet égard est sans doute C2 (Lecornec 1994a), orné d'une

Fig 3.4: Larmor-Baden (Morbihan), île de Gavrinis: la dalle C5 dans la chambre du dolmen; la partie sommitale a été tronquée à grands éclats, sans aucun égard pour le décor.

belle crosse en faux-relief disposée tête-bêche. La fouille a montré qu'en profondeur la dalle se prolongeait par un épaulement dont le pointement céphalique médian était brisé tandis que toute la partie inférieure de cette grande stèle anthropomorphe avait été emportée par une grande cassure oblique.

– On citera enfin le cas de l'Ile-longue à Larmor-Baden, à la fois complexe et indécis. A l'entrée du couloir, deux orthostates en vis-à-vis montrent chacun un grand signe en écusson, visible depuis l'extérieur et apparemment en situation primaire. Cependant, le plus élaboré orne une dalle (L2) grossièrement scutiforme et pouvant à la limite être considérée comme une ancienne stèle. Par contre, trois linteaux du couloir portent un décor qui, à en juger d'après les relations de fouille (Le Rouzic 1915), ne peuvent guère qu'avoir été en réemploi et nous renvoient au cas de figure suivant.

B 2 – *"Du sol au plafond"*

Dès 1965, J. L'Helgouac'h avait distingué, parmi les tombes à couloir et chambre simple, une série de quelque

26 chambres "à grand dallage". Le plus souvent, celui-ci est formé d'une ou deux grandes pierres plates apparemment banales mais, parfois, il s'agit manifestement de grandes stèles plates scutiformes couchées. C'est notamment le cas au Mané-Lud (Le Rouzic 1911) et au Petit-Mont (Lecornec 1994a) où les contours ont directement guidé l'implantation des orthostates et ainsi défini le plan sub-pentagonal de la chambre. Cependant, les réutilis-ations les plus nombreuses concernent les dalles de couverture. Les cas les plus spectaculaires sont bien sûr représentés par les grandes stèles en orthogneiss de Locmariaquer qui avaient en priorité attiré l'attention de J. L'Helgouac'h (1983). Là encore, deux types de situation peuvent être distingués, selon le degré de respect qui semble avoir entouré la pierre.

La dalle peut avoir été réutilisée dans son intégrité, même si elle était disproportionnée par rapport à son nouvel usage.

— Au Mané-Rutual, une stèle de 11m ne couvre ainsi que l'arrière-chambre de la tombe, et sur le tiers de sa longueur à peine. C'est d'autant plus remarquable que l'énorme signe en écusson qui orne la face aujourd'hui ventrale du monolithe se trouve en quasi-totalité sur la partie prolongeant la sépulture, au point qu'on peut se demander si celui-ci était bien noyé dans la masse d'un cairn aujourd'hui disparu ou s'il ne couvrait pas plutôt une sorte de *cella* indépendante laissant l'icône accessible. L'état actuel du monument, ruiné de longue date et drastiquement restauré avant-guerre, ne permet hélas pas de vérifier une telle hypothèse (dont on retrouvera plus loin le pendant à propos des allées-couvertes).

— A un moindre degré, le Mané-Lud voisin obéit à une logique similaire: la couverture de la chambre, dalle aujourd'hui brisée et tronquée, sans décor visible mais encore longue de près de 9m, déborde largement la chambre (sur le côté cette fois).

Il serait bien imprudent de qualifier de stèles réemployées toutes les dalles ornées figurant au plafond de sépultures mégalithiques même si le décor, qui ne peut en général être observé qu'en étant allongé sur le dos et se trouve bien souvent engagé dans les parois, nous semble en position aberrante. Quelques cas sont cependant flagrants comme la grande stèle servant de linteau dans le couloir du Petit-Mont II (Lecornec 1994a; 1997), dont le bris ne semble dû qu'à l'incrustation brutale d'un bunker dans le monument durant la dernière guerre. Dans la même veine, on peut également rappeler le linteau orné d'un écusson à l'entrée de Barnenez J (Giot 1987), la "hache-charrue" au plafond de la chambre de Kercado (sur une dalle au contour non dégagé) ou les deux petites stèles (dont l'une ornée de la seconde "hache-charrue" de ce monument) qui couvrent l'antichambre du Mané-Rutual.

Toute autre est la logique du dépeçage pour un réemploi utilitaire. Le cas le plus spectaculaire en est celui —désormais bien connu — de la grande stèle de 14m partagée entre les couvertures de la Table-des-Marchands,

de Gavrinis et, peut-être, du caveau d'Er-Grah à Loc-mariaquer (Le Roux 1985; 1995). Sur le premier site, on est encore dans une situation intermédiaire puisque le décor, quoique mutilé, a été laissé bien visible au plafond de la chambre quitte à surmonter une certaine difficulté technique (la dalle repose sur sa face la plus bombée). A Gavrinis au contraire, les considérations techniques semblent avoir prévalu sans vergogne: la pierre a été retournée pour que sa face plane serve de plafond, quitte à faire disparaître dans la masse du cairn un décor pourtant exceptionnel (mais sans doute devenu obsolète).

III – Dans les autres types de monuments

Les tombes à couloir du Néolithique moyen ne sont pas les seules concernées ; la réutilisation de stèles semble en effet avoir concerné très tôt d'autres architectures funéraires et avoir perduré assez longuement.

III A – Tertres et tumulus du Néolithique moyen

Dans la série des "tumulus géants" carnacéens, le Mané-er-Hroeg de Locmariaquer est célèbre depuis son exploration par la Société polymathique du Morbihan (Lefebvre et Galles 1863) pour le somptueux mobilier de son caveau central, mais aussi pour la petite stèle au décor très élaboré dont les fragments furent recueillis dans le blocage de celui-ci (notons au passage qu'une autre pierre, de dimensions et de décor comparables, donnée comme provenant du même site mais restée inédite, se trouverait dans une collection privée). Cependant, les réemplois du Mané-er-Hroeg ne s'arrêtent pas là; lors d'une consoli-dation du caveau en 1970, la couverture en fut dégagée, ce qui permit à P.-R. Giot de noter que ses deux dalles d'orthogneiss étaient en fait les deux moitiés d'un grand monolithe allongé qui avait été délibérément divisé.

Toute autre est la situation du "menhir aux serpents" qui, à Carnac, émerge du tertre du Manio II fouillé par Le Rouzic et Péquart en 1922. Les structures complexes qui y furent rencontrées peuvent être interprétées comme deux petits caveaux protégés par un cairn bas surmonté de superstructures en bois (Bailloud *et al.* 1995). C'est contre la plus orientale de ces sépultures que se dresse un monolithe de 4m de haut dont la base, protégée par le tertre, avait conservé cinq lignes serpentiformes gravées sur sa face occidentale (au pied de laquelle furent recueillies cinq lames de haches polies). Les conditions de la fouille de 1922 ne permettent cependant pas de savoir si le tertre est venu s'appuyer contre un menhir préexistant (et déjà assorti ou non de son dépôt de haches?) ou s'il s'agit d'un ensemble synchrone.

III B – Prolongements au Néolithique récent

Les liens entre stèles et tombes ne s'arrêtent pas au Néolithique moyen. Un monument coudé comme les Pierres-plates de Locmariaquer, construit sans doute à la fin du 4ème millénaire B.C., montre encore une grande dalle d'orthogneiss recouvrant la partie terminale de la chambre; il est cependant difficile de trancher ici entre la véritable réappropriation d'une pierre encore signifiante et la simple récupération d'un bloc à l'abandon. La situation de la "stèle aux cupules" aujourd'hui redressée à l'entrée du même monument est encore plus ambiguë, s'agissant d'un bloc de granite qui gisait à plat devant celui-ci avant sa restauration (Salmon 1893). Les tombes en "V" finistériennes de Plovan et Brennilis montrent l'une et l'autre un pilier non porteur au centre de la chambre, qui parait bien ressortir de la même logique que ceux évoqués plus haut à propos des tombes à couloir (L'Helgouac'h 1965, figs 68 et 69; Le Goffic 1994).

Il n'est pas jusqu'aux galeries funéraires du Néolithique final qui ne paraissent prolonger la vieille tradition du réemploi. Presque en face de l'entrée, dans la tombe à entrée latérale de Creac'h-Quillé en Saint-Quay-Perros, l'orthostate C15, orné d'un motif en "seins et collier" (L'Helgouac'h 1967b), semble représenter une forme fruste de statue-menhir tant son décor est proche de l'exemplaire du Trevoux (Le Roux 1998; 1999; Fig 3.5). Le rapprochement est d'autant moins incongru que l'on sait comment l'autre statue-menhir avérée de Bretagne, celle de Guidel, fut récupérée en morceaux parmi les pierres et fragments de meules qui formaient la chape d'un autre monument du Néolithique final (Giot 1960).

A propos des allées-couvertes armoricaines, on peut aussi noter combien la belle hache au manche pédiforme qui occupe le centre de la dalle septale au fond de la chambre du Mougau à Commana se trouve en position ostentatoire mais sans oublier que, dans le même monument, la paire de mamelons supérieure au moins de l'orthostate R2, partiellement engagée sous une table de couverture, ne saurait avoir été sculptée *in situ*. L'allée-couverte de Prajou-Menhir à Trebeurden nous procurera un dernier exemple de possible réemploi au Néolithique final. On sait que quatre des orthostates de sa cellule terminale sont richement décorés (L'Helgouac'h 1967a). La composition la plus élaborée (deux écussons quadrangulaires sommés chacun d'un rostre et accotés d'une palette) s'y déploie largement sur la grande dalle formant cloison avec la chambre principale (Fig 3.6). L'orientation de ce décor est normale, sur une surface verticale mais allongée horizontalement, et cohérente avec la structure générale du monument. Néanmoins cette dalle apparaît surdimensionnée, débordant de part et d'autre l'alignement des orthostates. Une telle disposition va à l'encontre de la "norme" dans ce type d'architecture où les dalles septales sont en général prises entre les parois latérales sans en interrompre la continuité. La question d'un réemploi mérite d'autant plus d'être soulevée que le signe en écusson quadrangulaire, en Armorique au moins, semble assez précisément lié aux pierres dressées : outre la spectaculaire stèle de Saint-Samson-sur-Rance (Le Roux à paraître), deux autres cas en ont été récemment recensés en Bretagne intérieure (Le Roux et Le Goffic 1996).

Fig 3.5: Saint-Quay-Perros (Côtes-d'Armor), tombe à entrée latérale de Crec'h-Quillé: orthostate-stèle orné d'une paire de seins et d'un "collier" face à l'entrée.

IV – Pour conclure

A l'issue de ce tour d'horizon, il convient tout d'abord de résister à la tentation de "voir des stèles partout". Dans la grande majorité des tombes mégalithiques armoricaines, rien de décisif ne vient plaider en ce sens et, même parmi les exemples cités, le lecteur aura perçu que bon nombre ne se situent qu'au niveau d'une "hypothèse de travail" restant à valider à la faveur d'une étude plus poussée. Néanmoins, les situations flagrantes sont assez nombreuses pour que le phénomène puisse être perçu comme une composante non négligeable du mégalithisme régional et pas simplement comme une curiosité ponctuelle.

On a vu au fil de ces pages que la présence – primaire ou en réemploi – de stèles dans les tombes mégalithiques s'observe dès la "première génération" de celles-ci, en plein 5ème millénaire B.C. pour devenir fréquente et volontiers spectaculaire dans le grand mégalithisme morbihannais à la charnière des 5ème et 4ème millénaires. On a vu aussi que le phénomène ne s'est pas cantonné aux tombes à couloir mais qu'il s'est aussi exprimé dans les grands tumulus carnacéens (Mané-er-Hroeg) et dans les tertres tumulaires (le Manio). On aura enfin noté que cette tradition a perduré sous une forme atténuée jusque dans les galeries funéraires du Néolithique final.

Fig 3.6: Trebeurden (Côtes-d'Armor), allée-couverte de Prajou-Menhir: le grand orthostate orné d'"écussons" et de "palettes" séparant la cella *de la chambre principale.*

Mais le phénomène ne s'arrête pas là. Dans le tumulus de Kersandy à Plouhinec (Finistère), la tombe centrale (au mobilier bien caractéristique de la "première série" des Tumulus Armoricains) était recouverte d'une grande dalle-idole scutiforme (Briard 1984). Tout le problème est d'apprécier dans quelle mesure ce réemploi – bien daté par le radiocarbone dans le deuxième quart du second millénaire B.C. – est encore assorti d'une connotation sacrée comparable à celle que l'on perçoit dans la plupart des situations comparables du Néolithique. La perduration des traditions techniques du mégalithisme dans l'architecture tumulaire des "petits princes d'Armorique" et les différents exemples de continuité culturelle que J. Briard a pu mettre en évidence, par exemple sur le site de Saint-Just entre bien d'autres (Briard *et al.* 1995), amènent à penser qu'une certaine vénération de la "Dame de Kersandy" par le "Sire de Plouhinec" et ses "exécuteurs testamentaires" du Bronze ancien devait être encore bien réelle, malgré les bouleversements techniques, sociaux et culturels ayant accompagné la mise en place de la première véritable culture du métal en Armorique.

Notes

1　Pour la description des décors évoqués dans cet article, il convient de se reporter aux deux ouvrages-clés que sont le *Corpus des signes gravés des monuments mégalithiques du Morbihan* (Péquart *et al.* 1927) et *The Megalithic Art of Western Europe* (Shee Twohig 1981) dont les appels n'ont pas été répétés pour ne pas alourdir le texte. Les références des dalles données renvoient à la nomenclature de ce dernier.

Bibliography

Bailloud, G., Boujot, C., Cassen, S. et Le Roux, C.-T. 1995 *Carnac. Les premières architectures de pierre.* CNMHS / CNRS-Editions, Paris.

Briard, J. 1984 *Les tumulus d'Armorique.* (coll. l'Age du Bronze en France 3), Picard, Paris.

Briard, J., Gautier, M. et Le Roux, G. 1995 *Les mégalithes et les tumulus de Saint-Just, Ille-et-Vilaine.* Document de Préhistoire **8**, CTHS, Paris.

Devoir, A. 1911 Essai d'interprétation d'une gravure mégalithique. Le grand support orné de la "Table des Marchands", *Bulletin de la Société archéologique du Finistère* **38**, 292–317.

Fouquet, A. 1874 Tombeau découvert près de la Haye en Saint-Gravé, *Bulletin de la Société polymathique du Morbihan* **18**, 122–241.

Gaillard, F. 1883 Rapport sur les fouilles aux dolmens de Port-blanc, Saint-Pierre-Quiberon, *Bulletin de la Société polymathique du Morbihan* **27**, 6–29.

Giot, P.-R. 1960 Une statue-menhir en Bretagne (ou le mystère archéologique de la femme coupée en morceaux), *Bulletin de la Société préhistorique française* **57**, 317–30.

Giot, P.-R. 1971 Informations archéologiques. Circonscription de Bretagne, *Gallia-Préhistoire* **14**, 339–61.

Giot, P.-R. 1987 *Barnenez, Carn, Guennoc.* Travaux du Laboratoire "Anthropologie, Préhistoire, Protohistoire et Quaternaire armoricains", Rennes.

Lecornec, J. 1994a *Le Petit Mont, Arzon, Morbihan.* Dossiers archéologique de l'Ouest, R.A.O., Rennes.

Lecornec, J. 1994b Les stèles et statues menhirs ou litholâtrie du Néolithique à l'Age du Fer, *Bulletin de la Société polymathique du Morbihan* **120**, 41–51.

Lecornec, J. 1997 Réflexions autour de Petit Mont à Arzon, Morbihan. In J. L'Helgouac'h *et al.* (dir.) Art et symboles du mégalithisme européen (actes du 2e colloque international sur l'art mégalithique, Nantes 1995) 125–32. *Revue archéologique de l'Ouest,* supplément **8,** Rennes.

Lefebvre, L. et Galles, R. 1863 Mané er Hroeck, dolmen découvert sous un tumulus à Locmariaquer, *Bulletin de la Société polymathique du Morbihan* **7,** 18–33.

Le Goffic, M. 1994 Le dolmen de Ti-ar-Boudiged en Brennilis, *Bulletin de la Société archéologique du Finistère,* **123,** 131–62.

Le Roux, C.-T. 1985 *Gavrinis et les îles du Golfe.* Guides archéologiques de la France 6, Ministère de la Culture / Imprimerie nationale, Paris.

Le Roux, C.-T. 1992 The Art of Gavrinis presented in its Armorican context and in comparison with Ireland, *Journal of the Royal Society of Antiquaries of Ireland* **122,** 79–108.

Le Roux, C.-T. 1995 *Gavrinis.* Gisserot, Paris.

Le Roux, C.-T. 1997 L'art mégalithique armoricain : pour les vivants, pour les morts, pour les esprits? In A. Rodriguez Casal (ed.) *O Neolitico atlantico e as Orixes do Megalitismo* (actes du colloque UISPP de Santiago 1996), 763–78. Universidade de Santiago de Compostela.

Le Roux, C.-T. 1998 Quelques réflexions sur l'art mégalithique d'Armorique et d'ailleurs, *Groupe vendéen d'Etudes préhistoriques* **34,** 52–00.

Le Roux, C.-T. 1999 Du menhir à la statue dans le mégalithisme armoricain. Actes du 2e colloque international sur la statuaire mégalithique, St. Pons 1997, *Archéologie en Languedoc* **22,** 237–54.

Le Roux, C.-T. 2003 L'art mégalithique armoricain face aux préhistoriens… et aux autres! In R. de Balbin Berhrmann y P. Bueno Ramirez (eds) *El Arte prehistorico desde los inicios del siglo XXI* (primer simposio internacional de Arte prehistorico de Ribadesella), 441–55. Asociacion cultural Amigos de Ribadesella.

Le Roux, C.-T. et Le Goffic, M. 1997 L'art des mégalithes en schiste de Bretagne centrale (actes du colloque de Nantes, 1995). En J. L'Helgouac'h *et al.* (dir.) Art et symboles du mégalithisme européen (actes du 2e colloque international sur l'art mégalithique, Nantes 1995) 133–48. *Revue archéologique de l'Ouest,* supplément **8,** Rennes.

Le Rouzic, Z. 1911 Dolmen à galerie et à grand dallage du Mané Lud, *Bulletin de la Société polymathique du Morbihan* **55,** 225–32.

Le Rouzic, Z. 1915 Dolmen à coupole et à galerie de l'Île-longue, *Bulletin de la Société polymathique du morbihan* **58.** 114–8.

Le Rouzic, Z. et Péquart, S.-J. 1923 (rééd. 1931) Carnac. Fouilles faites dans la région. Campagne 1922. Berger-Levrault, Nancy.

L'Helgouac'h, J. 1965 *Les sépultures mégalithiques en Armorique.* Travaux du Laboratoire d'Anthropologie, faculté des Sciences, Rennes.

L'Helgouac'h, J. 1967a Fouille de l'allée couverte de Prajou-Menhir en Trebeurden (Côtes-du-Nord), *Bulletin de la Société préhistorique française* **63,** 312–42.

L'Helgouac'h, J. 1967b La sépulture mégalithique à entrée latérale de Crec'h-Quillé en Saint-Quay-Perros (Côtes-du-Nord), *Bulletin de la Société préhistorique française* **63,** 659–98.

L'Helgouac'h, J. 1983 Les idoles qu'on abat… (ou les vissicitudes des grandes stèles de Locmariaquer), *Bulletin de la Société polymathique du Morbihan* **110,** 57–68.

L'Helgouac'h, J. 1997 De la lumière aux Ténèbres. En J. L'Helgouac'h *et al.* (dir.) Art et symboles du mégalithisme européen (actes du 2e colloque international sur l'art mégalithique, Nantes 1995), 107–23. *Revue archéologique de l'Ouest,* supplément **8,** Rennes.

Martin, A. 1911 Le dolmen de Kermarc à Languidic (Morbihan). Les dolmens à chambre circulaire et les dolmens à enceintes murales de l'Armorique, *Bulletin de la Société archéologique du Finistère* **38,** 88–118.

Minot, R.S. 1964 *Les monuments mégalithiques de l'Île-aux-Moines.* Société polymathique du Morbihan, Vannes.

Péquart, M., Péquart, S.-J. et Le Rouzic, Z. 1927 *Corpus des signes gravés des monuments mégalithiques du Morbihan.* Picard/ Berger-Levrault, Paris.

Salmon, P. 1893 La galerie couverte des Pierres-plates, *Revue anthropologique,* 17–9.

Shee Twohig, E. 1981 *The Megalithic Art of Western Europe.* Clarendon, Oxford.

4. Do you repair the homes of the Gods?

Frances Lynch

Today we are familiar with the concept of 'status' in prehistory, in fact it has become an almost universal context for explanation. In looking at the huge stone tombs of the Neolithic period in western Europe, and at the rather less stupendous but often striking monuments of the Bronze Age, it is easy for us to appreciate that they were designed to impress, even though we now see them in a ruined state. Excavation has also told us that their active history is usually a long one and that many may have been quite radically modified during this period of use, before natural decay and eventual damage took their toll. What has been less often discussed are the regular maintenance routines which must have been necessary to keep the monuments looking impressive and safe to enter and use. Or did this not matter – is it simply a modern concern, too anachronistic to be of value?

It gives me great pleasure to offer these few thoughts on this question to George Eogan whose own work has involved him so closely in the elucidation of these stone monuments and also in their repair and display to impress new generations of visitors. In particular it is presented in memory of a very scary crawl down the passage of the eastern tomb at Knowth, with George blithely commenting on the apparent deterioration of the structure since he had been through it the previous year! The situation wasn't helped by the failure of the torch halfway down!

Megalithic tombs are the product of very sophisticated engineering knowledge and a deep understanding of the properties of stone and the way in which it will behave, either as large blocks or as smaller drystone constructions. The absurdly time-consuming construction of Stonehenge reveals that those who worked in other traditions did not necessarily have that knowledge and points up the confidence of those who did.

We can work out the principles on which the buildings were erected but it is difficult to know the details of how the projects were managed, how many workers, how many directors, how long the work took, was it continuous, was it seasonal? The size of the workforce is relevant to the amount of 'administrative infra-structure' which would be needed, for a large number of people, like a mediaeval king's retinue, would soon eat out the resources of the locality, even if religious enthusiasm kept them going for some time. Though most monuments are built from local materials, some of the larger ones, such as Newgrange, contain elements brought from afar. The famous quartz and granite wall at Newgrange came from distant regions to the north and south of the Boyne and arrangements of a quite complex nature must have been made to bring that special stone to the site. The assembly of Edward I's workforce for castle building in Wales in the thirteenth century (Taylor 1961) demonstrates how efficient mediaeval administration could be, but that does pre-suppose a nationwide government structure in place. How far did the writ of those building Newgrange run?

In professional architectural matters the building of Newgrange demonstrates a similar forethought. The system of guttering over the passage shows that the problem of water ingress due to surface tension was anticipated and the solution worked out in advance. The cutting of the gutters was not a response to a problem observed once the passage was built, for a stone with a ready-cut gutter was eventually used as an upright stone at the entrance. The elaborate 'roofbox' and the slot through which the sun enters and strikes along the passage to the chamber is further evidence of the precision and attention to detail in the original construction of the monument which clearly envisaged that people would continue to visit it over a long period.

In view of this evidence for care and skill in construction it is all the more astonishing to see that K96, the kerbstone just 5m away from the entrance on the right hand side, fell forward at an early stage and was never re-erected (Fig 4.1; O'Kelly 1982, 68–9). The fall of this stone must have brought down a considerable length of the wall above it and created a scar across the monumental facade of the tomb where no visitor could fail to notice it. The evidence for this having happened at an early date is the cleanliness of the surface beneath it. No minor stones had fallen from the wall (as they did eventually all the way round) and there was no sign of a grass surface having developed, although regular stripping may have occurred

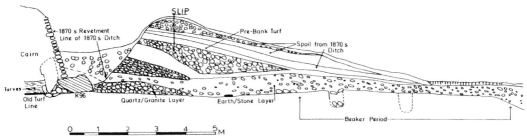

Fig 4.1: Newgrange. Section showing the fallen Kerbstone K96, old ground surface and slip of cairn. Reproduced from O'Kelly 1982 with permission.

(O'Kelly 1982, 127). In any case it happened during the period when there was active maintenance of the perimeter, but that maintenance did not include structural repair.

Perhaps as a result of this early disruption the quartz and granite wall had collapsed almost entirely by the time the cairn became fringed with hearths and informal settlement debris associated with the use of Beakers in about 2500 Cal. BC. Perhaps by then, some 600 years after the tomb was built, knowledge of the original profile of the cairn had been lost and the site, obviously still important as a focus for ritual, was not recognised as in decay. At Knowth, too, this late Neolithic period was one where there was a lot of activity around monuments in increasing disarray. My point, however, concerns the earlier period of limited damage that might perhaps have been repaired, and was not.

A similar situation seems to have occurred at Ti-ar-Boudiged, Brennilis, in Brittany where a kerbstone, not set into the ground but simply leaning against the side of the cairn, fell forwards at a time when Beaker pottery was in use. It was never set upright again, although it would have been simple to do so (Le Goffic 1994).

The tall facade stones of Irish Court Tombs are vulnerable to collapse but it is often difficult to pinpoint the time at which it happened. At Annaghmare, Co. Armagh, however, the fallen stone is overlaid by the deliberate blocking of the forecourt so it had clearly fallen forward at a time when the tomb was still being used/ visited by those who understood and venerated its primary role (Waterman 1965, 13). The blocking of forecourts seems to be a regular part of Neolithic rituals associated with these tombs, though we do not understand what it symbolised. It does not necessarily represent complete finality, but at Annaghmare those constructing the blocking obviously had no interest in setting the facade to rights before they started work.

It is difficult to know how Neolithic society would have measured spans of time. Obviously the year would have been a recognisable unit, but how far into the past or into the future would an individual's consciousness have stretched – and how far would a community's consciousness stretch? In Rome the cycle of the *Ludi Saeculares* began again when all those who had attended

the previous one had died. Perhaps some similar cycle might have punctuated the forward planning of the Neolithic. Back projection is less of a problem; it could be almost indefinitely extended by story telling. The individual lifespan would have been relatively short, yet they were building with permanence in mind. In wood-using traditions that permanence would only be gained after a number of regular stages had been gone through. How was the future ensured for a wooden chamber conceived as a final, permanent earthen long barrow? All this would suggest that the role of future generations was envisaged by the original builders and that their mind-set included a vision of the monument in a future period.

Ever since the 1960s archaeologists have realised that Neolithic tombs were modified, often in quite radical ways, during their period of active use. This normally involved the addition of extra chambers or changes to the cairn shape; sometimes within the same tradition and even planned for, as at Barnes Lower (Collins 1966), sometimes within an alien tradition reflecting the adoption of new ideas, as at Carnedd Hengwm South (Lynch 1976, 69–70). Obviously, therefore, there is no taboo against touching the house of the dead or the home of the ancestors once it has been constructed, and indeed this was necessary in some traditions, yet the idea of simple repair to elements visibly damaged is not easy to chronicle. In modern society perhaps the analogy is with cathedrals and other major churches where damaged and unfinished elements remain, and are acceptable for centuries, a situation which people would not accept in their homes.

Our traditional view of Bronze Age monuments is that they are not designed for such long-term interest but have more to do with the immediate celebration of an individual and his/her power. But in fact radiocarbon dates are showing that even seemingly simple mounds may have remained meaningful to their communities for up to a thousand years and to have been enlarged and changed on more than one occasion. It is equally relevant, therefore, to look at the question of maintenance and repair of these monuments too.

The simple mound of chalk, turves or stone is not a structure that needs very elaborate maintenance except to retain a profile and a colour distinction for a period. Certainly all have lost such finesse by now and it would

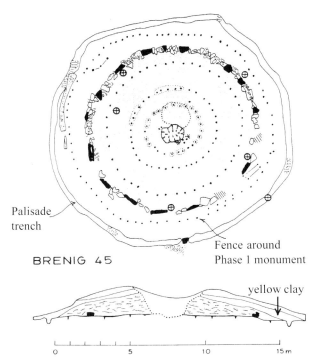

Palisade
trench

BRENIG 45

Fence around
Phase 1 monument

yellow clay

Fig 4.2: Brenig 45. Plan showing stake circles of which the outermost one was a free-standing fence. The section shows the final skin of yellow clay. Reproduced from Lynch 1993.

be difficult to judge how long they might have retained it in the Bronze Age. The elegant concave curves of the first stone mound at Trelystan I preserved beneath the turf enlargement reveal how carefully the surface of a cairn might be finished (Britnell 1982, fig 14, section FE) and the multiple stake fences around turf drums must surely relate to efforts to maintain a sharp profile.

Bright white chalk mounds in a green landscape make sense of the obsession with banks and berms which forms the element of architectural distinction in the Wessex Bronze Age. The experimental earthworks have shown that mounds and banks would have retained the whiteness longer than ditches (Jewell 1963) thereby intensifying the geometry. In other regions colour distinctions might be less sharp but excavations in Denbighshire have revealed that the barrows were given a final covering of yellow clay (Lynch 1993, 85). Eventually most of this outer skin tended to slip to the perimeter and, if not weeded, it is unlikely that it would remain vegetation-free for long.

One of the turf mounds in the Brenig valley, Brenig 45, which had a complex history of enlargement, was at one stage contained within a rather unstable kerb formed by small uprights with dry-walling between and topped by a scatter of stones set on the sloping surface of the mound (Fig 4.2). As shown by the scatter of stones outside this kerb, it was not a satisfactory edge and a metre or so outside there was a hurdle fence which enclosed the mound and some wooden features just outside it. It is tempting to suggest that this fence was set up to prevent animals and others from scrambling on the mound and

pulling down more of the unsatisfactory edging. At a later date the mound was enlarged further and given a solid palisade as its final kerb (Lynch 1993, 74). Here it would seem there was active concern to maintain the appearance of the monument and prevent further deterioration.

The interior of ring monuments of various kinds, stone circles, ring cairns and the like, might also be defined by colour variation which would need to be maintained. At Cefn Caer Euni I in Merioneth the interior of the kerb circle was spread with a uniform layer of imported yellow clay which would have helped to emphasise the form of the monument (Lynch 1986a, 88). At Brenig 44 the large interior space of the ring cairn was stripped of turf after the stone ring had been built and at that site it was possible to show that this bare yellow surface had been maintained by more than one stripping episode (Fig 4.3; Lynch 1993, 118). This was a monument that had a history of at least 500 years so, if the bare interior was important, it would certainly have needed maintenance. The stone ring was originally surrounded by a timber circle but this was removed when some of the uprights began to decay (some were rotten and left in the ground, others were still sufficiently robust to be removed entirely) and some of the stones had fallen from the ring. These changes would seem to have been a genuine refurbishment, rather than significant change, since rituals within the circle continued as before. At another similar monument on the slopes of Moel Goedog in Merioneth the interior was kept in a tidy state by the occasional addition of a thin layer of soil, rather than its subtraction (Lynch 1984, 16).

In the Bronze Age, therefore, despite the lack of grand constructions on the scale of Newgrange and Knowth, there seems to have been a concern with maintaining a clean and tidy appearance to the monuments, at least in north Wales.

Turning from artefacts in the landscape, subject to the effects of weather and gravity and the human desire for change, to artefacts in the hand and on the hearth, subject to the wear and tear of everyday use, one can see some oddities in the treatment of damage which merit some comment even if no firm conclusions can be reached.

Pottery is such a boon to archaeologists because it is so easily broken and frequently thrown away, either carelessly or with ceremony. Prehistoric pottery might still be usable when broken (*e.g.* Lynch 1993, 129) but was seldom repaired. There are some instances of large urns having been drilled for a thong to hold them together (*e.g.* Lynch 1984, 31–2), perhaps when biscuit dry rather than when fully fired, since drilling would then be difficult, but this is rare even when the pots represent a considerable investment of work (see Longworth 1984 *passim*). However there is one strange exception – a great deal of effort has been spent on the appalling jars from Simon's Ground, Dorset, sewn back together like a patchwork quilt (White 1982, G30, pl. 13)!

Repair of tools is not very commonly seen, perhaps because we seldom have the handles and other vulnerable

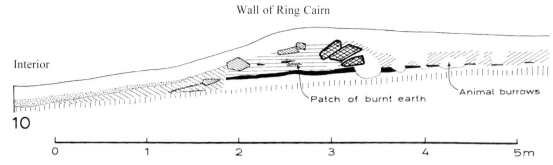

Fig 4.3: Brenig 44. Section 10 across ring cairn wall showing old ground surface cut by shaving of interior surface. Inner and outer banks (shown by diagonal hatching) were eventually built against the enclosing wall. Reproduced from Lynch 1993.

parts surviving. Stone and metal blades when broken are more often cut down and modified to some other purpose rather than mended in the true sense (*e.g.* Dowris no. 3, Eogan 1983, 120). Metal would usually have been melted down and all the cut up pieces in Late Bronze Age hoards are testimony to the frequency of this process. But occasionally there are pieces which have been carefully mended so that they can continue to fulfil their original role. A Ewart Park sword in Bangor Museum (Lynch 1986b, no. 126) and another from Park, Co. Meath (Eogan 1983, 113) have hilt plates neatly mended with run-on metal, a process which demands considerable skill. The mend is discreet, as one would expect today in such an operation where we hope that the damage will not be noticed.

We would judge such an attitude to be even more appropriate in the case of fine craftsmanship where the beauty of the piece would be disrupted by a visible patch or a re-worked seam. In the Early Bronze Age this is indeed the case. On the fine amber dagger pommel from Hameldon Down the tiny gold nails replicate the original work very carefully (Gerloff 1975, pl. 18, no. 194). In the Late Bronze Age sheet metalwork was frequently re-paired. Cauldrons must have been symbols of hospitality and wealth and, as such, were often offered to the gods but not before most of them had had heavy use and repair. These patches are normally quite straightforward, neither concealed nor flaunted, but simply functional.

However, on Iron Age pieces there are some surprisingly ostentatious patches, not only riveted to the outside but carrying ornament at variance to the original. Perhaps the most famous such piece is the Attic *kylix* from Klein Aspergle near Stuttgart, broken and mended and the cracks then covered with flamboyant gold foil (Megaw 1970, 60–1). It might not have been a very desirable cup in its homeland but by the time it had travelled to southern Germany it must have gained value and it was not thrown away. Its accident was not to be concealed but rather its recovery celebrated.

The elegantly decorated pony cap from Torrs, Kirkcud-brightshire, is perhaps the best known example from Britain. There are three patches on this cap (Atkinson

Fig 4.4: The Torrs Chamfrein. Reproduced from Atkinson and Piggott 1955 with permission of the Society of Anti-quaries.

and Piggott 1955, Fig 4.4). They are carefully shaped and decorated by engraving, a technique not found on the main piece. The style of decoration is similar to that on the associated drinking horns but it is impossible to guess what they might have belonged to originally. Another example is the decorated strip covering a gap in the seam of the trumpet from Llyn Cerrig Bach (Fox 1946, pl. XXXI). The original riveting is exceptionally neat and precise, yet attention is deliberately drawn to a fault in it. The Loughnashade trumpet has also got some interesting repairs (Raftery 1983, no. 781). There are several plain patches but one has a carefully cut wavy edge and one is D-shaped. The D-shaped patch appears again on the Ballyedmond Iron Age cauldron (Raftery 1983, no. 556) where one is elaborately decorated with small bosses. The D-shaped patch is relatively common and appears to be a semi-decorative device at a point where one might have expected an effort to conceal.

As at Klein Aspergle it may have become important to retain a visual record or memorial of the history of some especially potent objects, objects where artistic perfection was secondary to their long-standing role in family or political history. (I owe this insight to a comment made by Prof. Miranda Green at a conference where I first presented some of these ideas.) The crooked cross on the crown of St. Stephen of Hungary and the gash across the cheek of Our Lady of Czestochowa might be later examples.

Bibliography

Atkinson, R.J.C. and Piggott, S. 1955 The Torrs Chamfrein, *Archaeologia* **96**, 197–235.

Britnell, W.J. 1982 The excavation of two Round Barrows at Trelystan, Powys, *Proceedings of the Prehistoric Society* **48**, 133–201.

Collins, A.E.P. 1966 Barnes Lower Court Cairn, Co. Tyrone, *Ulster Journal of Archaeology* **29**, 43–75.

Eogan, G. 1983 *The Hoards of the Irish Later Bronze Age*. Dublin.

Fox, C. 1946 *A find of the Early Iron Age from Llyn Cerrig Bach, Anglesey*. National Museum of Wales, Cardiff.

Gerloff, S. 1975 *The Early Bronze Age Daggers in Great Britain and a Reconsideration of the Wessex Culture*. Prähistorische Bronzefunde VI. 2, Munich.

Jewell, P.A. 1963 *The Experimental Earthwork on Overton Down, Wiltshire*. London.

Le Goffic, M. 1994 Le Dolmen de Ti-ar-Boudiged en Brennilis, *Bulletin de la Société Archéologique du Finistère* **123**, 131–62.

Longworth, I.H. 1984 *Collared Urns of the Bronze Age in Great Britain and Ireland*. Cambridge University Press, Cambridge.

Lynch, F.M. 1976 Towards a Chronology of Megalithic Tombs in Wales. In G.C. Boon and J.M. Lewis (ed.) *Welsh Antiquity: Essays presented to H.N. Savory*, 63–79. National Museum of Wales, Cardiff.

Lynch, F.M. 1984 Moel Goedog Circle I, a Complex Ring Cairn near Harlech, *Archaeologia Cambrensis* **133**, 8–50.

Lynch, F.M. 1986a Excavation of Kerb Circle and Ring Cairn on Cefn Caer Euni, Merioneth, *Archaeologia Cambrensis* **135**, 81–102.

Lynch, F.M. 1986b *Catalogue of Archaeological Material in Bangor Museum*. Bangor.

Lynch, F.M. 1993 *Excavations in the Brenig Valley: A Mesolithic and Bronze Age Landscape in North Wales*. Cambrian Archaeological Monograph **5**, Cardiff.

Megaw, J.V.S. 1970 *Art of the European Iron Age*. Bath.

O'Kelly, M.J. 1982 *Newgrange, Archaeology, Art and Legend*, London.

Raftery, B. 1983 *A Catalogue of Irish Iron Age Antiquities*. Marburg.

Taylor, A.J. 1961 Castle-building in Wales in the later thirteenth century: the prelude to construction. In E.M. Jope (ed.) *Studies in Building History: Essays in Recognition of the work of B.H. St J O'Neil*, 104–33. London.

Waterman, D.M. 1965 The Court Cairn at Annaghmare, Co. Armagh, *Ulster Journal of Archaeology* **28**, 3–46.

White, D.A. 1982 *The Bronze Age Cremation Cemeteries at Simon's Ground, Dorset*. Dorset Archaeological and Natural History Society Monograph **3**.

5. Going round in circles? Understanding the Irish Grooved Ware 'complex' in its wider context

Alison Sheridan

Introduction

"It therefore appears that the Grooved Ware element at Brugh na Bóinne, particularly at Knowth, is more than just a ritual and material replacement and modification. It may have a wider significance, such as indicating the emergence of a new settlement pattern indicating a high status ritual tradition but of a different nature to that represented by passage tombs. It is not native but a complex that spread into Brugh na Bóinne. Its arrival appears to have diminished the importance of the passage tomb complex and led to its replacement...It is considered that the background to the Brugh na Bóinne Grooved Ware complex is in Britain, but from where has yet to be established." (Eogan and Roche 1999, 108, 109)

The first half of the third millennium BC was a time of significant change in parts of Ireland and Britain, with the widespread adoption of a new pottery style that had already been in use in Orkney (Grooved Ware), and of ceremonial practices that often featured the use of circular structures of timber, stone, earth or a combination of these materials. Our understanding of this time of change has been enhanced in recent years, both by new discoveries (*e.g.* of circular timber structures at Knowth, Co. Meath (Eogan and Roche 1997, 101–96, Appendix 2; 1999) and Ballynahatty, Co. Down (Hartwell 1998), and by reappraisals of Grooved Ware (Cleal and MacSween 1999), of timber circles (Gibson 1998) and of henges (Harding 2003; O'Brien in press). However, many questions remain as to the 'how?', 'why?' and 'when?' of this process of change.

As far as Ireland is concerned, the contribution made by George Eogan to the archaeology of this intriguing period cannot be overstated: it is thanks to George's work at Knowth that the existence of Irish Grooved Ware has received widespread recognition; his excavation of a well-stratified, Grooved Ware-associated timber structure there has helped to transform our understanding of activities in the Boyne Valley (Eogan 1991; Eogan and Roche 1994; 1997; 1999). The extract of his recent publication cited above shows, as ever, that George gets to the heart of the

matter and poses the most percipient and challenging questions. It is therefore with some trepidation, as well as with the warmest best wishes, gratitude and respect for a great scholar, that this author offers some comments on the Irish Grooved Ware 'complex' in its wider context. In attempting to understand this phenomenon, the importance of focusing not just on local-level changes but also on the wider picture – an approach exemplified *par excellence* by George's work on the Neolithic of the Boyne Valley (*e.g.* Eogan 1980) – will be underlined.

The Irish Grooved Ware 'complex'

In addressing the question 'What constitutes the Irish Grooved Ware "complex"?', it is not intended to present an exhaustive review of the evidence, as this has already been undertaken to a large degree by others (Eogan and Roche 1997, 101–222, Appendix 2; 1999; Brindley 1999a; 1999b; Roche and Eogan 2001). Essentially, the 'complex' has been loosely defined around the pottery itself, associated material culture and associated contexts, and each will be considered briefly below. This section will conclude with some comments regarding the overall nature and duration of the Irish Grooved Ware 'complex'.

Grooved Ware pottery

The existence of Grooved Ware in Ireland was first raised as a possibility by Sean P. Ó Ríordáin in 1951, in his discussion of pottery from the embanked stone circle at Grange, Lough Gur, Co. Limerick; but, as noted above, the idea did not gain widespread acceptance until Eogan's publication of the 'classic' example from Knowth tomb 6 (Eogan 1984, fig. 118; *cf.* Sheridan 1995, 15). Since then the number of Irish Grooved Ware findspots has risen steeply, and continues to rise, especially in those parts of eastern Ireland affected by the current road-building boom (H. Roche and A. Brindley pers comm.).

There is still some difference of opinion as to what constitutes Irish Grooved Ware, with Anna Brindley identifying its presence at 13 sites (plus one 'possible' at

Ballyvaston, Co. Antrim: Brindley 1999a, 24, 30, 32–3), and Eogan and Roche (1999) citing 12 definite findspots – not all matching the Brindley list – plus four 'possibles'. (The latter included the henge at Monknewtown, Co. Meath, but this has subsequently been ruled out: H. Roche pers comm.). The latest distribution map was published in 2001 (Roche and Eogan 2001, fig. 19), and comprised 17 findspots, but, as indicated above, this already needs to be revised.

Brindley has proposed a typological scheme for Irish Grooved Ware, eschewing the Longworth terminology (Wainwright and Longworth 1971) in favour of five 'types': the relatively highly decorated 'Kiltierney' and 'Knowth' types, which she tentatively dates to *c.* 3000 BC; the much plainer 'Dundrum-Longstone' and 'Donegore-Duntryleague' types, which appear to date to 2500/ 2400 BC; and the highly decorated 'Grange-Geroid Island' type, whose date is harder to estimate, not least because the two available radiocarbon dates fall below current standards of acceptability (Brindley 1999a, 31). All these types (excepting the 'Grange-Geroid Island' type, represented only by small sherds) have widespread parallels in Britain. The 'Dundrum-Longstone' type is by far the commonest, and this is the type associated with the Knowth timber circle and with other similar post/post-and-pit/pit circles (see below). It should be noted that although Brindley's argument for a mid-third millennium use for 'Dundrum-Longstone' type Grooved Ware seems valid, one must also consider the possibility that its use may have started earlier: comparable pottery appears to have been in use in Scotland slightly earlier in the third millennium BC at Balfarg, Fife (immediately pre-dating construction of the timber ring there: Mercer 1981, fig. 44 and 80–1; Henshall and Mercer 1981).

The question of the distribution and dating of British parallels for Irish Grooved Ware will be discussed further below.

Associated material culture

The question arises as to whether there is a distinctive set of artefact types or technologies that is mainly or exclusively connected with Grooved Ware in Ireland, as has been claimed to exist for parts of England (*e.g.* oblique arrowheads, including ripple-flaked and polished examples: Manby 1974; 1988, 59–64; 1999; Durden 1995; Edmonds 1995, 100; and see below for comments on maceheads). The answer would appear to be a qualified 'Yes', at least as far as oblique arrowheads and discoidal polished knives are concerned. The former – described by Green as 'Irish oblique arrowheads' (1980, 103) – have been found in direct or indirect association with Grooved Ware at Knowth (Dillon 1997, 170, 195), Newgrange (Lehane 1983, 146–50) and Grange (Woodman 1994, 213). Further examples, without ceramic associations, have been found at the henges at Monknewtown, Co. Meath, and the Giant's Ring, Ballynahatty, Co. Antrim (Woodman 1994, 213); in

the Boyne Valley (Brady 2002); at Lough Eskragh, Co. Tyrone (Waddell 1998, fig. 24); and at several locations in Co. Antrim, including in a hoard from Three Towns, along with hollow scrapers (Flanagan 1966). As Green has pointed out, however, "the Irish oblique series is not at all comparable" with British examples (Green 1980, 111), and no example has yet been found of the extremely fine ripple-flaked oblique arrowheads so characteristic of the Yorkshire 'industry'. This may indicate that the Irish oblique arrowheads were an echo, albeit in distinctively Irish form, of a British arrowhead type. As for polished discoidal flint knives, roughouts (indicating local manufacture) and fragments have been found at Newgrange (Lehane 1983, 162–5), and there is at least one further find, unassociated with pottery, from Toome, Co. Antrim (on display in the National Museum of Ireland).

As for other potentially distinctive aspects of the Grooved Ware-associated lithic repertoire in Ireland, the flint assemblage found in the Knowth timber circle is indeed remarkable, insofar as it was made from imported Antrim flint (unlike earlier and later flint assemblages at Knowth) and is characterised by a broad flake technique, creating broad and thick scrapers (Eogan and Roche 1999, 101–2). To a degree, the Knowth flint assemblage technology is echoed at the Grooved Ware findspots at Newgrange, nearby, and at the Grange enclosure, Co. Limerick (Eogan and Roche 1994, 328); and it may also echo the technology used to produce scrapers in late Neolithic Yorkshire (Manby 1999, 67–8). The porcellanite axehead found at the Knowth timber circle represents another import from Co. Antrim (Eogan and Roche 1997, pl. 11), but does not stand out as being significantly different in shape or treatment from other Neolithic axeheads of this material.

It has been claimed that some ovoid and pestle-shaped stone maceheads in Ireland and Britain, including the two examples found in the two passage tombs under the largest mound at Knowth (Site 1: Eogan and Richardson 1982), are a distinctive element within a Grooved Ware 'package'[1] (*e.g.* Roe 1968; Simpson 1996a; Cooney 2000, 18; *cf.* Simpson 1996b on antler maceheads). Parallels have been drawn between the motifs used on some of the elaborate 'Maesmawr' type ovoid maceheads – including the superb flint specimen found inside the eastern tomb at Knowth Site 1 – and those found on some Grooved Ware sites (A. Barclay 1999, 19 – albeit in a late third millennium context at Radley). The connections between these motifs and passage tomb 'art' have also been explored (*e.g.* Simpson 1988; Barclay 1999, 19; Brindley 1999b) and will be returned to below. In Scotland and especially Orkney, there does indeed seem to have been a link between some maceheads and Grooved Ware use. Macehead fragments have been found at the Grooved Ware settlements of Skara Brae, Rinyo and Barnhouse (Clarke *et al.* 1985, 58; Simpson and Ransom 1992), and the suspiciously high concentration of deliberately-broken pestle maceheads in Orkney (Callander 1931, 91, 93–5), almost all of which have been found on the narrow, 3.3km long stretch of land extending north-westwards from the Stones of Stenness henge, between the Lochs of Harray and Stenness, has invited the suggestion of a specific ritual practice by Grooved Ware users (D. Clarke pers comm.). Further south in Scotland, a link with Grooved Ware is suggested by the co-occurrence of ovoid maceheads with: i) a Grooved Ware bowl and two edge-polished flint knives in the 'Clyde' chamber tomb at Tormore on Arran, within 1.5km of the Machrie Moor timber and stone circles (Henshall 1972, 305), and ii) oblique and transverse arrowheads of non-local black flint, plus part of an edge-polished rectangular flint knife, in the 'Orkney-Cromarty-Hebrides' chamber tomb at Ormiegill North, Caithness (Highland: Davidson and Henshall 1991, 70, 129–30). In both instances – as indeed has been claimed for the Knowth maceheads (*e.g.* Simpson 1996a, 69) – these items have been regarded as late deposits within a pre-existing monument.

In Ireland, however, there has been no *direct* association of a macehead with Grooved Ware pottery, although the discovery of an 'Orkney pestle' macehead in Lough Gur, not far from several findspots of Grooved Ware, may tentatively suggest such a link (Simpson 1988, no. 17; Eogan and Roche 1999, illus. 11.9). Whether the Knowth maceheads – and indeed the other maceheads found in the Boyne Valley (Simpson 1988, nos 15, 16) – were contemporary with any of the Grooved Ware from Knowth remains unprovable but, as will be argued below, is a distinct possibility. What also seems likely is that macehead use in Ireland, or at least *awareness* of maceheads, may pre-date the appearance of Irish Grooved Ware. This is suggested by the presence of pendants shaped like miniature pestle and ovoid maceheads in several passage tombs (*e.g.* Loughcrew cairn R2 and Fourknocks I, Co. Meath, and Carrowkeel cairn K, Co. Sligo), in apparent association with the coarse decorated pottery ('Carrowkeel ware') that is often found in such contexts (Herity 1974, 285, 287, 290). This point will be returned to below.

A final element of material culture that should be mentioned in connection with the Irish Grooved Ware 'complex' is the enigmatic fired clay objects found in the timber circle at Knowth (Eogan and Roche 1997, pl. 12, fig. 37, 185–7). Parallels have been cited from Grooved Ware contexts in Yorkshire (Carnaby Top) and Wessex (Durrington Walls: Eogan and Roche 1997, 186); others have been found in other Grooved Ware contexts in Ireland (H. Roche pers comm.). Described as 'spindle whorls' (Wainwright and Longworth 1971, fig. 82) and as resembling loom weights (Eogan and Roche 1999, 102), and invariably found broken, it is quite possible that they were deliberately broken as part of the ceremonies that took place at these special sites (*cf.* deliberate breakage of some of the Knowth flint scrapers and also, probably, the pots). They are not sufficiently similar in shape to stone maceheads to be regarded as obvious

proxies for (or skeuomorphs of) them; they may have fulfilled another role, probably in the preparations for the feasting that almost certainly occurred at these sites. The Dineleys have suggested that large Grooved Ware tubs could have been used for brewing alcoholic beverages for feasting (2000): if this was so, then could these conceivably be weights for organic pot covers?

Associated contexts

The most distinctive characteristic of the Grooved Ware 'complex' in Ireland concerns the contexts in which it has been found. There seems to be a marked incidence of finds from special purpose ceremonial sites such as the aforementioned timber circular structures, and there is also at least one instance where Grooved Ware was deposited during funerary rites (at Kiltierney, Co. Fermanagh; it is uncertain whether the Grooved Ware found in Knowth passage tombs 6 and 18, and at Loughcrew cairn L, accompanied burials: *cf.* Roche and Eogan 2001, 127–8). Instances of demonstrably 'everyday' domestic use are limited to the settlements at Geroid Island and on Knockadoon on Lough Gur (the latter not on Brindley's list of Grooved Ware findspots). Elsewhere, at both Knowth and Newgrange it remains a moot point whether the 'extensive habitation layer' represents everyday occupation rather than activities connected with perhaps seasonal ceremonies: it is questionable whether there had been any ordinary settlement activity in these numinous surroundings, especially if the ceremonial post/post-and-pit/pit structures described below had been in contemporary use (*contra* Eogan and Roche 1994, 328 and O'Kelly 1983, 10–39). With other finds (*e.g.* Duntryleague, Co. Tipperary: Brindley 1999a, 33) it is difficult to ascertain the nature of the activities that led to Grooved Ware deposition.

i) Circular post/post-and-pit/pit structures
The timber-built (and post-and-pit, and pit-defined) circular ceremonial 'structures' with which Grooved Ware has been associated represent a wholly novel phenomenon in Ireland (but see below on the possible dating of earthen henges); and their proximity to pre-existing sacred sites within the passage tomb tradition cannot have been coincidental. As will be seen below, they are likely to date to *c.* 2600/2450 BC (Brindley 1999a, 31; Eogan and Roche 1999, 109). The sites comprise:
• The aforementioned timber circles with internal post settings from Knowth and Ballynahatty, together with further possible examples from Fourknocks (King 1990, 77) and Bettystown, both Co. Meath (Roche and Eogan 2001, 137–8; excavated, appropriately enough, by James Eogan (1999); and Balgatheran, Co. Louth, *c.* 8km north of the Boyne (*Archaeology Ireland* 56, 6). The overall dimensions of the Knowth and Ballynahatty structures are 8.37 x 7.15m and 11 x 11m respectively. At Ballynahatty, where two

construction phases were identified, the four central posts had each been 1m wide and an estimated 9.5m+ long, and the structure was deliberately burnt down; at Knowth, the timbers were allowed to rot.

• A large (90m diameter), complex, pit-and-post 'circle' at Newgrange, encompassing a small pre-existing passage tomb and comprising six concentric rings of close-set postholes and pits; two upright stones once stood close to the outermost ring at the southwest (O'Kelly 1983; Sweetman 1985). The outer ring had held substantial posts; ring 2 comprised clay-lined pits in which burning had taken place; ring 3 comprised a mixture of clay-lined 'burning' pits, non-clay-lined pits and postholes; and rings 4–6 consisted of small pits in which burnt animal remains (of butchery refuse parts, mainly from pig, but also from ox, deer, dog and sheep or goat) had been deposited. The arc of the outer ring intersects that of the 'Great Stone Circle' around the main Newgrange passage tomb, and Sweetman has argued (contra O'Kelly 1983) that the stone circle post-dates the pit-and-post circle (*cf.* Stout 2002, 36). However, as Bradley has pointed out (1998, 3–6), only further fieldwork can resolve any lingering confusion as to the relative date of these structures.

• Two smaller 'pit circles' at Newgrange, one (represented by two successive rings of pits *c.* 12m in diameter: Brindley 1999a, 33–4) inside the large pit-and-post circle and the other *c.* 50m to the west of the main passage tomb (Sweetman 1987). According to Sweetman, the latter started as a circle of large pits some 20m in diameter, clay-lined and with signs of burning in them (although not closely comparable with the clay-lined pits of the large circle at Newgrange). These were then filled in and succeeded by a circular roofed timber structure *c.* 13m in diameter (Sweetman 1987, figs 5, 6).

The Knowth circle was located close to the entrance to the eastern tomb in the massive Site 1 mound, while the large pit-and-post circle at Newgrange is very close to the main Newgrange passage tomb and echoes it in diameter. The Ballynahatty circle (BNH6), and the larger, apparently associated enclosure in which it lies (and which creates for it a sacred precinct, BNH5), is close to a simple passage tomb which may well date to the beginning of the fourth millennium (Sheridan 2003). It is also close to several cists containing 'Carrowkeel ware' bowls and unburnt and/or cremated human remains. Radiocarbon dates for some of these cremated bone deposits, and stratigraphic evidence relating to one cist, make it clear that these cists pre-dated the timber structures (A. Brindley and B. Hartwell pers comm.; Hartwell 1998, 44). The Giant's Ring henge is also in the vicinity, built to surround the passage tomb; given the topographical siting of the Ballynahatty timber structures, overlooking the henge (Hartwell 1998, 43), it seems likely that the henge was already in existence when they were built.

There is much uncertainty surrounding the original form and function of these structures, with Eogan and Roche favouring a roofed, non-funerary building for the Knowth circle (Bourke 1997), while Hartwell (1998, fig. 3.5) envisages an unroofed, enclosed exposure platform (*i.e.* for mortuary rites) for a structure with a markedly similar ground plan (*cf.* Gibson 1998, ch. 6). What commentators agree upon, however, is that feasting was an element of the associated ceremonies at or near these sites, with the remains of the feasts being deliberately inserted into some of the post-holes and pits.

The parallels that have been drawn between these sites and British structures include examples from southern England, with the Knowth timber circle being compared to slightly larger structures inside the 'super-henges' at Durrington Walls (Northern Circle) and Marden (Wainwright and Longworth 1971, figs 17, 87; Eogan and Roche 1999, 109). Even though the dating evidence for the Northern Circle at Durrington Walls is far from ideal (Gibson 1998, 34–5), it is at least possible that it is roughly contemporary with the Irish structures. Alex Gibson has suggested that the ovoid shape of the large Newgrange post-and-pit 'circle' may echo that of the timber circles at Durrington Walls South and Dorchester-on-Thames 3, and has hypothesised (not altogether convincingly) that the site might have been orientated on the midwinter sunrise – the same orientation as the main Newgrange passage tomb (Gibson 1998, 78). Whether or not this particular analogy is robust, one could point out that a further link with southern England is offered by the emphasis on pig remains at the Newgrange pit-and-post circle (and at Ballynahatty: Hartwell 1998, 43). This is reminiscent of Grooved Ware-associated feasting preferences in southern England (*e.g.* Durrington Walls: Wainwright and Longworth 1971, 188–91) and indeed also in Wales, as shown by lipid remains in the pottery (Dudd *et al.* 1999). The question of parallels will be returned to below.

ii) Other circular ceremonial structures: Grange and Longstone Cullen

The enclosure at Grange, Lough Gur, Co. Limerick, has been described by some as an embanked stone circle (*e.g.* Cooney 2000, 80) and discussed as an example of an Irish hengiform monument (Condit and Simpson 1998, 55). Although Grooved Ware is associated with it, and although the construction of the enclosure pre-dates Beaker-associated activity, the chronological relationship between the structure and the Grooved Ware is uncertain. Found in and under the bank, the Grooved Ware could pre-date the enclosure and be residual from earlier activities (as Brindley suggests: 1999a, 32); alternatively, Eogan and Roche have argued (1999, 108) that it was contemporary with the construction of the enclosure, being deliberately deposited opposite the entrance as a kind of 'foundation' deposit. For a radical new interpretation of the Grange monument see H. Roche (this volume).

Even more uncertainty surrounds the relative chronology of Grooved Ware and the enclosure at the 'hilltop henge' at Longstone Cullen, Co. Tipperary (Condit and Simpson 1998, 53, fig. 4.7), around 20km to the east of Lough Gur. Here, the largest assemblage of Grooved Ware yet found in Ireland was excavated (Roche and Eogan 2001, 138), but unfortunately the site remains unpublished, and there is a distinct possibility that the enclosure is of post-Neolithic date (*cf.* O'Brien's reassessment of the date of some other Irish hengiform sites: O'Brien in press). All that can be said is that the Grooved Ware definitely pre-dates Beaker activity at the site.

iii) Burial within a low stone circle at Kiltierney Deerpark, Co. Fermanagh

The Grooved Ware sherds from Kiltierney come from a multi-period cemetery for cremated remains, enclosed by a low stone circle around 10m in diameter with a discontinuous, stone-capped clay bank around part of its exterior; the excavators suggest it may be related to embanked stone circles (Daniells and Williams 1977). It lies close to the remains of a probable passage tomb cemetery, which may have been associated with a cursus-like structure. The Grooved Ware sherds were associated with a deposit of cremated bone in a rock-cut pit (Burial 4), to one side of the enclosed area. In the centre was a succession of two burials of cremated bone (Burial 7, the probable primary burial of the cemetery, underlying Burial 1), the lower one associated with beads of amber and ?stone, the upper one with three miniature macehead pendants and sherds of 'Carrowkeel' ware. This site is important as it suggests some continuity in funerary practice between the users of 'Carrowkeel' and Grooved Ware pottery, with the latter probably post-dating the former, but not necessarily by long.

The nature, date and duration of the Irish Grooved Ware 'complex'

From the opening quote to this article, it is clear that Eogan and Roche regard the appearance of Grooved Ware in the Boyne Valley as part of a significant change in the Boyne Valley social order, with the elite no longer deriving their power from the ancestral/cosmological authority vested in the passage tomb cemeteries. Instead, the new focus for ceremonial activities was provided by the various ceremonial structures outlined above (along with earthen henges). They do not go so far as to argue for the arrival of new people (although *cf.* Eogan 2003, 66 on 'passage tomb people' and 'Grooved Ware people'); but by emphasising the alien, British background to Grooved Ware and to the ritual structures, a significant injection of new ideas, if not new blood, is implied, with interchange between the Boyne Valley inhabitants and groups in western Britain being suggested as the conduit for the transmission of novel traditions and practices. A timescale for this change is not explicitly stated, but a relatively rapid change is implied. Some complexity to the process is suggested: "..it is

unlikely that there was a simple progression in Ireland from the passage tomb tradition to the Grooved Ware tradition" (Eogan and Roche 1999, 109).

In assessing the validity of this model, it is first necessary to examine the time frame within which such changes occurred, and the duration of the Grooved Ware 'complex'.

Eogan and Roche have argued, on the basis of direct and indirect stratigraphic evidence, that the period of use of Grooved Ware in the Boyne Valley post-dated the 'golden age' of these passage tomb cemeteries (when the massive tombs at Newgrange, Knowth and Dowth were constructed and used, in the final centuries of the fourth millennium BC), and pre-dated Beaker activity. Brindley, however, has argued for a degree of overlap with Beaker use around 2500/2400 BC, based partly on the 17 radiocarbon dates available for the Newgrange pit, pit-and-post and post structures and partly on the sinuous 'Grooved Ware-Beaker hybrid' vessel from Newgrange (1999a, 31, illus. 3.1.3).

Establishing an absolute chronology for Irish Grooved Ware use (and indeed for Grooved Ware use in general) is fraught with problems, not least of which is the presence of plateaux in the calibration curve around 4400, 4200 and 4000 BP, which create imprecision in dates covering the periods 3100–2900, 2850–2650 and 2600–2480 BC respectively (Brindley 1999a, 30; *cf.* Ashmore and MacSween 1998). Together with problems of non-association between the dated material and the pottery, old-wood effects, non-single-entity sample use and possible residuality of some charcoal, the extant dates cannot be taken as a wholly reliable guide (*cf.* the somewhat implausibly long currencies for Grooved Ware 'styles' in southern Britain: Garwood 1999, illus. 15.6). Nevertheless, from Brindley's careful evaluation of the available data, it seems likely that Irish Grooved Ware use was not a short-term phenomenon, but rather extended over half a millennium from *c.* 3000 to *c.* 2500–2400 BC – even though individual dated structures and features may have been short-lived. The incised Grooved Ware from the aforementioned burial at Kiltierney may, she argues, date to *c.* 3000 BC; this is not inconsistent with the dates cited for the incised Phase 2 assemblage from Pool, Orkney (Cowie and MacSween 1999, 54). The pit, pit-and-post and post circles at Knowth and Newgrange – and her 'Dundrum-Longstone' style of Grooved Ware which is associated with these – appear to date to the other end of the chronological spectrum, around 2600/2450 BC (Brindley 1999a, 32). Once more, this is not impossible if one considers the (admittedly broad) range of dates for similar, if mostly coarser Grooved Ware from the Links of Noltland in Orkney (Sheridan 1999; see also the comments above about early third millennium use of this kind of Grooved Ware at Balfarg henge). As for the 'Knowth' style pot from passage tomb 6 at Knowth (*cf.* Longworth's 'Clacton/Woodlands' style), while it must be admitted that the British comparanda appear to span over a millennium, between the late fourth millenium (at Barnhouse, Orkney: Ashmore and MacSween 1998; Jones 2000) and *c.* 2100 BC (Garwood 1999, illus. 15.6), it is nevertheless quite possible that this vessel at Knowth belongs towards the beginning of the Irish sequence, as Brindley suggests. For example, this kind of Grooved Ware has found not only at Barnhouse, but also in early third millennium BC contexts elsewhere in Orkney (*e.g.* Quanterness and the Stones of Stenness) and on the Scottish mainland (*e.g.* at Balfarg henge, where it was incidentally associated with the aforementioned plainer pottery comparable with Brindley's 'Dundrum-Longstone' type: Mercer 1981, fig. 43).

Given that Irish Grooved Ware use may well span half a millennium, then, how rapid and innovative was its adoption, and what was the timescale of the changes that are normally associated with its use?

In addressing these questions, unfortunately we do not have sufficient evidence on the dating of 'Carrowkeel ware' or other Middle Neolithic pottery to assess whether there was much chronological overlap between its use and that of Grooved Ware. 'Carrowkeel ware'-associated dates (which now include reliable dates from associated cremated remains, obtained from Tara and Ballynahatty) tend not to extend much after 3000 BC (A. Brindley, M. O'Sullivan and B. Hartwell pers comm.). However, there is some evidence to suggest that some Grooved Ware may have been used in a similar way to 'Carrowkeel ware', as a continuation of pre-existing traditions. This is indicated in the aforementioned Kiltierney cemetery, for whose Grooved Ware Brindley estimates a date of *c.* 3000 BC. It might also, arguably, be indicated in the deposition of Grooved Ware pots as either votive or funerary vessels inside passage tombs (at Knowth tombs 6 and 18, and at Loughcrew cairn L) – a practice echoed in the deposition of the two maceheads in the eastern and western tombs at Knowth site 1. (The plain macehead from the western tomb appears to have been burnt, as in a funeral pyre: Eogan and Richardson 1982, 125.)

Conversely, it appears that 'Carrowkeel ware' is associated with some of the changes in ritual practice that are normally linked, implicitly or explicitly, with Grooved Ware use. This is demonstrated by the presence of a 'Carrowkeel ware' bowl containing cremated human bones inside the earthen henge at Monknewtown in the Boyne Valley (Sweetman 1976); the pot must have been deposited after the henge had been constructed. Earthen henges, like the large pit-and-post structure at Newgrange, are often close to passage tombs and sometimes encompass them; some 13 are known from the Boyne region (Stout 1991; 2002), not counting a further probable example featuring an internal stone circle at Cloghalea, Dowth, Co. Meath (Stout 2002, fig. 39). Only two (at Monknewtown and the Giant's Ring, Ballynahatty, Co. Down) have been excavated; if Monknewtown is typical, their construction date should fall somewhere between the end of the fourth millennium and the late third

millennium, when secondary Beaker-associated activity was taking place (*cf.* the Grange embanked stone circle, where Beaker use was also secondary).

A final element that needs to be taken into account – leaving aside the problematic question of the date of the Great Stone Circle at Newgrange (see above) – is the possibility that one or two small passage tombs in the Boyne Valley (namely Site 2 at Knowth and site Z at Newgrange) were constructed after the major tombs at Knowth, Newgrange and Dowth had been built (Sheridan 1986, 27). In other words, the tradition of building passage tombs did not cease abruptly with these late fourth millennium mega-constructions.

Taking this all into consideration, one can *tentatively* propose the following model, which teases out the complexities alluded to by Eogan and Roche (1999,109) and posits a slightly more gradual transformation than they imply:

End of the fourth millennium – beginning of the third (say, between 3100/3000 and 2800 BC): continuing use of 'Carrowkeel ware' and continuing passage tomb construction for at least part of this period; construction of earthen henges (a novel practice), associated with 'Carrowkeel ware' at Monknewtown; probably also the construction of the Grange embanked stone circle (associated with Grooved Ware). Around 3000 BC: first use of Grooved Ware, at Kiltierney (within a pre-existing funerary tradition). Thereafter – either during this period or the next – deposition of Grooved Ware inside Knowth passage tomb 6, and possibly also at Knowth 18 and Loughcrew L. (As noted above, the 'Dundrum-Longstone' type Grooved Ware found in the latter two tombs could conceivably be as early as the pot from Knowth tomb 6, if the association between these variants of Grooved Ware at Balfarg is taken into account.) The deposition of the two maceheads in Knowth Site 1 could conceivably have taken place around the same time.

Early third millennium (say, c. 2800–2600 BC): Unclear, but presumably continuing use of Grooved Ware and henges; see comments above on the placing of deposits in passage tombs. 'Carrowkeel ware' presumably no longer in use.

Around 2600–2450 BC: Construction of circular pit, pit-and-post and post structures (probably accompanied by the so-called 'domestic' activities at Newgrange and Knowth); *floruit* of 'Dundrum-Longstone' Grooved Ware. Appearance of Beaker pottery towards end of this period, with Beaker-associated activities secondary to Grooved Ware-associated activities.

No doubt further and better radiocarbon dating (*e.g.* of the Kiltierney, Knowth and Monknewtown cremated bone) would help to clarify and correct this proposed scheme, even if the aforementioned plateaux in the calibration curve complicate matters.

In seeking to understand these changes, it is necessary to explore Ireland's links with Britain, starting with the oft-cited relationship with Orkney.

Links between Late Neolithic Ireland (especially the Boyne Valley) and Scotland (especially Orkney)

The existence of long-distance links between users of passage tombs in the Boyne Valley and Orkney has long been recognised (*e.g.* Piggott 1954, 217, 254–6, 328; Bradley and Chapman 1984; Renfrew 1985, 253; Sheridan 1986; Eogan 1992) and, in this author's opinion, their importance in accounting for the sequence of changes in both these areas cannot be overestimated.

It can plausibly be argued, for example, that the transformation in Orcadian passage tomb design from the somewhat simpler 'Orkney-Cromarty-Hebrides' type to the (generally) larger, more elaborate, 'Maes Howe' type (Henshall 1963, 121–34; Davidson and Henshall 1989, 37–51; Ashmore 2000a, 306) is due to the emulation of practices in the Boyne Valley around the end of the fourth millennium BC. The exotic Boyne Valley elements in the Orcadian tombs include the use of passage tomb 'art' in some tombs (and perhaps also the beliefs, symbolism and practices that lay behind these designs), and a concern with astronomical orientation at Maes Howe, which is aligned so that the setting midwinter sun penetrates along the passage and into the chamber. (At Newgrange, the same phenomenon occurs at midwinter sunrise). These exotic features are combined with some specifically Orcadian traits: for example, Grooved Ware was used in the Orcadian tombs, whereas 'Carrowkeel ware' was used in the Boyne Valley; there are no Irish parallels for the unusual-shaped stone objects found in the passage tomb at Quoyness (Davidson and Henshall 1989, fig. 28);[2] the large bone pins found in Orkney are of a different design from Irish mushroom- and poppy-headed pins; and the passage tomb art, though clearly similar, has some points of difference (Eogan 1992, 126).

In both Orkney and the Boyne Valley, the construction of large and elaborate tombs can be regarded as part of a process of competitive aggrandisement by local elites, who were harnessing the supernatural and ancestral authority vested in these 'houses of the dead' to enhance their worldly power (Sheridan 1986). In Orkney, this process can be seen taking place not only in the construction of passage tombs (and *par excellence* at Maes Howe), but also, arguably, in stalled cairns, as the massive example at Midhowe on Rousay suggests (Davidson and Henshall 1989, 146–8). The adoption of exotic elements in passage tomb design in Orkney would have added to the prestige and authority of the tomb builders, especially if 'exotic' were to be associated conceptually with 'supernatural'; the same applies to the exotic objects and designs in Boyne Valley tombs, which indicate links not only with Orkney but also with Brittany and Iberia (Sheridan 1986). Mary Helms (1993) has coined the term 'cosmological acquisition' for this use of exotic ideas and items, and Stuart Needham has used it effectively in describing relationships between the Early Bronze Age elites in Wessex and Brittany (Needham 2000).

This link between Orkney and the Boyne Valley could account for the aforementioned miniature macehead pendants seen in some Irish passage tombs which, like the pendant miniatures of Breton *haches à bouton*, evoke exotic prestige items (in this case, Orcadian maceheads: see Sheridan 1986). In other words, Irish passage tomb users might have been aware of Orcadian maceheads before any full-sized examples were actually in use in Ireland. Furthermore, it may be that some of the full-sized maceheads found in Ireland are imports from Orkney, or have an Orcadian link. The decorated Maes-mawr-type macehead from the eastern tomb at Knowth site 1 is clearly an import to Ireland (Eogan and Richardson 1982); and although the flint used to make it cannot have come from Orkney, the specific form of the spiral imagery has more in common with Orcadian passage tomb 'art' (*e.g.* at Pierowall, Westray: Barclay 1999, illus. 2.7) than with that found in the Boyne Valley (G. Eogan and E. Shee Twohig pers comm. George Eogan has reminded the author of a further Scottish *comparandum*, from Temple Wood stone circle in Argyll: Scott 1989, pl. 5, fig. 13).

Most importantly, this link between Orkney and the Boyne Valley can also account for Irish awareness of the existence of both Grooved Ware and of henges (or, at least, of one henge) around 3000 BC. As for the former, various parallels between Irish and Orcadian Grooved Ware have already been mentioned; the *comparanda* include assemblages dating to around the turn of the millennium (Ashmore and MacSween 1998, fig. 11.2). As for the latter, a suite of five dates recently obtained from animal bone at the base of the henge ditch at the Stones of Stenness in Orkney has confirmed that this monument (featuring a stone circle encircled by a penannular ditch with exterior bank) was in existence by 3100/3000 BC (Ritchie 1976; Ashmore 2000b, 124; 2001, 125). It may be that the henge-like ditch and bank surrounding the passage tomb at Maes Howe was also in existence at this time; unfortunately the available radiocarbon dates leave much to be desired (Davidson and Henshall 1989, 98). It must be admitted, however, that there are differences between the Stones of Stenness henge and Irish embanked enclosures: the latter lack the stone circle, and their banks were made by scarping the interior, rather than by digging ditches – a feature paralleled in (undated) southwest Welsh henges (Stout 1991, 254). Furthermore, the Grange embanked stone circle does not offer a closer parallel to the Stones of Stenness. It may be that such differences are analogous to the way in which Grooved Ware was initially used in Ireland: in other words, the adoption of a novelty involved a process of accommodation within local preferences.

Notwithstanding such discrepancies between the Stones of Stenness and Irish earthen henges, it remains a strong possibility that the *idea* of focusing ceremonial practices on 'open air' structures, rather than on passage tombs, was adopted in Ireland thanks to links with Orkney. The significance of this shift in practice has been much debated (*e.g.* Thomas 1991, 47–55; Harding 2003), and space does not permit a lengthy rehearsal here. Similarly, the extent to which henges and circles of timber and stone incorporate deliberate astronomical alignment cannot be discussed at length, other than to note that the Stones of Stenness do not seem to have an obvious alignment (Curtis 1976), whereas some other early third millennium stone circles and henges (*e.g.* Calanais, Stonehenge) definitely do seem to be aligned on lunar phenomena, particularly the major standstill positions; the reader is directed to Ruggles' authoritative study for further details (1999). Suffice it to say that henges and circles of timber and stone were probably foci for marking times that were significant to the community and that, in Orkney and Ireland, their proximity to pre-existing funerary monuments might indicate that ancestral authority may have been invoked during the ceremonies, rather than rejected in some ideological paradigm shift (*cf.* Pitts 2000).

If the adoption of 'open air' ceremonial structures and Grooved Ware in Ireland was due to links with Orkney around 3000 BC, this can be seen as part of a much broader process of expansion in the use of these new structures and this pottery type – a process affecting much of Britain (as shown, for example, in the first-phase monument at Stonehenge: Gibson 1998, 112–9; Harding 2003, 45–8). Once more, there is still much debate as to whether these novelties originated in, and spread from, Orkney (*e.g.* Harding 2003, 7–34). However, within Scotland at least, there appears to be clear evidence for a southward spread of these novelties. Along the western fringe of Scotland, from Lewis in the Outer Hebrides to Arran in the southwest, there is a thin but distinctive – and suggestive – scatter of Grooved Ware finds and of circles of timber or stone (see Fig 5.1 for details); at Machrie Moor, as at Temple Wood, a timber phase is succeeded by a stone phase.[3] The dating evidence, such as it is, suggests that this spread occurred around or shortly after 3000 BC, and the kind of Grooved Ware is fairly consistent, characterised by fineware bowls with incised decoration. The (main) stone circle at Calanais on Lewis, like stone circles 2 and 3 on Machrie Moor, Arran, is constructed of tall, narrow stones reminiscent of those used at the Stones of Stenness; and the aforementioned spiral design pecked into the stone circle at Temple Wood recalls Orcadian passage tomb 'art', as well as the design on the Knowth macehead. Such similarities with Orkney are arguably not coincidental.

Whether or not the use of fine incised Grooved Ware at the stone circle at Kiltierney Deerpark in Co. Fermanagh can be related to this particular chain of connections with Orkney (rather than to adoption from the Boyne Valley, where a more direct link with Orkney may have existed) is a moot point. Nevertheless, the general point – that the use of Grooved Ware and of 'open air' ceremonial structures is likely to have resulted from links with Orkney – offers a simple and plausible explanation for the observed changes in Ireland.

What about the sources of inspiration for the slightly later pit/pit-and-post and post structures? Here, attention needs to turn to Ireland's links with southern Britain.

Links between Ireland and southern Britain

Once more, space precludes a detailed consideration of the various links, but the following observations can be offered. As far as connections with Wales are concerned, there is clear evidence for contact at the time of the construction of the Boyne Valley passage tombs, during the late fourth millennium BC (reviewed in Sheridan 1986; 2003). This includes similarities between some 'Carrowkeel ware' (*e.g.* from Knowth and Townleyhall) and Welsh 'Peterborough Ware'; to the usual list of *comparanda* can be added a recent find of a near-complete, Irish-style 'Carrowkeel bowl' from Llanbedrgoch, Anglesey (Redknap 2003, 160; recognised as such by current author). This is dated by a radiocarbon date offering a *termini post quem* of 3490–3100 Cal. BC (Beta-90547, 4560±50 BP; M. Redknap pers comm.). As noted above, there is a superficial similarity in earthen henge design between Ireland and southwest Wales; but without further fieldwork in both countries, little can be inferred from this (*cf.* Darvill and Wainwright 2003).

Connections between Grooved Ware users in Ireland and Wales can perhaps best be described as 'tenuous' (see Gibson 1998, 16–18 and Gibson 1999 for details of Welsh Grooved Ware); and the timber circle at Sarn-y-bryn-caled, Powys, which shares some features in common with the timber circles from Knowth and elsewhere in eastern Ireland, is too late to have been a possible source of inspiration for their design (Gibson 1998, 106–8; figs 39, 74, 83, 94–5).

One returns to the structural and other similarities, already mentioned, between the Irish ceremonial structures and timber and pit circles in southern England. The closest structural similarity is that between the Knowth-type timber structures and the Northern Circle inside Durrington Walls. Otherwise, although there is a generalised link with the simple and complex timber circles of southern England (Gibson 1998), there are no precise matches. For example, the Newgrange pit-and-post structure does not offer a close parallel for the complex (and probably multi-phase) timber circles as seen, for example, at Woodhenge and Mount Pleasant (Gibson 1998, figs 69, 77; to judge from the admittedly unreliable dating evidence for Woodhenge, this site may post-date Newgrange in any case: Gibson 1998, 49). Similarly, although some parallels with some southern English Grooved Ware are evident, the Irish 'Dundrum-Longstone' type of Grooved Ware that is found here and in the other Irish timber/pit structures has its own distinctive characteristics. It is not matched assemblage-for-assemblage in the southern English sites, and it tends to be finer than much of the British Grooved Ware of comparable type. It may well be that the 'Dundrum-Longstone'

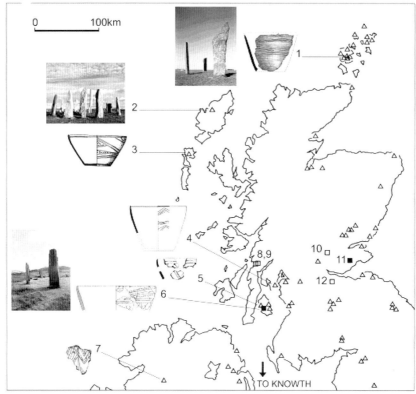

No	Site name	Site type	GW?	References & comments
1	Stones of Stenness, O	Henge with internal stone circle	Yes	Ritchie 1976
2	Calanais, Lewis	Stone circle* with central standing stone & possibly S stone row	Yes	Ashmore 1995. Other stone rows & avenue added later. Several other stone circles in area
3	Unival, N Uist	Orkney-Cromarty-Hebrides passage tomb: from high level in chamber deposits	Yes	Henshall 1972, 309 (14), 529-34. Secondary deposit in pre-existing tomb
4	Townhead, Rothesay, A&B	?Settlement	Yes	Mackay 1950
5	Tormore, Arran	Clyde chamber tomb (Tormore I): from outermost part of chamber	Yes	Henshall 1972, 305 (1), 371-3. Secondary deposit in pre-existing tomb, probably deposited alongside macehead & 2 edge-polished flint knives
6	Machrie Moor, Arran	Timber circles succeeded by stone circles	Yes	Haggarty 1991. Grooved Ware associated with site 1 timber circles. Several other stone circles in vicinity
7	Kiltierney Deerpark, Co Fermanagh	Cemetery of cremated remains within low stone circle	Yes	Daniells & Williams 1977
8	Upper Largie, A&B	Timber circle & avenue	No	Ellis forthcoming, *Proc Prehist Soc*
9	Temple Wood, A&B	Timber circle succeeded by stone circle	No	Scott 1989
10	N Mains, P&K	2 successive timber circles, subsequently enclosed within henge	No	G. Barclay 1983. Date for cremated bone under henge bank, obtained 2003 for NMS, confirms henge built several centuries after timber circle
11	Balfarg, Fife	Multiple concentric rings, possibly originally just a single ring; subsequently enclosed within henge	Yes	Mercer 1981
12	Cairnpapple, W Lothian	Timber circle within henge	No	G. Barclay 1999. Note: previous claims for presence of Grooved Ware incorrect

* The term 'circle' encompasses slightly oval settings, as here . Key: O = Orkney; A&B = Argyll & Bute; P&K = Perth & Kinross

Fig 5.1: Distribution of Grooved Ware (Triangles, dense in Orkney), and of timber circles of definite and probable Neolithic date (squares: filled - with GW; open: - without) in northern Britain and northern Ireland. Also shown are stone circles with particularly tall stones (see photographs). Sites featured in the text listed. Map based on Cowie and MacSween 1999, with additions. Photos: Historic Scotland, Crown copyright.

Grooved Ware evolved in Ireland from the repertoire that had been adopted from Orkney in previous centuries. A further possibility is that it could have been influenced by continuing links with Orkney at a time when (for example) the Links of Noltland site was occupied. Essentially, the impression gained from the structural and ceramic evidence is that people in eastern Ireland were aware of

developments in southern England around the middle of the third millennium, and chose to adopt some of the ritual practices and structures used there; but, as with the earlier phase of change described above, this was done within a local milieu. Whether, as Gibson has hinted (1998,78), there was any astronomical alignment of the Irish sites – as seems to have been the case with many of the southern

English sites (*e.g.* the solar, solstitial orientation of Woodhenge) – is a topic that will need proper investigation in the future.

Why should there have been an interest in, and contact with, southern England at this time? The answer may lie in the establishment (or re-emergence) of Wessex as a centre of power, rivalling or eclipsing that once held by the elites in the Boyne Valley and Orkney. This is reflected not only at Stonehenge, but also at other sites such as the 'mega-henges' at Avebury, Durrington Walls, Marden and Mount Pleasant, and at the various timber structures such as Woodhenge and the Sanctuary (see Harding 2003 for a recent review of the evidence). According to Harding, at least some of the mega-henges were in existence by (or from) 2600 BC. At Stonehenge, remodelling activities during the early-to-mid third millennium culminated, around 2550/2500 BC, in the replacement of a complex timber 'circle' with one built from stone, and a re-orientation of the site from a mainly lunar orientation (with gaps in the bank and ditch indicating the northern and southern maximum standstill positions of the moon in its 18.4 year cycle) to a mainly solar orientation (on midsummer solstice sunrise and midwinter solstice sunset: Ruggles 1999, 136–9; Harding 2003, 45–8). Given the nature and scale of such activities in Wessex, and the fact that communities in Britain and Ireland were clearly not isolated from each other, it is quite possible that inhabitants of eastern Ireland may have visited Wessex and adopted some of the practices and structures that they had seen there. Indeed, although it stretches the credibility of some of the author's colleagues, it may even be that even longer-distance connections existed during the mid-to-late third millennium BC. The design of the large Ring of Brodgar henge in Orkney is clearly different from that of the Stones of Stenness nearby, and although the site lacks an enclosing bank, the monumental rock-cut ditch and the numerous massive stones around its interior are reminiscent of the massive henge at Avebury in Wiltshire. Such contacts are not beyond the bounds of possibility, given that the Early Bronze Age grave goods from the Knowes of Trotty in Orkney indicate Orcadian contacts with Wessex early in the second millennium (Sheridan *et al.* 2003).

Conclusions

In one sense, Eogan and Roche are right to say that the appearance of Grooved Ware and associated structures and practices involved significant changes to society in the Boyne Valley. However, it is hoped that some idea of the probable complexity and timescale of this change has been conveyed here. In particular, a change in the axis of influence, from Orkney at the beginning of the third millennium to Wessex a few centuries later, has been proposed. It is not necessary to posit an influx of new settlers to account for any of the observed changes in the Boyne Valley (or elsewhere in Ireland), although of course some movement of people between areas must have taken

place. Rather, the changes can be seen as an active, deliberate and indeed selective adoption of exotic material culture and practices, undertaken against a background of local traditions, and evolving with a local dynamic.

Acknowledgements

The chief acknowledgement is to Helen Roche, for her patience, advice, information and encouragement. George Eogan is thanked for unwittingly sharing his opinion on the Knowth flint macehead; Anna Brindley, Barrie Hartwell, Muiris O'Sullivan and Mark Redknap are thanked for allowing me to mention unpublished radiocarbon dates; and the Society of Antiquaries of Scotland, along with individual authors and illlustrators, are thanked for permission to reproduce the pottery illustrations shown in Fig 5.1.

Notes

1   As with the flint objects, an exclusive association between ovoid and pestle maceheads and Grooved Ware cannot be claimed, since at least one ovoid macehead fragment (from Cam, Gloucestershire) has been found with Fengate Ware (Roe 1968, 158); and since two pestle maceheads are clearly of late second/early first millennium date, post-dating the use of Grooved Ware in the vicinity. The first is from the chamber tomb at Isbister in Orkney (Davidson and Henshall 1989, 71, 125-30), where one was found in a hoard placed on the cairn, accompanied by (*inter alia*) a V-perforated button of imported albertite (identification of material by Mary Davis for the National Museums of Scotland). The second is a miniature pestle macehead from Glenhead, near Doune, Perth and Kinross, found with the remains of a ?female aged 15-21 and a Food Vessel in a cist (Anderson 1883, 453; osteological identification by Hannah Koon for the National Museums of Scotland).

2   Although these odd-shaped stone objects are not paralleled in Ireland, it has been suggested (*e.g.* Piggott 1954) that there may be a connection, albeit distant, between the carved stone balls found in Orkney and northeast Scotland and the smooth stone balls found in some Irish passage tombs. The fact that some carved stone balls have been decorated with spiral designs, echoing passage tomb 'art', offers a further possible link.

3   This southward spread is also echoed on the Scottish mainland, for example at the Balfarg and North Mains henges (Mercer 1981; Barclay 1983 respectively). The pottery from Balfarg echoes Orcadian Grooved Ware fairly closely. At North Mains, it has just been demonstrated that the earthen bank and associated ditch were added several centuries after the main timber ring (A) was constructed, and thereby incidentally demonstrates that the building of earthen henges spans a millennium (*cf.* the dates for the Stones of Stenness). Cremated human bone from an unaccompanied deposit under the bank has been dated to 3665±45 BP (GrA-24007; 2140–1960 cal. BC at 1σ, 2200–1910 cal. BC at 2σ). Dating of the timber ring (Stenhouse 1983) has been complicated by the necessary adjustment of the standard deviations to ±110 years, but a date within the first half of the third millennium seems likely.

Bibliography

Anderson, J. 1883 Notice of urns in the Museum that have been found with articles of use or ornament, *Proceedings of the Society of Antiquaries of Scotland* **17**, 446–59.

Ashmore, P.J. 1995 *Calanais: the Standing Stones*. Stornoway.

Ashmore, P.J. 1997 'A list of Historic Scotland archaeological radiocarbon dates', *Discovery & Excavation in Scotland 1997*, 112–7.

Ashmore, P.J. 2000a Dating the Neolithic in Orkney. In A. Ritchie (ed.) *Neolithic Orkney in its European Context*, 299–308. Cambridge.

Ashmore, P.J. 2000b A list of archaeological radiocarbon dates, *Discovery and Excavation in Scotland* 1, 122–8.

Ashmore, P.J. 2001 'A list of archaeological radiocarbon dates', *Discovery & Excavation in Scotland* 2, 122–8.

Ashmore, P.J. and MacSween, A. 1998 Radiocarbon dates for settlements, tombs and ceremonial sites with Grooved Ware in Scotland. In A. Gibson and D.D.A. Simpson (eds) *Prehistoric Ritual and Religion*, 139–47. Stroud.

Ballin Smith, B., Donnelly, M. and McLellan, K. 1999 'Arran pipeline phase 1 (Kilmory parish)', *Discovery & Excavation in Scotland 1999*, 64.

Barclay, A. 1999 Grooved Ware from the Upper Thames Region In R. Cleal and A. MacSween (eds) *Grooved Ware in Britain and Ireland*, 9–22. Neolithic Studies Group Seminar Papers **3**, Oxford.

Barclay, G.J. 1983 Sites of the third millennium BC to the first millennium AD at North Mains, Strathallan, Perthshire, *Proceedings of the Society of Antiquaries of Scotland* **113**, 122–281.

Barclay, G.J. 1999 Cairnpapple revisited: 1948-1998, *Proceedings of the Prehistoric Society*, **65**, 17–46.

Bourke, E. 1997 Appendix 2. Towards a reconstruction of the Grooved Ware circular structure In G. Eogan and H. Roche 1997 *Excavations at Knowth (2): Settlement and Ritual Sites of the Fourth and Third Millennia BC*, 283–94. Royal Irish Academy Monographs in Archaeology, Dublin.

Bradley, R. 1998 Stone circles and passage graves – a contested relationship. In A. Gibson and D.D.A. Simpson (eds) *Prehistoric Ritual and Religion*, 2–13. Stroud.

Bradley, R. and Chapman, R. 1984 Passage graves in the European Neolithic – a theory of converging evolution. In G. Burenhult *The Archaeology of Carrowmore*, 348–56. Theses and Papers in North-European Archaeology **14**, Stockholm.

Brady, C. 2002 Earlier prehistoric settlement in the Boyne Valley, *Archaeology Ireland* **61**, 8–12.

Brindley, A. 1999a Irish Grooved Ware. In R. Cleal and A. MacSween (eds) *Grooved Ware in Britain and Ireland*, 23–35. Neolithic Studies Group Seminar Papers **3**, Oxford.

Brindley, A. 1999b Sequence and dating in the Grooved Ware tradition. In R. Cleal and A. MacSween (eds) *Grooved Ware in Britain and Ireland*, 133–44. Neolithic Studies Group Seminar Papers **3**, Oxford.

Callander, J.G. 1931 'Notes on (i) certain prehistoric relics in Orkney, (ii) Skara Brae, its culture and its period, *Proceedings of the Society of Antiquaries of Scotland* **65**, 78–84.

Clarke, D.V., Cowie, T.G. and A. Foxon 1985 *Symbols of power at the Time of Stonehenge*. Edinburgh.

Cleal, R. and MacSween, A. (eds) 1999 *Grooved Ware in Britain and Ireland*. Neolithic Studies Group Seminar Papers **3**, Oxford.

Condit, T. and Simpson, D.D.A. 1998 Irish hengiform enclosures and related monuments: a review. In A. Gibson, and D.D.A. Simpson (eds) *Prehistoric Ritual and Religion*, 45–67. Stroud.

Cooney, G. 2000 *Landscapes of Neolithic Ireland*. London and New York.

Cowie, T.G. and MacSween, A. 1999 Grooved Ware from Scotland: a review. In R. Cleal and A. MacSween (eds) *Grooved Ware in Britain and Ireland*, 48–56. Neolithic Studies Group Seminar Papers **3**, Oxford.

Curtis, G.R. 1976 Geometry and astronomy of the Stones of Stenness, Orkney. In J.N.G. Ritchie The Stones of Stenness, Orkney, *Proceedings of the Society of Antiquaries of Scotland* **107**, 48–50.

Daniells, M.J. and Williams, B.B. 1977 Excavations at Kiltierney Deerpark, County Fermanagh, *Ulster Journal of Archaeology* **40**, 32–41.

Darvill, T. and Wainwright, G. 2003 Stone circles, oval settings and henges in south-west Wales and beyond, *Antiquaries Journal*, **84**, 9–45.

Davidson, J.L. and Henshall, A.S. 1989 *The Chambered Cairns of Orkney*. Edinburgh.

Davidson, J.L. and Henshall, A.S. 1991 *The Chambered Cairns of Caithness*. Edinburgh.

Dillon, F. 1997 Lithic assemblage. In G. Eogan and H. Roche *Excavations at Knowth (2): Settlement and Ritual Sites of the Fourth and Third Millennium BC*, 161–84, 193–6. Royal Irish Academy Monographs in Archaeology, Dublin.

Dineley, M. and Dineley, G. 2000 From grain to ale: Skara Brae, a case study. In A. Ritchie (ed.) *Neolithic Orkney in its European Context*, 196–200. Cambridge.

Dudd, S.N., Evershed, R.P. and Gibson, A. 1999 Evidence for varying patterns of exploitation of animal products in different prehistoric pottery traditions based on lipids preserved in surface and absorbed residues, *Journal of Archaeological Science* **26**, 1473–82.

Durden, T. 1995 The production of specialised flintwork in the later Neolithic: a case study from the Yorkshire Wolds, *Proceedings of the Prehistoric Society* **61**, 409–32.

Edmonds, M. 1995 *Stone Tools and Society*. London.

Eogan, G. 1980 Objects with Iberian affinities from Knowth, Ireland, *Revista de Guimarães* **89**, 3–7.

Eogan, G. 1984 *Excavations at Knowth (1)*. Royal Irish Academy Monographs in Archaeology, Dublin.

Eogan, G. 1991 Prehistoric and early historic culture change at Brugh na Bóinne, *Proceedings of the Royal Irish Academy* **91**C, 105–32.

Eogan, G. 1992 Scottish and Irish passage tombs: some comparisons and contrasts. In N.M. Sharples and J.A. Sheridan (eds) *Vessels for the Ancestors*, 120–7. Edinburgh.

Eogan, G. 2003 The great mound at Knowth and the discovery of its passage tombs. In J. Fenwick (ed.) *Lost and Found: Discovering Ireland's Past*, 65–75. Wordwell, Bray.

Eogan, G. and Richardson, H. 1982 Two maceheads from Knowth, county Meath, *Journal of the Royal Society of Antiquaries of Ireland* **112**, 123–38.

Eogan, G. and Roche, H. 1994 A Grooved Ware wooden structure at Knowth, Boyne Valley, Ireland, *Antiquity* **68**, 322–30.

Eogan, G. and Roche, H. 1997 *Excavations at Knowth (2): Settlement and Ritual Sites of the Fourth and Third Millennia BC*. Royal Irish Academy Monographs in Archaeology, Dublin.

Eogan, G. and Roche, H. 1999 Grooved Ware from Brugh na Bóinne and its wider context. In R. Cleal and A. MacSween (eds) *Grooved Ware in Britain and Ireland*, 98–111. Neolithic Studies Group Seminar Papers **3**, Oxford.

Eogan, J. 1999 Recent Excavations at Bettystown, Co. Meath, *Irish Association of Professional Archaeologists Newsletter* **30**, 9.

Flanagan, L.N.W. 1966 An unpublished flint hoard from the Braid Valley, Co. Antrim, *Ulster Journal of Archaeology* **29**, 82–90.

Garwood, P. 1999 Grooved Ware in southern Britain: chronology and interpretation. In R. Cleal and A. MacSween (eds) *Grooved Ware in Britain and Ireland*, 145–76. Neolithic Studies Group Seminar Papers **3**, Oxford.

Gibson, A. 1998 *Stonehenge and Timber Circles*. Stroud.

Gibson, A. 1999 *The Walton Basin Project: Excavation and Survey in a Prehistoric Landscape 1993–7*. Council for British Archaeology Research Report 118, York.

Green, S. 1980 *The Flint Arrowheads of the British Isles*. British Archaeological Reports British Series **75**, Oxford.

Haggarty, A 1991 'Machrie Moor, Arran: recent excavations at two stone circles', *Proc Soc Antiq Scot* 121, 51–94, fiche 1:A4–A12.

Harding, J. 2003 *Henge Monuments of the British Isles*. Stroud.

Hartwell, B. 1998 The Ballynahatty complex. In A. Gibson and D.D.A. Simpson (eds) *Prehistoric Ritual and Religion*, 32–44. Stroud.

Helms, M.W. 1993 *Craft and the Kingly Ideal: Art, Trade, and Power*. Arizona.

Henshall, A.S. 1963 *The Chambered Tombs of Scotland. Volume One*. Edinburgh.

Henshall, A.S. 1972 *The Chambered Tombs of Scotland. Volume Two*. Edinburgh.

Henshall, A.S. and Mercer, R.J. 1981 Report on the pottery from Balfarg, Fife. In R.J. Mercer The excavation of a late Neolithic henge-type enclosure at Balfarg, Markinch, Fife, Scotland, 128–33, *Proceedings of the Society of Antiquaries of Scotland* **111**, 63–171.

Herity, M. 1974 *Irish Passage Graves*. Dublin.

Jones, A. 2000 Life after death: monuments, material culture and social change in Neolithic Orkney. In A. Ritchie (ed.) *Neolithic Orkney in its European Context*, 127–38. Cambridge.

King, H 1990 Fourknocks. In C. Manning and D. Hurl Excavations Bulletin 1980–84, *Journal of Irish Archaeology* **5**, 77.

Lehane, D 1983 The flintwork. In C. O'Kelly (ed.) *Newgrange, Co. Meath, Ireland: The Late Neolithic/Beaker Period Settlement*, 118–67. British Archaeological Reports British Series **190**, Oxford

Mackay, R.R. 1950 'Grooved Ware from Knappers Farm, near Glasgow, and from Townhead, Rothesay', *Proc Soc Antiq Scot* 84 (1949–50), 180–4.

MacSween, A. & Cowie, T.G. 1999 '[Grooved Ware gazetteer:] Scotland', *in* Cleal, R & MacSween, A (eds), 200–03.

Manby, T G 1974 *Grooved Ware Sites in Yorkshire and the North of England*. British Archaeological Reports British Series 9, Oxford.

Manby, T.G. 1988 The Neolithic in Eastern Yorkshire. In T.G. Manby (ed.) *Archaeology in Eastern Yorkshire*, 35–88.

Manby, T.G. 1999 Grooved Ware sites in Yorkshire and northern England: 1974–1994. In R. Cleal and A. MacSween (eds) *Grooved Ware in Britain and Ireland*, 57–75. Neolithic Studies Group Seminar Papers **3**, Oxford.

Mercer, R.J. 1981 The excavation of a late Neolithic henge-type enclosure at Balfarg, Markinch, Fife, Scotland, *Proceedings of the Society of Antiquaries of Scotland* **111**, 63–171.

Needham, S. 2000 Power pulses across a cultural divide: cosmologically driven acquisition between Armorica and Wessex, *Proceedings of the Prehistoric Society* **66**, 151–207.

O'Brien, W. in press (Con)fusion of tradition? The circle henge in Ireland. In A. Gibson, and J.A. Sheridan (eds) *Sickles and Circles: Britain and Ireland at the Time of Stonehenge*. Oxford.

O'Kelly, M.J. 1983 The Excavation. In C. O'Kelly (ed.) *Newgrange, Co. Meath, Ireland: The Late Neolithic/Beaker Period Settlement*, 1–54. British Archaeological Reports British Series 190, Oxford.

Ó Ríordáin, S.P. 1951 Lough Gur excavations: the great stone circle (B) in Grange Townland, *Proceedings of the Royal Irish Academy* **54**C, 37–74.

Piggott, S. 1954 *Neolithic Cultures of the British Isles*. Cambridge.

Pitts, M. 2000 *Hengeworld*. London.

Radley, A. 1993 'Upper Largie (Kilmartin parish)', *Discovery & Excavation in Scotland 1993*, 75.

Redknap, M. 2003 Llanbedrgoch: a Viking site on Anglesey, *Current Archaeology* **184**, 160–5.

Renfrew, A.C. 1985 Epilogue. In A.C. Renfrew (ed), *The Prehistory of Orkney*, 243–61. Edinburgh.

Ritchie, J.N.G. 1976 The Stones of Stenness, Orkney, *Proceedings of the Society of Antiquaries of Scotland* **107**, 1–60.

Roche, H. and Eogan, G. 2001 Late Neolithic activity in the Boyne Valley, Co. Meath, Ireland. In C.-T. Le Roux (ed.) *Du Monde des Chasseurs à Celui des Métallurgistes*, 125–40.

Roe, F.E.S. 1968 Stone maceheads and the latest neolithic cultures of the British Isles. In J.M. Coles and D.D.A. Simpson (eds) *Studies in Ancient Europe*, 145–72. Leicester.

Ruggles, C. 1999 *Astronomy in Prehistoric Britain and Ireland*. New Haven and London.

Scott, J.G. 1989 The stone circles at Temple Wood, Kilmartin, Argyll, *Glasgow Archaeological Journal* 15, 53–124.

Sheridan, J.A. 1986 Megaliths and megalomania: an account, and interpretation, of the development of passage tombs in Ireland, *Journal of Irish Archaeology* **3**, 17–30.

Sheridan, J.A. 1995 Irish Neolithic pottery: the story in 1995. In I.A. Kinnes and G. Varndell (eds) *'Unbaked Urns of Rudely Shape': Essays on British and Irish Pottery for Ian Longworth*, 3–21. Oxford.

Sheridan, J.A. 1999 Grooved Ware from the Links of Noltland, Westray, Orkney. In R. Cleal and A. MacSween (eds) *Grooved Ware in Britain and Ireland*, 112–24. Neolithic Studies Group Seminar Papers **3**, Oxford.

Sheridan, J.A. 2003 Ireland's earliest "passage" tombs: a French connection? In G. Burenhult and S. Westergaard (eds) *Stones and Bones: Formal Disposal of the Dead in Atlantic Europe during the Mesolithic–Neolithic Interface 6000–3000 BC*, 9–26. British Archaeological Reports International Series **1201**, Oxford.

Sheridan, J.A., Kochman, W. and Aranauskas, R. 2003 The grave goods from the Knowes of Trotty, Orkney: reconsideration and replication. In J. Downes and A. Ritchie (eds) *Sea Change: Orkney and Northern Europe in the Later Iron Age AD 300–800*, 176–88. Balgavies.

Simpson, D.D.A. 1988 The stone maceheads of Ireland, *Journal of the Royal Society of Antiquaries of Ireland* 118, 27–52.

Simpson, D.D.A. 1996a Irish perforated stone implements in context, *Journal of Irish Archaeology* **7**, 65–76.

Simpson, D.D.A. 1996b "Crown" antler maceheads and the Later Neolithic in Britain, *Proceedings of the PrehistoricSociety* **62**, 293–309.

Simpson, D.D.A. and Ransom, R. 1992 Maceheads and the Orcadian Neolithic. In N.M. Sharples and J.A. Sheridan (eds) *Vessels for the Ancestors*, 221–43. Edinburgh.

Stenhouse, M. 1983 'Radiocarbon dates from the North Mains sites', *in* G.J. Barclay, 1983 'Sites of the third millennium BC to the first millennium AD at North Mains, Strathallan, Perthshire', *Proc Soc Antiq Scot* 113, 259–60.

Stout, G. 1991 Embanked enclosures of the Boyne region, *Proceedings of the Royal Irish Academy* **91**C, 245–84.

Stout, G. 2002 *Newgrange and the Bend of the Boyne*. Cork.

Sweetman, P.D. 1976 An earthen enclosure at Monknewtown, Slane, Co. Meath, *Proceedings of the Royal Irish Academy* **76**C, 25–73.

Sweetman, P.D. 1985 A Late Neolithic/Early Bronze Age pit circle at Newgrange, Co. Meath, *Proceedings of the Royal Irish Academy* **85**C, 195–222.

Sweetman, P.D. 1987 Excavation of a Late Neolithic/Early Bronze Age site at Newgrange, Co. Meath, *Proceedings of the Royal Irish Academy* **87**C, 283–98.

Thomas, J. 1991 *Rethinking the Neolithic*. Cambridge.

Waddell, J. 1998 *The Prehistoric Archaeology of Ireland*. Galway.

Wainwright, G. and Longworth, I. H. 1971 *Durrington Walls: Excavations 1966–1968*. Reports of the Research Committee of the Society of Antiquaries of London **29**, London.

Woodman, P.C. 1994 Towards a definition of Irish Early Neolithic lithic assemblages. In N. Ashton and A. David (eds) *Stories in Stone*, 213–8. Lithic Studies Society Occasional Paper **4**, London.

6. Performance and place: The hoarding of axeheads in Irish prehistory

Gabriel Cooney

Introduction

One of George Eogan's many contributions to Irish archaeological studies has been his discussion and analysis of the phenomenon of hoarding in Irish pre-history. This is an aspect of prehistoric human behaviour that is relevant to much of his writing on the Bronze Age (*e.g.* Eogan 1964; 1965; 2000) and forms the focus of his major volume on *Hoards of the Irish Later Bronze Age* (1983). There not only is the evidence for the hoards from this period presented and assessed in detail but a critical assessment is made of the problems of Bronze Age hoards. This makes the work critical to our current interpretations of the Later Bronze Age in Ireland (*e.g.* Cooney and Grogan 1994; Waddell 1998) and also a key contribution to understanding the problem of the deliberate deposition of material in Bronze Age Europe (Bradley 1990, xv).

In this paper I want to develop two of the points made by Eogan in the *Hoards* volume. Firstly that hoards occur at various times throughout Irish prehistory (and history) and secondly that socketed bronze axeheads frequently occur in Later Bronze Age hoards in Ireland (Eogan 1983, 5, tables 2–9). This latter point is emphasised in his detailed catalogue and discussion of socketed bronze axes in Ireland (Eogan 2000). Here he noted that there are 43 associated finds of socketed axeheads of the Later Bronze Age, out of a total of around 160 hoards from this period. The vast majority of the hoards containing such axes, 38 out of the 43, occur in the latest (Dowris) phase of the period. This is interesting to compare with the occurrence of hoards containing earlier forms of axeheads in Irish prehistory.

In the Irish Early Bronze Age there is a dominance of flat and flanged bronze and copper axeheads in the fifty or so known hoards. Axeheads occur in 55 out of 60 (90%) of the hoards and account for more than three quarters of all the objects in such hoards (Harbison 1968, table 1; O'Flaherty 1995, 13). The basis for the consideration of hoards containing stone axeheads has long been Arm-strong's early paper (1918) when he discussed less than 20 such finds. However, recent consideration of such hoards as part of the research programme of the Irish Stone Axe Project (in Cooney and Mandal forthcoming) indicates that there are a significantly higher number, in excess of 60, than had previously been assumed. There are a number of points arising from this summary comparison of hoards containing axeheads from different periods in Irish prehistory that are interesting in themselves and merit further consideration.

Paths of enquiry

While a full assessment of the extent of evidence for hoarding in earlier Irish prehistory (Mesolithic and Neolithic periods) is awaited it is becoming clear that the deliberate deposition of material in the form of hoards is a significant feature of this time, as it is of the Bronze Age and Iron Age in Ireland. This is a point that has also been recognised in northwest Europe (*e.g.* Cordier and Bocquet 1998; Tilley 1996, 284–91). As in parts of Europe such as Scandinavia (Ebbesen 1993) the phenomenon of hoarding began in Ireland during the Mesolithic (Woodman 1978). From at least the Later Mesolithic, as indicated by the hoard of axes found during the excavation of Ferriter's Cove, Co. Kerry (Woodman *et al.* 1999, 63–5), stone axeheads were placed in hoards. From this time on axeheads, firstly of stone and then of metal, appear to have been seen as an appropriate type of object to be placed in hoards. Hence we can usefully take hoards containing axeheads as a focus in taking a long-term perspective on the phenomenon of hoarding in Ireland.

The apparent continuity of the significance of axeheads in hoards is interesting in the light of the fact that, certainly over the course of the Bronze Age (*e.g.* Eogan 1983, 5–7; O'Flaherty 1995, 18–9), there appear to have been particular periods when hoard deposition occurred, separated by times when it was far less common (Cooney and Grogan 1994, fig. 8.10). This raises the question of whether the continuation of placement of axeheads in hoards is representative of some sense of a long-term, enduring tradition or rather if we should see the deposition of axeheads in hoards as reflecting more directly the needs and social and economic character of the contemporary society (*e.g.* Needham 2001, 284). In this context we can usefully consider and critically evaluate the interpretation that the balance between the ceremonial/symbolic and the utilitarian roles of the axehead changed over time. The suggestion is that this was not so much to do with the switch from stone to metal or with the changing form of bronze axeheads, as with the widespread use of metal and growing diversity of object types in the Later Bronze Age, resulting in axes becoming primarily everyday tools (Bradley 1998, xxix).

It might be useful to begin by considering the wider context of the placement of axeheads in hoards by looking at the deposition of single axeheads. Hoards have been the subject of considerable work and interpretation, but single finds of the types of objects contained in hoards have in the past often been written off as stray finds and relatively little attention given to their context (see discussion in Cooney and Grogan 1994, 160). The recurring pattern that we see in the deposition of stone (Cooney and Mandal 1998, table 3.4), copper and bronze flat (and flanged) (Cooney and Grogan 1994, fig 6.3, based in information in Harbison 1969) and socketed bronze axeheads (Eogan 2000, 9–10) of significant numbers of single axeheads turning up in rivers, bogs and lakes is one indicator that many such objects were also deliberately deposited. Hence the act and context of deposition provides a key link between single and collective finds (Whittle 1988, 124–6). As O'Flaherty (1995, 12) suggested hoards containing axeheads may have been more closely related in the minds and intentions of the people who placed them in the ground to the deposition of single axeheads rather than to other contemporary hoards containing different kinds of objects.

The sheer number of stone axeheads, copper and bronze flat and flanged axeheads and socketed bronze axeheads is a remarkable feature of the archaeological record for Irish prehistory when compared with other areas which perhaps needs more careful consideration (indeed this is a comment that could be applied more broadly to other aspects of material record, certainly of the Irish Bronze Age, see Harding 1997, 167). There are over 20,000 stone axeheads (Cooney and Mandal 1998), over 2,000 flat and flanged axeheads (Harbison 1969) and again over 2,000 socketed axeheads (Eogan 2000). The significance of these numbers is borne out by a comparison with neighbouring areas. The density of finds of stone axeheads in Ireland is more than three times that of Wales/mid-west England and four times that of Scotland (see discussion in Cooney and Mandal 1995). Schmidt and Burgess (1981) recorded only 2,000 objects in their treatment of the entire range of Bronze Age axe types from Scotland and northern England (including palstaves which are not under discussion here) compared to well over 4,000 from Ireland. One implication from these figures is that axeheads would have been very important items of material culture in the minds and hands of people from the Mesolithic period onwards.

As mentioned above it has been suggested that with the increasing use and diversification of weaponry in the developed Bronze Age socketed axeheads may have lost symbolic status and become more mundane in role and function (*e.g.* Bradley 1990, 97). However, this misses out on the point that from the time when stone axeheads were first in use the ceremonial and utilitarian roles of axeheads were inter-mingled. For example, the very fact that we can recognise the signature of stone axeheads, flat and flanged copper and bronze axeheads and socketed bronze axeheads (and palstaves) on worked wood (O'Sullivan 1996, 341) demonstrates the day-to-day functionality of all of these axe types. Against this background perhaps we should be more cautious in assuming that socketed axeheads did not continue to have a wider symbolic and metaphoric importance. Indeed their occurrence in hoards could in itself be taken as an indicator of continued significance (Eogan 2000, 10). One could also draw attention to the similarity of the contents of some of the Later Bronze Age hoards containing axeheads with those of earlier date to suggest that there may have been similar intent in the minds of the people who deposited such hoards. As one example we can compare hoards consisting of pairs of axeheads; as in the case of the two stone axeheads found together in a bog at Killark, Co. Monaghan (Cooney and Mandal forthcoming), the two copper axeheads of Lough Ravel type found together in a limestone cleft at Clontoo, Co. Kerry (Harbison 1968, 45–6) and the two socketed bronze axeheads (apparently hafted) found in the vicinity of a bog at Calverstown, Co. Westmeath (Eogan 1983, 168; 2000; 217) (Fig 6.1).

Contents and contexts

In the contents of the hoards containing axeheads however we can also identify differences between the Later Bronze Age and earlier periods. In hoards containing stone axeheads the most common pattern is for two axes to have been deposited together. Over 50% of hoards containing stone axeheads consist of only axeheads. Of these 26 consist of two axeheads, 6 of three axeheads and 5 of between 4–19 axeheads (Cooney and Mandal forthcoming). Again in the case of Early Bronze Age hoards the most popular association within hoards is of axes with other axes only, this is the case for 60% of the hoards (O'Flaherty 1995, 15). Axes of a particular type are found in association with axes of the same or a closely related type. In contrast to this only two Later Bronze Age hoards consist exclusively of axeheads, one of them being the Calverstown hoard mentioned above. However, in 21 other hoards socketed axeheads were in association with only one other tool type. Some of these, with associations of axes and tools such as gouges, chisels and knives, appear to represent sets of wood-working tools (Eogan 2000, 7–8).

This does appear to represent a marked contrast with earlier patterns, but on the other hand it is possible to adzes. Recognising that the axehead may have had a more restricted functional usage in the Later Bronze Age, its continued potency and symbolic value may be indicated in the association between socketed axeheads and a wide range of other types (Eogan 2000, 7–8). For example, the Blackhills, Co. Laois hoard consisted of a socketed axe, a bronze sword and a plain leaf-shaped spearhead placed side by side, about a metre below the surface of a modern garden (Eogan 1983, 98; 2000, 217). This kind of hoard suggests that the socketed bronze axehead was in some cases seen as a weapon. The Blackhills hoard could also be seen as an example where the placement of the socketed axe (and the other objects) were actively and formally part of the rites involved in the deposition of the hoard, what Needham (2001, 291–2) has referred to as the *enactment*. In this context the new form of the axehead, *i.e.* the socket, is sometimes given significance, as in the case of hoards like that at Booltiaghadine, Co. Clare where the axehead acted as a container for a chisel and a razor (Eogan 1983, 65; 2000, 217).

In referring to hoards of axeheads above passing reference was made to their location and placement. There are in fact some striking parallels in the details of the placement and location of Later Bronze Age hoards containing axeheads and those containing older types of axeheads. One such pattern is the recurrence of a concern with marking the location of the hoard with a large stone, a clearly visible and recognisable marker. The Later Bronze Age hoard at Dreenan, Co. Fermanagh, for example, consisting of a sword, four plain leaf-shaped spearheads, the tip of a spearhead blade, an axehead (possibly more than one originally), a socketed hammer, a socketed knife and a lump of bronze, was discovered during the removal of a large rock (Eogan 1983, 83; 2000, 218). This can be compared with the Early Bronze Age hoard at Glenalla, Co. Donegal where four Ballyvalley type bronze axeheads were found under a large rock on high ground (Harbison 1968, 50). At Crovraghan, Co. Clare, two stone axeheads, two hammer stones, a possible hone and a nodular stone were found in a small cave or hollow beside a large stone close to the river Fergus (Mandal *et al.* 1991/2, 5; Cooney and Mandal forthcoming).

This brings up the wider question of context and the often discussed significance of the occurrence and relative proportions of hoards in wetland and dryland locations. O'Flaherty (1995, 24) made the observation that hoard deposition over the course of the Early Bronze Age seems to indicate an increasing concern with the placement of material in wetland locations. Discussing wider patterns Cooney and Grogan (1994, 138, 161–7) also pointed to the growing significance of deposition in rivers, bogs and lakes in the Middle and Late(r) Bronze Age. They suggested furthermore that different kinds of wetland places may have been chosen for different kinds of depositional activities. Tool hoards, which would include many of the hoards containing socketed axeheads, are the only category of hoard where dryland deposition was more

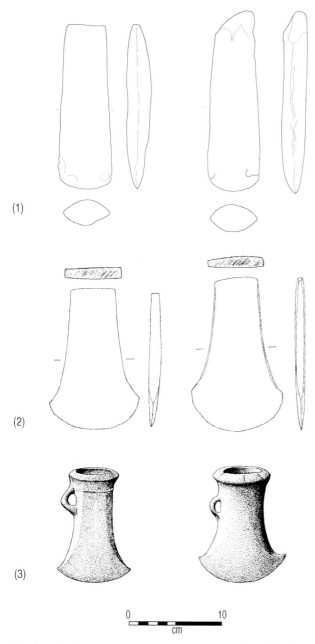

Fig 6.1: 1) The hoard of two stone axeheads from Killark, Co. Monaghan, 2) the hoard of two flat copper axeheads from Clontoo, Co. Kerry (after Harbison 1968), 3) the hoard of two socketed bronze axeheads from Calverstown, Co. Westmeath (after Eogan 2000).

read these kinds of hoards as containing wood-working objects, each with a specialised function, which in earlier times may have been carried out by one multi-functional object. Indeed this is reflected in the way in which we use the term 'stone axehead' to refer to a range of object types; axeheads, adzes, chisels and wedges and recognise that the same object can function, for example, as both an axe and an adze, depending on the way in which it is hafted (Cooney and Mandal 1998, 10). O'Sullivan (1996, 321) has commented that many Early Bronze Age metal axeheads could also have been used as wedges, chisels or

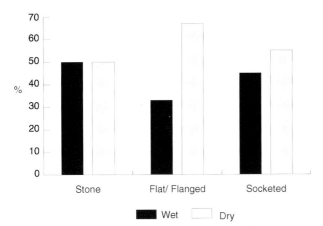

Fig 6.2: Comparison of the contexts of hoards containing stone axeheads (Cooney and Mandal forthcoming), flat/ flanged copper and bronze axeheads (Harbison 1968; O'Flaherty 1995) and socketed bronze axeheads (Eogan 2000).

popular than a wetland one (Cooney and Grogan 1994, 164, 167). I think it would be fair to say that most commentators have seen these trends as related to wider changes in the social dynamics of Bronze Age society. However, when the relevant statistics for the context of hoards containing stone axeheads are taken into account, it throws a different light on the issue (Fig 6.2). Using a crude wetland/dryland index and considering the data where the context of the hoard can be definitely identified, the figures for stone axehead hoards are 50%:50%, for Early Bronze Age hoards containing axeheads the figure is 33%:67% and for Late Bronze Age hoards containing socketed axeheads the figure is 45%:55% (data from Cooney and Mandal forthcoming; O'Flaherty 1995; Eogan 2000).

While the wetland hoards are dominated by deposition in bogs in all three cases, a significant number of hoards containing stone axeheads have been found in other wetland locations. Now it would appear that there was a greater focus on the deposition of hoards containing axeheads in wetlands before as opposed to during the Bronze Age. Indeed the pattern could be interpreted as lending some support to the notion of the changing status and importance of the axehead over time, from icon to mere wood-working tool. However, I have suggested above that we should be cautious about under-estimating the wider role of socketed axeheads. Perhaps we should be paying more attention to the relative stability in the ratio of wetland:dryland deposition over time. Acknowledging that it is a very crude indicator it is striking that the actual known number of hoards placed in bog which contain stone axeheads (15), Early Bronze Age flat and flanged axeheads (10) and Later Bronze Age hoards containing socketed axeheads (13) is so similar.

One might suggest here a greater element of continuity in practice and depositional behaviour than has previously been recognised. We have seen this above also in relation

to other practices, such as the marking of dryland hoards with a stone, or alternatively the marking out of a stone as special by the placement of a hoard. Bradley (1998, xviii) has pointed out that we have applied the wetland/dryland distinction too readily as a way of creating distinctions between different kinds of hoards when in reality all hoards should be interpreted in a similar framework (*e.g.* Vandkilde 1996, 33–9). Needham (2001) has argued this point very cogently pointing out that most if not all hoards can be regarded as ritual at some level but that this does not exclude a utilitarian aspect; ritual and utility should not be seen as mutually exclusive. What is important to characterise are the patterns of circulation of material, its deliberate deposition in the ground and the conditions in which it becomes appropriate to retrieve it. Looking at the process of deposition La Motta and Schiffer (2001, 44) argue that the deliberate placement of material below the ground can be seen in the context of people trying to effect linkages through these conduits to the natural and supernatural worlds.

A place for hoards

We can usefully develop this discussion by utilising the very long-term perspective afforded to us by considering hoards containing axeheads of stone, copper and bronze. Particularly in the Bronze Age hoards have tended to be seen as a particular category of depositional activity, increasingly set apart from other types of ceremony, such as funerary activity or the construction and use of monuments. It is the deposition of hoards containing metalwork that is seen as the focus of activity. And yet we now recognise, for example, that there were certain places in the landscape such as critical crossing points on major rivers like as the Shannon (Bourke 2001) that were repeatedly used as foci of deposition. So the commemoration or the marking of place would appear to have been a key factor in at least some forms of metalwork deposition.

Looking at hoards containing axeheads of different types it is clear that this concern with place would appear to be a long-term recurring feature. I have mentioned hoards that may have been deliberately placed at 'natural' stones but another example of this are the hoards at monuments such as the hoard of forty four flint artefacts consisting of thirty eight flakes, three axe roughouts, a plano-convex knife and a blank for a scraper found at the side of the socket for one of the court orthostats of the court tomb at Ballyalton, Co. Down (Evans and Davies 1934). A bronze flat axehead was placed with two pieces of raw copper immediately beside an upright to the northwest of the entrance to the wedge tomb at Toormore, Co. Cork (O'Brien 1999, 169–171). Looking at the hoards containing socketed axeheads there would not appear to be an obvious, immediate parallel. However, the hoard from Drumany (O'Brien), Co. Leitrim, containing a sword, a plain leaf-shaped spearhead and three socketed axeheads (Eogan 1983, 101) comes from a townland of some 31 hectares (126 acre) in which there is also a portal tomb and a wedge tomb (de Valera and O Nualláin 1972, 70–1; see also Cooney 1979). Without having the details of the exact relationship of the hoard and these monuments it would seem reasonable to suggest that the hoard was placed with reference to an area which had a long-term significance as an important locale in the landscape.

What I hoped to set out in this paper is the value of taking a long-term perspective in looking at the practice of depositing hoards in prehistoric Ireland and a focus on a particular artifact type. There are other points that could be developed, such as the intriguing implications of the continued use of stone axeheads in the Early Bronze Age (*e.g.* O'Brien 2001) and the later phases of the Bronze Age (*e.g.* Moloney *et al.* 1993). However, I wanted to conclude by coming back to the issue of the intention behind the placement of hoards containing axeheads in the ground and to link this with another of George Eogan's long-term research interests, the context and interpretation of megalithic art. Lewis-Williams (2002, 149) has discussed how we might see the rock on which such art was created as a 'veil', the interface between materiality and spirituality, with images of the other-world. In that sense both art and the placement of hoards, underground, in conduits to the other-world, could be viewed as the performance of ritual. Both are performed in a structured, formal way that materializes beliefs about the way the world works and relationships between people (*e.g.* Rappaport 1999, 27). We can understand then why they are central to our understanding of prehistoric societies and such fascinating foci of archaeological work.

Acknowledgements

My thanks to Barbara Leon for the illustrations. I am also grateful to Barbara Leon and Katharina Becker for their comments on an earlier draft of the paper.

Bibliography

Armstrong, E.C.R. 1918 Associated finds of Irish neolithic celts, *Proceedings of the Royal Irish Academy* 34C, 81–95.

Bourke, L. 2001 *Crossing the Rubicon: Bronze Age metalwork from Irish rivers.* Department of Archaeology, National University of Ireland, Galway

Bradley, R. 1990 *The passage of arms.* Cambridge University Press, Cambridge.

Bradley, R. 1998 Rereading The passage of arms. In *The passage of arms*, revised edition, xv–xxxii. Routledge, London.

Cooney, G. 1979 Some aspects of the siting of megalithic tombs in County Leitrim, *Journal of the Royal Society of Antiquaries of Ireland* 109, 74–91.

Cooney, G. and Grogan, E. 1994 *Irish prehistory: a social perspective.* Wordwell, Dublin.

Cooney, G. and Mandal, S. 1995 Getting to the core of the problem: petrological results from the Irish Stone Axe Project, *Antiquity* 69, 969–80.

Cooney, G. and Mandal, S. 1998 *The Irish Stone Axe Project. Monograph 1.* Wordwell, Dublin.

Cooney, G. and Mandal, S. forthcoming *The Irish Stone Axe Project. Monograph 2.* Wordwell, Dublin.

Cordier, G. and Bocquet, A. 1998 Le Dépôt de la Bégude-de-Mazenc (Drôme) et les dépôts de haches néolithiques en France. Note complémentaire, *Bulletin de la Société Préhistorique Francaise*, 221–38.

de Valera, R. and O Nualláin, S. 1972 *Survey of the Megalithic Tombs of Ireland, Volume III.* The Stationery Office, Dublin.

Ebbesen, K. 1993 Sacrifices to the powers of nature. In S. Hvass and B. Storgaard (eds) *Digging into the Past; 25 Years of Archaeology in Denmark*, 122–5. Royal Society of Northern Antiquaries and the Jutland Archaeological Society, Copenhagen and Moesgard.

Eogan, G. 1964 The Later Bronze Age in Ireland in the light of recent research, *Proceedings of the Prehistoric Society* 30, 268–351.

Eogan, G. 1965 *Catalogue of Irish bronze swords.* National Museum of Ireland, The Stationery Office, Dublin.

Eogan, G. 1983 *Hoards of the Irish Later Bronze Age.* University College, Dublin.

Eogan, G. 2000 *The socketed axes of Ireland.* Prähistorische Bronzefunde, Abteilung IX, Band 22. C.H. Beck, Munich

Evans, E.E. and Davies, O. 1934 Excavation of a chambered horned cairn at Ballyalton, Co. Down, *Proceedings of the Belfast Natural History and Philosophical Society* 1933–4, 79–103.

Harbison, P. 1968 Catalogue of Irish Early Bronze Age associated finds containing copper or bronze, *Proceedings of the Royal Irish Academy* 67C, 35–91.

Harbison, P. 1969 *The axes of the Early Bronze Age in Ireland.* Prähistorische Bronzefunde, Abteilung IX, Band 1, C.H. Beck, Munich.

Harding, A. 1997 Warfare: a defining characteristic of Bronze Age Europe? In J. Carman and A. Harding (eds) *Ancient Warfare*, 157–73. Alan Sutton, Stroud.

La Motta, and Schiffer, 2001 Behavioral archaeology: toward a new synthesis. In I. Hodder (ed.) *Archaeological theory today*, 14–64. Polity Press, Cambridge.

Lewis-Williams, D. 2002 *The mind in the cave.* Thames and Hudson, London.

Mandal, S., Cooney, G., O'Carroll, F. and Guinan, B. 1991/2 A review of the petrological techniques being utilised to identify, group and source Irish stone axes, *Journal of Irish Archaeology* 6, 1–11.

Moloney, A., Jennings, D., Keane, M. and MacDermott, C. 1993 *Excavations at Clonfinlough, Co. Offaly.* Irish Archaeological Wetland Unit Transactions 2, University College, Dublin.

Needham, S. 2001 When expediency broaches ritual intention: the flow of metal between systemic and buried domains, *Journal of the Royal Anthropological Institute* 7, 275–98.

O'Brien, W. 1999 *Sacred Ground: Megalithic Tombs in coastal south-west Ireland.* Department of Archaeology, National University of Ireland, Galway.

O'Brien, W. 2001 Bronze Age copper mining in Ballyrisode hill, *Mizen Journal, Mizen Archaeological and Historical Society* 9, 5–15.

O'Flaherty, R. 1995 An analysis of Irish Early Bronze Age hoards containing copper or bronze objects, *Journal of the Royal Society of Antiquaries of Ireland* 125, 10–45.

O'Sullivan, A. 1996 Neolithic, Bronze Age and Iron Age woodworking techniques. In B. Raftery *Trackway excavations in the Mountdillon bogs, Co. Longford 1985–91*, 291–342. Irish Archaeological Wetland Unit Transactions 3, Crannóg, Department of Archaeology, University College, Dublin.

Rappaport, R.A. *Ritual and religion in the making of humanity.* Cambridge University Press, Cambridge.

Schmidt, P.K. and Burgess, C.B. 1981 *The axes of Scotland and northern England.* Prähistorische Bronzefunde, Abteilung IX, Band 7, C.H. Beck. Munich.

Tilley, C. 1996 *An ethnography of the Neolithic: early prehistoric societies in southern Scandinavia*. Cambridge University Press, Cambridge.

Vandkilde, H. 1996 *From stone to bronze: the metalwork of the late Neolithic and earliest Bronze Age in Denmark*. Jutland Archaeological Society, Aarhus.

Waddell, J. 1998 *The prehistoric archaeology of Ireland*. Galway University Press, Galway.

Whittle, A. 1988 *Problems in Neolithic archaeology*. Cambridge University Press, Cambridge.

Woodman, P.C. 1978 *The Mesolithic in Ireland*. British Archaeological Reports, British Series **58**, Oxford.

Woodman, P.C., Anderson, E. and Finlay, N. 1999 *Excavations at Ferriter's Cove, 1983–95: last foragers, first farmers in the Dingle Peninsula*. Wordwell, Dublin.

7. Little and Large: Comparing Knockroe with Knowth

Muiris O'Sullivan

This paper draws attention to some interesting comparisons between Knowth and Knockroe, a passage-tomb site excavated by the author in county Kilkenny. Although the entire Knockroe complex is no larger than the bigger satellites at Knowth, it is remarkably similar to the large Knowth tumulus in many of its features. The close comparisons with the Boyne Valley, including Newgrange too, are so compelling that they appear to go beyond mere coincidence.

Towards the end of 1989, George Eogan suggested to me that I should consider an archaeological excavation of the passage tomb at Knockroe, county Kilkenny, with a view to addressing some of the ambiguities emerging from the Carrowmore excavations (Burenhult 1980, 114–5; Caulfield 1983). Being a decorated site, located away from the Meath-Sligo axis, Knockroe might show whether the construction phase of passage tombs was as short as the Boyne Valley results suggested or more extended as Göran Burenhult was claiming. In due course, with the aid of research grants from the Royal Irish Academy, four seasons of excavations were conducted at the county Kilkenny site, enriched by discussions with George during and arising from his visits.

Although known since the nineteenth century the Knockroe site had escaped attention throughout the greater part of the twentieth century, in spite of the intense research conducted into megalithic monuments generally in this period. It was not until the mid-1980s that the significance of the site was recognised, when it was published as one of a small group of megalithic tombs distributed loosely across the landscape from the pinnacle of Slievenamon Mountain in south county Tipperary to the rounded summit of Kilmacoliver, an eminence of modest elevation in south county Kilkenny (Ó Nualláin and Cody 1987). These sites overlook the valley of the Lingaun river, a tributary of the Suir, and would appear to be linked in a general way with another scatter of monuments, located on hills flanking the Aherlow river, a tributary entering from the other side of the Suir to the west.

At the time of its re-discovery, the megalithic tomb at Knockroe was overgrown with trees, so that only the western tomb, part of the kerb and an enigmatic concentration of stones on the eastern side were visible. Its most distinctive feature was the existence of megalithic art on many of the structural stones (O'Sullivan 1987). By a strange irony, Knockroe would ultimately prove to have so many similarities with Knowth in particular that any notion of it being an intermediate site between the Boyne Valley structures and those in other parts of Ireland would be difficult to sustain. In any case, the dating of the Carrowmore sites has been discussed again in detail by Berg (1995), while the chronological subtleties of the complex have been recognised in Burenhult's more recent work (pers. comm.).

What makes the similarities between Knowth and Knockroe so interesting is the obvious differences in scale and regional context that can be recognised between the two complexes. Knowth is situated in the geographical heartland of the passage tomb tradition in Ireland, with Newgrange and Dowth as close neighbours, and the Loughcrew complex only forty kilometres distant. Knockroe, by contrast, is a peripheral site in national terms. Some of the other megaliths in the Lingaun group do not appear to be standard passage tombs (O'Sullivan 1993, 14–5) and the nearest known other decorated complex is Baltinglass Hill in county Wicklow, some sixty kilometres to the northeast. In scale, the large tumulus at Knowth dominates the eighteen satellite mounds that surround it, and is the most westerly of the three focal monuments that crown prominent ridges in the Boyne Valley. The cairn at Knockroe, by contrast, approximates in size to the larger Knowth satellites and has no known satellites of its own (Fig 7.1). It is located on the side of a valley rather than on a summit (Fig 7.2) and, bearing in mind the spatial analysis of Irish passage-tomb complexes conducted by Cooney (1990), occurs towards the eastern end of the Lingaun group. The distance from one end of the Boyne Valley group to the other is no more than about two kilometres whereas the distance from the cairn on the summit of Slievenamon to the Baunfree site at the summit of Kilmacoliver is about thirteen kilometres (Fig 7.3). An even greater contrast emerges when it is recognised that as many as forty sites occur in the Boyne Valley group whereas there are at most six sites in the Knockroe group (O'Sullivan 1993, 14–17). Prior to the commencement of the archaeological excavations, only the artwork set Knockroe apart from the other sites in the Slievenamon/

Lingaun region. Even then, however, the total number of decorated stones at Knockroe (*c*. 30) amounts to considerably less than 10% of the total at Knowth.

And yet there are uncanny resemblances between Knockroe and the large focal monuments in the Boyne

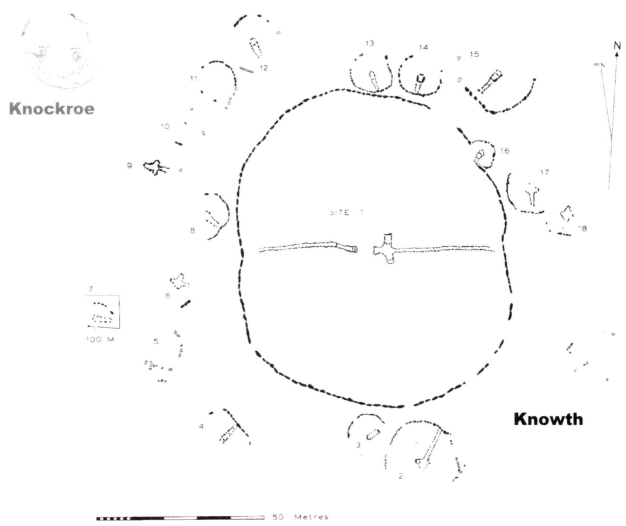

Fig 7.1: Overall plan of Knowth (after Eogan 1986) with plan of Knockroe at approximately the same scale.

Fig 7.2: View of Knockroe complex from the south. The passage-tomb site, located on the south-facing slope of the Lingaun valley, is visible beyond the second hedgerow.

Fig 7.3: Looking west to Slievenamon mountain (far distance) from the back of the chamber at the Baunfree site, located on the summit of Kilmacoliver Hill.

Valley, specifically Knowth and to a lesser extent Newgrange. In terms of its location relative to the nearby river, the cairn at Knockroe occurs on the eastern side of the Lingaun at a point where the east-flowing waterway turns to the south (Fig 7.4). This equates almost exactly to the spatial relationship between Knowth and the Boyne

Fig 7.4: Aerial view of Knockroe passage tomb in its landscape setting, with the deep valley of the Lingaun on the right and the grass-covered Kilmacoliver Hill in the distance (Photograph: Michael Herity).

(Eogan 1986, 13, fig. 2). An added point of comparison is the occurrence of a ford on the river in both cases, within a few hundred metres of the passage tomb complex (see Stout 1997, 303, for Knowth). It could be argued, of course, that these points of comparison are mere coincidences, although the manner in which Baltinglass Hill, for example, overlooks the river Slaney and many other passage tombs occur close to waterways suggests that the position of these monuments in relation to the respective rivers may be deliberate symbolic statements.

In any case, the more convincing parallels between Knockroe and the larger Boyne monuments are seen in the realms of morphology, art and ritual. Like the large tumuli at Knowth and Dowth, the tumulus at Knockroe, although considerably smaller in scale, incorporates two passage tombs. Of the two Boyne Valley comparisons, however, Knowth is the closer. Here, as at Knockroe, the tombs are entered from opposite sides of the mound, although the Knowth tombs lie almost back-to-back on the east-west diameter whereas the Knockroe tombs are entered from the southeast and southwest respectively, with a considerable expanse of cairn between them. Interestingly, however, in the case of both Knowth and Knockroe, the western tomb is relatively simple in plan whereas the eastern tomb is cruciform (Fig 7.5). The

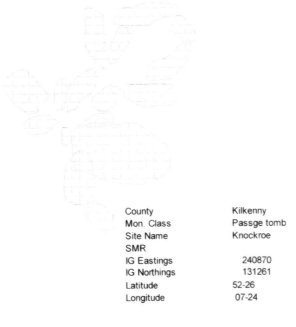

County	Kilkenny
Mon. Class	Passge tomb
Site Name	Knockroe
SMR	
IG Eastings	240870
IG Northings	131261
Latitude	52-26
Longitude	07-24

Line/Point	Magnetic Brg.	Observed Alt.	Latitude	Azimuth	Sun Dec Cen	Sun Dec UL	Sun Dec LL	Remarks
axis	238.00	3	52.43	230.93	-20.34	-20.11	-20.58	Western Tomb
limit	242.00	3	52.43	234.93	-18.28	-18.05	-18.51	Western Tomb
limit	230.00	3	52.43	222.93	-24.19	-23.94	-24.43	Western Tomb
axis	128.00	3	52.43	120.93	-16.07	-15.84	-16.30	Eastern Tomb
limit	143.00	3	52.43	135.93	-23.66	-23.42	-23.90	Eastern Tomb
limit	120.00	3	52.43	112.93	-11.60	-11.38	-11.82	Eastern Tomb

Fig 7.5: Plans of western and eastern tombs at Knockroe, showing their measured alignments. On Midwinter Day, the eastern tomb is aligned to the rising sun and the western tomb is aligned to the setting sun (Data and diagram: Frank Prendergast).

Fig 7.6: View of the forecourt in front of the western tomb at Knockroe, defined by upright quartzite stones flanking the entrance. Notice the line of comparatively large stones running from the foot of the supporting wooden stake on the right to the fallen capstone, lying on the platform towards the right.

Knowth tombs are the more regular in shape, however, the western chamber being quadrilateral (Eogan 1986, 43, fig. 23) and the eastern tomb a polygonal chamber with recesses at the cardinal points (Eogan 1986, 35, fig. 17). The chamber of the west tomb at Knockroe is polygonal in plan (O'Sullivan 1997, 33, fig. 37) and the cruciform shape of the eastern tomb is achieved in a relatively complex manner, the lateral recesses opening off the passage and, in the absence of an end recess, the polygonal chamber acting as the inner end of the cruciform plan (O'Sullivan 1995, 16, fig. 3).

At Knockroe, the western tomb is aligned to the setting sun on mid-winter day and the eastern tomb appears to be aligned on the rising sun that morning (Fig 7.5). It has been suggested that the Knowth tombs are aligned to the rising and setting sun at the spring and autumn equinox, but this claim has not been described or demonstrated with any conviction. On the other hand, the alignment of the Newgrange tomb on the winter solstice has received general acceptance. Solar alignments are claimed with varying degrees of authority and conviction at a number of passage tombs and other prehistoric monuments in Ireland and beyond, but it is interesting that both the Newgrange and Knockroe alignments occur on midwinter day, the former at the rising of the sun and the latter at both the rising and setting. Although Newgrange is aligned to the rising sun on midwinter day and Maes Howe is apparently aligned on the setting sun that same day, alignments on both the rising and setting sun that day appears to be a unique feature of the Knockroe monument.

Preoccupation with the movement of the sun, identified above in the solstice alignments, is reflected in yet another point of comparison between Knockroe and the Boyne Valley. Measurements taken by the writer in 1980 indicate that the sequence of kerbstones along the perimeter of the large tumulus at Knowth is not haphazard. There is a

general, although not rigid, increase in the lengths of the kerbstones from the north and south towards the east and west sides of the mound (O'Sullivan 1998, 45). The shortest stones occur in a sequence along the northern side of the perimeter and the longest kerbstone on both the east and west side is the one located directly in front of the respective tombs. The distribution of artwork appears to follow this pattern. About ninety of the one hundred and thirty kerbstones are decorated with megalithic art and the only unbroken sequence of stones without megalithic art is the sequence of unusually short kerbstones on the northern side. In the circumstances, it is interesting that nine of the ten decorated kerbstones at Knockroe lie south of the tombs (O'Sullivan 1998, 46). The exception, a kerbstone located directly across the cairn from the west tomb, features two short arcs of picking and is the least extensively decorated of the ten kerbstones bearing artwork. The distribution pattern of the artwork along the kerb appears to be intentional in the sense that kerbstones of green sandstone, the material with which megalithic art appears to be most closely associated at both Knockroe and the Boyne Valley, are themselves concentrated along the southern side of the kerb. As if to emphasise the close relationship between artwork and choice of stone, the most distinctive artistic arrangement on the Knockroe kerb is found on kerbstone S2, a lone fine-grained green sandstone in a sequence of decorated coarse-grained green sandstones.

As at Knowth, the significance of the tomb entrances is reflected in the arrangement of kerbstones. The incurved façade flanking the west tomb at Knockroe consists of light grey quartzite blocks, standing on end, which, in colour, texture and the complete absence of artwork, contrast with the green sandstone kerb-stones found elsewhere (Fig 7.6). The three sill stones dividing the chamber are also blocks of quartzite. A further small collection of undecorated quartzite blocks occurs along the kerb in front of the east tomb, while the sill stones and a minority of the orthostats in the east tomb are also of quartzite. It is striking, in this context, that the pillar standing in front of the west tomb at Knowth is identified as quartzo-sandstone (Eogan 1986, 65). This pillar occurs in a row of unusual boulders and nodules located in front of the tomb, traversing its long axis. At Knockroe, too, a line of stones occurred on the platform in front of the west tomb, traversing the line of the tomb (Fig 7.6). One of the stones in this collection was a nodule of granite, the only piece of granite identified at Knockroe and further distinguished through its identification as Galway granite, a non-local intrusion into this area of Ireland. Moreover, in the vicinity of both the eastern and western tombs, the collapsed perimeter of the cairn was marked by a comparative profusion of quartz (O'Sullivan 1993, 11, fig. 3). The occurrence of this phenomenon at Newgrange and Knowth has been recorded by O'Kelly (1982) and Eogan (1986). As O'Kelly claimed in the case of Newgrange, some of the quartz at Knockroe appears to have collapsed from above the kerbstones (O'Sullivan 1993, 12–13). Again, the discovery of three sandstone balls at the entrance to the east tomb at Knockroe mirrors the profusion of water-rolled stones recorded in front of the kerb around the entrances at Newgrange and Knowth.

A common feature amongst Irish cruciform passage tombs is the relative emphasis given to the right-hand recess. It tends to be slightly bigger and sometimes more elaborate than the left-hand recess. In the focal cairns of the Boyne Valley, the emphasis on the right-hand recess is unusually pronounced. At Newgrange, for instance, it is in the right-hand recess that a unique pair of basins occur, one resting on the other, and an unusually elaborate arrangement of megalithic art is found on the capstone. In the case of Dowth, the right-hand recess of the northern, cruciform, tomb is also distinguished from the left-hand equivalent by its size, elaborate design and artwork. The most impressive right-hand recess of all occurs in the east tomb at Knowth. Here, the entrance to the recess is marked by a pair of jambs, a feature that is unknown in the case of either the left-hand or end recess. A substantial basin, magnificently shaped and elaborated decorated, occurs in the right-hand recess and this compartment is further distinguished by the impressive artwork on the backstone and the corbel overlying it. The discovery of the decorated mace-head at the entrance to this recess is further proof of its pre-eminence. At Knockroe, too, the right-hand recess of the east tomb is distinguished by some unique features, of which the most obvious is the Carrowkeel pot discovered in the fill (O'Sullivan 1995, 26). Although this pot was crushed, its upper portion missing, it is a rare example of a relatively complete Carrowkeel vessel occurring *in situ*. The fact that it rested in the right-hand recess might be taken as an accident of discovery, were it not for the manner in which the backstone of this recess is also distinguished. What sets this stone apart from the other orthostats in the tomb is the large natural hollows in its face (Fig 7.7). In general, an unusually large proportion of the structural stones employed in passage tombs feature cupmarks, natural hollows and other anomalies, the frequent occurrence of which appears to reflect the symbolic importance of such stones in the passage tomb tradition. Even within the chamber at Gavrinis, in Brittany, the surface of orthostat 18 is interrupted by a horizontal array of three deep pits separated by strap-like causeways (Le Roux 1985, 85). Below this arrangement, the decoration features spirals, an unusual occurrence in Brittany but a distinctive feature of Irish megalithic art. Accordingly, there may be some significance in the location of stones marked by distinctive natural features. In terms of symbolism, the hollowed stone at the back of the right-hand recess in the east tomb at Knockroe may be as important as the decoration in the equivalent recesses at Newgrange and Knowth. Likewise, the occurrence of the Carrowkeel pot at Knockroe may be as ideologically significant as the distinctive basins at Knowth and Newgrange.

Fig 7.7: View into the northern, right-hand recess of the east tomb at Knockroe, showing the distinctive natural hollows in the backstone.

With only a single exception the orthostats and surviving roof stones in the western tomb at Knockroe are green sandstones. The exception is orthostat 11, a pink sandstone located beside the inner sill stone, on the south side of the chamber. This is the most intriguing upright in the tomb. It is awkward from a structural viewpoint, being warped and asymmetrical in form, especially at the lower end where it thickens considerably to one side. By comparison with the other orthostats it is exceptionally tall, to the extent that a special matching orthostat appears to have been added outside the northern side of the chamber, a stone rising to a similar height as the pink orthostat on the south side, presumably so that the overlying roof stone could rest horizontally on this pair. Such a complicated arrangement, designed to facilitate the inclusion of the pink sandstone, implies that the stone in question was deemed to be very important. In the absence of any obvious structural value, the stone would appear to have been included for its symbolic value. Its location beside a sill stone may also be significant. Each of the two sides of the western tomb at Knowth consists of a sequence of approximately forty orthostats.

One of these is orthostat 49, located on the right-hand side directly inside the outermost of the three sill stones in the tomb. The orthostat bears a design that, although not unique in compositional terms, is singularly impressive in an aesthetic sense and has often been interpreted as a stylized anthropomorphic image (Eogan 1986, fig. 11). Bearing in mind the numerous other similarities between Knowth and Knockroe noted above, it is tempting to speculate whether the pink sandstone beside the sill stone in the west tomb at Knockroe corresponds in some symbolic way with the anthropomorphic design beside the sill stone in the western tomb at Knowth. Both occur on the right hand side. Anthropomorphic images in other passage tombs appear to be located at similar transition points in the structures.

In the light of the many comparisons discussed above, it is not surprising that the closest parallels for some of the artwork at Knockroe are to be found in the Boyne Valley and specifically at Knowth. Only in the larger tumuli of the Boyne Valley, for example, is art of a similarly impressive scale found along the kerb, there being more decorated stones along the one kerb at Knockroe than are known in total amongst the kerbs of the twelve decorated sites in the Loughcrew complex. At a more detailed level, the array of serpentiform lines on kerbstone S2 at Knockroe finds no comparisons in Ireland other than on some of the kerbstones at Knowth. Similarly, the tightly coiled linear designs on orthostats 8 and 10 in the western tomb at Knockroe find no parallels in Ireland, except possibly in the tombs at Knowth. Beyond the megalithic artwork, it is interesting that fragments of a decorated bone object recovered from the western tomb at Knockroe appear to be the fragmentary remains of a large pin bearing an inscribed chevron design. Only three other examples of this pin type are known in Ireland, two from Knowth and one from Fourknocks I (Eogan 1986, 143, fig. 58).

In scale, diversity and overall archaeological richness, Knockroe is a relatively minor site by comparison with Knowth. There are many characteristic at Knowth that are not shared at Knockroe; there are many characteristics at Knockroe that are unique to that site; and there are a few characteristics at Knockroe that compare more closely with Loughcrew than the Boyne Valley. That said, however, it is Knowth that provides the closest parallels for many of the more impressive features at Knockroe. It is easier to identify these comparisons than to explain them. To suggest that the designers of the enormous complex at Knowth were trying to imitate a relatively isolated site in county Kilkenny is probably to invite ridicule. In any case, there are no *prima facie* grounds for such a claim. And yet, the temptation to interpret Knockroe as a smaller replica of Knowth runs into many obstacles, not least the lack of a detailed chronological sequence for the two complexes. Even the existence of radiocarbon determinations, notably in the case of Knowth, does not provide the level of detail that would be required, because of the wobbles along this part of the calibration curve. It also stretches reason to suggest that the designers of both complexes happened by chance to produce incredibly similar solutions to various problems of design, construction and ritual usage.

The most reasonable explanation that can be offered is that Knockroe was constructed at a time when the focal tumulus at Knowth was already in existence or at an advanced stage of planning and design. The designers at Knockroe, while following their own specific agenda, incorporated a number of features that appear to be echoes of the Knowth complex, as if the identification with Knowth represented by these echoes was an exceptionally significant gesture. In historical times, there are many instances of such acts of identification. The layout of most church buildings, for example, reflect the general theological world-view and relevant cultural *milieu* in which they were constructed, but some individual church buildings might also reflect ideas deliberately borrowed from another ecclesiastical site. In this as in other spheres of life, it is often the structure at the centre of the tradition, whether in Rome, London or Athens, that provides the inspiration for elements at the periphery. Was it likewise in the case of the Irish passage tomb tradition? In the case of Knockroe, for example, the similarities with the Boyne Valley might be interpreted as expressions of identification, perhaps even of identity. It would appear that the relationship with the Boyne Valley in this case took a different turn from that recognised at Loughcrew.

The feast of discovery at Knowth over the past forty years is a measure of George Eogan's energy, single-mindedness and perseverance. His constant flow of publications setting out the various findings has been remarkable in an era when the publishing of excavation reports has fallen behind schedule. The challenge for the future, however, is to maintain the flow of publications into the next generation of Knowth scholarship. Having feasted on the richness of the Knowth complex, archaeologists are now challenged to assess this vast array of material in the light of emerging insights and discoveries elsewhere. While comparative discussions of the type set out here are less exciting than the wonder of primary exploration, they help to identify the patterns that give meaning to the original discovery. They also provide the accumulated indicators from which conclusions about the complexity of Neolithic society can best the drawn.

Bibliography

Bergh, S. 1995 *Landscape of the Monuments: A Study of the Passage Tombs in the Cúil Irra Region, Co. Sligo, Ireland.* Central Board of National Antiquities, Stockholm.

Burenhult, G. 1980 *The Archaeological Excavations at Carrowmore, Co. Sligo, Ireland: Excavation Seasons: 1977–79. Theses and Papers in North-European Archaeology*, University of Stockholm.

Caulfield, S. 1983 The Neolithic settlement of North Connaught. In T. Reeves-Smyth and F. Hammond (eds) *Landscape Archae-*

ology in Ireland, 195–215. British Archaeological Reports British Series **116**, Oxford.

Cooney, G. 1990 The place of megalithic tomb cemeteries in Ireland, *Antiquity* **64**, 741–53.

Eogan, G. 1986 *Knowth and the Passage-Tombs of Ireland.* Thames and Hudson, London.

Le Roux, C.-T. 1985 *Gavrinis et les Îles du Morbihan: Les Mégalithes du Golfe.* Guides Archéologiques de la France 6, Ministère de la Culture, Imprimerie nationale, Paris.

O'Kelly, M.J. 1982 *Newgrange: Archaeology, Art and Legend.* Thames and Hudson, London.

Ó Nualláin, S. and Cody, E. 1987 Passage Tombs in the Suir Valley region, *Journal of the Royal Society of Antiquaries of Ireland* **117**, 69–83.

O'Sullivan, M. 1987 The art of the Passage Tomb at Knockroe, county Kilkenny, *Journal of the Royal Society of Antiquaries of Ireland* **117**, 84–95.

O'Sullivan, M. 1993 Recent investigations at Knockroe Passage Tomb, *Journal of the Royal Society of Antiquaries of Ireland* **123**, 5–18.

O'Sullivan, M. 1995 The eastern tomb at Knockroe, *Old Kilkenny Review: Journal of the Kilkenny Archaeological Society* **47**, 11–30.

O'Sullivan, M. 1997 On the meaning of megalithic art, *Brigantium* **10**, 23–35.

O'Sullivan, M. 1998 Retrieval and revision in the interpretation of megalithic art. In C. Jones and C. Hayden (eds) *The Archaeology of Perception and the Senses*, 37–48. Archaeological Review from Cambridge **15**(1), Cambridge University Press, Cambridge.

Stout, G. 1997 The Bend of the Boyne, County Meath. In F.H.A., Aalen, K. Whelan, and M. Stout, *Atlas of the Irish Rural Landscape*, 299–315, Cork University Press.

8. Exotic materials in the Early Bronze Age of Southeastern England

Timothy Champion

In November 2001 a metal-detectorist prospecting in a field at Woodnesborough, near Sandwich, Kent, in southeastern England, found a small crumpled object of sheet metal. It turned out to be a gold cup of Early Bronze Age date, and an important addition to the small class of such items known in western Europe. The Ringlemere cup, as it is now known from its findspot, was a most unexpected discovery, and not the least surprising thing about it was its location in East Kent, an area not normally associated with rich or exotic finds of this period. The aim of this paper is to explore the regional context of the cup within Kent and more widely within southeastern England in the light of some other recent discoveries. It is a particular pleasure to be able to offer such a contribution to this volume in honour of George Eogan, that master of Bronze Age metalwork scholarship, whose work includes a study of the goldwork of Britain and Ireland (Eogan 1994). Another, much earlier work, on Late Bronze Age metalwork (Eogan 1964), formed an essential part of my own introduction to the archaeology of Ireland, and it was a pleasure therefore eventually to meet its author. His friendship over many years, exemplified by his ready willingness to show generations of our English students around the excavations at Knowth, has been greatly appreciated.

Exotic materials in Early Bronze Age Kent

The prehistoric period in Kent has, on the whole, not received the same level of attention as the Roman and Anglo-Saxon. The latest published review of the Bronze Age (Champion 1982) adopted a rather negative and pessimistic tone about the quantity and quality of evidence available, but recent years have seen considerable progress. Grinsell's discussion of the Bronze Age barrows of Kent (1992) documented the limited evidence available from excavations, but was compiled before recent aerial photographic evidence was available and seriously underestimated the number of barrows that must originally have existed. Development work in Kent, especially road and rail construction, has led to the excavation of over twenty barrows in Kent in the last two decades, though

few are yet published. This evidence is beginning to transform our knowledge of the period (Fig 8.1).

The Ringlemere cup (Varndell and Needham 2002) was found in a plough-damaged barrow, which survives as a barely visible mound. It presumably derives from a burial in the barrow, though its nature is unknown. The barrow was built in a place that had already seen Late Neolithic activity. Flints and pottery, especially Grooved Ware, were found in the material making up the barrow mound and in pits, suggesting that the place had a long history of significance.

Other nearby sites which have produced exotic materials include Monkton, on the Isle of Thanet in northeast Kent, where road improvements cut through a large barrow cemetery (unpublished excavations by Canterbury Archaeological Trust). The barrows had been ploughed out, but the cemetery was known from aerial photographs. The roadworks affected ten barrows, and a series of burials from the Beaker period to the Middle Bronze Age were revealed. Among the burials was an inhumation accompanied by a Beaker and 217 small disc beads of jet, which would originally have comprised all or part of a necklace. Analysis has confirmed that the beads are made of true jet, almost certainly from Whitby in Yorkshire. Another barrow in the cemetery produced a jet bead and a copper alloy bead from the fill of the ditch; these probably derived from a burial, or possibly two different burials, which had originally been deposited in the barrow before being ploughed out.

There are two other known finds of jet close to Monkton and also on the Isle of Thanet. A Beaker burial in a ploughed-out barrow at Manston, northwest of Ramsgate (Perkins and Gibson 1990), contained a flint knife and a V-perforated jet button. On the western edge of Ramsgate itself, at Chalk Hill, works for the new approach road to the harbour (unpublished excavations by Canterbury Archaeological Trust) revealed a Neolithic causewayed enclosure (Dyson *et al.* 2000), and only 60 metres outside the outer ditch another ploughed-out barrow contained a further Beaker burial with a jet pendant.

Another exotic material found in Kent is *faience.*

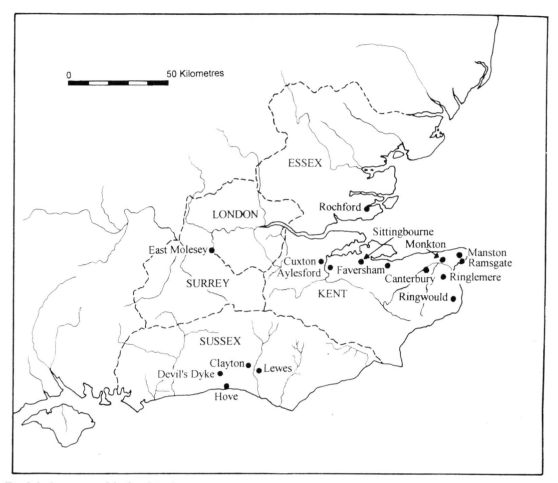

Fig 8.1: Location of finds of Early Bronze Age gold, amber, jet, shale and faience in southeastern England.

Nineteenth-century excavations (Woodruff 1874) of a pair of barrows on the chalk downland above Ringwould, near Deal, produced a series of burials in the western one. A group of four small pits were cut down into the chalk bedrock below the barrow mound, each containing an inverted urn placed over the cremated bone. One of these burials included a Wessex biconical urn inverted over an incense cup and another small vessel, which had in turn been placed on top of the cremated remains, among which were found three segmented beads and one oblate bead of *faience* (Woodruff 1874, 21–25 and Pl. II, 3, 4, 6).

These finds of gold, jet and *faience* all occur in a small area of East Kent, within about 15km of each other. The pattern can be augmented by the evidence of early copper alloy metalwork; although the distribution is not so tightly clustered, there is a considerable concentration in East Kent, especially when seen in comparison to the rest of southeastern England. Among the burials excavated during road construction at Monkton were two further Beaker inhumations which each contained a small bronze bracelet. Exact parallels are hard to find, but they clearly belong in the Migdale-Marnoch tradition (Britton 1963, 263–279, esp. 271 and 274) or to Metalwork Assemblage III (MA III), characterised by the presence of ornaments such as bracelets (Needham *et al.* 1985, iii).

Other metal finds include tanged copper daggers from East Kent, found at Sittingbourne, Faversham and Canterbury (Gerloff 1975, nos 5, 13, 17). These are spread out along the northern coastal region, but there is also a small cluster of copper alloy objects in the Medway valley, represented by finds of dagger blades at Aylesford and Cuxton (Gerloff 1975, nos 86, 103, 110), to which can now be added a further find from the River Medway itself (Kelly 1987, 356).

Kent in its regional context

This distribution of gold, jet, faience and copper alloy objects, found from the Medway valley eastwards and especially in the easternmost part of the county, must be placed in a wider regional setting to establish whether it is a markedly clustered concentration or part of a much wider pattern in the region. To provide that regional context, similar finds have been documented for the southeastern region of England, comprising Sussex, Surrey, London and Essex (Fig 8.1). The evidence available from this region has been reviewed, using county surveys such as those for Essex (Buckley 1980; Bedwin 1996), Surrey (Bird and Bird 1987), London (Kendall 2000) and East Anglia (Glazebrook 1997), as well as catalogues of material such as those of gold (Taylor 1980; Eogan 1994), *faience* (Beck and Stone 1935), amber (Beck and Shennan 1991), copper alloy daggers (Gerloff 1975), Beakers (Clarke 1970) and collared urns (Longworth 1984), supplemented by personal (and probably patchy) knowledge of more recent discoveries.

In Essex, there is only one find of relevance, an important but inadequately published cremation burial from Rochford, near Southend, originally found in 1914 (Erith 1963; Couchman 1980, 40; Beck and Shennan 1991, 168). The cremation, which may have been contained in a collared urn, was accompanied by a necklace comprising eleven amber beads, two shale beads with gold sheeting, and a further four gold sheets.

There are no comparable finds in Surrey, while in the Greater London district there is only one. A double cremation burial under a ploughed-out barrow excavated at East Molesey (Brown and Cotton 2000, 85) contained three segmented *faience* beads.

In Sussex, on the other hand, there are rather more relevant finds. The most famous of these is the amber cup from a grave group found in a barrow at Hove in 1856 (Curwen 1954, 152–3, pl. XIII; Gerloff 1975, no. 183; Clarke *et al.* 1985, 277, no. 97 and fig. 4.45). An inhumation burial in a tree-trunk coffin was accompanied by a stone battle-axe, a whetstone pendant, a bronze dagger and the amber cup. Amber was also found in a bowl barrow excavated in the early nineteenth century at Oxsettle (or Oxteddle) Bottom, Lewes (Curwen 1954, 157, fig. 42; Longworth 1984, no. 562, pl. 197e). This contained a cremation burial in a collared urn, accompanied by a bronze ring, a boar's tusk, a bone pin and a number of beads and pendants, which were in all probability originally parts of a necklace; these comprised one quoit pendant and two segmented beads of *faience*, two amber beads, and at least sixteen items of jet.

Two other finds from Sussex complete this brief catalogue. A Beaker burial at Beggar's Haven, Devil's Dyke, contained parts of a necklace comprising copper and lignite beads (Grinsell 1931, 39; Curwen 1954, 150, pl. XI, 3–4; Clarke 1970, no. 991), while a single *faience* quoit pendant was found in an urn at Clayton Hill, near Lewes (Beck and Stone 1935; Curwen 1954, 157, fig. 43).

There is thus a small cluster of finds in East Sussex, and only very occasional finds anywhere else in southeastern England. This picture is confirmed by the pattern of copper and bronze daggers catalogued and mapped by Gerloff (1975). Apart from a number of such objects from the River Thames (*e.g.* nos 16, 146, 148, 151), there is a single find from Teddington (no. 102) in the Thames valley to the west of London not far from East Molesey, and two others from Sussex (nos 159 and 183), including the example from Hove found with the amber cup mentioned above. Otherwise, the southeast of England is devoid of finds.

Though the purpose of this investigation is to emphasise the existence of hitherto unrecognised regional groups, it is worth noting that many of the finds of exotic materials noted here conform to a pattern beginning to be identified in Beaker and Early Bronze Age burials elsewhere. Woodward (2000, 100–122) has noted that many of the finds of beads cannot have been survivals from complete objects, but may rather represent fragments of composite necklaces or carefully selected groups of individual items with special significance to their owner. Even the 217 jet beads from Monkton would have extended to a length of little more than 20cm, and may have originally, before burial, been only part of a longer string. Similarly, the collections of items from Rochford and Oxteddle Bottom, Lewes, seem unlikely ever to have been used as a single necklace.

Clusters and continuity

It has long been recognised that the distribution of such materials as copper, gold, jet, amber and *faience* in the British Early Bronze Age is a highly clustered one. Piggott's (1938) classic study of this material concentrated on the evidence from Wessex and saw such burials as representing a 'Wessex culture'. With further research it is clear that other concentrations of wealth existed in the Bronze Age, and particular attention has been given to regions such as the Peak District, Yorkshire and parts of Scotland (*e.g.* Clarke *et al.* 1985). It is becoming increasingly obvious, however, that in addition to these very large clusters there are other areas of Britain that show lesser concentrations of some or all of these materials. Against the background, demonstrated above, of a very low density of finds of such materials throughout the southeast of England, the concentrations in Sussex and in East Kent stand out, suggesting that Bronze Age societies there shared some of the cultural practices seen most plentifully in Wessex and also shared access to some of these exotic raw materials.

Other finds in the East Kent region emphasise the connection with Wessex and the shared traditions. The burial at Ringwould which included the *faience* beads also contained a small pottery vessel of the type known as an 'incense cup'. These are best known from richer graves in the Wessex region. Other examples are known in Kent from Luddington Wood between Bekesbourne and Littlebourne, near Canterbury, and from barrow sites at Tilmanstone and Lord of the Manor, Ozingell, near Ramsgate on Thanet (Perkins n d, 18 20). Other fragments of such vessels have been found at Monkton and at Castle Hill, Folkestone. It is interesting to note that another example of such an accessory vessel was found in Sussex at Clayton Hill, not far from the *faience* pendant mentioned above (Curwen 1954, 157, fig. 44). Another important find linking Kent and Wessex is a pair of bone tweezers found in the White Caps barrow at Whitfield, north of Dover, again during road works (unpublished excavations by Canterbury Archaeological Trust). Such tweezers are most commonly associated with Wessex graves (Proudfoot

1963, 424–425) and found exclusively in Wessex and the Upper Thames Valley with this exception.

Although the quantity and quality of the objects is of a very different order, it can be seen that the East Kent region shares many of the traits best seen in Wessex. It should be seen as a distinct regional group, as also should the East Sussex finds. Quite why the distribution of these materials is so clustered in the Early Bronze Age, and quite why the clusters are where they are, are difficult questions to answer. The cluster in Kent is particularly interesting for the diversity of the material represented and for its long-lasting existence. The burials and objects discussed could have been deposited over a period of as long as four or five hundred years. One factor that may have been important in this particular case is Kent's geographical location, strategically placed at the shortest crossing of the English Channel and at the junction of the Channel and the North Sea. These maritime links are seen very clearly in some of the finds from Monkton: the jet from Whitby has been described above, while another burial contained a Trevisker urn from Cornwall (Gibson *et al.* 1997). The most likely means of these arriving in Kent would have been by boat along the coast. The clearest evidence of the importance of maritime transport at this time is the Bronze Age Dover boat (Clark forthcoming). It is interesting to note that when the Dover boat was finally deposited in its resting place in a backwater of the River Dour, it was accompanied by a placed deposit of another exotic raw material, shale from Kimmeridge in Dorset.

Another important factor in the location of these rich burials in Kent may be the continuity of the significance of place. Thomas (1991, 145–177) has shown how in certain parts of the landscape of Wessex and the Upper Thames Valley Early Neolithic long barrows and causewayed enclosures acted as a focus for the location of later monuments such as henges and round barrows. It is possible that something similar was happening in Kent. Recent excavation and aerial photography has documented the existence, previously unsuspected, of causewayed enclosures, but there is still no persuasive evidence for the henges.

There are two certain and two probable causewayed enclosures in Kent (Oswald *et al.* 2001). Two of these lie in the East Kent zone of rich burials described earlier. The barrow with the Beaker burial and jet pendant at Chalk Hill, Ramsgate, was immediately outside the ditches of one of the excavated examples, which had at a later date been crossed by a pair of parallel ditches, possibly representing a cursus (Dyson *et al.* 2000). The other site at Tilmanstone, suspected from air photographs, is in the heart of the area containing many of the burials described above, close to the barrows containing one of the incense cups and only about 5km from Ringlemere. There is, of course, a long time lag between the construction of the causewayed enclosures in the fourth millennium and the deposition of the burials early in the second. The

enclosures would, however, have marked significant places in the landscape and their ditches may have remained visible for a very long period. The proximity of the barrow and the enclosure at Chalk Hill, Ramsgate, may not be purely coincidental, and the pits with Grooved Ware at Ringlemere suggest a much longer period of activity on the site before its use for a human burial. There is also evidence for long continuity of respect and activity after the Bronze Age burials. The barrow at Manston containing the Beaker burial and perforated jet button also had a series of small pits dug into it, each containing a carefully placed lump of flint and a sherd of Late Bronze Age pottery. This activity must have taken place at least a millennium after the burial.

Although no exotic materials such as gold, jet or *faience* have been found in the Medway valley, it was noted above that there is a concentration of early copper and copper alloy daggers there. Here too it is tempting to think that their location may reflect the long-term significance of the middle Medway region. It has the largest concentration of Neolithic monuments in south-eastern England. There are two groups of megaliths which, though now ruinous, were once some of the largest and most impressive of early Neolithic funerary monuments anywhere in the country (Ashbee 1993; 1999; 2000). The western group comprises three certain monuments, Addington and the Chestnuts close to each other and Coldrum a short distance to the north (Ashbee 1998); two others may have existed close to Coldrum, but they are now reduced to a long spread mound of chalk and a line of sarsen stones respectively. The other cluster lies at the foot of the scarp slope of the North Downs east of the Medway. It comprises four certain monuments and two possible ones; Kit's Coty House (Ashbee 2000, 328, pl. II) is perhaps the best known monument in Kent. Not far from this group is the early Neolithic house excavated at White Horse Stone during the building of the Channel Tunnel Rail Link (Glass 1999, 192, fig. 2); this clearly had a long significance after its initial construction, as deposits of Peterborough and Grooved Ware pottery show. Only a short distance to the north, on the side of the Medway valley is another possible Neolithic causewayed enclosure at Burham (Oswald *et al.* 2001). As in the far east of Kent, there may be difficulties in the very long time span involved from the construction of the early Neolithic monuments to the deposition of the Bronze Age burials, but the geographical proximity of these finds is striking. It may also be significant that Grooved Ware, which is not at all common in Kent, has been found in the pits at the Ringlemere barrow and in a pit at the site of the Neolithic house at White Horse Stone.

The evidence for prehistoric Kent is growing rapidly, and it has been possible here to do no more than indicate the patterns that are beginning to emerge and to suggest some lines for future enquiry. It is a sobering thought that, of all the evidence from Kent discussed here, only the ruined megaliths, some of the daggers and the

Ringwould barrow were known more than fifteen years ago; all the rest are more recent discoveries. There is every reason to expect that future work will bring as many surprises. In the meantime, it can be proposed that there was a distinct regional group of wealthy burials of the Early Bronze Age in East Kent, with a particular focus in the very easternmost part of the county; something similar may have happened in the Medway valley, but the evidence is less clear. These people had access to the same exotic materials as are seen in greater abundance in better known regions such as Wessex and shared many of the same practices associated with the deposition of objects in graves. The location of these clusters of deposits was in all probability influenced by long-term respect for places in the landscape, already marked by the prior existence of major Neolithic monuments.

Acknowledgements

I am grateful to the Canterbury Archaeological Trust, and especially to Paul Bennett, Peter Clark and Tim Allen, for information about recent excavations as yet unpublished. The views expressed here are my own responsibility.

Bibliography

Ashbee, P. 1993 The Medway megaliths in perspective, *Archaeologia Cantiana* **111**, 57–111.

Ashbee, P. 1998 Coldrum revisited and reviewed, *Archaeologia Cantiana* **118**, 1–43.

Ashbee, P. 1999 The Medway megaliths in a European context, *Archaeologia Cantiana* **119**, 269–284.

Ashbee, P. 2000 The Medway megalithic long barrows, *Archaeologia Cantiana* **120**, 319–345.

Beck, C. and Shennan, S. 1991 *Amber in prehistoric Britain*. Oxbow, Oxford.

Beck, H.C. and Stone, J.F.S. 1935 Faience beads of the British Bronze Age, *Archaeologia* **85**, 203–252.

Bedwin, O. (ed.) 1996 *The archaeology of Essex: Proceedings of the 1993 Writtle conference*. Essex County Council Planning Department, Chelmsford.

Bird, J. and Bird, D.G. (eds) 1987 *The archaeology of Surrey to 1540*. Surrey Archaeological Society, Guildford.

Britton, D. 1963 Traditions of early metalworking in the later neolithic and earlier Bronze Age in Britain: Part 1, *Proceedings of the Prehistoric Society* **29**, 258–325.

Brown, N. and Cotton, J. 2000 The Bronze Age. In M. Kendall (ed.), *The archaeology of Greater London: an assessment of archaeological evidence for human presence in the area now covered by Greater London*, 81–100. Museum of London, London.

Buckley, D.G. (ed.) 1980 *Archaeology in Essex to AD 1500*. Council for British Archaeology Research Report **34**. Council for British Archaeology, London.

Champion, T.C. 1982 The Bronze Age in Kent. In P. Leach (ed.), *Archaeology in Kent to AD 1500*, 31–39. Council for British Archaeology, London.

Clark, P. (ed.) forthcoming *The Dover Bronze Age boat*. English Heritage, London.

Clarke, D.L. 1970 *Beaker pottery of Great Britain and Ireland*. Cambridge University Press, Cambridge.

Clarke, D.V., Cowie, T.G. and Foxon, A. 1985 *Symbols of power at the time of Stonehenge*. Her Majesty's Stationery Office and the National Museum of Antiquities of Scotland, Edinburgh.

Couchman, C. 1980 The Bronze Age in Essex. In D. Buckley (ed.), *Archaeology in Essex to AD 1500*, 40–46. Council for British Archaeology, London.

Curwen, E.C. 1954 *The archaeology of Sussex*. Methuen 2nd ed. London.

Dyson, L., Shand, G. and Stevens, S. 2000 Causewayed enclosures, *Current Archaeology* **168**, 470–472.

Eogan, G. 1964 The Later Bronze Age in Ireland in the light of recent research, *Proceedings of the Prehistoric Society* **30**, 268–351.

Eogan, G. 1994 *The accomplished art: gold and gold-working in Britain and Ireland during the Bronze Age*. Oxbow, Oxford.

Erith, F. 1963 The Rochford gold necklace and the Middle Bronze Age in Essex, *Colchester Archaeological Group Bulletin* **6**(1), 2–5.

Gerloff, S. 1975 *The early Bronze Age daggers in Great Britain and a reconsideration of the Wessex Culture*. Beck, Munich.

Gibson, A., MacPherson-Grant, N. and Stewart, I. 1997 A Cornish vessel from farthest Kent, *Antiquity* **71**, 438–441.

Glass, H.J. 1999 Archaeology of the Channel Tunnel Rail Link, *Archaeologia Cantiana* **119**, 189–220.

Glazebrook, J. (ed.) 1997 *Research and archaeology: a framework for the eastern counties, 1: resource assessment*. East Anglian Archaeology Occasional Paper **3**. Scole Archaeological Committee for East Anglia, Norwich.

Grinsell, L.V. 1931 Sussex in the Bronze Age, *Sussex Archaeological Collections* **72**, 30–68.

Grinsell, L.V. 1992 The Bronze Age round barrows of Kent, *Proceedings of the Prehistoric Society* **58**, 355–384.

Kelly, D. 1987 Archaeological notes from Maidstone Museum, *Archaeologia Cantiana* **104**, 350–367.

Kendall, M. (ed.) 2000 *The archaeology of Greater London: an assessment of archaeological evidence for human presence in the area now covered by Greater London*. Museum of London, London.

Longworth, I.H. 1984 *Collared urns of the Bronze Age in Great Britain and Ireland*. Cambridge University Press, Cambridge.

Needham, S.P., Lawson, A.J. and Green, H.S. 1985 *British Bronze Age Metalwork, Associated Finds Series: A1–6, Early Bronze Age Hoards*. British Museum, London.

Oswald, A., Dyer, C. and Barber, M. 2001 *The creation of monuments: neolithic causewayed enclosures in the British Isles*. English Heritage, Swindon.

Perkins, D.R.J. n d *The Isle of Thanet Archaeological Unit: interim excavation reports 1977–1980*. Isle of Thanet Archaeological Unit, Ramsgate.

Perkins, D.R.J. and Gibson, A. 1990 A Beaker burial from Manston, near Ramsgate, *Archaeologia Cantiana* **108**, 11–27.

Piggott, P. 1938 The Early Bronze Age in Wessex, *Proceedings of the Prehistoric Society* **4**, 52–106.

Proudfoot, E.V.W. 1963 Report on the excavation of a bell barrow in the parish of Edmondsham, Dorset, England, 1959, *Proceedings of the Prehistoric Society* **29**, 395–425.

Taylor, J.J. 1980 *Bronze Age goldwork of the British Isles*. Cambridge University Press, Cambridge.

Thomas, J.S. 1991 *Rethinking the neolithic*. Cambridge University Press, Cambridge.

Varndell, G. and Needham, S. 2002 New gold cup from Kent, *PAST (Newsletter of the Prehistoric Society)* **41**, 2–4.

Woodruff, C.H. 1874 On Celtic tumuli in east Kent, *Archaeologia Cantiana* **9**, 16–30.

Woodward, A. 2000 *British barrows: a matter of life and death*. Tempus, Stroud.

9. The construction of funerary monuments in the Irish Early Bronze Age: a review of the evidence

James Eogan

One of my father's main areas of research, certainly the one that was most obvious to me spending long enjoyable summers at Knowth, is in monuments and monumentality. His field research has been principally concerned with passage tombs. It is notable that as one crosses the period boundary from the Neolithic to the Early Bronze Age the focus of research changes from monuments to artefacts, individual graves and technology. This paper, which attempts to straddle that boundary, is offered with thanks for the many hours enjoyed excavating (and socialising) at Knowth and for the numerous field trips to other monuments in Meath and beyond.

Almost 1,400 Early Bronze Age graves have been identified in Ireland, of this number 563 have been found in or at 325 monuments of various types (Table 9.1). Two patterns are apparent from examination of this data, firstly that a considerable number of monuments, principally barrows and cairns, were constructed in this period and secondly that significant numbers of earlier monuments were re-used in this period as places of burial.

Monument type	Percentage of all known examples with secondary EBA burials
Court tombs	4
Portal tomb	2
Passage tombs	14
Linkardstown-type graves	71
Wedge tombs	5

Table 9.2: Frequancy of secondary Early Bronze Age burials at Neolithic burial monuments.

While this paper will focus on Early Bronze Age barrows and cairns it is worth noting that significant patterns are also apparent within the re-use of earlier monuments. Early Bronze Age burials have been found in secondary positions at passage tombs and Linkardstown-type graves in disproportionate numbers when compared to the number of the same types of burials found at other types of Neolithic burial monuments (Table 9.2).

The study of all aspects of Early Bronze Age burial practices is impeded by the poor standards of recording (cf. Waddell 1990; Mount 1997). The majority of monuments at which Early Bronze Age burials have been identified were investigated before 1930 (Fig 9.1) and information on the form of the monument in which the burials were placed is generally recorded in a cursory fashion. While standards improved greatly from the 1930s even after that date there are instances where details of individual sites are scanty. It is notable that while the quality of archaeological excavation and recording techniques improved through the 20th century the number of excavations at Early Bronze Age burial monuments has decreased (Fig 9.2). While the numbers have risen in the last decade to the levels seen in the 1940s and '50s, as a result of developer-funded excavation, as a proportion of all excavations carried out in this decade the numbers have declined. The study of Early Bronze Age burial monuments in Ireland has never reached a critical mass due to the lack of a systematic programme of investigation.

Monument type	Number
Barrows	91
Cairns	88
Passage tombs	32
Wedge tombs	27
Standing stones	17
Court tombs	16
Ring ditches	14
Possible monuments	13
Ring barrows	9
Linkardstown-type graves	5
Stone circles	3
Ring cairns	3
Portal tombs	3
Unclassified megaliths	2
Henges	2
Total	325

Table 9.1: Monuments at which Early Bronze Age burials have been found.

Fig 9.1: Date of the first report of investigations at barrows and cairns.

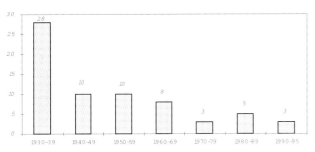

Fig 9.2: Number of excavations at barrows and cairns (post-1930).

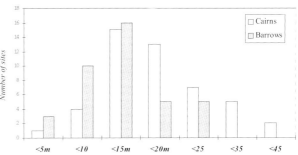

Fig 9.3: Maximum recorded diameters of barrows and cairns.

	Townland	County	Form	Diameter
1.	Mullyknock	Fermanagh	cairn	27.4m
2.	Killarah	Cavan	cairn	28m
3.	Annaghkeen	Galway	cairn	30m
4.	Edenagarry	Down	kerbed cairn	30.4m
5.	Lodge	Galway	cairn	40.5m
6.	Sheehinny	Fermanagh	cairn	42.7

Table 9.3: Cairns >25m in maximum external diameter.

Notwithstanding reservations as to the quality of the available data the following observations can be made about the form of barrows and cairns in which Early Bronze Age burials have been found.

Plan

The overwhelming majority of the barrows and cairns constructed in the Early Bronze Age are round in ground plan, only two barrows are recorded as being oval. One is a kerbed example at Loughfad, Co. Donegal, under which a segmented cist was found (Raftery 1942, 122); the other, "a small oval nipple" which covered two cists one of which contained a crouched inhumation accompanied by a bowl and a boar's tusk at Barrettstown, Co. Westmeath (Wilde 1857–61).

Dimensions

Generally the dimensions of Early Bronze Age barrows and cairns are poorly recorded. The diameters are more often recorded than the heights. Due to a variety of human and natural factors the present dimensions of a monument may be quite different to those when it was constructed. The maximum diameter of 47 barrows and 39 cairns has been established. The greatest numbers of sites in both categories are between 10m and 14.99m in maximum diameter, however, the distribution of the diameters of monuments in each category is not identical (Fig 9.3). A greater proportion of barrows (74%) are less than 15m in diameter, while 58% of cairns are greater than 15m in

maximum diameter. This difference can be explained in two ways, firstly cairns are often added to in field clearance and are more likely to spread over time, in contrast earthen barrows are more easily eroded, through natural agencies and agricultural practices such as ploughing. The numbers of small barrows are also skewed by the presence of the seven monuments that form the Carrowjames cemetery, Co. Mayo.

At the other end of the scale it is notable that the largest Early Bronze Age burial monuments are cairns, six of which are recorded to have been over 25m in maximum diameter (Table 9.3). Three of these cairns seem to have been built specifically to cover Early Bronze Age burials: Mullyknock, Co. Fermanagh, Annaghkeen, Co. Galway, and Lodge, Co. Galway. At 'Ballyheady Cairn', Killarah, Co. Cavan, and Sheehinny, Co. Fermanagh, the burials recorded were found in peripheral positions, at 'Knock-iveagh Cairn', Edenagarry, Co. Down, the cremated bones of a child and an adult, accompanied by a bowl, were found in the body of a cairn, under which was also found sherds of Neolithic pottery (Collins 1957). It is not certain that these three monuments were built to specifically cover the Early Bronze Age burials found in them. While none of these cairns approach the size of the mega-passage tombs, they do compare in size to the majority of Sheridan's "Stage 4" passage tombs (Sheridan 1985–6).

Kerbs

Kerbs are known at twenty-one cairns and eight barrows which covered Early Bronze Age burials (Table 9.4) and as with the earlier megalithic tombs they served three functions:

Townland	County	Monument	Primary ceramic associations
1. Ballyvennaght	Antrim	cairn	bowl
2. Drumbare	Antrim	cairn	"cinerary urns" †
3. Linford	Antrim	cairn	"plain...urn" †
4. Moyadam	Antrim	cairn (with fosse(?))	"urns" †
5. Tobernagee	Antrim	cairn	beaker†
6. Ballon Hill	Carlow	barrow(?) *	vase † & cordoned urn †
7. Coolnatullagh	Clare	cairn	-
8. Coolhill	Cork	barrow *	vase
9. Curraghbinny	Cork	cairn	-
10. Moneen	Cork	barrow (with fosse)	beaker pottery
11. Ballydullaghan	Derry	cairn	bowl
12. Gortacloghan	Derry	cairn	-
13. Gortacloghan	Derry	cairn	unclass. vessel (sherd)
14. Slaghtneill	Derry	cairn	"urn" †
15. Kilmonaster Middle	Donegal	cairn	-
16. Loughfad	Donegal	oval barrow	-
17. Edenagarry	Down	cairn	Neolithic pottery †
18. Cavancarragh	Fermanagh	barrow	bowl †
19. Inisheer	Galway	barrow	cordoned urn
20. Ballynorig West	Kerry	cairn *	-
21. Rathmore West	Kildare	barrow *	-
22. Coolgrange	Kilkenny	cairn	-
23. Cush	Limerick	barrow	bowl
24. Knockadoon	Limerick	cairn	plain coarse urn
25. Carrickredmond	Louth	cairn	"urns" †
26. Cashel	Mayo	barrow	vase †
27. Knock North	Mayo	cairn	vase †
28. Ballyeeskeen	Sligo	cairn	unclass. vessel
29. Donaghanie	Tyrone	cairn	bowl †

Table 9.4: Early Bronze Age burial monuments with kerb (Notes: *: *doubtful kerb;* †: *doubtful association).*

1. defining the area of the monument
2. forming a facing to the mound or cairn
3. revetting the material of which the monument was constructed, be it earth or stone

The nature of the kerb can only be described with certainty in 12 cases. Two types of kerb can be recognised. The first is a boulder kerb, where the edge of the monument is defined by a contiguous line of large stones. The second is a kerb-wall where the edge of the monument is defined by a coursed drystone wall. Both types of construction are known in the Neolithic and may have no more significance than the availability of suitable stones. Boulder kerbs have been recorded at nine sites (Table 9.5).

The average maximum heights recorded for the kerbs encircling these sites is 0.71m; they range from a maximum height of 1.06m, at Moneen, Co. Cork, to a minimum of 0.45m recorded at Tobernagee, 'Lyles Hill', Co. Antrim. In general the kerb stones seem to have been erected in shallow pits or just laid on the pre-construction surface, in some cases it is reported that individual kerb-stones were supported by packing-stones (Tobernagee; 'Cornacleary', Ballydullaghan, Co. Derry; Circle P, Knockadoon, Co. Limerick). A kerb-wall which was reportedly up to four courses high enclosed a cairn at Curraghbinny, Co. Cork, though there is some doubt as to whether this feature revetted the edge of the cairn originally, as it was located some distance inside the recorded edge of the monument it might originally have

Townland	County
1. Tobernagee	Co. Antrim
2. Moneen	Co. Cork
3. Ballydullaghan	Co. Derry
4. Gortacloghan (both cairns)	Co. Derry
5. Edenagarry	Co. Down
6. Coolgrange	Co. Kilkenny
7. Cush	Co. Limerick
8. Knockadoon	Co. Limerick

Table 9.5: Early Bronze Age burial monuments with boulder kerbs.

been an internal feature of the cairn, the excavator interpreted the material outside the kerb as cairn slip (Ó Ríordáin 1933). The kerb of a cairn at Knockadoon was reportedly composed of two courses of stones at some points, in general though it was built of single boulders. A kerb of limestone slabs revetted by a kerb wall was found at Coolnatullagh, Co. Clare (Eogan 2003). The nature of the kerbs reported at Loughfad, Co. Donegal, Cashel, Co. Mayo, and Ballyeeskeen, Co. Sligo, cannot be described with certainty.

Fosses

Seventeen barrows reportedly had a fosse around the base of the mound (Table 9.6); the cairn recorded at Moyadam, Co. Antrim, might have been encircled by a fosse though

	Townland	County	Width	Depth	Primary artefactual associations
1.	Moneen	Cork	0.91m *	0.3m	beaker (?)
2.	Carrowbeg North "1"	Galway	4.27m	1.2m	Bronze razor
3.	Carrowbeg North "2"	Galway	0.46m	0.3m	plano-convex flint knife
4.	Nurney Demesne	Kildare	-	-	"urns"
5.	Doonmoon	Limerick	1m	0.6 *	-
6.	Killineer	Louth	-	-	-
7.	Burren	Mayo	0.9m	-	-
8.	Carrowjames "1"	Mayo	1.73m *	0.3m *	bronze razor
9.	Carrowjames "2"	Mayo	1.8m *	0.45m	cordoned urn, bronze razor
10.	Carrowjames "3"	Mayo	2.1m *	0.45m	cordoned urn, bronze razor
11.	Carrowjames "5"	Mayo	1.2m	0.65m	-
12.	Carrowjames "6"	Mayo	0.95m *	0.65m *	-
13.	Carrowjames "7"	Mayo	1.7m	0.7m	-
14.	Carrowjames "9"	Mayo	1.2m	0.8m	bronze fragments
15.	Longstone	Tipperary	-	-	?
16.	Crannogue	Tyrone	-	-	-
17.	Crannogue	Tyrone	-	-	-

Table 9.6: Barrows enclosed by fosses (and the recorded dimensions of the fosses) (Note:*: averaged measurement).

the original report of the discoveries at this site is imprecise (Herity 1974, 222). From a functional point of view a fosse would have provided the material for the construction of the barrow, for this reason the lack of fosses recorded around cairns can be explained, the material for their construction being gathered off the surface of the land rather than being dug from it. However, fosses have not been found enclosing all excavated barrows (*e.g.* Annaghkeen and Pollacorragune, Co. Galway, Cashel and Corrower, Co. Mayo, Fourknocks "Site 3", Co. Meath *etc.*) so it is likely that the excavation of a fosse had a particular social and ritual context beyond the functional.

Generally barrows and their enclosing fosses seem to have been contemporary. The one definite exception is Moneen where no firm association can be made between the digging of the fosse and the construction of the kerbed barrow which sits eccentrically within it, while the excavator believed the fosse to predate the barrow the authors of a more recent study have reversed the sequence (O'Kelly 1952; Brindley *et al.* 1987/8). Nine of the remaining barrows enclosed by fosses are found in a relatively small area in north Co. Galway and south Co. Mayo. In this area these monuments seem to be associated with a particular funerary ritual, namely cremation of single adult males accompanied by pottery of the cordoned urn tradition and/or bronze blades that are interpreted as razors. In all cases the fosses enclosing these sites seem to have been annular and the material from the ditch seems to have been used to construct the internal mounds. Little is known about the other sites, a cordoned urn was found in a slab-covered pit dug on top of the barrow at Killineer, Co. Louth, however, it does not seem to be a primary association, a fosse was recognised around this site in field survey (Buckley and Sweetman 1991, 51). The construction of a barrow at Doonmoon, Co. Limerick seems to have taken place in a single operation, however, the chronological and cultural context of this

monument is not clear, a possible beaker pottery kiln was found about 6m southwest of the barrow but no link was established between these features (Gowen 1988, 52–4). In the absence of published accounts of the excavations at Longstone, Co. Tipperary, and Crannogue, Co. Tyrone, it is not possible to assess these sites adequately.

Discussion

The principle external morphological traits of barrows and cairns that cover Early Bronze Age burials are similar. They are round in plan, the majority are between 10m and 20m in diameter and one-in-four is defined by a fosse (only barrows) or a kerb (predominantly cairns). The incidence of enclosing elements such as kerbs and fosses is likely to increase with careful excavations and field survey, though a number of excavated sites that do not have such features indicate that they were not an integral part of all Early Bronze Age monuments.

While the differences between ritual practice in Later Neolithic and the Early Bronze Age are frequently stressed, for instance burial in monuments *vs.* burials in flat cemeteries, communal burial *vs.* individual burial, the construction of barrows and cairns as places of burial in the Early Bronze Age can be seen as a continuation of certain aspects of the traditions of monumentality in the foregoing Neolithic period.

These monuments compare in scale with the majority of passage tombs, though they lack the complex structural elements of the earlier monuments. While it appears that the Early Bronze Age saw a greater emphasis on the individual in society, examination of the monuments erected in this period indicates that the logistics required for their construction are likely to have required a considerable amount of communal effort. A number of these sites are enclosed by kerbs, though these might be termed sub-megalithic in comparison with the kerbs around passage tombs, the concept is the same. Barrows and cairns acted as *foci* of communal burial, albeit in a different way than chambered tombs, it is probable that they were also locations at which non-funerary rituals were carried out.

Though not dealt with in this paper barrows and cairns are also known to have been built in close proximity to one another to form cemetery groupings and like some passage tombs are sited in prominent locations in the landscape. In this context the disproportionate numbers of Early Bronze Age burials in secondary positions at passage tombs and Linkardstown-type graves can be interpreted as a conscious decision in the second millennium BC to adapt the use of architectural styles and concepts established in the fourth millennium BC.

Acknowledgements

This paper is based on part of an MA thesis submitted to University College Dublin in 1996. I would like to thank my supervisor Dr. Gabriel Cooney for encouragement and advice in completing the research. I would like to thank the editors for their invitation to contribute to this volume and for their patience.

Bibliography

Brindley, A.L., Lanting, J.N. and Mook, W.G. 1987/8 Radiocarbon dates from Moneen and Labbacallee, County Cork, *Journal of Irish Archaeology* **4**, 13–20.

Buckley, V.M. and Sweetman, P.D. 1991 *Archaeological survey of County Louth*. The Stationery Office, Dublin.

Collins, A.E.P. 1957 Trial excavations in a round cairn on Knockiveagh, Co. Down, *Ulster Journal of Archaeology* **20**, 8–28.

Eogan, J. 2003 Excavations at a cairn in Coolnatullagh townland, Co. Clare, *North Munster Antiquarian Journal* **42**, 113–150.

Gowen, M. 1988 *Three Irish gas pipelines: new archaeological evidence in Munster*. Wordwell Ltd., Dublin.

Herity, M. 1974 *Irish passage graves, Neolithic tomb-builders in Ireland and Britain 2500 BC*. Irish University Press, Dublin.

Mount, C. 1997 Early Bronze Age burial in south-east Ireland in the light of recent research, *Proceedings of the Royal Irish Academy* **97C**, 101–93.

Ó Ríordáin, S.P. 1933 Excavation of cairn in Townland of Curraghbinny, Co. Cork, *Journal of the Cork Historical and Archaeological Society* **38**, 80–84.

O'Kelly, M.J. 1952 Excavation of a cairn at Moneen, Co. Cork, *Proceedings of the Royal Irish Academy* **54C**, 121–159.

Raftery, J. 1942 Finds from three Ulster counties. *Ulster Journal of Archaeology* **5**, 120–31.

Sheridan, A. 1985–6 Megaliths and megalomania: an account, and interpretation, of the development of passage tombs in Ireland, *Journal of Irish Archaeology* **3**, 17–30.

Waddell, J. 1990 *The Bronze Age burials of Ireland*. Galway University Press, Galway.

Wilde, W.R. 1857–61 [Barrettstown, Co. Westmeath], *Proceedings of the Royal Irish Academy* **7**, 89–91.

10. Middle Bronze Age burial traditions in Ireland

Eoin Grogan
For George with warmest regards and gratitude

Introduction

The processes, procedures and ceremonials associated with the treatment of the dead are some of the most illuminating aspects of prehistoric societies. Indeed, the archaeological study of the Neolithic and Early Bronze Age periods in Ireland has often been dominated by concerns about funerary ritual and funerary sites. In part this reflects the reality that a large percentage of the available evidence for these periods is associated with aspects of burial processes, although, in relation to the Neolithic at least, it also reflects a particular fascination with the monumental aspect of the burial monuments.

Several important studies concerning aspects of the Bronze Age funerary record have been published. These include work on Early Bronze Age burials (Waddell 1990; Doody 1986) and Early Bronze Age funerary vessels (Ó Ríordáin and Waddell 1993), regional studies in North Leinster (Cooney 1987), South Leinster (Mount 1997a; Kilfeather 1991) and North Munster (Grogan 1989), as well as cemetery studies (*e.g.* Mount 1995; 1997b; 1998). This provides a very comprehensive database for the period and a significant proportion of the record has been dated through a research programme based in Groningen (*e.g.* Brindley *et al.* 1987/88; Brindley and Lanting 1991/92; 1998).

Despite this body of comprehensive research little attention has been devoted to the burial record of the latter part of the Bronze Age apart from general descriptions (Cooney and Grogan 1994; Raftery B., 1981; Waddell 1998). There is, however, a growing body of information that places many burials in this period and suggests that distinctive Middle and Late Bronze Age traditions can be identified in Ireland. Amongst the more extensive examples are the cemeteries at Altanagh, Co. Tyrone (Williams 1986), and Carrig, Co. Wicklow (Grogan 1990), and several dated sites discovered during the construction of the Limerick Gas Pipeline (Gowen 1988; Grogan 1988a). During the 1990s many new sites have been excavated (*e.g.* Reed 2000; Dunne 1998a; 1998b; Stevens 1998a).

The term Middle Bronze Age has only been used intermittently to refer to this period in Ireland except in relation to metalworking traditions (*e.g.* Eogan 1964; Herity and Eogan 1977, 159–81). Reports on burials have occasionally used the term although the exact chronological reference has not always been clear-cut (*e.g.* Raftery 1938–39; 1940–41). There has been a dramatic increase in the wider archaeological evidence during the past fifteen years principally from work on large-scale construction enterprises such as pipelines, roadworks and mining (*e.g.* Gowen 1988; Grogan 1988a; Gahan 1997; Read 2000; Gowen *et al.* 2000). The review of this broader evidence, the increase in more accurate dating, and a re-examination of the metalwork, have emphasised the wealth and diversity of the period and the identification of several important developments that provide it with a significant character (Cooney and Grogan 1994; Ramsey 1995; Brindley 1995; Baillie 1995). Nevertheless, there is considerable continuity with both the preceding Early and the succeeding Late Bronze Age and forms part of a seamless period of overall Bronze Age development.

In chronological terms the period begins *c.* 1600 BC at a time when the technological developments of Eogan's (1964) Omagh and Killymaddy phases become current. These include the introduction of two-piece stone moulds allowing for the casting of the first socketed implements, including rapiers and palstaves (Burgess 1980, 126–9; Eogan 1964, 268–72). In this study the Middle Bronze Age encompasses the period beginning towards the end of the Arreton/Inch Island metalworking stage and continuing through the succeeding Acton Park/Killymaddy phase into the Bishopsland/Taunton stage (Burgess 1980, 122–9, 149–55; Herity and Eogan 1977, 153–64, 167–9), that is what has previously been termed 'MB 1' and 'MB 2' (Butler 1981, 351: table) which appears to span the period from *c.* 1600–1200 BC.

Early Bronze Age funerary background

A brief summary of earlier traditions is relevant as most of the significant aspects of Middle Bronze Age burial customs reflect a very strong element of continuity. From

Pottery type	Flint scraper	Flint arrow	Plano-convex	Flint blade/flake	Bead	Bone pin	Bone toggle	Bronze Dagger	Bronze razor	Bronze awl	Boar's tusk	Battle/mace	Stone axe	Faience	Jet beads	Amber beads	Other	Non-ceramic	Other pot	Total
Bowls	4	2	3	8	0	0	0	2	1	1	2	0	0	0	0	0	3	26	9	35
Vases	3	0	3	4	0	4	0	3	0	1	0	0	0	1	0	0	2	21	16	37
Vase Urns	0	0	4	5	1	2	1	2	1	0	0	0	0	0	0	0	1	17	13	30
Encrusted Urn	0	0	5	1	0	2	1	0	0	0	0	0	0	0	0	0	1	10	20	30
Collared Urns	0	2	3	0	1	1	0	2	0	0	0	2	0	0	0	0	1	12	6	18
Cordoned Urns	1	0	1	7	2	7	3	0	15	0	0	2	1	6	0	0	0	45	13	58
Coarse vessels	3	0	0	0	1	0	0	0	0	0	0	0	0	0	0	0	1	5	1	6
No pottery	4	3	7	12	2	3	3	1	9	2	3	0	1	1	4	2	7	64	0	64
Total	15	7	26	37	7	19	8	10	26	4	5	4	2	8	4	2	15	15	78	278

Table 10.1: Gravegoods and associations in the Early and Middle Bronze Age.

the burial record the period can be divided into five main phases.

1. Crouched inhumations or cremations in short cists accompanied by bowls. At least some of the crouched inhumations in cists without gravegoods (27+ examples), many of them in cemeteries that contain bowl burials, belong to this stage

2. Cremations or occasional inhumations with vases or bowls. Non-ceramic grave goods are infrequently included during these two stages; these predominantly consist of flint flakes, blades, scrapers or arrowheads (Table 10.1). Four graves with bronze daggers and bowls or vases, six with plano-convex flint knives, two with boar's tusks, and two with bronze awls may belong to towards the end of phase 2. In excess of 170 short cists, and 30 pits, contained no pottery but came from contexts, such as cemeteries, that indicate an Early Bronze Age date. Graves without ceramic evidence produced other gravegoods including daggers (1 example), plano-convex knives (7), boar's tusks (3) and bronze awls (3). Other burials, including both inhumations and cremations in pits and cists, without other gravegoods appear from their occurrence in cemeteries with more closely dateable graves to date to this period also.

3. Gradually vase urns ('enlarged food vessels', and 'encrusted urns') and later collared urns, all generally inverted, replaced vases and bowls as ceramic accessories. These urn burials were sometimes placed in short rectangular, or occasionally compartmented, cists but increasingly pits or stone edged pits became the most frequent grave type. The urns were occasionally accompanied by vases, and by smaller accessory vessels (biconical or 'pygmy' cups, or miniature vases). Other gravegoods remained scarce but daggers (4 burials) and plano-convex flint knives (13 burials) further indicate continuity in burial customs. Towards the end of this stage cordoned urns also appear in burials. A small number of associations, including one example with a vase urn and one with bowls, indicate that bronze razor-knives were introduced during this period and some (rare) associations between cordoned urns and vases, vase and collared urns support this view. Four burials with stone battleaxes, two with collared and two with cordoned urns, may also belong to this phase. A single association of a vase with a *faience* bead also indicates that material that became more widespread in the following period had already been introduced during the latter stages of the Early Bronze Age. With the exception of an inhumation associated with a vase urn (Oldtown, Co. Kildare), and that with two bowls and a razor-knife from Keenoge, Co. Meath, all of the burials in this stage appear to have been cremations.

4. In the early stages of the Middle Bronze Age cordoned urns become the dominant ceramic type. These burials occur in cemeteries containing earlier graves, and in new cemeteries. While there is an increase in the number of gravegoods these largely consist of three items, *faience* beads (6 burials), bone pins (7) and bronze razor knives (15)(Table 10.1). The custom of including other vessels as accessories also continues. It appears that there were also large numbers of burials without pottery in this period and some of these are dated by the occurrence of razor-knives in 9 graves. There are several wealthy burials from this period including those at Tara, Co. Meath, Castlemartyr, Co. Cork, and Carrig 2, Co. Wicklow (Table 10.3).

5. Inurned burial now contained in coarse flat-bottomed domestic vessels continues. However, the burial tradition of the developed Middle Bronze Age is characterised by simple pits containing token cremations occasionally accompanied by sherds of coarse domestic pottery. There is a general absence of gravegoods. The burials occur in a wide variety of contexts but barrows, ringditches and unenclosed pit cemeteries are widespread. This tradition continues to the end of the Bronze Age.

Early – Middle Bronze Age transitions

By the end of the Early Bronze Age burials contained in cordoned urns form the dominant tradition. Other pottery

Site	primary burial	Burial No.	County	Site Type	Grave type	Rite	Pottery	Position	Razor	Faience	Other Gravegoods cal. BC (2 sigma)	Individuals/ Age/Sex	Reference
Keenoge	EBA	3	Mh.	Flat cemetery	Pit	cInh	b b	⇔ ?		ψ	Flint arrowhead, blades, scraper; paved floor	?	
Ballyduff	EBA		Wx.	Single grave	Cist	Cr	v	∨	0			A♂, A♀	
Laheen	EBA		Dl.	Single grave	Pit	Cr	©	⇐			B, v sherd	?	K21
Ballintubbrid	EBA		Wx.	Single grave	Pit	Cr	©	⇐			B, burnt flint chip	A	K58
Tullymurry	EBA		Dn.	?	?	?	©	?	?		With B?	?	K31
Castleboy, Tara		22	Mh.	Passage tomb mound	Pit	Cr	©	⇐			v⇐, B, ▲	?	K37, W 128
Corkagh, Kilskeery	EBA		Ty.	Ringditch	Cist	Cr	m©	⇔			With ©, bc, v	A♂, A♀	W 138
Inisheer	EBA		G	Mound	Cist	Cr	©	?			m©, bronze pin/awl	?	K26
Knockadea	EBA	2	Li	Flat cemetery	Cist	Cr	©	⇐			m©	?	K32
Tullyveagh	EBA		Ty.	?	?	Cr	©	?			m©	?	K50
Knockoneill	N		Dy.	Court tomb	Pit	Cr	m©	⇐			bc, urn sherds also		
Knockboy	EBA		An.	Mound?	Pit	Cr	©?	?		◉	bc		
Longstone Cullen	N		Ti.	Enclosure	Pit	Cr	©	⇐		0	pc		
Harristown	LN	5	Wa.	Wedge tomb	Pit	Cr	©	⇔			bc	ch	K52
		2			Pit	Cr	©	⇐	ψ	◉	I ring headed	YA♂	K53
Tara	N		Mh.	Mound	Pit	Inh			ψ	0000	Amber, jet and bronze beads	Ad♂	
Monasterboice	EBA		Lh.	Single grave	Cist	?	©sh	?			Tievebulliagh axe		
Kilcroagh	EBA	2	An.	Flat cemetery	Pit	Cr	©pl	⇐	ψ	0	1745-1941	A♀/Ad	
	EBA	1	Li.	Flat cemetery	Pit	Cr	©	⇐		●	●bronze, ●stone	A♂, A♀	
Carrig 2	EBA	C3	Ww.	Cist cairn	Pit	Cr	©	⇐	ψ	00★		A, A♀	
		D5			Pit	Cr	©	⇐	ψ		Animal bones, 1226-1525	A♂, A, Ad, ne	
Castlemartyr			Co.	Single grave, cave	Pit ?	Inh					Gold plates, amber beads	A	
Cush 4	EBA	2	Li.	Flat cemetery	Pit	Cr	©	⇔	ψ			ch	K30
		1	Li.		Pit	Cr	©	⇐	ψ		Flint fabricator	?	K29
Carrowjames 2	EBA	1	Ma.	Barrow	Pit	Cr	©	⇐	ψ			A♂	K41
Carrowjames 3	EBA	1	Ma.	Barrow	Pit	Cr	©	⇐	ψ			A	K42
Carrowjames 1	EBA	1	Ma.	Barrow	Pit	Cr			ψ			A ch	
Reardnogy More	EBA	2	Ti	Flat cemetery	Pit	Cr			ψ			A♀?	
Hill of Rath	EBA	1	Lh.	Flat cemetery	Pit	?	©	⇐	ψ		I flint scraper, whetstone, flat polished stone	?	K39 W 111-3
Carrowbeg North 1	EBA		G	Ringbarrow	Pit	Cr			ψ		Pit cut through pyre	A♂	
Pollacoragune	EBA		G	Ringbarrow	Pit	Cr	©	⇐	ψdec			?	K27
Kilmore	EBA	C	Wm.	Mound	Pit	Cr			ψψ			A, Ad, inf	
Glenaree	EBA		Li.	Single grave	Pit	Cr	©	⇐	ψ			?	K31
Urbalreagh	EBA	1	An.	Ringditch	Pit	Cr	©	⇐	ψ?			A♂	K7
Rahinashurock	EBA	2	Wm.	Flat cemetery	Pit	Cr			ψ		I Bone toggle	A♂	
Gortereghy			An.	Single grave	Pit	Cr.	©	⇐	ψ			?	K4
Castleconor	EBA		So.	Tumulus	?	Cr			ψ		No further details	?	
Nr Newcastle	MBA		Ww.	Single grave	Cist	Cr	-	-	ψ			?	W 166
Knockast	EBA	18	Wm.	Cemetery mound	Prot	Cr			ψ		◈	A♂	
		36			Pit	Cr	©	⇐	ψ			eldA	K57
		14		Cemetery mound	Prot	Cr	v©pl	⇐	ψd		v⇐	YA♂	
Altanagh	EBA	171	Ty.	Flat cemetery	Pit	Cr	©	⇐			●pottery, bronze boss, 1526-1735	A♀	
Altmore	EBA	2	Ty.	Cairn	?	?	'urn'		ψ			?	
Donaghmore	EBA		Ty.	Single grave	Pit	Cr	©	?			I	?	K46
Killyneill	EBA		Ty.	Gravel ridge	Pit	Cr	©	⇐			Bone toggle	?	K48
Killinchy	EBA	1	Dn.	Flat cemetery	Pit	Cr	©	⇐			'curved bone needle'	?	K24
Killycreen/Glarryford			An.	?	?	?	©pl	?			◈◈ I perforated	?	K5 W 47
Carrigeens			So.	?	Cist	Cr	©	⇐			Bone toggle, cowrie (Trivia sp.) shells	Ad	Exc 1992

b bowl	v vase	v© vase urn	© collared urn	pc pygmy cup	◈ plano-convex flint knife	0 faience segmented	ψ bronze razor/knife
© cordoned urn	©pl plain	m© miniature	s© small urn	bc biconical cup	B stone battleaxe/macehead	◉ quoit	▲ bronze dagger
⇐ inverted	⇒ upright	∨ on side	Cr cremation	Inh inhumation	I bone pin	● bead (stone or bone)	★ star	K Kavanagh 1973/76, cat. No.
A Adult	eld elderly	A♀ Adult female	A♂ Adult male	Ad Adolescent	ch Child	ne Neonate	Y young	• simple bead	W Waddell 1990, p. no.

Table 10.2: Rich burials from the end of the Early Bronze Age and the beginning of the Middle Bronze Age.

Pottery type	⇕ Cist - Inhumation	⇑ Pit - Inhumation	⇑ Cist - Cremation	⇑ Pit Cremation	⇓ Cist - Inhumation	⇓ Pit - Inhumation	⇓ Cist - Cremation	⇓ Pit Cremation	> Cist Inhumation	> Cist Cremation	> Pit Cremation	Total with full details	Inhumation in cist	Cremation in cist	Inhumation in pit	Cremation in pit	Inhumation	Cremation
Bowls	30	3	20	2	1	0	1	2	9	3	1	72	76	67	23	11	100	87
Vases	5	0	29	2	2	0	5	2	0	3	0	48	17	71	0	6	18	84
Vase Urns	0	0	0	1	1	0	18	20	0	1	0	41	0	26	1	24	1	55
Encrusted Urn	0	0	1	3	0	0	22	30	0	1	0	57	0	32	0	36	0	71
Collared Urns	0	0	0	3	0	0	4	14	0	0	1	22	0	4	0	20	0	25
Cordoned Urns	0	0	1	10	0	0	2	36	0	0	1	50	0	8	1	61	1	96
No pottery													53	98	18	12	72	115

Table 10.3: Grave types, vessel disposition and funerary rite in major ceramic groups.

types continued to be deposited occasionally. A small number of vases associated with cordoned urns indicate the survival of aspects of earlier customs albeit that the vases in these contexts, as at Knockadea, Co. Limerick (Power 1931), are clearly influenced by cordoned urns (Brindley 1980, 201). Although pottery of the vase tradition had gone out of use early in the Middle Bronze Age several funerary sites indicate continuity from the Early Bronze Age right through into the later phases of the Middle Bronze Age and beyond (see below).

During the later part of the Early Bronze Age a phase of comparatively rich burials emerge: this extends into the Middle Bronze Age (Table 10.2). The deposition of these burials clearly began in the Early Bronze Age. This is indicated by the date from Kilcroagh 2 (Williams *et al.* 1991–92: 1745–1941 cal. BC, GrN-15378, 3510±35 BP) and the association of a pygmy cup with the Longstone urn (see Table 10.1; Peter Danaher pers comm.). Dates from Carrig C4, and Altanagh, Co. Tyrone (F169, F170, F171), suggest that these burials continued in use up to perhaps as late as 1400 BC. At Keenoge, Co. Meath, grave 3 contained two bowls, flint blades and a scraper in addition to a bronze razor (Mount 1997b). The bowls and the crouched inhumation refer back to an earlier burial tradition while the razor may represent one of the first examples of an artefact that occurs frequently in this period and the succeeding Middle Bronze Age. A similar suggestion can be made for the vase burial accompanied by a *faience* bead from Ballyduff, Co. Wexford, and for the dagger grave at Castleboy, Tara, Co. Meath, that produced an inverted vase and a stone battleaxe (Table 10.2). There are three other burials containing battleaxes or maceheads (Table 10.2), as well as two poorly documented examples from a megalithic chamber at Ballynahatty, Co. Down (Waddell 1990, 75–6). Other burials in this group may include Knockast 14, Co. Westmeath, a plain vase urn with an inverted vase and a bronze dagger or razor (Hencken and Movius 1934), and a plain cordoned urn with a bone pin and two plano-convex flint knives, at Killycreen/Glarryford, Co. Antrim, and the burial at Corkagh, Co. Tyrone, which was associated with an inverted vase ('encrusted') urn containing a miniature cup, an upright miniature collared urn, and an inverted vase. The association of smaller accessory vessels with several cordoned urn burials continues an element of the vase tradition. These pots include miniature cordoned urns as well as biconical cups.

The Middle Bronze Age: razor-knife and faience burials (Table 10.2)

To date fourteen cordoned urns have produced burials associated with small bronze razors or knives, while an unidentified urn and a razor were found at Altmore, Co. Tyrone (Binchy 1967; Kavanagh 1976, 324; 1991). A further eight cremations contained razors but no pottery while an extended inhumation burial at Tara, Co. Meath (Ó Ríordáin 1955), also produced a razor. Amber beads came from both Tara and the inhumation associated with gold plates from a cave at Castlemartyr, Co. Cork. The human remains of razor-accompanied burials have been identified in 17 cases representing 26 individuals. Of these 8 were adult males, 7 were 'adults' and there are three adult females – including one from Reardnogy More, Co. Tipperary (Waddell 1969). Although there are 7 adolescents and children in only one instance (Cush 4, Co. Limerick, burial 2, Rynne and O'Sullivan 1967) does a grave not contain the remains of an adult. Adults, and to a lesser extent adult males, also predominate among those

buried in cordoned urns (without razors) and of the 36 individuals (from 31 graves) from burials with some anatomical analysis 30 were adults and of these 13 were adult males and 8 were adult females. A particular emphasis on adult males is most apparent in the burials consisting of a single individual in an inverted urn (see Table 10.4).

Among the burials in cordoned urns several have produced other gravegoods including grave D2 at Carrig (three *faience* beads), and Harristown, Co. Waterford, grave 2 (*faience* bead, perforated bone pin; Hawkes 1941), and a burial at Hill of Rath, Co. Louth (perforated bone pin, perforated whetstone, flat polished stone, flint thumb scraper; Kavanagh 1976). Two cordoned urns at Kilcroagh, Co. Antrim (Nos 1, 2; Williams *et al.* 1991–92), also produced *faience* beads. One of these (No. 2) was in a plain upright urn. The Castleboy, Tara, burial contained four *faience* beads (Ó Ríordáin 1955, 168, pl. 23:5). A cremation pit at Longstone, Co. Tipperary, produced a Pygmy Cup and a segmented *faience* bead (Peter Danaher pers comm.).

There are a number of other trends that develop during this period. Cordoned urns without further decoration are recorded from 8 burials, including Knockast, Co. Westmeath, (burial 15, Hencken and Movius 1934) and a second at Kilcroagh (No. 3), but are also known from settlement sites, for example Lough Gur Circles K and L, and Sites C and D (Ó Ríordáin 1955; Grogan and Eogan 1987). They indicate a general trend away from ceramic decoration, apparent from an earlier period with collared urns, which characterises the later part of the Middle, and the whole of the Late, Bronze Age (Brindley 1995, 8). In the period after *c.* 1500 BC there may have been a phase when the tradition of inverting urns over burials gradually gave way to less rigid concern with inversion and many vessels were placed in an upright position (Table 10.3). Adding to Waddell's (1990, 14) figures of cordoned urns with recorded positions 42 were inverted, 11 were upright and two were placed on their sides.

Funerary continuity: cemeteries and complexes

The gradual developments outlined above including the trend away from specially produced funerary pottery should be seen against a continuity in some specific aspects of burials traditions. Cemeteries with their beginnings in the Early Bronze Age, such as Carrig, Carrowjames (Raftery J. 1938–39; 1940–41), Cush (Sites 1–3, Ó Ríordáin 1940), the Mound of the Hostages, Castleboy, Tara, and Knockast, remained active. Other sites and megalithic tombs widely in use during this period had been started in the Neolithic. These include the Hill of Rath where a probable flat cemetery produced a number of urn burials (Waddell 1990, 111–3; Kavanagh 1973; 1976). More recent excavation nearby have revealed a complex of prehistoric ritual/funerary activity including depositional and cremation pits containing Western

Pottery type	A♂	A♀	A	YA	Ad	Child	Infant	Total	Adults	Child	Child %	Inhumation	Cremation
Bowl	27-6	6-3	10-8	1-0	3.1	13-8	0	86	61	25	29	60	26
Vase	2-5	3-2	1-11	2-4	5	3-5	1-1	45	30	15	33	12	33
Vase Urns	3	1	9	1	1	7	2	24	14	10	44	0	24
Encrusted Urns	5	6	7	5	-	7	1	31	23	8	26	0	31
Collared Urns	1	2	2	-	1	3	3	12	5	7	58	0	12
Cordoned Urns	17	10	11	2	4	6	1	51	40	11	23	0	51
Coarse vessels	8	1	17	-		3	2	31	26	5	16	0	31
No pottery	11-4	11-10	2-29	2	2-2	13-10	5-6	107	69	38	36	44	63
								387	268	119	31	116	271
Cordoned ⇔∨	2	2	2	-	1	2	-						
Cordoned ⇐	3	2	2	-	1	0	1						
Cordoned ⇐ singleton	10	3	6	0	2	-	-						
Cordoned ⇔∨ singleton	1	3	-	2	-	4	-						
Cordoned unknown	1	-	1	-	-	-	-						
Total (51)	17	10	11	2	4	6	1						
Cordoned ψ	4	2	4	-	2	2	-						
ψ No pottery	3	1	3	-	2	2	-						

Table 10.4: Major funerary pottery types and the age and gender ranges. In columns 2–8 the first figure in bold (where present) represents inhumation; other figures are cremations. Figures represent only those burials where age and gender have been identified. In the bottom section cordoned urns burials are compared where the grave contain the remains of multiple or single (singleton) individuals.

Pottery type	Polygonal Cist	Cist	Pit	Inverted	Upright	On side	Sherds[1]
Bowls	5	156	38	7	57	13	16
Vases	4	92	9	9	39	3	6
Vase Urns	8	24	28	48	1	1	9
Encrusted Urn	11	18	39	58	4	1	7
Collared Urns	4	4	23	23	4	1	2
Cordoned Urns	1	10	65	42	11	2	6
Coarse vessels	0	1	30	8	7	2	30
No pottery	11	160	30	-	-	-	-

Table 10.5: Middle-Late Bronze Age burials from megalithic tombs and related sites

Neolithic, decorated Middle Neolithic, Grooved Ware and Beaker pottery (Duffy 2002). While the nature of the early prehistoric activity is unclear two cremation pits nearby produced sherds from the same cordoned urn, while two further pits contained cremations and sherds of coarse pottery. A large number of megalithic tombs, including Harristown, Altanagh, Lough Gur, and Moylisha, Co. Wicklow, were used for burial and other depositions during the Middle Bronze Age (Tables 10.6, 10.7; see O'Brien 1993; 1999). This persistence in the importance of earlier sacred places suggests strong bonds with social and landscape histories as well as the continuation of local burial traditions.

The developed Middle Bronze Age

Other developments are evident in the wider ritual of the period with a greater emphasis on the votive offering of bronzes in wetland sites. This may be connected with the general dis-improvement in the climate that occurred around this time (*e.g.* Burgess 1980, 131, 239, 350–1;

Cooney and Grogan 1994, 133–42; Baillie 1995). The widespread use of *fulachta fiadh* becomes a feature of the landscape (see Buckley 1990; Hodder and Barfield 1991; Brindley *et al.* 1989/90), as do wooden trackways in wetland areas (*e.g.* Raftery 1990; 1996; Moloney *et al.* 1993). During this phase coarse domestic vessels, both inverted and upright, enter the burial record and by *c.* 1500–1400 BC have replaced cordoned urns completely. The evidence from Lough Gur suggests that this was also the case on domestic sites, with decoration becoming much less common. Inurned burials, contained in coarse domestic vessels, continue to be deposited, as at Cush 3, burial 5, Knockast burials 1 and 5, and Carrowjames, Tumulus 4, Co. Mayo (Table 10.6). Increasingly, however, burials contain sherds of broken vessels generally representing only a small portion of the pot. Other gravegoods are scarce although flint flakes and animal bones were deposited in some graves. A feature of this period is the reduction of the proportion of the body represented in burials (see below). Established cemeteries or funerary complexes, as at Altanagh, Carrig, Carrow-

Site	Primary use	Burial No.	County	Monument Type	P = pit	Rite	Pottery	Disposition	Other deposits/ Location of burial	Age/gender	Reference	C-14 Cal. BC
Cooradarrigan	MBA		Co.	Boulder burial	P	?	-				O'Brien 1992	1266-1426
Drombeg	MBA	1	Co.	Stone circle	P	Cr	★	Br?			Fahy 1959	794-1124
		2			P	Cr	-					
Bohonagh	MBA		Co.	Stone circle	P	Cr	-	-	Mound		Fahy 1961	
Reenascreena South	MBA		Co.	Stone circle	P	Cr	-	-			Fahy 1962	
Labbacallee	LN		Co.	Wedge tomb		Inh ?	★+	Br?	Chamber	A, ch	Leask and Price 1936	
Largantea	LN		De.	Wedge tomb			©sh	-	Chamber		Herring 1938	
Loughash	LN		Ty.	Wedge tomb			★		Chamber		Davies 1939	
Kilhoyle	LN		De.	Wedge tomb			★		Chamber			
Baurnadomeeny 1	LN		Ti.	Wedge tomb		Cr	★		Cairn		O'Kelly 1960	
Harristown	LN	4	Wa.	Wedge tomb		Cr	★ sh		Cairn	A	Hawkes 1941	
		1			P	Cr	©	∨		YA		
		6				Cr	-	-		?		
		7			P	Cr	-			A♂		
Moylisha	LN		Wi.	Wedge tomb		Cr	★+	Br?	m	?	Ó h-Iceadha 1946	
Lough Gur	LN		Li.	Wedge tomb		?	★		m		Ó Ríordáin and Ó h-Iceadha 1955	
Ballykeel	N		Ar.	Portal tomb			3★+	B?	Chamber	?	Collins 1965	
Kilfeaghan	N		Do.	Portal tomb			★+	Br?	Chamber		Collins 1959	
Kiltiernan	N		Dn.	Portal tomb			★©	Br?	Chamber		Ó h-Eochaidhe 1957	
Legland	N			Court tomb					Chamber		Davies 1939-40	

★ coarse pottery   © cordoned urn   sh sherds only   ∨ vessel on side   Br? Vessel broken before deposition
m spearhead mould

Table 10.6: Middle-Late Bronze Age burials from megalithic tombs and related sites.

Period Material	Altar, Co.	Labbacallee, Co.	Largantea, Dy.	Loughash, Ty.	Lough Gur, Li.	Moneen, Co.	Moylisha, Ww.	Moytirra, Ww.	Toormore	Baurnadomeeny, Ti.	Kilmashogue, Du.	Kilhoyle, Dy.	Clontygora	Harristown, Wa.	Ballynahatty, Dn.	Drimnagh, Du.	Ballymacaldrack	Ballymarlagh	Knockroe, Kk.	Altanagh, Ty.
Neolithic	■	■			■†	■†									■†					■
Beaker		■	■	■	■	■†	■		■											
EBA									■											
food vessel			■†	■†	■†	■†								■		■†	■	■	■	
vase urn		■								†	■	■								
MBA									■†					■						■
cordoned urn		■	■†	■†ψ	■									■ψOl	■	■+				■
coarse ware		■†	■ψ		■									■†						
metal/mould				■■m		■□m	■□m	■◆?	■O											
LBA	■				■				■											
Iron Age	■																			
Early Historic	■																			
Medieval	■								■											
Early modern	■				■															
Modern	■																			

■ Recorded event   ψ razor-knife   ◆ sword/rapier   □m spearhead mould   ■m palstave mould   O EBA hoard
† Definite evidence for burial   0 faience

Table 10.7: Event histories in Irish megalithic tombs and related sites.

james, Cush, Knockast, Kilcroagh, and the Hill of Rath, have produced some coarse vessel burials and these, and other sites, frequently contain unaccompanied, and frequently unprotected, cremations of this period. There were 23 such cremations at Knockast, for example. A large number of new cemeteries, many consisting of clusters of unmarked pits, were established at this stage. The burial traditions forming during this period continue right through to the end of the Bronze Age and only those burials that have been dated through radiocarbon or association are included in this paper (see below).

Burial rites: broken, crushed and comminuted

Almost uniquely in Irish prehistory inhumation forms a significant part of the burial record during the earliest part of the Bronze Age. While bowl food vessels accompanied the vast majority of these burials there are also a number of instances of unaccompanied inhumations in cists (Cooney and Grogan 1994). Cremation is re-established as the dominant rite in the period after the demise of bowls as funerary ware and is the sole rite in relation to vases, vase urns, encrusted urns, collared and cordoned urns. While the majority of Early Bronze Age burials are those of individuals there is a very significant minority that contain multiple burials (Cooney 1987; Grogan 1989; Cooney and Grogan 1994; Mount 1995; 1997a). Although the research on this aspect of the record is confined to the regional studies cited above there appears to be a greater incidence of multiple burials associated with cordoned urns. This is of particular interest as these vessels continue in use for a considerable period after the other cinerary urn types fade from the record and they form a significant part of the Middle Bronze Age funerary evidence.

It is evident that throughout prehistory the body could go through several stages of treatment during the funerary process. These include excarnation prior to the final deposition of the surviving skeletal material, possible excarnation prior to cremation, temporary inhumation followed by exhumation and cremation, immediate cremation followed by a period of temporary burial or storage prior to final deposition, and cremation at death followed immediately by final burial. During the Neolithic and Early Bronze Age it seems that cremation was followed by the careful extraction of all or most bones from the pyre, the washing of the skeletal remains and their reduction to smaller fragments by pounding or crushing. In many documented examples a significant portion of the skeletal remains were present in the final burial and this included many small bones, such as metatarsals and metacarpals, and well as teeth separated from the jaw. This suggests that reasonable care and attention was given to the extraction of bones from the pyre and that the burial of the 'whole' person was an essential part of the burial tradition. This does not mean that the complete physical remains were present even in the majority of burials. However, it does show that it was clearly considered appropriate to obtain a substantial and representative portion of the skeleton for burial.

Substantial burials, containing large portions of the deceased, also occur during the Middle and Late Bronze Age. However, a significant feature of the burials of this period is the contrasting sharp reduction in the quantity of bones generally present in burials (O Donnabháin 1988). Many individuals are represented only by a few bone fragments and often these are comminuted, that is reduced through severe crushing and pounding to tiny fragments often no more that 5mm in length. In this context it is worth noting that bones that have been crushed regularly survive as the comparatively large fragments (often containing individual pieces up to 10cm in length) and retain sharp edge fractures. Pounded bones have generally lost their structure and are more prevalent to further post-depositional decomposition. Many reports refer to tiny fragments of unidentifiable bone material that has a typically smooth dusty texture. These remains, often referred to as 'token burials', can consist of only a few grammes of bone and generally represent less than 1% of the cremated skeleton. These burials also often contain some portion of the pyre: it appears as though a small portion of the pyre material containing bone was removed and pounded and this comprised the remains ultimately deposited in the grave.

A small number of inhumations date to this period and include the burials at Tara and Castlemartyr. At Adamstown, Co. Limerick, a large central pit, apparently covered by a canopy, produced the lower mandible of an adult male possibly from a disarticulated or disturbed burial (Grogan 1988c). Whether this constituted the remnant of one part of a long process of burial ceremony, *e.g.* the temporary burial of an individual prior to exhumation, cremation and final reburial, is a matter of speculation but, in this context the Adamstown burial is of importance as it may reveal part of a complex funerary rite that is represented at other sites only by the final burial. In this regard it might be suggested that elaborate funerary processes and rituals provided a series of contexts within which the dead were honoured and their role and status in life was commemorated. This contrasts with the provision of gravegoods as the principal means of establishing the status of the dead and those in control of burial during the earlier Bronze Age.

Possible pyres or crematoria have been identified at a few sites including Carrowbeg North 1, Co. Galway (Willmot 1939), and Ballyvelly (Dunne 1999).

Bodyless burials?

A number of excavated funerary sites in east Limerick have produced no evidence for human remains; these include 4 barrows at Mitchelstowndown West (Daly and Grogan 1993), 8 barrows on an enhanced natural platform at Duntryleague, and several barrows in the Lissard-Ballynamona complex (Ó Ríordáin 1936; Grogan 1989). Clearly the very small quantities of bone representing many burials of this period would be difficult to identify, particularly if deposited, for example, like some of the burials in the surrounding ditch at Shanaclogh, Co. Limerick (Gowen 1988). Nevertheless, it is possible that funerary monuments commemorated the dead without the inclusion of their remains.

Graves, markers and monuments

Although rectangular cists were occasionally used in the Middle and Late Bronze Age in general burials were contained in pits, or in small polygonal or square cists. The latter most commonly consist of stone lined pits and are often associated with inverted urns. Small cists (*c.* 0.30m by 0.30m) have been recorded at many sites; these generally contain unaccompanied cremations as at Baurnadomeeny, Co. Tipperary (O'Kelly 1960), Monknewtown, Co. Meath (Sweetman 1976), Lough Gur, Co. Limerick (Cleary 1995), and Moylisha, Co. Wicklow (Ó h-Iceadha 1946). The majority of burials are, however, contained in pits. Occasionally these were covered by small capstones.

Some form of identifiable marker or monument indicated the location of most burials.

a. Standing stones at Carrig E, Carrowjames, and Ballybeen, Co. Antrim (Mallory 1984). Timber posts at Killoran (Stevens 1998a; 1998c, Sites 6 and 10), Ballynamuddagh, Co. Wicklow (Deevy 2002), New Downs, Mullingar, Co. Westmeath (Dennehy 2002), Ballyconneely, Co. Clare (Read 2000), Richardstown, Co. Louth (Byrnes 2000, 222).

b. Burials placed in existing megalithic tombs, either deposited in the burial chambers, or in secondary graves in the mound or cairn (see Table 10.5).

c. Burials contained in barrows or ringditches (Grogan 1989; Cooney and Grogan 1994).

d. Burials contained in cairns, ringcairns and kerbed cairns: Carrig, Carnkenny, Co. Tyrone (Lynn 1973–74), Lough Gur Circle P (Grogan and Eogan 1987).

d. Enclosed flat cemeteries: Shanaclogh and Duntryleague, Co. Limerick (Gowen 1988).

e. Caves: Lough Gur (Cleary 1995), Castlemartyr.

f. Burials contained in boulder burials (Table 10.6; O'Brien 1992)

g. Burials within stone circles (Table 10.6)

Unmarked burials? Flat cemeteries and single pits

A number of apparently unmarked burials have been identified although by their nature these are usually found either accidentally or through the monitoring of large projects such as road building or pipeline construction. The first significant identification of these types of burials occurred during excavations on the Limerick Gas Pipeline (Gowen 1988; Grogan 1988) when they were located both as apparently isolated burials and within more formal funerary landscape such as barrow cemeteries. Since then similar burials have been identified in very large numbers singly or in flat cemeteries. Examples include large clusters, as at Ballyconneely, Co. Clare (Read 2000); and Killoran within the Derryville-Lisheen complex, Co. Tipperary (Gowen *et al.* 2000; Stevens 1998, Site 10). Smaller groups, consisting of 2–10 sites, have been excavated at Knocksaggart, Co. Clare (Tarbett-Buckley and Hull 2002), Cherrywood, Co. Dublin (Site 19, O'Donovan 1999; Ó Néill 2000), Sheephouse, Co. Kildare (Nelis 2002), Killoran, Co. Tipperary (Stevens 1998b, Site 4), Ballyvelly 1 and 2, Co. Kerry (Dunne 1999), Bricketstown, Co. Wexford (Elder 2002), and Site 2, Ballyhenry, Co. Antrim (McManus 2002, 2). The site at Mitchelstowndown North, Co. Limerick (Grogan 1988b), is a good example of these sites. Here 7 small pits contained token cremations each consisting of very small quantities of comminuted bone. The cremations had been mixed with what appeared to be material from a pyre and this formed a putty-like lining to the pits. Some of the burials were then partly sealed with a clean clay capping. This treatment of the burials has been noted at other sites including Killoran Site 10. Sherds of coarse

pottery accompanied two burials at Mitchelstowndown and each of the pits contained the remains of an adult; No. 1 also produced the bones of a neonate.

Although reports are available for only a few of these recently excavated cemeteries the very small quantity of bone recovered from most burials supports the view established for the county Limerick sites that these almost exclusively contain the remains of a single adult (O Donnabháin 1988; Grogan 1988a; 1989). This provides a contrast with the cordoned urns of the early Middle Bronze Age and suggests a trend towards more exclusive, if apparently less spectacular, burial customs.

Isolated pit burials?

Simple, often unaccompanied, cremations from many cemeteries have already been referred to. Single, apparently isolated, burial pits have also been recorded although many of these have been within relatively narrow construction corridors. Middle-Late Bronze Age burial pits have been identified at New Downs, Co. Westmeath (Dennehy 2002), Richardstown, Co. Louth (Byrnes 2000, 222), Site 6, Castle Upton, Co. Antrim (Gahan 1997), Sarsfieldstown, Co. Meath (Lynch 1998), as well as beneath and within the enclosure at Johnstown South, Co. Wicklow (Fitzpatrick 1998). Many of these consist of simple isolated pits containing finely burnt and comminuted cremations. At Ballynatona the remains of six vessels were recovered. Spittle 3 produced two pots, one of urn size and the other smaller and of finer ware than the other Limerick coarse vessels (Gowen 1988). At Raheen burial pit 11 had a fill of black silt with abundant charcoal; there was no pottery but the remains were human. At Spittle 3 the base of the pit was filled with charcoal rich soil containing flecks of cremated bone. The pit at Duntryleague 19 (B), perhaps an outlier to the funerary complex at Duntryleague 9 and 10 (see above), seems to have contained a token burial; at least one of the pots was inverted and set against an upright slab.

The majority of these simple cremations are, however, found in cemeteries and in several areas single pits, and small groups of 2–3 burials, have been found within more extensive complexes. In the Mitchelstowndown-Raheen area of southeast Limerick an extensive landscape contains funerary and secular components. The burial record consists of barrow cemeteries, single barrows, pit clusters and single pits; examples of each of these have been dated to the Middle Bronze Age (Gowen 1988; Grogan 1988a; 1988b; 1989; Cooney and Grogan 1994, 129–32; Daly and Grogan 1993; Ó Ríordáin 1936). While there are particular concentrations of activity, for example at Duntryleague, Lissard, Mitchelstowndown North and East, Raheen and Raheenamadra, overall the individual elements combined with the evidence for settlement sites suggests that this was a highly organised and integrated landscape and that none of the burials were 'isolated'. Similar evidence has come from the Killoran (Ó Néill

1998; Gowen *et al.* 2000), Cherrywood, and Bally-conneely areas.

General Discussion

Two principal phases have been identified for the Middle Bronze Age burial tradition. The first, dating to *c.* 1500–1300 BC, is dominated by cordoned urns although graves without ceramics were also current. Another feature is the presence of a large number of comparatively wealthy burials containing accessory vessels, bronze razors, or *faience* beads, as well as other more occasional grave-goods of amber, gold, bone and bronze. Similarities in grave construction, vessel deposition, and burial rite, as well as the occurrence of many of these burials in earlier cemeteries, underline the strength of continuity with Early Bronze Age traditions. The second phase (*c.* 1300–1000 BC) is characterised by the introduction of coarse domestic vessels, sometimes represented by sherds or sometimes as complete vessels acting as containers, and a general absence of gravegoods. Single token cremations of adults in pits appear to predominate. Although earlier cemeteries continued to be used the majority of graves occur in new cemeteries or barrows, or within extensive funerary landscapes containing a variety of burial sites. Two important features can be identified in the development of burial traditions in this stage. The first is the gradual reduction in the extent of human remains deposited. Cremation continues to the dominant rite although unburnt, and apparently disarticulated, bone occurs at a small number of sites. Many burials contain only a portion of the human skeleton. It is not clear if this represents selective extraction from the pyre or the cremation of selected remains following a period of decay and disarticulation. Many other deposits consist of only token remains and these burials usually contain comminuted bone that had been reduced by pounding or rolling into tiny (≤5mm) fragments (O Donnabháin 1988). The apparent absence of any bone has been noted at a number of other sites (*e.g.* Daly and Grogan 1993; Ó Ríordáin 1936). The second feature is the disappearance of burials that distinguish their occupants through associated artefacts. The minimalism of this tradition is therefore reflected through the small quantities of both human remains and pottery sherds contained in many graves, and especially by the dominance of unaccompanied token cremations. This contrasts with the wider archaeological record with the increase in emphasis on artefact, including hoard, deposition especially in wetland contexts (Eogan 1983; Cooney and Grogan 1994; 133–42). There also appears to be an increase in the construction of funerary monuments, including barrows, ringditches, boulder burials and cairns, sometimes occurring in large clusters. During this period and the succeeding Late Bronze Age, other monuments that were at least occasionally used for burial include stone circles and boulder burials, as well as earlier megalithic tombs. It is clear that differentiation in status was no longer mediated through the provision of elaborate gravegoods although it is possible that some individuals were distinguished through the special construction of substantial burial monuments, or by the deposition of their remains in earlier monuments. The focus for the establishment and display of status appears to have moved towards increased material wealth, elaborate personal ornamentation and the deposition of artefacts, principally in wetland locations (Cooney and Grogan 1994, 133–42).

While far more research is required, especially on the huge number of sites currently entering the record from large-scale linear construction sites such as roads and pipelines, it appears that burials of this period may be far more numerous than those of the Early Bronze Age. The simplicity of the graves and the minimalism of the burial rite contrasts with the comparative opulence of earlier funerary customs, and the dramatic increase in the material wealth of contemporary societies. This contrast between the affluence of at least some social groups, and the evidence for an increased emphasis on the display of wealth amongst the living, and the paucity and simplicity apparent treatment of the dead, was to increase during the Late Bronze Age.

The burial traditions established in the Middle Bronze Age, including rite, funerary processes, deposition and association, as well as a wide range of burial site types, continue through to the end of the Irish Bronze Age. In the Late Bronze Age a number of large scale ceremonial enclosures, including The Grange Stone Circle, Lough Gur, (Ó Ríordáin 1936; Roche this volume), Circle O, Lough Gur (Grogan and Eogan 1987), Lugg, Co. Dublin (Kilbride-Jones 1950), and Coolalough, Co. Limerick (Cross and Grogan 1995), Johnstown, Co. Wicklow (Fitzpatrick 1998), also contain evidence for funerary related activity.

Bibliography

Baillie, M. 1995 Dendrochronology and the Chronology of the Irish Bronze Age. In J. Waddell and E. Shee Twohig (eds) *Ireland in the Bronze Age,* 30–7. The Stationery Office, Dublin.

Binchy, E. 1967 Irish Razors and Razor-Knives of the Middle Bronze Age. In E. Rynne (ed.) *North Munster Studies: Essays in commemoration of Monsignor Micheal Moloney,* 43–60. Thomond Archaeological Society, Limerick.

Brindley, A. 1980 The Cinerary Urn tradition in Ireland – an alternative interpretation, *Proceedings of the Royal Irish Academy* **80**C, 197–206.

Brindley, A. 1995 Radiocarbon, Chronology and the Bronze Age. In J. Waddell and E. Shee Twohig (eds) *Ireland in the Bronze Age,* 4–13. The Stationery Office, Dublin.

Brindley, A. and Lanting, J. 1991/92 Radiocarbon Dates from the Cemetery at Poulawack, Co. Clare, *Journal of Irish Archaeology* **6**, 13–17.

Brindley, A. and Lanting, J. 1998 Radiocarbon Dates for Irish Trackways, *Journal of Irish Archaeology* **9**, 45–67.

Brindley, A., Lanting, J. and Mook, W.G. 1987/88 Radiocarbon dates from Moneen and Labbacallee, County Cork, *Journal of Irish Archaeology* **4**, 13–20.

Brindley, A.L., Lanting, J.N. and Mook, W.G. 1989/90 Radio-carbon Dates from Irish Fulachta Fiadh and Other Burnt Mounds, *Journal of Irish Archaeology* **5**, 25–33.

Buckley, V. (ed.) 1990 *Burnt Offerings*, 18–23. International Contributions to Burnt Mound Archaeology, Dublin.

Burgess, C. 1980 *The Age of Stonehenge*. J.M. Dent and Sons Ltd., London.

Butler, J.J. 1981 Review (*The Age of Stonehenge*, C. Burgess), *Proceedings of the Prehistoric Society* **47**, 350–3.

Byrnes, E. 2000 Richardstown, Co. Louth. In I. Bennett (ed.) *Excavations 1999*, 221–2. Wordwell, Dublin.

Cleary, R. 1995 Later Bronze Age settlement and prehistoric burials, Lough Gur, Co. Limerick, *Proceedings of the Royal Irish Academy* **95**C, 1–92.

Collins, A. 1959 Kilfeaghan Dolmen, Co. Down, *Ulster Journal of Archaeology* **22**, 31–32.

Collins, A. 1965 Ballykeel Dolmen and Cairn, Co. Armagh, *Ulster Journal of Archaeology* **28**, 47–70.

Cooney, G. 1987 *North Leinster in the earlier prehistoric period*. Unpublished PhD Thesis, National University of Ireland.

Cooney, G. and Grogan, E. 1994 *Irish Prehistory. a social perspective*. Wordwell, Dublin.

Cross, S. and Grogan, E. 1995 Coolalough, Co. Limerick. In I. Bennett (ed.) *Excavations 1994*, 55–6. Wordwell, Dublin.

Daly, A. and Grogan, E. 1993 Excavation of four barrows in Mitchelstowndown West, County Limerick, *Discovery Programme Reports* **1**, 44–60. The Discovery Programme/Royal Irish Academy, Dublin.

Davies, O. 1939 Excavations at the Giant's Grave, Loughash, *Ulster Journal of Archaeology* **2**, 254–68.

Davies, O. 1939–40 Excavations at Legland Horned Cairn, *Proceedings of the Belfast Natural Historical and Philosophical Society* 1935–36, 16–24.

Deevy, M. 2002 Ballynamuddagh, Bray, Co. Wicklow, Bronze Age pits and structures. In I. Bennett (ed.) *Excavations 2000*, 363–4. Wordwell, Dublin.

Dennehy, E. 2002 Area E, New Downs, Mullingar, Co. Westmeath. In I. Bennett (ed.) *Excavations 2000*, 348. Wordwell, Dublin.

Doody, M. 1986 *Bronze Age Burials in Munster*. Unpublished MA thesis, National University of Ireland.

Duffy, C. 2002 Hill of Rath, Co. Louth, Prehistoric complex. In I. Bennett (ed.) *Excavations 2000*, 231–3. Wordwell, Dublin.

Dunne, L. 1998a Mounthawk 1, Tralee, Co. Kerry. In I. Bennett (ed.) *Excavations 1997*, 87–88. Wordwell, Dublin.

Dunne, L. 1998b Late Bronze Age burials in County Kerry, *Archaeology Ireland* **44**, 4.

Dunne, L. 1999 Ballyvelly, Tralee, Co. Kerry. Flat cemetery and crematoria. In I. Bennett (ed.) *Excavations 1998*, 00–00. Wordwell, Dublin.

Elder, S. 2002 Bricketstown, Co. Wexford, Possible prehistoric flat cremation cemetery. In I. Bennett (ed.) *Excavations 2000*, 350–1. Wordwell, Dublin.

Eogan, G. 1964 The Later Bronze Age in Ireland in the light of recent research, *Proceedings of the Prehistoric Society* **14**, 268–350.

Eogan, G. 1983 *Hoards of the Irish Later Bronze Age*. University College, Dublin.

Fahy, E.M. 1959 A recumbent-stone circle at Drombeg, Co. Cork, *Journal of the Cork Historical and Archaeological Society* **64**, 1–27.

Fahy, E.M. 1961 A stone circle, hut and dolmen at Bohonagh, Co. Cork, *Journal of the Cork Historical and Archaeological Society* **66**, 93–104.

Fahy, E.M. 1962 A recumbent-stone circle at Reenascreena South, Co. Cork, *Journal of the Cork Historical and Archaeological Society* **67**, 59–69.

Fitzpatrick, M. 1998 Johnstown South enclosure, Co. Wicklow. In I. Bennett (ed.) *Excavations 1997*, 199–200. Wordwell, Dublin.

Gahan, A. 1997 A Course on Irish prehistory – excavations at Castle Upton, Templepatrick, Co. Antrim, *Archaeology Ireland* **40**, 29–30.

Gowen, M. 1988 *Three Irish Gas Pipelines: New Archaeological Evidence in Munster*. Wordwell, Dublin.

Gowen, M., Casparie, W., Caseldine, C., Geary, B., Hatton, J., Stuijts, I., Reilly, E., Owens, B., Murray, C., Stevens, P., Ó Néill, J. and Cross, S. 2000 *Wetland and landscape archaeology in County Tipperary: The Lisheen Archaeological Project*. Margaret Gowen and Company Ltd., Dublin.

Grogan, E. 1988a The pipeline sites and the prehistory of the Limerick area. In M. Gowen *Three Irish Gas Pipelines: New Archaeological Evidence in Munster*, 148–57. Wordwell, Dublin.

Grogan, E. 1988b Unenclosed cremation pit group (Mitchelstowndown North, Co. Limerick). In M. Gowen *Three Irish Gas Pipelines: New Archaeological Evidence in Munster*, 98–102. Wordwell, Dublin.

Grogan, E. 1988c Curvilinear ditch, pits and associated features (Adamstown, Co. Limerick). In M. Gowen *Three Irish Gas Pipelines: New Archaeological Evidence in Munster*, 94–8. Wordwell, Dublin.

Grogan, E. 1989 *Settlement and society in north Munster during the Neolithic and Earlier Bronze Age*. Unpublished PhD Thesis, National University of Ireland.

Grogan, E. 1990 Bronze Age Cemetery at Carrig, Co. Wicklow, *Archaeology Ireland* **16**, 12–14.

Grogan, E. and Eogan, G. 1987 Lough Gur excavations by Seán P. Ó Ríordáin: further Neolithic and Beaker habitations on Knockadoon, *Proceedings of the Royal Irish Academy* **87**C, 299–506.

Hawkes, J. 1941 Excavations of a megalithic tomb at Harristown, Co. Waterford, *Journal of the Royal Society of Antiquaries of Ireland* **71**, 130–47.

Hencken, H. O'N. and Movius, H. 1934 The Cemetery-Cairn at Knockast, *Proceedings of the Royal Irish Academy* **41**C, 232–84.

Herity, M. and Eogan, G. 1977 *Ireland in Prehistory*. Routledge and Keegan Paul, London.

Herring, I. 1938 The Cairn Excavation at Well Glass Spring, Largantea, Co. Londonderry, *Ulster Journal of Archaeology* **1**, 164–88.

Hodder, M. and Barfield, L. (eds) 1991 *Burnt Mounds. Hot Stone Technology*, Sandwell.

Kavanagh, R. 1973 The Encrusted Urn in Ireland, *Proceedings of the Royal Irish Academy* **73**C, 507–617.

Kavanagh, R. 1976 Collared and Cordoned Urns in Ireland, *Proceedings of the Royal Irish Academy* **76**C, .293–403.

Kavanagh, R. 1991 A reconsideration of razors in the Irish Earlier Bronze Age, *Journal of the Royal Society of Antiquaries of Ireland* **121**, 77–104.

Kilfeather, A. 1991 *Patterns in Early Bronze Age society: a study of aceramic grave goods in Ireland*. Unpublished MA thesis, National University of Ireland.

Kilbride-Jones, H. 1950 The excavation of a composite Early Iron Age monument with "Henge" features at Lugg, Co. Dublin, *Proceedings of the Royal Irish Academy* **53**C, 311–32.

Leask, H. and Price, L. 1936 The Labbacallee Megalith, Co. Cork, *Proceedings of the Royal Irish Academy* **43**C, 77–101.

Lynch, P. 1998 Sarsfieldstown, Co. Meath. In I. Bennett (ed.) *Excavations 1997*, 144–5. Wordwell, Dublin.

Lynn, C. 1973–74 The excavation of a ring-cairn in Carnkenny, Co. Tyrone, *Ulster Journal of Archaeology* **36–37**,17–31.

McManus, C. 2002 IDB (NI) Industrial Development Site, Ballyhenry, Co. Antrim. In I. Bennett (ed.) *Excavations 2000*, 2–3. Wordwell, Dublin.

Mallory, J.P. 1984 The Long Stone, Ballybeen, Dundonald, County Down, *Ulster Journal of Archaeology* **47**, 1–4.

Moloney, A. Jennings, D., Keane, M. and McDermott, C. 1993 *Survey of the Raised Bogs of County Longford.* Irish Archaeological Wetland Unit Transactions **1**, Crannóg Publications, Dublin.

Mount, C. 1995 New research on Irish Early Bronze Age cemeteries. In J. Waddell and E. Shee Twohig (eds) *Ireland in the Bronze Age*, 97–112. The Stationery Office, Dublin.

Mount, C. 1997a Early Bronze Age burial in south-east Ireland in the light of recent research, *Proceedings of the Royal Irish Academy* **97C**, 101–93.

Mount, C. 1997b Adolf Mahr's Excavations of an Early Bronze Age Cemetery at Keenoge, County Meath, *Proceedings of the Royal Irish Academy* **97C**, 1–68.

Mount, C. 1998 Five Early Bronze Age cemeteries at Brownstown, Graney West, Oldtown and Ploopluck, County Kildare, and Strawhill, County Carlow, *Proceedings of the Royal Irish Academy* **98C**, 25–99.

Nelis, D. 2002 Northern Motorway Site No. 3, Sheephouse, Co. Meath, Prehistoric enclosure. In I. Bennett (ed.) *Excavations 2000*, 265. Wordwell, Dublin.

O'Brien, W. 1992 Boulder-burials: a later Bronze Age megalith tradition in South-West Ireland, *Journal of the Cork Historical and Archaeological Society* **97**, 11–35.

O'Brien, W. 1993 Aspects of Wedge Tomb Chronology. In E. Shee-Twohig and M. Ronayne (eds), *Past Perceptions: The Prehistoric Archaeology of South-West Ireland*, 63–74. University College, Cork.

O'Brien, W. 1999 *Sacred Ground. Megalithic Tombs in Coastal South-West Ireland.* Bronze Age Studies **4**, Department of Archaeology, National University, Galway.

O Donnabháin, B. 1988 Report on the osseous remains from sites on the ....gas pipelines. In M. Gowen *Three Irish Gas Pipelines*, 192–5. Wordwell, Dublin.

O'Donavan, E. 1999 Cherrywood and Laughanstown, Co. Dublin. Prehistoric/post-medieval. In I. Bennett (ed.) *Excavations 1998*, 00–00. Wordwell, Dublin.

Ó h-Eochaidhe, M. 1957 Portal Dolmen at Kiltiernan, Co. Dublin, *Proceedings of the Prehistoric Society* **10**, 221.

Ó h-Iceadha, G. 1946 The Moylisha Megalith, Co. Wicklow, *Journal of the Royal Society of Antiquaries of Ireland* **76**, 119–28.

O'Kelly, M. 1960 A Wedge-shaped Gallery Grave at Baurnadomeeny, Co. Tipperary, *Journal of the Cork Historical and Archaeological Society* **65**, 85–115.

Ó Néill, J. 1998 Killoran. Unenclosed later prehistoric settlement. In I. Bennett (ed.) *Excavations 1997*, 173–74.Wordwell, Dublin.

Ó Néill, J. 2000 Cherrywood Science and Technology Park, Cherrywood, Co. Dublin. Archaeological landscape. In I. Bennett (ed.) *Excavations 1999*, 00–00. Wordwell, Dublin.

Ó Ríordáin, B. and Waddell, J. 1993 *The Funerary Bowls and Vases of the Irish Bronze Age.* Galway University Press, Galway.

Ó Ríordáin, S.P. 1936 Excavations at Lissard, Co. Limerick, and other sites in the locality, *Journal of the Royal Society of Antiquaries of Ireland* **66**, 173–85.

Ó Ríordáin, S.P. 1940 Excavations at Cush, Co. Limerick, *Proceedings of the Royal Irish Academy* **45C**, 83–181.

Ó Ríordáin, S.P. 1951, Lough Gur Excavations: The Great Stone Circle (B) in Grange Townland, *Proceedings of the Royal Irish Academy* **54C**, 37–74.

Ó Ríordáin, S.P. 1955 A Burial with Faience beads at Tara, *Proceedings of the Prehistoric Society* **21**, 163–73.

Ó Ríordáin, S.P. and Ó h-Iceadha, M. 1955, Lough Gur Excavations: The Megalithic Tomb, *Journal of the Royal Society of Antiquaries of Ireland* **85**, 34–50.

Power, P. 1931 Some Recent Antiquarian Finds in Munster, *Journal of the Royal Society of Antiquaries of Ireland* **61**, 55–60.

Raftery, B. 1981 Iron Age Burials in Ireland. In D. Ó Corráin (ed.) *Irish Antiquity*, 173–204. Tower Books, Cork.

Raftery, B. 1990 *Trackways through time.* Headline Publishing, Rush.

Raftery, B. 1996 *Trackway Excavations in the Mountdillon Bogs, Co. Longford, 1985–1991.* Irish Archaeological Wetland Unit Transactions **3**, Crannog Publications, Dublin.

Raftery, J. 1938–39 The tumulus cemetery of Carrowjames, Co. Mayo; Part I – Carrowjames I, *Journal of the Galway Archaeological and Historical Society* **18**, 157–67.

Raftery, J. 1940–41 The tumulus cemetery of Carrowjames, Co. Mayo; Part II – Carrowjames II, *Journal of the Galway Archaeological and Historical Society* **19**, 16–85.

Ramsey, G. 1995 Middle Bronze Age metalwork: are artefact studies dead and buried. In J. Waddell and E. Shee Twohig (eds) *Ireland in the Bronze Age*, 49–62. The Stationery Office, Dublin.

Read, C. 2000 Neolithic/Bronze Age cemetery site at Ballyconneely, Co. Clare, *Archaeology Ireland* **54**, 28–9.

Rynne, E. and O'Sullivan, J. 1967 Two Urn Burials from Cush, Co. Limerick, *North Munster Antiquarian Journal* **10**, 103–7.

Stevens, P. 1998a Killoran 6, Co. Tipperary. In I. Bennett (ed.) *Excavations 1997*, 172. Wordwell, Dublin.

Stevens, P. 1998b Killoran 4, Co. Tipperary. In I. Bennett (ed.) *Excavations 1997*, 173. Wordwell, Dublin.

Stevens, P. 1998c Killoran 10, Co. Tipperary. In I. Bennett (ed.) *Excavations 1997*, 174–5. Wordwell, Dublin.

Sweetman, P. 1976 An earthen enclosure at Monknewtown, Slane, Co. Meath, *Proceedings of the Royal Irish Academy* **76C**, 25–73.

Tarbett-Buckley, C. and Hull, G. 2002 Ballycasey to Dromoland Road Improvement Scheme. In I. Bennett (ed.) *Excavations 2000*, 15. Wordwell, Dublin.

Waddell, J. 1969 Two Bronze Age Burials from Reardnogy More, Co. Tipperary, *North Munster Antiquarian Journal* **12**, 3–5.

Waddell, J. 1990 *The Bronze Age Burials of Ireland.* Galway University Press, Galway.

Waddell, J. 1998 *The Prehistoric Archaeology of Ireland*, Galway University Press, Galway.

Williams, B. 1986 Excavations at Altanagh, County Tyrone, *Ulster Journal of Archaeology* **49**, 33–88.

Williams, B., Wilkinson, J. and Magee, R. 1991–92 Bronze Age burials at Kilcroagh, County Antrim, and Faience beads in Ireland, *Ulster Journal of Archaeology* **54–5**, 48–60.

Willmot, G.F. 1939 Two Bronze Age Burials at Carrowbeg North, Belclare, Co. Galway, *Journal of the Galway Archaeological and Historical Society* **18**, 121–40.

11. Irish gold artefacts: Observations from Hartmann's analytical data.

R. Warner

Introduction

We are indebted to George Eogan for his published work on the goldwork of the Irish Bronze Age, pulled together in his masterly *The Accomplished Art* (Eogan 1994). Through his work and that of a few others (notably Joan Taylor) we have available to us in published form a reliable typology, chronology and contextual and cultural framework for the prehistoric gold artefacts of the British Isles, and particularly of Ireland.

This corpus of archaeological information has, for many years, been complemented by a database of a different kind that has the potential to add significantly to our understanding of ancient Irish gold. In the 1960s and 1970s Axel Hartmann persuaded the curators of many of Europe's great archaeological museums to allow him to sample their prehistoric gold artefacts. In 1970 and 1982 he published, in two dense volumes, the results of his chemical analyses of over 4000 objects, including almost all that had been found in Ireland. He also subjected the analyses to a statistical process from which he identified a number of analytical groups, which he recognised had some value as chronological, geographical and cultural discriminators (Hartmann 1979). The baffling 'statistical' method by which Hartmann arrived at his analytical groups and concern about the reliability of his data have resulted in his conclusions (and his data) being largely ignored. Unfortunately no-one would now have access to the level of sampling that Hartmann had, for curators, faced with an apparently widespread opinion that the analysis of their gold objects had been virtually worthless, will not readily allow further sampling to be undertaken.

Hartmann measured the silver content of his gold samples sometimes by specific gravity and sometimes by wet chemistry, and quoted the result as a percentage of the total content (by weight). He then analysed for the copper, tin and some other trace elements (lead, bismuth, nickel, zinc and platinum for instance) using Optical Emission Spectroscopy, quoting the results either quantitatively as a percentage of the gold (not of the total) or qualitatively as a 'trace' (present in quantities that were at the limit of detection by his equipment) or 'not detected'

(below that limit). In the following discussion I will show that artefact types indeed group closely on their levels of tin and copper, which could not happen unless Hartmann's measurements had a reliability and precision significantly better than their overall spread. This alone should be sufficient to give archaeologists faith in his data.

Recently the opportunity has arisen to test Hartmann's data using more modern technology – Inductively-Coupled Plasma Mass-Spectrometry (ICPMS; in Perth, Western Australia), X-ray Fluorescence Spectroscopy (XRF; in the National Museum of Ireland) and Electron Probe Micro-Analysis (EPMA; in the School of Earth-Sciences in Leeds). Hundreds of Irish samples returned from the Hartmann project, and many whole objects, have been re-analysed (mostly by XRF), and the results compared with Hartmann's. We have found, as expected, that the accuracy of Hartmann's silver data is poor. Where Hartmann gives silver at around 3%, 15% or 35% we can be confident that these figures show low, medium and high, silver content. But we may not, from his silver values, safely draw fine distinctions. On the other hand the group-means of the silver obtained from his data, for the various types, are found to be within two percent of the means obtained by the recent re-analysis. The copper values recently obtained, on the other hand, correlate very well with Hartmann's values, and are within the range of variability of copper in most artefacts. The tin values (checked by EMPA only, on a few samples) are also in fairly good agreement. Because I am confident in using Hartmann's copper data, I feel equally confident in accepting his tin data. Hook and Needham (1989) undertook a similar test and were also persuaded that Hartmann's data were usable.

A few archaeologists have used Hartmann's results to characterise gold objects or cultures, with some success. 'Ternary' plots have been used (for instance by Taylor 1980 and Northover 1989) to analyse and display the patterns. This method, while better than Hartmann's histogram method, is unsatisfactory in view of the unreliability of Hartmann's silver values. In the discussion that follows I will update, and expand upon, a paper of

1993 in which I used only binary plots of copper against tin (Warner 1993). The axes in the charts that follow have been transformed by the power of two-thirds and the percentages of the copper and tin have been converted from Hartmann's '% of gold' to a more useful '% of total'. I will indicate silver values as required, using the newly obtained data where this is available, and Hartmann's where it is not (for instance, for non-Irish artefacts). Finally, although I will make a number of observations about patterns in the data I will leave it to authorities on the Bronze Age (which I am not) to draw archaeological conclusions.

The 'core' groupings (Fig 11.1)

In Fig 11.1 I illustrate a particular feature of Hartmann's data – its ability to distinguish between typological and chronological groups of artefacts on the basis of the concentrations of tin and copper. The recently obtained measurements of the silver content show that it is also occasionally a good discriminator. The groups or hoards shown here were chosen to typify the general prehistoric gold traditions in Ireland, especially as outlined by Taylor (1980) and Eogan (1994). I have given labels to these groups (following Warner 1993) that roughly coincide with, or fall within, groups identified by Hartmann.

The so-called *sun-discs*, the earliest gold objects of the Irish Early Bronze Age (Taylor 1979), almost all lie together in the bottom left of the diagram, having both low copper (less than 0.5%, mean 0.3%) and low tin (less than about 0.035%, mean 0.01%). The silver mean is 12%. I will refer to this core group as 'D-gold', with the warning that not all the discs lie within it. The copper and, especially, tin values are close to Hartmann's limit of detection and are possibly within the range of these metals in natural gold in the British Isles (this is a subject that will be addressed elsewhere). The *Derrinboy hoard* (Eogan 1983a, no. 24) defines the goldwork of the Middle Bronze Age (the Bishopsland phase of Eogan's Later Bronze Age), and its values are tightly clustered around a mean of 1.0% copper and 0.13% tin. The mean silver value for this group, 11%, is not significantly different from that of the sun-discs. I shall call this core group 'B-gold'. The *four-flanged torcs*, which belong to the general class of *bar-torcs*, and are also of Middle Bronze Age date (*contra* Warner 1993; discussion below), show a tight cluster in their values – around 5% copper and 0.3% tin. Their mean silver content is 16%. These values are all significantly higher than those for the Derrinboy hoard and, although the two groups are of similar date, this is quite clearly a completely different gold type, which I shall call 'F-gold'. The *gorgets*, of Late Bronze Age date (Eogan 1994, 82ff), also cluster tightly – around 6% copper and 0.14% tin (the tin value is virtually the same as that for the earlier B-gold). Its mean silver content is 13%. This I shall call 'G-gold'. Quite clearly copper is a major intentional additive for both the F-gold and the G-

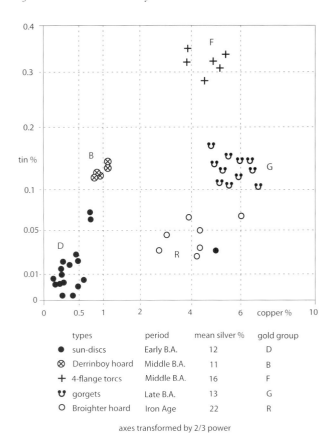

types	period	mean silver %	gold group
● sun-discs	Early B.A.	12	D
⊗ Derrinboy hoard	Middle B.A.	11	B
+ 4-flange torcs	Middle B.A.	16	F
℧ gorgets	Late B.A.	13	G
○ Broighter hoard	Iron Age	22	R

axes transformed by 2/3 power

Fig 11.1: The core groups, D, B, F, G and R.

gold, as it also seems to be for the objects of the *Broighter hoard*, included to illustrate Iron Age gold. These objects are firmly away from those of the other groups, but are rather loosely distributed around 4% copper and 0.04% tin. This 'R-gold' differs particularly from the earlier groups in its high silver (a mean of 22%) and the presence of platinum (never found in Irish objects before this period). It must be borne in mind that while some of the Broighter artefacts are probably of Irish manufacture, others are certainly Roman, even Mediterranean, the implications of which I shall explore on another occasion.

In the graphs that follow I include, where appropriate, the foci (the means) of some of the groups described above in order to aid visual location and comparison.

Early Bronze Age (Figs 11.2 and 11.3)

Fig 11.2a shows the range of values for the most distinctive class of ornament from the Irish Early Bronze Age, the *lunula* (Taylor 1980). The mean copper value for these objects, 0.03%, is the same as that that of the sun-discs (D-gold), and the mean silver value of 10% is not significantly different. The ranges in these two elements are also comparable, only two lunulae and three discs exceeding 0.5% copper. The surprise comes in the great variability of the tin in the lunulae, the range of which runs from less than 0.001% (undetected) to 0.35%. In other words the lunulae differ considerably from the sun-

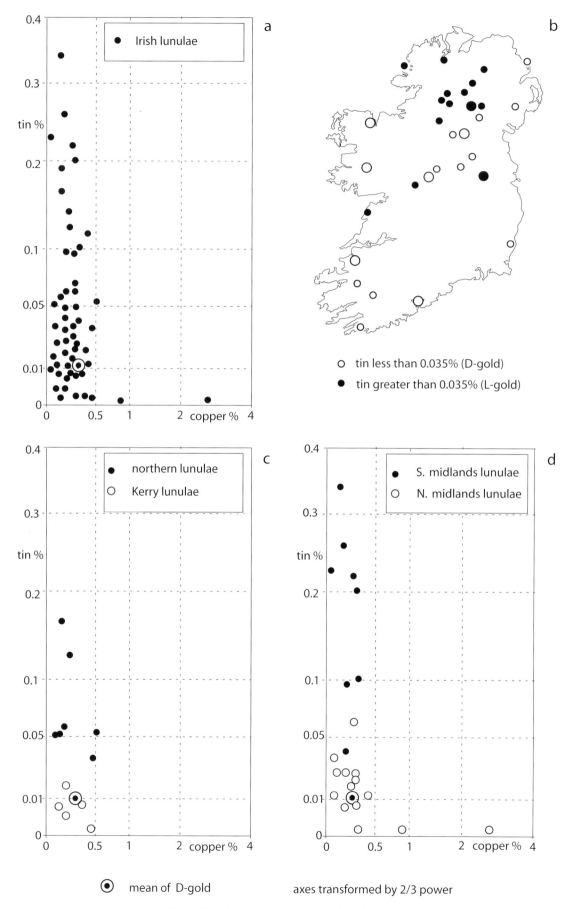

Fig 11.2: Irish Early Bronze Age lunulae (gold-L).

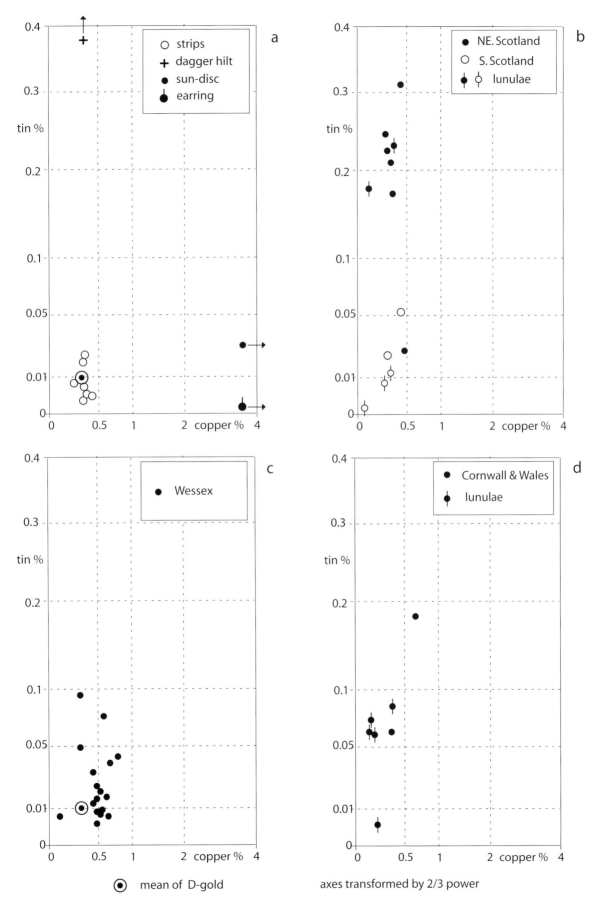

mean of D-gold   axes transformed by 2/3 power

Fig 11.3: Early Bronze Age: other Irish, & British.

discs in the range of their tin values. No obvious structure or modality can be seen in the distribution on the chart – the gap at around 0.08% is unlikely to indicate a real division. For this reason I am inclined to see the lunulae as belonging to a single gold-group whose silver and copper matches D-gold, but whose tin runs from the low of D-gold to high values. Nevertheless I shall, for now, class those lunulae that have copper less than 0.5% and tin less than 0.035% as D-gold and call those with higher tin 'L-gold', resisting the temptation to further subdivide the L-gold. No meaningful pattern emerges between the various typological sub-classes of the lunulae (classical, plain, unaccomplished, provincial – Taylor 1980). However, something interesting is seen when we indicate their general provenances. As we see on Figs 11.2c and 11.2d all the lunulae from Co. Kerry are D-gold. A zone that I have called the 'north-midlands' (which includes the north-east coast) can also be identified as containing only low-tin (mostly D-gold) lunulae. On the other hand an area (the north-west of Ireland) and a narrow zone (the 'south-midlands') have produced only lunulae of L-gold, the former with tin bunching around 0.05% and with a maximum at 0.2%, and the latter concentrated between 0.2% and 0.25% tin, with a maximum at 0.35%. The geographical pattern is well illustrated by the map (Fig 11.2b), on which I have shown only closely-provenanced artefacts (lunulae, sun-discs and *strips*). The *sun-discs* and the *strips* (see Fig 11.3a) have tin values commensurate with the geographical zones (as defined by the lunulae) in which they lie. Furthermore, the Topped Mountain gold-decorated *dagger hilt* (indicated on chart 3a), which has a very high tin value of 0.5%, was found within the northern high-tin area.

The silver values that have been obtained by the recent re-analysis programme indicate that almost all the Early Bronze Age objects are made of gold of a very similar silver value, perhaps even of a single (though not necessarily Irish) origin, and the presence of high tin has not yet been demonstrated in accessible natural gold from the British Isles. I offer, with great caution, the suggestion that the geographical tin-level zones tell us not about the gold source(s) but about workshop practices. I suggest that one or two workshops, somewhere in the north, added (intentionally or as part of the process of manufacture) a small amount of tin. Some support for this idea is given by the interesting fact that the four high-copper (above 0.8%) Early Bronze Age artefacts (two lunulae, one disc and the Deehommed earring) are all low-tin and lie within their proper tin-level zones – indicating the addition of copper as a local alternative to the addition of tin.

Further evidence for this workshop suggestion is provided by the lunulae and other Early Bronze Age objects from Britain, from the standpoint of their copper/tin values (Fig 11.3b–d). The mean silver for the Scottish Early Bronze Age is 9%, and the same for the Scottish lunulae (Hartmann's data). For the Cornish lunulae the mean silver is 10%. These values are in accord with the mean for the Irish lunulae, so a common gold source cannot be ruled out. The copper values are also within the same range as for Ireland. But a pattern strikingly similar to that we have seen in Ireland appears in the British tin values. In 'north-east' Scotland (north of the Forth-Clyde line) all but one of the artefacts are 'high tin' (L-gold), clustering around 0.2% – very similar to the cluster identified for the Irish 'south-midlands'. All the objects from 'southern Scotland' (south of the line) are low tin (D-gold), comparing closely with the Irish north-midlands. The separation between these Scottish tin values is more clearly marked than for Ireland. The middle ground appears to be taken by Cornwall and Wales, whose artefacts have their tin clustering around 0.07% – L-gold, very like that from the Irish 'northern' zone. This might be taken as support for an Irish origin for the lunulae were it not that the other objects from those areas fall into the same value groups. In particular the Orkney sun-discs are firmly in the appropriate high tin group, contrasting with the very low tin of almost all of the Irish discs. A workshop explanation is again indicated here.

Lastly, I would draw attention to the plot for the objects from the Wessex graves (Fig 11.3c; see Taylor 1999). The group is not dissimilar in its tin values to the Irish north-midlands material, and its mean silver is absolutely identical to the Irish D-gold. However, the plot shows that the copper values concentrate slightly higher than those of the same date for Ireland, around 0.5%. Furthermore, very low copper and tin are both missing in the Wessex gold, which perhaps implies slight local addition of both, rather than the use of a naturally copper- and tin-rich gold. If so, a common origin for the Irish and Wessex raw gold is a possibility.

The Middle Bronze Age (Fig 11.4)

On Fig 11.4a I show again the B-gold core objects, but add *bracelets* of the *twisted* and *ribbed* varieties and *tress-rings* – all of which belong to the same cultural *facies* as Derrinboy – and plain bracelets associated with those (Eogan 1994, 50ff). The fairly tight clustering of these artefacts around the B-focus on the chart is very noticeable, indicating a clear signature for these particular Middle Bronze Age objects at about 1.0% copper and 0.14% tin (see also Northover 1989). I shall indicate the general environs of each of my core gold groups by the use of an asterisk (Warner 1993). The gold of the objects analytically associated with the B-gold will therefore be called B*-gold. Its silver mean of 10% is not distinguishable from that of the Early Bronze Age and the same gold source might be indicated. I am advised that a natural gold alone could not produce such a tight tin-copper cluster at such high levels of each. The addition of tin and copper is a likely explanation, and the tightness of the results shows us that this could not have been accidental or fortuitous. I will discuss a possible mechanism to explain this below.

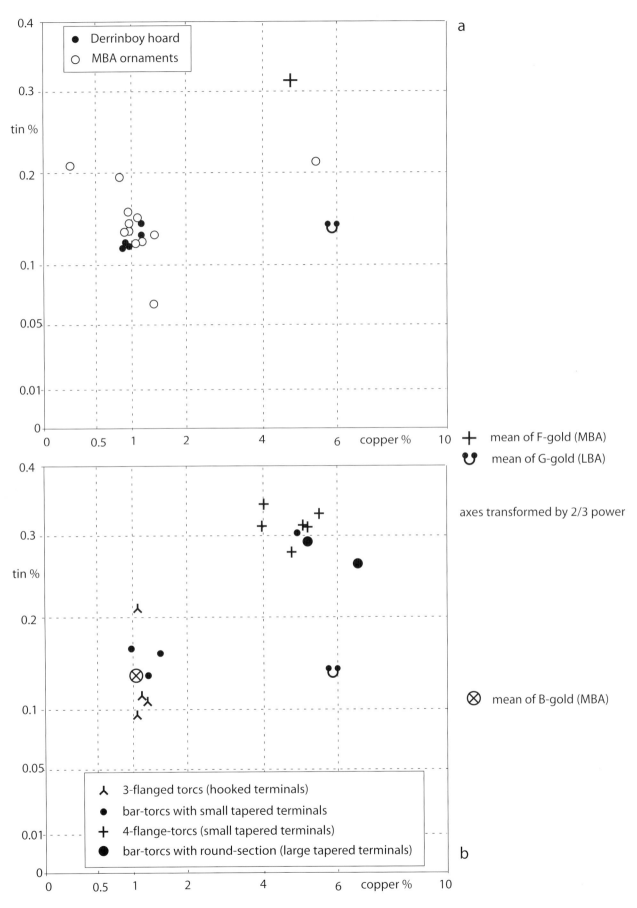

Fig 11.4: Middle Bronze Age (gold-B and gold-F).

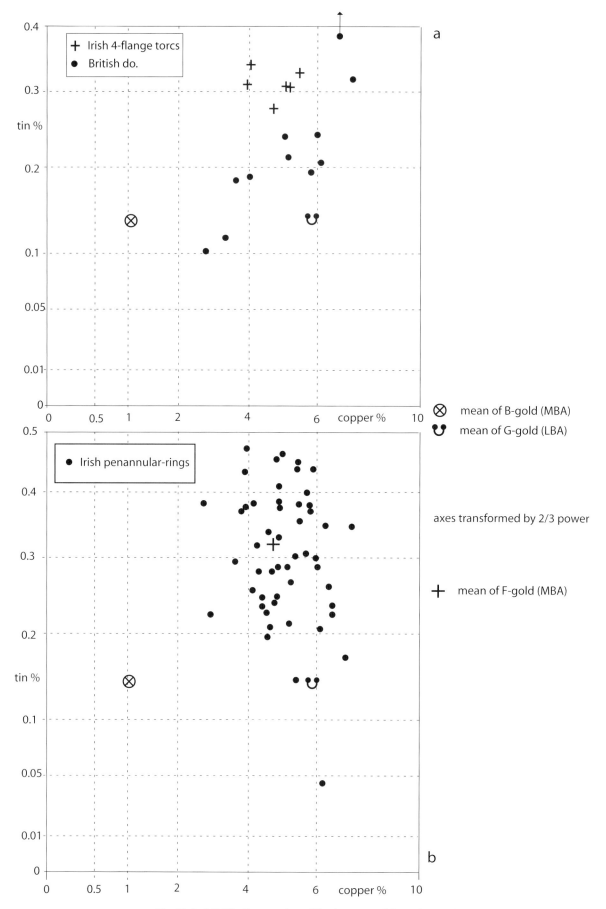

Fig 11.5: Middle Bronze Age (F* objects and British torcs).

We now come to Fig 11.4b. One of the most distinctive and spectacular Bronze Age artefacts is the *bar-torc*, of which there is a large number, from Ireland and from Britain. The typology, chronology and gold content of these objects have been discussed by Northover (1989). All bar-torcs have recurved terminals, some in the form of hooks, some 'tapered' ('trumpet' shaped') – the latter coming in small and large forms. The bars themselves can have round, triangular or square cross-sections or might have three or four longitudinal flanges, and might or might not be twisted. The Irish bar-torcs have been subdivided in different ways by different writers, and the following subdivision is just one more. I have divided the analysed Irish torcs into the following sub-classes – three-flanged torcs, which all have hooked terminals; four-flanged torcs, which all have small tapered terminals; non-flanged bar-torcs with small tapered terminals and circular-section bar-torcs with large tapered terminals. The connection between all the groups is clear, either through their terminals or the existence of flanges, and all date to the Middle Bronze Age.

The three-flange torcs fall into the B* group, and their mean silver (10%) is not inconsistent with this conclusion. Three of the non-flanged torcs with small tapered terminals also lie with that group, but one is in quite a different place, near the F-gold focus. It will be seen on Fig 11.4a that a bracelet, from a hoard whose other members are in the B*-group, also lies in this area. The F-gold is defined by the four-flange torcs, and close to these on our chart are the two round-section bar-torcs with large tapered terminals. The F-gold is spectacularly different from the B-gold to which it is so closely linked by the visual character of its artefacts. The mean values for the B* group, 10% silver, 1% copper and 0.13% tin, have become 16%, 5% and 0.32% respectively. It is absolutely clear that the intentional addition of copper and tin is the only explanation of the enhanced levels of these metals. We might also conclude that a new high-silver gold source is being exploited. But the ratio of the standard-deviation to the mean for the silver in these artefacts is the same (0.1) as for the copper and the tin, and must give us at least a suspicion that the silver is also an intentional addition (see also Northover 1989, 129). I shall return to this below. The distinction between the two Middle Bronze Age gold-types (B and F) has been addressed by Northover (1989) who shows that those object types that fall into my group B* are contemporary with the Taunton phase of the English Middle Bronze Age while the four-flange torcs (F-gold) date to the later Penard phase.

Fig 11.5a shows an interesting distinction between the Irish four-flange torcs and those from Britain (the Continental ones have a similar signature to the British). Although the non-Irish torcs have mean values for silver and copper (18% and 5%) that are similar to the Irish, and also have a high (0.24%) tin value, they do not coincide on the diagram with the Irish ones. Neither do they show the tight clustering on the chart that is so distinctive of my Irish Bronze Age core gold-groups. The British torcs display, on the contrary, a correlation between the copper and tin. The relationship is Sn = 0.036 Cu, and the correlation has a less than 5% probability of arising by chance. An addition of bronze having a Cu:Sn ratio of about 30:1 is strongly indicated. No such correlation is seen in any of the Irish data.

On Fig 11.5b I show *penannular rings* (often called *ring-money* or *hair-rings*), which are particularly common in Ireland. Only the Irish rings are shown – the British rings having a different analytical signature. Most of these rings are made of foil over a copper or tin core, but some are solid gold. It will be seen that the rings form an extensive cloud around the F-gold focus, with much greater variation than the torcs that define F-gold (they are therefore F* objects). The mean values for the rings (see also Fig 11.6a) are silver 18%, copper 5% and tin 0.3% – which do not significantly differ from the core-group means. Some of these rings have narrow bands of silver or silver-alloy pressed into them, giving a striped effect. These silver-alloy bands are difficult to avoid in analysis and have caused a few analysed rings to give over-high silver values. They also provide evidence for the availability of pure silver to the metalworkers responsible for this group of artefacts and we might recall the suggestion made above – that the heightened silver of the F/F* group might have been additive rather than indicating a high-silver source. The very clear implication here that the penannular rings must date to the Middle Bronze Age, assuming that to be the date of the F-gold (that is, of the four-flange torcs), is quite at odds with the archaeological evidence that puts these rings into the Dowris phase of the Late Bronze Age (Eogan 1997). I can offer no explanation of this contradiction (but see Northover 2000).

The Late Bronze Age (Fig 11.6)

The recognition of the cloud (F*) of small objects surrounding the F-gold focus defined by large, high-quality objects is even more obvious with the G-gold (defined by the gorgets). Gorgets are dated to the Dowris phase of the Late Bronze Age and in Fig 11.6a I show the copper-tin mean values for the other important object types belonging to that phase. It will be noted that all except the penannular rings (see above) lie very close to the G focus (the silver mean values are also very close), and support the notion that all these types are the products of a single gold industry (G* group), the mean values of which are silver 13%, copper 6.5% and tin 0.14%. Although the level of tin is not significantly different from that for B-gold, the significantly higher silver level implies a different gold source. There can no doubt that the copper and tin were intentionally added (not in the form of bronze, there being no correlation between the copper and the tin), continuing the tradition certainly present in the F-

R. Warner

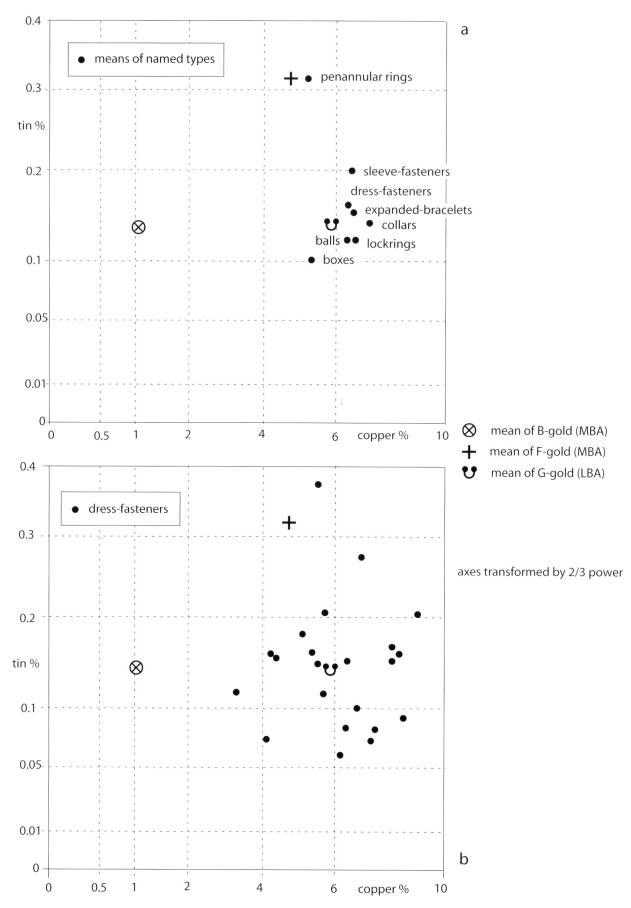

Fig 11.6: Late Bronze Age (G* objects).

gold production. On Fig 11.6b will be seen the plot of one of the Dowris phase types – the dress-fasteners. They cluster round the gorgets of G in the same way that the penannular rings clustered around the four-flange torcs of F, each group having a mean almost identical to the core-mean but with greater variability.

This brings me to a brief discussion of the relationship between the core objects of F and G and their associated (F* and G*) clusters. I suggest that small amounts of natural gold were being enriched with copper (and perhaps with tin) to the target level required by that particular tradition (workshop?). Whether this addition was weighed, or judged by the colour of the resultant gold alloy, is a question I am unable to answer, but it would be a hit-and-miss affair that would result in a wide spread of tin and copper levels. Any small objects made from these 'ingots' would echo this variability, and give us the extensive clouds that we have noted for the smaller objects (rings, sleeve-fasteners, bracelets and so-on). It can be shown that the larger an object is – that is the more pieces of gold that were melted together and used in its manufacture – the closer its concentration in each constituent will be to the group mean. The means of the values for all three metals for a number of large objects will be the same as those for a number of small objects, but the variability will be far less – precisely as we see in these charts. The failure of the L-gold lunulae to cluster is probably because the tin was added not to any small 'ingots' but to the final melt for each lunula.

The 'enigma' of the ribbon torcs and the Iron Age (Fig 11.7)

Argument has raged over the date of those simple, twisted strips of gold called ribbon torcs, particularly common in Ireland but also found in Scotland and Wales (Eogan 1983b). The archaeological evidence is ambiguous – one was found with a three-flanged torc of certain Middle Bronze Age date (Coolmanagh), and two others were found associated with Iron Age objects. Majority opinion holds that most are of Middle Bronze Age date but that some might be Iron Age. Both the Coolmanagh torcs are of B*-gold, as are three other Irish ribbon torcs and the three ribbon torcs from Wales (the Heyope hoard). On the other hand the rest of the Irish ribbon torcs have a totally different fingerprint, matching instead the R-gold defined by the Broighter hoard, including a platinum trace in most of them. Platinum is present in many Continental Iron Age gold objects, but has not been found in Bronze Age Irish artefacts. It can therefore be said without fear of contradiction that while a very few ribbon torcs (which have simple hook terminals, as noted by Northover in 1989) are certainly Middle Bronze Age the majority (mostly with knobbed terminals) are Iron Age. There can be no possible connection between these two groups (this is discussed in greater detail in Warner 2003).

Platinum is found also in the Scottish torcs, which share

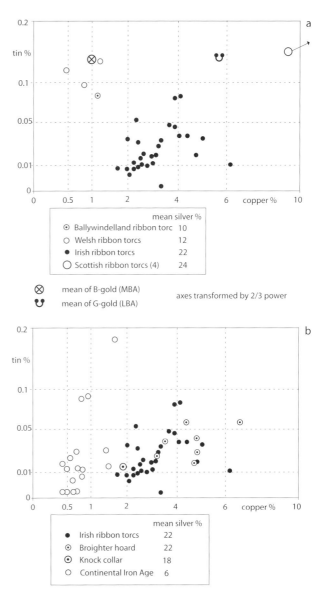

Fig 11.7: Ribbon torcs and the Iron Age.

their high silver value (around 24%) with the Irish ribbon torcs but differ from them in their high levels of tin (0.2% mean) and copper (an extraordinary 19% mean). There can be no doubt that the Scottish ribbon torcs are also Iron Age and no doubt at all that the copper in those of both Ireland and Scotland has been intentionally added. Whether the high silver value of these insular Iron Age objects reflects an intentional addition or a high-silver source I cannot say, except to observe that high-silver natural gold has been discovered in Scotland (inf. from R. Chapman). In view of the Continental Iron Age origin of most of the Irish Iron Age metalwork it comes as something of a surprise to discover that the gold ornaments from that milieu analysed by Hartmann, and shown on Fig 11.7b, have such a different fingerprint to the Irish ones. They all have much lower silver (the mean is 6%) and copper (the mean is 0.8%) and most have lower tin (mean 0.03%). It is of some interest that the Continental typological parallels for the Broighter and Knock collars (both of which fall into the Irish group on the three metals) have typical Continental fingerprints. These two collars are, therefore, as has been suspected on typological and artistic grounds, of Irish manufacture.

Note and acknowledgements

The recent work of sample re-analysis to which I have alluded is part of a project that includes a study of British natural gold (the Prehistoric Gold Research Project – See Taylor 1999). Although the subject of this paper does not form any part of the research plan of that project, I am grateful to the other members of the project for much advice and help.

Bibliography

Eogan, G. 1983a *Hoards of the Irish Later Bronze Age*. University College, Dublin.

Eogan, G. 1983b, Ribbon torcs in Britain and Ireland, in A. O'Connor and D. Clarke (eds) *From the Stone Age to the 'Forty-Five'*, 87–126. John Donald Ltd., Edinburgh.

Eogan, G. 1994 *The Accomplished Art. Gold and Gold-Working in Britain and Ireland during the Bronze Age*, Oxbow Monographs **42**, Oxford.

Eogan, G. 1997 'Hair-rings' and European Late Bronze Age society, *Antiquity* **71**, 308–320.

Hartmann, A. 1970 *Prähistorische Goldfunde aus Europa*. Studien zum den Anfängen der Metallurgie **3**, Gebr. Mann Verlag, Berlin.

Hartmann, A. 1979 Irish and British gold types and the west European counterparts. In M. Ryan (ed.) *The Origins of Metallurgy in Atlantic Europe*, 215–228. Proceedings of the Fifth Atlantic Colloquium, Dublin.

Hartmann, A. 1982 *Prähistorische Goldfunde aus Europa II*. Studien zum den Anfängen der Metallurgie **5**, Gebr. Mann Verlag, Berlin.

Hook, D. and Needham, S. 1989 A comparison of recent analyses of British Late Bronze age goldwork with Irish parallels, *Jewellery Studies* **3**, 15–24.

Northover, J.P. 1989 The gold torc from St. Helier, Jersey, *Annual Bulletin of the Société Jersiaise* **25**, 112–137.

Northover, J.P. 2000 Ring money: the problem child of Bronze Age gold, *Beiträge aus der Mineralogie*, Geochemie, Lagerstättenforschung, Archäometrie, Archäologie und *Denkmalpflege*, 299–304. München.

Taylor, J. 1979 The relationship of British Early Bronze Age goldwork to Atlantic Europe. In M. Ryan (ed.) *The Origins of Metallurgy in Atlantic Europe*, 229–250. Proceedings of the Fifth Atlantic Colloquium, Dublin.

Taylor, J. 1980 *Bronze Age Goldwork of the British Isles*. Cambridge University Press, Cambridge.

Taylor, J. 1999 Gold reflections. In A.F. Harding (ed.) *Experiment and Design*, 108–115, Oxford.

Warner, R. 1993 Irish prehistoric goldwork: a provisional analysis, *Archaeomaterials* **7**, 101–113.

Warner, R. 2003 Old letters and new technology – the Ballyrashane gold hoard, in J. Fenwick (ed.) *Lost and Found*, 151–164. Wordwell, Dublin.

12. Pit 119: Rathgall, Co. Wicklow

Barry Raftery
For George, with warmest regards

Introduction

Rathgall in southwest Co. Wicklow is an impressive, multivallate hillfort covering a total area of 7.30ha (Fig 12.1). Eight seasons of excavation by the writer, between 1969 and 1978, have shown that the site was a place of considerable human activity, at varying intervals, from the Neolithic to the Medieval period (Raftery 1970a; 1970b; 1971; 1973; 1976. Full report pending). Most intensive and, indeed, extensive was activity which took place there in the late second and early first millennia BC. Dating to this period the excavation revealed evidence for domestic, industrial, sepulchral and, perhaps also, for more formally ritual activity. Postholes and pits occurred in all areas excavated, and four ring-ditches of differing size and form were also uncovered. Bronze Age Rathgall was undoubtedly an extraordinarily significant focus of human activity.

In all parts of the excavated area many thousands of coarse, handmade potsherds were found and there can be no doubt that these were of local fabrication. Several thousand clay mould fragments, and two almost complete crucibles (as well as further fragments) from the site indicate that bronze casting was clearly of particular importance. At least five discrete zones of industrial activity could be isolated. A small, sharp-edged chisel of bronze from the site may well have been used for metal engraving.

Other bronze objects came from the site, as well as objects of gold, and no fewer than 87 glass beads that represent one of the largest concentration of glass beads of this period from any contemporary European site. Ongoing research on this material points to important contacts between the occupants of Rathgall and the wider European Bronze Age.

More than 200 pits were examined in the course of the excavation. These varied considerably in size and depth and, indeed, it must be admitted that the precise original function of the majority remains unclear: the temptation to dismiss them with the blanket term "rubbish pits" is clearly facile. A particularly interesting example, however, one that stands apart from the rest, is Pit 119 in Sq. 35.

Pit 119

Around the inner perimeter of the central stone enclosure, and partly underlying it, excavation revealed a ditch of V-section (Fosse 1), 65cm to 85cm in depth below the boulder clay (Fig 12.2). It enclosed a circular area 33–34m in internal diameter. Off-centre within this a narrow, vertical-sided trench, with an entrance gap in the east, enclosed a circular area 15m in diameter. Numerous pits and postholes occurred both within, and outside, this enclosure but it was clearly evident that these did not belong to a single phase. Pit 119, one of the largest of the pits, lay within the enclosure.

The pit (Figs 12.2, 12.3) first came to light after the ubiquitous, brown humus covering the site had been removed and the yellow boulder-clay had been reached. The first indication of its presence was in the form of a thin band of black, organic material, forming a regular, flattened-oval area, with north-south orientation and with dimensions of 1.85m by 1m. The black oval enclosed an area of clean, yellow soil from which the upper portion of a sizable boulder projected. The black streak, generally 3–5cm in width, was damaged and partly removed in the west in an area of rabbit disturbance. Here a rabbit burrow, filled with brown humus, extended as far as the boulder before veering away to the south. This disturbance added to initial uncertainty as to the character of this feature.

Upon investigation it became evident that the yellow material was extremely fine and was entirely without stones. In its natural state this would hardly have been the case so that it is likely that the soil had been carefully prepared, perhaps even sieved, before packing it around the boulder.

With the removal of the yellow filling the character of the pit became clear. It was 33cm deep and had regular, almost vertical sides and a flat, carefully dug, base. The boulder had been placed directly on top of a thick, black, basal layer that extended upwards around the sides of the pit to form a continuous, unbroken lining. It was thus evident that the black streak that had been initially visible on the surface, was the upper edge of this black lining. Upon excavation it was revealed that the latter had a

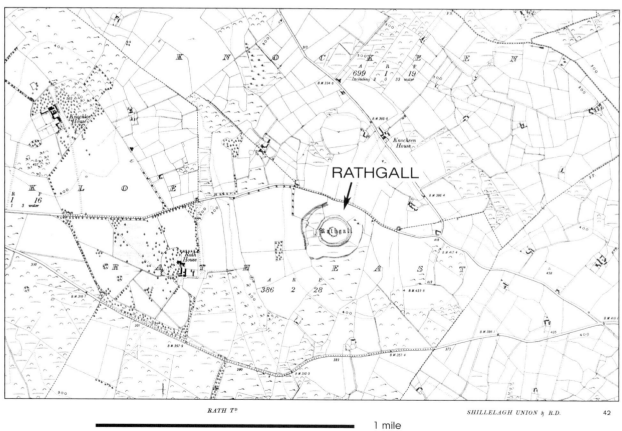

Fig 12.1: Location of the hillfort at Rathgall, Co. Wicklow.

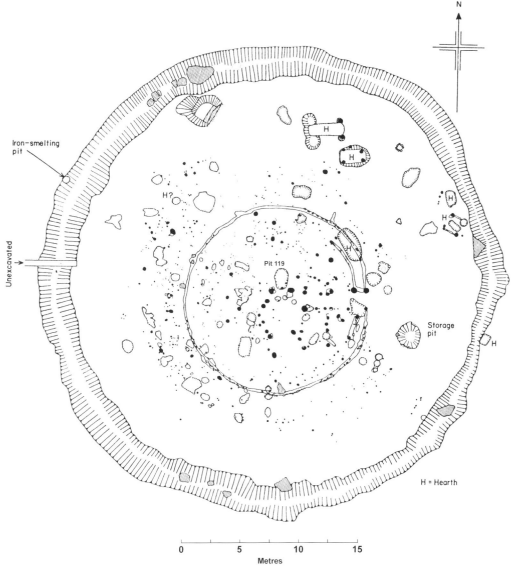

N

Fig 12.2: The V-sectioned ditch (Fosse 1) showing Pit 119 in the centre of the enclosure.

maximum thickness of 8cm at the base thinning somewhat to the lip of the pit, as noted above. The manner in which the black material adhered to the sides and base of the pit clearly indicated that it represented a former, organic lining. This was almost certainly basketry, positive evidence for which was revealed in one of the larger pits (Pit 118, Sqs 17/18).

The boulder, an erratic of local granite, filled slightly less than half the pit. It was flat-sided and was more or less rectangular in plan and sections. Its regular proportions give the clear impression of deliberate rather than random selection. It was 87cm in length, 54cm in width and 37cm in height. When it was lifted, it was clearly evident that there was nothing whatever, not even the slightest hint of silting, between it and the black layer. It had been placed directly on the organic lining, as had the yellow fill, which had been carefully packed around the boulder. The digging of the pit, the creation and

insertion of the lining feature and its final filling were thus, without question, part of a single, deliberate act.

The purpose of this carefully created feature became evident with the discovery of a small, penannular metal ring at the centre of the pit which came to light after the removal of the boulder. It had sunk a few centimetres into the black basal lining but this was evidently a secondary event and originally it had lain on top. A small quantity of finely burnt human bones was concentrated around the ring, mostly on the surface of the black lining, but a few had sunk slightly. Again it was evident that the bones had originally been carefully placed on the surface of the organic lining.

Examination of the bones by the late Professor E. R. Erskine, Department of Pathology, Trinity College Dublin, has identified them as those of an infant of uncertain sex. It appeared that the surviving remains represented only portion of the burnt infant. This allowed

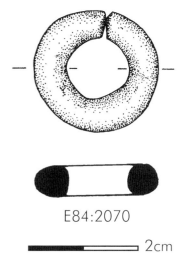

E84:2070

2cm

Fig 12.3: The gold foil covered ring from Pit 119.

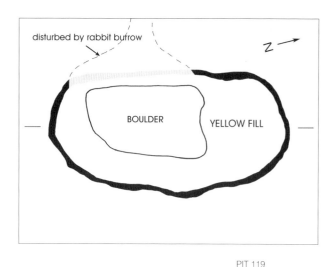

PIT 119

CREMATED BONES AND GOLD RING

1 m

Fig 12.4: Plan and section of Pit 119.

for the possibility that a token deposit rather than a formal burial might be represented. It should be borne in mind, however, that the small, soft bones of an immediately post-natal infant would not necessarily survive in their entirety so that a formal burial cannot here be ruled out. At any rate there can be no doubt that the pit was specifically created for the deposition of the bones and the accompanying ring. There are no indications that the pit had ever been used for any other purpose.

The Ring

The ring (E84:6070; Figs 12.3; 12.4) was carefully made to form an almost exact circle its external diameter being 1.05cm by 1.1cm. Internally, the ring scarcely deviates from a diameter of 5.5mm and it maintains a consistent thickness of 2.5mm. It is not quite circular in section for around its interior it is very gently flattened, creating overall a barely perceptible D-shaped section. The ring-ends virtually touch but one face displays an almost imperceptible slope outwards from the other. It is not quite flush with the latter projecting very slightly outwards beyond its outer edge. Similarly, under high magni-fication, it can be seen that the same face, on the interior, also has a minute internal stagger. Such differences are, however, negligible and the tiny ring has evidently been made with very considerable care and precision.

All around the outer circumference of the ring nu-merous tiny, haphazard scratches occur. These are only evident under magnification. In general they extend transversely across the surface but a few are longitudinal, especially near the ends of the ring.

The ring appeared initially to be of solid gold. Detailed examination, however, indicates a core of base metal with a very fine gold cover, a feature which Coffey (1918, 70) regarded as evidence of ancient forgery! The core shows as a greyish black material. It is probably either copper or lead but this remains to be established by scientific

analysis. The likelihood is, however, that it is copper. The surface cover is gold foil of exceptional thinness, so thin, in fact, that it almost looks as if it had been painted on. Around the inner surface of the ring neither junction nor overlapping ends of foil are discernable. Such might have been removed by some sort of fine hammering or pressure welding, but tiny, irregular zones of wear where the gold is missing, mainly around the flattened inner surface, but also (less frequently) around the sides, might suggest that an original seam has been obscured by wear. The gilding of the little ring has, however, been executed with very considerable skill and detailed scientific analysis is necessary to establish with confidence the technique employed.

Context

Stratigraphy in the central area where the pit was found is particularly complex and problems in this regard are greatly exacerbated by the deep, intensive spade culti-vation that has taken place throughout the entire area within the inner, stone enclosure. It is evident, however, that there is considerable overlap of pits and postholes, and this can be taken as indicating continuous and, indeed, intensive Bronze Age activity in this area. In this regard there is an important point of reference as the circular bedding trench that encloses Pit 119 was dug through several pits, most particularly through the fill of Hearth 1 in Sq. 25, one of the largest hearths uncovered on the site.

Owing to the extremely problematical nature of the stratigraphy it is difficult, to establish, with any degree of confidence, the relationship between Pit 119 and the other features uncovered in the central enclosure. The concentration of most of the larger pits in the south-eastern zone of the enclosure is worthy of note and judicious juggling of the larger postholes allows the isolation of a small, oval of free-standing posts concentrated in the area south of the pit which might be seen as representing some sort of a mini-enclosure. Such a feature might conceivably be related to whatever activities were associated with the deposition of the ring and the bones in the pit. Similarly, it could be that the two postholes that flank Pit 119 in the south (which are among the deepest in the inner enclosure) represent a monumental feature of some sort associated with the burial. In the context of the available evidence, however, speculation of this sort is of little value and is, indeed, potentially misleading as it is now virtually impossible to establish the relationships to one another of individual postholes.

Perhaps more meaningful is the position of Pit 119 within the large ditched enclosure (Fosse 1). While the pit is obviously situated off-centre within the 15m enclosure, even allowing for the unavoidably irregular edges of the surrounding ditch it is, in fact, in the almost precise centre of the enclosure which was formed by the latter. Indeed, in 1971, it was only when the final section of the central baulk was being removed, on the very last day of the excavation, that the pit was excavated and the burial deposit found. It is therefore possible that the central location of Pit 119 within the large enclosure indicates a relationship between these two features. Thus the possibility exists that Fosse 1 was specifically dug to enclose Pit 119.

The question of the relationships with each other of the various features occurring within and outside the enclosure formed by Fosse 1 is, however, extremely complex and cannot be pursued here. This will be examined in detail in the forthcoming monograph on the Rathgall excavations. In the present discussion, however, it is important to note the radiocarbon date of 1290–1040 Cal. BC (GrN-27101) for the black lining material in Pit 119. Material from Hearth 1, already referred to above, (which is obviously earlier than the bedding trench) yielded a date of 2810±105 BP (D-134). This is, however, an early (1973) Trinity College Dublin age determination that unfortunately, calibrates to a disappointingly wide date-range of 1400–800 Cal. BC (information courtesy R. B. Warner). The date is, nonetheless, firmly in the Middle to Late Bronze Age and is entirely in keeping with the overall dating for the site. This is, obviously, a question that will be analysed in detail in the full report.

In reference to the nature of the lining of Pit 119, at Mitchelstowndown North, Co. Limerick (Gowen 1988), 7 small pits contained token cremations each consisting of very small quantities of comminuted bone. The cremations had been mixed with what appeared to be material from a pyre and this formed a putty-like lining to the pits. Some of the burials were then partly sealed with a clean clay capping. This treatment of the burials has been noted at other sites including Killoran Site 10 within the Derryville-Lisheen complex, Co. Tipperary (Stevens 1998). Sherds of coarse pottery accompanied two burials at Mitchelstowndown and each of the pits contained the remains of an adult; No. 1 also produced the bones of a neonate. There are two radiocarbon dates from Mitchelstown, 1428–1264 Cal. BC and 1416–1224 Cal. BC.

Discussion

This small ring from Rathgall is one of two such rings from the site. The second ring (E84:8000), like the first, has a core of base metal with a gold foil covering. Unlike that from Pit 119, however, it appears not to have been a deliberate deposit. It came from the north-west corner of Sq. C1, in an area of black material, immediately to the east of the late stone enclosure, which was extraordinarily rich in occupation debris.

Small penannular rings of the type here under discussion belong to a well-known and much studied group (most comprehensively, Eogan 1997 but also Eogan 1964; 1994; Hartmann 1970; Taylor 1980; Northover 2000; Varndell 2001). These rings are principally found in Ireland and in various parts of Britain, with a small number occurring in northwest Europe (Northover 2000, 303, table 2). Ireland, now with almost 130 known examples, has yielded considerably more than those from all the other areas combined. Unfortunately, no fewer than 88 of the Irish examples are unprovenanced. Where information concerning their find circumstances is forthcoming, apart from the Rathgall examples and a recent, unpublished specimen from Ballypriorbeg, Co. Tyrone, all are from hoards of varying types (Eogan 1997, 317–8). In Britain, too, only a small number are from helpful contexts. On the European mainland such rings are clustered, with only occasional outliers, in a discrete zone in Belgium, the Netherlands and northeast France (Eogan 1997, fig. 1). The French examples include those from cremation deposits, a significant number of the Belgian examples are likely also to have been from burials (Warmembol 1999, 39ff.).

Toupet (1979; 1982; 1983), in a detailed consideration of cremation cemeteries at Longuesse, Val d'Oise and Villeneuve-St.-Germain, Aisne, both in northwest France, drew attention to the presence of several burials containing gold rings of the type here under discussion. He made direct comparison between them and the Rathgall find. The French sites in question, which Toupet dated to the end of the local Bronze Age (though without greater precision), do consist of cremation deposits enclosed by circular ditches, as is the case at Rathgall. They also, however, display structural features that are quite distinct from the Irish burial. The unburnt nature of the Rathgall ring may also be significant. The relationship between Toupet's "Groupe de Longuesse" and the Rathgall burial is thus uncertain. Moreover, though few in number and lacking a gold ring, burials of the Late Bronze Age in Ireland comparable with that from Rathgall (although on an admittedly more modest scale) have been found. Ballybeen, Co. Down is one example though the available radiocarbon date (900–775 Cal. BC) is some centuries more recent than the Rathgall example here under discussion (Mallory 1984; Mallory and McNeill 1991, 138–9).

Despite what has been written concerning these rings, their dating is by no means as tight as is sometimes assumed, especially in view of the fact that the overwhelming majority are without association. Increasingly there are indications that the earliest examples, belonging to the end of the second millennium BC, are considerably older than has been hitherto allowed. Thus, for example, a ring from Mucking in Essex (Bond 1988) is considered by Northover (2000, 302) to belong in a local, Penard Phase context beginning in the thirteenth/twelfth centuries BC, and for two frequently quoted Scottish finds, from Ballymashannar and Covesea he now suggests dates "starting around the end of the eleventh century BC and finishing in the eighth century BC" (Northover 2000, 303). He concludes that the development of these rings "started in the Penard phase of the Middle Bronze Age and they flourished during the Ewart Park phase of the Late bronze Age" (Northover 2000, 303).

The ring from Rathgall Pit 119 is important as it supports an early dating for these objects. Apart for the date for the pit itself, a large number of other dates from the site are in keeping with this early dating. To these Rathgall dates should be added the recent dating of the ring referred to above, from the main occupation layer of a circular house discovered at Ballypriorbeg, Co Tyrone. The date is 1373–1019 Cal. BC, and there are six other dates from the same site, none of which is more recent than 1000 Cal. BC (I. Suddaby pers. comm.).

Such early dates are in keeping with the development of modern research and the reassessment of the dating of the later phases of the insular Bronze Age (Needham 1996). Rathgall fits in with this trend for, to date, the site has produced no fewer than fourteen dates between 1380 Cal. BC and Cal. 1000 BC, from a variety of contexts. In addition, though work on the clay moulds from the site is ongoing, it has been possible to recognize, among the diagnostic fragments, those which were probably for the manufacture of tongued chapes and there is one sizable fragment which can only have been for casting a palstave (Raftery 1971, pl. XLVII:c). A bronze bladed implement from an early phase at the site may be the remains of a small rapier.

It cannot be emphasized too strongly that Bronze Age Rathgall was without question a site of exceptional importance in the centuries centring on 1000 Cal. BC.

Although the excavation, strangely, failed to identify any clear house plans, there is solid evidence that a population of some size occupied the hilltop at this time on a permanent basis. As earlier noted, large quantities of coarse potsherds were found in most areas of the site, associated with all the principal features uncovered, leaving little room to doubt that Bronze Age Rathgall was occupied by a predominantly native population. But at the same time, there are indications that some elements of the surviving material culture display links with the wider world outside.

Obviously, in this short paper, such matters can only be dealt with in the most cursory manner. It is important to note here, however, that high silver content of the Rathgall ring, for example, is a feature rare in Irish gold of pre-Iron Age date (see Hartmann 1970), but is of potential significance as a similarly high silver content has been recognized in two twisted gold ear-rings from Castlereagh, Co. Roscommon (TEIA 1979, 49, Pl. 3; IK 1983, 80–1, Kat. 7, 8; Hartman 1970, Au 966, 967; Taf. 25). Such ear-rings, apart from occasional examples in south-east England and coastal areas of France, occur only in the east Mediterranean. Hawkes (1961) regarded them, and other comparable examples in the west, as evidence of trading contacts with the east in the thirteenth or twelfth centuries BC. This view is not favoured today (*e.g.* Eogan 1994, 59; Taylor 1980, 65; Hartmann 1970, 30) notwithstanding the presence of comparable objects in the Carpathian region (Eogan 1994, 59). It has not been proven to be wrong. Taylor (1980, 66), for example writes "Little can be said to refute Hawkes, but none of the rings can be dated as all are isolated finds…". Eluère (1980; quoted in Eogan 1994, 59) went further, suggesting that these Irish objects might even be modern imports from west Africa, a suggestion which, however, can now be disregarded, especially in view of their gold content.

The possibility of a distant East Mediterranean element in the genesis of this small group of gold earrings, while of course in no way proven, is interesting as a Mediterranean background has also been mooted for the tiny gold rings of the type here under discussion. In Egypt large numbers of small, penannular gold rings occur which appear to have been wig-rings used as amulets, often accompanying the dead. Thus, for Hawkes (1961, 468) the introduction of the so-called "hair-ring" from Egypt to Ireland was clear: "as Mycenean loot passed on into the Western trade".

Nobody denies that the Egyptian rings closely resemble the Irish rings such as that from Rathgall, Pit 119. Taylor (1980, 65), for example, wrote that "their close correspondence to the British (*sic*) rings is, indeed, uncanny". Nonetheless, she rejects the view for "to bring the rings in one non-stop trip to the British Isles seems impossible…" (Taylor 1980, 65). Eogan, most recently, revisited the matter of possible Egyptian elements in the development of these rings in the west (1997, 310). Like Taylor, an apparent chronological gap of several centuries between the insular and the Egyptian rings of necessity ruled out an Egyptian connection. He wrote, however, that "the origin of hair-rings presents a puzzle as there are no definite forerunners in Europe" (Eogan 1997, 308).

The matter thus remains open but the time-span of the Egyptian rings needs critical examination. They were certainly known in the Eighteenth Dynasty, and continued into the Nineteenth Dynasty (which ended in 1185 BC) and now, with the current back- dating of the earliest of these rings in the west, a Mediterranean background cannot be discounted. Of course, there can, at least for the moment, be no certainty in this and, indeed, Taylor's skepticism may be justified (1980, 69).

The very exceptional nature of Rathgall is, however, clear, a point particularly stressed by the seemingly exotic group of glass beads from the site, no fewer than 87 of which have come to light (Raftery and Henderson 1987). Analysis of the glass content points strongly to eastern Switzerland or northern Italy as their place of origin (Henderson 1988; see also Grogan and Eogan 1987). One of the Rathgall beads had been elaborately and exquisitely mounted on a tiny tube of gold with an incredibly fine ring of twisted gold wire attached at each end. A comparable pendant from a bog at Milmorane, Co. Cork, consisted of a large amber bead, mounted, like the Rathgall object, on a gold tube with four rings of finely twisted gold wire at each end. The object was found with a second amber bead but, more interesting, is the suggestion that tiny splinters of a glass bead were present in the bog when found (Mitchell 1944, 15; GaI 1981, 43). The superbly made gold and glass pendant from Rathgall is a magnificent piece, perhaps made by an Irish gold-worker, using an imported bead. Milmorane, too, could be of local fabrication in this instance using amber from the Baltic.

Eogan wrote most recently that "the origin of hair-rings presents a puzzle as there are no definite forerunners in Europe" (1997, 308). With the convincing early dating for Irish "ring money", at Rathgall and Ballypriorbeg, the Irish and Egyptian dates begin to coalesce. In view of the gold of the ring and the exotic material from Rathgall and, indeed, the obviously exceptional, high-status character of the site as a whole, it might thus be interesting to revisit the notion of Mediterranean links. Indeed, in considering the superbly manufactured Irish gold "lock-rings" Eogan wrote, in the absence of exact prototypes "it may be that the type stemmed from advanced metallurgical centres, possibly in the Mediterranean area" (1969, 111).

East Mediterranean or north African links need not be seen as outlandish today, certainly no more outlandish than a north African Barbary Ape from Iron Age Navan Fort in Co. Armagh (Raftery, in Waterman 1997, 121–5). Nor are such suggestions any more bizarre than the recent discovery of what appear to be Linear B letters engraved on an amber nodule from a mid-fourteenth century BC occupation site at Bernstorf, Lkr. Freising, in southern Germany (Gebhard and Rieder 2002).

Acknowledgements

The author is grateful to Ms Mary Cahill for generous assistance and advice on the subject of Later Bronze Age gold; to R.B. Warner for his invaluable comments on the Rathgall gold and for his assistance in interpreting the radiocarbon dates; to I. Suddaby for information on the Ballypriorbeg ring, and for permission to refer to the date. The author is also grateful to Ms Ursula Mattenberger for Figs 12.1 and 12.3. Finally, thanks are due to George Eogan who was, as always, generous with his help and advice, though he probably didn't know the purpose of my questioning!

Bibliography

Bond, D. 1988 Excavation at the North Ring, Mucking, Essex: a Late Bronze Age enclosure, *East Anglian Archaeology*, Report **43**, 14.

Coffey, G. 1918 *The Bronze Age in Ireland*. Hodges, Figgis and Co., Dublin.

Eluère, C. 1980–1 Réflexions à propos de 'boucles d'oreilles' torsadées en or de types connus à l'Age du Bronze, *Antiquités Nationales* **12–13**, 34–9.

Eogan, G. 1964 The Later Bronze Age in the light of recent research, *Proceedings of the Prehistoric Society* **30**, 268–351.

Eogan, G. 1969 'Lock-Rings' of the Late Bronze Age, *Proceedings of the Royal Irish Academy* **67C**, 93–148.

Eogan, G. 1994 *The accomplished art: gold and gold-working in Britain and Ireland during the Bronze Age (c. 2300–650B.C.)*. Oxbow Books, Oxbow Monographs, Oxford.

Eogan, G. 1997 'Hair-rings' and European Late Bronze Age Society, *Antiquity* **71**, 308–320.

Ga I 1981 *Gold aus Irland*. Exhibition Catalogue, Haasmüller, Frankfurt.

Gebhard, R. and Rieder, K.H. 2002 Zwei bronzezeitliche Bernstein-objekte mit Bild- und Schriftzeichen aus Bernstorf (Lkd. Freising), *Germania* **80**, 115–133.

Gowen, M. 1988 *Three Irish Gas Pipelines: New Archaeological Evidence in Munster*, Wordwell, Dublin.

Grogan, E. and Eogan, E. 1987 Lough Gur Excavations by Seán P. Ó Ríordáin: Further Neolithic and Beaker Habitations on Knockadoon, *Proceedings of the Royal Irish Academy* **87C**, 299–506.

Hartmann, A. 1970 *Prähistorische Goldfunde aus Europa*. Studien zu den Anfängen der Metallurgie **3**, Gebr. Mann Verlag, Berlin.

Hawkes, C.F.C. 1961 Gold earrings of the Bronze Age: east and west, *Folklore* **72**, 438–474.

Henderson, J. 1988 Glass production and Bronze Age Europe, *Antiquity* **62**, 435–51.

IK 1983 *Irische Kunst aus drei Jahrtausenden: Thesaurus Hiberniae*. von Zabern, Mainz.

Mallory, J.P.1984 The Long Stone, Ballybeen, Dundonald, Co. Down, *Ulster Journal of Archaeology* **47**, 1–4.

Mallory, J.P. and McNeill, T.E. 1991 *The Archaeology of Ulster from Colonization to Plantation*. Institute of Irish Studies, The Queen's University of Belfast, Belfast.

Mitchell, G.F. 1944 The Relative Ages of Archaeological Objects Recently Found in Bogs in Ireland, *Proceedings of the Royal Irish Academy* **50C**, 1–19.

Needham, S. 1996 Chronology and periodisation in the British Bronze Age, *Acta Archaeologica* **67**, Supplementa 1, 121–140.

Northover, J.P. 2000 Ring money: the problem child of Bronze Age gold, *Münchener Geologische Hefte* **28**, 299–304.

Raftery, B. 1970a The Rathgall Hillfort, County Wicklow, *Antiquity* **44**, 51–54.

Raftery, B. 1970b A Decorated Strap-end from Rathgall, Co. Wicklow, *Journal of the Royal Society of Antiquaries of Ireland* **100**, 200–211.

Raftery, B. 1971 Rathgall, Co. Wicklow: 1970 excavations, *Antiquity* **45**, 296–298.

Raftery, B. 1973 Rathgall: a Later Bronze Age burial in Ireland, *Antiquity* **47**, 293–5.

Raftery, B. 1976 Rathgall and Irish Hillfort problems. In D.W. Harding (ed.) *Hillforts: Later Prehistoric Earthworks in Britain and Ireland*, 339–357. Academic Press, London.

Raftery, B. and Henderson, J. 1987 Some glass beads of the Later Bronze Age from Ireland, *Marburger Studien zur Vor- und Frühgeschichte* **9**, 39–53.

Stevens, P. 1998 Killoran 10, Co. Tipperary. In I. Bennett (ed.) *Excavations 1997*, 174–5. Wordwell, Dublin.

Taylor, J.J. 1980 *Bronze Age goldwork of the British Isles*. Cambridge University Press, Cambridge.

TEIA 1979 *Treasures of Early Irish Art, 1500 B.C. to 1500 A.D.* Metropolitan Museum of Art, New York.

Toupet, C. 1979 *Une necropole à incinérations à Longuesse, Val d'Oise*. Service departmental d'archéologie du Val d'Oise, rapport des fouilles 95011. Cergy-Pontoise.

Toupet, C. 1982 *La nécropole protohistorique de l'Languesse – Val d'Oise: mode et rituel funeraires.* Service départmental d'archéologie du Val d'Oise, Cergy-Pontoise.

Toupet, C. 1983 *Enclos funeraires et structures d'habitat en Europe du nord-ouest*. Table Ronde du C.N.R.S., Rennes 1981, 242–261.

Warmembol, E. 1999 Le soleil des morts: Les ors protohistoriques de Han-sur-Lesse (Namur, Belgique), *Germania* **77**, 39–69.

Waterman, D.M. 1997 *Excavations at Navan Fort 1961–1971.* (Completed and edited by C.J. Lynn), Northern Ireland Archaeological Monographs **3**, Department of the Environment for Northern Ireland, The Stationery Office, Belfast.

Varndell, G. 2001 Ringing the changes: when terminology matters, *Antiquity* **75**, 515–6.

13. Moynagh Lough, Co. Meath, in the Late Bronze Age

John Bradley

The remarkable archaeological site at Moynagh Lough was discovered by George Eogan. It lies just over a quarter of a mile southwest of the village of Nobber, County Meath. The lake was drained around 1850 and all that survives today is a small pool, 200 metres long and 50 metres wide. The archaeological site was an earthen mound on the north side of the pool. In 1977 the landowner decided to reclaim some of the boggy ground that constituted the bed of the old lake. He bulldozed the mound and spread the earth across the marshy field. In the process, large quantities of animal bones were uncovered and, fortunately for Irish archaeology, the landowner immediately stopped removing the mound. When George Eogan visited the site it was evident that it was the remains of a crannog, or artificial island, a monument type generally dated to the period between 500 and 1000 AD. The crannog was so destroyed that one month of excavation was thought sufficient for the task. It was not appreciated at the time that crannogs are like icebergs – nine-tenths can lie below the surface. What commenced in 1980 as a four-week excavation continued almost every summer until 1998. It was anticipated that material from the first millennium AD would be present but the discovery of several layers of prehistoric activity, which predated the crannog, was completely unexpected. This paper concentrates on the Late Bronze Age material, which I trust will be of interest to Professor Eogan.

The site was first inhabited in the Later Mesolithic (*c.* 4300 BC) and from the time that settlement was abandoned the climate appears to have gradually deteriorated, becoming wetter and wetter. By about 2000 BC the level of the lake waters had risen considerably and the Mesolithic surface was covered by a layer of brown, open-water mud, varying in thickness from 10 to 60cm. Around 1900 BC, however, there was a period of climatic improvement. Areas, which had formerly been wet, dried out and were available once more for occupation and people came out to the small island in the lake. The surface was still somewhat wet because their initial activity consisted of the deposition of timber and stones, which formed the foundation for a habitation layer that extended over a surviving area of 12m by 8m. The layer had been removed on the south side by the bulldozing that led to the discovery of the site but the remains of two houses were present. House 1 was the earlier of the two. It was of circular plan with a diameter of 6m. The house-wall consisted of thirteen posts spaced approximately 90cm from each other while the posts themselves ranged in diameter from 6cm to 16cm. The occupation layer consisted of charcoal and peat that averaged 6cm in thickness. The finds from this structure were few and comprised pieces of burnt flint and grain. House 2 was round in plan with a diameter of 6.8m. Its wall was formed with twenty posts spaced approximately 85cm from one another, while the posts themselves had an average diameter of 10cm. The occupation layer, consisting of lenses of charcoal, peat and brushwood reached a maximum thickness of 15cm. The artefacts recovered included sherds of decorated, cordoned pottery from at least twelve vessels, rounded scrapers, barbed-and-tanged arrowheads, pointed bone objects, rubbing stones and fragments of saddle querns. A series of posts, running in an east-west direction, was found at a distance of 4m from the houses. These may have formed part of an enclosing palisade but because this area was under water it was impossible to confirm this hypothesis. A radio-carbon determination of 3460±35 BP (GrN-11442, calibrated 1881–1685 Cal. BC;) was obtained from the occupation layer. Very few occupation sites of Early/Middle Bronze Age date are known in Ireland but the settlements that have most in common with Moynagh Lough are Cullyhanna, County Armagh, and Downpatrick, County Down (Hodges 1958; Pollock and Waterman 1964).

From about 1600 BC the climate seems to have deteriorated but during the Late Bronze Age the site dried out and became available once more for settlement. By this time, the Mesolithic platforms and the Early/Middle Bronze Age activity had been transformed by the action of lake-water into an east-west running ridge. It was on this ridge that the Late Bronze Age occupation concentrated. Two stages of activity were present. The initial

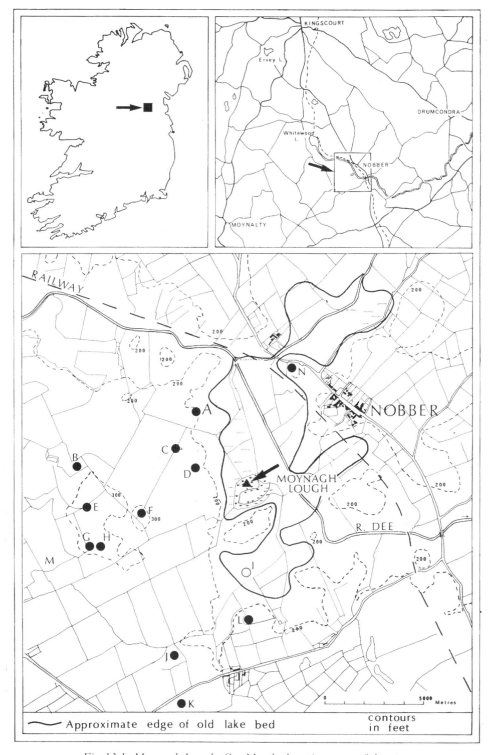

Fig 13.1: Moynagh Lough, Co. Meath: location map of the site.

stage consisted of four stone spreads whose function was probably to provide patches of firm ground on the exposed lake mud. In addition there were two open-air hearths and the remains of a circular structure about 6.5 m across with a hearth placed slightly off-centre. Despite the presence of a hearth and associated ash spills, this structure had no occupation layer and, consequently, it does not appear to have been used as a house. Finds from this level included two quernstones, a bone spindle whorl, sherds of coarse pottery, and a bronze "hair-ring". This level was subsequently covered by a layer of stones, mostly heat-cracked, intermixed with charcoal and debris. The layer varied in thickness from 15–30cm and produced all of the remaining artefacts. A radiocarbon determination

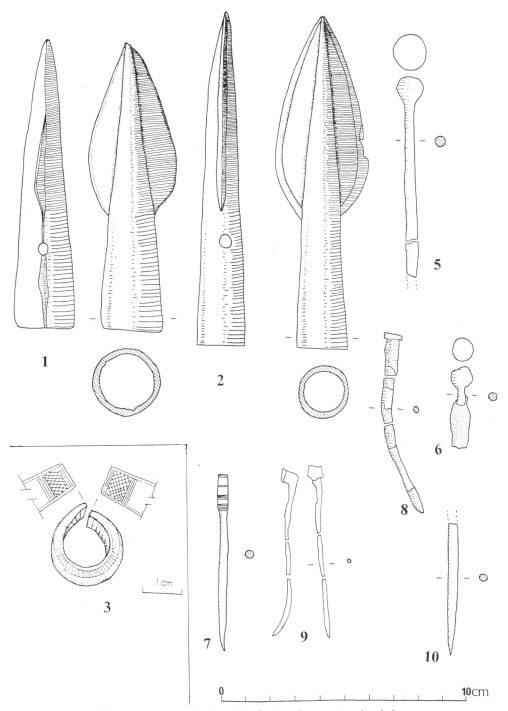

Fig 13.2: Moynagh Lough, Co. Meath, Late Bronze Age level: bronzes.

of 2650±80 BP (GrN-12359, 893–791 Cal. BC;) was obtained from this level, while a floating timber yielded a dendrochonological date of 922±9BC (Q4383).

Finds

Bronze

Fifteen bronze objects were present. These consisted of eight pins, two tweezers, two spearheads, a penannular ring, a disc, and a rod. The individual number of bronzes is greater than that from any other Irish Later Bronze Age settlement site but more significant, undoubtedly, is the difference in range. Tweezers have been recovered from Rathtinaun, Co. Sligo, and Rathgall, Co. Wicklow, while penannular rings (of gold) have also been found at both sites. A flesh-hook was present at Ballinderry 2, Co. Offaly, while a sword, sunflower pin and an axehead were discovered on the foreshore at Knocknalappa, Co. Clare. Spearheads, however, have not been discovered before

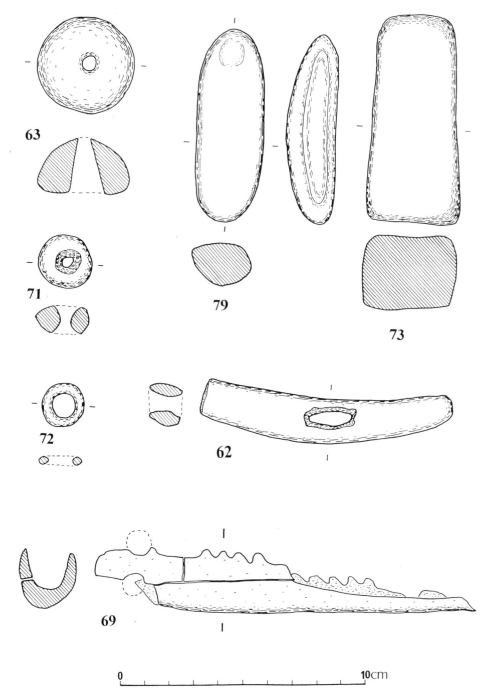

Fig 13.3: Moynagh Lough, Co. Meath, Late Bronze Age level: objects of stone and bone.

on settlement sites but all things considered it is probably the range of pins that makes the Moynagh Lough group of bronzes exceptional. All dimensions given below are in millimetres.

Spearheads
The spearheads were found some 10m apart and appear to have been casually lost. In both cases there was no trace of a spear-shaft but, since the objects were found on the crest of the ridge and well above the water table, it is

possible that these could have disintegrated in antiquity. Accordingly it is not clear if the spearheads were hafted or not when lost.

1. Leaf-shaped, socketed, spearhead with bevelled edges. Slight corrosion. Two lateral pegholes were placed 9mm below the blade. The socket was repaired with a small rectangular bronze patch, placed internally. L. 134; W. of blade 38; Ext. diam. of socket 22.
2. Leaf-shaped, socketed, spearhead with bevelled edges. Slight corrosion. Two lateral pegholes were

placed immediately below the blade and a casting seam runs down the socket from them. L. 114; W. of blade 34; Ext. diam. of socket 23.

"Hair-ring"

3. Thick penannular ring of D-shaped cross-section tapering towards the terminals. It consists of a bronze sheeting placed over a lead core; it has a central longitudinal seam and was evidently hammered into position. The sides are decorated with a band of incised ornament, consisting of diagonal scores, placed within two concentric lines. The terminals are decorated with an incised rectangular panel which links the two lateral sets of ornament. The panel is marked off from the body of the ring by four incised straight lines and the panel itself is decorated with a cross-hatched design comprising nine or ten criss-crossing diagonal lines on one terminal but with no more than seven on the other. The tip of the panel is bounded by two incised horizontal lines. "Hair-rings" of gold have been found on the Late Bronze Age settlement sites of Rathgall, Co. Wicklow, and Rathinaun, Co. Sligo, and Eogan (1997) has suggested that these objects functioned as status symbols, indicating that the wearer was a person of rank or, at least, of local significance. Av. diam. 18; max. diam. 21; T. 6 tapering to 2 at the terminals.

Pins

4. Pin with an evenly expanded head and round cross-section. The shank is 3mm thick immediately below the head and broadens to 3.5mm about two-thirds of the way down before tapering towards the tip. It was found in two pieces and had been broken in antiquity. L. 114; diam. of head 6.

5. Globular-headed pin with a round cross-section, missing its tip. Slight corrosion. L. of shank 70; T. of shank 4; T. of head 11; H. of head 10.

6. Globular-headed pin of rounded cross-section. Corroded. L. of shank 73; T. of shank 3; T. of head 8; H. of head 6. Found together with no. 8.

7. Pin with a slightly expanded, elongated head decorated with a series of lightly-incised horizontal lines, grouped together in bands. Slight corrosion. Rounded cross-section. L. 71; T. 3.5.

8. Nail-headed pin of rounded cross-section. Found together with no. 6. L. 70. T. of shank 3.5; Diam. of head 7.

9. Pin with head placed at right angles to the shank. The head consists of a short cylinder terminating in a flat face with slightly flared edges. Rounded cross-section. L. 68; T. of shank 2; dims of head 6x6. There is a similar looking object from the hoard at Derry-hale, Co. Armagh (Eogan 1983, 59 and fig. 23.16).

10. Shank of a bronze pin missing its head. Oval cross-section tapering to the point. Corroded. L. 52; T. 3.5x2.

11. Shank of a bronze pin missing its head. Round cross-section. L. 87; T. 3 tapering towards the tip.

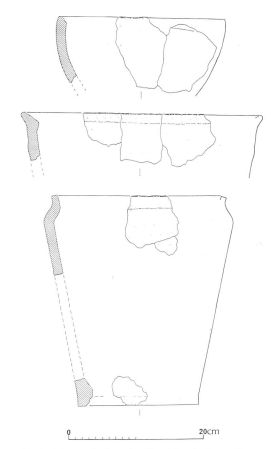

Fig 13.4: Moynagh Lough, Co. Meath, Late Bronze Age level: pottery.

Tweezers

12. Tweezers, similar to the example from the Rathtinaun hoard but smaller (Eogan 1983, 151 and fig. 84.1). L. 49; W 4 tapering to 3 at the loop; W. of head 2.5.

13. Tweezers. L. 52. W 6 tapering to 5 at the loop. It is possible that this object was deposited in early medieval times because it was found at the junction of the Late Bronze Age and early medieval levels.

Other bronze objects

14. Circular disc. Slightly corroded. Diam. 22; T. 7.

15. Rod with rounded cross-section, curved at one end. Slightly corroded. L. 45; T. 3.5.

Amber

Thirty-two amber beads and part of a ring were present. One of the beads (17) was a spacer but the remainder were graduated and, when suspended, would have presented a sub-trapezoidal form to the viewer. The beads tended to be disc-shaped with a cylindrical perforation (unless otherwise stated) usually placed slightly off centre. Some cylindrical beads were also present. The beads ranged in size from a diameter of 6mm to 14mm and it is likely that all derive from necklaces. Many of the beads had nibble-marks that may have resulted from the pressure of the vice in which they were held during manufacture. Thirteen of the beads were broken or fragmentary.

Three shades of amber were present. The most common was a translucent reddish-brown amber which displays a shattered or cellular structure when held to the light. There was also a slightly paler, translucent, reddish-brown amber with little or no shattering, and an opaque orange amber.

Amber has been found on a number of settlement sites of this period, including Rathgall, Co. Wicklow (Raftery 1976, 346) but the number of beads at Moynagh Lough is high in comparison to the five known from Knocknalappa, Co. Clare, the two from Ballinderry 2, Co. Offaly, and the single example from Clonfinlough, Co. Offaly (Hencken 1942, 13; Raftery 1942, 56–8; Moloney *et al.* 1993). Similar numbers of beads are known from hoards, however, such as Tooradoo, Co. Limerick, Rathtinaun, Co. Sligo, and Banagher, Co. Offaly (Eogan 1983, 104–5, 115–116, 151–2). The size and shape of the Moynagh examples can be almost exactly paralleled in the hoards from near Portlaoise, Co. Laois, and Ballycurrin, Co. Mayo, but it is noteworthy that none of the large globular beads present in these hoards was recovered at Moynagh Lough (Eogan 1983, 100–1, 107–8 and pl. ii).

Ring
16. Half of a round-sectioned ring with central and transverse perforations. The main perforation is hourglass shaped while the transverse perforation is cylindrical. The surfaces are slightly flattened at the mouths of the transverse perforation. It would seem to be an amber version of the bronze rings known from hoards such as Ballytegan, Co. Laois, and Annagh, Co. Roscommon (Eogan 1983, 98 and fig. 51: nos 19–21, 143 and fig. 61d: nos 2–3). Est. diam. 20; T. 8.5; diam. of main perf. 8.5.

Beads
17. Quarter of a spacer bead with a central cylindrical perforation off of which there are lateral and transverse perforations. The lateral perforation was cylindrical while the transverse one is of hour-glass form. Amber beads with transverse perforations are present in the hoards from Ballycurrin Demesne, Co. Mayo, and Cogran, Co. Offaly (Eogan 1983, 108, 116). Est. diam. 15; est. diam. of central perf. 3; diam. of lateral perf. 2; diam of transverse perf. 2.5 tapering to 1.
18. Reddish-brown translucent bead fragment. Est. diam. 16; T. 7.
19. Reddish-brown translucent bead fragment. Est. diam. 14; T. 10 tapering to 7.
20. Orange ovoid bead. Diam. 13.5 x 12.5; T. 7 tapering to 3; diam. of perf. 7.
21. Reddish-brown, fractured, bead fragment. Est. diam. 13.5; surviving T. 7.

22. Orange bead. Diam. 13; T. 9 tapering to 7.5; diam. of perf. 4.
23. Reddish-brown, fractured, bead. Diam. 12.5; T. 6.5 tapering to 6; diam. of perf. 4.
24. Reddish-brown, fractured, bead. Diam. 11; T. 7.5 tapering to 6.5; diam of perf. 5.
25. Reddish-brown, translucent, bead. Diam. 11; T. 6.5 tapering to 5; diam. of perf. 4.
26. Bead with faceted sides giving it a sub-hexagonal cross-section. Diam. 10; T. 5.5; diam. of perf. 3.
27. Bead. Diam. 9.5; T. 5.5 tapering to 5; diam. of perf. 3.5.
28. Reddish-brown translucent bead missing a small piece. Diam. 9.5; T. 5.5 tapering to approx. 4 where broken; diam. of perf. 4.5.
29. Reddish-brown, fractured, bead with slightly faceted sides. Diam. 9; T. 3.5; diam. of perf. 3.
30. Reddish-brown, fractured, bead. Diam. 9; T. 6 tapering slightly; diam. of perf. 4.5.
31. Reddish-brown, translucent, bead with slightly faceted sides. Diam. 9; T. 4 tapering to 3.5; diam. of perf. 3.
32. Reddish brown, translucent bead with some fracturing. Diam. 9; T. 5 tapering to 4.5.
33. Half of a bead. Est. diam. 9; T. 6; diam of perf. 4.
34. Reddish-brown, translucent, bead. Diam. 8; T. 3 tapering slightly; diam. of perf. 4.
35. Half of a reddish-brown, fractured, bead of oval cross-section. Est. diam. 8; diam. of perf. 4.
36. Half of an orange bead. Diam. 8; T. 3 tapering to 2; diam. of perf. 3. Found in uncontexted spoil but the form and the nibble marks suggest that it is of Late Bronze Age date.
37. Slightly damaged reddish-brown, fractured, cylindrical bead. Diam. 7.5; T. 5; diam. of perf. 4.
38. Reddish-brown, translucent, bead. Diam. 7.5; T. 4 tapering to 3; diam. of perf. 3.
39. Opaque orange bead. Diam. 7; T. 3 tapering to 2; diam. of perf. 3.
40. Bead. Diam. 7. T. 3.5 tapering to 2.5; diam. of perf. 3.
41. Reddish-brown, fractured, bead in two fragments. Est. diam. 7; diam. of perf. 4; T. 4 tapering to 3.
42. Orange bead. Diam. 6.5; T. 2.5 tapering to 2; diam. of perf. 2.
43. Reddish brown, translucent, cylindrical bead. Diam. 6; T. 4 tapering to 3; diam. of perf. 3.
44. Bead fragment probably of oval cross-section originally. L. 22.
45. Reddish brown, fractured, bead fragment probably of ovaloid cross-section. L. 10; T. 9.
46. Reddish-brown, translucent, bead fragment. Est. diam. 13; surviving T. 5.5; est. diam. of perf. 3; F217.
47. Reddish-brown, translucent, bead fragment. T. 7.
48. Bead fragment. T. 6.

Glass
49. Half of a light green-blue/turquoise bead with a

cylindrical perforation. The glass is different from that found in early medieval levels and is noticeably more vessiculated as well as having a striated surface which presumably resulted from the manufacturing process. Diam. 14; T. 11; diam of perf. 4.

Lignite and Shale

Parts of five bracelets, six beads and two rings were present.

Bracelets

50. Part of a shale bracelet. The surviving piece is a sliver with a semi-circular cross-section but it was probably rounded originally. It is decorated with three slightly recessed panels a little over 11mm wide. Est. diam. 110. T. 5. Found in three fragments some 8m apart.
51. Fragment of a highly polished lignite bracelet. Rounded cross-section. The ends display saw-marks suggesting that the piece was deliberately broken. Found in two fragments some 14m apart. Ext. diam. 109; T. 11.5.
52. Shale bracelet sliver of semi-oval cross-section but probably rounded originally. L. 52.
53. Lignite bracelet fragment. Oval cross-section. L. 51; T. 10.
54. Lignite bracelet sliver chipped at one end suggesting deliberate damage. L. 31; present T. 4.

Beads

The beads are circular in profile with a cylindrical perforation unless otherwise stated.

55. Cylindrical bead of lignite. Diam 12; T. 8 tapering to 7.5; diam. of perf. 4.
56. Lignite bead. The perforation is expanded and faceted on one side while the other is flat. Diam. 12; T. 4 tapering to 3.5.
57. Ovoid bead. The perforation expands slightly at both ends. The front of the bead has traces of two lightly incised lines that may be due to the process of manufacture. Diam. 11.5 x 10.5; T. 8.
58. Lignite bead with sub-trapezoidal cross-section. The perforation was placed slightly off centre indicating that it was probably hung as part of a necklace. Diam. 10; T. 4.5 tapering to 3.5; diam. of perf. 3.
59. Lignite bead sliver. Diam 25; T. 4; diam. of perf. 7.

Rings

60. Half of a shale ring. Est. diam. 29; T. 3.
61. Sliver from a lignite ring with central and transverse perforations. Diam. 19; T. 5; diam. of central perf. 10; est. diam. of transverse perforations 6.

Bone and Antler

Nine bone objects were recovered.

Cheek-piece

62. The surface has been smoothed by rubbing and is pierced by an elliptically-shaped perforation. It lacks the characteristic triple perforation identified by Britnell (1976, 24) but a similar piece is known from Ballinderry 2 (Hencken 1942, 15 and fig. 5.667). L. 99; av. T. 11.5; perf. 22 x 9.

Spindle-whorls

63. From cattle talus or metacarpal. Conical perforation. Diam. 39; T. 20; diam. of perf. 12 tapering to 6.
64. From cattle talus or metacarpal. Cylindrical perforation. Diam. 47; T. 16; diam. of perf. 10.

Pins

65. Pig fibula pin lacking its tip. L. 90.
66. Point of a bone pin. L 59. W. 6.5 tapering towards the point. T. 3.
67. Bone point, perhaps the tip of a pin. L. 45; W. 9 tapering towards the point; T. 5.
68. Bone point, perhaps the tip of a pin. L. 62; W. 9 tapering to the point; T. 4.

Comb

69. An unusual handled-comb for which there are no known parallels.

Other bone pieces

70. Rectangular bone piece with a cylindrical perforation; beside it is a shallow depression where an earlier attempt was made to drill a hole. The surface is covered with parallel striations suggesting that it was sawn. At the broken end there are traces of an incised score that may have been made preparatory to breaking the piece. L. 25; W. 11 expanding to 13 at the broken end; T. 3 tapering to 1.5 at the tip which has traces of an indentation.

Stone

Two stone spindle-whorls (71–2), six rubbing stones (73–78), two burnishers (79–80), and fragments of over twenty-two saddle-querns (81–102) were found.

Pottery

Several hundred sherds of coarse pottery were recovered but these seem to derive from no more than five or six individual pots.

Discussion

In terms of comparisons, the clearest structural parallels are with Knocknalappa, County Clare, and Killymoon, County Tyrone (Raftery 1942; Grogan *et al*. 1999; Hurl 1995; 1999). These sites were also located in wetland situations and they show similarities in construction. In particular they share the presence of a spread of burnt stones containing a range of artefacts and occupation debris. At Moynagh Lough much of the debris is domestic in function. The number of quernstones, however, is exceptional. The ornaments and bronzes indicate that the inhabitants were of high status, while the amber, imported from Scandinavia, was almost certainly a prestige item. It is the spearheads, however, which provide the clearest indication that the Moynagh dwellers were people of some standing. They hint at the presence of warriors or hunters (and by this period the two were probably synonymous), while their casual loss reflects the affluence of the owners. Despite the domestic nature of the finds, there is an element of ritual also. The vast majority of the artefacts were found scattered through a layer of debris that had was not connected with any structure on the site. The impression is gained of feasting and the subsequent scattering of debris. The heat-cracked stones almost certainly derive from an off-site *fulacht fiadh*, several of which have been noted in and around the former lakebed of Moynagh Lough. Two explanations suggest themselves. Firstly, that the layer of burnt stones and debris was derived from elsewhere and thrown down to form a foundation for a structure that was never built. This could explain why fragments from the same jet bracelets were found so far apart. Secondly, that the material is simply the leftover of meals and festivities had on or near the site. Of the two explanations, it is the second that seems to me to provide the most satisfactory solution, particularly because of the parallels with Knocknalappa and Killymoon. It is unlikely that all three sites were simply foundation levels and, if they were, why is it that archaeologists have not found a completed structure? As to the jet bracelet fragments they may simply have been discarded in this manner once the items broke.

What we are looking at on all three sites is, I believe, the full evidence. Why would people gather in the Late Bronze Age to cook food using hot stones, grind grain and possibly other plants, break jewellery and/or lose it, and lose weapons? The weapons are perhaps easiest to explain as lost in the course of fowling, although it would have to be a big bird that would be worth hitting with one of those implements. The simplest explanation, it seems to me, is that the evidence is connected with ritual activity. The shallows at Moynagh Lough was a place where people assembled and ate preparatory to depositing offerings in the lake. Such offerings may have been simply a joint of meat rather than the fine metalwork that we often associate with such activities. Whether this is true or not is impossible to say. The analysis of the animal bones may require an alternative interpretation and further work may perhaps reveal votive depositions or an off-site habitation. In the meantime we may be thankful to Professor Eogan for discovering this site, ensuring that it was excavated, and, through his writings and encouragement, providing us with so much to think about.

Bibliography

Bradley, J. 1991 Excavations at Moynagh Lough, County Meath, *Journal of the Royal Society of Antiquaries of Ireland* 121, 5–26.

Britnell, W.J. 1976 Antler cheek-pieces of the British Late Bronze Age, *Antiquaries Journal* **54**, 24–34.

Eogan, G. 1983 *Hoards of the Irish Later Bronze Age*. University College, Dublin.

Eogan, G. 1984 *Excavations at Knowth (1)*. Royal Irish Academy Monographs in Archaeology, Dublin.

Eogan, G. 1997 "Hair-rings" and European Late Bronze Age society, *Antiquity* **71**, 308–20.

Grogan, E., O'Sullivan, A., O'Carroll, F. and Hagen, I. 1999 Knocknalappa, Co. Clare: a reappraisal, *Discovery Programme Reports* **5**, The Discovery Programme/Royal Irish Academy, Dublin.

Hencken, H. O'N. 1942 Ballinderry crannog no. 2, *Proceedings of the Royal Irish Academy* **47**C, 1–76.

Hodges, H.W.M. 1958 A hunting camp at Cullyhanna Lough near Newtown Lough, Co. Armagh, *Ulster Journal of Archaeology* **21**, 7–13.

Hurl, D. 1995 Killymoon – New light on the Late Bronze Age, *Archaeology Ireland* **34**, 24–27.

Hurl, D. 1999 More light on Killymoon, *Archaeology Ireland* **50**, 5.

McCormick, F. 1986 Interim report on the animal bones from Moynagh Lough, *Ríocht na Midhe* **7**, 86–90.

Moloney, A., Jennings, D., Keane, M. and McDermott, C. 1993 *Excavations at Clonfinlough County Offaly*, Irish Archaeological Wetland Unit Transactions **2**, Crannóg Publications, Dublin.

O'Sullivan, A. 1998 *The Archaeology of Lake Settlement in Ireland*, Discovery Programme Monographs **4**, The Discovery Programme/Royal Irish Academy, Dublin.

Pollock, A.J. and Waterman, D.M. 1958 A Bronze Age habitation site at Downpatrick, *Ulster Journal of Archaeology* **27**, 31–58.

Raftery, B. 1976 Rathgall and Irish Hillfort problems. In D.W. Harding (ed.) *Hillforts: Later Prehistoric Earthworks in Britain and Ireland*, 339–357. Academic Press, London.

Raftery, J. 1942 Knocknalappa Crannog, Co. Clare, *North Munster Antiquarian Journal* **3**, 53–72.

14. The Gold Beads from Tumna, Co. Roscommon

Mary Cahill

In thinking of a subject which would show due recognition of the immense contribution which George Eogan has made to the study of Irish prehistory, and, in particular, to the study of Bronze Age gold, one is faced with a difficult challenge. His work has covered so much that there seems to be little left to explore. However, in checking through some of his publications I found that, somehow, the gold beads[1] from Tumna, Co. Roscommon, had not been published. This gave me an opportunity to look at this interesting and unique group of objects (Fig 14.1).

Discovery, collection and publication history

The first published reference to the discovery of 'ancient gold balls', was in *The Dublin Penny Journal* in 1834. A brief description and a drawing were published (Figs 14.1 and 14.2).[2] The article noted that eleven balls of pure gold had been left at the Journal's office by George McDermot, of 17 Sackville Street.[3] They had been found by two of his tenants in "finishing, or, what is generally called landing potatoes, about twelve inches under the surface, near the ruins of an old chapel, and a fort, on the western banks of the Shannon, near Carrick."[4] The article noted that they had been exhibited at the Royal Irish Academy where it was suggested that they were ornamental beads for the neck of a priest or prince of the ancient Irish. The total weight was recorded as twenty ounces eight pennyweights. The discovery was also briefly noted in Lewis' *Topographical Dictionary of Ireland* (1837, 660) where Tumna is recorded as the findplace. Tumna is also recorded as the findplace on a Plunkett watercolour of a group of gold ornaments from the Academy's collection including two of the gold beads. This painting is now in the National Museum, Copenhagen.[5]

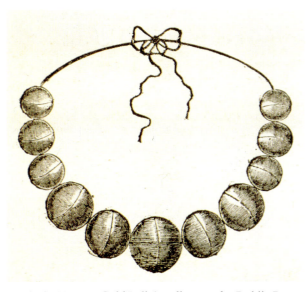

Fig 14.2: 'Ancient Gold Balls' as illustrated in Dublin Penny Journal 1934.

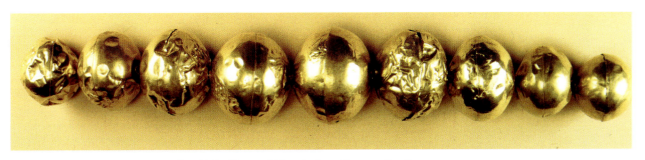

Fig 14.1: Nine gold beads from Tumna, Co. Roscommon.

Fig 14.3: Lough Eidin at Tumna, Co. Roscommon.

In his 1859 catalogue of bronze antiquities Sir William Wilde described a Late Bronze Age bronze sword[6] which he noted was found at Tumna on the Boyle water, Co. Roscommon (Fig 14.3),[7] "in the same townland with (sic) the hollow golden balls of which there are six in the Academy's collection". This information had been communicated to Mr. William T. Mulranny, Commissioner of Public Works, by Mr. Richard A. Gray, an engineer based in the Drainage Office, Kinnegad, on December 1st 1851. This letter, published in the *Proceedings of the Royal Irish Academy,*[8] states that the sword was found in the same townland as seven golden balls already in the Academy, viz. Tumna, in the county of Roscommon.

Wilde, in his catalogue of the gold ornaments in the Academy's Museum (1862, 35), neglected to mention the townland name and described the findplace as "near Carrick-on-Shannon, in the county of Leitrim". Wilde also states that the objects came into the possession of Mr. West before "they were distributed amongst several collections prior to the formation of the Academy's Museum". He continues

"several are now much battered but when found it is said that they were smooth and perfect. It is apparent that a necklace formed of these eleven balls must have descended as low as the breast. Research does not aid our inquiries as to what class they were worn by, whether chieftain, Druid-priest, or king, but their ostensible use was that of a necklace of the largest and most gorgeous description".

The next published reference to the objects is in a note on a megalithic tomb by W. F. Wakeman (1887–8, 111) who described the discovery as follows

"It appears that about thirty or forty years ago Mr. Edward Hayden, a farmer, who still lives close to Carrick-on-Shannon, was digging on the opposite side of the hill to that on which the tomb or altar is situated, and he found close to the surface eight hollow balls, varying from two to three inches in diameter, and each having an aperture pierced through its shell. These balls, or beads, a Dublin goldsmith pronounced to be

formed of gold, and they were purchased by him from Mr. Hayden for the sum of £70. They were supposed by the finder to have been in some way connected with the ancient churches of the place, possibly as the necklace of a memorial statue, or carved figure of a saint. It is probable, however, that their date is older than the introduction of Christianity to Ireland. They were disposed of in Dublin, and in all likelihood at present preserved amongst the golden glories of ancient Erin, which so excite wonder and admiration of all visitors to the Museum of the Royal Irish Academy. I may add, in conclusion, that I am not without hope of being able to identify at least a portion of this interesting' find', and of figuring the relics in the pages of our Journal."

George Coffey (1912–13, 449–450) also had occasion to refer to the gold balls. During the course of a visit to Mr. H. G. B. Clements, Killadoon House, Celbridge, Coffey was shown a gold object which he recognised "as one of the eleven balls which were found at Carrick-on-Shannon in 1834". Mr. Clements showed Coffey an undated letter (but believed to be about 1835) written by his ancestor, the Earl of Leitrim,[9] to his wife. The Earl wrote

"I have not yet made my entire confession with respect to my extravagance yesterday in Dublin. It consisted in buying an antique Irish ornament, lately found in Roscommon, a large golden ball about the size of a lemon; there were thirteen of them, all different sizes, but diminishing gradually, hollow and perforated, as if intended to be strung, from which it is conjectured that they must have been worn as an ornament around the neck. I met with it, or rather them, at West's......., and the price of the one I bought .... was £9."

In turn the discovery was also described by Armstrong (1920, 37–38, 86) but his account is mostly derived from Wilde and Coffey and he, too, records the objects as being from near Carrick-on-Shannon. This was followed in more recent publications with the exception of Waddell (1998, 236) who had picked up the Wakeman reference and recorded the provenance as Tumna, Co. Roscommon. As Wilde and Armstrong would have been the most commonly used sources the accepted provenance has, therefore, since 1862 been 'near Carrick-on-Shannon'. For this reason in 1968, Mr. Oliver Snoddy, Assistant Keeper, Art and Industry Division, National Museum of Ireland, began corresponding with a number of people in the Leitrim/Roscommon area in an effort to identify the findplace of the gold beads. One of his correspondents, Mr. Farrell McElgunn, Carrick-on-Shannon, responded with the following information. He had consulted with the County Registrar who informed him that "the place where the find was made was the churchyard at Toomna, 1½ miles from Carrick on the banks of the Boyle River".

Mr. Michael O'Callaghan,[10] Boyle, Co. Roscommon, made exhaustive enquiries and reported in 1968 that the traditional story of the finding was as follows

"A group of men, a *meitheal*, were working with George McDermott, a small farmer, at Tumna, when one of them turned up a sod and found a number of gold objects. Mr. McDermott gathered them up and in the evening gave a gold object to each man working with him. Sometime later an Excise man from Carrick-on-Shannon visited a house in the area and found children playing with a gold object. He inquired where it came from and was told the story of the find at Tumna. He then arranged to have all the finds collected and when this was done he sent them to the Museum."

Although there is some confusion in these various accounts, it is clear that a find was made in 1834 at Tumna, Co. Roscommon, consisting of eleven or thirteen large gold beads. The *Dublin Penny Journal* account is contemporary and ought to be the most reliable if, in fact, Mr. McDermot visited the offices himself. It also seems most likely that all the beads in his possession were acquired by Mr. West, the jeweller, at that time based in Capel Street. From Mr. West's hands the beads disappeared into private collections and with the passage of time most found their way into Museum collections. In 1839 the British Museum purchased one bead from Messrs Franklin.[11] By 1862, when Wilde published his gold catalogue, seven beads had been acquired for the Museum of the Royal Irish Academy. In 1841 Major Sirr died and with the purchase of his collection the Academy acquired two of the gold beads.[12] By 1842 the Academy had managed to collect sufficient funds to purchase the collection made by Dean Dawson from his widow and thus acquired two more beads.[13] One was bought from Mr. West in 1862 for £9.8.0.[14] Another was bought, according to the Antiquities Committee Minute Book, from Dr. Todd in January 1862.[15] This had been previously in the possession of Sir Francis Hopkins, Bart., Co. Westmeath. There is no information available on the purchase or acquisition by the Academy of the seventh bead.

Between 1862 and 1975 no further acquisitions were made. However, in 1975, the National Museum of Ireland acquired a collection of six gold ornaments from the representatives of the late Colonel H. T. W. Clements, Killadoon, Celbridge, Co. Kildare. This collection included the gold bead recorded by Coffey (1912–13).[16] Finally, in 1990, another bead, together with other gold objects, was acquired from the Duke of Northumberland.[17] In a manuscript catalogue of the collection of antiquities kept at Alnwick Castle, it is recorded that the gold bead in the Duke's collection was acquired from the collection of Mr. Robert Chambers Walker[18] "by whom it is stated to have been selected as the most perfect though the smallest of the series". The author of the catalogue, Albert Way, drew attention to the similarity between the beads from Tumna and a set of gold beads found under a cairn at Chesterhope Common, Rigsdale, Northumberland. A sketch shows sixteen beads of graduating size each of

which appears to have been formed of two parts. The weight is recorded as 7 pennyweights indicating that these beads are very small.

As noted previously, the *Dublin Penny Journal* refers to the discovery of eleven beads and again, as it seems plausible that, as Mr. McDermot was present or in the immediate vicinity of the discovery, the correct number is eleven rather than thirteen. However, an examination of all the surviving beads (see below) suggests that thirteen may be the correct figure. It has not been possible to trace the missing bead(s) but as one survived in a private collection as late as 1990 there is still some hope that one or more may yet come to light.

Description

The gold beads from Tumna are unique in the Irish record of gold artefacts. Although there are several other finds of Late Bronze Age gold beads recorded, none of these is comparable either in size or form. Sheet gold was used extensively in Ireland in the Late Bronze Age but the form in which it is used in the beads from Tumna is unique and cannot be paralleled in Britain or western or northern Europe. By comparison with the skill levels required to make other sheet gold objects such as gorgets or earspools, they may appear somewhat crude but this impression is not correct. Each half has been very skilfully raised from a small ingot and where possible to measure, the sheet varies from 00.01 to 00.04mm in thickness. The perforation has been punched from the interior leaving a slightly raised rim on the outer surface. Each bead is formed by overlapping the edge of one half over the other. The join was achieved by fusing the overlapping edges around the circumference. The area of overlap is up to 6.50mm in the larger beads. As there is no evidence for the use of a solder, it is assumed that fusing was the technique used, *i.e.* both surfaces were heated to the point where a bond formed on joining the surfaces together. There is no completely intact join present except for the beads which were restored in the 19th century using modern white solder, not all of which has remained in place. The original fusing in not continuous, the fusion bonding has been effected irregularly at a number of places along the circumference.

When newly made each complete bead was of flattened spherical form. Each hemisphere is perforated at its highest point from the interior leaving a slightly raised ridge. These perforations indicate that they were intended to be strung and to function as beads. The beads vary from 9.72 to 6.80cm in maximum diameter. The decrease in the maximum diameter of the long axis from pair to pair is variable, the bead closest to the centre bead (Bead 1) diminishing by 0.58cm (see Appendix 2).[19] The pairs numbered 2 and 3, diminish by 0.34cm from one another while pairs 3 and 4 diminish by 0.20cm. There is a more noticeable decrease of 0.62, 0.68 and 0.50cm between pairs 4, 5, 6 and 7, respectively.

There is also a variation in weight but the weights do not always decrease with the decrease in diameter. The heaviest weighs 73.38g (NMI W30) while the lightest (NMI 1990:80) weighs 38.43g.[20] However, the heaviest (NMI W30) is the not the largest (NMI W31). Pairs 2 and 6 are each very close in weight while there is some variation amongst the other surviving pairs, *e.g.* pair 3 are very close in size but there is a variation in weight of over 1.7g. These variations are not significant and have been caused by slight discrepancies in the cutting of ingot fragments to size before raising the sheet, the aim of the goldsmith being to produce pairs matching in size rather than weight. By using the available weights it can be calculated that a complete necklace of thirteen would have weighed in or around 772 grammes (24.82 troy ounces). This is a significant amount of gold, the equivalent, in Late Bronze Age terms, of at least three gorgets.

Four beads have been extensively restored while the other six are in their original condition and show differing degrees of damage in the form of dents and dinges. Two are now in two parts while the remainder are joined either by the original method or by modern restoration using a white metal solder. One has suffered severe discolouration caused by excessive heat in an undated but modern attempt to join the two sections. Some of the restoration is more than what would be deemed appropriate today. This has caused some difficulty in measuring the objects accurately but what follows is a suggested arrangement based on an examination of the dimensions and weights of the individual objects.

Assuming the largest surviving bead to be the central bead (Bead 1 - W31) by comparing the diameters of the remaining nine it can be seen that they fall into three pairs, beads 2a and 2b (W31A and W30), 3a and 3b (BM 1839.3–27.1 and 1975:231) and 6a and 6b (W29 and W28).[21] The remaining three beads, 4a (W32), 5a (W33) and 7A (1990:80) do not have a close enough matching bead amongst those that survive. This strongly suggests that three beads are missing, Beads 4b, 5b, and 7b. If this is correct it follows that there were originally thirteen rather than eleven beads found as indicated by some of the early reports of the discovery. As these reports also suggest that the beads were distributed amongst the finders, this may account for the loss of three beads. Arranged thus in pairs on either side of the largest bead, the remaining beads form a necklace of graduated beads similar to, although more grandiose than, the necklaces that are usually formed of amber beads. In fact, the closest parallels for the Tumna gold beads are to be found in the corpus of Late Bronze Age amber beads from Ireland and Britain. The largest surviving Irish amber bead, from Cashel, Co. Armagh (NMI 1906:131), is 6.70cm in maximum diameter. The smallest bead from Tumna is 6.80cm (1990:80) in maximum diameter. Figs 14.4 and 14.5 show that both are very similar in plan and section demonstrating the clear intention of the goldsmith to replicate the form of the amber bead in another material.

The similarity of the sheet gold technique to that of the Dowris period goldsmiths, and also the form of the beads, confirms their manufacture during that period.

Discussion

When the gold beads are compared to the largest recorded examples of amber beads it is seen that there are some striking similarities. Beck and Shennan (1991) in their discussion of amber beads from Britain categorise beads as (amongst other variables) small, medium and large. According to their general classification beads over 2.00cm in diameter are regarded as large. Any beads over 2.00cm may be regarded as exceptional. Any bead approximating in size to the smallest bead from Tumna is, therefore, even more exceptional (Figs 14.4 and 14.5). The corpus of British beads (Beck and Shennan 1991, 143–194) records very few beads of annular or globular form over 4.00cm in diameter. One, a modified amber pebble from Burythorpe, Yorkshire, is of Early Neolithic/Middle Neolithic date; two from Simonside, Northumberland, which measure 5.30 and 5.50cm in diameter are suggested to be Late Bronze Age in date; in Scotland a perforated amber disk 4.40cm in diameter was found at Biggar, Lancarckshire; an amber ring 4.8cm in diameter was found at Lochryan, Wigtownshire. No dates are proposed for the Scottish examples. One bead is recorded from Llangadfan, Montgomery, Wales, which is 4.3cm in diameter.

Although relatively scarce in Britain, there is a significant number of very large amber beads known from Ireland. At least fifteen discoveries of single beads have been recorded ranging in size from 4.00cm to 6.81cm in maximum diameter (Appendix 3 and Fig 14.6). Others of 4.00cm or more are incorporated into necklaces usually being the largest bead in the set and occupying the centremost position with smaller beads arranged in pairs on either side.[22] These beads tend to be of flattened spherical form with a straight perforation through the shorter axis. The resemblance of the largest amber beads to the sheet gold beads from Tumna is remarkable. Their manufacture seems to have been a goldsmith's attempt to reproduce in sheet gold the form and character of the large amber beads.

In antiquity amber was traded from the Baltic area to the east, west and south of Europe and beyond over many thousands of miles by sea and land routes. What commodity or commodities may have been traded from Ireland in exchange is not known but it seems clear from the quantity that has survived that a well-established trading network existed. Amber was a valuable and desirable exotic material that reached Ireland through a trading system that ultimately reached across the North Sea to the Baltic.[23] Its rarity would have restricted its availability to a privileged minority.

Whether amber was imported as a raw material into Ireland or as finished beads is unclear. To date there is no

Fig 14.4: Gold bead (NMI 1990:80), Tumna, Co. Roscommon, and amber bead from Cashel, Co. Armagh (NMI 1906:131).

Fig 14.5: Gold bead (NMI 1990:80), Tumna, Co. Roscommon, and amber bead from Cashel, Co. Armagh (NMI 1906:131).

evidence for the working of amber on any prehistoric site from Ireland although amber was worked in Ireland during the Viking period as evidenced by the debitage recovered from excavations in Dublin, dated to the tenth and eleventh centuries. It must be assumed that amber used in eighth and ninth century brooches and other fine ecclesiastical metalwork (although in very small quantities) was also worked *in situ* as it had to be customised to the particular requirements of each object. The lack of evidence for Late Bronze Age amber working in Ireland must be counterbalanced by the lack of evidence from Denmark for the use of amber during the same period.[24] This suggests that the beads were being produced locally rather than being imported as finished objects.[25] Kristiansen's observation (1998, 233–240, note 3) in a discussion of the economic and social factors that influenced the use of large quantities of amber in southern Europe from 750–450 BC explains the paucity of manufactured amber in the Baltic during this period. Amber was no longer seen as a prestige material in Denmark having been replaced in the Bronze Age by metal. Its value was in its usefulness

as a commodity to be traded for other exotic, prestige goods. Its abundance made it cheap locally and thus it became devalued.

Amber and other similar resinous materials[26] have been used by many societies since prehistoric times, although, for example, copal (another type of resinous material, less valuable than amber) is not believed to carry the same protective power. Amber is still regarded as a desirable commodity in cultures to which it is foreign because its colour and electrostatic qualities imbue it with a value way beyond its value as a, merely, decorative material as it is believed to have strong magical or apotropaic qualities. These include protection against the evil eye and a range of diseases including poor eyesight. An additional factor for many ethnic peoples for whom amber is an important material is its colour. Yellow Baltic amber, in particular, was very highly prized amongst the people of Tibet and Nepal. Although amber from Burma (known as burmite) is available in these regions it is not as highly prized as Baltic amber. Hannelore Gabriel (1999, 124) records the following

Fig 14.6: Selection of large amber beads from Ireland.

Fig 14.7: Tibetan officials wearing ceremonial costume and necklaces of amber beads at New Year ceremonies, Lhasa, Tibet, 1946. (Copyright Pitt Rivers Museum, Oxford).

"Rare, but especially noteworthy because of their size and value are amber necklaces, sometimes brown with age, that Nyinba women wear for ceremonial occasions. The large Baltic amber beads, so cherished by all Tibetan peoples, have survived in quantity only in remote parts of Nepal, especially in the far west . ..... here it is still possible to see long strands of Baltic amber beads up to 5 cms in diameter."

Hugh Richardson, a British civil servant who spent many years in Tibet, has published a photograph taken in 1946 of Tibetan government officials dressed in New Year ceremonial costume wearing long strings of graduated amber beads which reach to below waist level (Fig 14.7). He described (1993, 14–16) the officials as wearing

"ornaments of unusual size - great circular golden turquoise studded charm boxes, a heavy turquoise pendant earring in the right ear and in the other a long golden bar covered in slabs of turquoise which reached down to the waist and had to be held in the hand. There were also necklaces of large coral beads and one of huge amber beads, some as big as a golf ball."

He notes further that "these precious possessions ......

are known as the *ringen,* 'the Ancient Ornaments', and are kept in the Potala Treasury." Their use was confined to certain special occasions such as the celebration of the King's New Year and they could only be worn by the highest officials. At the end of the ceremonies the precious ornaments were meticulously checked by a member of the cabinet before being returned to their storage place. Although Richardson describes some of the beads as being as large as golf balls, his photograph suggests that some were much bigger than that and the largest beads are comparable in size to the largest of the Tumna gold beads. In the photograph it is possible to see that between each bead a separator of cloth or some soft material is placed in order to protect the beads from damage that would otherwise be caused by the movement of the beads against one another.

Baltic amber was also used for jewellery in Africa where, in addition to its desirability for personal adornment, its magical and amuletic powers were much prized. In writing about the jewellery used by north African peoples Angela Fisher (1984, 230) notes that

"The Berbers have enjoyed the benefits of a rich trade with Europe, the Middle East and West Africa. As a result they have incorporated into their fine silver jewellery bold unfashioned lumps of amber, chunks of coral and lumps of amazonite. Amber, highly prized both for its colour and medicinal powers, came from the Baltic Sea and, to a lesser extent, from the Atlantic coast of Morocco. Since Hippocrates' time it has been thought to cure a variety of ailments including gonorrhoea, earache, poor sight, fevers and hysteria. In the oasis towns of the south it is an important component of 'lunar paste' a sticky greyish ointment made with spring water and musk sold in earthenware pots at markets and recommended by a *taleb* (a magician with curative powers) for specific beneficial or evil purposes".

Conclusion

The beads from Tumna are the only beads in gold of their type and size to have survived from Ireland. However, their form is clearly derived from the larger amber beads of flattened spherical form which are very well represented in the Irish record. Worn together as a neck ornament they are an extravagant, ostentatious statement produced, perhaps, with the intention of surpassing or eclipsing the impact of a collection of large amber beads in a way which might only be matched by the wearing of a gold collar such as a gorget (which given their restricted distribution may not have been available in the north-western region of Ireland) or an impressive bronze collar such as the one from near Roscommon town (NMI W1; Eogan 2001, 231–240). Another reason for their production may have been the unavailability of amber to make a necklace of large beads. Gold may have been deemed a suitable replacement and in replicating the form of amber beads in an even grander style may have been held to carry the same potent magic that has been for so long associated with the prestigious and exotic substance. Their final abandonment close to a large body of water in a place which may well have been underwater at the time of deposition is another episode in the ritual renunciation of a valuable, and in this case, unique form of personal ornament.

Acknowledgements

I would like to acknowledge the following colleagues for their comments and advice during the preparation of this paper Brian Clarke, Aideen Ireland, Cathy Feeney Johnson, Flemming Kaul, Raghnall Ó Floinn, and Maeve Sikora. I am also indebted to Valerie Dowling, Senior Photographer, and Margaret Lannin, Senior Technical Assistant, National Museum of Ireland. Fig 14.7 is reproduced by kind permission of the Pitt Rivers Museum, University of Oxford.

Notes

1   Although most often referred to as 'balls', the term 'beads' is preferable as the objects are perforated. See further below on this point.

2   The full text from the journal is reproduced in "Roger Chambers Walker", Aideen M. Ireland 2002 *Journal of Irish Archaeology* **11**. 147–87. Ireland (forthcoming).

3   Now O'Connell Street, Dublin. As 17 Lower Sackville Street was the premises of Hoyte and Flood, Drug, Spice and Colour Merchants it is more likely that George McDermott was staying at 17 Upper Sackville Street, the premises of the Waterford Hotel and Coach Office.

4   Carrick-on-Shannon, Co. Leitrim.

5   I am grateful to Maeve Sikora for this information.

6   NMI Reg. No. W39. This object was presented by R. A. Grady C.E.

7   The Boyle water is a tributary of the Shannon which it enters at Carrick-on-Shannon having flowed through Lough Gara, Lough Key and Lough Eidin. The townland of Tumna (pronounced Toomna) is on OS 6" Sheets 7 and 11, parish

Tumna, barony Boyle, county Roscommon. The inventory of Recorded Monuments and Places notes RO007-087, 08701-5, Ecclesiastical remains, church, graveyard and altar and RO007-086 , an earthwork site on the banks of Lough Eidin adjacent to the town of Carrick-on Shannon.

8   Vol. 5, 1850-53, xxxiv–xxxvi.

9   This is Nathaniel Clements, 2nd Earl of Leitrim, whose seat was at Manorhamilton, Co. Leitrim. He died on 31 December 1854.

10   Former editor of the Roscommon Herald.

11   BM Reg. No. 1839.3–27.1. The British Museum paid £9.13.0 to Messrs Franklin, the London dealers.

12   NMI Reg. Nos W32, W 33.

13   Dean Dawson died in 1840. NMI Reg. Nos W29, W 30.

14   NMI Reg. No. W28.

15   NMI Reg. No. W31A.

16   NMI Reg. No. 1975:231. The collection also included a gold lunula, a gold dress-fastener, a gold foil-covered penannular ring, a gold sleeve-fastener and a gold bracelet. No provenances have been recorded for these objects. NMI Reg. Nos 1975:229–30; 232–4. It now seems likely that these objects and others acquired from other members of the Clements family in 1967 by the National Museum may have been the original collection of the Earl of Leitrim.

17   NMI reg. No. 1990:80.

18   Ireland as in note 2.

19   For descriptive purposes in the following paragraphs the largest bead is called Bead 1 while each pair of beads on either side is termed Bead 2a, 2b *etc.* even where the matching pair may be missing. The figures quoted are calculated by subtracting the larger figures in each set from one another.

20   The weights recorded include the modern solder present in the following W31; 1975:231; 1990:80. The amounts are minimal.

21   See catalogue for detailed measurements.

22   See for example Tooradoo, Co. Limerick, Meenwaun (Banagher), Co. Offaly, Cogran, Co. Offaly, Mountrivers, Co. Cork, Derrybrien, Co. Galway. I would like to thank Cathy Feeney Johnson for allowing me access to her unpublished thesis on prehistoric amber from Ireland.

23   See Eogan (1999, 84) for a discussion of possible routes.

24   Dr. Flemming Kaul has advised me that Bronze Age amber beads of 4.00cm diameter or more are quite exceptional in Denmark.

25   Eogan (1999, 81) has calculated the number of finds of amber beads from Ireland as up to 3,500 individual beads. He also notes that this is a minimum figure as many beads have been lost. For example, a cutting from the *Limerick Chronicle* (precise date unknown but *c.* 1840) preserved in one of John Windele's scrapbooks records that "a countryman, in the act of cutting turf mould in a bog near Tipperary, dug up a string of amber beads, of uncommonly large size, and two gold rings, measuring six inches in circumference; also a small gold chalice or vase; all in a perfect state of preservation. The bead (*sic*) is a rare antique the like not having been used by any religious community in this country, it is thought, for centuries. These articles were purchased by a jeweller of our city." The number of surviving beads from Britain is much less partly due to deposition in environments which are inimical to amber.

26   For a discussion of amber and related materials see Ross 1998.

Bibliography

Anon. 1834 *Dublin Penny Journal*. Dublin.

Armstrong, E.C.R. 1920 *Catalogue of Irish Gold Ornaments in the Collection of the Royal Irish Academy*. The Stationery Office, Dublin.

Beck, C. and Shennan, S. 1991 *Amber in prehistoric Britain*. Oxbow Monograph **8**, Oxford.

Coffey, G. 1912–13 Two unpublished lunulae and other objects, *Proceedings of the Royal Irish Academy* **30**C, 449–450.

Eogan, G. 1999 From Skane to Scotstown; some notes on amber in Bronze Age Ireland. In A.F. Harding (ed.) *Experiment and Design – archaeological studies in honour of John Coles*, 75–86. Oxbow Books, Oxford.

Eogan, G. 2001 A composite Late Bronze Age chain object from Co. Roscommon. In W.H. Metz *et al.* (eds) *Patina – Essays presented to Jay Jordan Butler*, 231–240. Amsterdam.

Feeney, C. 1976 *Aspects of Irish amber finds*. Unpublished MA Thesis, University College, Dublin.

Fisher, A. 1984 *Africa Adorned*. H. Abrahms, New York.

Gabriel, H. 1999 *Jewelry of Nepal*. H. Abrahms, London.

Kristiansen, K. 1998 *Europe before history*. Cambridge University Press, Cambridge.

Lewis, S. 1837 *A topographical dictionary of Ireland*. London.

Richardson, H. 1993 *Ceremonies of the Lhasa Year*. Serindia Publications, London.

Ross, A. 1998 *Amber – the natural time capsule*. The Natural History Museum, London.

Waddell, J. 1998 *The archaeology of prehistoric Ireland*. Galway University Press, Galway

Wakeman, W.F. 1887–8 On a cromlech-like altar, or monument, at Tumna, Co. Roscommon, *Journal of the Royal Society of Antiquaries of Ireland* **18**, 107–111.

Wilde, W.R. 1859 *A descriptive catalogue of the antiquities of animal materials and bronze in the museum of the Royal Irish Academy*. Hodges, Smith and Co., Dublin.

Wilde, W.R. 1862 *Catalogue of the antiquities of gold in the museum of the Royal Irish Academy*. Hodges, Smith and Co., Dublin.

Appendix 1

Catalogue of gold beads from Tumna, Co Roscommon, arranged by registration number. Dimensions in cm

BM 1839.3-27.1 is complete and unrestored. The surfaces are much dented. The original join is complete over *c.* 2/3 of the circumference. The apex of both hemispheres has been pierced from the inside leaving a small rim of metal on the outer surface.
D 8.80 x 7.02; Wt. 60.30g.

W28 is complete and intact but in a very battered condition. The original join is complete over *c.* 1/3 of the circumference. The apex of both hemispheres has been pierced from the inside leaving a small rim of metal on the outer surface.
Dimensions are approximate due to distortion.
D 7.21 x 6.80; D of perforations 0.59 x 0.53 and 0.64 x 0.64; T 0.02; Wt. 44.68g.

W29 is complete with both sections still attached over majority of circumference. One area seems to have been prised away from the join and there is no evidence of solder on either surface. Many dents and dinges in surface. The apex of both hemispheres has been pierced from the inside leaving a small rim of metal on the outer surface.
D 7.30 x 5.70; D of perforations 0.60 x 0.56 and 0.63 x 0.61; T 0.02-0.03; Wt. 45.44g.

W30 is complete but much crumpled and misshapen; does not seem to have been restored. The original join between both sections of the bead has survived in three places. The apex of both hemispheres has been pierced from the inside leaving a small rim of metal on the outer surface.
D 9.00 x 7.36; T 0.02-0.04; D of perforations 0.58 x 0.61 and 0.60 x.0.68; Wt 73.38g.

W31 is in two separate pieces. There is evidence of three modern soldered joins which have not held. One area is discoloured where the metal was heated in order to apply modern solder. It has been restored but retains evidence of creases and crumples of ancient damage. The apex of both hemispheres has been pierced from the inside leaving a small rim of metal on the outer surface.
D 9.72 x 8.28; T of sheet 0.02-0.04; D of perforation 0.62 x 0.60 and 0.57 x 0.57; Wt. 71.77 g.

W31A is complete. It seems to have been partly restored and rejoined. The visible surfaces near the edges have been flattened and straightened. The remainder appears to have had the original dents smoothed out but not fully restored. The apex of both hemispheres has been pierced from the inside leaving a small rim of metal on the outer surface. There are a number of small pointed protuberances on the surface as if punched by a small punch from the interior. Perhaps the impression of some objects introduced into the interior.
D 9.14 x 8.07; T 0.02-0.03 only measurable at perforation. D of perforation 0.68 x 0.72 and 0.80 x 0.59 (distorted); Wt. 72.97g.

W32 is complete but dented and crumpled in appearance. The original join between both sections of the bead has survived in three places. The apex of both hemispheres has been pierced from the inside leaving a small rim of metal on the outer surface.
D 8.60 x 7.50; D of perforations 0.59 x 0.62 and 0.54 x 0.58; T 0.20-0.40; Wt. 62.50g.

W33 is complete, both sections still attached over half the circumference. Several large and small dents in surface with areas of raised dots as if punched from inside. The apex of both hemispheres has been pierced from the inside leaving a small rim of metal on the outer surface.
D 7.98 x 6.3; D of perforations 0.60 x 0.61 and 0.57 x 0.57; T 0.03-0.04; Wt. 58.18g.

1975:231 is complete but has suffered extensive restoration and been joined with solder causing serious discolouration of the metal. One large tear in the sheet. The apex of both hemispheres has been pierced from the inside leaving a small rim of metal on the outer surface.
D 8.70 x 6.90; D of perforations 0.60 x 0.54 and 0.63 x 0.66; T only measurable at one point 0.35; Wt. 62.07g.

1990:80 is in two separate pieces and has been restored. There is evidence of a modern soldered join which has not held. The apex of both hemispheres has been pierced from the inside leaving a small rim of metal on the outer surface.
D 6.80 x 6.10; D of perforations 0.55 x 0.58 and 0.48 x 0.47; T 0.11-0.30; Wt. 38.43g.

Appendix 2

Summary of dimensions (cm) and weights of the gold beads (arranged as possible pairs) from Tumna, Co. Roscommon

Number	Diameter	Weight g	Number	Diameter	Weight g
1. **W31**	9.72 x 8.28	71.77			
2a. **W31A**	9.14 x 8.07	72.97	2b **W30**	9.00 x 7.36	73.38
3a. **BM 1839.3-27.1**	8.80 x 7.02	60.30	3b. **1975:231**	8.70 x 6.90	62.07
4a. **W32**	8.60 x 7.50	62.54g	4b. present whereabouts unknown		
5a **W33**	7.98 x 6.30	58.18	5b. present whereabouts unknown		
6a. **W29**	7.30 x 5.70	45.44	6b. **W28**	7.24 x 5.84	44.6
7a. **1990:80**	6.80 x 6.10	38.43	7b. present whereabouts unknown		

Appendix 3

Provisional list of single finds of amber beads of 4.00cm diameter or more from Ireland arranged by county

County	Townland	Reg. No.	Max. Diameter (cm)
Armagh	Cashel	NMI 1906:131	6.70
Cavan	Marahill	NMI 1962:245	4.60
Cavan	Skeagh Bog	NMI 1937:2633-42	4.49
Cavan	Tonymore	NMI Wk. 630	4.15
Clare	Knocknalappa	NMI E30:31	4.50
Derry	Garvagh	UM 1962:260	4.50
Limerick	Kilmallock	NMI 1903:252	5.76
Sligo	Leitrim South	NMI 1945:84	4.20
Tyrone	near Ballygawley	BM 1845.12-26.49	5.70
Ireland		NMI 1907:54	4.06
Ireland		NMI 1882:103	4.95
Ireland		NMI RSAI 52	6.50
Ireland		NMI Wk. 694	4.40
Ireland		NMI 1882:149	6.57
Ireland		NMI Wk. 701	5.20

15. The Dating of the Embanked Stone Circle at Grange, Co. Limerick

Helen Roche

Throughout my long association with George Eogan, first as a student and then the many years working together at Knowth, I have learned many valuable lessons; the importance of research and publication, the willingness to question established theories and to accept criticism bravely. These are the essential objectives by which George himself has lived by during his career in archaeology. It is a privilege to regard George as my mentor and I offer the following reinterpretation of the Grange Stone Circle to him in appreciation, admiration and friendship.

The impressive site at Grange was excavated by Seán P. Ó Ríordáin in 1939 (1951, 37–74), and it remains one of the most impressive and enigmatic prehistoric sites in Ireland. It is located about 1km to the west of the Knockadoon peninsula on the far side of the lake, set in an archaeologically rich landscape (Fig 15.4) that has produced a wealth of prehistoric information, both monumental and artefactual, extending from the earliest stages of the Neolithic up to the Iron Age.

Outline of the construction and site history of Grange

The Grange enclosure (Fig 15.1) consists of a circle of contiguous orthostats contained by a surrounding earthen bank, enclosing an internal area some 47m in diameter. The narrow stone-lined entrance (Fig 15.1; Fig 15.2: section KL), located in the north-east, is dominated by two enormous portal stones, c. 2m in height, which are mirrored on the opposite side of the site by two equally large stones. In the absence of a ditch it appears that material for the bank was acquired from the immediate surrounding area. Excavation revealed that after the construction of the bank, the erection of the orthostats and the packing of stones within the sockets, a thick layer of gravely clay, averaging 45cm thick, was spread over the entire interior space creating a level higher than that on the exterior of the enclosure. The old ground surface, sealed beneath this covering contained features and an abundant quantity of artefacts, mainly pottery.

The number of features uncovered was limited and consisted of a post-hole in the exact centre of the circle, which Ó Ríordáin (1951, 44) interpreted as representing the point from which the circumference of the inner bank was marked. Two hearths were found in close proximity in the northwestern area of the interior. One consisted of an area of burning but the second contained two stones set on edge that were the remains of a stone edging around the hearth. Portions of five trenched enclosures were also found (Fig 15.1), four were circular in plan and one had squared corners. Although these trenches were only visible at the level of the old ground surface the only associated artefacts recovered were portions of clay pipes, leading Ó Ríordáin (1951, 45) to argue that they dated to the seventeenth century and may have represented huts or tents possibly associated with military activity in the area at that time.

Limited areas of the bank were excavated (Fig 15.2). The cutting on the western side of the site, behind orthostats 67 and 68, showed that there were two lenses of dark charcoal-rich material within the bank. Ó Ríordáin (1951, 47) suggested that these were turf lines that represented the resting places of the workers as they built the bank. Similar turf lines were found in the other cuttings through the bank. The original ground surface was uncovered beneath the bank and an area of burning was found within this layer on the southern side.

Ó Ríordáin's analysis and dating of the material assemblage

A varied and interesting range of artefacts was found within the interior of the site, in and around the orthostat sockets as well as within and beneath the bank. The majority consists of pottery, which Ó Ríordáin identified as representing Early and Late Neolithic wares (his Class I and Class II), Grooved Ware, Late Neolithic/Early Bronze Age Beaker pottery and Early Bronze Age Food Vessels. Three bronze objects were found consisting of part of a circular object, possibly a bracelet, a short length of a possible awl, and a U-sectioned piece of sheet bronze that Ó Ríordáin (1951, 48) interpreted as a mounting,

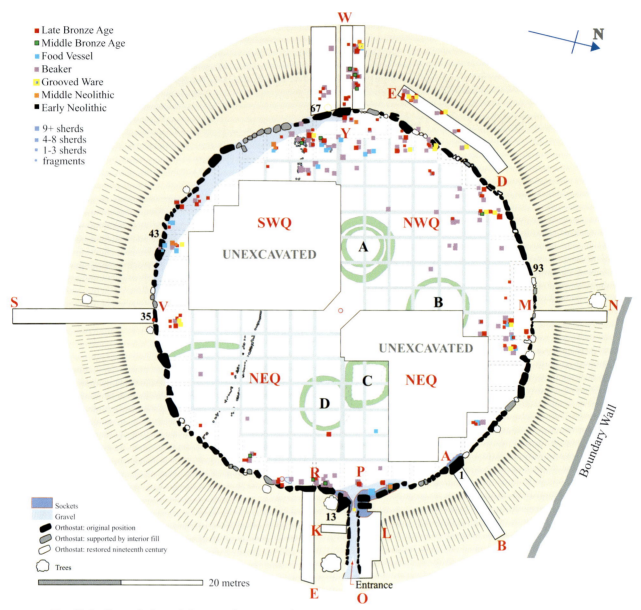

Fig 15.1: Ground plan of Grange, Co. Limerick. Showing areas of excavation and distribution of pottery.

possibly for a dagger sheath. The mounting came from the old ground level and the other two objects came from near the bottom of the fill in the entrance. Up to 400 flint and chert pieces (the latter representing only about 20 examples) were found in the interior of the site, mainly from the original ground surface but some apparently from the overlying clay fill and the turf-lines under the bank at the west. These included hollow-based, transverse and barbed-and-tanged arrowheads, thumb-nail scrapers and knives (Ó Ríordáin 1951, 49: fig. 3). A complete felsite axehead was found on the original ground surface near the orthostats in the North West Quadrant. A fragment of another felsite axe was found associated with the hearth beneath the bank on the southern area of the site and a second fragment (greenstone) came from the gravel packing inside the orthostats in the South West Quadrant.

Three bone points and a range of animal bones representing cattle, sheep/goat, pig, horse, dog, red deer and some bird bones were also found.

Unburnt human bone was recovered from three separate areas. A tibia and humerus of an infant were found in the bank on the west side of the site. Bones including portions of the skulls of two adults were found in the fill in the North West Quadrant. There was no evidence for formal burial and it is possible that burials pre-dating the construction of the site were disturbed (Ó Ríordáin 1951, 67–8).

Ó Ríordáin interpreted the site as having been constructed as one unit. As not all the bases of the orthostats actually reached the old ground level he logically surmised that they could only have remained in position with the support of the surrounding bank and the interior packing.

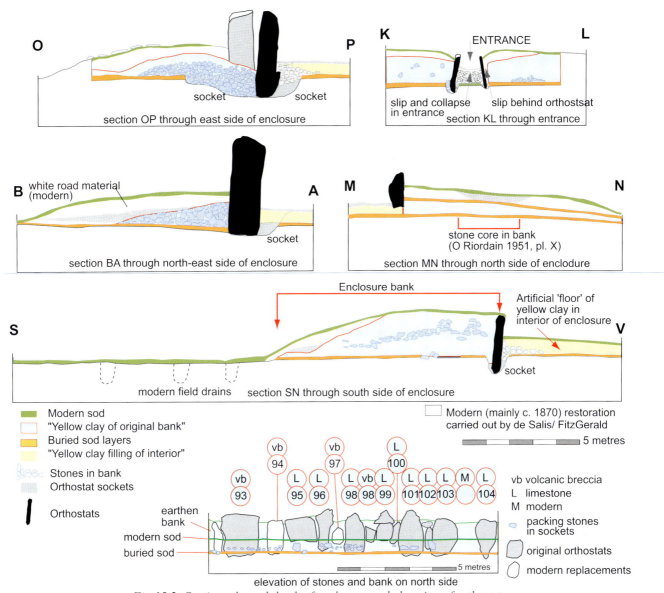

Fig 15.2: Sections through bank of enclosure and elevation of orthostats.

He also considered the different types of pottery to have been largely in contemporary use. He regarded the Early Neolithic bowls (Class 1) as a late surviving group on the site being contemporary with Beaker and Food Vessel. He suggested that a group of sherds with grooved decoration had affinities with British Grooved Ware pots. This was an important identification as it was the first time Grooved Ware was recognised in Ireland, a point that is often overlooked. Regarding the Beaker and Food Vessels he rightly saw British parallels for the Beaker assemblage, but again saw both pottery types as being in contemporary use on the site (Ó Ríordáin 1951, 68–72). However, it is his interpretation and identification of 'Class II' ware that is one of the main concerns in this paper.

This pottery, which Ó Ríordáin (1954, 375–7, 451–2, 455–6) had already uncovered at nearby sites at Knockadoon, was described as either barrel or bucket shaped

coarse, flat-based vessels. Because stratigraphically they appeared in layers associated with early Neolithic carinated bowls, Ó Ríordáin concluded that both types were in contemporary use and were pre-Beaker in date. He regarded the Grange finds as confirmation of his premise that Class II ware occurred in both Neolithic and Early-Middle Bronze Age contexts. At Grange he observed a spatial difference between Beaker and Food Vessel sherds and Class II, in that the former were mainly found in the interior and within the sockets, while the latter were mainly found either beneath or within the surrounding bank. He regarded the presence of Class II as representing "the more ordinary domestic wares which occurred here side by side with highly decorated vessels" (Ó Ríordáin 1951, 68). In broader terms he interpreted this situation as representing close cultural contacts during the Neolithic and Early Bronze Age, especially with

Orcadian Grooved Ware pottery, which in the 1950s was thought to be of Early Bronze Age date (Ó Ríordáin 1951, 68–69).

He pointed out that this undecorated coarse pottery could indeed be confused with other pottery types, for example, cinerary urns; however, he considered that Class II was "providing part of the ancestry of the cinerary urn". He also argued against the findings of similar ware found in megalithic tombs where they were identified as dating to the Late Bronze Age or Iron Age periods, concluding that "An acceptance of the early date of coarse sherds found in megalithic tombs obviates in many instances the necessity to postulate extraordinarily late dating or long usage or, as has sometimes been the case, to do violence to the stratigraphical evidence" (Ó Ríordáin 1951, 69).

Subsequent interpretations

It should be emphasised that the above summary outlining Ó Ríordáin's interpretation of his excavation at Grange was published over fifty years ago, without the benefit of radiocarbon dating or a greater understanding of the chronological development of Irish prehistoric pottery. Yet, despite the fact that it is now obvious that the pottery types at Grange represent well over two thousand years of activity, in examining current literature and even with developments in dating and new evidence from more recent excavations it is surprising that this interpretation of Grange, with few exceptions, is still broadly accepted to the present day. All of the textbooks published since the late 1980s place the construction of this site firmly, and without question, in the late Neolithic period, with obvious later activity represented by the presence of Food Vessels. Although having clear affinities with stone circles, it is placed within the same tradition as the embanked enclosures in the Boyne Valley (Harbison 1988, 94; O'Kelly 1989, 137–139; Cooney and Grogan 1994, 89; Waddell 1998, 112; Cooney 2000, 84). In more specialist papers the same interpretation is accepted (Condit and Simpson 1998, 55; Cleary 2000, 123–124). Yet, as far back as 1961 the concept of Class II ware was questioned by Case (1961, 206–8). In his report on the hillfort at Freestone Hill, Co. Kilkenny, Raftery (1969, 92), recognised the similarity between the coarse flat-based pottery on that site and that at Knockadoon, questioning if it might not date to the Iron Age, the date then believed for the Freestone Hill material. It should be noted that shortly afterwards, as a result of his excavations at Rathgall, Co. Wicklow, Raftery realised that this type of pottery most definitely dated to the Late Bronze Age. More recently Sheridan, in her paper on Irish Neolithic pottery suggested the possibility of Class II ware actually representing Grooved Ware (1995, 17). Sheridan pointed out the difficulties in accepting the identification of "Lough Gur Class II pottery" as being contemporary with Class I (early Neolithic) and Class Ia (middle Neolithic) wares. Although accepting that coarse flat-based pottery

(Class II) was securely stratified in pre-Beaker contexts, she went on to suggest "an identification of this material as Grooved Ware now seems reasonable in view of the discoveries elsewhere". That is also the conclusion that this author arrived at while carrying out research for an MA thesis (Roche 1995, 129). I will admit to approaching this site with the absolute confidence that Ó Ríordáin's Class II ware would prove to represent Grooved Ware pottery. This seemed a perfectly reasonable assumption in the then current climate where two recognized Grooved Ware sites had recently been uncovered, the timber circles with associated pottery at Ballynahatty, Co. Down, and Knowth, Co. Meath (Hartwell 1998, 32–44; Eogan and Roche 1997). My assumption was also encouraged by the fact that the earliest published reference for the presence of Grooved Ware in Ireland was in Ó Ríordáin's excavation at Grange (1951, 62–63). However, the pottery did not conform to this neat theory. Grooved Ware certainly formed part of the assemblage but the majority of the 'Class II' ware proved to be indisputably Late Bronze Age coarse ware (Roche 1995).

To date, Kelly (1978, 23–26) has presented the most virulent and convincing reassessment of the dating of coarse flat-based pottery, specifically the assemblages from Knockadoon, Lough Gur, Co. Limerick. This is an important paper as the pottery sequence devised by Ó Ríordáin at the Knockadoon sites directly influenced his interpretation of the pottery sequence at Grange. In this paper Kelly questions Ó Ríordáin's interpretation of the stratigraphical evidence from the Knockadoon excavations. His main thesis was that there was little evidence to prove that Class II dated to earlier than the Middle or Late Bronze Age and that because of the thinness of the soil and lack of well-defined stratigraphy on a site which obviously had a long history of habitation activity, a mixing of artefacts from different archaeological ages is not hard to understand. He even refers to sites that produced similar ware including hillforts, crannogs and ringforts (Kelly 1978, 26). He argues that the pottery sequence at Knockadoon was mainly based on the material from Site C (Ó Ríordáin 1954, 321–384), where stratification occurred, whereas elsewhere it was poorly defined with later activity confusing the situation. Kelly interpreted the yellow layer revealed in the 1949 excavations as actually separating the earlier Class I and Class Ia wares from the Class II ware. He also points out that apart from some Beaker and Food Vessel sherds the only dateable artefact found in association with Class II ware was a nail-headed pin, which was pointed out by Ó Ríordáin (1954, 361) himself as having parallels with a Late Bronze Age example from Heathery Burn Cave in Durham. Ó Ríordáin (1954, 323) seemed to have dismissed this find saying that nothing could be later than Beaker, despite further finds of another nail-headed pin, a socketed bronze axehead and a Class 1 razor from the above disturbed layer. Kelly points out that the majority of the small amount of pottery from the Neolithic house site (Site A)

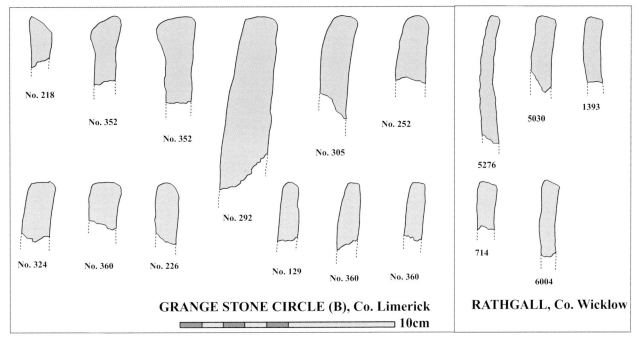

GRANGE STONE CIRCLE (B), Co. Limerick

RATHGALL, Co. Wicklow

10cm

Fig 15.3: Sections of Late Bronze Age coarse ware from Grange, Co. Limerick and Rathgall, Co. Wicklow.

belonged to Class 1. He goes on to say that pottery and later finds were also found in the upper unstratified levels. He suggests that it is not unlikely that the examples of Class II were incorporated because of later activity. Regarding sites showing evidence for successive habitation, for example Sites D and F, Kelly explores the theory that Class II ware overlay both Neolithic and Beaker material. At Site D, where two successive houses were found, Kelly points out that the associated pottery consisted almost exclusively of Class I and Class Ia. This again suggests that the small amount of Class II ware could have been incorporated by the digging of pit at a later stage of activity. Above this a Beaker level occurred over the early Neolithic level. Above this terrace walls and a stone house were constructed and Class II ware was found banked against the walls and also associated with the house. In addition associated evidence for metalworking in the form of moulds and crucibles was found. These included moulds for a looped palstave and a looped socketed spearhead, as well as another nail-headed pin.

Kelly's reassessment of Class II ware from the Knockadoon sites emphasised that the only secure associations were of Middle and Late Bronze Age date (Kelly 1978, 25). He also pointed out quite rightly that there was no mixing of Class II ware with other pottery types on single period sites (Sites B, G, H and F; Ó Ríordáin 1954), whereas Class II was found with other pottery types only on sites that also had Later Bronze Age levels.

The Grange coarse pottery

The Late Bronze Age sherds at Grange (Fig 15.3) range from a relatively fine degree of coarseness to extremely coarse sherds, varying from 8mm to 19.2mm thick. The surviving remains of up to twenty-one individual pots are represented. The rims are unexpanded and flat, unexpanded and rounded and internally bevelled. The finer wares are compact with relatively fine inclusions and an effort has been made to smooth the exterior surface. The coarser wares are friable and crumbly in texture with uneven surfaces where inclusions protrude through the surface. All are undecorated, flat-based and either barrel or bucket-shaped. Carbonised accretions are present on both the exterior and interior surfaces of many pots, showing that at some stage they were used for cooking, either of a domestic or ritual nature. Although much of the Late Bronze Age pottery at Grange is of finer quality than that found on most known Late Bronze Age sites, it is far from unique. Similar quality pots are present in the Rathgall hillfort assemblage (Fig 15.3) and from a burial at Carrig, Co. Wicklow (Grogan 1990, 12–14). Closely related pottery comes from several habitation sites on the Knockadoon peninsula, 500m to the east (Ó Ríordáin 1954; Grogan and Eogan 1987; Cleary 1995a).

In this paper I will demonstrate that the embanked stone circle at Grange represents a Late Bronze Age ritual site and that 'Class II' ware there is not Neolithic in date, and that wherever it occurs, whether at Knockadoon, Grange or elsewhere, it represents a regionalized version of either Middle Bronze Age domestic cordoned urns or Late Bronze Age coarse ware.

Grange Stone Circle: a re-interpretation

Because of the diversity of pottery types found on the site it is tempting to suggest that it was constructed in stages,

Pottery	Number of sherds	Old ground surface beneath bank	Turf layers within bank	Old ground surface within enclosure	Within sockets of orthostats
Early Neolithic carinated bowls	40	•	•	•	•
Middle Neolithic globular bowls	36	•		•	
Late Neolithic Grooved Ware	1160	•	•	•	
Final Neolithic Beaker	1231	•		•	•
Early Bronze Age Food Vessels	206	•		•	•
Middle Bronze Age cordoned urns	371	•		•	•
Late Bronze Age coarse ware	1073	•	•	•	•

Table 15.1: Distribution of pottery types at Grange, Co. Limerick. It is important to note that out of a total number of 4117 sherds, 2697 are only small fragments and crumbs. The above sherd count does not include the reconstructed Beaker vessel at present on display in the National Museum of Ireland.

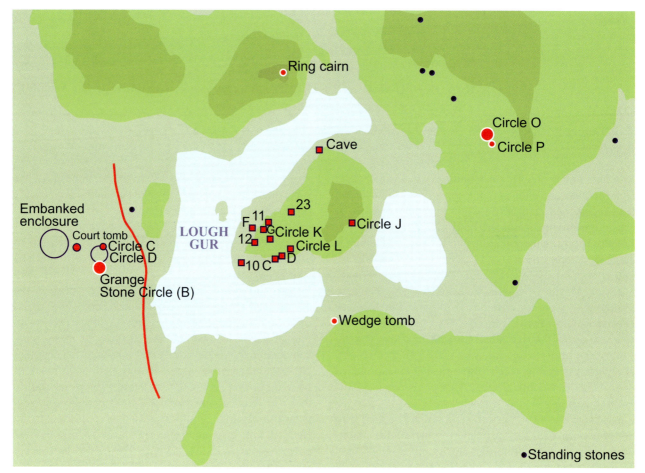

Fig 15.4: Location map of prehistoric sites in the immediate Lough Gur area.

initially the stone circle with the surrounding bank representing a later addition. However, it is difficult to argue against Ó Ríordáin's overall interpretation of the constructional sequence of the site, in that the erection of the monument appears to have been planned and constructed in a single, lengthy operation. His arguments are convincing, mainly that in order for the orthostats to remain upright the support of the bank was needed, as well as the sockets and packing stones. Excavation revealed that the sockets, and the packing stones behind the orthostats, penetrated well into the core of the bank

(Fig 15.2: section SV). In addition the absence of interference with the structure of the bank, which would have been necessary to insert the stones of the circle, points to a single planned procedure. The yellow fill that was spread over the interior of the site also had an important role to play in the overall construction as not only did it form an even surface but was also necessary to support small uprights and orthostats without sockets (Fig 15.2: lower section).

Thus, in accepting that the site represents a single phase of construction, what about the broad range of pottery types present and which type represents contemporaniety with the construction of the site? Over 4000 sherds (Table 15.1) were found during the excavation, mainly consisting of fragments. They represent Early Neolithic carinated bowls, Middle Neolithic globular bowls, Late Neolithic Grooved Ware, Final Neolithic Beaker, Early Bronze Age Food Vessels, Middle Bronze Age cordoned urns and Late Bronze Age coarse ware. In examining the distribution of the pottery (Table 15.1) it can be seen that all types are found in most contexts with the main concentrations tending towards the north western area of the site. Ó Ríordáin placed considerable emphases on the presence of Beaker pottery within the sockets of the orthostats as determining the date of the site. However, as almost all pottery types were found in sockets it seems more likely that sherds were merely incorporated while backfilling was taking place. The range of pottery types found at Grange spans a period of time of some 2600 years of activity. Clearly not all are contemporary with the construction of the site and as pottery was not found in the covering layer of yellow fill in the interior, the vital sherds in determining the date of construction are the most recent examples beneath the bank on the old ground surface. They are of course, coarse flat-based pots (Ó Ríordáin's Class II) dating to the Late Bronze Age. As they represent the latest type of pottery on the site, and if it is accepted that the site was constructed as a single operation, Grange must date to the Late Bronze Age period. The presence of earlier types of pottery on the site, especially the large quantity of Beaker sherds (although most are tiny fragments), obviously represents protracted activity in this special place. Although it is not possible to say whether the earlier evidence at Grange represents religious/ritual or secular events, one is inclined to suggest that the construction of the impressive Late Bronze Age enclosure was a result of an enduring tradition of a particular sacredness at this specific place.

Conclusions

Grange was a site of great importance, most likely of a ritual nature, from possibly as far back as the Early Neolithic period. A re-examination of the pottery and the structural history of the monument clearly illustrates that the site as we view it today was constructed during the Late Bronze Age period. The so-called Class II ware is comparable to pottery securely dated at hillforts such as Rathgall, Haughey's Fort, Co. Armagh, Mooghaun, Co. Clare, and Dun Aonghasa, Co. Galway (Raftery 1995; Mallory 1991; 1995; Grogan 1999; forthcoming; Cotter 1996). Although it has been accepted for some time that Class II ware at the Knockadoon sites represents Late Bronze Age pottery (Cleary 1995a; 1995b), it is still possible to read that this pottery, has a long history dating back to the Neolithic (Cleary 2000, 129), even though identical pottery has been securely dated to the Late Bronze Age period. Despite this general acceptance of

coarse flat-based pottery as representing part of the Late Bronze Age assemblage, the Late Neolithic date for Grange has not been challenged.

Grange is not, of course, an isolated site. Within the immediate vicinity on the west side of Lough Gur there are several other ritual monuments including a possible court tomb, an embanked enclosure, standing stones and two stone circles (Ó Ríordáin 1951, 37–40, fig. 1). This area was clearly a sacred place over a considerable period in prehistory and the residual Neolithic, Beaker and Early Bronze Age pottery incorporated into the fabric of the enclosure may represent ritual activity at this location. The human remains, although not apparently representing burials on site may reflect a role in funerary or dedication rituals for the Grange monument. The deliberate placing of human bone, especially skull or skull fragments, in Late Bronze Age wet and dry sites is a relatively common act in Ireland. Three skulls were placed under the floor of the house at Ballinderry 2, Co. Offaly, and a jawbone was found in a pit close to a ring-ditch at Adamstown, Co. Limerick (Cooney and Grogan 1994, 146–48). The deposition of human remains in Late Bronze Age contexts is also a known practice in Britain (Brück 1995, 245–264). The four small enclosures in the interior at Grange appear to be ringditches and are comparable to that at Monknewtown, Co. Meath, which has a phase of Middle to Late Bronze Age burials long post-dating the embanked enclosure (Sweetman 1976). It is unlikely, as Ó Ríordáin suggested, they date to the seventeenth century as such disturbance would surely have been detected in the overlying fill which had been spread over the interior surface during the Late Bronze Age. In addition to the habitation sites at Knockadoon, on the opposite side of the lake at Lough Gur there are two further sites with affinities to Grange that can certainly be dated to the Late Bronze Age (Fig 15.4). Circle P is a kerbed cairn that contained a pit with two Late Bronze Age coarse pots, each containing cremated bone. 30m to the north is Circle O, an embanked stone circle enclosing a kerbed cairn (Grogan and Eogan 1987). Although there are no associated finds at this site the similarity to both Grange and Circle P would indicate that it dates to the Late Bronze Age. The Late Bronze Age decorated shield found in the lake at Lough Gur is another example of the wider ritual activities in the landscape in this area during the Late Bronze Age (Waddell 1998, 242: ff. 105). Another site similar to Grange is Ballynamona (Hospital), Co. Limerick (O'Kelly 1943, 178, fig. 10), and further afield there are embanked stone circles at Castleruddery and Boleycarrigeen, Co. Wicklow (Grogan and Kilfeather 1997). Other related monuments with similar pottery include the ceremonial enclosures at Lugg, Co. Dublin (Kilbride-Jones 1950), and Johnstown, Co. Wicklow (Fitzpatrick 1998).

There can no longer be any doubt that plain coarse flat bottomed pottery is securely dated to the Late Bronze Age and is identified at a selection of securely dated sites of this period. It is time to remove Grange and related monuments from the Final Neolithic henge tradition and to regard the embanked stone circles as a Late Bronze Age phenomenon.

Acknowledgements

I wish to express my thanks to Eoin Grogan for his many helpful comments and to Barry Raftery for allowing me to refer to the Rathgall pottery assemblage. Part of this research was funded by the Irish Research Council for the Humanities and Social Sciences.

Bibliography

Brück, J. 1995 A place for the dead: the role of human remains in Late Bronze Age Britain. *Proceedings of the Prehistoric Society* **61**, 245–277.

Case, H. 1961 Irish Neolithic Pottery: distribution and sequence, *Proceedings of the Prehistoric Society* **27**, 174–233.

Cleary, R.M. 1995a Later Bronze Age Settlement and Prehistoric Burials, Lough Gur, Co. Limerick, *Proceedings of the Royal Irish Academy* **95**C, 1–92.

Cleary, R.M. 1995b Irish Late Bronze Age pottery: a preliminary technological assessment. *Kungl. Vitterhets Historie och Antikvitets Akademien Konferenser* **34**, 77–90. Stockholm.

Cleary, R.M. 2000 The potter's craft in prehistoric Ireland with specific reference to Lough Gur, Co. Limerick. In A. Desmond, G. Johnson, M. McCarthy, J. Sheehan and E. Shee Twohig (eds) *New Agendas in Irish Prehistory*, 119–134. Wordwell, Dublin.

Condit, T. and Simpson, D. 1998 Irish Hengiform Enclosures and Related Monuments: a Review. In A. Gibson and D. Simpson (eds) *Prehistoric Ritual and Religion,* 45–61. Sutton Publishing, Stroud.

Cooney, G. 2000 *Landscapes of Neolithic Ireland.* Routledge, London and New York.

Cooney, G. and Grogan, E. 1994 *Irish Prehistory: A Social Perspective.* Wordwell, Dublin.

Cotter, C. 1996 Western Stone Fort Project. Interim Report 1994, *Discovery Programme Reports* **4**, 1–14. The Discovery Programme/Royal Irish Academy, Dublin.

Eogan, G. and Roche, H. 1997 *Excavations at Knowth 2.* Royal Irish Academy, Dublin.

Fitzpatrick, M. 1998 Johnstown South enclosure, Co. Wicklow. In I. Bennett (ed.) *Excavations 1997*, 199–200. Wordwell, Dublin.

Grogan, E. 1990 Bronze Age Cemetery at Carrig, Co. Wicklow, *Archaeology Ireland* **16**, 12–14.

Grogan, E. 1999 Excavations at Mooghaun South, 1995, Interim report, *Discovery Programme Reports* **6**, 125–130. The Discovery Programme/Royal Irish Academy, Dublin.

Grogan, E. and Eogan, G. 1987 Lough Gur excavations by Seán P. Ó Ríordáin: further Neolithic and Beaker habitations on Knockadoon, *Proceedings of the Royal Irish Academy* **87**C, 299–506.

Grogan, E. and Kilfeather, A. 1997 *Archaeological Inventory of County Wicklow.* Office of Public Works, Dublin.

Harbison, P. 1988 *Pre-Christian Ireland: From the First Settlers to the Early Celts.* Thames and Hudson. London.

Hartwell, B. 1998 The Ballynahatty Complex. In A. Gibson and D. Simpson (eds) *Prehistoric Ritual and Religion*, 32–44. Sutton Publishing, Stroud.

Kelly, E. 1978 A Reassessment of the Dating Evidence for Knockadoon Class II pottery, *Irish Archaeological Research Forum* **V**, 23–26.

Kilbride-Jones, H. 1950 The excavation of a composite Early Iron Age monument with "Henge" features at Lugg, Co. Dublin, *Proceedings of the Royal Irish Academy* **53**C, 311–32.

Mallory, J. 1991 Excavations at Haughey's Fort: 1989–1990, *Emania* **8**, 10–26.

Mallory, J. 1995 Haughey's Fort – Macha's Other Twin, *Archaeology Ireland* **31**, 28–30.

O'Kelly, M.J. 1943 A Survey of the Antiquities in the Barony of Small County, County Limerick. Part II, *North Munster Antiquarian Journal* **4**, 169–84.

O'Kelly, M.J. 1989 *Early Ireland: An Introduction to Irish Prehistory.* Cambridge University Press. Cambridge.

Ó Ríordáin, S.P. 1951 Lough Gur Excavations: The Great Stone Circle (B) in Grange Townland, *Proceedings of the Royal Irish Academy* **54**C, 37–74.

Ó Ríordáin, S.P. 1954 Lough Gur Excavations: Neolithic and Bronze Age Houses on Knockadoon. *Proceedings of the Royal Irish Academy* **56**C, 297–459.

Raftery, B. 1969 Freestone Hill, Co. Kilkenny: an Iron Age hillfort and Bronze Age cairn, *Proceedings of the Royal Irish Academy* **68**C, 1–108.

Raftery, B. 1995 The Conundrum of Irish Iron Age Pottery. In B. Raftery (ed.) *Sites and Sights of the Iron Age*, 149–156. Oxbow Monograph **56**, Oxford.

Roche, H. 1995 *Style and Context of Grooved Ware in Ireland.* Unpublished MA thesis. University College Dublin.

Sheridan, A. 1995 Irish Neolithic pottery: the story in 1995. In I. Kinnes and G. Varndell (eds) *'Unbaked Urns of Rudely Shape': Essays on British and Irish Pottery for Ian Longworth*, 3–21. Oxbow Monograph **55**. Oxford.

Sweetman, P.D. 1976 An Earthen Enclosure at Monknewtown, Slane, Co. Meath, *Proceedings of the Royal Irish Academy* **76**C, 25–72.

Waddell, J. 1998 *The Prehistoric Archaeology of Ireland.* Galway University Press, Galway.

16. Goldener Zierrat, Goldblechkalotten und Goldblechkegel der Bronze- und Urnenfelderzeit Alteuropas

Peter Schauer

"Had the Irish monarchs or provincial kings crowns?" Diese Frage stellte der Vizepräsident der Royal Irish Academy, Sir William R. Wilde 1862 sich und der wissenschaftlichen Gemeinschaft[1] anhand einer 1692 gefundenen Goldblechkalotte, die 1723 in der englischen Übersetzung von G. Keatings (1570–1644) "History of Ireland" abgebildet wurde.[2] Die wissenschaftliche Frage danach, ob Angehörige sozialer Führungsschichten der Bronze- und Eisenzeit Mittel- und Westeuropas goldene "crowns" oder "hats" trugen, ist infolge einschlägiger Neufunde oder Neuerwerbungen unerwartet aktuell (Fig 16.1–16.2). In diesen Sachzusammenhang gehört auch goldener Zierrat als Schmuck zeremonialer Gewänder der europäischen Bronze- und Urnenfelderzeit, wie er kürzlich erstmals nahezu vollständig geborgen werden konnte[3] (Fig 16.1). George Eogan, der Jubilar, hat sich vor einigen Jahren selbst mit hier in Betracht kommenden Goldgegenständen und deren Herstellung in England und Irland ausführlich befaßt.[4]

Die seit dem 18. Jahrhundert als "crowns" oder "hats" bezeichneten irischen Goldblechfunde sind heute verschollen oder eingeschmolzen, so daß sich Sabine Gerloff bei dem Versuch "die traditionelle [sic!] Meinung, daß die Kegel kostbare Kopfbedeckung oder Kronen darstellen, wieder zu rehabilitieren"[5] auf zeitgenössisch gefilterte, quellenkundliche Überlieferung stützen mußte. Im wesentlichen basiert ihre Argumentation auf einer überlieferten und einer von ihr gemachten Beobachtung: Die Tatsache "daß sie [die Goldblechkalotten] von denen, die sie ursprünglich gesehen und beschrieben haben, als "Hüte" erkannt wurden[6] [kann] dafür [ins Feld geführt werden], daß die Bleche auf einen Kopf gepaßt haben". "Deren zentraler Mittelbuckel spricht gegen eine Verwendung als Schale, und die konische, spitz zulaufende Form (der Goldblechkalotte von Bearnán Eile [Devil's Bit], Irland) entspricht ebenfalls nicht den bauchigen Umrissen bekannter Goldschalen".[7] Über die Zeitstellung der irischen Goldblechkalotten ist nichts sicheres in Erfahrung zu bringen. Soweit die Ziermuster der sog. "Comerford crown" von Bearnán Eile (Devil's Bit Mountain), Co. Tipperary, in der englischen Übersetzung

von Keatings Werk von 1723 zutreffend wiedergegeben sind, könnte es sich um jungbronze- oder früheisenzeitliche Punzabdrücke handeln.[8] Mit Frau Gerloff kann man annehmen, daß die beiden Goldblechkalotten von Axtroki b. Escoriaza, part. Vergara (Prov. Guipúzcoa)[9] mit dem Randsaum nach unten, respektive auf der Mündung stehend zu denken sind, da nur so der eingepunzte Wasservogel-Zierstreifen als "unendliche" Figurenfolge erkennbar wird. Dagegen wird man der Verfasserin darin nicht zwangsläufig folgen wollen, daß die Goldblechkalotte von der "Playa de Leiro" bei Rianxo, part. Padrón, Prov. La Coruña[10] wegen des "auf der Spitze befindlichen Dorn, wie bei einer preußischen Pickelhaube, ... ohne Zweifel als eine Kopfbedeckung" identifiziert wird.[11] Einschlägige archäologische Befunde stellen diesen Deutungsvorschlag infrage. Goldblechkalotten und Goldblechbecher sind danach in "bergender" Funktion durchaus überliefert. Daher mag der Dorn auf der Goldblechkalotte von der "Playa de Leiro" ebenso auch als Halterung (Griffdorn) für eine Handhabe aus organischem Material gedient haben. In diesem Sinne lassen sich zumindest die folgenden Befunde deuten:

1) Der Goldbecher von Gölenkamp (Dm 14,0 cm, Gew. 255 g), Lkr. Grafschaft Bentheim, Niedersachsen[12] soll mit "schwarzer Erde" gefüllt gewesen sein, die nach naturwissenschaftlicher Analyse mit Knochenresten eines verbrannten Menschen vermischt gewesen ist.[13] Das Goldblechgefäß war über die Mündung eines groben Tongefäßes gestülpt, das mit "weißem Sand" gefüllt gewesen sein soll.

2) Die große Goldschale von Zürich-Altstetten[14] (Dm 25,0 cm, Gew. 910 g) lag "mit der Öffnung nach unten auf einem flachen Stein von 50 cm Durchmesser. Durch ein übergestülptes graues Tongefäß war sie von dem umgebenden humuskiesigen Erdreich geschützt. Das Innere der Schale soll mit einer staubartigen weißlichen Masse (Asche?) gefüllt gewesen sein.[15]

3) Die Goldblechgefäße von Albersdorf, Kr. Ditthmarschen, Schleswig-Holstein[16] – ein spitzbodiger (Dm 7,5 cm, Gew. 80 g) und ein kalottenartiger

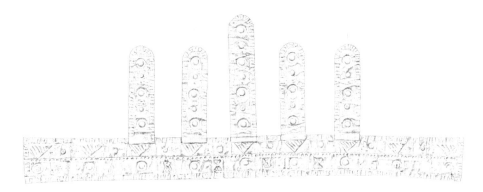

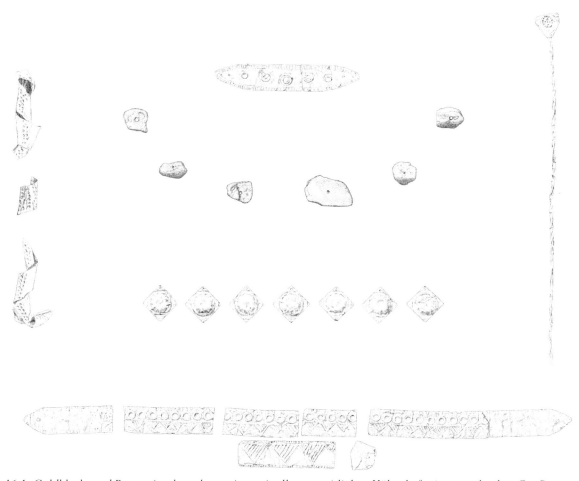

Fig 16.1: Goldblech- und Bernsteinschmuck aus einer mittelbronzezeitlichen Höhenbefestigung nahe dem Gut Bernstorf bei Kranzberg, Lkr. Freising, Oberbayern (nach R. Gebhard). M. 1:4.

Becher (Dm 9,5 cm, Gew. 25 g) lagen – der kalottenartige Becher über das andere Goldblechgefäß gestülpt – in einem mit Asche gefüllten und mit flachen Steinen umstellten Tongefäß.

4) Als kapselartige Behältnisse mit den Mündungen aufeinander gefügt, waren die Goldblechbecher von Unterglauheim, Lkr. Dillingen, Bayerisch Schwaben (Dm je 8,5 cm, Gew. 41 bzw. 51 g) und von Ladegård, Haderslev Amt, Dänemark[17] (Dm 10,2 bzw. 10,3 cm, Gew. 58,8 bzw. 59,9 g), die Substanzen aus organischen Materialien, darunter Brandreste von Knochen und Asche, einschlossen.

Auch der Goldblechkegel von Schifferstadt, Kr. Ludwigs-hafen, Rheinland-Pfalz, barg eine unbekannte Substanz, die "vielleicht mit Asche vermischt war". Er wurde aufrecht stehend auf einer Platte aus gebranntem Lehm in einer eigens hergerichteten Grube aufgefunden.[18]

Die von S. Gerloff herangezogenen Goldblechkalotten lassen sich also nicht ohne weiteres als kostbare Kopf-bedeckungen ("skull caps") definieren. Dagegen wurde eine derartige Deutung für den Goldblechkegel von Schifferstadt seit seiner Auffindung 1835 diskutiert.[19] Die dafür maßgeblichen Argumente sollen unter Berück-sichtigung der Berliner Goldblechkegel-Neuerwerbung (Fig 16.2) erneut knapp zusammengefaßt werden:[20]

Die Goldblechstärke des Schifferstadter Kegelschaftes beträgt zwischen 0,20 und 0,25 mm. Die Krempe ist dagegen erheblich dünner auf eine Stärke zwischen 0,08 und 0,13 mm getrieben.[21] Am Fuß der Schifferstadter Kalottenpartie war ein ehemals nicht sichtbarer stabilisier-ender, von Goldblech umhüllter Bronzereif eingearbeitet. Er wurde entfernt, um das ihn umlappende Goldblech auszuschmieden. Danach wurden zwischen Krempe und Kegelstumpf gegenüberliegend zweimal zwei Löcher wohl mit einem spitzen runden Dorn eingestochen.[22] Im Kegelinneren steht an dieser Stelle ein scharfgelappter Grat heraus, dessen Kanten im Restaurierungsbericht von E.Foltz (Römisch-Germanisches Zentralmuseum, For-schungsinstitut für Vor- und Frühgeschichte) als glanzlos: "matt" bezeichnet werden.[23] "Auch die Schmutzauflage verläuft stellenweise um die Kanten herum, so daß kein Zweifel darüber besteht, daß die Löcher alt sind und wohl schon in der Bronzezeit eingestochen wurden."[24] Alle Beobachtungen sprechen dafür, daß das Randblech des ursprünglich krempenlosen Schifferstadter Goldblech-kegels nach Entfernung des stabilisierenden Bronzereifes auf ein Drittel bzw. nahezu die Hälfte (0,08 – 0,13 mm) der ursprünglichen Materialstärke (0,20 – 0,25 mm) ausgeschmiedet worden ist. Die dabei aufgetretenen handwerkstechnischen Schwierigkeiten wurden bereits geschildert.[25]

Auch ist auf den frappanten Unterschied der Ver-zierungsmuster auf dem Kegel und auf der sekundär dünn ausgeschmiedeten Krempe hingewiesen worden.[26] Nach alldem halte ich es für ausgeschlossen, daß der Schiffer-stadter Kegel bereits vor der "Umarbeitung" eine Krempe aufgewiesen hat.[27]

Unter dem Eindruck des mittelbronzezeitlichen Gold-blechfundes nahe dem Gut Bernstorf bei Kranzberg, Lkr. Freising, Oberbayern[28] (Fig 16.1) scheint es mir überdies nicht ausgeschlossen, daß die von außen in den Schiffer-stadter Goldblechkegel paarweise eingestochenen Löcher eine Fixierung des Kultgegenstandes mittels Stiften aus organischem Material oder aus Metall – zweifellos nicht auf einem Menschenkopf – ermöglichen sollten.[29]

Da "die Ziermuster auf der Krempe [des Berliner Goldblechkegels] von unten im Positiv sichtbar sind"[30] vermutet W. Menghin, "der Huttragende habe sich von erhabener Warte aus gezeigt"[31] (Fig 16.2). Folgte man

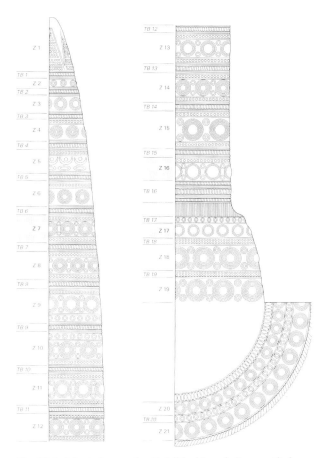

Fig 16.2: Musterkanon des Goldblechkegels "vermutlich aus Süddeutschland". Museum für Vor- und Frühgeschichte, Stiftung Preußischer Kulturbesitz Berl in (nach W. Menghin). M. 1:2.

dieser Argumentation, dann hätte der Betrachter auf den Träger des "Schifferstadter Beispiels [an dem] die Muster auf der Krempe allerdings oberseitig positiv zu sehen" [sind][32] herabgesehen.

Über den Berliner Goldblechkegel (Fig 16.2) läßt sich nun auch der sekundär ausgeschmiedete Krempenrand des Schifferstadter Exemplares rekonstruieren. Der Kö-niglich-Bayerische General-Commissär v. Stengel fand bei der Nachuntersuchung des Fundplatzes "Bruchstücke eines Kupferdrahtes auf, über welchen der Rand des Hutkranzes gerändert war, um ihm Festigkeit zu geben."[33] Mit Blick auf das Berliner Fundstück einerseits und auf den geglätteten "diagonal gerieften Krempenrand"[34] der Schifferstadter Goldtreibarbeit andererseits wird man annehmen dürfen, daß deren Krempenblech einst einen tordierten Bronze(?)ring umhüllte (dessen Reste nach der Auffindung des Objektes entfernt worden sind bevor der Krempenrand dann "geglättet" wurde).

Im Falle der beiden Goldblechkegel von Avanton und Ezelsdorf[35] muß entgegen W. Menghin[36] offen bleiben, ob die beiden Goldarbeiten ehemals "Krempen" aufwiesen. Im Falle des Avantoner Exemplares gibt es dafür nicht den geringsten Anhaltspunkt und beim Ezelsdorfer Fund-stück tragen die dafür beigezogenen Nachweise nicht.[37]

W. Menghin ist insoweit zuzustimmen, daß wohl auch verzierte Goldblechstücke an der Kegelbasis des Ezelsdorfer Fundstückes vor der Vergrabung des Gegenstandes entlang einer horizontalen Linie im Blech abgeschnitten worden sind.[38]

Es trifft auch zu, daß eine 4,5 mm lange und 0,019 mm[!] dünne Goldfolie einst ein Bronzestäbchen von 32 mm Länge und noch 2,8 mm x 1,4 mm Stärke, das an einem Ende flach ausgeschmiedet ist, ummantelte.[39] Vier weitere Goldflitterstückchen (0,019 mm dünn) werden eine ähnliche Funktion erfüllt haben, ohne jedoch zum 0,078 mm starken Kegelgoldblech zu gehören. Es gibt keinerlei Anhaltspunkte dafür, daß das Bronzestäbchenfragment und die Goldfolienstückchen (0,019 mm!) als Reste "der verlorenen Hutkrempe des Goldblechkegels von Ezelsdorf"[40] aufzufassen sein könnten.

Für einschlägige Deutungsversuche darf daher festgehalten werden:

1) Trotz "Kopfgrößendurchmesser" und "Pickelhauben"-Dorn lassen sich keine verläßlichen Beweise dafür beibringen, daß Goldblechkalotten von sozial Führenden der Bronze- und Urnenfelderzeit im Rahmen kultischer Handlungen getragen worden wären. Goldblechkalotten bedecken u.a. nach überlieferten archäologischen Befunden vielmehr organische Substanzen.

2) Der Goldblechkegel von Schifferstadt wurde erst im Zuge einer "Überarbeitung" mit einer hutartigen geränderten Krempe versehen und dürfte in beiden Fassungen allenfalls einen Pfahl oder ein menschengestaltiges Holz(?)bildwerk (vgl. Befund von Bernstorf) geziert haben.

3) Es gibt keine Anhaltspunkte dafür, daß die Goldblechkegel von Avanton und Ezelsdorf je mit "Krempen" ausgestattet gewesen wären.

4) Der Goldblechfund von Bernstorf, Gde. Kranzberg, Lkr. Freising, Oberbayern, (Fig 16.1) macht erstmals anikonische oder menschengestaltige, geschmückte, hölzerne(?) (und andere organische Materialien?) Kult- und/oder Zeremonial- bzw. Pfahlbildwerke mindestens seit der mittleren Bronzezeit Mitteleuropas wahrscheinlich. Die Deutung goldenen Zierrates, von Goldblechkalotten und der Goldblechkegel der Bronze- und Urnenfelderzeit wird dadurch erheblich erweitert.

Der Schifferstadter, Ezelsdorfer und der Berliner Goldblechkegel (Fig 16.2) sind ehemals aufrecht stehend vergraben worden, wie die Befundrekonstruktionen ergeben haben. Nach dem ursprünglichen Erhaltungszustand zu urteilen, muß das Berliner Exemplar gefüllt vergraben worden sein, vom Schifferstadter Kegel ist überliefert, daß "an Ort und Stelle noch Bruchstücke von der Erde zu finden war, womit der Kopf des Hutes ...... gefüllt war. Vielleicht ist diese Erde auch mit Asche vermischt."[41] Ähnlich wie manche kalottenartigen Gefäße und Schalen (s.S. 112ff) scheinen die aufrecht stehend

vergrabenen Goldblechkegel auch bergende Funktion wahrgenommen zu haben.

Wie R. Gebhard dargelegt hat, weisen die meisten der Bernstorf-Goldbleche ungefähr die Wandstärke der Goldblechkegel von Berlin (0,06 mm) und Ezelsdorf (0,078 mm) auf. Die Fragilität des Bernstorfer goldenen Zierrats und daran nachgewiesene Brandspuren ließen den Autor vermuten, daß es sich um die "Schmuckausstattung eines lebensgroßen Bildwerkes handelt, die nach einem Brandereignis rituell vergraben wurde.[42] In diesem Zusammenhang wäre auch eine entsprechende Deutung für die späturnenfelderzeitlichen Goldkegel zu überlegen: als Bekrönung oder Hut einer Göttergestalt."[43] Auf mögliche Vorbilder für solche Bildwerke, auch aus Holz, menschengestaltig oder anikonisch aus dem ägäischen Raum während minoisch-mykenischer bis archaischer Zeit wies er in diesem Zusammenhang hin.

Freilich sind mit goldenem Zierrat geschmückte Holzfiguren aus der Bronzezeit Mitteleuropas bislang unbekannt.[44] Aus England und aus dem früheisenzeitlichen Italien gibt es aber immerhin bemerkenswerte hölzerne Bildwerke, die an jungbronze- und früheisenzeitliche Kult- oder Ritualfiguren denken lassen. So werden fünf aus Kiefernholz roh herausgearbeitete Kriegerfiguren, die in einem hölzernen Bootsmodell verankert aus der Gezeitenmündung des Humber nahe Roos Carr, Holderness, Yorkshire, geborgen worden sind, aufgrund hölzerner Miniatur-Rundschilde in die jüngere Bronzezeit (10.–8. Jh. v. Chr. Geburt) datiert. Eines der Bildwerke wies eine Augeneinlage aus Quarzitkiesel auf.[45] Ähnliche Bootsmodelle mit bronzenen Figuren liegen aus dem jüngerbronzezeitlichen Nordischen Kreis im westlichen Ostseeraum z.B. von Fårdal, Nordjütland, Dänemark[46] und Grevensvaenge, Seeland, Dänemark[47] (wohl Periode V nach O. Montelius) vor.

Die Augen des kleinen Frauenbildnisses von Fårdal sind mit Goldblech belegt und damit wie im Falle des einen Kriegerbildnisses von Roos Carr, Holderness, stark betont ("göttlicher Blick").[48] Als Miniaturausgaben von Kultfiguren mit betonter Augendarstellung dürfen auch die beiden Männerbildnisse mit Hörnerhelmen und großen Kultäxten von Grevensvaenge, Seeland,[49] gelten.

Daß die Sitte, hölzerne Kultfiguren zu verfertigen in Alteuropa weit älter ist, als die jüngere Bronzezeit, belegt ein androgynes Eschenholzbildwerk aus Somerset, England, das J. Coles als "neolithic god-dolly" bezeichnet und seinerzeit in das jüngere Neolithikum bzw. in die Kupferzeit (14C-Datum einer darüberliegenden Holzplanke im Moor: 2890 BC ± 100) datiert hat.[50] Es handelt sich wohl um das noch 15,5 cm hohe Oberteil einer Pfahlfigur, die kopfüber in den Morast eines Moor-Bohlenwegunterbaues gerammt war.

Für uns soll es als *pars pro toto* der Vielzahl von unbekannt gebliebenen weil aus organischen Materialien gefertigten und daher vergangenen, metallzeitlichen Ritual- und Kultbilder jeder Größe gelten.

R. Gebhard hat im Zusammenhang seines Deutungsvorschlages für den Bernstorfer Goldfund (Fig 16.1) auf Vorbilder für mögliche mitteleuropäische Kultbilder der Bronze- und Urnenfelderzeit u.a. aus dem ägäischen Raum verwiesen, der mit den Küstenregionen Westasiens und insbesondere dem hethitischen Großreich während mykenischer Zeit in Kontakt stand.[51]

In der hethitischen Religiosität und der Vorstellung von Tod und Jenseits spielt das eigens verfertigte Ritualbildnis des verstorbenen Königs, wie uns die von H. Otten übersetzten Tontafelaufzeichnungen aus der Büyük-kale-Burg (Ausbauzeit des 13. Jhs. v. Chr. Geburt) der Reichshauptstadt Bogazköy mitteilen, während der vierzehntägigen Toten- und Trauerfeier eine besondere Rolle:[52] Am Morgen nach der Einäscherung des Toten werden am Verbrennungsplatz die Umrisse eines menschlichen Körpers mit Früchten (Rosinen, Oliven) ausgelegt. In diese Körperkontur werden unbekannte Substanzen eingebracht und es wird Bier hinzugegossen.

Am siebten Tag der Bestattungsfeierlichkeiten wird von einem wohl aus dauerhaftem Material verfertigten Sitzbild des Toten berichtet, das von Klagefrauen aus dem "Steinhaus" (Wohnstatt des Toten während der Feiern) geleitet und auf einen Wagen gesetzt wird, wobei umfangreiche Opfer dargebracht werden.

Am achten und neunten Tag des Totenrituals wird mit dem Bild des Toten verfahren wie mit seinen verbrannten Gebeinen: es wird vom Wagen genommen und in ein bereits errichtetes Zelt verbracht, wo es – wohl prächtig geschmückt – auf einen goldenen Sessel gesetzt wird. Reiche Opfer schließen sich vor dem Bild an. Am Abend wird zusätzlich ein Bild des Toten aus Früchten gemacht.

Wiederum mit reichen Opfern vor dem Ritualbild des Toten beginnt der zwölfte Tag. Es wird auf einen Wagen gesetzt, hinter dem Klagefrauen wie bei einem Leichenzug schreiten und an einen anderen Ort gebracht. Am dreizehnten Tag werden dem Sitzbild des Verstorbenen Brote in den Schoß gelegt und der Tote wird darum gebeten, seinen Nachfolgern nicht zu zürnen und ihnen gewogen zu sein. Gleichfalls am dreizehnten Tag findet eine Kulthandlung statt mit sogenannten Lahanzana-Vögeln, wohl im spirituellen Sinne Mittler zwischen der Götterwelt und den Menschen. Lebende Lahanzana-Vögel werden durch ein Fenster in das "Steinhaus" hineingehalten.

Für die Deutung des Goldblechfundes von Bernstorf (Fig 16.1) z.B. dürften die ausgeführten Ritualhandlungen mit künstlich aus Wolle, Teig oder Holz hergestellten Lahanzana-Vogelbildnissen von Interesse sein: 10 davon sind teilweise mit Silber plattiert, bei fünfen sind die Köpfe mit Gold belegt. Die Vogelbildnisse werden unter Wehklagen verbrannt und das sie schmückende Gold und Silber wird anschließend im "Steinhaus" deponiert. Ob mit dem zweifellos kostbar bekleideten und geschmückten Sitzbild des Toten ebenso verfahren wurde, läßt sich der fragmentarischen hethitischen Tontafeltext-Überlieferung nicht entnehmen.

Auch an den Bernstorf-Befunden scheinen sich rituelle Handlungen ablesen zu lassen bei denen vermutlich eine kostbar bekleidete und geschmückte, zumindest teilweise aus Holz (und Wachs?) gemachte Ritualfigur ohne ihren Goldschmuck verbrannt wurde. Die goldenen Trachtbestandteile sind anschließend in Lehm (Ton/Sandgemisch) eingebettet nahe einem Tor innerhalb der Höhenbefestigung von Bernstorf vergraben worden.[53]

In diesem Zusammenhang läßt sich erneut auf das hethitische Totenritual Bezug nehmen: Am Morgen nach der Einäscherung des Toten findet u.a. eine rituelle Handlung statt während der eine "weise" Frau die beiden Schalen einer Handwaage mit unterschiedlichen Substanzen füllt. In die eine Schale legt sie Silber, Gold und edle Steine, in die andere Lehm und Mörtel. Daran schließt sich ein Wechselgespräch zweier "weiser" Frauen an, das mit der Frage beginnt, wer den mit Namen gerufenen Toten herbeibringen soll.[54]

Da die Inhalte beider Waagschalen – einerseits Gold, Silber und Edelsteine, andererseits Lehm und Mörtel – im rituellen Geschehen der hethitischen Bestattungsfeierlichkeiten verwendet wurden, mußten sie anschließend zwingend der profanen Nutzung durch Versenkung, Vergrabung oder Vernichtung entzogen werden. Auch aus der bronzezeitlichen Ägäis ist, wie aus Westasien, die Sitte, geweihte Gegenstände mit Ton oder Lehm zu ummanteln und an heiligen Plätzen oder in Heiligtümern zu vergraben, geläufig.[55] Der Bernstorf-Befund belegt nun, daß dieser Brauch auch während der mittleren Bronzezeit Zentraleuropas geübt wurde.

Der oberbayerische Fundplatz läßt überdies eine, über weitere Zwischenstationen aufrecht erhaltene Verbindung zur spätbronzezeitlichen Ägäis erkennen: Zwei gravierte Bernsteinobjekte mit Schriftzeichen wurden – eingebettet in einem Lehm-Sandgemisch – im Herbst 2000, nur wenige Meter von dem früher geborgenen Goldblechfund entfernt, entdeckt (Fig 16.3).

Auf dem einen, 3,2 cm breiten, dreieckigen Bernsteinplättchen ist ein stilisiertes Männergesicht mit spitz zulaufendem Kinnbart eingeritzt. Auf der Rückseite des Bildträgers sind drei eingegrabene Piktogramme, darunter eine Speichenraddarstellung erkennbar. Bei dem zweiten, ovalen Bernsteinstück handelt es sich um eine Petschaft mit Siegelbild und rückseitiger Befestigungshandhabe. In deren Durchbohrung fanden sich noch zwei Goldblechreste, die vermutlich von der ehemaligen Aufhängevorrichtung an einem Faden oder einer Schnur, stammen. Das Siegelbild gliedert sich in zwei Zonen: im unteren Bildfeld erstreckt sich eine Darstellung über die gesamte Breite der Petschaft, die formal an das in Bernstorf aufgefundene Goldblechdiadem erinnert. Darüber sind drei Linear B-Schriftzeichen eingraviert, die in der Bedeutung >> pa-nwa-ti << oder im Siegelabdruck >> tinwa-pa << vermutlich eine Namensnennung, zu lesen sind.[56]

Auch die Ergebnisse der Röntgenfluoreszenzanalysen des Bernstorfer Goldes verweisen auf Westasien, das östliche Mittelmeergebiet oder die Ägäis als Ursprungsregionen des Rohmaterials bei dem es sich um nahezu

1   2a   2b

Fig 16.3: Zwei gravierte Bernsteinobjekte (1–2 a.b) mit Schriftzeichen aus einer mittelbronzezeitlichen Höhenbefestigung nahe dem Gut Bernstorf bei Kranzberg, Lkr. Freising, Oberbayern (nach. R. Gebhard u. K.H. Rieder). M. 1:1.

reines Gold handelt.[57] Um diesen Reinheitsgrad erreichen zu können, mußte das Gold mittels der sogenannten Zementation unter Zugabe u.a. von Salz geschieden werden, ein Verfahren das nach allem was die Rohstoff-forschung darüber weiß, nicht in Mitteleuropa zuhause war, wo geringfügig "verunreinigtes" Fluß- oder Berggold verarbeitet worden ist.

Bezogen auf die jüngst vorgebrachten, einlinigen Deutungsvorschläge für Goldblechkegel und –kalotten als zeremonielle Kopfbedeckungen von "bronzezeitlichen Priesterkönigen", die "als Herren der Zeit" verehrt worden seien, kann nicht genug darauf hingewiesen werden, daß Ritus und Kultgeschehen aus komplexen Prozessen von Kognition und Traditionsbewußtsein erwachsen. Sie sind ihrem Wesen nach zwangsläufig vieldeutig, zumal dann, wenn sie aus der Dürftigkeit einschlägiger, aufgrund von Überlieferungsbedingungen vielfach gefilterter archäo-logischer Quellen erschlossen werden sollen.

Dem Befund von Bernstorf kommt deshalb in dieser Hinsicht besondere Bedeutung zu. Erstmals scheinen dadurch Schlußfolgerungen auf die Existenz großer (lebensgroßer?) anikonischer oder menschengestaltiger ritueller Bildwerke aus organischen Materialien im bronzezeitlichen Mitteleuropa begründet zulässig. Bern-storf weist damit auch auf jüngere Kompositbildnisse im eisenzeitlichen Grabkult Italiens hin, deren körperähnliche Form aus Bronzeblech oder Holz geklittert war. Diese Oberkörperfiguren sind ehemals mit plastischen Model-lierungssubstanzen überfangen, mit Perücken versehen, bekleidet und geschmückt gewesen.[58] Aus villanova-zeitlichen Anfängen sind sie, wie die Kopfkapsel aus einem Grab von Marsiliana d'Albegna, Etrurien[59] zu erkennen gibt, herzuleiten und bilden dann eine der Grundlagen zur Entstehung der etruskischen Groß-plastik.[60]

Notes

1   P. Schauer, Die Goldblechkegel der Bronzezeit. Ein Beitrag zur Kulturverbindung zwischen Orient und Mitteleuropa. *Monographien Röm.-Germ. Zentralmus* 8 (1986) 2 (dort sind alle hier besprochenen Goldgegenstände, abgesehen von den Neufunden, abgebildet).

2   S. Gerloff, Bronzezeitliche Goldblechkronen aus Westeuropa. In: A. Jockenhövel (Hrsg.), *Festschrift für Hermann Müller-Karpe zum* 70. Geburtstag (1995) 161ff.

3   R. Gebhard, Der Goldfund von Bernstorf. *Bayer. Vorgeschbl.*

64, 1999, 1ff. – Ders., Der Goldfund von Bernstorf – Zubehör eines Kultbildes der älteren Bronzezeit. In: *Das arch. Jahr in Bayern* 1999 (2000) 22ff. – Ders. u. K.H. Rieder, Zwei gravierte Bernsteinobjekte aus Bernstorf. In: Ebd. 2000 (2001) 44ff. – L. Wamser u. R. Gebhard (Hrsg.), Gold. Magie-Mythos-Macht. Gold der Alten und Neuen Welt. *Ausstellungs-katalog der Archäologischen Staatssammlung München* (2001) 20 Abb. 11; 230ff. Nr. 40; 41. – R. Gebhard u. K.H. Rieder, Zwei bronzezeitliche Bernsteinobjekte mit Bild- und Schreftzeichen aus Bernstorf (Lkr. Freising). Germania 80, 2002, 115ff.

4   G. Eogan, The accomplished art. Gold and gold-working in Britain and Ireland during the Bronze Age (*c.* 2300-650 BC). *Oxbow Monograph* 42 (1994).

5   Gerloff a.a.O. (Anm. 2) 159.

6   Ebd. (Anm. 2) 164.

7   Ebd. (Anm. 2) 165.

8   Schauer a.a.O. (Anm. 1) 51.

9   S. Gerloff gibt als Fundort der Goldblechkalotten Atroxi an. Veröffentlicht sind die Goldgegenstände dagegen als Funde aus Axtroki, Prov. Guipúzcoa (vgl. Schauer a.a.O. [Anm. 1] 20,31,36-38,40,42, Taf. 40, 1-2. – V. Pingel, Die vorge-schichtlichen Goldfunde der Iberischen Halbinsel. *Madrider Forschungen* 17 (1992) 249 Nr. 97 Taf. 87, 1-2; mit älterer Lit. – Gerloff a.a.O. [Anm. 2] 173ff. Abb. 6; 7,1).

10   Schauer a.a.O. (Anm. 1) 34, 40, 51, 54 Taf. 40,3. – Pingel a.a.O.(Anm. 9), 309 Nr. N3 Taf. 98, 13. – Gerloff ebd. (Anm. 2) 175ff. Abb. 7,2

11   Gerloff a.a.O. (Anm. 2) 172.

12   W. Menghin u. P. Schauer, Der Goldkegel von Ezelsdorf. Kultgerät der späten Bronzezeit. Die vor- und frühgeschicht-lichen Altertümer im Germanischen Nationalmuseum Heft 3 (1983) 72f. Abb. 32-32a. – Schauer a.a.O. (Anm. 1) 54 Taf. 32,2.

13   J. Grüß, Ergebnisse der biologischen Archäologie. For-schungen und Fortschritte. Nachrichtenblatt der Deutschen Wissenschaft und Technik 15, 1939, 60f. – Schauer a.a.O. (Anm. 1) 54.

14   Menghin u. Schauer a.a.O. (Anm. 12) 125f. Abb. 56. – Schauer (Anm. 1) 54 Taf. 41,2.

15   Schauer (Anm. 1) 54.

16   Menghin u. Schauer a.a.O. (Anm. 12) 77ff. Abb. 34. – Schauer a.a.O. (Anm. 1) 52 Taf. 38,5.

17   Menghin u. Schauer a.a.O. (Anm. 12) 91ff. Abb. 39. – Schauer a.a.O. (Anm. 1) 54 Taf. 34,1.

18   Schauer a.a.O. (Anm. 1) 52.

19   Ders. ebd. (Anm. 1) 2ff., 24, 30, 45.

20   W. Menghin, Der Berliner Goldhut und die goldenen Kalend-arien der alteuropäischen Bronzezeit. *Acta Praehistorica et Archaeologica* 32, 2000, 31ff. (mit älterer Lit. S. 35 Anm. 20 und den einschlägigen Abbildungen). – Ders., Der "Berliner Goldhut". In: Wamser u. Gebhard (Hrsg.) a.a.O. (Anm. 3) 56ff.

21 Schauer a.a.O. (Anm. 1) 24.

22 Ebd. (Anm. 1) 3 Abb. 2;24.

23 Ebd. (Anm. 1) 80.

24 Ebd. (Anm. 1) 80.

25 Ebd. (Anm. 1) 24.

26 Ebd. (Anm. 1) 24.

27 Dagegen Menghin (2000) a.a.O. (Anm. 20) 67.

28 Vgl. Anm. 3.

29 Vgl. Anm. 2 und 20.

30 Menghin (2000) a.a.O. (Anm. 20) 67.

31 Ebd. (Anm. 30).

32 Menghin (2000) a.a.O. (Anm. 20) 68.

33 Schauer a.a.O. (Anm. 1) 24.

34 Menghin (2000) a.a.O. (Anm. 20) 50.

35 Schauer a.a.O. (Anm. 1) 26ff.

36 Menghin (2000) a.a.O. (Anm. 20) 51ff.

37 T. Springer, Der Goldkegel von Etzelsdorf-Buch – ein Meisterwerk bronzezeitlicher Goldschmiedekunst. In: *Götter und Helden der Bronzezeit* (1999) 177 Abb. 2. – Menghin (2000) a.a.O. (Anm. 20) 53ff.

38 Menghin ebd. (Anm. 20) 57f.

39 Schauer a.a.O. (Anm. 1) 82. – Menghin ebd. (Anm. 20) 56.

40 Menghin ebd. (Anm. 20) 56.

41 Schauer a.a.O. (Anm. 1) 2 Anm. 16.

42 Gebhard (1999) (Anm. 3) 17.

43 Ebd. (Anm. 42).

44 Ebd. (Anm. 42).

45 S. Piggott u. G.E. Daniel, *A picture book of ancient British art* (1951) Taf. 30. – J.V.S. Megaw, *Art of the European Iron Age: A study of the elusive image* (1970) No. 284. – Ders. u. D.D.A. Simpson, *Introduction to British Prehistory from the arrival of homo sapiens to the Claudian invasion* (1979) 322f. Abb. 6.42.2.

46 H.C. Broholm, Anthropomorphic Bronze Age Figures in Denmark. *Acta Archaeologia.* 18, 1947, 198 Abb. 4, a-b.

47 R. Djupedal u. H.C. Broholm, Marcus Schnabel og bronce-alderfundet fra Grevensvaenge. *Aarbøger* 1952, 44ff. Abb. 8-12.

48 Vgl. P. Schauer, Spuren orientalischen und ägäischen Einflusses im bronzezeitlichen Nordischen Kreis. *Jahrb. Röm.-Germ. Zentralmus.* 32, 1985, 123ff. Taf. 10,5; 16,4; 18,2; 19,1.4.

49 Schauer a.a.O. (Anm. 48) Taf. 10,5.

50 J. Coles, A Neolithic God-dolly from Somerset, England. *Antiquity* 42, 1968, 275ff. Taf. 40.

51 Gebhard (1999) a.a.O. (Anm. 3) 17. – Vgl. auch W. Helck, *Die Beziehungen Ägyptens und Vorderasiens zur Ägäis bis ins 7. Jahrhundert v. Chr.* (1979) besonders 150ff.

52 H. Otten, Hethitische Totenrituale. Deutsche Akademie der Wissenschaften zu Berlin. *Institut für Orientforschung* 37 (1958).

53 Gebhard (1999) a.a.O. (Anm. 3) 1ff.

54 Otten a.a.O. (Anm. 52).

55 Vgl. G. Zahlhaas, Orient und Okzident. *Ausstellungskatalog Prähist. Staatsslg.* 28 (1995) VIII-8. – Dies., In: Wamser u. Gebhard (Hrsg.) a.a.O. (Anm. 3) 232f. Nr. 42.

56 Gebhard u. Rieder (2000) a.a.O. (Anm. 3). – Wamser u. Gebhard (Hrsg.) a.a.O. (Anm. 3) 232 Nr. 41 mit Abb.

57 Gebhard (1999) a.a.O. (Anm. 3) 9f.

58 F. Prayon, Die Anfänge großformatiger Plastik in Etrurien. In: Archäologische Untersuchungen zu den Beziehungen zwischen Altitalien und der Zone nordwärts der Alpen während der Frühen Eisenzeit Alteuropas. *Regensburger Beiträge zur Prähistorischen Archäologie* 4 (1998) 191ff.

59 Prayon ebd. (Anm. 58) 200f. Abb. 10.

60 Ebd. (Anm. 59).

17. Hallstatt Fascination: 'Hallstatt' buckets, swords and chapes from Britain and Ireland

Sabine Gerloff

For nearly half a century, George Eogan's studies of the chronology (1964; 1974) and foreign relations (1990; 1995) of the Late Bronze Age in Ireland have contributed greatly towards our understanding of the significant role Ireland played not only within the Bronze Age of the Atlantic West, but also within the European Bronze Age as a whole. These contributions, together with his classic monographs on Irish swords (1965), later Bronze Age hoards (1983), Irish/British goldwork (1994) and socketed axes (2000), have influenced and facilitated future research on the material cultures of the Late Bronze Age not only in Ireland, but also in other parts of Europe. When, in the 1980s, the present writer was engaged in her research on Atlantic buckets and cauldrons, she, too, profited from George's vast knowledge and his kind personal assistance. Also, after this study had been submitted as a habilitation thesis in 1991, George acting as a referee, he continued giving valuable advice and suggested amendments for the final publication. As this is still with the publishers, the writer may be permitted to give here a brief summary of the origin, typology and chronology of Late Bronze Age buckets; a summary concerning the cauldrons of Leeds' (1930) Class A has appeared elsewhere (Gerloff 1986).

The present contribution, however, will not only treat the buckets, which until Hawkes and Smith's (1957) classic study were believed to be of Hallstatt or Etruscan origin, but will also discuss the origin of the Hallstatt swords of Gündlingen type, these being one of the characteristic features of the earliest Iron Age in Britain and Ireland. These so-called 'Hallstatt' swords are traditionally believed to have originated on the continent and been introduced to Britain and Ireland by invading Celtic warriors, a notion first proposed by Déchelette (1913, 723f). It was eagerly taken up in Britain and Ireland during the 1920s and 1930s, when, for instance, Crawford (1922, 27) and Peake (1922, 85ff) were followed by Evans (1931, 209), Kendrick and Hawkes (1932, 151f) and Mahr (1937, 395 ff), who all believed that invasions of Hallstatt 'sword bearers' were connected with the celticisation of the west during the close of the Bronze Age, which was

seen as contemporary with the Hallstatt period on the continent (*cf.* Savory 1948; Champion 1982; Waddell 1991). But first we shall discuss Atlantic 'Hallstatt' buckets. In his classic paper Leeds (1930, 24ff) connected their introduction in common with that of other Late Bronze Age types with movements of a "…..migrating folk, unquestionably Keltic who descended from the western alpine region on the east of England."

'Hallstatt' and 'Etruscan' buckets from Britain and Ireland, their history of research

John Evans, the founder of British Bronze Age studies and chronology, was the first to assign insular buckets and cauldrons to the Late Bronze Age. He realized that handle fragments from these large bronze vessels occasionally occurred in Late Bronze Age founders' hoards in England and Scotland. As most of these hoards also included flange-hilted, leaf-shaped swords and socketed axes, his type fossils of the Late Bronze Age, he was able to assign the hoards to that period (Evans 1881, 409ff, 469ff), which he believed to have lasted until the beginning of the Celtic Iron Age or La Tène period between 500 and 400 BC. Evans suggested that the conical buckets were probably earlier in date than the spheroidal cauldrons and compared the Dowris buckets to "identical bronze urns from the cemetery at Hallstatt, of which several appear to be of Etruscan fabric" (1881, 412). He did not, however, regard the Irish and British examples as actual imports, because he realized that their handle structures differed from those of their continental counterparts, and he argued that Irish or British smiths might have imitated the continental buckets. When connecting the Irish and British buckets with similar vessels found at Hallstatt, which in turn were derived from Etruria, Evans proposed views that were also to become fashionable on the Continent. Lindenschmit (1881), Müller (1897) and Montelius (1910) each proposed an ultimate Etruscan/ Italian origin, not only for the bronze vessels from Hallstatt, but also for most others known from central, northern and western Europe. This concept of Italian primacy was also advocated by Childe (1930, 231) when he declared Irish and British buckets to have been imported from Italy. In 1935 (160f) he described insular buckets as local hybrids of Italian/Hallstatt bodies and 'Hellenic' handles, the latter perceived as copies of tubular spool-like handle attachments of Greek cauldrons (*dinoi*) of the Geometric period, which Leeds (1930) believed to have been the prototypes of insular cauldrons of his Class A. In trying to trace the origin of insular buckets, Leeds, too, adhered to traditional beliefs, arguing that they were modelled on Etruscan and Hallstatt *situlae* and dated their beginnings to the second quarter of the seventh century BC (1930, 25f). As late as the middle of the twentieth century the concept of an Etruscan/Hallstatt origin was still proposed in the latest edition of Macalister's *The Archaeology of Ireland* (1949, 217), which stated that the buckets of the 'Hallstatt Culture' in Ireland were of 'North Italian origin'.

The concept of a Hallstatt period in Ireland was formulated by Armstrong in 1922 when he listed typical 'Hallstatt types' imported into Ireland, among them twenty-four bronze swords, one iron sword, seven winged chapes and seven buckets. His *The Early Iron Age or Hallstatt Period in Ireland*, published posthumously in 1924, provided the first comprehensive catalogue of all the Atlantic bronze vessels found in Ireland, updating Wilde's (1857–61) inventory, which had listed mainly the vessels in the collection of the Royal Irish Academy (today National Museum of Ireland) in Dublin. Armstrong accepted the current view that the 'bucket-shaped cauldrons' were probably imported and, following Evans (1881), he related them to similar vessels of ultimate Etruscan origin from the Hallstatt cemetery. Armstrong assigned buckets and cauldrons to the transitional period between the Bronze and Iron Ages, which he believed to be contemporary with the continental Hallstatt period. His most important contribution to the study of Atlantic bronze vessels, however, was his division of the cauldrons into two typological series, which formed the basis for Leeds' (1930) classic division into Classes 'A' and 'B', which is still valid today.

It was in Britain, and not on the continent, that the dominant role of Etruscan Italy in the origin of sheet-bronze vessels was first questioned. As early as 1924, in his *Villanovans and Early Etruscans* Randall-MacIver stated, "…it is impossible to credit the Etruscans with the invention of this remarkable technique. It is more natural to regard this entire new development of bronze working either as the spontaneous invention of native Villanovans or else the result of an inspiration derived from their neighbours in Central Europe or the Balkans" (1924, 26). He was, however, unable to cite any definite central or southeastern European prototypes for the Italian vessels. These were provided two years later by V. G. Childe (1926, 132; also 1929, 375 f), who proclaimed basins with cruciform or T-shaped handle-attachments (*Kreuzattaschenbecken*), small bronze cups, and decorated

bronze buckets of Type Hajdúböszörmény – all known from Bronze Age Hungary – to be ancestral to equivalent Iron Age vessels in Italy and central Europe. Childe did not, however, relate any of those Hungarian vessels to our Atlantic buckets and cauldrons, believing them, as stated above, to derive from the 'Etruscan situlae'.

Randall-MacIver's and Childe's theories were not immediately adopted on the continent. Åberg, in the first two volumes of his *Bronzezeitliche und früheisenzeitliche Chronologie* (1930 and 1931), still maintained Italian primacy. Only in the fifth volume did he come to regard Hungary and not Italy as the ultimate home of all European bronze vessels (Åberg 1935, 49ff). He illustrated and cited a small situla-shaped bucket in the Hungarian hoard from Kurd, which he dated to Montelius Period III, with similar bucket fragments found in the hoards of Privina Glava, Serbia, and Bizovac, Croatia, as possible prototypes for all Iron Age buckets and situlae (Åberg 1935, 54). It was to be Gero von Merhart who in 1952, in his classic paper *Studien über einige Gattungen von Bronzegefäßen*, firmly established the Danubian and early Urnfield background of nearly all sheet-metal vessels of both late Urnfield and early Hallstatt date. In that paper he was also the first to connect the Irish-British buckets with these Danubian buckets, which he coined 'Typ Kurd' (von Merhart 1952, 29ff). Von Merhart realized that most of the continental Urnfield 'Kurd buckets', which he assigned to the early Urnfield period of Ha A, were mainly found in Hungary and Romania, whereas the later Urnfield examples dated to Ha B, which are far fewer in number, occurred further west. His Iron Age examples of Ha C and Ha D were shown to have an even more westerly distribution, being absent altogether from Danubian southeast Europe and more frequently found in an area stretching from the foot of the southeastern Alps in the east to Ireland in the west and Italy in the south (von Merhart 1952, 32, map 5). Von Merhart placed all the Irish and British vessels in his latest group of Hallstatt Kurd buckets. He did so reluctantly, because on typological grounds he saw them as related more closely to the continental Urnfield examples than to the more angular-shaped Iron Age buckets. However, he did not feel competent to question the authority of Leeds, who had dated the insular buckets to the seventh century BC and connected them with the Hallstatt and Etruscan cultures of the continental Iron Age, a view still current in discussions of continental Iron Age buckets and *situlae* during the 1960s (Kimmig 1962–63, 90) and even 1970s (Desittere 1974, 130f). As these two vessel types are often confused, it is important to point out that the term '*situla*' was applied by von Merhart to – and should be reserved for – only those vessels which have a single mobile arc-shaped handle (*Bügelhenkel*), like the handle on a modern bucket (1952, pl. 16–21, 1–5). Merhart's buckets (*Eimer*) were distinguished by two fixed strap-shaped handle-carriers (*Bandhenkel*), often holding annular ring-handles (*ibid.*, pl. 21, 6–11.22) . Buckets appeared during the early Urnfield period and lasted into the Hallstatt period, whereas situlae appeared only in Ha C and continued into early La Tène (*ibid.*, 36.ff; also Kimmig 1962–63).

Hawkes, too, still advocated an Etruscan origin for insular buckets in 1947 (Dudley and Hawkes 1947, 10). Ten years later, however, influenced by von Merhart, Hawkes and Smith, in their classic paper (1957, 137ff), rejected the traditional theories of an ultimate Etruscan/Hallstatt origin for insular buckets and derived them instead from his group of Late Urnfield vessels. They were the first to realize that insular buckets can be divided into two distinct series, the 'Kurd bucket' with continental-style strap-handles *(Bandhenkel)* and the 'native bucket' with ribbed tube-shaped attachments, like those on insular cauldrons. Hawkes and Smith believed the Kurd buckets, characterized by their continental handle-attachments and base-plates, were imported into Britain towards the middle of the eighth century BC, being earlier in origin than Class A cauldrons and native buckets, which they believed appeared around 700 BC. Although Hawkes and Smith must have realized that the most similar Urnfield buckets – from southeastern Europe – the progenitors of their first group, were dated much earlier than 700 BC, they could not assign a similar date to the insular Kurd buckets, as there was no new evidence which could connect them with a period before the latest phase of the insular Bronze Age, known now as the Dowris phase in Ireland (Eogan 1964) and Ewart Park in Britain (Burgess 1968). Hawkes and Smith's theories on the origin and date of insular buckets were soon adopted and incorporated in more recent discussions of these vessels (Eogan 1964, 299f; Burgess 1969; O'Connor 1980, 192f).

One of the most recent discussions of insular buckets and cauldrons appeared in 1987, when C. S. Briggs (with M. Holland) provided an updated list of insular buckets. He also discussed the Kurd buckets on the continent, showing their most western occurrences on his distribution map of continental buckets and cauldrons (Briggs 1987, 162). In his group of comparable buckets from the western part of the continent, he included some vessels which should not be classified as Kurd buckets, but which belong to the later types of the *Rheinische Situla* and related vessels, as defined by Kimmig (1962–63) and Bouloumié (1977), dated mainly to Ha D and early La Tène. When relating the continental buckets to those from Ireland and Britain, Briggs noticed considerable differences both in construction and deposition, believing the continental examples to have come mostly from rich Hallstatt burials (Briggs 1987, 172). He presumably referred to the continental Iron Age buckets and *situlae*, which do indeed come from burials. He does not, however, mention the find-circumstances of the continental Urnfield buckets. Those – apart from the small Kurd bucket found at Hart in Bavaria (Müller-Karpe 1956; Jacob 1995, no. 305) – have never been found in burials, but, like our insular buckets, were either found singly or came from 'scrap' or founders' hoards. Briggs, therefore, found it difficult to relate the continental buckets to those from Ireland and

Britain or to accept the insular Kurd buckets as true imports and hence he concluded that, "while enjoying a common family origin, the insular bucket series is largely developed indigenously" (Briggs 1987, 165). He rejected Hawkes' terminology and twofold classification into 'imported' and 'native' buckets and proposed labelling the two series A and B. As to the origin of insular bronze vessels, he believed them, in common with other early European sheet-bronze artefacts, to have been modelled on leather prototypes.

Around the time Briggs published his article, the present writer gave a preliminary report on her studies (Gerloff 1986), in which she related the British Kurd buckets to the larger variant of Kurd buckets, Patay's (1990, 37–40) Variant Hosszúpályi (Fig 17.1). This Variant and not the smaller Kurd buckets were seen to be the immediate ancestors of insular buckets (below). The ultimate origin of the west European and Danubian multi-sheet bronze buckets was seen in Mycenaean Greece, where such vessels were already known from the Shaft-Grave period (Matthäus 1980, nos 1–13) and where single-sheeted cauldrons – often attached to a tripod and similar in shape and size to both south-east European cauldrons and early Insular ones – appeared in Late Mycenaean times between the fourteenth and thirteenth century BC (Matthäus 1980, nos 74–78). At Mycenae, too, we find the earliest prototypes for multi-sheet buckets, mostly dating to the Shaft Grave period (Matthäus 1980, nos 189–204). These Mycenaean vessels were not, of course, regarded as the immediate forbearers of our Atlantic ones, only as their ultimate ancestors. In contrast to previous views, the route of contact between the Mediterranean and the far west of Europe was not seen to have been through the western Mediterranean, but to have led across the continent, *via* the Danube and across France to southern Britain and Ireland. The latter has produced Class A cauldrons only of more advanced type, the earliest Class A vessels being confined to southern England. Although Ireland has produced the greatest number of complete multi-sheet Atlantic vessels, it cannot be regarded at present as the home of the earliest vessels, nor was it necessarily their main production centre. The scarcity of complete vessels in other parts of Atlantic Europe, such as southern Britain, Atlantic France and Iberia, should perhaps be viewed as reflecting different deposition practices there and need not necessarily represent the true currency of such vessels in those areas during the Late Bronze Age. Only very recently two Irish/British-style Class A cauldrons have come to light in western France. A fragmentary Class A0 vessel was found next to a Rosnoën hoard at Saint-Ygeaux in Brittany (Fily 2003) and a single find of an intact Class A 2 cauldron, apparently with an iron rim enforcement was found at Ouzilly-Vignolle, Vienne (Pautreau and Soyer 2001–2002). Whereas the former belongs to the very beginning of the Late Bronze Age, the latter – with a counterpart in a handle fragment of a Class A2 cauldron in the Vénat

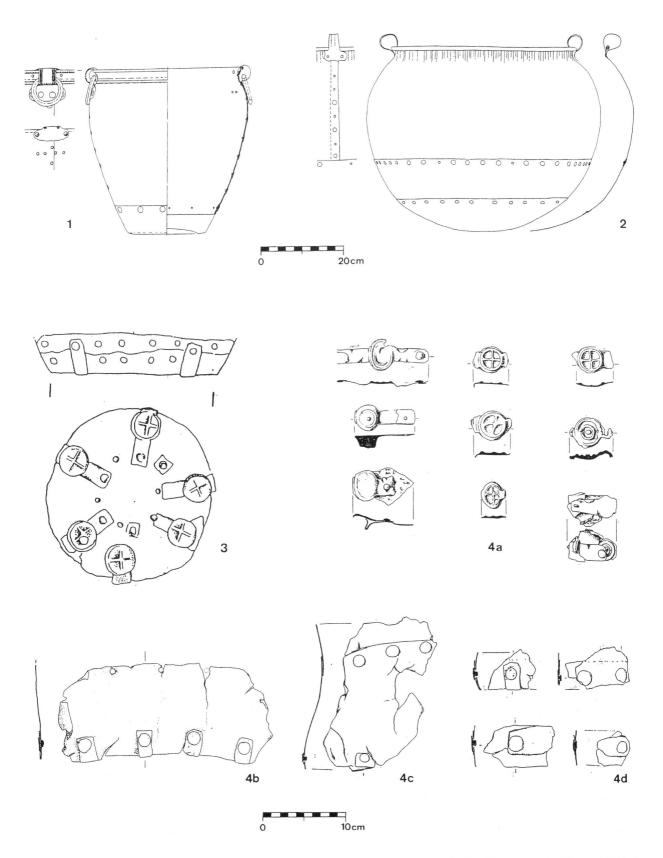

Fig 17.1: Late Bronze Age buckets and cauldrons from south-east Europe. 1. Hosszúpályi, Hungary (after Patay 1990). 2. Sipbachzell, Austria (after Höglinger 1996). 3. Buza, Romania (after Soroceanu and Buda 1978). 4a–d. Škocjan, Croatia (after Teržan and Mihovilič forthcoming). Scale: Fig 17.1.1–2: 1:8. Fig 17.1.3–4: 1:4.

hoard (Gerloff 1986, 100, pl. 12ii,d) – belongs to its very end.

Whereas in 1986 we were unable to cite very close or securely-dated Danubian parallels for our earliest insular cauldrons of Types Colchester and Shipton-on-Cherwell, we now have a very good prototype in a multi-sheet cauldron, discovered in 1987 at Sipbachzell in Austria (Höglinger 1996). This cauldron (Fig 17.1,2), – which in common with our insular vessels of Class A – originally consisted of a dished bottom-sheet and two wall-sheets. Its base was later repaired with a fourth large dished sheet. The cauldron contained a founders' hoard of the early Urnfield period. The intentionally broken bronzes included early Urnfield types, as for instance, 300 sickle fragments of Type Uioara, fragments of flange-hilted swords of Type Nenzingen, of median-winged axes, of knives of Baiersdorf and Riegsee types, as well as sheet fragments from further vessels including strap handles and possibly of body armour all dating to Bronze D/Ha A1. This dating confirms that proposed by the writer in 1986 for our earliest insular cauldrons of Type Colchester, which were assigned to the early Penard phase. This chronology early in the Late Bronze Age can now be substantiated by a radiocarbon date obtained from wooden remains inside the socket of the fleshook from Feltwell, Norfolk, discovered inside a Type Colchester cauldron. The wooden sample (OxA-10859) was dated to 3013±36 BP, calibrating with 95% probability to 1390–1120 cal BC (Bronk Ramsey *et al*. 2002, 41). In contrast to our earliest cauldrons, the initial appearance of insular buckets is still difficult to establish, nor is it certain whether they should be regarded as imports or – in common with our earliest cauldrons (Type Colchester and Shipton: Gerloff 1986, 88 ff, figs 6–7) that have insular multiple-ring handle-carriers – were modelled on Danubian prototypes.

The two Atlantic bucket series

Hawkes and Smith (1957) introduced the term 'Atlantic' when discussing insular cauldrons, they did, however, not extend this term to insular buckets, as they believed their first group of 'Kurd buckets' to have been imported from southeastern Europe. For the sake of convenience, however, we should also label all multi-sheet insular buckets as 'Atlantic', in order to distinguish them from closely related continental examples. Atlantic cauldrons and buckets show a similar distribution pattern (Gerloff 1986, fig. 12), having been found in comparable circumstances in Ireland, Britain and Atlantic France. Also, in common with cauldrons, most buckets from Ireland, Wales and to some extent those found in northern Britain, were deposited complete, whereas the great majority of examples from southern Britain and nearly all from France were deposited as fragments. The intact examples, with the possible exception from Dowris, were always deposited singly and have come from wet places like rivers, lakes, bogs or fens, whereas the great majority of

fragments have come from founders' hoards. There are as yet no finds of complete Atlantic buckets from the Iberian Peninsula, although it is possible that some large sheet fragments in the museum of Porto which show rows of rivets-holes may have been part of a bucket (Schubart 1961, 45, fig. 13 D1-2) and that some of the numerous small vessel fragments found on the Peninsula may have been part of buckets, rather than of cauldrons.

In common with cauldrons of Class A, Atlantic buckets are invariably constructed of three sheets, which consist of a tub-shaped base and two wall-sheets, the latter being joined by vertical seams placed under each of the two handle attachment which have inserted ring-handles. The buckets have a truncate-conic body, their height varies from 325mm and 485mm and their capacity from 20 to about 35 litres. Apart from some buckets of our Danubian-style series, there is no set pattern for the overlap of sheets in the upper ring but the upper ring always fits inside the base. The rivets always have large flat internal heads and small heads on the interior. The base of the lower sheet generally takes the form of an omphalos surrounded by one, occasionally two foot-rings worked in the sheet. The angle of base and sides and the foot-ring are generally reinforced by cast base-plates, which are decorated and riveted to the base and lower wall of the bucket.

As the bodies of all the buckets are of identical construction and mostly of very similar shape they are extremely difficult to classify. Their most distinctive features are provided by the various styles of handle-attachment and base-plates, which provide the basis for their classification into two series, each comprising several types. The first series, Hawkes' and Smith's imported group of buckets, is characterized by strap-shaped handle attachments or ring carriers (*Bandhenkel*) typical of the southeast European Kurd and Hosszúpályi buckets and should, therefore, be referred to as 'Danubian-style series'. As on their southeast European counterparts, their ring-carriers are riveted to the body and form a loop between the rim and shoulder; at rest the ring-handles fall *outside* the body of the vessel. In our second 'Hiberno-British' series, Hawkes' and Smith's group of native buckets, the cast, ribbed or ridged, arc-shaped tubular handle-attachments or ring carriers are cast over the rim and inner face of the neck, so at rest, the ring-handles fall *inside* the rim. As already noted by Evans, the tubular ribbed handle-attachments are clearly related to, and probably derived from, those of Atlantic cauldrons of Class A; they have no continental counterparts. In both series of buckets the ring-handles are nearly always of lozengic cross-section and have diameters of between 80 and 100mm. This is in contrast to most ring-handles of cauldrons that have rounded or ribbed cross-sections and diameters that are generally over 100 mm. This distinguishing feature proves useful in identifying rings found singly or with only part of their attachment as having been part of a bucket or a cauldron.

In addition to Hawkes' and Smith's classification by

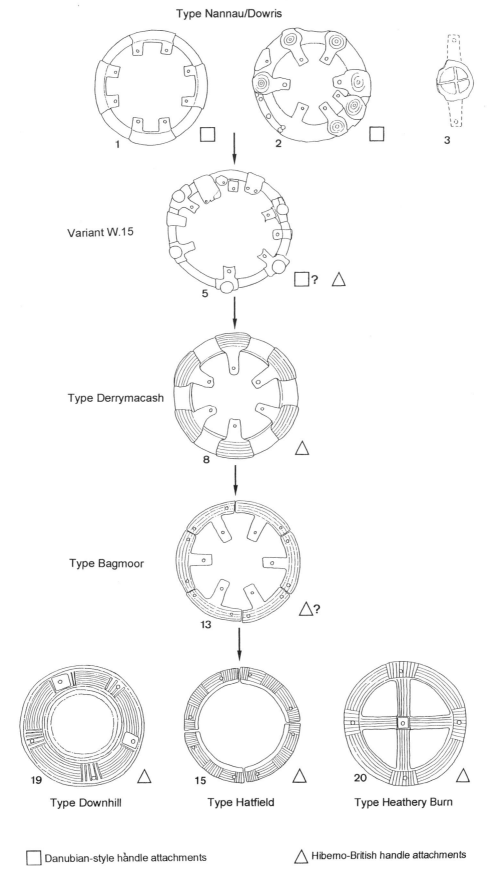

Fig 17.2: Evolution of base plates of Atlantic buckets. Numbers refer to Appendix. Not to scale.

type of handle-attachment, there are further distinct differences between the two series, which confirm the buckets' division into these two definite groups. Whereas the buckets with Danubian-style strap-handles are often supplied with southeast European style base-plates in the form of a set of tabbed round discs, those with native Hiberno-British handles show a different mode of base-protection (Fig 17.2). Here, the foot-ring and the angle between base and wall are protected by a broken or continuous ring of ribbed plates, which are not round but form a complete circle or segments of a circle to fit the outline foot-ring. The latter plates as yet have no Bronze Age parallels in continental Europe, but recall strengthening devices found on continental Iron Age vessels of Kurd and related types which will be discussed below (p. 133ff). We shall first turn to Hawkes' and Smith's group of imported 'Kurd' buckets, our Danubian-style series.

Danubian-style buckets (Appendix, Nos 1–7)

As can be seen on the distribution map (Fig 17.5), most Danubian-style buckets are known from Ireland (Nos 2, 4–7), one has come from Wales (No. 1), close to the Irish Sea, and a single base-plate fragment was included in a founders' hoard from the southern shore of the River Thames in Surrey (No. 3). The latter is the only example certainly to have been found with association, the bucket from Dowris (No. 2) probably being part of a multiple-period deposit. Danubian-style buckets are distinguished by continental-style strap-shaped handles attachments in the shape of a turned 'H' and by individual base-plates in the form of the handle (Nannau, No. 1; Fig 17.3,2) or by small tabbed discs, one tab being riveted to the foot-ring, the other bent over the angle of base and wall and attached to the lower wall of the vessel (Dowris, No. 2, Fig 17.3,1). These buckets can be divided into two types: Plain buckets of Type Nannau-Dowris (Nos 1–5) and decorated buckets of Type Cape Castle (Nos 6–7). All have or had primary Danubian-style strap-handles and/or base-plates. The original handle carriers of an unprovenanced Irish bucket (No. 5), here named 'W.15' after Wilde's (1857–61) accession number, may have been of Danubian type and it is included with our undecorated buckets of Type Nannau-Dowris. Its base-plates (Fig 17.2,5) are similar to those from Dowris, but also show affinities to the rectangular plates of the Hiberno-British Type Derry-macash (Fig 17.2,8) This bucket may, therefore, be regarded as a transitional variant (Variant W.15) and may be placed between Danubian-style and Hiberno-British buckets.

The two decorated buckets of Type Cape Castle, include two vessels from Ireland (Nos 6–7), which also display Danubian-style strap-handles, but of modified form. They are more tubular and reminiscent of the attachments of 'native' buckets. Also, in one of the buckets, Cape Castle (No. 7), the attachment shows ribs and in common with Hiberno-British examples, the ring-handles fall to the interior of the vessel (Fig 17.3,4). One bucket has no base-plates (No. 6), whereas the primary plates of the eponymous vessel appear to have been tabbed (Fig 17.3,4). It now has a secondary Hiberno-British base-ring of Type Heathery Burn (below). In contrast to all other Atlantic buckets which are plain, the shoulder of the two Type Cape Castle vessels show an embossed decoration in a manner similar to continental buckets of Type Hajdúböszörmény (Patay 1990, 40ff). Whereas the latter primarily show embossed figurative patterns of the 'Bird-sun-barque' (*Vogelsonnenbarke*) motif, the insular examples display non-figurative geometric patterns of horizontal rows of differently sized bosses bordered by embossed pendant triangles, the latter design also being known from a Danubian bucket (Patay 1990, no. 64).

As most vessels of our Danubian-style vessels are single finds, the authenticity of the Dowris hoard having been questioned (Coles 1971), it is extremely difficult to date them. However, on the basis of typology and that of metal-compositions (Northover in Gerloff forthcoming), Type Nannau-Dowris should to be regarded as the earlier of the two Danubian-style types. It should, therefore, include our earliest Atlantic buckets. Although its only associations, those of the Egham base-plate (No. 3), belong to the Carp's Tongue horizon and suggests a Ewart Park date for their deposition, the continental evidence (below) certainly suggests that tabbed Danubian-style base-plates are much earlier in their beginnings. When Hawkes and Smith (1957, 137ff) related our Danubian-style vessels to buckets of Type Kurd, they cited a tall 'Kurd bucket' from Hosszúpályi (Fig 17.1,1), which Patay later (1990, 37ff) assigned to a 'taller' variant of Type Kurd, named after this vessel. On typological grounds, however, Patay's 'Variant Hosszúpályi' ought to be seen as a type in its own right. In common with our Atlantic buckets, these buckets reach heights of just over 40cm, always have two strap-shaped handle attachments which may still show inserted ring-handles and are invariably constructed of three sheets: a tub-shaped base sheet and two wall-sheets. The smaller Kurd buckets, between 15 and 20cm high, only have one wall sheet and their strap-shaped handle(s) never show inserted rings. Some, as for instance Dresden-Dobritz (Coblenz 1952; von Brunn 1968, 316f), only have a single handle. Most importantly, Kurd and Hosszúpályi buckets presumably had different functions. The smaller Kurd 'bucket', which is between 15 and at most 20cm tall, may have been used four pouring in the manner of a jug or served as a large mug or communal drinking cup. The taller Hosszúpályi examples, on the other hand, are true buckets and should have functioned as ceremonial containers for some precious, presumably alcoholic, drink which may have been withdrawn and served by the smaller Kurd 'bucket'.

Whereas in continental Europe Kurd vessels may occur side by side with larger Hosszúpályi buckets, in Ireland and Britain the smaller Kurd type has yet not been discovered and only the larger Hosszúpályi-style bucket

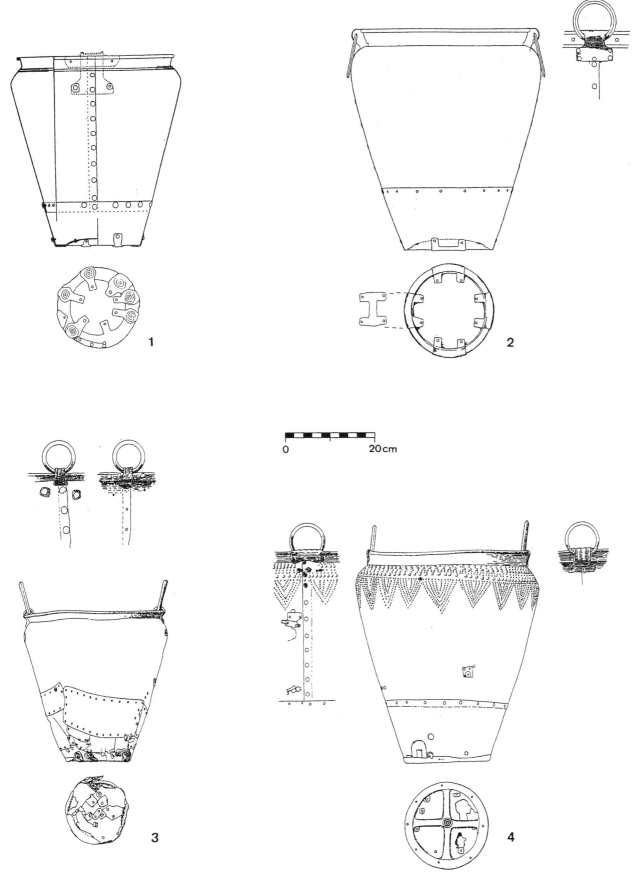

Fig 17.3: Atlantic buckets with primary Danubian-style fittings. 1. Dowris, Ireland (App. No. 2). 2. Nannau, Wales (App. No. 1). 3. Ireland (App. No. 4). 4. Cape Castle. Ireland (App. No. 7). Scale: 1:8.

seems to be predominant. In both, Atlantic and southeast European buckets the mode of construction is identical. They are made of a high-walled tub-shaped bottom section, strengthened by a foot-ring, and a pair of rectangular wall sheets that are joined by two vertical seams placed below each handles. The seams in both western and eastern examples are about two centimetres wide; the rivets in both are equally spaced, showing large round heads hammered flush to the outside and small nail-heads on the inside. The most striking invariable feature in their construction is the mode of joining the wall sheets. Along both of the vertical seams the left sheet always overlaps the right. This mode of overlap is standard on all southeastern Hosszúpályi buckets (Patay 1990, 34) and occurs on all insular undecorated examples which display or had primary Danubian strap-handles, namely those of our Type Nannau-Dowris (Nos 1–2, 4), whereas in Danubian-style buckets of Type Cape Castle (Nos 6–7) and on all buckets with 'native' handles, the method of joining the wall sheets is not standardised. In common with all Class A cauldrons, the latter buckets show seams which overlap right over left; or, left over right in one, and right over left in the other. It is possible, therefore, that our Danubian-style buckets of Type Nannau-Dowris were manufactured by continental metal workers, either locally or on the continent. They may thus represent true imports, whereas Type Cape Castle, in common with all Hiberno-British buckets and insular cauldrons – should certainly be of local manufacture.

In the absence of associations it is still difficult to date insular Danubian-style buckets in their own right. We, therefore, have to rely on the date of their continental parallels. In southeast Europe Hosszúpályi buckets either occur singly or in vessel hoards, their fragments, however, are included in securely dated founders' hoards that have been dated to the early Urnfield period of Bronze D and Ha A1 (Patay 1990, 39f). We should now turn to the base-plates that are typical of our Danubian-style vessels. The H-shaped base-plates from Nannau (No. 1; Fig 17.3,2) are unique, they have no counterparts in Britain nor on the continent. They may have been made from blanks of Danubian-style handle attachments. The tabbed, disc-shaped plates from Dowris (No. 2; Fig 17.2,2) and the single plate from Egham (No. 3; Fig 17.2,3), however have exact prototypes in southeast Europe. Although tabbed base discs can as yet only be connected with one intact bucket of Type Hosszúpályi, Püspökladány in Hungary (Patay 1990, no. 55), they should, however, be associated with this type, which has mainly survived in fragments. Base-plates are not known from the small Kurd buckets, nor have they yet been identified on buckets of Type Hajdúböszörmény. It seems obvious that base strengthening devices were only necessary for large buckets, these having a greater capacity and therefore being much heavier when filled.

The closest parallels to our base-plates from Egham have come from the fragmentary base section of a vessel

from a hoard at Buza, Romania (Soroceanu and Buda 1976). The tub-shaped base has six tabbed discs (Fig 17.1,3) which are decorated with a raised cross and are identical to the piece from Egham (Gerloff 1986, 104 pl. 10.iii [Buza], pl. 12.ii [Egham]). The Buza hoard, which also contained fragments of buckets of Type Hajdúböszörmény and two basins of von Merhart's Group B1, can be securely dated to Ha B1. Further base discs, some identical to those from Buza and Egham, were included among the numerous Late Bronze Age finds from the cave deposit at the 'Fliegenhöhle' at Škocjan (St. Kanzian) near Trieste, in Istria (Szombathy 1913, 154ff figs 116–121; Hawkes and Smith 1957, 139f, fig. 3D). The plates discovered at this site (Fig 17.1,4a) also include some that bear the concentric circle motif seen on the Dowris discs, others show a single dished circle as on the unprovenanced Irish bucket 'W.15' (No. 5; Fig 17.2,5). Unfortunately, the discs from Škojan cannot be securely dated as the numerous bronze finds from the cave, mostly fragmented, cover the whole duration of the Urnfield period. Among the bronzes were more than one thousand burnt vessel fragments weighing 17.6kg (Szombathy 1913, 160f). They included fragments from Hajdúböszörmény buckets, basins with cruciform handle attachments and numerous plain sheets with remains of vertical and horizontal seams as well as of strap handles and strengthening base tabs (Fig 17.1,4b–d), which should be assigned to Hosszúpályi buckets. Although the latter most commonly occur in southeastern Europe, some examples have come from more western parts of the continent, thus bridging the gap between the Danubian plain, Britain and Ireland. One large, folded fragment of an undecorated bucket has been dredged, together with other early Urnfield scrap metal finds, from the River Rhône at Geneva (Primas 1995, 218, fig. 13). A more or less complete example, still retaining its handles, has come from the lake site settlement of Zürich-Wöllishofen, Haumesser (Primas 1995, fig. 14), which has mostly yielded bronze finds belonging to Ha A2 and Ha B1 and been dendro-dated from the mid- eleventh century BC to the mid tenth (Becker *et al.* 1985, 43).

Hosszúpályi buckets should, therefore, have been current from the beginning of the Urnfield period, Bronze D/ Ha A1, when their fragments appear in many Danubian hoards and should certainly have lasted until Ha B1. With the exception of a Hosszúpályi bucket fragment from a founders' hoard at Seeboden on the Millstädter See in Carinthia (Müller-Karpe 1959, pl. 145A) and two Italian fragments from the late Villanova Culture (below, p. 135), there are as yet no continental finds which definitely date to the latest Urnfield phase of Ha B2/B3, *i.e.* to the later tenth and ninth centuries BC. It is only during the eighth century BC when Hosszúpályi buckets or the so-called 'Kurd buckets' reappear at the very beginning of the continental Iron Age. At this time, however, they ceased to be deposited in hoards, but are placed in richly furnished graves, both in Italy and in more central and

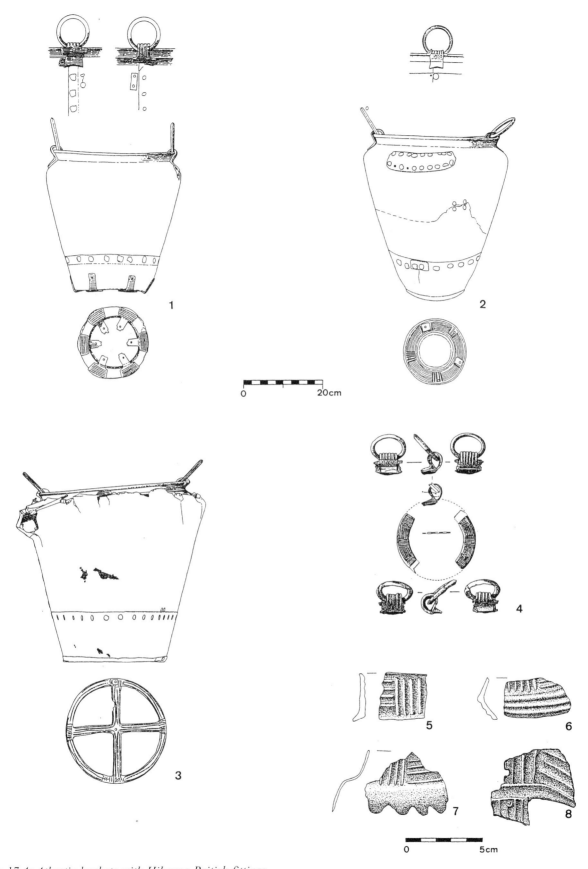

Fig 17.4: Atlantic buckets with Hiberno-British fittings
1. Derrymacash, Ireland (App. No. 8). 2. Downhill, Ireland (App. No. 19). 3. Dervock, Ireland (App. No. 22). 4. Hatfield, England (App. No. 14). 5. South Cadbury hillfort, England (App. No. 16). 6. Bonneville, France (App. No. 18). 7. Vénat, France (App. No. 17). 8. Graville-St.-Honorine, France (App. No. 23). Scale: Fig 17.1.1–4: 1:8. Fig 17.1.5–8: 1:2.

western parts of continental Europe (below, p. 133ff). It was these latter examples that were seen to have contributed to the concept of a 'Hallstatt period' in Britain and Ireland (above, p. 119ff).

To conclude our section on Danubian-style Atlantic buckets we can state that they were certainly modelled on continental prototypes, the earliest examples (Type Nannau-Dowris) possibly having been imported from southeastern Europe some time during the last quarter of the second millennium BC. As our earliest Atlantic cauldrons were seen to date to the early Penard phase, it seems likely that both Danubian derived vessel forms, buckets and cauldrons, were introduced at a similar time, *i.e.* during the British Penard phase, when other continental types of prestigious metal work, such as bronze shields (Needham 1979) and the earliest flange-hilted swords of Nenzingen/Reutlingen Type (Gerloff 1980/81; Colquhoun and Burgess 1988, nos 59–61) reached southern Britain. The question whether our earliest buckets were actual imports from the continent may only be answered after comparing their individual metallurgy. Although nearly all insular buckets and cauldrons have been analysed (see Northover in Gerloff forthcoming), comparable data are yet not available from the continent. On typological grounds, however, it is clear, that only insular buckets of Type Nannau-Dowris may possibly represent true imports, whereas our decorated Cape Castle vessels should be viewed as local imitation (above, p. 125). The latter cannot date earlier than the Wilburton phase, their embossed decoration being reminiscent of Hajdúböszörmény buckets, which date to Ha B1. Both types of Danubian-style buckets should, however, have survived into the insular Ewart Park/ Dowris phases, as some (Nos 4, 5, 7) show secondary fittings that are typical of Hawkes' and Smith's second series of native buckets which are connected with this phase and will be discussed below.

Hiberno-British buckets (Nos 8–31)

Hiberno-British buckets of the second series have handle-attachments in the form of cast tubular holders, strengthened by three to seven ribs, reminiscent of handle carriers of Class A cauldrons. Their ring handles fall to the inside of the vessels. The handles and attachments have either survived complete, being still attached to buckets or were deposited as fragments, the latter frequently being included in founder's hoards. In common with Danubian-style buckets and all Class A cauldrons, Hiberno-British buckets are made of three sheets, a tub-shaped base sheet, riveted to the outside of two wall sheets. In contrast to Type Nannau-Dowris of the former, the wall sheets of Hiberno-British buckets show no standardized mode of overlap in their vertical seams. As they are all of very similar dimension and construction, they can only be distinguished by their different types of base-plates. These differ from those found on buckets with Danubian-style handles in that they are adapted to the circular outline of

the foot-ring. Either they are forged and tabbed, their centre pieces being segments of an open or closed circle (Fig 17.2,8,13), or they consist of a flanged ring which was cast in segments (Fig 17.2,15) or as a continuous ring (Fig 17.2,19, 20). These differences enable us to divide Hiberno-British buckets into several types. As already noted by Hawkes, insular base strengthening devices seem to present a continuous typological and technological sequence, which originated in the separate, tabbed discs of Danubian-style buckets and terminated in the closed rings of Hiberno-British buckets of Types Hatfield, Downhill and Heathery Burn (Dudley and Hawkes 1947, 10).

Type Derrymacash plates (Nos 8-12; Fig 17.2.8 and 17.4.1) appear to be the earliest among the baseplate types of the Hiberno-British buckets series as they are closest in style to the tabbed discshaped plates of Danubianstyle buckets, the plates of bucket W.15 (No. 5, Fig 17.2.5) representing elements both forms (above, p.125). Type Derrymacash plates are known from two or three complete buckets (Nos 8,11,12) of which the eponymous vessel is the only surviving one. They also occur on a detached bucket base from the Dowris assemblage (No. 9) that produced two further detached plates (No. 10). Derrymacash base-plates appear mainly Ireland, the two lost English examples (Nos 11–12) having been discovered not far from the Irish Sea (Fig 17.6). Type Derrymacash base-plates represent a technological advance in that they are now adapted to the circular outline of the foot-ring which they partially cover, thus offering additional reinforcement and protection for this most vulnerable area of the vessel. However, there was obviously still room for improvement. Type Derrymacash plates only cover sections of the foot-ring and protect the weak angle between base and body only at intervals. Quoting Hawkes: "What was desired was a continuous protection for the lowest part of the vessel in its weakest points, namely for the angle between base and wall and for the base itself" (Dudley and Hawkes 1947, 10).

The first step in this direction are the T-shaped plates of Type Bagmoor (No. 13; Fig 17.2,13) known by a set of six individual angled plates from the eponymous founders' hoard in Lincolnshire. The plates cover the whole area of the foot-ring, thus approaching the closed circle of Type Hatfield. They are flanged at their outer edge, again similar to those of Type Hatfield, but show a single inner tab that was riveted to the base in the manner of Danubian-style plates and those of Type Bagmoor. In common with Type Bagmoor the plates show four concentric grooves and, as in Type Hatfield, there are lateral rivets in the plates, which attach them to the base. This structure although an improvement on Type Derrymacash did, however, still have its weaknesses, in that it was forged and still made use of tabs, features which will be seen to have been abandoned in the cast, flanged rings of Types Hatfield, Downhill and Heathery Burn which were riveted directly to the base (Fig 17.2,15, 19–20).

Fig 17.5: Distribution of Atlantic Danubian-style and Hiberno-British buckets. Numbers refer to Appendix.

In Type Hatfield (Nos 14–18) the ring, marked by alternating sections of circumferential and radial grooves, consists of four segments of a continuous circle, each comprising a little less than a full quarter circle (Fig 17.2,15). The eponymous hoard from Hatfield also contained bucket handles and five- and six-ribbed handle-attachments (No. 14; Fig 17.4,4), presumably from the same vessel as the base-plates. These clearly belong to the Hiberno-British series and it can be fairly safely assumed that all buckets with base-rings of this type belonged to this series, as do the handles of the related vessels of Types Downhill and Heathery Burn (below). There are no complete vessels with base-plates of Type Hatfield. The plates have either survived intact, as in the eponymous hoard and on a detached bucket base from Little Houghton (No. 15; Fig 17.2,15), or they were deposited as small fragments, as at South Cadbury (No. 16, Fig 17.4,5) and in the French founders' hoards of Vénat (No. 17, Fig 17.4,7) and Bonneville (No. 18, Fig 17.4,6). The surviving fragments are too small as to assign them to Type Hatfield with an absolute degree of certainty, their decoration and the locations of their find-spots, however, suggest that they belonged to this type, rather than to Types Downhill and Heathery Burn. Whereas intact rings of Type Hatfield have so far only been discovered in southern Britain, intact rings of Types Downhill and Heathery Burn are confined to northern Ireland and Scotland (see Fig 17.6).

Type Downhill (No. 19) only represented by the eponymous vessel that has six-ribbed Hiberno-British handle attachments, constitutes a type in it own right (Fig 17.4,19). Its base-ring shows affinities with Type Hatfield as well as Heathery Burn. Here the segmented base-plates of Type Hatfield have become fused to a continuous ring, reminiscent of Type Heathery Burn, but lacking its spokes. The vessel was found singly in northern Ireland.

Type Heathery Burn (Nos 7.20–22) shares with Type Downhill a base-ring in the form of a complete circular casting. This, however, is bridged by four radial spokes meeting at right angles at the centre of the base. It is known from four complete vessels. Whereas the base-wheel of the eponymous English vessel (No. 20) and those from Cardross, Scotland (No. 21) and Dervock, Ireland (No. 22) seem to be the original base strengthening devices, the base-wheel from the original Danubian-style bucket from Cape Castle, Ireland (No. 7), appears secondary. The three others (Nos 20-22) from northern Britain and Ireland have primary Hiberno-British handle attachments (see Fig 17.6) distinguished by six to seven ribs. They are among the largest of the Atlantic bucket group, their capacity being about 35 to 40 litres. Their shoulders – in common with continental Iron Age buckets – appear more angular than in the preceding types. Whereas the Scottish bucket from Cardross (No. 21) and the Irish vessel from Dervock (No. 22) were single deposits, the eponymous bucket from Heathery Burn (No. 20) has come from a cave in Co. Durham, where it was

discovered among numerous metal finds. These, however, were scattered over the whole length (160m) of the cave and need not have been deposited simultaneously. Whereas all insular base-rings of Type Heathery Burn have survived intact, a fragment may be identified from the French coast of the Channel, where it comes from the founders' hoard at Graville-St.-Honorine near Le Havre (No. 23, Fig 17.4,8). This piece, originally described an *objet de garniture* (Dubus 1912, 21), is only 58mm in length and, therefore, very difficult to attribute. Its angled form and arrangement of radial and concentric grooves are typical of base-rings of Type Hatfield, fragments of which we have identified in two other French hoards (Nos 17–18). However, it shows vestiges of a possible spoke and should therefore rather be included in Type Heathery Burn. Also, B. O'Connor has recently identified a fragmented base-plate in the Gilmonby hoard, which he assigns to Type Heathery Burn (*cf.* No. 26).

We should now consider the date of Hiberno-British buckets and that of their individual types. In common with Danubian-style buckets and with cauldrons, nearly all intact buckets of the Hiberno-British series are single finds and, therefore, extremely difficult to date. Apart from the doubtful associations at Dowris and Heathery Burn, no complete bucket has been found in association although diagnostic handle and base-plates fragments have survived in founders' hoards of the Ewart Park phase, which may be early or late within the phase.

Whereas we were able to distinguish a typological sequence of base-plate styles (Fig 17.2), the handles appear more uniform. They do, however, differ in that the arched tubular holders show a varying number of ribs, ranging from three to seven. A secondary three-ribbed Hiberno-British handle attachment appears on an un-provenanced bucket from Ireland (No. 4), which originally had primary Danubian-style strap handles, suggesting that the replacement took place when both series of handle attachments were in use, possibly at the transition from Wilburton to Ewart Park phase. The eponymous bucket from Derrymacash (No. 8) shows a handle attachment with four corrugations; four also occur on the Hiberno-British handle fragments from the hoard at Gilmonby (No. 26) and the handle from Duddingston Loch (No. 24), which was found with other bronzes while dredging for shell-marl. Although both these finds contain bronzes mainly of the Ewart Park phase, the presence of Wilburton spearheads with lunate openings in both finds, and that of a Wilburton sword at Duddingston Loch and perhaps an early Ewart Park example at Gilmonby may suggest an early date within Ewart Park, at least for some of the hoard's components. It is possible, therefore, that Hiberno-British handle attachments with three or four ribs – also present on the complete bucket from Derrymacash with its individual base-plates reminiscent of Danubian-style plates – may have appeared earlier than handle attachments with five or six ribs, fragments of which are mainly included in hoards with Carp's Tongue material

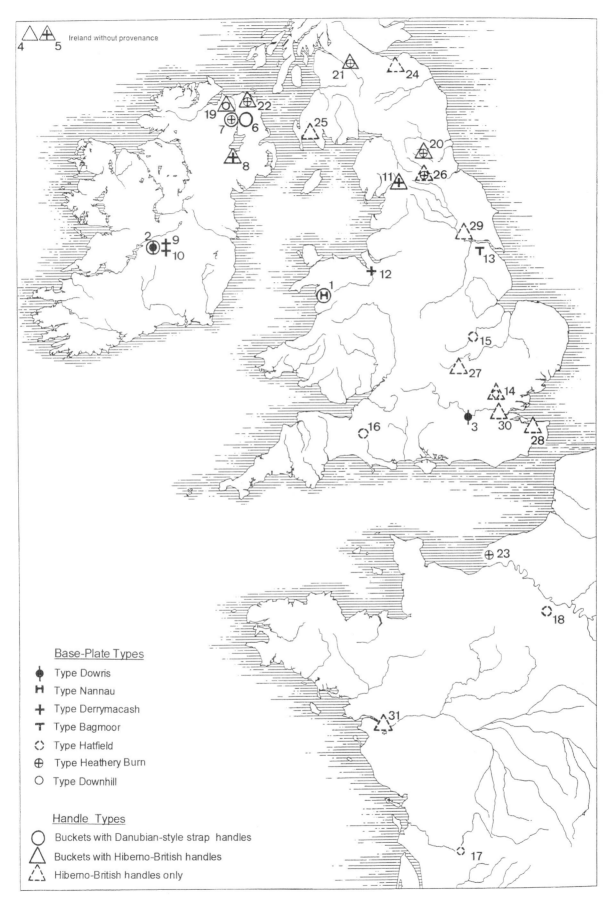

Fig 17.6: Distribution of Danubian-style and Hiberno-British buckets. Numbers refer to Appendix.

(Nos 14, 27–28, 30) and which are typical of buckets with cast base-rings of Types Hatfield, Downhill and Heathery Burn. The cast base-ring fragments from the Gilmonby, assigned to Type Heathery Burn (above), were associated with a four-ribbed handle attachment (*cf.* No. 26). The base and handle fragments, however, need not have come from the same vessel, but may suggest that the Gilmonby hoard was deposited at time when cast base-plates had been adopted. We should now return to the typology of the base-plates, for it appears that their typological sequence also represents a chronological one. The close typological connection of the individual tabbed base-plates of Type Derrymacash with Danubian-style plates suggests an overlap of both series. The metal composition of the fragmentary Dowris bucket displaying base-plates of Type Derrymacash (No. 9), does not rule out, that it may have been manufactured during the Wilburton or contemporary Irish Roscommon phase (Northover in Gerloff forthcoming). In common with Type Derrymacash, the individual base-plates of Type Bagmoor may possibly date early within the Ewart Park phase and be of pre Carp's Tongue date. Although most of the metal types from the Bagmoor hoard (Davey 1973, nos 386–416) can be securely dated to the Ewart Park phase, its plain spearheads occur in both Wilburton and Ewart Park hoards, whereas a spearhead with lunate opening in its blade is primarily found in Wilburton hoards and does not generally occur in Carp's Tongue assemblages.

On the evidence of the Hatfield hoard and the Heathery Burn deposit, the eponymous cast and flanged base-rings, both found with five- and six-ribbed handle attachments, clearly belong to the Carp's Tongue horizon of Ewart Park phase. The Hatfield founders hoard included Carp's Tongue forms and segments of base-rings of the eponymous type (Nos 17–18) and fragments of cast base-rings were included in the French Carp's Tongue hoards from Vénat, (No. 17) Bonneville (No. 18) and Graville (No. 23). Recently, G. Cordier (1996, 20, fig. 6.8) has identified a Gündlingen hilt fragment (possibly of Thames sword?) in the hoard of Petit-Villatte, Cher, which – although not containing any bucket fragments – has yielded cauldron fragments of Class BO (Gerloff forthcoming), the latter also included in other French hoards which have yielded fragments of Ewart Park and Carp's Tongue blades. On the evidence of two calibrated radiocarbon dates from the Egham hoard (see No. 3), the deposition of British Carp's Tongue hoards can be assigned to the ninth and early part of the eighth century BC. Earlier dates for bag-shaped chapes (Needham *et al.* 1997, nos Dob 3 and 16), traditionally connected with Carp's Tongue swords, do not necessarily indicate an earlier date for Carp's Tongue hoard, as was suggested by Needham (*et al.* 1997, 95). It will be argued below, that bag-shaped chapes are not part of the genuine Carp's Tongue complex, but should rather be connected with British Ewart Park swords, which – in common with bag-shaped chapes – have prototypes in the British Wilburton period (see below, p. 141).

The cast base-rings of Type Hatfield, Downhill and Heathery Burn connected with the Carp's Tongue horizon of the final Bronze Age should have survived into the British Llyn Fawr phase, which has produced 'Hallstatt swords' of Gündlingen type, fragments of which having come been diagnosed in the hoards from Vénat and Graville, which were seen to have produced base-ring fragments of Type Hatfield and Heathery Burn. According to Alcock (1971) the South Cadbury base-plate fragment of Type Hatfield (No. 16) may originally have been part of a 'scrap' hoard, which included Late Bronze Age as well as early Iron Age forms. Among the latter are swan neck pins and an early Ha C razor of Type Feldkirch/Bernissart (Jockenhövel 1980, no. 661), a type which according to Jockenhövel (1980, 175) may have its origins in southern Britain. The Vénat hoard contained fragmentary wheel fittings of Type Bad-Homburg, which also appear in other French Carp's Tongue hoards (Pare 1987). Similar fittings have come from the cave at Heathery Burn, which has also produced the eponymous bucket. But more importantly, Type Bad Homburg fittings were associated with a Gündlingen sword in the Bavarian burial of Wehringen, traditionally dated to Kossack's (1959) Ha C1, but now believed to belong to a transitional horizon between Ha B3 and C (Pare 1987). This phase, coined HA C0 or Ha C1a is characterized by Gündlingen swords, now believed to be earlier than Mindelheim swords. The latter, previously believed to be contemporary with the former, both being assigned to Kossack's traditional Ha C1, are now believed to belong to the later horizon, Ha C1 or C1b (Pare 1998, 298f; Hennig 2001, 88ff). The Wehringen burial of the earlier Gündlingen phase has yielded a dendro-date of 778±5 BC (Friedrich and Hennig 1995). This date is just within the range of the cal BC dates obtained for the deposition of the Egham Carp's Tongue hoard (see No. 3), supporting the belief that the deposition of Carp's Tongue bronzes is a later feature of the Ewart Park phase and continued into a period in which Gündlingen swords started to appear at the turn from the ninth to the eighth century BC. In both Britain/Ireland and central Europe this period should have witnessed the beginning of the early Iron Age. Some of our later Atlantic buckets should therefore be contemporary with continental examples of the earlier Hallstatt period that were traditionally seen as the progenitors of all Atlantic buckets.

Continental Iron Age buckets and their relation to Atlantic buckets

In contrast to Atlantic and Urnfield buckets, both groups having come from hoards or found singly, nearly all continental Iron Age buckets were associated with burials. They are part of the funerary equipment of some of the richest tombs of the Hallstatt and Etruscan Culture. Their distribution stretches from the Netherlands in the west to Slovenia in the east, most examples having been found

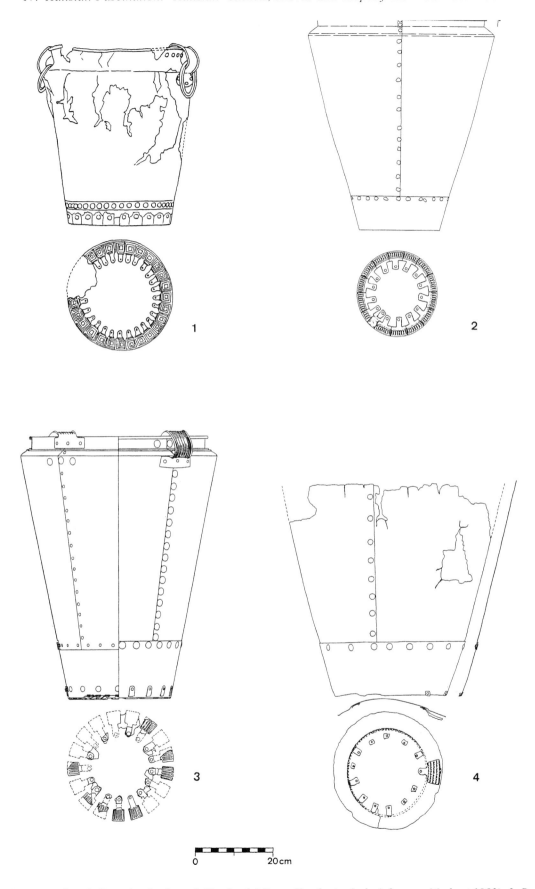

Fig 17.7: Continental early Iron Age buckets. 1. Tomba del Duce, Vetulonia, Italy (after von Merhart 1952). 2. Burial 504, Hallstatt, Austria (after Prüssing 1991).   3. La Côte-St.-André, France (after Chapotat 1962). 4. Choryn, Poland (after Gedl 2001). Scale 1:8.

south of the Danube (Egg 1985, fig. 39). They are still constructed in the Urnfield tradition in that they display a tub-shaped base section which was riveted to the wall of the vessel and have strap-shaped *Bandhenkel* (Fig 17.7, fig 1.3). Whereas all insular buckets, in common with larger Urnfield examples, have two wall-sheets and two handles, continental Iron Age examples frequently display more than two wall-sheets and handles. Significantly, strap-handles do not occur on those insular buckets which are closest in time to the continental Iron Age examples displaying them. There are further distinguishing features: continental Iron Age buckets may be twice as tall as Atlantic examples, the former reaching heights of up to 80cm, whereas the latter – in common with continental Urnfield buckets – are at most 45 cm tall. It follows that none of our insular buckets can be derived from continental buckets of the Hallstatt or Etruscan Culture. As was demonstrated above, the typology of Atlantic buckets, especially that of their base-plates, mirrors a continuous sequence from early forms, derived from continental buckets of the earlier and middle Urnfield Culture, and evolves into purely native forms of the insular latest Bronze and early Iron Age.

Having established that Atlantic buckets do not closely compare with continental Iron Age examples, we should consider the evidence of their base-strengthening devices which are a distinctive feature not only of insular and continental Urnfield buckets, but also of Iron Age vessels. Base-plates occur only on those vessels that still display the Urnfield-style, riveted-on base rather than a crimped-on one (*Falzboden*). The latter device was only introduced during the later Hallstatt period and became standard in early La Tène, when vessels with a riveted-on base ceased to be produced. The latter is not only typical of all Iron buckets as defined by von Merhart (above, p. 120), but also distinguishes those *situlae* and bucket-shaped vessels without handles (*grifflose Situlen)* which do not display the more usual Iron Age form of a cramped-on base. In Britain and Ireland all buckets were seen to have the Urnfield style riveted-on base and most display base-plates. *Situlae* and handle-less vessels typical of the continental Iron Age are here virtually unknown. In common with base-plates of Hiberno-British buckets, continental Iron Age plates differ from their Urnfield predecessors in that the plates are now adapted to the outline of the foot-ring, they either cover it completely or protect it at close intervals (Fig 17.7). In common with Urnfield plates, continental Iron Age plates may be attached by two or one lateral tab. They resemble our Hiberno-British plates of Types Derrymacash and Bagmoor, in that their centre section is also adapted to the outline of the foot-ring. This similarity was already noticed by Leeds (1930, 20) and subsequently stressed by von Merhart (1952, 30). On continental vessels tabbed plates seem to have been abandoned by Ha D, when continuous rings (*cf.* Prüssing 1991, no. 101) or sections of rings (*cf.* Jacob 1995, Nos 307.309), riveted directly

to the foot-ring became common. These latter plates are undecorated and appear sufficiently different to our cast and flanged base-rings of Types Hatfield, Downhill and Heathery Burn, that they need not concern us here.

On the continent, tabbed plates are well known from Etruscan tombs, where they appear on at least two Kurd buckets from Vetulonia, one certainly found in the well-known *Tomba del Duce.* It has 24 (from originally 30) small angular plates decorated with raised ribs of concentric squares covering the entire foot-ring (Fig 17.7,1; Montelius 1910, pl. 186, 11; Randall-MacIver 1924, 113, 123, pl. 22). Apart from appearing on buckets, Vetulonia-style plates also occur on *situlae* and handle-less vessels in other Etruscan tombs of the Orientalising period beginning in the later eighth century BC and continuing into the seventh (Cerchiai 1988). Base-plates have as yet not been identified on Italian vessels of earlier periods. Although buckets or their fragments already appear in protovillanovan hoards of the earlier Late Bronze Age, the earliest Iron Age examples come from later Villanovan tombs, from which two fragmentary examples are known. They were found at Bologna, Benacci Caprara 39 (Brizio 1889, pl. 1.19) and Veii 1036 (Müller-Karpe 1959, pl. 36–38), both having survived without their base. So we do not know if they originally displayed base-plates. Müller-Karpe assigned the tombs to Bologna/Veii late II (Peroni's 1994: *I Ferro 2b*), believing this phase to be contemporary with his Ha B3 in central Europe, dating it to the late eighth century BC (Müller-Karpe 1959, 6. 88. 242f). According to calibrated radiocarbon dates (Peroni 1994) and in particular new dendro-dates from central Italy (Njiboer *et al.* 1999/2000) and central Europe (Wehringen), the absolute dates of this phase should now be raised by 50 to 70 years (see also Pare 1998), thus dating it to the earlier eighth century BC. It should therefore be contemporary with the newly established central European phase of Ha CO/Ha C1a, whereas the Orientalising phase of the Etruscan period (Peroni's *I Ferro 3*) should be paralleled with Ha C1/Ha C1b and Ha C2 (Tomedi 1999, 662f. fig. 1).

Von Merhart (1952), when discussing Etruscan buckets and *situlae*, believed these to have been modelled on central European prototypes of the Hallstatt Culture. The central European Hallstatt buckets are indeed very similar to the Italian ones, also displaying rings of individual, tabbed base-plates. These plates appear, for instance, on a tall bucket from La Côte-Saint-André, Dép. Isère, France, which displays 17 Vetulonia style base-plates covering the foot-ring at intervals (Fig 17.7,3). It comes from a tumulus, possibly from a cremation burial, and was associated with four bronze wheels of Late Urnfield type (Chapotat 1962). Vetulonia type base-plates are also known from a *situla* found in a princely tomb at Frankfurt-Stadtwald, Germany (Jacob 1995, no. 313) and from two vessels without handles from Hallstatt, burials 504 and 507 (Fig 17.7,2; Prüssing 1991, no. 94). Their most northern appearance is on a damaged vessel from Choryn in Poland (Fig 17.7,4; Gedl 2001, no.44), its plates being closest to those of our insular Types Derrymacash and Bagmoor.

Although the latter Hiberno-British plates show certain resemblances to the above listed continental examples in that they are tabbed and have centre-sections adapted to the outline of the foot-ring, there are, however, differences and they are by no means identical. All continental sets include a far greater number of individual plates or segments and consequently their centre-section is much smaller than of that of insular examples. Furthermore, the decoration of the plates in both groups varies. Most continental examples show a pattern of radial ribs that are arranged at a right angle to the outline of the foot-ring, or are in concentric squares, as on the bucket from Vetulonia. They thus contrast to the concentrically grooved insular plates which only appear on a single continental vessel, namely on the bucket from Choryn, If we consider the date of the continental examples displaying tabbed plates, it is evident that they are later in their beginnings than our insular plates of Types Derry-macash and Bagmoor (Fig 17.2,8, 13), the beginnings of which should date to the Ewart Park phase, possibly even early within it (Blackmoor phase). Type Derrymacash and Bagmoor plates should, therefore, be contemporary with Ha B2/B3 of the latest continental Bronze Age. This phase, however, has as yet not produced any vessels distinguished by base-plates, buckets being virtually unknown in Ha HaB2/B3 contexts. This may be due to deposition practices, as it seems unlikely that the production of buckets ceased during this period, considering that all Iron Age buckets still show the Urnfield-type handles, riveted-on base and tabbed base-plates.

Among the earliest continental Iron Age buckets is the tall vessel from Choryn which has survived without its rim section, its handle structure being unknown (Fig 17.7,4). It was found with a bronze amphora of Jockenhövel's (1974) Type Gevelinghausen-Seddin, conventionally dated to the transition of Ha B3 to Ha C or later eighth century BC. According to newly available dendro-dates for Ha B3 and early Ha C this absolute date should now be raised and the Choryn vessel be connected with Ha CO/Ha C1a of the earlier eighth century BC. Likewise, the bucket from La Côte-Saint-André, found with Late Bronze Age wheels of Type Coulon and originally dated to the transition from Bronze to Iron Age (Chapotat 1962), has now been assigned to the Gündlingen phase of Ha C0/ C1a (Pare 1987; 1992). Type Coulon wheels are closely connected to the bronze wheel fittings of Type Homburg. The latter, apart from appearing in several Ha B3 and Carp's Tongue hoards, have been discovered in the burial at Wehringen, here associated with a Gündlingen sword. The preserved wooden felloes of the La Côte-Saint-André wheels have been dendro-dated to 745–735 BC (Boquet 1990, 36f) and provide us – in addition to Wehringen – with a dendro-date for this early Hallstatt phase. Ha B0/ Ha C1a should, therefore, have occupied the first two or

three quarters of the eighth century BC. It was followed by the Mindelheim phase (Ha C1/C1b) of the later eighth and earlier seventh century BC, this having produced the above cited vessels from Frankfurt-Stadtwald and Hallstatt, both associated with Mindelheim swords, the former in bronze, the latter in iron.

Continental Iron Age buckets found nearest to Britain have come from three barrows in Holland, two found close to the banks of the Rhine. None of them are recorded to have base-plates. They were found at Barloo (Byvanck 1946), Oss (Moddermann 1964) and Rhenen (Heeringen 1998–99). Whereas the vessel from Barloo has no recorded associations, the latter two, associated with cremations, appeared in Hallstatt contexts. Their types of horse harness and wagon fittings are typical of the 'classic' Mindelheim phase of Ha C1, the burial from Oss also having produced an eponymous iron sword.

Thus, on present evidence, the earliest continental Iron Age vessels bearing base-plates, Choryn and La Côte-St.-André, can be assigned to Ha CO/Ha C1a of the early and mid eighth century BC. They have come from the periphery of the Hallstatt Culture. These buckets and the base-plates which they display should be later in their beginnings than the comparable Atlantic ones of Types Derrymacash and Bagmoor, the latter possibly predating cast base-rings which have been found in a few Carp's Tongue hoards. In the Late Bronze Age of Atlantic west, unlike the continent, we have witnessed a typological evolution from the tabbed round strengthening plates of early Urnfield tradition to the tabbed rectangular plates or base-rings which either cover the foot-ring in sections or cover it completely. These latter designs are also typical of continental Iron Age plates. Schauer (1972) suggested contacts between the Late Atlantic Bronze Age and the earliest phase of the continental Iron Age when he derived bronze Gündlingen swords from late versions of continental examples of insular Ewart Park swords. Base-plates fragments of Hiberno-British buckets were seen to be associated with fragments of Gündlingen and Ewart Park swords in French Carp's Tongue hoards, suggesting a time of overlap between hoards of the latest Atlantic Bronze Age and the earliest burials of the Hallstatt Culture in central Europe. It may, therefore, be no coincidence that the base-plates of the Polish bucket from Choryn (Fig 17.7,4) contemporary with the earliest Hallstatt phase that is characterized by Gündlingen swords, have their closest parallels in Atlantic plates of Types Derrymacash and Bagmoor.

Gündlingen swords and winged chapes

Hallstatt or Gündlingen swords of bronze were seen as prime evidence for Celtic 'invasions' into Britain and Ireland. Their distribution ranges from Bohemia/Bavaria in the east to Ireland in the west, but they occur most frequently in areas west of the Rhine and Alps, with dense concentrations in the Thames valley, the Benelux coun-

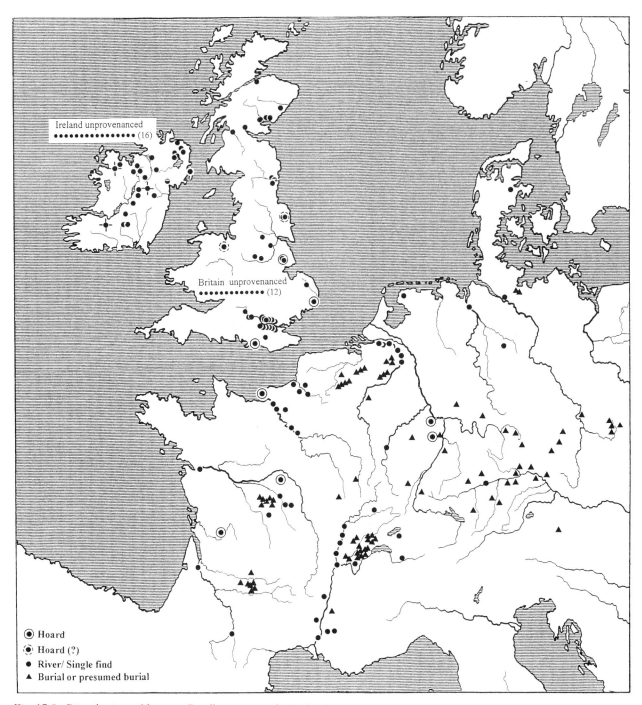

Fig 17.8: Distribution of bronze Gündlingen swords. Ireland after Eogan (1965), Britain after Colquhoun and Burgess (1988) and Continent after Schauer (1971) and Gerdsen (1986) with additions (Schauer's continetal Muschenheim type omitted, cf p. ##).

tries, the Jura and southwest France as shown in Fig 17.8. Here we have mapped Schauer's (1971) types Steinkirchen and Weichering (Fig 17.9.2a–b), as these occur in Britain and Ireland as well as in continental Europe: they are the most common forms in western Europe. We have also included Type Lengenfeld (Fig 17.9.2c) although it is not known from Britain, there are a few examples from Ireland. We have omitted Schauer's Muschenheim Type (Fig 17.9.2d) as this is only known

from the continent, where it was also produced in iron. Muschenheim swords show some typological features – a single rivet-hole in shoulder and tang, occasionally a rivet-hole at the side of the pommel-piece – of some iron Gündlingen as well as of most Mindelheim swords. The great majority of the latter were produced in iron and belong to the 'classic' phase of Ha C. Apart from one iron example found in the Llyn Fawr deposit, Mindelheim swords are unknown in Britain, where all 'Hallstatt

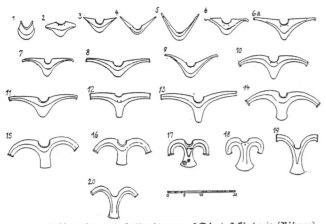

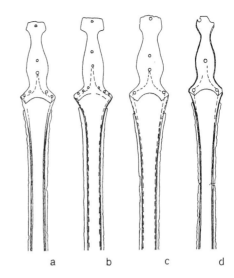

1

2

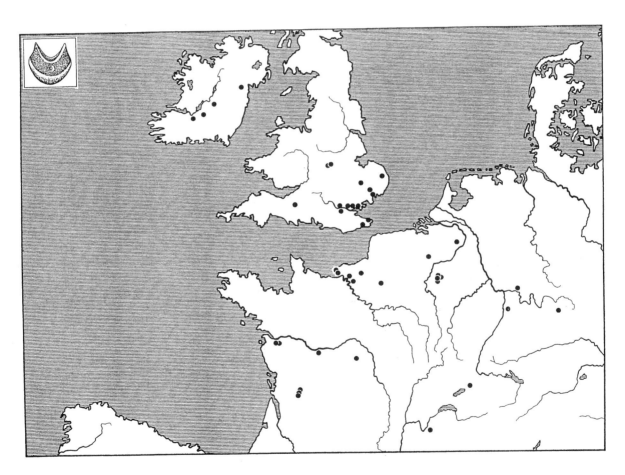

3

Fig 17.9: 1. 'Evolution' of early winged chapes (after Rieth 1942). –2. Gündlingen sword types after Schauer (1971): a) Type Steinkirchen, b) Type Weichering, c) Type Lengenfeld, d) Type Muschenheim. –3. Distribution of bag-shaped chapes (after Hein 1992) with addition (Potterne, Wiltshire).

swords' are bronze Gündlingen types. Whereas the insular examples, in common with those from northwestern France, are nearly all single finds, frequently retrieved from rivers, examples found east of the Rhine and Rhône and in the Benelux countries are generally associated with burials: cremations east of the Rhine and in Belgium, inhumations in east, central and southwestern France. Several continental finds outside northern France, however, have also come from rivers, especially the Maas and the Rhône. Most river finds cluster on both sides of the English Channel in the lower reaches of the Thames, Seine, Somme and Maas, while further southwest two examples have come from the mouths of the Loire and Garonne. The hoards from Ferring, near Worthing, on the coast of Sussex and Graville on the mouth of the Seine, both with fragments of Gündlingen swords, face each other across the Channel. The west European distribution pattern of Gündlingen swords mirrors that of British Thames swords in the Atlantic west (*cf.* Cowen 1967, 415, map F) and suggests that both types entered the continent from across the Channel, continuing their way inland by river. On our map (Fig 17.8) we have indicated all examples individually: the clusters in France and Benelux are explained by several examples coming from one cemetery.

The relative chronology of continental Gündlingen swords, which Reinecke (1911, 315ff) connected with Ha B, but were later attributed to Hallstatt C by Kimmig (1940, 103ff) and Ha C1 by Kossack (1959), has been reassessed by Pare (1987). He assigned them to a horizon transitional between Ha B3 and Ha C, now termed Ha C0 or C1a, followed by the Mindelheim phase of Ha C1 or C1b characterized by the above cited eponymous iron sword. Usually found without associations apart from other swords or chapes, insular Gündlingen swords are difficult to date. Their chronology has been based on that of their continental counterparts and assigned to a phase contemporary with Ha C on the continent (Cowen 1967), called Llyn Fawr in Britain (Burgess 1968). Gündlingen swords were generally not included in hoards of the Ewart Park phase of the latest British Bronze Age: one fragmentary blade is known to have been found in association with a socketed axe of the Carp's Tongue complex at Boyton in Suffolk (Burgess 1979) and a fragment of a Gündlingen sword hilt found near the nucleus of a Ewart Park hoard from North Tuddenham, Norfolk, has recently been reported (CMAL 2003, 27, fig. 17; not included in our Fig 17.8).

In Atlantic France, however, possible Gündlingen sword fragments were associated with Carp's Tongue swords in the hoards from Vénat and Graville-St.-Honorine, while a fragment of a Gündlingen hilt has recently been identified in the hoard from Petit-Villatte (Cordier 1996, 20, fig. 6.8). These hoards also contain fragments of Carp's Tongue and Ewart Park swords, bag-shaped chapes, Class A2 cauldron handles and presumed base-ring fragments of late Hiberno-British buckets (*cf.*

Nos 17, 3). Briard has also listed other Ha C material found in some Carp's Tongue hoards (1965, 239). It is, therefore, possible that more Gündlingen blade fragments may yet be identified among the 'scrap' material of other founders' hoards of the latest Bronze Age in the Atlantic west. The early Iron Age hoard from Wattenheim (Alsenborn) in the Palatinate, Germany, produced fragments of a Gündlingen sword, a detached iron strap handle possibly from an early Iron Age Kurd bucket, and a west European linear-faceted axe (Cowen 1967, 397, fig. 6.10; Kibbert 1984, pl. 98C–99). Linear-faceted axes, together with axes of Type Sompting, are characteristic of the British Llyn Fawr phase, their main distribution centre being in southern Britain (O'Connor 1980, 321ff, map 76). The Wattenheim piece, significantly found in a hoard and not a burial, has a very good parallel in the British hoard from Ferring, West Sussex, where a nearly identical axe was also associated with fragments of a Gündlingen sword (Huth 1997, 275, pl. 37). Further, two blank castings (from different moulds) of Gündlingen swords were probably included in a scrap hoard (partly lost) which also contained an Atlantic axe with rib-and-pellet decoration and was found on the Scharlachberg at Bingen on the west bank of the Rhine (Cowen 1967, Nos 51, 52, pl. 55,.3). Kibbert (1984, 130) has connected this axe (his no. 616) with Briard's Armorican Type Brandivy (1965, 248f). Several Armorican axes have been discovered in Carp's Tongue hoards, thus again demonstrating the overlap or interaction of Atlantic forms of the latest Bronze Age with those of the earliest Iron Age.

Gündlingen swords show many typological features of insular Ewart Park swords and the latter seem to be their closest Bronze Age relations. There are as yet no comparable Bronze Age prototypes from continental Europe. The exact chronological relationship between late versions of Ewart Park swords (Colquhoun and Burgess' 'south-eastern step 4' or Cowen's Thames Type) and swords of Type Gündlingen has been a subject of controversy. Cowen believed Thames swords to be devolved versions of Ewart Park swords that incorporated features of imported Gündlingen swords, these 'cavalry' swords having been 'invented' in southern Germany/ Bohemia in response to mounted warriors, the so-called 'Thraco-Cimmerians' from the east (Cowen 1967, 412f). In contrast to Cowen, Briard (1965, 205f) had classified British Ewart Park sword fragments from the Breton hoards at Kerlouan, St.-Père-en-Retz and Prairie de Mauves – the latter also included a Hiberno-British bucket handle (No. 31) – as '*protohallstattienes*' (Briard 1965, fig. 71.4–8). In this group he also included a Thames sword (Briard 1965, fig. 71.3), thus implying that those swords should be regarded as the prototype of the Hallstatt bronze sword, a notion previously put forward by Naue in 1903, who illustrated a Ewart Park sword from Switzerland as the immediate ancestors of a Gündlingen blade (Naue 1903, 27 pl. 11, 7–8). This hypothesis was also taken up by Schauer (1971; 1972), who reversed Cowen's sequence and derived Gündlingen swords from swords of Thames Type. In common with Cowen, however, he believed Gündlingen swords to have originated on the continent, where he identified several examples of the British Thames Type, which he believed to have been ancestral to all Gündlingen swords. Schauer's theories were strongly opposed by Burgess (1979, 277ff) who demonstrated that many of Schauer's continental Thames swords were in fact ordinary Ewart Park swords. This controversial topic has since been thoroughly discussed by O'Connor (1980, 243ff) and Warmenbol (1988, 244ff), who both favoured Schauer's propositions – as O'Connor stated: "There is no obvious origin for Gündlingen swords in central Europe" (O'Connor 1980, 246).

As there are still no convincing prototypes for Thames or Gündlingen swords from the continent, Schauer's sequence 'Ewart Park-Thames-Gündlingen' is acceptable. His and Cowen's theory of a continental origin, however, is not. It seems unlikely that a few exported Thames swords should have stimulated the production of so many Gündlingen swords, with the 'new' Gündlingen (or transformed Thames) sword then being reintroduced into Britain and Ireland. It seems much more likely that the transformation from Ewart Park via Thames to Gündlingen took place in Britain itself, in the Thames area of south-east England during the later Ewart Park phase in the later ninth century BC, when Carp's Tongue bronzes must still have been current. This would explain the occasional associations of Gündlingen swords with Carp's Tongue material. It is also significant that Britain has only produced Gündlingen swords of the continental types which were not copied in iron (Types Steinkirchen and Weichering), suggesting that these types appeared – in Britain and on the continent – earlier than the continental types also known in iron (Lengenfeld and Muschenheim; for illustrations of rather 'neglected' iron examples see Rieth 1942, fig. 16).

In southeast Britain we see a clear evolution from continental-style flange-hilted and leaf-shaped swords of the earlier Urnfield period (Nenzingen, Hemigkofen and Erbenheim types) via insular Clewer, Limehouse, Taplow, Teddington and Wilburton forms to Ewart Park, Thames and finally Holme Pierrepoint and Gündlingen swords (*cf.* Colquhoun and Burgess 1988, pl. 10–110), a typological sequence already noted by Champion (1982, 41) and not witnessed in continental Europe. Some 'ordinary' Ewart Park swords of step 1 to 3 already incorporate elements of Thames (and Gündlingen) swords and their typology often gets confused, as noted by Burgess when discussing Schauer's proposition. For instance numerous Ewart Park swords of step 2 and 3 already show signs of the spiked butt-end on the midrib (*cf.* Colquhoun and Burgess 1988, pl. 43–47, 68–76), spiked butt-ends being typical of Gündlingen swords. Some Ewart Park step 1, 2 and 3 swords already have notched pommel-pieces (Colquhoun and Burgess 1988, nos 281, 289, 395, 498, 583) or narrow, relatively high ones (nos 490, 516–517A,

592, 587, the latter already with a Gündlingen-style square pommel-piece preserved in bone), while others exhibit pin rivets or tiny rivet holes (nos 280, 282, 287, 298, 389, 501, 511, 512, 517), or have no hilt flanges (nos 280, 286, 288, 491, 513). Some of these features – notched terminals (nos 196–197) and pin rivets (no. 213) – already appear on Wilburton swords. It is therefore not surprising that Abels (2000, 23, pl. 13.1) identified the Ewart Park sword from the Heunischenburg in Franconia as a Thames sword, although it has some good parallels among early (step 1and 2) Ewart Park weapons (*cf.* Colquhoun and Burgess 1988 nos 286, 297, 381, 780). Cowen distinguished his hybrid and Thames types (Colquhoun and Burgess 1988 southeastern step 4) as combining leaf-shaped blades of Ewart Park form with Gündlingen-style hilts, all cast in one. His composite type has a Ewart Park blade to which a separate Gündlingen-type hilt was cast on, the sword being remade from two fragments. As Cowen noted himself (1967, 411), "there is no clearer evidence of the contemporary existence of the two types." Whereas Cowen believed his Thames, composite and hybrid types were created after the 'novel' Gündlingen swords entered southern Britain, we take the view that Gündlingen swords arose out of the Thames type in the Thames valley itself, the main distribution centre of both Thames and Gündlingen swords. The beginnings of the former should predate the beginning of the latter, although both forms may have overlapped for some time. It is generally assumed that Thames swords do not appear in Late Bronze Age hoards, but as their blade fragments are indistinguishable from those of Ewart Park swords, and numerous Ewart Park blade fragments occur in Late Bronze Age hoards, it is possible that some of those blades had hilts of Thames type, which, as shown above, had gradually evolved out of native forms.

The notion of an insular origin for Gündlingen swords may be supported if we consider the origins of wing-shaped chapes, traditionally connected with Gündlingen swords. Winged chapes also lack prototypes on the Continent, but they resemble bag-shaped chapes to which wing-shaped ends have been added. The similarity between bag-shaped and winged chapes was noted long ago by Montelius (1908, 154, figs 146–148, 198) and Déchelette (1913, 274), followed by Rieth, who illustrated a typological sequence (1942, 26, fig. 15). That sequence is most clearly represented in Britain and Ireland. Rieth's evolution begins with an Irish bag-shaped piece, continues via boat-shaped examples which develop into chapes with straight, slightly drooping or swept-back wings, and ends with chapes whose wings curve down (Fig 17.9.1). Rieth connected all these chapes with Ha C, whereas Kossack (1959, 15) related the bag-shaped examples to the Late Bronze Age and all winged examples to his phase Ha C1. In contrast to Kossack and also Cowen (1967, 400f), Rieth believed the chapes with straight to swept-back wings, predominantly found in western Europe (Kossack 1959, pl.151A), preceded the type with down-turned wings, found mainly in central Europe (Kossack 1959, pl. 151B). According to the new chronology of Hallstatt C, Rieth's earlier chapes, namely the boat-shaped form and examples with straight- or swept-back wings, most commonly found in western Europe and frequently accompanied by Gündlingen swords, can now be assigned to Ha C0 or C1a, whereas the chapes with down-turned wings, typically associated with Mindelheim swords and found further east, belong to Ha C 1 or Ha C1b. Significantly, the eponymous continental swords from Steinkirchen and Weichering, which we believe are early among Gündlingen swords (above), have been found with boat-shaped chapes (Schauer 1971: Typ Neuhaus) which are early in Rieth's typological sequence (*cf.* Fig 17.9.1, Nos 2, 3, 6), being closest in form to the bag-shaped type of the Late Bronze Age, whereas the chape found with the eponymous Muschenheim sword (Fig 17.9,17) – which we assumed to belong to the latest type of Gündlingen swords – has down-turned wings generally found with iron Mindelheim swords and unknown from Ireland and Britain.

Bag-shaped chapes, recently discussed by Hein (1992), are predominantly an Atlantic form traditionally connected with the Carp's Tongue horizon of the latest Bronze Age (Kendrick and Hawkes 1932, 125). They occur in Atlantic areas peripheral to the Carp's Tongue complex and are certainly more common in southeastern Britain and Ireland than in Atlantic France (Fig 17.9,3). Apart from a peripheral example in the hoard from Prairie de Mauves, Nantes (*cf.* No. 31), they are completely absent from Brittany, the major centre for Carp's Tongue hoards. In addition to fragments of Carp's Tongue swords, the hoards with bag-shaped chapes nearly always also contain fragments of Ewart Park (or Thames?) swords, as for instance Nos 3, 17, 23, 30 and 31 in the Appendix below. Further bag-shaped chapes are known from Ireland, yet Ireland has produced no Carp's Tongue swords, but numerous Ewart Park types: the Dowris assemblage (No. 2), for example, contains swords only of Ewart Park type. Bag-shaped chapes can definitely be connected with the latest phase of the British/Irish Bronze Age and may have been derived from British/Irish short, tongue-shaped chapes of the preceding Wilburton phase (O'Connor 1980, 190). They should, therefore, be regarded as an indigenous British form of the Ewart Park phase rather than part of the French Carp's Tongue complex, as already envisaged by George Eogan, when he wrote: "...it is, therefore, possible that the bearers of Class 4 (Ewart Park and Thames) swords tipped their scabbards with Class 3 (bag-shaped) chapes" (1965, 170). We therefore suggest that winged chapes – in common with Gündlingen swords – evolved in the Atlantic West, the area of their most frequent distribution and of typological prototypes. They certainly did not originate in the western provinces of the Urnfield Culture, as suggested by Kossack (1959, 15), nor can Gündlingen swords be derived from southern Germany, as proposed by Cowen and Schauer (1972, 268f). The most likely

location for the origin of both winged chapes and Gündlingen swords is southeastern Britain or, less likely, Ireland. Those regions produced Ewart Park, Thames and Gündlingen swords and they have also yielded bag-shaped chapes (Eogan 1965, fig. 94; O'Connor 1980, 546f) as well as early winged ones (Cowen 1967, 453). The gradual transition from Late Bronze to Early Iron Age swords and chapes is there most clearly represented.

Bag-shaped chapes – in common with Thames swords – may have continued into a period which saw the introduction of Gündlingen swords, the latter generally connected with early wing-shaped chapes. This implies that both forms should have overlapped. In the Carp's Tongue hoards of Graville, Vénat and Petit-Villatte bag-shaped chapes were associated with fragments of Gündlingen and Ewart Park blades (above, p. #). At Han-sur-Lesse in Belgium four bag-shaped chapes come from the same location as three British Thames swords, all retrieved from the bed of the River Lesse (Mariën 1975, fig. 1; Warmenbol 1988, 247). Gündlingen swords possibly occur with bag-shaped chapes at Weert in Holland (Warmenbol 1988, 247 no.13, pl. 3.3), and certainly at Chavéria in France (Vuaillat 1977, 45, figs 16–17; O'Connor 1980, 190). At Court-St.-Etienne, Belgium (Mariën 1975, no. CSE 7, fig. 7) a Gündlingen sword was associated with a chape that O'Connor (1980.) describes as intermediate between the Late Bronze Age bag-shaped and early Iron Age Neuhaus type. This surely suggests that Atlantic Late Bronze Age forms must have overlapped in time with those of the earliest Iron Age on the continent. In Britain, bag-shaped chapes – like later forms of Hiberno-British buckets (above, p. ##) and possibly other Late Bronze Age forms – should certainly have survived into the beginning of the Llyn Fawr phase when bronzes were still deposited in hoards, although more frequently in areas – such as Wessex – with fewer Ewart Park hoards. Late Bronze Age forms also occur occasionally in settlements that have yielded Iron Age material, such as Mountbatton near Plymouth (Cunliffe 1988), South Cadbury (No. 16) and Potterne near Devizes in Wiltshire (Lawson 2000). Among its late Bronze Age forms Potterne has produced a bag-shaped chape (Gingell 2000, 193, figs 73, 76) decorated with three concentric-circle ornaments that has an exact parallel in the French Carp's Tongue hoard from Déville-lès-Rouen (O'Connor 1980, fig. 63). Late Bronze and Early Iron Age forms are rarely associated in hoards, as at the hillfort at Danebury in Hampshire, where earlier Bronze Age types were also present in the hoard (Cunliffe and O'Connor 1979).

From the above it is abundantly clear, that 'Hallstatt sword-bearers' may finally be laid to rest in peace in their continental graves, their ghosts no longer needing to haunt western archaeologists. They never invaded the west nor did they bring 'Hallstatt' forms to Britain and Ireland or introduce an early Celtic language. We have seen that 'Hallstatt' buckets, chapes and swords developed from insular Late Bronze Age forms. Whereas the chapes may be related to native forms of the Wilburton phase, the earliest ancestors of buckets and Gündlingen swords must be sought in the Penard phase, when they evolved from continental prototypes of the earlier Urnfield period. Although our buckets and swords have their ultimate origin in continental forms, these were not transmitted at the beginning of the Iron Age, but half a millennium earlier at the beginning of the Late Bronze Age, when types that have been associated with the 'Celticisation' of the west were really introduced. It is not necessarily coincidental that the earliest insular cauldron, from Colchester in Essex (Hawkes and Smith 1957), the Hiberno-British bucket fragment (No. 16) and spectacular Type Yetholme shield from South Cadbury in Somerset as well as other Late Bronze and Early Iron Age metal types – including the tip of a winged chape – from Navan Fort in Ireland (Waterman 1997, figs 37– 41), have all come from sites that were dominant Celtic strongholds in later prehistoric and early historic times. As John Waddell (1991) has pointed out, 'Celticisation' was a Bronze Age and not an Iron Age process. It is likely that some of our 'Hallstatt sword-bearers' had their roots in the Late Bronze Age Celtic or Proto-Celtic Atlantic west and introduced 'Hallstatt forms', such as Gündlingen swords, winged chapes and crescentic single-edged razors of Type Feldkirch/Benissart (above, p. ##) – and possibly novel strengthening plates for buckets – to more central parts of Europe, where they or their kinsmen contributed to the rise and wealth of the Hallstatt Culture during the earlier eighth century BC. In western central Europe, Hallstatt swords occur near some of the most famous Celtic *Fürstensitze*, such as the Mont Lassois, the Hohenasperg and the Heuneburg with their surrounding, opulently furnished graves. Zürn (1970, 127f), followed by Gerdsen (1986, 76), suggested that 'Hallstatt sword-bearers' were the ancestors of the aristocratic elite who were to occupy those sites during the later phases of the Hallstatt Culture. Perhaps one of the sources of their wealth was that they – in common with their sword-bearing ancestors – acted as continental middlemen in the trade in Atlantic tin and possibly also in Irish gold, controlling its distribution along the Rhine, Seine, Rhône and Danube. As already during the Bronze Age, gold and tin must still have been in high demand during the ensuing Hallstatt period of the continental Iron Age, whose most prestigious metalwork was made of gold while its buckets, situlae, cauldrons, body armour and – last but not least – the Hochdorf *kline* were still produced in bronze.

Appendix: Atlantic buckets

Plain Danubian-style buckets of Type Nannau-Dowris

1. *Nannau*, Merionethshire, Gwynedd, Wales.– Single find (*c.* 1881).– Largely complete bucket with H-shaped handle attachments and four base-plates in shape of handles; bucket may possibly be identical with a lost bucket found in 1826 in peat bog at Arthog, Gwynedd, Wales (below, No. 35).– Nat. Mus.Wales Cardiff (65.49).– Hawkes and Smith 1957, 132–4, 142, fig. 1, pl. 20.a–b; Hemp 1960; Bowen and Gresham 1967, 126–7, pl. 7; Savory 1980, 58, 114–5, no. 256, pl. 6a; Briggs 1987, 164f; Briggs and Holland 1987, 183, no. 1 ('Arthog').– Figs 17.2,1; 17.3,2.

2. *Dowris,* Co. Offaly, Ireland.– From multiple deposit (*cf.* Coles 1971) found during 1820s.– Complete bucket, handles missing, traces of original Danubian-style strap-handles, 6 disc-shaped tabbed base-plates with traces of 7th century Assoc. (selection): bucket fragments (Nos 9–10 below), Class A1 cauldron of Type Tulnacross, Class A2 cauldron handle attachments of Type Portglenone, Ewart Park swords and sword fragments, bag-shaped chape.– Brit. Mus. London (54. 7–14. 313).– Cooke 1848–50, 425, no. 1; Brit. Mus. Guide 1904, 29f, fig. 4.2 (illustrated with the Type Portglenone cauldron handle mistakenly attached); Armstrong 1924, 109; Leeds 1930, 18, 36, no. 9; pl. 8.2; von Merhart 1952, 29–34; pl. 18.2; Hawkes and Smith 1957, 134–137, 142, 145–146, fig. 2.3E; Eogan 1964, 300, fig. 13; Eogan 1983, 130, no. 94, fig. 72; Briggs and Holland 1987, 186, no. 10; Gerloff 1986, 111, pl. 12.iic (for cauldron handle).– Figs 17.2,2; 17.3,1.

3. *Egham,* Petters Sportsfield, Surrey, England. – From founders' hoard, recovered during 1976–77 excavations of LBA/EIA (?) ritual /settlement site near southern bank of River Thames.– Part of ring handle and of tabbed disc-shaped base-plate of Dabubian style.– Assoc. (selection): Type Portglenone handle attachments of Class A 2 cauldron (Gerloff 1986, no. 22), Ewart Park and Carp's Tongue sword fragments, bag-shaped chape.– two radiocarbon dates (BM-1624N): 2630±70 BP and (BM-2596): 2610 ±60 BP (95% prob. between 895–760 Cal BC (Needham *et al.* 1997, 95).– Brit. Mus. London (Petters Sportsfield excav. coll.).– Needham 1986a, 54, pl. 17, fig. 38, no. 84; Needham 1990, 63ff; Briggs and Holland 1987, no. 18.– Fig 17.2,3.

4. *Ireland.–* Single find with bog patina (pre 1900).– Complete, but much repaired bucket with secondary 3-ribbed Hiberno-British handle attachments and traces of primary Danubian-style strap handles; traces of (?)4 original Danubian-style base-plates).– Nat. Mus. Ireland Dublin (1901. 57).– Wright 1900–02, 285 with fig.; Armstrong 1924, 110; Leeds 1930, 16, 36, no. 13; Hawkes and Smith 1957, 145–6; Briggs 1987, 165; Briggs and Holland 1987, no. 21.– Fig 17.3,3.

5. *Ireland.–* Single find with bog patina (pre 1855).– Largely complete bucket with 6-ribbed Hiberno-British handle attachments and possible traces of primary Danubian-style attachments, 6 original base-

plates with 4 secondary strap repairs on junction between base and wall.– Nat. Mus. Ireland Dublin (W.15).– Mallet 1855, 324f, no. 14 (for metal analysis); Wilde 1857–1861, 531, no. 15, fig. 409; Evans 1881, 412, fig. 512; Armstrong 1924, 110; Leeds 1930, 36, no. 12, pl. 8.1; Hawkes and Smith 1957, 145; Briggs 1987, 165: Briggs and Holland 1987, no. 20.– Fig 17.2,5.

Decorated Danubian-style buckets of Type Cape Castle

6. *Bann Valley,* Co. Antrim, Ireland.– Single find (?) with bog/water patina (pre 1856).– Complete bucket decorated with geometric pattern of repoussé bosses, flanged strap-handles of Danubian style, no base-plates.– Mus. York.– Briggs 1987, 162ff, fig. 6; Briggs and Holland 1987, no. 3.

7. *Cape Castle Bog, Armoy,* Co. Antrim, Ireland.– Single find (?) from bog (pre 1881).– Complete bucket, shoulder decorated with pattern of repoussé bosses, secondary ribbed strap-shaped handle attachments; traces of six tabbed primary base plates, secondary base-ring in form of spoked wheel of Type Heathery Burn.– Hunt Mus. Limerick.– Evans, 1881, 412–3, fig. 513; Armstrong 1924, 110; Leeds 1930, 36, no. 6; Hawkes and Smith 1957, 142, 153; Doran 1978, 5f, pl. 1.2; Briggs 1987, 165, pl. 2; Briggs and Holland 1987, no. 4.– Fig 17.3,4.

Hiberno-British buckets of Type Derrymacash

8. *Derrymacash,* Co. Armagh, Ireland.– Single bog find (1896) 90m from the south of Lough Neagh.– Complete bucket with 4-ribbed Hiberno-British handle attachments and 6 base-plates of Type Derrymacash; according to Hawkes and Smith bucket may have had primary Danubian-style strap attachments. – Nat. Mus. Ireland Dublin (1898.114).– Dugan 1897, 437f with fig.; Armstrong, 1924, 111, fig. 7; Leeds 1930, 35, no. 8, pl. 8.3; Hawkes and Smith 1957, 144f; Eogan 1964, 300 fig. 13; Briggs 1987, 165; Briggs and Holland 1987, no. 7.– Figs 17.2,8; 17.4,1.

9. *Dowris,* Whigsborough, Co. Offaly, Ireland.– Complete base sheet with 5 (of originally 8) base-plates of Type Derrymacash.– Assoc. see No. 2 above.– Brit. Mus. London (54.7–14.314).– Cooke 1848–50, 425, no. 2; Leeds 1930, 35, no. 10, pl. 8.4; Hawkes and Smith 1957, 145f; Eogan 1983, 130, no. 95, fig. 72; Briggs and Holland 1987, no. 11.

10. *Dowris,* Whigsborough, Co. Offaly, Ireland.– Two possible base-plates of Type Derrymacash, more slender than other base-plates of this form and they may have served another function.– Assoc. see No. 2 above.– Brit. Mus. London (54.7–14.315).– Leeds, 1930, 35, no. 12; Hawkes and Smith 1957, 145f.;

Eogan 1983, 130, no. 96; Briggs 1987, 165; Briggs and Holland 1987, no. 12.

11. *Ravenstonedale,* Westmoreland, England.– Single bog find (1774).– Complete Hiberno-British bucket (lost) with 6 base-plates of Type Derrymacash.– accurately described by Nicholson and Burn (1777, 529), but never illustrated.– Clough 1969, 23f

12. *Coddington,* Cheshire, England.– Single find (before 1718) .– Complete bucket (lost) with 8 base-plates of Type Derrymacash or possibly Bagmoor; form of handle-attachments unknown, possibly Hiberno-British as handles are to outside of vessel .–Illustrated by William Stukeley in manuscript (Society of Antiquaries, London: Soc. Ant. MSS. 265, p. 30), a different version by Lort appears in Soc. Ant. MSS. 264, p. 9.– Stukeley 1725, vol. I, Iter III, 56; Stukeley 1726, vol. I, Iter III, 59; Hawkes and Smith 1957, 148, note 1; Briggs 1977, 90f, fig. 1, pl. 22 (for full discussion of MS sources); Briggs 1987, 165; Briggs and Holland 1987, no.6.

Hiberno-British bucket fragment of Type Bagmoor

13. *Bagmoor,* Burton-upon-Stather, Lincolnshire, England.– Hoard from quarry (1933).– Six base-plates of Type Bagmoor forming a complete circle.– Mus. Scunthorpe (B52).– Dudley and Hawkes 1947, 8ff, fig. 2, pl. 1; Dudley 1949, 95ff, figs. 34–35; Hawkes and Smith 1957, 139ff; Inv. Arch. GB. 23.1; Davey 1973, 94 fig. 42; Briggs 1987, 165; Briggs and Holland 1987, no. 2.– Fig 17.2,13.

Hiberno-British bucket fragments of Type Hatfield

14. *Hatfield Broad Oak,* Essex, England.– Founders' hoard (1893).– Two Hiberno-British 5/6-ribbed handle-attachments with ring-handles and two base-plates of Type Hatfield.– Mus. Colchester (151.94).– Laver 1898, 172ff; Beaumont 1903, 266 (described as cauldron handles) figs 28–29 and 32; Leeds 1930, 16f; 35, no. 3; Hawkes and Smith 1957, 145, 152f; Davies 1979, 149ff, nos 1–4, fig. 8.1; Briggs 1987, 162; Briggs and Holland 1987, no. 15, figs 5–6.– Fig 17.4,4.

15. *Little Houghton,* Northamptonshire, England.– Single find (1984).– Tub-shaped base sheet with 4 base-plates of Type Hatfield, each representing approximately a quarter segment of a circle.– Mus. Northampton.– Needham 1986b, 374ff– Fig 17.2,15.

16. *South Cadbury hillfort,* Somerset, England.– Found among unstratified LBA/EIA bronzes during excavations.– Small fragment of base-plate probably of Type Hatfield, possibly Type Downhill.– EIA bronzes include swan-necked pins and early Ha C razor.– Yetholme shield recently discovered in silt-filled ditch just below hillfort.– Glasgow University (excav. coll. 095/80).– Alcock 1971, 1ff;, Alcock

1972, 113–17; Alcock 1980, 654ff; Jockenhövel 1980, no. 661 (for Ha C razor); Briggs 1987, 165; Briggs and Holland 1987, no. 19 with fig.; Coles *et al.* 1999, 34, fig. 5 (for shield).– Fig 17.4,5.

17. *Vénat,* Angoulème, Dép.Charente, France.– Founders' hoard in pottery vessel from bank of River Charente (1893).– Small fragment of base-plate probably of Type Hatfield or possibly Downhill (so far not identified as base-ring fragment), surviving decoration of 4 radial and 4 circumferential grooves.– Assoc. (selection): Fragment of handle attachment of Class A2 Type Portglenone cauldron (Gerloff 1986, no. 24), sword fragments of Carp's Tongue, Ewart Park and Gündlingen type, bag-shaped chapes and wheel fittings of Pare's (1992) Type Bad Homburg.– Mus. Angoulème.– George and Chauvet 1895, pl. 21, no. 261; Coffyn *et al.* 1981, 178, pl. 52.9 (pl. 2.12 for Gündlingen fragment); Pare 1992, 43.– Fig 17.4,7.

18. *Bonneville,* Civry-la Forêt, Dép.Seine-et-Oise, France.– Founders' hoard (1895).– Small fragment of base-plate, probably of Type Hatfield or possibly Downhill, although described by Forrer (1896) as vessel fragment, it has not been identified as base ring fragment; angled fragment has full height of wall flange, on base-strip remains of 5 radial and 2 circumferential grooves.– Assoc. (selection): fragments of Ewart Park and Carp's Tongue swords.– ex Forrer coll. – Mus. Essen, Germany.– Forrer 1896, 33, pl. 21, fig. 37; Gaucher 1981, 380f, fig. 103 D.10. – Fig 17.4,6.

Hiberno-British bucket of Type Downhill

19. *Downhill,* Magilligan, Co. Derry, Ireland.– Single find with bog-patina (pre 1914).– Listed by Armstrong (1924), Leeds (1930) and Hawkes and Smith (1957) as an unprovenanced Irish find; vessel located by Corcoran (1965) and provenance established by Rynne (1967).– Complete bucket with 6-ribbed Hiberno-British handle fittings and spoked base-ring found before 1914, patina suggests bog find.– Hunterian Mus. Glasgow (B.1914.344).– Armstrong 1924, 110; Leeds 1930, 36, no. 14; Hawkes and Smith 1957, 145, 148; Corcoran 1965, 12ff, fig. 1, pl. 11–14; Rynne 1967, 109f; Briggs 1987, 162; Briggs and Holland, 1987, no. 9.– Fig 17.2,19 and Fig 17.4,2.

Hiberno-British buckets of Type Heathery Burn

20. *Heathery Burn Cave,* Stanhope, Co. Durham, England.– Found (1872) close to mouth of the cave, other LBA bronze finds scattered over whole length of cave (160m).– Heavily damaged bucket (now mounted on fibre glass) with 5/6-ribbed Hiberno-British handle fittings and spoked base-ring.– Brit. Mus. London (WG 1271).– Evans 1881, 412; Greenwell 1894, 95f with fig.; Brit. Mus. Guide 1920, 46; Leeds 1930, 35, no. 2; Hawkes and Smith 1957, 148ff,. fig. 5; Britton and Longworth 1967; Briggs 1987, 165; Briggs and Holland 1987, no. 16, figs 5–6.– Fig 17.2,20.

21. *Cardross,* Flanders Moss, Stirlingshire, Scotland.– Single find with bog patina from corner of small earth-work (found in early 19th century).– Complete bucket with 7-ribbed Hiberno-British handle fittings and spoked base-ring.– Nat. Mus. Scotland, Edinburgh (DU 11).– Anderson 1887–88, 36ff, fig. 1; Leeds 1930, 22, 35, no. 4 fig. 8; Hawkes and Smith 1957, 145, 151; Coles 1962, 29; Briggs 1987, 162; Briggs and Holland 1987, no. 5, fig. 5.7.

22. *Dervock, Belleisle Bog,* Co. Antrim, Ireland.– Single find from bog (pre 1880).– Damaged bucket with 6-ribbed Hiberno-British handle fittings and spoked base ring.– Ulster Mus. Belfast (1911.141).– Evans 1907–9, 128, fig. 7; Armstrong 1924, 110; Deane 1925, 10f, fig. 5; Leeds 1930, 35, no. 7; Hawkes and Smith 1957, 142, 145; Briggs 1987, 165; Briggs and Holland 1987, no. 8.– Fig 17.4,3.

23. *Graville-Sainte-Honorine,* Le Havre, Dép. Seine Maritime, France.– Founder's hoard from at mouth of Seine (19th cent.).– Small section of (so far unidentified) base-ring of with remains of one spoke, rivet-hole at join of ring and spoke.– Assoc. (selection): Fragments of Carp's Tongue (Dubus 1912, pl. 4.2–4), Ewart Park (Dubus 1912, pl. 4.1.12–13) and Gündlingen (Dubus 1912, pl. 4.7) swords, two bag-shaped chapes (Dubus 1912, 8–9) and cast ribbed tube, possibly fragment of wheel or wagon fitting (Dubus 1912, pl. 4.36).– Mus. de L'Homme, Paris (formerly Dubus collection).– Dubus 1912, 21 pl. 5.5fi (*objet de garniture)*; O'Connor 1980, 398 ff– Fig 17.4,8.

Hiberno-British handle fragments

24. *Duddingston Loch,* Duddingston, Edinburgh, Midlothian, Scotland.– From (?) Crannog (1778).–Fragment of bucket comprising 3-ribbed Hiberno-British handle-attachment and ring-handle, dull gold brown water patina.– Found during dredging operations together with other 'broken' bronzes including Wilburton spearhead and Ewart Park swords.– Nat. Mus. Scotland, Edinburgh (DQ 1).– Wilson 1863, I, 348ff, fig. 50 (left); Stuart 1865, 161–2; Evans 1881, 409, 465; 142; Montelius 1908, 150f fig. 189 (with metal analysis of handle); Callander 1922–3, 361; Leeds 1930, 35, no. 5; Hawkes and Smith 1957, 145, 189; Coles 1962, 29, 88; Briggs 1987, 165; F 1987, 186, no. 13; Colquhoun and Burgess 1988, 52, no. 234; pl. 177–178A (for sword fragments).

25. *Dowalton Loch,* Monreith, Wigtonshire, Scotland.– From crannog (1863).– Fragment of bucket comprising ring-handle, 4-ribbed handle-attachment, part of rim reinforcement and some sheet metal.– Nat.

Mus. Scotland, Edinburgh (HU 5).– Lovaine 1863, 90, 93, fig. 6; Maxwell 1865, 109 ff; Stuart 1865, 121; Coles 1962, 29, 88.

26. *Gilmonby,* Bowes, Co. Durham, England.– Founders' hoard (1980).– Fragment of 4-ribbed handle attachment and 2 fragments of circular ring-handle(s); B. O'Connor has recently also identified base ring section of Type Heathery Burn among contents of hoard.– Mus. Barnard Castle.– Coggins and Tylecote 1983; Briggs 1987, 165; Briggs and Holland 1987, 186 no. 14; base ring fragment not published, B. O'Connor pers comm.

27. *Meldreth,* Cambridgeshire, England.– Founders' hoard (1880) near Meldreth Railway Station.– Fragment of 5-ribbed handle-attachment (incorrectly referred to in Brit. Mus. Guide [1904 and 1920] as coming from a cauldron), 1 ring-handle, possible fragment of 2nd handle-attachment.– Assoc. (selection): Fragments of Ewart Park and Carp's Tongue swords.– Brit. Mus. London (80.11–24.37–38).– Evans 1881, 172, 411, 424, 466; Brit. Mus. Guide 1904, 39; Brit. Mus. Guide 1920, 45; Leeds 1930, 15f, 35 no. 1; Hawkes and Smith 1957, 144–5.189; O'Connor 1980, 192; Briggs 1987, 165; Briggs and Holland 1987, no. 17; Colquhoun and Burgess 1988, 81–2, no. 404, pl. 169A (for swords).

28. *Minnis Bay,* Birchington, Isle of Thanet, Kent, England.– Founders' hoard (1938).– Fragment of 5/6-ribbed handle-attachment, identified by Hawkes and Smith (1957) as part of Class B1 cauldron handle; fragment, however, has wrong profile for cauldron attachment, is ribbed in the manner of bucket attachments and is clearly from a vessel with a neck of much smaller radius than that of a cauldron.– Assoc. (selection): Fragments of Ewart Park and Carp's Tongue swords and bag-shaped chape.– Brit. Mus. London (1961.10–6.63).– Worsfold 1943, 28ff, pl. 12.37; Hawkes and Smith 1957, 185; Cunliffe 1974, 34f., fig. A.4; O'Connor 1980, 384ff., figs 59–60; Briggs 1987, 165; Colquhoun and Burgess 1988, 126 pl. 167.C.

29. *Vale of York,* Yorkshire, England.– Presumably 19th century find.– Two circular ring-handles with 6-ribbed handle attachments identified as cauldron handles (Briggs 1987), but attachments are clearly from a bucket, being very similar to those from Dervock (above, No. 22) and the possible fragment from Gray's Thurrock I (below, No. 30), all being characterised by six ridges or ribs.– Mus .York (1242.1948).– Briggs 1987, 165, 183.

30. *Grays Thurrock I,* Essex, England.– Founders' hoard (1906).– Fragment of 6-ribbed arch, possibly from handle-attachment of bucket and two small sheet fragment with flat-headed rivet, possibly from same vessel.– Assoc. (selection): Fragments of Carp's Tongue and Ewart Park swords and 2 bag-shaped chapes.– Mus. Colchester (2362.11).– Butcher 1922,

105ff with fig.; Hawkes and Smith 1957, 145; O'Connor 1980, 380f, fig. 56; Colquhoun and Burgess 1988, 77f, pl. 166 D (swords).

31. *Prairie de Mauves*, Nantes, Dép.Loire Atlantique, France.– Founders' hoard from bed of River Loire (1881).– Handle-attachment of bucket, 3-ribbed arch with lateral flanges, survived with fragments of sheet and rim reinforcement; classified by Hawkes and Smith (1957) as part of a Class B1 cauldron handle; this identification continued by Schubart (1961), Briard (1965) and Briggs (1987); the shape of the arch and mouldings and the width and small radius of the rim, however, indicate that the attachment comes from a bucket (Gerloff 1986, 100).– Assoc. (selection): Fragments of Carp's Tongue and Ewart Park swords, two bag-shaped chapes, possible wheel fittings of Type Bad Homburg and a socketed leather working knife of EIA type (O'Connor 1980, 239).– Mus. Nantes (881–12–393). –Untitled communication in *Revue Archéologique* 1881, 2, 185f; Hawkes 1952, 110, fig. 8.2; Hawkes and Smith 1957, 182, 185; Schubart 1961, 49, fig. 7; Briard 1965, 235f, 315, no. 365, fig. 75.3; Jockenhövel 1980, pl. 86; Gerloff 1986, 100; Briggs 1987, 162.

32. *Vénat,* Angoulème, Dép.Charente, France.– Possible (but unlikely) fragments of ribbed bucket handle-attachments in form of arch with angular ribs; hitherto not identified as vessel fragments, but as those as of ribbed necks of socketed axes (Coffyn *et al.* 1981).– See No. 17.– Mus. Angoulème.– George/Chauvet 1895, pl. 23, fig. 297; Coffyn *et al.* 1981, pl. 51, nos 22, 24–25.

Ring handles

The following rings have the dimensions and section typical of bucket ring-handles. The diameter of cauldron ring-handles nearly always exceeds 100mm, whereas that of buckets is always less than 100mm. The following rings have diameters of 76 and 78mm which is within the size range for bucket handles; if their section is recorded, it is of lozenge form, the latter again typical of buckets rings and hardly ever found on those of cauldron.

33. *La Guerche*, Dép. Ille-et-Vilaine, France.– Founders' hoard (1891).– Possible ring-handle of bucket (diam. 78mm, lozengic cross section), identified as bracelet (Briard 1965).– Mus. Antiqu. Nat. St.– Germain-en-Laye.– Briard 1965, 313, no. 298; Briard 1985, 74, fig. 2.5.

34. *Chrishall/Elmdon*, Essex, England.– Founders' hoard (1843–44).– Possible ring-handle (lost), diam.74mm, cross-section unknown.– hoard included handle fragment of Class A2 Type Portglenone cauldron and fragments of Ewart Park and Carp's Tongue swords.– Neville 1848, 3 no. 1 with fig.; Clarke 1872–73, 280 ff; pl .4A; Evans 1881, 117, 283, 426, 467; Gerloff 1986, 111, no. 21, pl. 12ii, b (for cauldron handle).

Lost bucket of unknown Type

35. *Arthog*, Llangelynin Gwynedd, Wales.– Single find ? (1826).– Described by Lewis (1840) as 'a copper urn', apart from measurements (18.4" deep, diam. 14.2" at mouth and 11.2" at base) no description or illustration; Hemp (1960) equates measurements with those of the Nannau bucket (above, No. 1); although most of measurements agree quite closely, the base diameter of the Nannau bucket is 195mm against the recorded *c*. 290mm for the Arthog bucket. Lewis 1840 (under 'Llangelynin'); Hemp 1960, 356ff; Bowen and Gresham 1967, 126f; for further bibliography see No. 1.

Acknowledgements

I am very grateful to Peter Northover, who – in the 1980's – was of immense help when compiling an extensive catalogue of all Atlantic vessels (to appear in full in the forthcoming PBF volume) and examining their constructions. His metallurgical analyses and discussions will be included in the forthcoming PPF volume. I am also deeply indebted to Brendan O'Connor who went over the present text and not only polished my English but also provided valuable comments and informed me of new (some unpublished) and recently republished finds relevant to this study. Thanks are also due to Ingeborg Hohenester (proofreading) and Irene Seeberger (illustrations). Last but not least I would like to thank those students from Erlangen University, who endured a seminar on the transition from Bronze- to Iron Age in central and western Europe, their essays, lively discussions and comments also contributed greatly to this paper.

Bibliography

Abels, B.-U. 2002 *Die Heunischenburg bei Kronach. Eine späturnenfelderzeitliche Befestigung*. Regensburger Beiträge zur Prähistorischen Archäologie **9**, Bonn.

Åberg, N. 1930–1935 *Bronzezeitliche und früheisenzeitliche Chronologie 1–5*. Stockholm.

Alcock, L. 1971 Excavation at South Cadbury Castle, *Journal of the Royal Society of Antiquaries* **51**, 1–7.

Alcock, L. 1972 *By South Cadbury is that Camelot....?. The excavations of Cadbury Castle 1966–1970*. London.

Alcock, L. 1980 The Cadbury castle sequence in the first millennium BC, *Bulletin of Board of Celtic Studies* **28**, 654–718.

Anderson, J. 1887–88 Notice of a bronze bucket-shaped vessel or cauldron, exhibited by H.D. Erskine, Esq. of Cardross, *Proceedings of the Society of Antiquaries of Scotland* **22**, 36–42.

Armstrong, E.C.R. 1922 Note on the Hallstatt period in Ireland, *Journal of the Royal Society of Antiquaries* **2**, 204–207.

Armstrong, E.C.R. 1924 The Early Iron Age or Hallstatt Period in Ireland, *Journal of the Royal Society of Antiquaries of Ireland* **54**, 1–14, 109–127.

Beaumont, G.F 1903 Early Man. In J. Chalkley-Gould (ed.) *The History of the County of Essex 1*, 261–274. Victoria County History, London.

Becker, A., Billamboz, A., Egger, H., Gassmann, P., Orcel, A. and Ruoff, U. 1985 *Dendrochronologie in der* Ur- und Früh-geschichte. *Die absolute Datierung von Pfahlbausiedlungen nördlich der Alpen im Jahrringkalender Mitteleuropas*. Basel.

Boquet, A. 1990 Le char de la Côte Saint-André. *In Les premiers princes celts*, 35–37. Exhibition catalogue, Musée Dauphinois, Grenoble.

Bouloumié, B. 1977 Situles de bronze trouvées en Gaule (VIIeIVe siècles av. J.-C.), *Gallia* **35**, 3–8.

Bowen, E.G. and Gresham, C.A. 1967 *From the earliest times to the Native Princes. The History of Merioneth 1*. Dolgellau.

Briard, J. 1965 *Les dépôts bretons et l'Âge du Bronze Atlantique*. Rennes.

Briard, J. 1985 *Les premiers cuivres d'Armorique – une ré-estimation*. In *Palaéometallurgie de la France atlantique, Ages du Bronze II*, 71–79. Rennes.

Briggs, C.S. 1977 A Roman camp kettle of copper, *Journal of the Royal Society of Antiquaries* **57**, 90–91.

Briggs, C.S. 1987 Buckets and cauldrons of the Late Bronze Age of north-east Europe: a review. In C.J. Blanchet (ed.) *Les relations entre le Continent et les Îles Britanniques à l'Âge du Bronze*, 161–187. Actes du colloque de Bronze de Lille, Paris.

Briggs, C.S. and Holland, M. 1987 Buckets in the British Isles. Appendix 2 in C.S. Briggs Buckets and cauldrons of the Late Bronze Age of north-east Europe: a review. In C.J. Blanchet (ed.) *Les relations entre le Continent et les Iles Britanniques à l'Âge du Bronze*, 183–187. Actes du colloque de Bronze de Lille, Paris.

British Museum Guide 1904 *A guide to the antiquities of the Bronze Age*. London.

British Museum Guide 1920 *A guide to the antiquities of the Bronze Age*. 2nd edition, London.

Britton, D. and Longworth, I.H. 1967 *Late Bronze Age finds in the Heathery Burn Cave*. Inventaria Archaeologia Great Britain **9**, GB 5, London.

Brizio, E. 1889 Bologna- Scavi dell'arcaica necropoli italica nel predico già Benacci, ora Caprara, presso Bologna negli anni 1887–88, *Notizie degli Scavi di Antichità* 1889, 288–333.

Bronk Ramsey, C. *et al.* 2002 Radiocarbon dates from the Oxford AMS System: Archaeometry datelist 31, *Archaeometry* **44**, 3 Suppl. 1, 1–149.

Brunn, W.A. von 1968 *Mitteldeutsche Hortfunde der jüngeren Bronzezeit*. Berlin.

Burgess, C.B. 1968 The later Bronze Age in the British Isles and north-western France, *The Archaeological Journal* **125**, 1–45.

Burgess, C.B. 1969 Chronology and terminology in the British Bronze Age, *Journal of the Royal Society of Antiquaries* **49**, 22–29.

Burgess, C.B. 1979 A find from Boyton, Suffolk, and the end of the Bronze Age in Britain and Ireland. In C.B. Burgess and D. Coombs (eds) *Bronze Age hoards. Some finds old and new*, 269–282. British Archaeological Reports British Series **67**, Oxford.

Burgess, C.B. and Coombs, D. (eds) 1979 *Bronze Age hoards. Some finds old and new*. British Archaeological Reports British Series **67**, Oxford.

Butcher, C.H. 1922 A hoard of bronzes discovered at Grays Thurrock, *Journal of the Royal Society of Antiquaries* **2**, 105–108.

Byvanck, A.W. 1946 *De vorgeschiedenis van Nederland*, Leiden 4.

Callander, J.G. 1922–23 Scottish Bronze Age hoards, *Proceedings of the Society of Antiquaries of Scotland* **57**, 123–166.

Cerchiai, L. 1988: La situle de type Kurd découverte dans la tombe 4461 de Pontecagno. In: Les Princes Celtes et la méditerrané. Rencontres de L' École du Louvre (Paris)103–110.

Chapotat, G. 1962 Le char processionel de la Côte-Saint-André, *Gallia* **20**, 34–78.

Champion, T. 1982 The myth of Iron Age invasions in Ireland. In: B. Scott (ed.) *Studies on Early Ireland. Essays in honour of M.V. Duignan*, 39–44. Belfast.

Childe, V.G. 1926 Two Bronze hoards from Hajdusámson, nr. Debreczen, *Man* **26**, 31–32.

Childe, V.G. 1929 *The Danube in prehistory*. Oxford.

Childe, V.G. 1930 *The Bronze Age*. Cambridge.

Childe, V.G. 1935 *The prehistory of Scotland*. Edinburgh.

Clarke, J. 1872–73 Notes on objects in the Mayer Collection relating to Essex, with an account of the discovery of celts and war implements, *Transactions of the Lancashire and Cheshire Antiquarian Society* **25**, 271–284.

Clough, T.H. McK. 1969 Bronze Age metalwork from Cumbria, *Transactions of the Cumberland and Westmoreland Antiquarian and Archaeological Society* **49** (N.S.), 1–39.

CMAL *The Council for Museums, Archives and Libraries 2003, Portable Antiquities Scheme: annual report 2001/02–2002/03*. London.

Coblenz, W. 1952 Der Bronzegefäßfund von Dresden-Dobritz, *Arbeits- und Forschungsberichte zur Sächsischen Bodendenkmalpflege* **2**, 135–161.

Coffyn, A., Gomez, J. and Mohen, J.-P. 1981 *L'apogée du Bronze Atlantique. Le dépôt de Vénat. L'Âge du Bronze en France 1*. Paris.

Coggins, D. and Tylecote, R.F 1983 *The Gilmonby, Co. Durham: bronze hoard*. Bowes Museum Archaeological Reports **2**, Barnard Castle.

Coles, J.M. 1962 Scottish Late Bronze Age metalwork: typology, distributions and chronology, *Proceedings of the Society of Antiquaries of Scotland* **93**, 16–134.

Coles, J.M. 1971 Dowris and the Late Bronze Age of Ireland: A footnote, *Journal of the Royal Society of Antiquaries of Ireland* **101**, 164–165.

Coles, J.M., Leach, P., Minnitt, S., Tabor, R. and Wilson, A. 1999 A later Bronze Age shield from South Cadbury, Somerset, England, *Antiquity* **73**, 33–48.

Colquhoun, I. and Burgess, C.B. 1988: *The swords of Britain*. Prähistorische Bronzefunde IV, 5, München.

Cooke, T.L. 1848–50 On bronze antiquities found at Dowris in the King's County, *Proceedings of the Royal Irish Academy* **4**, 423–450.

Corcoran, J.X.W.P. 1965 A bronze bucket in the collection of the Hunterian Museum, University of Glasgow, *Journal of the Royal Society of Antiquaries* **45**, 12–17.

Cordier, G. 1996 *Le dépôt de l'Âge du Bronze Final du Petit-Villatte à Neuvy-sur-Barangeon (Cher) et son contexte regional*. Joué-Lès-Tours.

Cowen, J.D. 1967 The Hallstatt sword of bronze; on the continent and in Britain, *Proceedings of the Prehistoric Society* **33**, 377–454.

Crawford, O.G.S. 1922 A prehistoric invasion of England, *Journal of the Royal Society of Antiquaries* **2**, 27–35.

Cunliffe, B.W. 1974 *Iron Age communities in Britain*. London/Boston.

Cunliffe, B.W. 1988 *Mountbatton, Plymouth. A prehistoric Roman port*. Oxford University Committee for Archaeology Monograph **26**, Oxford.

Cunliffe, B and O'Connor, B. 1979 The late Bronze Age hoard from Danebury, Hampshire. In C.B. Burgess and D. Coombs (eds) *Bronze Age hoards. Some finds old and new*, 235–244. British Archaeological Reports British Series **67**, Oxford.

Davey, W. 1973 Bronze Age metalwork from Lincolnshire, *Archaeologia* **104**, 51–127.

Davies, G.D. 1979 Hatfield Broad Oak, Leigh, Rayne, Southchurch: Late Bronze Age hoards from Essex. In C. B. Burgess and D. Coombs (eds), *Bronze Age hoards. Some finds old and new*, 149–172. British Archaeological Reports British Series **67**, Oxford.

Deane, A. 1925 Prehistoric Ulster antiquities: the Bronze and early Iron Ages, *Belfast Municipal Museum Quarterly Notes* **50**, 1–19.

Déchelette, J. 1913 *Manuel d'Archéologie Préhistorique, Celtique et Gallo-Romaine II, 2: Premiér Âge du Fer ou Époque de Hallstatt*. Paris.

Desittere, M. 1974 Quelques considérations sur l'âge du bronze final et le premier âge du fer en Belgique et dans le sud des Pays-Bas, *Helinium* **14**, 105–134.

Doran, P. 1978 The Hunt Museum, *North Munster Antiquarian Journal* **20**, 3–16.

Dubus, A. 1912 Époque de Bronze. Carte et tableau analytique de la répartition du bronze dans la Seine-Inférieur, *Bulletin de la Société Géologique de Normandie* **31**, 1–35.

Dudley, H.E. 1949 *Early days in northwest Lincolnshire*. Scunthorpe.

Dudley, H.E. and C.FC. Hawkes 1947 The Bagmoor founder's hoard, *The Archaeological Journal* **103**, 8–11.

Dugan, C.W. 1897 Interesting 'find' in the Montiaghs, Co. Armagh, *Journal Royal Society of Antiquaries of Ireland* **27**, 437–438.

Egg, M. 1985 Die hallstattzeitlichen Hügelgräber bei Helpfau-Uttendorf in Oberösterreich. *Jahrbuch des Römisch-Germanischen Zentralmuseums Mainz* **32**, 323–393.

Eogan, G. 1964: The later Bronze Age in Ireland in the light of recent research, *Proceedings of the Prehistoric Society* **30**, 268–351.

Eogan, G. 1965 *Catalogue of Irish Bronze Swords*, National Museum of Ireland, Dublin.

Eogan, G. 1974 Regionale Gruppierungen in der Spätbronzezeit Irlands, *Archäologisches Korrespondenzblatt* **4**, 319–327.

Eogan, G. 1983 *Hoards of the Irish Later Bronze Age*, University College, Dublin.

Eogan, G. 1990 Possible connections between Britain and Ireland and the east Mediterranean region during the Bronze Age. In *Orientalisch Ägäische Einflüsse in der Europäischen Bronzezeit. Monographien des Römisch- Germanischen Zentralmuseums Mainz* **15**, Bonn.

Eogan, G. 1994 *The accomplished art: Gold and Gold working in Britain and Ireland during the Bronze Age*. Oxbow Monographs **42**, Oxford).

Eogan, G. 1995 Ideas, People and Things: Ireland and the External World during the Later Bronze Age. In J. Waddell, and E. Shee Twohig (eds) *Ireland in the Bronze Age*, 128–136. The Stationery Office, Dublin.

Eogan, G. 2000 The socketed bronze axes in Ireland. *Prähistorische Bronzefunde* IX, 22, Stuttgart.

Evans, E. 1931: The Late Bronze Age in western Europe, *Man* **31**, 207–211.

Evans, E. 1907–09 Untitled communication. *Proceedings of Society of Antiquaries of London* 22 (2nd ser.), 121–29.

Evans, J. 1881 *The ancient bronze implements, weapons and ornaments of Great Britain and Ireland*. London.

Fily, M. 2003 *Le Bronze Final I en Bretagne: le site à dépôts de Saint-Ygeaux dans les Côtes d'Armor, mémoire de maîtrise sous la direction de Michèle Casanova, direction scientifique de Maréva Gabillot*. Rennes 2,

Fischer, U. 1979: Ein Grabhügel der Bronze- und Eisenzeit im Frankfurter Stadtwald. Schriften des Frankfurter Museums für Ur- und Frühgeschichte 4 (Frankfurt/Main).

Forrer, R. 1896 Der Depotfund von Bonneville. Strasbourg.

Friedrich, M. and Hennig, H. 1995 Dendrochronologische Untersuchungen der Hölzer des hallstattzeitlichen Wagengrabes 8 aus Wehringen, Lkr. Augsburg und andere Absolutdaten zur Hallstattzeit. *Bayerische Vorgeschichtsblätter* **60**, 289–302.

Gaucher, G. 1981 *Sites et cultures de l'Âge du Bronze dans le Bassin Parisien*. Paris.

Gedl, M. 2001 *Die Bronzegefäße in Polen*. Prähistorische Bronzefunde II, 15, Stuttgart.

George, J. and Chauvet, G. 1895 Cachette d'objets en bronze découverte à Vénat, commune de Saint-Yrieix, près Angoulème. Rapports présentés à la Société Archéologique et Historique de la Charente. *Bulletin et Mémoires de la Société Archéologique et Historique de la Charente 1895*, 141–143.

Gerdsen, H. 1986 *Studien zu den Schwertgräbern der älteren Hallstattzeit*. Mainz.

Gerloff, S. 1980–81 Westeuropäische Griffzungenschwerter in Berlin. Zu chronologischen Problemen der britischen Spätbronzezeit. *Acta Praehistorica et Archaeologia* 11–12, 183–216.

Gerloff, S. 1986 Bronze Age Class A cauldrons: typology, origins and chronology, *Journal of the Royal Society of Antiquaries of Ireland* 116, 84–115.

Gerloff, S. forthcoming Atlantic cauldrons and buckets. *Studies in typology, origin and function of multi-sheet vessels of the Late Bronze and Early Iron Age in western Europe*. With a contribution on their construction and metallurgy by P. Northover. Prähistorische Bronzefunde II. Stuttgart (in press).

Gingell, C.J. 2000 Copper alloy objects. In A.J. Lawson, Potterne 1982–5: Animal husbandry in later prehistoric Wiltshire, 186–193, *Wessex Archaeology Report* 17, 186–193.

Greenwell, W. 1894 Antiquities of the Bronze Age found in the Heathery Burn Cave, County Durham, *Archaeologia* 54, 87–114.

Hawkes, C.FC. 1952 Las relaciones atlánticas en el Bronze final entre la Peninsula Ibérica y las Islas Británicas con respecto a Francia, Europa Central y el Mediterránea, *Ampurias* 14, 81–119.

Hawkes, C.FC. and Smith, M.A. 1957 On some buckets and cauldrons of the Bronze and Early Iron Ages, *Journal of the Royal Society of Antiquaries* 37, 131–198.

Heeringen, R.M. 1998–99 Burial with Rhine view: Hallstatt situla grave on the Keurheuvel at Rhenen. *Berichten van den Rijksdients voor het Ouheidkundig Bodemonderzoek te Amersfoort* 43, 69–97.

Hein, M. 1992 Ein Schneidenbeschlag vom Heiligenberg bei Heidelberg – Zur Typologie endbronzezeitlicher und früheisenzeitlicher Ortbänder (Ha B2/B3-Ha C). *Jahrbuch des Römisch-Germanischen Zentralmuseums Mainz* 36 (1), 301–326.

Hemp, W.J. 1960 The tale of a bucket, *Journal of the Merionethshire Historical Record Society* 3–4, 353–359.

Hennig, H. 2001 *Gräber der Hallstattzeit in Bayerisch-Schwaben*. Monographien der Archäologischen Staatsammlung München 2, Stuttgart.

Höglinger, P. 1996 *Der spätbronzezeitliche Depotfund von Sipbachzell/OÖ*. Linzer Archäologische Forschungen, Sonderheft 16, Linz.

Huth, C. 1997 *Westeuropäische Horte der Spätbronzezeit. Fundbild und Funktion*. Regensburg/Bonn.

Jacob, C. 1995 *Metallgefäße der Bronze- und Hallstattzeit in Nordwest-, West- und Süddeutschland*. Prähistorische Bronzefunde II, 9, Stuttgart.

Jockenhövel, A. 1974 Eine Bronzeamphore des 8.Jhdts. v.Chr. von Gevelinghausen, Kr. Meschede (Sauerland). *Germania* 52, 16–58.

Jockenhövel, A. 1980 *Die Rasiermesser in Westeuropa*. Prähistorische Bronzefunde VIII, 3, München.

Kendrick, T.D. and Hawkes, C.F.C. 1932 *Archaeology in England and Wales 1914–1931*. London.

Kibbert, K. 1984 *Die Äxte und Beile im mittleren Westdeutschland II*. Prähistorische Bronzefunde IX, 13 München.

Kimmig. W. 1940 *Die Urnenfelderkultur in Baden. Untersucht auf Grund der Gräberfunde*. Römisch-Germanische Forschungen 14, Berlin.

Kimmig, W. 1962–63 Bronzesitulen aus dem Rheinischen Gebirge, Hunsrück-Eifel, Westerwald, *Berichte der Römisch-Germanischen Kommission* 43–44, 31–106.

Kossack, G. 1959: *Südbayern während der Hallstattzeit*. Römisch Germanische Forschungen 24, Berlin.

Laver, H. 1898 Founder's hoard at Hatfield Broad Oak, *Transactions of the Essex Archaeological Society* 6 (N.S.), 172.

Leeds, E.T. 1930 A bronze cauldron from the River Cherwell, Oxfordshire, with notes on cauldrons and other bronze vessels of allied types, *Archaeologia* 80, 1–36.

Lewis, S. 1840 *A topographical dictionary of Wales*. London.

Lindenschmit, L. 1881 *Die Altertümer unserer heidnischen Vorzeit* 3. Mainz.

Lisle du Dréneuc, P. de 1903 Catalogue du Musée Archéologique de Nantes (Nantes[3]).

Lovaine (Duke of Northumberland) 1863 On the recent discovery of lacustrine human habitations in Wigtonshire. *Transactions of the British Association for the Advancement of Science*. Newcastle-upon-Tyne. Reprinted in Archaeological and Historical Collections relating to Ayrshire and Galloway 5, 1863, 79–99.

Macalister, R.A.S. 1949 *The archaeology of Ireland*. 2nd edition, London.

Mahr, A. 1937 New aspects and problems in Irish prehistory, *Proceedings of the Prehistoric Society* 3, 262–436.

Mallet, J.W. 1855 Report on the chemical examination of antiquities, *Transactions of the Royal Irish Academy* 22, 313–324.

Mariën, M. 1975 Épées de bronze «proto-hallstattiennes» et hallstattiennes découvertes en Belgique, *Helinium* 15, 14–35.

Matthäus, H. 1980 *Die Bronzegefäße der kretisch-mykenischen Kultur*. Prähistorische Bronzefunde II,1, München.

Maxwell, W. 1865 Collection of articles found exploring a Crannog, or artificial island in Dowalton Loch, Wigtonshire, *Proceedings of the Society of Antiquaries of Scotland* 6, 109–111.

Merhart, G. von 1952 Studien über einige Gattungen von Bronzegefäßen. In *Festschrift des Römisch-Germanischen Zentralmuseums zur Feier seines hundertjährigen Bestehens*, 1–71. Mainz.

Modderman, P. 1964 The Chieftains Grave of Oss reconsidered. *Bulletin Antieke Beschafing* 39, 57–62.

Montelius, O. 1908 The chronology of the British Bronze Age. *Archaeologia* 61, 97–162.

Montelius, O. 1910 *La Civilisation Primitive en Italie depuis l'Introduction des Métaux. 2. Italie Centrale*. Stockholm.

Müller, S. 1897 *Nordische Altertumskunde*. Strasbourg.

Müller-Karpe. H. 1956 Das urnenfelderzeitliche Wagengrab von Hart a. d. Alz, Oberbayern, *Bayerische Vorgeschichtsblätter* 21, 46–75.

Müller-Karpe. H. 1959 Beiträge zur Chronologie der Urnenfelderzeit nördlich und südlich der Alpen, *Römisch-Germanische Forschungen* 22, Berlin.

Naue, J. 1903 *Die vorrömischen Schwerter aus Kupfer, Bronze und Eisen*. München.

Needham, S.P. 1979 Two recent British shield finds and their Continental parallels, *Proceedings of the Prehistoric Society* 45, 111–134.

Needham, S.P. 1986a The metalwork. In M. O'Connell *Petters Sports Field, Egham. Excavations of a Late Bronze Age/Early Iron Age site*, 22–59. Surrey Archaeological Society Research Volume 10.

Needham, S.P. 1986b A Bronze Age bucket base from Little Houghton, Northamptonshire, *Journal of the Royal Society of Antiquaries* 66, 374–376.

Needham, S.P. 1990 *The Petters Late Bronze Age metalwork. An analytical study of Thames Valley metalworking in its settlement context*. British Museum Occasional Papers 70, London.

Needham, S.P., Bronk Ramsey, C., Coombs, D., Cartwright, C., and Pettitt, P. 1997 An independent chronology for British Bronze Age metalwork: the results of the Oxford Radiocarbon accelerator programme, *Archaeological Journal* 154, 55–107.

Neville, R. 1848 *Sepulchra Exposita, or an account of the opening of some barrows with remarks upon miscellaneous antiquities discovered in the neighbourhood of Audley End*. Saffron Walden, Essex.

Nicholson, J. and Burn, R. 1777 *The history and antiquities of the counties of Westmoreland and Cumberland 1*. London.

Nijboer, A.J., van der Plicht, J., Bietti Sestieri, A.M. and de Santis,

A. 1999–2000 A high chronology for the Early Iron Age in Central Italy, *Palaeohistoria* **41/42**, 163–176.

O'Connor, B. 1980 *Cross-channel relations in the later Bronze Age.* British Archaeological Reports International Series **91**, Oxford.

Pare, C.F.E. 1987 Wagenbeschläge der Bad Homburg Gruppe und die kulturgeschichtliche Stellung des hallstattzeitlichen Wagengrabes von Wehringen, Kreis Augsburg, *Archäologisches Korrespondenzblatt* **17**, 467–482.

Pare, C.F.E. 1992 *Wagons and wagon-graves of the early Iron age in Central Europe.* Oxford.

Pare, C.F.E. 1998 Beiträge zum Übergang der Bronze- zur Eisenzeit in Mitteleuropa. Teil I: Grundzüge der Chronologie im östlichen Mitteleuropa (11.–8. Jahrhundert v.Chr.), *Jahrbuch des Römisch-Germanischen Zentralmuseums Mainz* **45** (1), 293–433.

Patay, P. 1990 *Die Bronzegefäße in Ungarn.* Prähistorische Bronzefunde II, 10. Stuttgart.

Pautreau J.-P. and Soyer, C. 2001–2002 Chaudron en bronze de l âge du Fer découvert à Ouzilly-Vignolles, Vienne (France), *Aquitania* **18**, 403–410.

Peake, H.J.E. 1922 *The Bronze Age and the Celtic world.* London.

Peroni, R.1994 *Introduzione alla protostoria italiana.* Roma/Bari.

Primas, M. 1995 Stand und Aufgabe der Urnenfelderforschung in der Schweiz. In *Beiträge zur Urnenfelderzeit nördlich und südlich der Alpen*, 201–224. Monographien des Römisch-Germanischen Zentralmuseums Mainz **35**, Bonn.

Prüssing, G. 1991 *Die Bronzegefäße in Österreich.* Prähistorische Bronzefunde II, 5, Stuttgart.

Randall-MacIver, R. 1924 *Villanovans and early Etruscans.* Oxford.

Reinecke, P. 1911 Grabfunde der zweiten Hallstattstufe aus Süddeutschland (Juli 1908). In *Die Altertümer aus unserer heidnischen Vorzeit* 5, 315–323. Mainz.

Rieth, A. 1942 *Die Eisentechnik der Hallstattzeit.* Mannus Bücherei **8**, Leipzig.

Rynne, E. 1967 The bronze bucket in the Hunterian Museum, *Journal of the Royal Society of Antiquaries* **47**, 109–110.

Savory, H.N. 1948 'The sword bearers'. A reinterpretation, *Proceedings of the Prehistoric Society* **14**, 155–176

Savory, H.N. 1980 *Guide Catalogue of the Bronze Age collections.* National Museum of Wales, Cardiff

Schauer, P. 1971 *Die Schwerter in Süddeutschland, Österreich und der Schweiz I.* Prähistorische Bronzefunde IV,2, München.

Schauer, P. 1972 Zur Herkunft der bronzenen Hallstattschwerter, *Archäologisches Korrespondenzblatt* **2**, 261–270.

Schubart, H. 1961 Atlantische Nietenkessel von der Pyrenäenhalbinsel, *Madrider Mitteilungen* **2**, 35–54.

Soroceanu, T. and Buda,V. 1978 Der Bronzegefäßhort von Buza (Kr.Cluj), *Dacia* NS **22**, 99–106.

Stuart, J. 1865 Notices of a group of artificial islands in the Loch of Dowalton, Wigtonshire and of other artificial islands or 'crannogs' throughout Scotland, *Proceedings of the Society of Antiquaries of Scotland* **6**, 114–131.

Stukeley, W. 1725 *Itinerarium Curiosum.* London.

Stukeley, W. 1776 *Itinerarium Curiosum.* 2nd edition, London.

Szombathy, J. 1913 Altertumsfunde aus Höhlen bei St.Kanzian im österreichischen Küstenlande, *Mitteilungen der Prähistorischen Kommission Wien* **2** (2), 127–169.

Teržan, B. and Mihovilič, B. forthcoming *Depoji pozne bronaste dobe na Slovenskem III-Depo iz Musje jame pri Skocjanu.*

Tomedi, G. 1999 Eliten und Dynastien in der späten Urnenfelderzeit und Hallstattzeit im Südostalpenraum. In *Eliten der Bronzezeit. Ergebnisse zweier Kolloquien in Mainz und Athen*, 661–681. Monographien des Römisch-Germanischen Zentralmuseums Mainz **43**, 2, Bonn.

Vuaillat, D. 1977 *La necropole tumulaire de Chaveria (Jura).* Paris.

Waddell, J. 1991 The celticization of the West: an Irish perspective. In C. Chevillot and A. Coffyn (eds) *L'Âge du Bronze Atlantique. Actes du Ier colloque du Parc Archéologique de Beynac*, 349–366. Beynac-et-Cazenac.

Warmenbol, E. 1988 Broken bronzes and burned bones. The transition from Bronze to Iron Age in the Low Countries, *Helinium* **28**, 244–270.

Waterman, D.M. 1997 *Excavations at Navan Fort 1961–71.* Completed and edited by C.J. Lynn. Northern Ireland Archaeological Monographs **3**, Belfast).

Wilde, W.R. 1857–61 *A descriptive catalogue of the antiquities of animal materials and bronze in the museum of the Royal Irish Academy.* Dublin.

Wilson, D. 1863 *Prehistoric Annuals of Scotland* Vol. 1 (London, Cambridge, Edinburgh).

Worsfold, F.H. 1943 A report on the Bronze Age site excavated at Minnis Bay, Birchington, Kent, 1938–40, *Proceedings of the Prehistoric Society* **9**, 28–39.

Wright, E.P. 1900–02 Notes on some Irish Antiquities deposited with the Academy, *Proceedings of the Royal Irish Academy* **22**, 283–288.

Zürn, H. 1970 *Hallstattforschungen in Nordwürttemberg.* Stuttgart.

18. Von West nach Ost?
Zur Genese der Frühbronzezeit Mitteleuropas

Albrecht Jockenhövel

Spätestens seit den Arbeiten von Ernst Sprockhoff (1941) und Jay Jordan Butler (Butler 1963) wissen wir um die Bedeutung der westeuropäischen Frühbronzezeit für den mitteleuropäischen Raum (vgl. auch Laux 1995). Die Beziehungen werden anschaulich belegt zum Beispiel durch das Vorkommen von goldenen Lunulae von Irland über die Britischen Inseln bis in das westliche Mitteleuropa. Es sind entweder direkte Importe oder kontinentale (*provincial*) Nachahmungen (Taylor 1980; Herrmann 1999). Letztere wurden ihrerseits in Mitteleuropa sogar im "geringer wertigen" Kupfer imitiert bzw. umgeformt (Reim 1995). Spätestens seit der Arbeit von Rüdiger Krause wissen wir auch, dass offenbar Westeuropa, d. h. die Britischen Inseln und Irland, aber auch die Bretagne, die alte Armorica, in der Frühbronzezeit als Zinnlieferant für Mitteleuropa in Frage kommt: In einem im älteren Abschnitt der südwestdeutschen Frühbronzezeit, d. h. vor der klassischen Stufe Bz A2 (= Stufe Langquaid) belegten Gräberfeld von Singen (Südbaden) fanden sich einige pointilléverzierte Dolchklingen mit einem recht hohen Zinnanteil (Krause 1988, 59, Abb. 21; 242 ff. bes. 244). Die besten Parallelen zu den Pointillé-Dolchklingen liegen von den Britischen Inseln und aus der Bretagne vor (Gerloff 1975), so dass die Vermutung auf der Hand liegt, dass nicht nur zinnhaltiges Kupfer (so die Dolche von Singen), sondern auch reines Zinn – trotz seiner Empfindlichkeit durch äußere Einflüsse (Zinnpest, Kälte usw.), die seine Überlieferung stark beeinträchtigen – aus westeuropäischen Lagerstätten nach Mitteleuropa gelangte und dort wesentlich zum Aufkommen der Bronzetechnologie beitrug. Aus den Zinnlagerstätten Mitteleuropas, besonders dem Sächsischen Erzgebirge (Bartelheim und Niederschlag 1998) und dem Fichtelgebirge sowie aus weiteren Lagerstätten, liegen immer noch keine montan-archäologischen oder metallanalytische Anhaltspunkte für ihre frühbronzezeitliche Ausbeutung vor. Viel besser steht es im Grunde auch nicht um die Verhältnisse in Westeuropa selbst, wo vor allem Cornwall als Heimatland des bronzezeitlichen Zinns gilt (Penhallurick 1986). In seinen unzähligen neuzeitlichen Zinnseifen, den "streamworks", wurden zwar auch bronzezeitliche Objekte geborgen.

Jedoch belegen sie für die Bronzezeit nicht zwingend eine auf das Zinnwaschen zielgerichtete Tätigkeit, sondern können durchaus sekundär in die Seifen gelangt sein, d. h. als Flussdeponierungen oder als Beigaben in später abgespülten Gräbern oder als verlagerte Güter aus Siedlungen. Es gibt bisher nur einen Befund einer frühbronzezeitlichen Zinngewinnung in Cornwall: In einem Ringwall-Grabhügel bei Caerloggas Down fanden sich eine fragmentierte Dolchklinge vom Typ Camerton-Snowshill (Gerloff 1975) und mehrere Stücke Zinnschlacke (Penhallurick 1986, 177 f. 221, Abb. 79). In diesem Zusammenhang sei bemerkt, dass als Nebenprodukt der alluvialen Flussseifen Cornwalls auch Gold gewonnen wurde, so dass vielleicht auch der frühbronzezeitliche Goldreichtum Westeuropas (zuletzt Eogan 1994), der bis in die Glockenbecherzeit zurückgeht, auf dem Hintergrund gemeinsam ausgebeuteter Alluvial-Sekundärlagerstätten zu suchen ist.

Die enge Nachbarschaft von Gold-, Silber-, Kupfer- und Zinnlagerstätten in der Bretagne, Südwestengland und Irland, wozu noch im Südosten Englands Lagerstätten baltischen Bernsteins kommen (Beck and Shennan 1991), macht diese ganze Zone zu einem "Eldorado" der Frühbronzezeit Europas und ist, was den Reichtum an Erzlagerstätten betrifft, nur noch mit den Verhältnissen auf der Iberischen Halbinsel vergleichbar (Monteagudo 1977). Alle diese frühbronzezeitlichen Kostbarkeiten Westeuropas sind auf der berühmten Halskette von Exloërmond, Gem. Odoorn (Drenthe; Niederlande) aufgefädelt, die übereinstimmend der Frühbronzezeit zugewiesen wird (Fig 18:1): Sie besteht aus einem Bronzeblechröhrchen, 25 Zinnperlen, 14 Bernsteinperlen und vier segmentierten Fayenceperlen (zuletzt Butler 1990, 54 ff. Nr. 1 Abb. 4). Edel- und Buntmetalle sowie Bernstein kommen in überreichem Maße auch in den frühbronzezeitlichen Gräbern der südenglischen Wessex-Fazies (Gerloff 1975) und der Armoricanischen Gruppe (Briard 1984) vor. In diesem Zusammenhang weise ich besonders auf die beiden bekannten Miniatur-Stabdolche aus den wessexzeitlichen Gräbern von Hengistbury Head (Dorset) und Wilsford G8 (Wiltshire) (Clark *et al.* 1985, 123 f. Abb. 4.55–56) hin: In einen kleinen Schaft aus

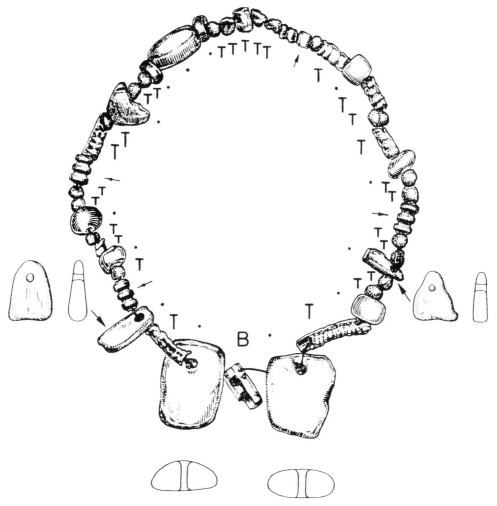

Fig 18.1: Exloërmond, Gem. Odoorn (Drenthe, Niederlande). Kette aus Bronzeröhren (B), Zinnperlen (T), Fayenceperlen (Pfeile) und Bernsteinperlen (nach J. J. Butler 1990). M. 1:1.

Bernstein ist jeweils eine kleine Kupfer- bzw. Bronzeklinge eingelassen. Wie allgemein bekannt, sind gerade die Stabdolche eines der wichtigsten überregionalen Kennzeichen der europäischen Frühbronzezeit (Lenerzde Wilde 1991). Sie verbanden sowohl formal als auch funktional unterschiedlichste Kulturgruppen zwischen der Iberischen Halbinsel und Mitteleuropa. Hinter ihrer Verwendung standen nicht nur waffentechnische, sondern vor allem auch ideologisch-symbolische Gemeinsamkeiten, die nur auf einer weitgespannten frühbronzezeitlichen Interaktion bzw. Kommunikation beruhen konnten.

I

Die umfangreichste Fundgruppe der frühbronzezeitlichen Objekte, die von den Britischen Inseln und/oder Irland auf den Kontinent gelangten, stellen jedoch die sog. "anglo-irischen" Flachbeile und Randleistenbeile dar. Sie kommen auf dem europäischen Festland in West- und Mitteldeutschland und in Südskandinavien (Dänemark, Südschweden, Nordfrankreich, in Belgien und den

Niederlanden, in West- und Norddeutschland) vor (Fig 18.7). Ihre Anzahl beträgt ca. 60–70 Stücke. Schon Megaw und Hardy (1938) sowie Butler (1963) konnten herausarbeiten, dass diese "anglo-irischen" Beile offenbar in zwei Richtungen auf den Kontinent über den Kanal und die Nordsee auf das europäische Festland gelangten: einmal über die Nordsee nach Dänemark und nach dem westlichen Ostseegebiet (bis Südschweden), zum anderen über den Kanal in Richtung Nordfrankreich, Belgien und Niederlande nach West- und Mitteldeutschland. Unter ihnen sind die Beile vom weit gefaßten Typ Ballyvalley am zahlreichsten, die sich durch eine typische trapezförmige Umrißform und eine – häufig – geometrische Verzierung auszeichnen (Harbison 1969, 78 ff.). Ohne Zweifel wurden solche Beile in Irland selbst hergestellt oder ihre kontinentalen Vergleichsstücke gehen auf sie zurück, sei es als Import, sei als Nachahmung (unter Einfluß der lokalen Beilproduktion) (Butler 1963; 1995/1996; Vandkilde 1996). Harbison vermutete, dass auf dem Kontinent einige von ihnen sogar von irischen Bronzeschmieden selbst hergestellt wurden (Harbison 1969, 180).

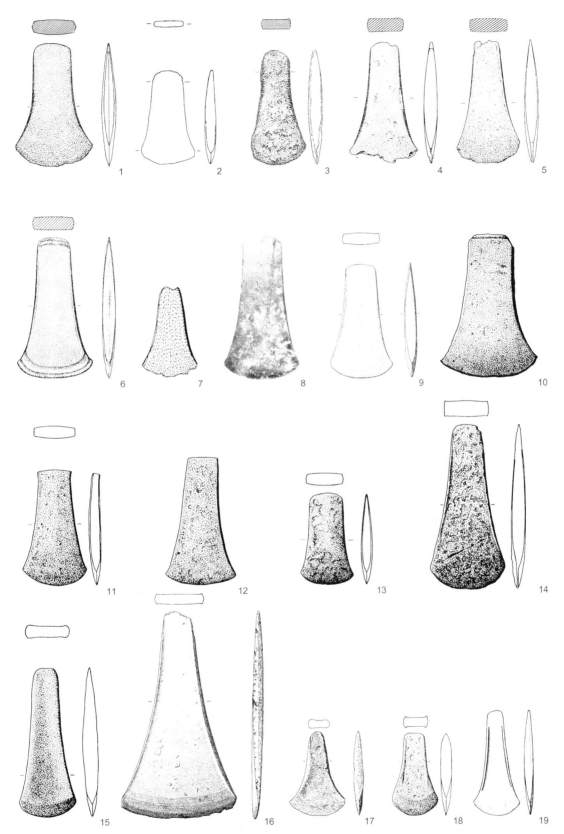

Fig 18.2: "Anglo-irische" Beile und ihre Derivate vom europäischen Festland (NL Niederlande; B Belgien; F Frankreich; D Deutschland; DK Dänemark; S Schweden): 1 Wageningen (NL). – 2 Arnheim (NL). – 3 Haler (NL). – 4 Hapert (NL). – 5 Drouwen (NL). – 6 Wijchen (NL). – 7 Bacouël (F). – 8 Fredsø (DK). – Pelleshave (DK). – 10 "Düsseldorf" (D). – 11 "Mainz" (D). – 12 Pirmasens (D). – 13 Rhein bei Mainz (D). – 14 Herchen (D). – 15 Uffeln (D). – 16 Øndrup Mark (DK). – 17 Holmlands Klit (DK). – 18 "Rheinland" (D). – 19 Rekem (B). – Kupfer/Bronze. – (1–6 nach Butler, 7 nach Blanchet, 8. 9. 16. 17 nach Vandkilde, 10–15. 18 nach Kibbert; 19 nach Mariën). – M. 1:3.

Wenn auch die relative Chronologie des *Early Bronze Age* auf den Britischen Inseln und Irlands mangels typenreicher geschlossener Funde aus Gräbern und Horten noch weiter diskutiert wird (Burgess 1980; Needham *et al.* 1997), ist die irische Abfolge nach Burgess (1980) in sieben Phasen (*stages*, benannt nach kennzeichnenden Hortfunden) durchaus plausibel und nachvollziehbar. *Stage 1 (Castletownroche)* und *Stage 2 (Lough Ravel)* gehören in einen auf die Megalithzeit folgenden Zeitabschnitt, der in Irland (und auf den Britischen Inseln) mit der Glockenbecherkultur zeitlich und kulturell zu verknüpfen ist. Mit *Stage 3 (Frankford)* befinden wir uns, wie das Aufkommen von Stabdolchen zeigt, bereits in einem typischen frühbronzezeitlichen Zeitmilieu, das seine genetische Fortsetzung in *Stage 4 (Killaha)* findet. Mit *Stage 5 (Ballyvalley)* und *Stage 6 (Scrabo Hill)* erreichen wir die Vor-Wessex-Zeit und Wessex-Zeit, während *Stage 7 (Derryniggin)* als späteste älterbronzezeitliche Phase Irlands gilt, die zur Mittelbronzezeit überleitet. *Stage 7* kann über die südenglische *Arreton-Ebnal-Phase* (Burgess 1980) mit dem kontinentalen *Sögel-Wohlde-Horizont* parallelisiert werden. Innerhalb dieser Abfolge gehören die verzierten "anglo-irischen" Beile überwiegend in die Ballyvalley- und Scrabo Hill-Phase, d. h. in die *Stages 5 und 6*. Diese relative Abfolge wurde unlängst auch durch "typologieunabhängige" Methoden, d. h. 14C-Daten bestätigt (Needham *et al.* 1997).

Die zeitliche Position der auf den Kontinent gelangten "anglo-irischen" Beile ist nicht immer exakt zu bestimmen, da es sich bei ihnen zumeist um Einzelfunde handelt. Der Zusammenfund eines solchen *Stage 6*-Beiles (O'Brien 1994, 204 ff. pl. 52) mit jungaunjetitzischem Formengut im Hortfund Nr. 2 von Dieskau (Mitteldeutschland) (von Brunn 1959, Taf. 16,3; Otto und Witter 1952, Nr. 397) (Fig 18.3,11) läßt immerhin eine relative Einordnung in die Stufe Bz A 2 nach P. Reinecke zu. Dank der Dendrodatierungen der Aunjetitzer Fürstengräber von Helmsdorf und Leubingen ist eine absolute Datierung von Teilen der Stufe Bz A2 in das 19. und 18. Jahrhundert v. Chr. vertretbar (zuletzt Czebreszuk und Müller 2001). Die untere Grenze des "anglo-irischen" Importes von Randleistenbeilen dürfte der altbekannte Hortfund von Hausberge in Ostwestfalen markieren, der ein "britisches" Absatzbeil mit schildförmiger Rast (*shield-pattern*) und regionaltypisches Formengut der Sögel-Wohlde-Fazies enthält (Sudholz 1964, 109; Kibbert 1980, 189 ff. 192 Nr. 468 Taf. 68, C), so dass eine Datierung dieses Hortes in die Stufe Bz B, d. h. die beginnende Mittelbronzezeit naheliegt, die mit der englischen Arreton-Ebnal-Phase zu parallelisieren ist. Damit dürfte die untere Grenze dieser "anglo-irischen" Flach- und Randleistenbeil-Importe um ca. 1500/1400 v. Chr. zu ziehen sein.

Auffälligerweise korrespondiert diese Zeitspanne, d. h. die erste Hälfte des 2. Jahrtausends v. Chr., mit der Hochblüte der in den letzten Jahrzehnten durch die englisch-walisische und irische Montanarchäologie ans Licht geförderten Kupferbergwerke, von denen bisher ca. 30 Abbauorte lokalisiert und teilweise archäologisch untersucht werden konnten (vgl. O'Brien 1994; 1995; 1996; 1999). Nach den in großer Zahl vorliegenden 14C-Datierungen begann ihre Abbautätigkeit bereits in der zweiten Hälfte des 3. Jahrtausends (Ross-Island [Kerry, Irland]), d. h. in der Zeit der frühen Glockenbecher-Fazies und der letzten imposanten Ausbauphasen von Stonehenge, und erreichte ihr Maximum in der ersten Hälfte des 2. Jahrtausends. Offenbar kam der derzeit nachweisbare irische und britische Bergbau spätestens am Beginn der dortigen Jungbronzezeit *(Bishopsland-/Penard-Phase)* zum Erliegen und die Bronzeversorgung wurde ab dieser Zeit durch Importe von Rohkupfer, Fertigprodukten oder Schrott vom Kontinent sichergestellt (Northover 1999), wovon die Inhalte von jungbronzezeitlichen Schiffswracks Zeugnis ablegen (Muckelroy 1981; Rohl and Needham 1998).

In den walisischen und irischen Bergwerken waren folgende Kupfererze zugänglich bzw. wurden abgebaut (O'Brien 1996; Ottaway 1994, 71 ff.): Great Orme (Wales: Chalkopyrit, Kupferkarbonat [meist Malachit, auch Azurit], gediegenes Kupfer, Bleiglanz); Cwmystwyth (Copa Hill, Mittel-Wales: Chalkopyrit); Alderley Edge (England: Malachit, Azurit, Kupfersulfide); Mount Gabriel (Cork, Irland: Fahlerz [Tetraedrit, Tennantit], Malachit); Ross Island (Kerry, Irland: im Westteil der Abbaustelle Chalkopyrit, arsenreiches Fahlerz [Tennantit]; im Ostteil Chalkopyrit, Galenit, Sphalerit, geringeres Vorkommen von Fahlerz). In Relation zur zeitlichen Abfolge der Bergwerke und der Fertigprodukte zeigt sich, dass am Beginn der irischen Metallurgie eine Gewinnung von Kupfermetall aus sulfidischen Erzen steht, das zudem noch einen mehr oder weniger hohen Anteil an Arsen (z. B. Tennantit), Antimon (z. B. Tetraedrit) und Silber (also typische Bestandteile von Fahlerzen) aufweist. Dies korrespondiert mit den bisher für die Britischen Inseln ermittelten Metallgruppen (Northover 1980), denn die älteste Kupfersorte Irlands und der Britischen Inseln wird durch kupferne Gegenstände mit relevanten Anteilen von Arsen, Antimon und Silber gekennzeichnet ("Sorte A" nach Northover). Nach derzeitigem Forschungsstand kommt lediglich das Bergwerk von Ross Island als Erzlieferant in Betracht (O'Brien 1995; 1996). Diese auf Fahlerzen basierende Metallsorte verschwindet nach Northover (1980, 1982, 1999) um ca. 1900 v. Chr., als neue Kupfersorten mit oder ohne Verunreinigungen ("Sorte B": Arsen und Nickel; "Sorte C": geringe Verunreinigungen; "Sorte D": Arsen, Antimon, Nickel, Silber; "Sorte E": Arsen, Antimon, Nickel; "Sorte F": Arsen, Silber; "Sorte G": Nickel) aufkamen. Möglicherweise stammen einige Kupfersorten aus Erzen, die aus Bergwerken wie Mount Gabriel, Great Orme, Crmystwyth oder Alderly Edge kommen. Nach neueren Bleiisotopie-Untersuchungen kommt aber auch ein bisher unbekannter, noch nicht lokalisierter frühbronzezeitlicher Bergbau in

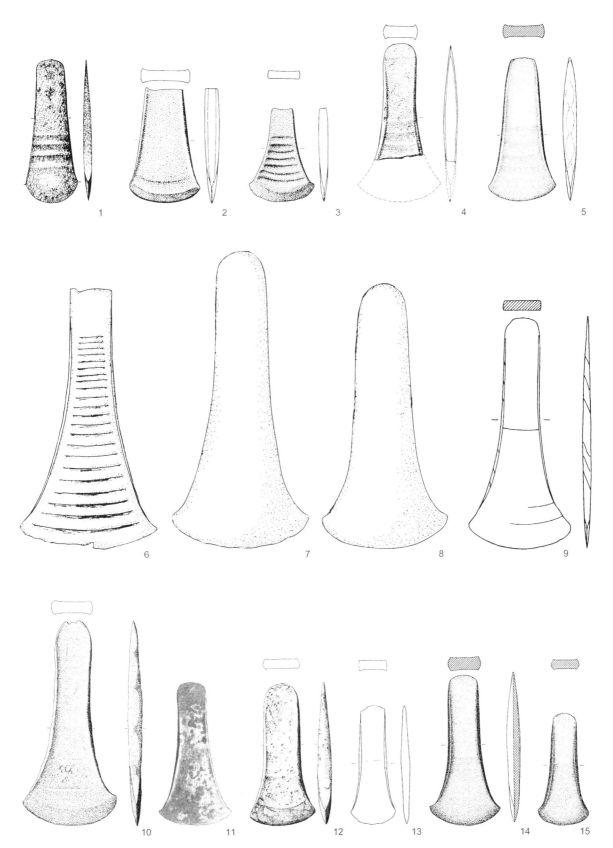

Fig 18.3: "Anglo-irische" Beile und ihre Derivate vom europäischen Festland (NL Niederlande; B Belgien; F Frankreich; D Deutschland; DK Dänemark; S Schweden): 1 Borest (F). – 2 Ahausen (D). – 3 Ronnenburg (D). – 4 Sassenberg (D). – 5 Nijmwegen (?) (NL). – 6–8 Skivarg (S). – 9 Fåborg (DK). – 10 Selchausdal (DK). – 11 Dieskau (D). – 12 Nähe Davrup (DK). – 13 Grott Haasdal (NL). – 14 s'Hertogenbosch (NL). – 15 Gemert (NL). – Kupfer/Bronze. – (1 nach Blanchet, 2–4 nach Kibbert, 5. 13–15 nach Butler, 6–10 nach Oldeberg, 10. 12 nach Vandkilde). – M. 1:3.

Albrecht Jockenhövel

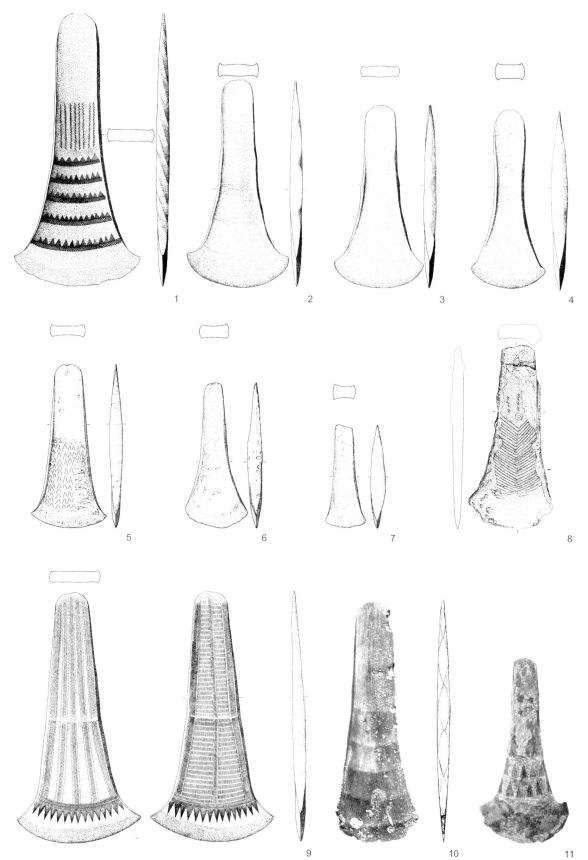

Fig 18.4: "Anglo-irische" Beile und ihre Derivate vom europäischen Festland (NL Niederlande; B Belgien; F Frankreich; D Deutschland; DK Dänemark; S Schweden): 1–4 Store Hoddinge (DK). – 5–7 Lumby Torp (DK). – 8 Vaux-sous-Chévremont (B). – 9 Selchausdal (DK). – 10 Gallemose (DK). – 11 Löddeköppinge (S). – Kupfer/Bronze. – (1–7. 9 nach Vandkilde, 8 nach Gob, 10 nach Megaw/Hardy, 11 nach Forssander). – M. 1:3.

Cornwall selbst in Betracht: Drei Stabdolche, ein Flachbeil und eine Dolchklinge aus verschiedenen Fundorten Süd- und Westenglands sowie Wales lieferten eine zinnfreie Kupfersorte mit einer typischen Silber-Kobalt-Nickel-Arsen-Wismuth-Verunreinigung, die zudem uranhaltig ist. Ein solcher typischer radioaktiver "Fünf-Metall"-Fingerabdruck ist nur für ganz wenige Kupferlagerstätten Europas signaturgleich, die allesamt variskischer Genese sind. Sie erstrecken sich von Cornwall und Devon über die Bretagne, das Massif Central und die Vogesen und bis zum Harz und dem Erzgebirge. In Cornwall liegen entsprechende Lagerstätten in der Umgebung von St. Austell und in der Region um das Bodmin Moor (Budd *et al.* 2000).

In der Nähe der Kupfermine vom südwestirischen Mount Gabriel wurde aus einem Megalithgrab vom Wedge-Typ bei Toormore (Kerry) ein kleiner Metallhort geborgen, der offenbar erst nach der Nutzung des Kollektivgrabes niedergelegt wurde (O'Brien 1994, 217 ff.). Eine frühbronzezeitliche Aktivitätsphase im bzw. am Grab wird durch zwei 14C-Datierungen (1730–1412 BC bzw. 1870–1450 BC) angezeigt. Der Metallhort besteht aus zwei kleinen Klumpen Rohkupfer und aus einem verzierten bronzenen Flachbeil vom Typ Ballyvalley, dessen Zinnanteil 10,32% beträgt. Die chemischen Analysen legen für die Gegenstände die gleiche Kupferquelle nahe. Das Kupfer weist als kennzeichnende Verunreinigungen Arsen und Silber (As > Ag) auf, was der Gruppe F1 nach Northover entspricht (Northover 1980). Nach derzeitigem Forschungsstand stammt das verwendete Kupfer jedoch nicht aus einer Mine des nahe gelegenen Mount Gabriel, denn diese ist durch arsenfreie Kupfererze gekennzeichnet (O'Brien 1994, 222, 263; O'Brien 1999; 1999a), sondern aus einer anderen, bisher unbekannten Lagerstätte. Man kann aus diesem Befund lernen, dass bei gegebener Zeitgleichheit die enge räumliche Nachbarschaft von Bergwerk, Rohmaterialien und Fertigprodukten ohne Einsatz moderner Analytik zu Fehlschlüssen führt, wie z. B. zur Existenz einer angeblich geschlossenen archäometallurgischen Kette.

Die Analysen des Flachbeiles von Toormore und verwandter Beilformen, wie Typ Ballybeg und Typ Ballyvalley (Harbison 1969, 32 ff.) belegen das Aufkommen von echten Zinnbronzen (Zinnanteil um ca. 10% Sn) während *Stage 3* (Frankford) und *Stage 4* (Killaha) in Irland und auf den übrigen Britischen Inseln, d. h. einige Zeit *vor* der klassischen Wessex-Zeit. Es wurde offenbar arsen-antimon-silberhaltiges Kupfer mit Zinn legiert (Northover 1980; 1982). Völlig neue Metallsorten erscheinen in Westeuropa dann in den folgenden Phasen der Frühbronzezeit (*Stages 5 und 6*) mit Arsen-Silberhaltigen ("Sorte F"), Arsen-Nickel-haltigen ("Sorte B") Bronzen oder mit fast reinen Zinnbronzen (ohne die oben genannten Elementanteile). Diese Vielfalt geht in der Mittelbronzezeit der Britischen Inseln zurück, wo vor allem nickelhaltige Zinnbronzen weiterhin für die britische Mittelbronzezeit typisch sind.

II

Zu den wichtigen frühbronzezeitlichen Hortfunden Südskandinaviens – vom überragenden Hortfund von Pile (Gem. Tygelsjö, Schonen) (Vandkilde 1996, Abb. 75; Oldeberg 1974, 125 f. Nr. 832) abgesehen – gehört der Fund von Store Heddinge (Præsto Amt) mit seinen vier Randleistenbeilen (Fig 18.4,1–4), davon eines vom gleichnamigen Typ (Fig 18.4,4), zwei "pseudo-irischen" Beilen (Fig 18.4,2.3) und einem "echten" anglo-irischen Beil mit reicher Verzierung (Fig 18.4,1) (Vandkilde 1996, 80 Abb. 64). Diese drei zuletzt genannten Beile zeichnen sich neben ihrem gerundeten, dünnen Nacken alle durch einen trapezförmigen Umriss und ausladende Schneiden aus, ein wichtiges Merkmal zur Abgrenzung anglo-irischer Beile von den übrigen kontinentalen Beilen. Hinzu kommt auch die auf dem unteren Beilkörper eingepunzte Verzierung oder gehämmerte Facettierung. Zu den reichverzierten Beilen dieser Gruppe gehören die beiden Prunkbeile mit seitlichen Ösen von Ahneby (Kr. Schleswig-Flensburg) (Fig 18.5,1) und von Ulstrup (Fig 18.5,2) (Vandkilde 1996, 89 Abb. 74) sowie das totalverzierte Beil von Selchausdal (Fig 18.4,9) (Vandkilde 1996, 88 Abb. 73, oben), die alle dem irisch-britischen Beiltyp Scrabo Hill nahestehen (Harbison 1969; Schmidt and Burgess 1981, 64 f.). Das zweite, öhrlose Beil aus dem Hort von Ulstrup (Fig 18.5,3) (Butler 1963, 31 Taf. 3, b) hat gleichfalls spezifische Merkmale des Typs Scrabo Hill, dem auch das reichverzierte Beil von Löddeköpinge (Schonen) (Montelius 1927 Nr. 782; Forssander 1936, Taf. 37, 3; Oldeberg 1974, Nr. 483) zuzurechnen ist (Fig 18.4,11). Auch aus dem berühmten Hort von Pile (Schonen), der fast alle in der Frühbronzezeit Südskandinaviens gebräuchlichen Beilformen – sei es als einheimische Arbeiten oder als Importe bzw. deren Nachahmungen – in sich vereint und über den die meisten Beiltypen Südskandinaviens miteinander verknüpft sind, liegt ein "anglo-irisches" Beil vor (Montelius 1927, Nr.789; Vandkilde 1996, 90 Abb. 75, E) (Fig 18.6,4). In einem weiteren Hort, dem von Lumby Torp (Vandkilde 1996, Nr. 3C Abb. 32) (Fig 18.4,5–7), fand sich ein anglo-irisches Beil vom Typ Falkland (Schmidt and Burgess 1981, 63) (Fig 18.4,5) zusammen mit einem Beil vom Typ Gallemose und einem Halbfabrikatbeil vom Typ Lumby Torp (Vandkilde 1996, 91). Neben weiteren Einzelfunden (Vandkilde 1996, 83 f. Abb. 67 Nr. 259: Selchausdal [Fig 18.3,10]; Flenstofte [ebd. Nr. 260] [Fig 18.5,8]; Fåborg [ebd. Nr. 261] [Fig 18.3,9]), darunter viele Funde aus Mooren, sind "pseudo-irische" Beile in den Horten von Fjälkinge (Schonen) (Oldeberg 1974, Nr. 152; Vandkilde 1996, 86 Abb. 71) (dort zusammen mit einem Langquaid-Randleistenbeil) (Fig 18.6,5.6) und Skivarp (Schonen) (Vandkilde 1996, 85 Abb. 70, Mitte) (Fig 18.3,6–8) sowie im Hort von Västra Frolunda (Västergotland) enthalten (Oldeberg 1974, Nr. 2405; Vandkilde 1996, 84) (Fig 18.6,1). Zwei weitere "anglo-irische" Beile bzw. ihre Derivate liegen von Ørndrup Mark (Mors) (Vandkilde 1996, 86 Abb. 72, Nr. 262) (Fig 18.2,16) und

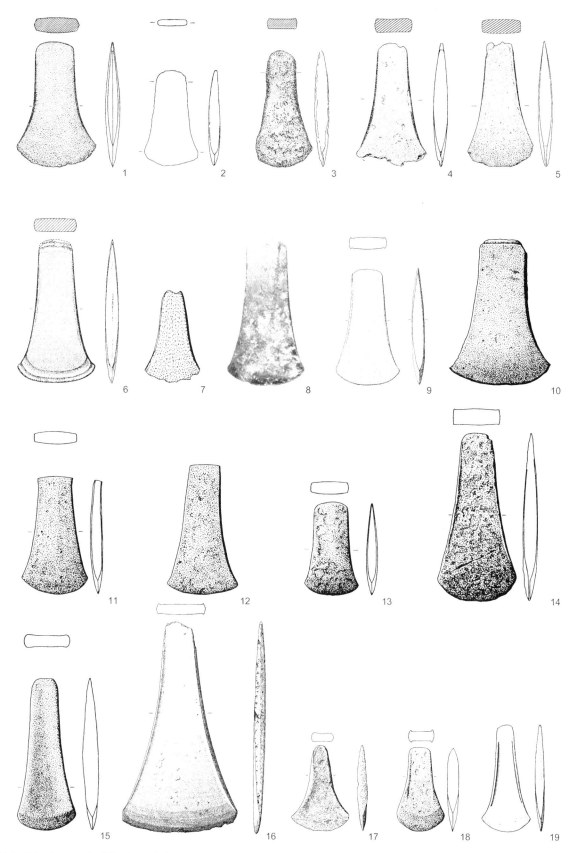

Fig 18.5: "Anglo-irische" Beile und ihre Derivate vom europäischen Festland (NL Niederlande; B Belgien; F Frankreich; D Deutschland; DK Dänemark; S Schweden): 1 Ahneby (D). – 2.3 Ulstrup (DK). – 4 Haren (NL). – 5 Pontavert (5). – 6 Boulogne-sur-Mer (F). – 7 Frankenthal (D). – 8 Flenstofte (DK). – 9 Wessmer (D). – Kupfer/Bronze. – (1–3. 8 nach Vandkilde, 4.9 nach Butler, 5 nach Blanchet, 6 nach Megaw/Hardy, 7 nach Kibbert). – M. 1:3.

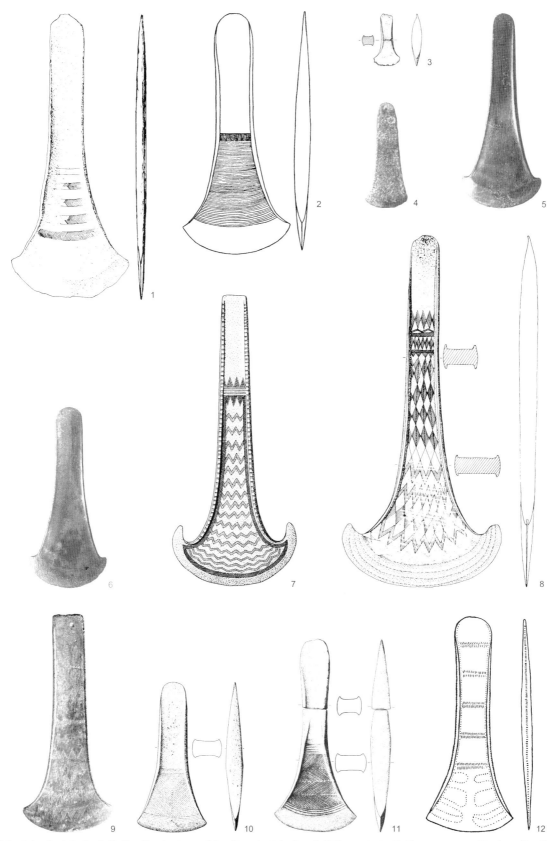

Fig 18.6: "Anglo-irische" Beile, Derivate und im "anglo-irischen" Stil verzierte Beile vom europäischen Festland (NL Niederlande; B Belgien; F Frankreich; D Deutschland; DK Dänemark; S Schweden): 1 Väster Frölunda (S). – 2 Flenstofte (DK). – 3 Aalter (B). – 4 Pile (S). – 5. 6 Fjälkinge (S). – 7 Sorèze (F). – 8 Mareuil-sur-Ourcq (F). – 9 Schweta (D). – 10 Jarløse. – 11 Æbelnæs. – 12 Griefstedt. – Kupfer/Bronze. – (1 nach Oldeberg, 2. 4–6. 10. 11 nach Vandkilde, 3 nach de Laet; 7 nach Coutil, 8 nach Blanchet, 9 nach Billig; 12 nach Megaw/Hardy). – M. 1:3.

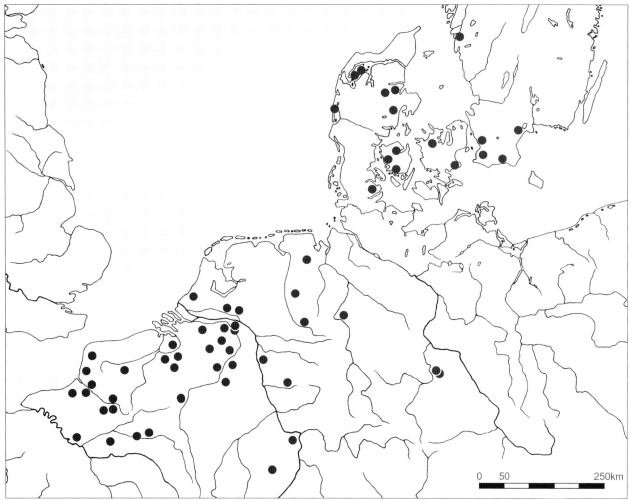

Fig 18.7: Verbreitung der "anglo-irischen" Beile und ihrer Derivate auf dem europäischen Festland (ohne Typdifferenzierung) (nach Vandkilde, Oldeberg, Butler, Laux, Kibbert, Verlaeckt, Blanchet u. a.) (Entwurf A. Jockenhövel).

in Miniaturform von Holmsland Klit (Ringkøbing) (Vandkilde 1996, Nr. 268) (Fig 18.2,17) vor, letzteres dem irischen Typ Killaha (Harbison 1969, 24 ff.) ähnlich. Die größte Gruppe der "anglo-irischen" Beile bilden mit neun Exemplaren in Dänemark die sog. *"anglo-irish developed bronze flat axes"* (Type A10 nach Vandkilde 1996, 87), die nach Vandkilde den Typen Ballyvalley, Glenalla, Falkland und Scrabo Hill entsprechen bzw. nahe stehen. Es handelt sich um die Beile von Selchausdal (Vandkilde 1996, Nr. 265: Typ Scrabo Hill) (Fig 18.4,9), "Nähe Davrup" (ebd. Nr. 263) (Fig 18.3,12), Palleshave (ebd. Nr. 264) (Fig 18.2,9), Ulstrup (ebd. Nr. 266 A. B: Typ Scrabo Hill) (Fig 18.5,2.3), Store Heddinge (ebd. 80 Abb. 64 Nr. 227) (Fig 18.4,1–3), Lumby Torp (ebd. 59 Abb. 32 Nr. 3C: Typ Scrabo Hill) (Fig 18.4,5–7), Gallemose (Megaw and Hardy 1938, Taf. 55, b; Vandkilde 1996, Nr. 175) (Fig 18.4,10); Ahneby (Kr. Schleswig-Flensburg [Deutschland]) (Vandkilde 1996, 89 Abb. 74) (Fig 18.5,1), Pile (Schonen [Schweden]) (Fig 18.6,4) und Löddeköpinge (Montelius 1927, Nr. 782; Forssander 1936, Taf. 37, 3; Oldeberg 1974, Nr. 483) (Fig 18.4,11).

Zum südlichen "Import-Strom" "anglo-irischer" Beile gehören Nordfrankreich, Belgien, die Niederlande, Westfalen und Niedersachsen sowie ihre angrenzenden Gebiete (Butler 1963; Butler 1995/1996; Sudholz 1964; Laux 2000, 50 ff.; Kibbert 1980; Blanchet 1984). Auch in diesen Gebieten konnte die Forschung zwischen echten Importen und Nachahmungen unterscheiden, wobei diese Beile zudem noch den Anstoß zur Produktion einer Regionalform in den Niederlanden und am Rhein gaben, dem Typ Emmen (Butler 1995/1996; Kibbert 1980, 101 ff., Laux 2000, 26 f.) der durch alpines Singen-Kupfer geprägt ist (Butler 1995/1996). Am Anfang der Kontakte stehen Flachbeile vom Typ Migdale in den Niederlanden (Butler 1995/1996, 172 ff.: Arnhem [Fig 18.2,1], Drouwen [Fig 18.2,5], Haler [Fig 18.2,3], Hapert [Fig 18.2,4], Wageningen [Fig 18.2,1], Wijchen [Fig 18.2,6]), Nordfrankreich (Bacouël: Blanchet 1984, 127 f. Abb. 53,7 [Fig 18.2,7]) und Westdeutschland ("Düsseldorf": Osborne 1887, 64 Taf. 8,2; Kibbert 1980, 75 Nr. 52 [Fig 18.2,10]). Diese Beile sind typologisch und relativchronologisch älter als die folgenden Beile der Typen Killaha, Ballyvalley,

Falkland, Aylesford und Scrabo Hill. Aus Belgien sind insbesondere die Beile von Geraardsbergen, Waasmunster, Baasrode, Wichelen, Gent (Verlaeckt 1996, 19 f.), Vaux-sous-Chèvremont (Gob 1980) (Fig 18.4,8), Hastière und Rekem (Fig 18.2,19) zu nennen, aus den Niederlanden die von Gemert (Fig 18.3,15), Groot Haasdal (Fig 18.3,13), Haren (Fig 18.5,4), s'Hertogenbosch (Fig 18.3,14) und Nijmwegen (?) (Fig 18.3,5) (Butler 1995/1996, 177 Nr. 26 Abb. 10,a; Nr. 25 Abb. 10,a; 178 Nr. 28 Abb. 10,b; 178 Nr. 27 Abb. 10,a), aus Nordfrankreich die Beile von Les Essarts-Varimpré, "Somme", Conchil-le-Temple, Lille, Condé-sur-Aisne, Banthelu, Masnières, Umgebung von Abbeville und Amiens (je ein Beil), Borest (Fig 18.3,1), Pontavert (Fig 18.5,4) und Boulogne-sur-Mer (drei Beile) (Fig 18.5,6) (alle kartiert bei Blanchet 1984, 145 f. Abb. 67) sowie aus Westdeutschland von Ahausen (Laux 2000, 50 f. Nr. 151 Taf. 9 [Fig 18.3,2]), Ronnenberg (Laux 2000, 50 Nr. 150 Taf. 9, 150 [Fig 18.3,3]), Sassenberg (Kibbert 1980, 108 Nr. 114 Taf. 10 [Fig 18.3,4]), aus Mainz (Kibbert 1980, 76 Nr. 53; 78 Nr. 61 Taf.6;7) (Fig 18.2,11.13), Pirmasens (Kibbert 1980, 76 Nr. 54 Taf. 6) (Fig 18.2,13), Herchen (Kibbert 1980, 76 f. Nr. 56 Taf. 7) (Fig 18.2,14), Uffeln (Kibbert 1980, 77 Nr. 57 Taf. 17) (Fig 18.2,15), Wessmar (Butler 1963, 35 Abb. 5) (Fig 18.5,9) und Dieskau (von Brunn 1959, Taf. 16,3) (Fig 18.3,11).

III

Falls relevante Metallanalysen vorliegen, zeichnen sich die meisten der "anglo-irischen" Beile durch einen hohen Zinnanteil aus (Butler 1963, 39 ff.; Butler 1995/1996; Zinn-Klassen 5 und 6: Vandkilde 1996, 30. 169 ff.), während ihre "Pseudo"-Ausprägungen meist einen deutlich geringeren Zinnanteil aufweisen (Vandkilde 1996, 87 f.). Zudem ist das Kupfer der "echten", wohl importierten anglo-irischen Beile weitgehend frei von Verunreinigungen (entspricht den SAM-Materialgruppen E00/E00-FC; E01/E01A; C2D/C5; FG). Es bleibt aber nach wie vor offen, wo die auf dem Kontinent aufgefundenen anglo-irischen Beile gefertigt wurden, denn ihre Materialzusammensetzung weicht erheblich von ihren britischen Vorbildern ab, die sehr häufig aus der Kupfer-"Sorte A" bestehen (Northover 1982, 230), die der SAM-Gruppe E11 entspricht (Vandkilde 1996, 85 Abb. 69). Man muß also entweder an eine noch unbekannte Rohstoffquelle auf den Britischen Inseln (z. B. Schottland, Nordengland) oder an die Existenz von britischen Handwerkern auf dem Kontinent denken (Butler 1963, 207 f.; Harbison 1969), die nach ihrem ureigenen Stil Beile aus kontinentalem Metall fertigten. Dies mag besonders ab dem Zeitpunkt der Fall gewesen sein, als ihnen eventuell von den Britischen Inseln mitgebrachtes Werkstattmetall, was gewichtsmäßig jedoch nur in beschränktem Umfang der Fall gewesen sein dürfte, als Ausgangsstoff ausging (Vandkilde 1996, 91). Sie fügten jedoch Zinn in hoher Konzentration (bis über 10 % Sn) hinzu (von Brunn 1959;

Butler 1963), was in der lokal-kontinentalen Beil-Produktion noch nicht üblich war. In diesem Zusammenhang ist auch das vielzitierte bronzene (ca. 14% Zinn enthaltene) Randleistenbeil aus dem mitteldeutschen Hortfund 2 von Dieskau (Sachsen-Anhalt) zu sehen, das in seinem Beilkörperumriss und seiner Verzierung unübersehbare anglo-irische Züge aufweist (Fig 18.3,11). Nach einer verfeinerten Beiltypologie gehört es dem vor allem in Mittelengland verbreiteten Typ Falkland (Schmidt and Burgess 1981, 62 f.) an, dem auch ein Beil aus dem Hort von Lumby Tarp (Vandkilde 1996, fig. 32 Nr. 3C) (Fig 18.4,5) zuzurechnen ist. Auch auf das Ballyvalley-Beil von Wichelen (Belgien) mit seinem Anteil von 39,72% Zinn sei besonders hingewiesen (Verlaeckt 1966, 121 f. Nr. 271).

Wenn wir den Fundbestand quantitativ zusammen-fassen, liegen aus ca. 500 Jahren nur etwa 60–70 Beile "anglo-irischer" Prägung vom Kontinent vor (Fig 18.7). Sie machen zwar nur einen relativ geringen Anteil an dem Gesamtbestand der frühbronzezeitlichen Flach- und frühen Randleistenbeile aus, ihr morphologischer Einfluß auf die einheimische Beilproduktion wurde aber stets betont (vgl. Kibbert 1980; Butler 1963; 1995/1996; Vandkilde 1996). Aber nicht nur in ihrer formalen Gestalt sind sie für die frühbronzezeitlichen Menschen Mitteleuropas erkennbar gewesen, sondern auch in ihrem Aussehen, denn sie unterschieden sich durch ihre durchgängig hohen Zinnan-teile auch optisch von den kontinental-einheimischen Beilen. Ästhetisch wirkten sie "andersartig" oder "frem-dartig"; wegen ihres hohen Zinnzusatzes haben sie sicher auch einen anderen Klang. Vielleicht lag hierin der Reiz zur Kopie oder Nachahmung dieser Beile, der ja auch in der Übernahme der reichen "anglo-irischen" Verzierung auf kontinentalen Beilen spürbar ist, denen teilweise der Charakter von "haches d'honneur" (Coutil 1935) oder "Prunkbeilen" (Billig 1957) zuerkannt wird (Fig 18.6,1–2.7–9.12). Man benötigte jedoch auf dem Kontinent das Zinn. Ohne Zweifel ist die klassische Zinnbronze auf den Britischen Inseln früher belegt als in Mitteleuropa (zuletzt Pare 2000). Das dortige Experimentieren mit Kupfer und Zinn belegen auch einige frühbronzezeitliche *"tin-plating"*-Flachbeile der Britischen Inseln, die eine weißliche Oberfläche aufweisen (Kinnes *et al.* 1979). Die Zinn-Lagerstätten in Cornwall lagen in der Frühbronzezeit jedenfalls näher vor der Haustür als Zinn-Lagerstätten im Vorderen Orient oder die unlängst in Zentralasien entdeckten Zinnminen, die in das 3. Jahrtausend v. Chr. zu datieren sind (Parzinger und Boroffka 2003).

Bei der innovativen Rolle Englands und Irlands für die frühbronzezeitliche Metallurgie, besonders der Zinn-Bronze, und bei der Bedeutung der Kulturbeziehungen zum Kontinent müssen wir fragen, ob nicht auch in der Metallversorgung der zentralmitteleuropäischen Früh-bronzezeit Kupfer aus Westeuropa eine gewisse, bisher noch nicht klar erkannte Rolle spielte. Möglicherweise ist dieses Kupfer in Form von Fertigprodukten oder als Barren, beides können auch Beile gewesen sein (analog den Neyruz- und Salezbeilen am Hochrhein: Krause 1988; Krause und Pernicka 1998), in den mitteleuropäischen Metallkreislauf eingespeist worden. Bisher ist es aber noch nicht gelungen, den "genetischen Fingerabdruck" des irischen, walisischen oder nordwestenglischen Kupfers in den unzähligen Fertigprodukten der Frühbronzezeit Mitteleuropas, besonders der großen Aunjetitzer Metall-horte, zu entdecken – eine Herausforderung für die moderne Analytik. Wenn wir diese Möglichkeit noch auf das Zinn erweitern, wäre erneut zu fragen, ob das frühbronzezeitliche Westeuropa mit seinen ergiebigen Kupfer- und Zinnlagerstätten nicht doch eine größere Rolle in der Genese der Frühbronzezeit Mitteleuropas, vor allem auch bei dem Aufkommen der Zinn-Bronze-Technologie, gespielt hat, jedenfalls in größerem Ausmaße als wir bisher im archäologischen Fundbestand einschließlich der Aussagen der Metallanalysen feststellen können.

Bibliography

Bartelheim, M. und Niederschlag, E. 1998 Untersuchungen zur Buntmetallurgie, insbesondere des Kupfers und Zinns, im sächsisch-böhmischen Erzgebirge und dessen Umland, *Arbeits- und Forschungsberichte zur sächsischen Bodendenkmalpflege* **40**, 8–87.

Beck, C. and Shennan, S. 1991 *Amber in prehistoric Britain*. Oxbow Monograph **8**, Oxford.

Billig, G. 1957 Das Prunkbeil von Schweta. Ein Beitrag zur Herstellungstechnik und zum Verwendungszweck der früh-bronzezeitlichen Randbeile in Mitteldeutschland, *Arbeits- und Forschungsberichte zur sächsischen Bodendenkmalpflege* **6**, 185–316.

Blanchet, J.-C. 1984 *Les premiers Métallurgistes en Picardie et dans le nord de la France. Chalcolithique, Age du Bronze et début du premier Age du Fer*. Paris.

Briard, J. 1984 *Les tumulus d'Armorique*. (coll. l'Age du Bronze en France **3**), Picard, Paris.

Brunn, W. A. von 1959 *Bronzezeitliche Hortfunde I. Die Hortfunde der frühen Bronzezeit aus Sachsen-Anhalt, Sachsen und Thüringen*. Berlin.

Budd, P., Haggerty, R., Ixer, R.A., Scaife, B. and Thomas, R.G. 2000 Copper deposits in south-west England identified as a source of Copper Age metalwork. (http://www.archaeotrace.co.uk/stories/provenance.html).

Burgess, C. 1980 *The Age of Stonehenge*. J.M. Dent and Sons Ltd., London.

Butler, J.J. 1963 Bronze Age Connections across the North Sea. A Study in Prehistoric Trade and Industrial Relations between the British Isles, the Netherlands, North Germany and Scandinavia *c*. 1700–700 BC, *Palaeohistoria* **9**, 1963.

Butler, J.J. 1990 Bronze Age metal and amber in the Netherlands (I). *Palaeohistoria* **32**, 47–110.

Butler, J.J. 1995/1996 Bronze Age metal and amber in the Netherlands (II:1). Catalogue of flat axes, flanged axes and stopridge axes, *Palaeohistoria* **37/38**, 159–243.

Clark, D.V., Cowie, T.G. and Foxon, A. (eds.) 1985 *Symbols of Power at the time of Stonehenge*. National Museum of Antiquities of Scotland, Her Majesty's Stationery Office, Edinburgh.

Coutil, L. 1935 Haches d'honneur de l'Age du bronze à formes anormales et ornées de gravures, *Bulletin Société Préhistorique Français* **32**, 380–385.

Czebreszuk, J. und Müller, J. 2001 *Die absolute Chronologie in Mitteleuropa. 3000–2000 v. Chr.* Poznan/Bamberg/Rahden.

Eogan, G. 1994 *The Accomplished Art. Gold and Gold Working in Britain and Ireland during the Bronze Age (c. 2300–650 BC)*. Oxbow Monographs **42**, Oxford.

Forssander, J.E. 1936 *Der ostskandinavische Norden während der ältesten Metallzeit*. Lund.

Gerloff, S. 1975 *The Early Bronze Age Daggers in Great Britain and a Reconsideration of the Wessex Culture*. Prähistorische Bronzefunde VI, 2, München.

Gob, A. 1980 Une hache décorée du bronze ancien découverte à Vaux-sous-Chèvremont (Liège), *Helinium* **20**, 59–62.

Harbison, P. 1969 *Axes of the Early Bronze Age in Ireland*. Prähistorische Bronzefunde IX, 1, München.

Herrmann, F.-R. 1999 Eine irische Goldlunula aus Hessen. In: *Festschrift für Günter Smolla*, 267–270. Wiesbaden.

Ixer, R.A. and Pattrick, R.A.D. 2003 Copper-arsenic ores and Bronze Age mining and metallurgy with special reference to the British Isles. In P.T. Craddock and J. Lang (eds.) *Mining and Metal Production through the Ages*, 9–20. London.

Kibbert, K. 1980 *Äxte und Beile im mittleren Westdeutschland I*. Prähistorische Bronzefunde IX, 10, München.

Kinnes, I.A., Craddock, P.T., Needham, S. and Lang, J. 1979 Tin-plating in the Early Bronze Age: the Barton Stacey axe, *Antiquity* **53**, 141–143.

Krause, R. 1988 *Die endneolithischen und frühbronzezeitlichen Grabfunde auf der Nordterrasse von Singen am Hohentwiel*. Stuttgart.

Krause, R. and Pernicka, E. 1998 Frühbronzezeitliche Kupfersorten im Alpenvorland und ihr archäologischer Kontext. In C. Mordant, M. Pernot, and V. Rychner (eds.) *L'atelier du bronzier en Europe*, 191–202. Comité des Travaux historiques et scientifiques, Paris.

Laux, F. 1995 Westeuropas Bedeutung für die Bronzezeit Niedersach-sens. Zum Übergang von der Sögel-Wohlde Zeitstufe zur älteren Bronzezeit. In: A. Jockenhövel, (ed.) *Festschrift für Hermann Müller-Karpe zum 70. Geburtstag*, 85–101, Bonn.

Laux, F. 2000 *Äxte und Beile in Niedersachsen I (Flach-, Randleisten- und Absatzbeile)*. Prähistorische Bronzefunde IX, 23, Stuttgart.

Lenerz-de Wilde, M. 1991 Überlegungen zur Funktion der frühbronzezeitlichen Stabdolche, *Germania* **69**, 25–48.

Megaw, B.R.S. and Hardy, E.M. 1938 British Decorated Axes and their Diffusion during the Earlier Part of the Bronze Age, *Proceedings of the Prehistoric Society* **4**, 172–307.

Monteagudo, L. 1977 *Die Beile auf der Iberischen Halbinsel*. Prähistorische Bronzefunde IX, 6, München.

Montelius, O. 1927 *Minnen från vår Forntid*. Stockholm.

Mordant, C., Pernot, M. and Rychner, V. (eds.) 1998 *L'atelier du bronzier en Europe du XXe au VIIIe siècle avant notre ère: 1 Les analyses de composition du métal: leur rapport à l'archéo-logie de l'Age du Bronze; 3 Production, circulation et consom-mation du bronze*. Travaux historiques et scientifiques, Paris.

Muckelroy, K. 1981 Middle Bronze Age trade between Britain and Europe: a maritime perspective, *Proceedings of the Prehistoric Society* **47**, 275–297.

Needham, S., Ramsay C.B., Coombs, D., Cartwright, C. and Pettitt, P. 1997 An Independent Chronology for British Bronze Age Metalwork: the Results of the Oxford Radiocarbon Accelerator Programme, *The Archaeological Journal* **154**, 53–107.

Northover, P. 1980 Bronze in the British Bronze Age. In W.A. Oddy (ed.) *Aspects of early metallurgy*, 63–70. London.

Northover, P. 1982 The analysis of Welsh Bronze Age metalwork. In H. Savory (ed.) *Guide catalogue of the Bronze Age collection*, 229–243. Cardiff.

Northover, P. 1999 The earliest metalworking in Southern Britain. In: *The beginnings of Metallurgy*, 211–225. Bochum.

O'Brien, W. 1994 *Mount Gabriel. Bronze Age Mining in Ireland*. Galway University Press, Galway.

O'Brien, W. 1995 Ross Island and the origins of Irish-British metallurgy. In J. Waddell and E. Shee Twohig (eds) *Ireland in the Bronze Age*, 38–48. The Stationery Office, Dublin.

O'Brien, W. 1996 *Bronze Age Copper Mining in Britain and Ireland*. Risborough.

O'Brien, W. 1999 Resource availability and the metal supply in the insular Bronze Age. In: *The beginnings of Metallurgy*, 227–235. Bochum.

O'Brien, W. 1999a Arsenical copper in early Irish metallurgy. In: *Metal in Antiquity*, 33–42. Oxford.

Oldeberg, A. 1974 *Die ältere Metallzeit in Schweden 1*. Stockholm.

Osborne, W. 1887 *Das Beil und seine typischen Formen in vorhistorischer Zeit. Ein Beitrag zur Geschichte des Beiles*. Dresden.

Ottaway, B. 1994 *Prähistorische Metallurgie*. Espelkamp.

Otto, H. and Witter, W. 1952 *Handbuch der ältesten vorgeschichtlichen Metallurgie in Mitteleuropa*. Leipzig.

Pare, C.F.E. (ed.) 2000 *Metals make the world go round. The supply and circulation of metals in Bronze Age Europe*. Oxbow, Oxford.

Parzinger, H. und Boroffka, N. 2003 *Das Zinn der Bronzezeit in Mittelasien 1. Die siedlungsarchäologischen Forschungen im Umfeld der Zinnlagerstätten*. Mainz.

Penhallurick, R.D. 1986 *Tin in Antiquity. Its Mining and Trade throughout the ancient World with particular reference to Cornwall*. London.

Reim, H. 1995 Ein Halskragen aus Kupfer von Dormettingen, Zollernalbkreis (Baden-Württemberg). In A. Jockenhövel (ed.) *Festschrift für Hermann Müller-Karpe zum 70. Geburtstag*, 237–248. Bonn.

Rohl, B. and Needham, S. 1998 *The circulation of metal in the British Bronze Age: the application of lead isotope analysis*. British Museum Occasional Paper **102**, London.

Schmidt, P.K. and Burgess, C.B. 1981 *The Axes of Scotland and Northern England*. Prähistorische Bronzefunde IX, 7, München.

Sprockhoff, E. 1941 Niedersachsens Bedeutung für die Bronzezeit Westeuropas. Zur Verankerung einer neuen Kulturprovinz. *Bericht der Römisch-Germanischen Kommission* **31(2)**, 1–138.

Sudholz, G. 1964 *Die ältere Bronzezeit zwischen Niederrhein und Mittelweser*. Münster.

Taylor, J.J. 1980 *Bronze Age Gold Work of the British Isles*. Cambridge University Press, Cambridge.

Vandkilde, H. 1996 *From stone to bronze: metalwork of the late Neolithic and earliest Bronze Age in Denmark*. Århus.

Verlaeckt, K. 1996 *Between river and barrow, a reappraisal of Bronze Age metalwork found in the Province of East-Flanders (Belgium)*. Oxford.

19. On Bronze Age Swords, their production and function

Henrik Thrane

The sword is, in my opinion, the best logo or symbol for the Bronze Age, much better than the famous Trundholm Sun Wagon chosen by the Council of Europe, because the sword became universal to all European Bronze Age cultures by its practical and symbolical properties. George Eogan's study was concerned with typology and technology (Eogan 1965) and was followed by many studies, mainly in the Prähistorische Bronzefunde series. Still, the understanding of the variability and the reasons behind the development of constantly fresh types has received little attention. I cannot hope to redress the balance but maybe I can point to a few issues of interest not only to the recipient of this Festschrift, restricting myself, however, to the Nordic Bronze Age. Even if we concede that Ireland has more bronze swords than any other country according to Harding (2000, 280) I maintain that Denmark has the largest number of burial swords and of swords *per* km^2 (c. 0.05, judging by Aner and Kersten 1972ff., Table 19.1). Actually, we should compare the near contemporary Class 1, *i.e.* the 42 Ballintober swords (Eogan 1965) with the 2600 Danish (including Scania and Schleswig) period I–III swords to grasp the comparative situation.

The multitude of swords all over Europe (Harding 2000, table 8.1) must persuade even the most sceptical prehistorian that business was meant. All our inherited knowledge of the use of swords in the Iron Age, Middle Ages and later must lead us to affirm this proposal. That the sword was given a number of extra roles as insignia of knighthood or royalty, display of rank *etc.* during these periods should not distract from its principal role as a vital piece of the armoury of the Bronze Age.

Scandinavian research has been rather hesitant to accept Bronze Age warfare as a proper issue. Certainly weaponry roused the curiosity right from the beginnings of archaeological research but not even the most astute archaeologist went beyond a purely antiquarian attitude. Actually, this was not restricted to Scandinavian research (Keegan 1993, 90f). The presence of weapons was accepted but how they were used and what they might signify was not discussed. It would have gone against the general understanding of the Bronze Age as a Golden Age in harmony with nature to speak of warfare.

Warfare is a sensitive issue in Prehistory. Conflict there was, no doubt, and violence was used in what sometimes looks like indiscriminate slaughter and overkill (Keegan 1993, 121f). Whether wars were fought during the Bronze Age and how is not easily definable but indirectly, through the symbolism of the warrior not least by the sword, the ideal of warfare is present (1).

Production

Immediately after the opening of Nordic sword production

Region	area km^2	swords	sword/ km^2	km^2/ sword	tumuli	tumuli with bronzes	tumuli with swords
Zealand	7514	457	0.06	16.4	9465	642	321
Bornholm	588	45	0.07	13.06	1140	92	38
Lolland-Falster	1797	48	0.03	37.4	1003	60	25
Fyn	3474	150	0.04	23.2	1651	159	79
Jutland	26255	1027	0.04	25.56	incomplete data		
South Slesvig	4136	288	0.07	14.4	5460	459	143
North Slesvig	3972	251	0.06	15.8	6604	621	225
Scania	11283	216	0.02	25.56	incomplete data		
Total	**72392**	**2482**					

Table 19.1: Sword count for periods I–III, based on Aner and Kersten volumes I–XI; Broholm 1943; Sprockhoff 1931; 1934, Baudou 1960.

with the workshop that produced the Valsømagle and related swords at the end of period I (Ottenjahn 1969, 2ff; Vandkilde 1996, 236ff) diversity begins to unfold and throughout periods II and III we observe a bewildering multitude of sword types. This no doubt reflects several factors such as local traditions and preferences as well as social choices but also, and perhaps foremost, experiments to solve the main problem of bronze swords – and indeed of any sword. It is all very well to produce a good blade but if the joining of blade and hilt is not solid enough the risk of severing the fragile hilt from the heavy blade is imminent. It is not so much the blade that was at risk as the organic or hollow bronze hilt. Needless to say this could be critical in a proper fight, leaving the warrior defenceless.

The early swords show the tradition from the Bell Beaker daggers through the Wessex and Aunjetitz traditions. Indeed the early swords are recognizable as prolonged daggers in their technical features as well as in the initial lengths. Soon, however, swords like the Apa type and contemporary blades reached proper sword lengths (Harding 1995, 5f) and from then on the swords inspired the dagger production rather than vice versa – indeed daggers were sometimes made from shortened swords. Apart from the cosmetic solution called "Rahmen-griff" which was just a parenthesis in sword production (Sprockhoff 1934, 35) we see three main solutions. The first is the "Griffplatte" with either a rounded or an angular proximal end of the blade, attached to the hilt by rivets. The second is the tanged blade (with "Griffangel") continuing the blade in a long and narrow, rod like part that was encased by an organic hilt. The third is the grip tongued ("Griffzunge") hilt where the continuation of the blade is flanged and as broad as the organic parts of the hilt that are riveted to the tongue.

The swords with bronze hilts, the solid hilted swords which loom so prominently in the Nordic finds (Ottenjahn 1969), were only rarely cast in one with the blade, as some of the earliest specimens demonstrate. All sorts of variations of "Griffplatten" or tangs are known and even some half-tongue-like upper ends of the blade were not uncommon, *e.g.* in the octagonally hilted swords. From a purely technical point of view it was a great waste of energy to produce swords that would have doubtful qualities in combat. The grip tongue sword presented a good solution, given that the wooden or bone (or ivory) pommel and halves of the grip itself were fastened solidly enough to the tongue – by two or more rivets. Obviously it was a viable technical arrangement as it was one that persisted from the Early Bronze Age through the Hallstatt period, and in marginal areas even later (5th–4th cent BC at Sindos in Macedonia). With a good bulging pommel the control of the sword even in heavy slashing was secured (Fig 19.1; Boye 1894–6 pl. V, 4 and Aner and Kersten no. 4740A; Sprockhoff 1931, Taf. A, 7; Tor-brügge 1995, Abb.1 – with excellent analytic maps, illustrating the widespread use of the Hallstatt sword).

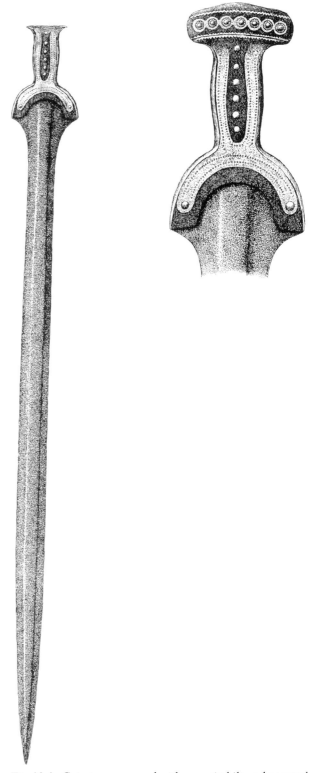

Fig 19.1: Grip tongue sword with organic hilt and pommel from period II oak coffin, Muldbjerg, Hover parish, West Jutland, length 72cm (after Boye 1896, pl. V).

Ultimately it was the simpler solution with the tang continued through the grip and secured on top of the pommel which, persisting through the Late Bronze Age urnfield types, became the iron La Tène sword and has

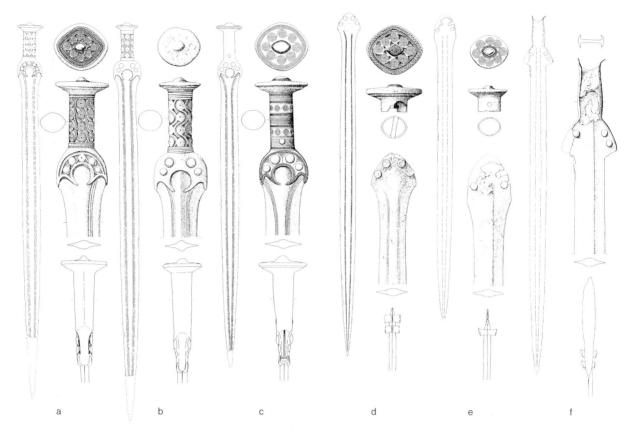

Fig 19.2: Swords found bundled at the edge of a bog at Åstofte, Asnæs parish Northwest Zealand. All three main types of period II are represented, a – c. fully hilted, d – e. with Griffplatte, f. grip tongue. Note that nearly all tips are missing and notches on the edges, Kristiansen has promised a study of this find. (After Aner and Kersten II, 1976, Taf. 29–30).

remained the permanent solution wherever swords are still made or used. When the two better technical options were known at least by the Middle Bronze Age, why all the different types of alternative solutions that we have from the Nordic and Tumulus and Urnfield cultures in most of Europe? It was not just an experimental phase that had to be gone through, the experiments lasted through periods II and III. Why did the experimenting cease and uniformity begin with the Late Nordic Bronze Age (Period IV)? Why was it necessary for each generation to find its own solutions? Is it because sword production was a local affair (Ottenjahn 1969)? But swords were the most international fashion-regulated types throughout the Bronze Age. Were then other desires more important than making swords fit for fight? And what purpose does a weapon serve if it does not give the necessary reliability to its user? Or are we altogether asking the wrong questions? Are our ideas of how the swords were used at all relevant to the demands and uses of the past?

It has long been customary to lament the small size of the hilts, thus hinting that the bronze swords were useless in fighting. Also it has been said repeatedly that the weight of the swords was wrong (Harding 2000, 278). The starting point for the interpretation was what modern fencing procedures tell us about how swords can be used.

This may not be the most fruitful approach. Instead the starting point should be that swords were developed from daggers in order to get a more efficient, *i.e.* longer and stronger, pointed weapon with sharp edges so that damage could be inflicted from a slightly more advantageous distance from the opponent. The logical use would be a continuation of the dagger, *i.e.* stabbing or thrusting – as we see Mycenaean rapiers handled on the stelae and signet rings. From the original hold of the weapon with the whole hand, which rather limits the range of the thrusting movements, a displacement of the hand so that the forefingers steered the top of the blade would be an improvement. This is what was suggested for the Early to Middle Bronze Age solid hilted swords (Müller 1898, 222; Bridgford 1997, 105). In this interpretation these swords represent an advantage in fighting technique.

Only much later in the Bronze Age was it apparently realized that these long sharp edges might be more suitable for cutting human skin and flesh through protective clothing and leather and the cut-and-thrust sword came into being (Harding 2000). Though this remained an Urnfield and Hallstatt culture phenomenon I wonder if the broad blades of period IV in the North do not represent a local version of this new fighting manner. They had certainly dropped the less stable hilt forms by then. Nearly all research has focused upon the hilts because they give the most multivaried starting points for typological studies. The grip, the pommel and the shoulders each have their own discrete set of morphological and decorative elements that develop seemingly rather independently. Yet, blades were the lethal part of the swords and should be treated as the important elements that they are. The problem for our normal typological analyses is that the swords that we have in our museums may be secondary products. Blades may change hilts or vice versa (Quillfeldt 1995, nos 3 and 307). This is just as true for Bronze Age swords as it has been for private and military swords to the present day. We can sometimes see damage which must have been repaired by changing blade or hilt and part of the problems of fixing the status of, for example, octagonal hilted swords, whether imported or locally copied, arise from the fact that local blades were added to imported hilts.

The constant change in the Nordic sword production reflects two aspects: 1. A continuous influence from Central Europe and 2. a continuous experimenting with technical problems. The latter were hardly handled just for technological reasons but must reflect a need for improvement and adaptation to the demands from the men who were to wield the swords. This of course presupposes that the swords were functional and not just for display but had a general offensive and ultimately lethal function as true weapons. If not there would be no need for so much emphasis on the solution of the main problem of the junction of blade with hilt. Thus we are led to our true dilemma – what was the role of the sword in warfare during the Bronze Age? Yet for generations we have acknowledged the presence of the swords – and other weapons – but no conclusion was drawn. It was left to arms historians to examine the probable use of these swords. The conclusion was that they were capable weapons, albeit not used exactly like later iron/steel swords.

We still face the ambiguity of the evidence. We have a lot of weapons but practically no other sources indicating the use of violence, let alone warfare, but a definite stand is not immediately apparent from the sources. Here I shall look at functional aspects of the Nordic swords in order to see what they may contribute to our understanding of warfare or peace in the Nordic Bronze Age. Only recently was a direct critical observation of the blades from periods II and III undertaken and the images of weaponry on rock carvings were also taken up (*e.g.* Nordbladh 1989). Kristian Kristiansen (1984) suggested that it was possible to distinguish a whole range of degrees of re-sharpening of the edges from peripheral to extensive. He still owes us a thoroughly documented study of the indications of fighting style, like the attempt by Gebühr for the Iron Age (1980). The total (re-) grinding down of the blade surface, eliminating even the central rib with its flanking grooves ("Blutrillen") is such a radical measure that it can hardly have been desirable from an aesthetic point of

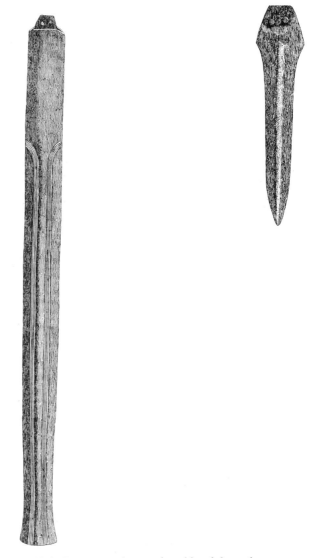

Fig 19.3: Dagger with sword scabbard from the grave at Borum Eshoj (Boye 1896, pl. X).

view (*cf.* the completely worn down grip tongue sword converted into dagger Aner and Kersten no. 3559D). These features we may regard as decoration. The curvature of the upper ends of these flanking grooves is a chronologically sensitive typological element that shows that it was considered important. It was certainly not necessary to design the faint grooves and ridges as carefully as we see them on the good blades. The midrib no doubt strengthened the blade and was a combination of practical demands and aesthetics. The practical need must have overridden the aesthetic wishes when the decorative elements were ground away, indicating that it was more important to have a proper weapon than a nice showpiece. Such strong hammering and filing could only be necessary after combat heavy enough to leave the cutting edges scarred and battered by the hitting and parrying of opposing swords. Some swords still have cuts of some depth preserved and these could hardly be repaired by simple hammering and grinding while keeping the original cutting edge. Incidentally, the cuts still extant on some blades contradict the interpretation of the arms historians. Stabbing alone could hardly account for even the smaller cuts not to mention the higher level of damage. Needless to say, preservation conditions are crucial for such analyses and careful distinction between pre- and post-depositional damages is a prerequisite.

The conclusion from the small sample of reliable observations is that the bronze swords in question had been used against each other or against other weapons with equally sharp edges – spears? It may still be worth considering whether the primary role of swords was in duels, whether ritualised or genuine. In spite of their number swords can hardly have been every man's property. There are, however, other swords in what looks like mint condition (Aner and Kersten *passim*; Quillfeldt 1995) – again a small sample because of the post-depositional corrosion and damages. Apparently swords could have very different life-stories. If there was a functional relationship between effectivity and typology we would expect the functionally best types to show the heaviest damages, *i.e.* the grip tongue and tanged swords should be the most re-sharpened types. According to Kristiansen (1984) the grip tongue and the octagonally hilted swords were more sharpened. Observations of cuts on the edges just below the hilt are quoted which seem to belie the idea of stabbing as the fencing technique – but what may happen in the heat of the moment? He also states that the tips were often bent or broken off but that the period III swords show more use of slashing which would accord with the trend in period IV (Fig 19.2). Breaking a sword blade does not seem to be an easy affair, judging by the swords which have been bent 180 degrees without breaking (Aner and Kersten no. 4132 and 4861). Does that mean that all broken off blades had been deliberately broken as part of the deposition rites or could fights be so violent that a blade could break during the action – at the hilt?

A somewhat ambiguous attitude to the decorative features seems to have ruled. Although the hilt may have the most refined and complicated decoration and technical execution as a result, we may think, of a desire to display the command of good craftsmen and design, these features were sometimes deliberately obscured or hidden before the sword was buried (Boye 1896, pl. XX, 2; Aner and Kersten no. 3313 Trevad). There are other graves with a blade without proper hilt but a wrapping simulating a hilt (Aner and Kersten no. 1515 – similar re-use no. 1781). Here there was no question of providing the dead with a useful weapon. A suggestion was enough, just as it was in the young man's oak coffin in Borum Eshøj (Fig 19.3; Boye 1896 pl. X, 3–4) where a full size wooden scabbard (71 cm long) contained only a dagger. Pia fraus is the reason normally given for this case which is only revealed because of the preservation conditions in the iron pan-encased tumuli.

Burials

Although a lot of information can be gleaned about function and production from the swords themselves this is not enough to place them in their proper cultural setting. The study of context is crucial and because of the custom of burying swords with the dead during periods I – III with heavy emphasis on II–III (and rather rarely during periods IV – V) in South Scandinavia it presents a good approach. Again it should be remembered, however, that well documented contexts are not that abundant, they represent at most between 0.8% and 21% of the known burials with swords.

As in so many other respects the burial complexes within this group of closed burial finds are highly varied. This is true of the sword graves as well. I count a minimum of about 2400 of them. We have burials with just the sword left, the organic equipment being lost. Other swords come from graves with rich equipment of bronze and gold – in the famous oak coffins supplemented by the marvellous textiles and furniture (Boye 1896) which give us an idea of what is normally lost. Between the extremely rich and the poor sword graves is a whole range of combinations with weapons, tools and ornaments. The evidence is thus radically different from the Irish situation (Bridgford 1997).

Within this broad spectre of combinations the swords themselves add to the confusion. They occur in a variety from very plain to very complicated and highly ornate specimens. The rules governing their place in the context hierarchy is not easy to understand. The problem seems to be that there are so many individual situations that the rules can only be applied at a very general level. We need to go at least one step further in detailed analyses than just establishing the combinations of weapon types, sword, axe, spear. The associated types are needed to place the sword burials in a wider societal context.

The purpose of this paper is not to present a new thesis on the role of swords or other elements of Bronze Age weaponry but rather to examine some aspects of the swords, resuming earlier studies of the objects themselves. There is still a need for in-depth analyses of the swords and their contexts. The baffling number of swords from the Nordic Bronze Age indicates an emphasis on what we must call the martial aspects of life and society. The challenge is to understand these aspects in the context of a society otherwise dominated by peaceful activites linked to agriculture and a possessive attitude to land expressed by the thousands of tumuli and by the very sword graves so dominant in our image of these monumental mounds.

How these many graves may fit into a ranked, multi-tiered society organised according to the chieftainship model taken over from the neo-evolutionism of social anthropology remains a central issue in our Bronze Age studies. The Nordic Bronze Age may present better opportunities for this task than the Irish Bronze Age with its less complete sources (Waddell and Shee Twohig

1995). I hope that we shall be able to improve our understanding beyond the still rather simple or (too) optimistic interpretations of the moment. The approach all too sketchily presented here is but one of the many needed for this purpose.

Note

1. This paper stems from a project on War and Society funded by the Danish Research Council for the Humanities, jointly managed by the departments of Ethnography and Social Anthropology and Prehistoric Archaeology at Moesgård, Aarhus University. The final volume is Ton Otto, Henrik Thrane and Helle Vandkilde (eds) *Warfare and Society from an Archaeological and Social Anthropological Perspective*, Århus (2003).

Bibliography

Aner, E. and Kersten, K. 1972–2002 *Die Funde der älteren Bronzezeit des nordischen Kreises in Dänemark, Schleswig-Holstein und Norddeutschland I– XI*. Neumünster.

Baudou, E. 1960 *Die regionale und chronologische Einteilung der jüngeren Bronzezeit im Nordischen Kreis*, Stockholm.

Boye, V. 1896 Trouvailles de Cercueils en Chene de l'Age du Bronze en Denmark. Copenhagen.

Brandherm, D. and Sicherl, B. 2001 Überlegungen zur Schwertproduktion der späten Urnenfelderzeit, *Archäologisches Korrespondenzblatt* **31**, 223–41.

Bridgford, S.D. 1997 Mightier than the Pen? (an Edgewise Look at Irish Bronze Age Swords). In J. Carman (ed.) *Material Harm*, 95–115. Glasgow.

Eogan, G. 1965 *A Catalogue of Irish Bronze Swords*. National Museum of Ireland, The Stationery Office, Dublin.

Gebühr, M. 1980 Kampfspuren an Schwertern des Nydam-Fundes. In T. Krüger and H.G. Stephan (eds) *Beiträge zur Archäologie Nordwestdeutschlands und Mitteleuropa*, 69–84. Hildesheim.

Harding, A.F. 1995 *Die Schwerter im ehemaligen Jugoslawien*, Prähistorische Bronzefunde IV, 14. Stuttgart.

Harding, A.F. 2000 *European Societies in the Bronze Age*. Cambridge University Press, Cambridge.

Kristiansen, K. 1984 Krieger und Häuptlinge in der Bronzezeit Dänemarks, *Jahrbuch des Römisch-Germanischen Zentralmuseums Mainz* **31**, 187–208.

Müller, S. 1898 *Vor Oldtid*. København.

Nordbladh, J. 1989 Armour and Fighting in the South Scandinavian Bronze Age. In T.B. Larsson and H. Lundmark (eds) *Approaches to Swedish Prehistory*, 323–33. British Archaeological Reports International Series **500**, Oxford.

Ottenjahn, H. 1969 *Die nordischen Vollgriffschwerter der älteren und mittleren Bronzezeit*, Römisch-Germanischen Forschungen **30**. Berlin.

Quillfeldt, I. von 1995 *Die Vollgriffschwerter in Süddeutschland*, Prähistorische Bronzefunde IV,11. Stuttgart.

Sprockhoff, E. 1931 *Die germanischen Griffzungenschwerter*, Römisch-Germanischen Forschungen **5**. Berlin.

TOMBA (database of European sword graves from Bronze and Early Iron Age) www.rgzm.de

Torbrügge, W. 1995 Die frühe Hallstattzeit (Ha C) in chronologischen Ansichten und notwendige Randbemerkungen I, *Jahrbuch des Römisch-germanischen Zentralmuseums* **38**, 223–463. Mainz 1991.

Vandkilde, H. 1996 *From Stone to Bronze*. Århus.

Waddell, J. and Shee Twohig, E. (eds) 1995 *Ireland in the Bronze Age*. The Stationery Office, Dublin.

20. A Long Distance Connection in the Bronze Age: Joining Fragments of a Ewart Park Sword from two Sites in England

Richard Bradley and Deborah Ford

Introduction (Richard Bradley)

Every few months I see George Eogan in a library in Oxford and we have a cup of coffee together. I look forward to these meetings and to our conversations about archaeology. What has been happening on either side of the Irish Sea? Some of our encounters have been particularly memorable. I recall the occasion when we found that, quite independently, we had both discovered similar designs inside passage tombs – mine were in Orkney and George's were in the Boyne Valley. I had planned to write more about them here, when I learned of a surprising discovery in the English Midlands. It was exactly the sort of find that I would be telling George about over coffee, so it seemed appropriate to make it the subject of this paper. Not only is it the kind of information in which he has always taken an interest, it relates directly to his early studies of Bronze Age swords.

A Ewart Park sword from Hanford and Trentham, Staffordshire (Richard Bradley and Deborah Ford)

How can one sword come from two sites? There have been cases in which parts of the same object have ended in separate collections, but in this case two halves of the same weapon were found in different places.

The lower section was discovered by a metal detectorist at Trentham in Staffordshire (SJ 8540) and most of the remainder was located by the same method thirteen years later. This came from Hanford, three kilometres away (SJ 8742). The finders did not know one another. The sites are on hilltops on either side of the River Trent and they are intervisible. Examination of the find spot at Hanford showed that the upper portion of the sword had been just below the surface and had not been buried in a pit or similar feature. Neither section of the artefact was directly associated with other objects, but a Middle Bronze Age socketed spearhead, a Roman terret and other later metalwork (medieval and post medieval) have been found on the hill at Hanford, which includes a series of springs (Ford *et al.* 1998).

The sword (Fig 20.1) is in reasonably good condition, although the point is rather worn. There are no signs of deliberate damage apart from the breaks that divide the sword into three portions (part of the hilt is missing). The blade fracture left a jagged edge and the two surviving fragments fit together exactly, leaving no room for doubt that they were parts of the same object. Both are in a similar state of preservation, but the edges of this fracture are more rounded in the lower section of the sword, suggesting that it may have circulated for longer – or have been handled more intensively – than the other piece. Enough remains of the weapon to show that it was a Ewart Park sword, although it would be difficult to assign it to one of the subgroups proposed by Colquhoun and Burgess (1988). Recent work suggests that the most likely date for the Ewart Park phase was between about 920 and 800 BC (Needham *et al.* 1998).

Interpretations

Finds of broken swords are very common, although they tend to occur in hoards rather than as single finds. This particular discovery is unusual, for here it seems as if parts of the same weapon were deposited in separate locations. Their association with hilltops (and in one case with a group of springs) recalls the contexts of other finds in Late Bronze Age Europe (Harding 2000, 309–20). There is also the striking feature that the two hills are on either side of a major river which contains numerous weapons in its lower reaches, especially in Nottinghamshire and Lincolnshire (Scurfield 1997; Davis 1999).

There are three main ways of interpreting the intentional breakage of Bronze Age swords.

1.   It is possible that objects were deliberately destroyed when their period of use was over. An elaborate artefact like a sword might have been disabled to prevent its continued circulation, perhaps when the original owner had died. That would certainly account for the damage done to some of the swords found in Continental graves (Gerdsen 1986), and it would also explain why so much of the weaponry deposited in

the Thames had been damaged before it was committed to the water (York 2002). That idea could not account for the erosion on the fractured surface of the sword tip from Trentham. This suggests that it had continued to circulate for some time after the weapon was broken.

2. Another explanation is that objects might be reduced to fragments as a preliminary to recycling the metal. This applies to the collections known as founders' hoards, some of which have been interpreted as lost or abandoned stores of raw material. It is certainly true that metal analysis provides abundant evidence for the recycling of discarded objects (Mordant, Pernot and Rychner 1998), but that would not explain the evidence from Hanford and Trentham, where both parts of the same sword still survive. Nor would it provide any reason why they should have been deposited in apparent isolation, and on separate sites.

3. A third possibility is that certain kinds of objects were divided into units of standard weight and were used as ingots (Pare 1999). There is certainly some evidence for a system of weights in Late Bronze Age Europe, and Sommerfeld (1994) has pursued this hypothesis in a detailed study of the hoards containing broken sickles. As his research makes clear, the same kind of system could have involved the subdivision of sword blades. That hypothesis is especially tempting as it has already been suggested that the poor quality socketed axes made in northwest France at the end of the Bronze Age may have been intended as ingots (Briard 1965, 270–1). In South Scandinavia, Malmer (1992) has suggested that a series of figurines were also made according to a prescribed system of weights, and a rather similar system has been postulated for the Iberian Peninsula (Ruiz-Gálvez 2000).

The last two hypotheses can, of course, be combined. Smiths may have divided entire objects into fragments according to a system of weights. They may also have employed those weights in preparing metal for recycling, but again that would not account for the unusual character of these two finds. Are there other factors to take into consideration?

Perhaps the most important point is that once the sword had been broken its parts seem to have been treated separately. There are indications that the lower section had become more worn than the remainder of the weapon. Perhaps it had been handled more often or it circulated over a longer period, after which both parts were deposited on separate sites. Is there any indication that this happened in other cases?

In the corpus of British Bronze Age swords there is a disparity in the representation of fragmentary weapons. Among single finds of Ewart Park weapons hilt fragments outnumber the lower part of the blade in a ratio of approximately 2.5: 1 (Colquhoun and Burgess 1988). For earlier swords the ratio is virtually the same, and among

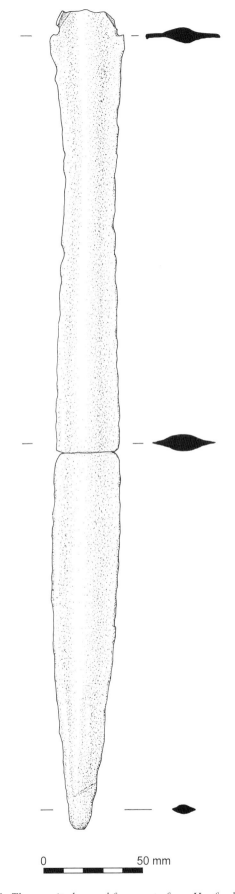

0   50 mm

Fig 20.1: The reunited sword fragments from Hanford and Trentham, Staffordshire. Drawing: Noel Boothroyd.

the later Carps Tongue swords it is even wider. There are obvious objections to this kind of analysis – the hilts of swords are easier to recognise then their blades, and this may lead to their preservation and publication – but they do not explain the evidence from well-recorded hoards. In this case it is clear that all the metalwork has been identified, and yet the proportions in which these parts of the weapons are represented are similar to those among the single finds. Here the ratio of hilt sections to the lower blade is 2:1 among the Ewart Park swords. It is virtually the same among earlier swords, and in the Carps Tongue tradition it remains unchanged. This cannot reflect the durability of these different components, for among the older dirks and rapiers the disparity is significantly reduced (Burgess and Gerloff 1981); in this case the ratio among the single finds is only 1.5: 1. In George's own study of Irish swords (Eogan 1965) the numerous examples of Class 4 show a ratio of hilt section to lower blade of only 1.1:1.

Such evidence implies that the parts of broken swords might have been treated in different ways during the Late Bronze Age. Some fragments continued to circulate or were deposited with a certain formality, whilst others disappear from the record, perhaps because they were melted down. This happened in some periods more than in others and the Irish evidence clearly shows that practice varied widely, even within these islands.

Reference to Continental sources reveals a similar situation. Sometimes it is unclear whether all the surviving fragments have been published, yet it seems remarkable that in major corpora of swords the ratio of hilt sections to the lower blade is generally between 1:1 – the situation in Hungary (Kemenczei 1989; 1991) – and 5:1 – that in Southern Germany, Austria and Switzerland (Schauer 1971; Krämer 1985). In each case the different parts of these weapons appear in similar proportions in the local hoards. The same imbalance is seen in the large collection of Late Bronze Age hoard finds studied by Huth (1997) in Western Europe, but again it is not a universal pattern. In former Yugoslavia, for example, this pattern is reversed, and in the later hoards from that region the lower sections of sword blades are better represented than their hilts (Harding 1995). Again the evidence suggests that cultural selection was important.

It seems as if the separate parts of Bronze Age swords may have possessed a different significance once their original role as weapons was at an end. How else can we account for the survival of so many hilts and upper blades compared with the lower section? This was a widespread pattern in Bronze Age Europe, but it was by no means universal. One possibility is that the hilt was thought to be more directly associated with the original owner. It may have been preserved as a relic whilst the rest of the artefact was treated as raw material.

Again that cannot provide the entire explanation for the finds from Hanford and Trentham. It may be true that the two parts of the sword were treated as separate artefacts. They may even have been used in different ways, and yet the manner of their deposition suggests that in people's minds they were still connected to one another. Each fragment was placed on a hilltop on either side of a major river. Neither seems to have been accompanied by any artefacts, and the two sites were visible from one another. These were two halves of the same object: is it too much to suppose that they were deposited as parts of the same transaction?

Recently John Chapman (2000) has described a similar situation in the archaeology of southeast Europe. He summarises his interpretation in this way:

> "Two people who wish to establish some form of social relationship or conclude some kind of transaction agree on a specific artefact appropriate to the interaction in question and break it in two or more parts, each keeping one or more parts as a token of the relationship .... The fragments of the object are then kept until reconstitution of the relationship is required, in which case the part(s) may be deposited in a structured manner" (Chapman 2000, 6).

He describes this relationship between people and objects by the term 'enchainment'. His study runs from the Mesolithic period to the Copper Age, but he illustrates the same principle with a number of examples that extend from the Classical world to the Middle Ages. It would be wrong to seize upon this model simply because other interpretations are inadequate, but it could account for a number of features of the Staffordshire finds which still pose serious problems. If swords were broken up as a source of raw material, why were both halves of this particular example left intact and deposited on different sites? If objects were reduced to fragments in conformity with a system of weights, it does not explain why these pieces have survived. Moreover, it seems as if the separate parts of Bronze Age swords may have possessed a different significance once their role as weapons was at an end, but in this case each section was deposited in a similar location.

Chapman's notion of 'enchainment' provides one way of accounting for the preservation of both parts of the same weapon. It also allows the fragments to have circulated independently. All these are possibilities that are already present in the archaeological literature. Where it breaks new ground is in postulating the reunion of the separate fragments through the act of deposition. That is surely the implication of these two finds from the English Midlands. Even after the sword had been broken, the relationship between the two parts remained an important concern: so much so that in the end both were placed in the ground in a similar manner. The link between them was emphasised by the sites that were chosen for the purpose, for both were found on hilltops that could be seen from one another.

We have drawn upon George Eogan's study of Irish Bronze Age swords in the course of this paper, but it would be wrong to give the impression that it is merely a catalogue, for he was one of the first scholars writing in English to realise that the deposition of prehistoric metalwork cannot be taken for granted. It poses special problems of interpretation, and many of these have still to be resolved. The joining fragments of the Staffordshire sword add yet another element to an already complicated picture. We hope that George will find this evidence as intriguing as we do ourselves.

Acknowledgements

We must thank Noel Boothroyd for allowing us to use his drawing of the sword.

Bibliography

Briard, J. 1965 *Les dépôts Bretons et l'Age du Bronze Atlantique.* Laboratorie d'anthrolopogie préhistorique de la Faculté des Sciences de Rennes, Rennes.

Burgess, C. and Gerloff, S. 1981 *The Dirks and Rapiers of Great Britain and Ireland.* C.H. Beck, Munich.

Chapman, J. 2000 *Fragmentation in Archaeology. People, Places and Broken Objects in the Prehistory of South Eastern Europe.* Routledge, London.

Colquhoun, I. and Burgess, C. 1988 *The Swords of Britain.* C.H. Beck, Munich.

Davis, R. 1999 Bronze Age metalwork from the Trent Valley: Newark, Notts, to Gainsborough, Lincs, *Transactions of the Thoroton Society of Nottinghamshire* **103**, 25–48.

Eogan, G. 1965 *Catalogue of Irish Bronze Swords.* National Museum of Ireland, The Stationery Office, Dublin.

Ford, D., Goodwin, J., Boothroyd, N., Abby, R., Cook, B. and Youngs, S. 1998 A prehistoric Excalibur and other artefacts of divers dates: a catalogue of selected finds from Staffordshire recovered through metal detecting. *West Midlands Archaeology* **41**, 36–48.

Gerdsen, H. 1986 *Studien zu der Schwertgräbern der älteren Hallstattzeit.* Von Zabern, Mainz.

Harding, A. 1995 *Die Schwerter im ehemaligen Jugoslawien.* Franz Steiner, Stuttgart.

Harding, A. 2000 *European Societies in the Bronze Age.* Cambridge University Press, Cambridge.

Huth, C. 1997 *Westeuropäische Horte der Spätbronzezeit. Fundbild und Funktion.* Universitätsverlag, Regensberg.

Kemenczei, T. 1989 *Die Schwerter in Ungarn 1.* C.H. Beck, Munich.

Kemenczei, T. 1991 *Die Schwerter in Ungarn 2.* Franz Steiner, Stuttgart.

Krämer, W. 1985 *Die Vollgriffschwerter in Österreich und der Schweiz.* C.H. Beck, Munich.

Malmer, M. 1992 Weight systems in the Scandinavian Bronze Age, *Antiquity* **66**, 377–88.

Mordant, C., Pernot, M. and Rychner, V. (eds) 1998 *L'atelier du bronzier en Europe, tome 1: Les analyses du métal: leur apport à l'archéologie de l'Age du Bronze.* Comité des Travaux historiques et scientifiques, Paris.

Needham, S., Bronk Ramsay, C., Coombs, D., Cartwright, C. and Pettit, P. 1998 An independent chronology for British Bronze Age metalwork: the results of the Oxford Radiocarbon Accelerator Programme, *Archaeological Journal* **154**, 55–107

Pare, C. 1999 Weights and weighing in Bronze Age Central Europe. In *Eliten in der Bronzezeit*, 421–514. Römisch-Germanischen Zentralmuseums, Mainz.

Ruiz-Gálvez, M. 2000 Weight systems and exchange networks in Bronze Age Europe. In C. Pare (ed.) *Metals Make the World Go Round. The Supply and Circulation of Metal in Bronze Age Europe*, 267–79. Oxbow, Oxford.

Schauer, P. 1971 *Die Schwerter in Süddeutschland, Österreich und der Schweiz 1.* C.H. Beck, Munich.

Scurfield, C. 1997 Bronze Age metalwork from the River Trent in Nottinghamshire. *Transactions of the Thoroton Society of Nottinghamshire* **101**, 29–57.

Sommerfeld, C. 1994 *Gerätegeld Sichel. Studien zur monetären Struktur bronzezeitlicher Horte in nördlichen Mitteleuropa.* Walter de Gruyter, Berlin.

York, J. 2002 The life cycle of Bronze Age metalwork from the Thames, *Oxford Journal of Archaeology* **21**, 77–92.

21. Bronzes in a context: rock carvings of Scandinavia

John Coles

The contribution of George Eogan to European Bronze Age studies has been immense. Much of his original work has concerned the metalwork traditions in both bronze and gold, and his publications and their many citations reflect his profound achievements in bringing to notice the variety and spread of the weapons, tools and ornaments that help to identify the European Bronze Age in all its complexities.

Bronzes, the product of metallurgical workshops both large and small, have great variety both in shape, hence suitability for typological analysis, and in association, where found in graves or hoards. On occasion, and sometimes in abundance, they or their residues are found in settlements, and thereby gain immeasurably in context. But a vast majority of bronze weapons and tools occur, insofar as our records now attest, as individual finds or in hoards, in association only with other bronzes. Thereby divorced from their original places in the hands of Bronze Age people, they are for us reduced in impact to admiration and analysis as works of craftsmanship, to conjecture about their places of disposal, and to debate about their original purpose and function in the societies that created them.

In the north European Bronze Age, metal objects have an additional focus for attention, although this has not so often been explored in depth. In southern Scandinavia there exists some thousands of rock carvings, and among them a number in which the weapons and tools of the Bronze Age are depicted. In theory, such representations should offer us a unique opportunity to study some of the contextual evidence for bronzes that is otherwise rare.

Rock carvings have an advantage in being immovable, so the objects represented are fixed in place, the art produced at that place, unlike metal objects that could be, and were, traded or otherwise moved over distances to perhaps gain new and different values. In addition, the carved representations are generally associated with a variety of other images on the sites, many of them contemporaneous in production but even if not then clearly linked by proximity and position. The whole carved site has its own identity within a landscape of the Bronze Age, with its own distributions of settlements, burial monu-

ments, field and forest and sea, and its whole geographical base identified ever more closely by modern studies.

The representation of Bronze Age objects upon a wholly inert inorganic medium offers a number of useful pieces of evidence for us. The precise character of the artifact, a sword, axe, helmet, ard or boat, can be clearly expressed and remains unaltered in shape. The organic elements of the object, its wooden haft for example, can be carved in some detail (Fig 21.1). The ways in which

Fig 21.1: Axe-bearer at Simris. All photos copyright John Coles.

Fig 21.2: *Ard scene at Västra Östergård.*

Fig 21.3: *Rubbing of a cart and team at Frännarp. John Coles.*

objects were worn, carried, sheathed or brandished are often expressed on the rocks. The association by number and variety of representations can be clearly seen, and by such associations we may come to some views about the circumstances of use, or performance, of objects that otherwise, as individual bronzes in our museums, we can hardly dare to guess. All of this leads us to a better conception of the significance of the metalwork of the Bronze Age in the north, and perhaps by extrapolation to other areas of northern and western Europe. And, finally, we may glimpse on the rocks some elements of the organic material culture of the Bronze Age, the wooden tools, boats and carts, perhaps clothing and decorative panels, that otherwise rarely survive the passage of time and the processes of decay and elimination.

What follows here is but a brief commentary on the evidence from the rock carvings, and a full statistical account is not yet possible, essentially because not all of the relevant carved sites are published in such a way that the details of the artifacts can be clearly seen. Nonetheless, the body of evidence is impressive and it may well be that the parameters are defined and the overall structure clear enough to stand scrutiny.

Above all else, it is weaponry and the elements of display and parade that are most abundantly represented

on the rocks. Of domestic equipment – the pots, baskets, clothes and plant foods – there is little that is visible. There are no clear houses or barns, and only a few patterns that might be field systems or maps of land holdings. Of sheep or goats there is not much sign, few fish or the nets used to catch them, but plenty of boats are shown, and in great and elaborate detail. It is as if the ordinary mundane objects of life could be ignored within the repertoire of the carvers.

However, more complex or complicated objects, involving craftsmanship and ingenuity, were often represented on the rocks. Ards are shown either as static or in use with draught animals, and the detail on carvings such as those from Aspeberget, Valla Östergård (Fig 21.2) and Stenbacken (Bohuslän) is sufficient to allow efforts at re-creation and testing. Carts and wagons are more abundantly represented than is generally acknowledged, and often shown with pairs of horses attached (Fig 21.3). The array of carts at Frännarp (Skåne) is probably the most detailed of all, but the wagons at Rished, and the postulated sun-carriage at Backa (Bohuslän) with its bronze and gold Trundholm model connections, are also significant. Isolated designs of wheel-crosses are likely to represent the wheelwright's art although other discs may well have had different connotations. Carts, wagons

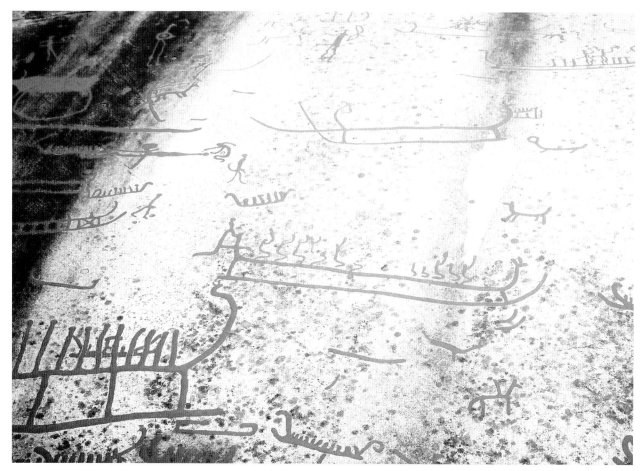

Fig 21.4: Boat carvings at Vitlycke.

and wheels were essentially made of wood, with few metal attachments, and from a few wetsites in the north and west of Europe there have been recovered wooden pieces of such complex artefacts.

The greatest conundrum, however, is the abundance of carvings of boats, and the extreme rarity of such important objects from the actual artifactual record. Although many logboats have been recovered from bogs, lakes and other wet deposits, they are barely represented as rock carvings; instead, the artists depicted elaborately curved boats that must have been plank-built, with high stem and stern posts, as examples from Vitlycke (Bohuslän) (Fig 21.4) and Simris (Skåne) attest. Of real boats in the artifactual record there are but a few, the North Ferriby (England) boats as prime examples, and now the Dover boat adds useful information. Later in time is the Hjortspring (Denmark) boat, which is closer in intentional appearance to the carved boat images, such as those at Litsleby (Bohuslän), than are the English earlier Bronze Age wooden craft.

The question of the chronological patterning of the carvings of boats has been addressed through their representation on small bronzes, such as razors, that bring a measure of dating through typology and association – a neat reversal of the normal circumstances of context (Kaul

1998). In addition, the remarkable discovery of carvings on a kerb of stones internal to an Early Bronze Age burial mound at Sagaholm in Sweden offers further opportunities to date certain rock carvings (Goldhahn 1999).

So the rock carvings add considerably to our information about the capabilities and preferential designs of Bronze Age craftsmen for such crucially important objects, in cultivation of the land, in land transport, and in travel by waterway, in other words, in significant actions within Bronze Age societies.

When we turn to the weaponry of the Bronze Age and its representation on the rocks, we are faced with a number of tantalizing problems and possibilities. Some of the rock carving areas of northern Europe have little more than carvings of cupmarks and boats, perhaps with some discs and simple unsexed human images here and there. Other areas, however, possess great variety and abundance of images of weapons and other prestigious items, often associated with humans and human groups. The detail sometimes exhibited allows relatively good dating on the basis of typology and association. For example, the wide-bladed crescentic axes on the sites at Simris (Skåne) and Flyhov (Västergötland) are probably of the earlier Bronze Age, and the narrow-bladed axes at Aspeberget (Bohuslän) may well be of a later period. Axes may be shown

Fig 21.5: Part of major panel of carvings at Fossum.

hafted but unheld, but as often they are carved as part of a design or small scene, held by humans probably on land and sometimes on boats; the site of Fossum (Bohuslän) (Fig 21.5) has a variety of these axemen, large and small, on land and on sea. Their wide-bladed axes have a straight haft and are mostly held high above the heads of warriors who sometimes face one another in bellicose mode.

Axemen do not threaten quadruped animals, but spearmen are sometimes shown attacking animals. The spears on sites such as Fossum, Karlslund and Litsleby (Bohuslän) are leaf-shaped and slender, and attached by socket to long thin spearshafts. They are shown held by phallic warriors as if ready for the throw or thrust, and occasionally a spear may transfix an animal. Several disc-bodied humans have spear-like arms at Finntorp (Bohuslän).

Male warriors may have axes and sword scabbards, or spears and scabbards, but they are not shown with both axe and spear, so the emphasis is always on the single weapon held generally in one hand. Sword scabbards, shown protruding at an angle from the backsides of the humans, are not ever, I think, associated with a sword-bearing warrior. For some reason, humans do not brandish swords at one another or at the world in general; their scabbards are sufficient evidence of their power. Bronze swords of the northern lands are often found in graves, and the visible amount of wear upon them suggests that

the sword was perhaps an emblem to be passed to the next generation, and not to be displayed and identified on the rocks. On several major sites in Östergötland, however, swords are defiantly carved upon the rocks, in association with shield-like designs, boats and animals, so here the display of the sword, as an image itself, was not curtailed. Elsewhere the scabbard alone carried the weight of responsibility and prestige, and winged chapes on some are probably indicative of a later Bronze Age date, as at Järrestad (Skåne) and Svenneby (Bohuslän), associated at Svenneby with a shield-bearer and a human with club or hammer.

The representation of shields is difficult to identify from the large number of discs that appear in the carvings. Where multiple circular designs are contained within the disc, perhaps these indicate the concentric ribs of shields, as seen at Ekenberg (Östergötland), but a more positive identification can be seen at Hede (Fig 21.6) and Svenneby (Bohuslän) where warriors with sword scabbards carry shields. There are probably of the later Bronze Age on the basis of shield form and scabbard type.

One type of weapon is not well represented in the metalwork of the Bronze Age, for obvious reason. Wooden bows dating to the Bronze Age have been recovered from wet deposits, and a few are shown on the carved rocks, as isolated bowmen, at Häljesta (Västman-

Fig 21.6: Part of panel at Hede, with shield-bearer.

land) or as confrontational pair, with dogs, at Hamn (Bohuslän). These bowmen do not wear sword scabbards, nor do they have quivers of arrows shown. Males with clubs, presumably of wood although possibly of metal, are occasionally seen in the rock carvings, but the details are not clear enough for categorization. The scabbard-wearing phallic human at Kasen Lövåsen (Bohuslän) has a particularly impressive club or hammer, and is an altogether formidable, perhaps malevolent, figure.

A large number of humans are shown with small or practically non-existent heads surmounted by horns. The presumptive dancer from Smörsten, and scabbard-wearer from Bottna Olskroken, and the trio from Kalleby (Fig 21.7) (all Bohuslän) appear to be wearing horned helmets of the kind found in bronze at Viksø in Denmark. More common are males with squared upper bodies, probably wearing body armour, perhaps sheet leather or along the lines of the sheetmetal armour from Marmesse (France).

A particular feature of many boat carvings are the single and sometimes several curved stroke lines over the gunwale, perhaps indicating that bronze horns or lurs were being carried and sounded. Greater detail and more certain identity is provided by sites such as Kalleby (Fig 21.7) (Bohuslän) where humans are shown holding and blowing the lurs, of a shape reminiscent of the Brudevaelte (Denmark) great bronze lurs. These provide a later Bronze Age date for the Kalleby carvings, which also include horned helmets and body armour.

It will be clear from the above that bronze objects

depicted on the rocks are not utilitarian or common varieties. Axes where shown are large and are held in threatening positions. Spears have long shafts and are equally hostile. Males often wear sword scabbards and on rare occasions the hilt of the sword is shown, but otherwise this emblem of prestige and power is hidden from direct view. The horned helmets, body armour, great lurs, and very occasional neckrings or earrings on extremely large humans at Litsleby and Backa (Bohuslän), all are indicative of prestige, display and control. They may have been created on the rocks as part of human ceremonies or as representations made of, or for, the gods of the Bronze Age, or a combination of factors that we cannot now comprehend. The carvings set out an element and a concept of Bronze Age society that does not accord well with much of our other archaeological evidence, of farming settlements, industrial activities and established territories.

The increasing evidence for fortified settlements of the Bronze Age in many parts of Europe suggests that matters may not have been quite as stable as we are often led to believe. There are likely to have been many undercurrents, and actions, that we cannot recognise. At the present time, the known settlements and other places of Bronze Age activity have not yielded the amount of wealth in metal that we might expect to see, and they provide no real guide to the systems of belief or assertions of power that the rock carvings, the pictures, suggest. The metal objects themselves, impressive products,

Fig 21.7: Lur-blowers with horned helmets and body armour at Kalleby.

specialised workshops, and extensive trading networks, suggest a more complex state of affairs that the industries of stone, bone and clay might indicate on settlements. It is as if there was a higher level of aspiration, of social stature for some, of other-world powers that had to be acknowledged, by metal deposition in special places, and by the representation of the extreme powers of forces that lay outside normal human behaviour. To placate such powers was an imperative, and where wealth in metal existed then it could be offered; where such wealth was not available, in the north, then elaborate ceremonies and carvings could be substituted.

However, this explanation, often advanced, does not acknowledge the immense concentration of complex rock carving sites in a relatively small area of northern Bohuslän. Other factors must have been at work here, bringing people from the south and east in periodic visits for dedication and affirmation. The elucidation of such activities is a current theme of research. In the future, expansive studies of locations, contexts and associations, chronological precisions and detailed analyses of the

images may well help to refine our understanding of the carvings as part of Bronze Age societies. Meantime, this paper, offered to my long-time friend and colleague George Eogan may pose more questions than answers; yet it is just such questions, from a different angle, that George has pursued through his own work on the European Bronze Age.

Bibliography

Many of the rock carvings identified in the paper are illustrated in these books:

Burenhult, G. 1973 *The Rock Carvings of Götaland*, Acta Archaeologica Lundensia **8**.
Coles, J. 1990 *Images of the past. A guide to the rock carvings and other ancient monuments of northern Bohuslän*. Uddevalla.
Goldhahn, J. 1999 *Sagaholm – hällristningar och gravritual*. Jönköping.
Hygen, A-S. and Bengtsson, L. 2000 *Rock Carvings in the Borderlands*. Bohuslän and Ostfold. Sävedalen.
Kaul, F. 1998 *Ships on Bronzes. A study in Bronze Age religion and iconography*. Copenhagen.

22. Bronze Age rotary spits: finds old and new, some false, some true

Colin Burgess and Brendan O' Connor

Une broche à rôtir articulée, trouvée à Amathonte de Chypre, pose des problèmes de datation par rapport à celle communément admise pour les modèles analogues en usage en Occident et en Sardaigne pendant le Bronze Final.

> Gomez 1991, 369

Les auteurs qui, ces dernières années s'intéressèrent aux broches à rôtir, s'accordent à leur attribuer une fonction rituelle liée aux «repas sacrés» similaire et complémentaire de celles des chaudrons et des crochets à viande en bronze.

> Vilaça 1990, 168

"Holmes, is there any point to which you would wish to draw my attention?"
"Why, to the curious incidence of carp's tongue in Portugal."
"But carp's tongue did nothing in Portugal!"
"That was the curious incidence, my dear Watson."
With apologies to Arthur Conan Doyle and *Silver Blaze*

The instruments termed *broches à rotir articulées* by French writers, here more succinctly *rotary spits,* have frequently been discussed in the literature (*e.g.* Almagro Gorbea 1974; Mohen 1977; Coffyn 1985; Chevillot 1989, 161–2; Vilaça 1990; Gomez 1991; Mederos 1996). These publications have added steadily to the number of finds, and extended the distribution eastwards to Cyprus (Karageorghis and Lo Schiavo 1989). Such questions as chronology, distribution, origins, and function have regularly been touched on, but there has been a tendency to repeat uncritically the catalogue of finds from one publication to the next. The aim of this survey is to add some new finds, remove others which appear in many of the published lists, to return to the problem of chronology, highlighted by Gomez' remarks at the head of this paper, and to attempt to set these instruments in their Bronze Age context. We cannot here, alas, deal with the question of technology, which requires scientific examination beyond our means. What follows we offer to our old friend George Eogan, one of the last of the great bronze specialists, whose work has enlightened all who have come after.

Terminology (Fig 22.1)

Rotary spits, typically 55–90cm in length, are characterised by a long, square/rectangular-sectioned *shank* or *shaft* (*tige* in the French publications), tapering to a *point*. At the other end is a ring terminal on the end of a much shorter round-sectioned *grip*, which may be straight or may expand slightly, but normally ends in a trumpet-shaped expansion. The spirally ribbed grip of the Monte Sa Idda example (no. 7) is unique at the moment. The trumpet expansion divides the grip from the rotary mechanism. This consists of a short, round-sectioned *spindle*, around which a *hook-holder ring* rotates. This ring is frequently ribbed or corrugated around its circumference. On one side it has a protruding tab or tongue, perforated to take the square-sectioned pendant double hook. This is sometimes missing, leaving the holes. Mounted on the ring opposite this hook tab is a decorative figure of a bird or animal. Usually more certain identification is not possible, but the Port-Sainte-Foy bird (no. 12) is almost certainly an eagle (Fig 22.2; Chevillot 1989, 161, and pers. comm.), though doves or something similar appear more normal. In most cases the animals are undistinguished quadrupeds, but the example from Challans (no. 9) is surmounted by a fine stag's head.

Beyond the hook-holder ring, the other side of the spindle is stopped by the trumpet mouth of a short circular-sectioned piece, which forms the *shank holder*. This is frequently bobbin or reel-shaped, with its other end also a trumpet expansion. From this end protrudes the long shank (see the Ste.-Marguerite fragment, no. 13, Fig 22.3).

It will be clear from the above that rotary spits are of complex construction, put together from a number of separate pieces. To complicate the question of manufacture even more, at least one bears signs of a terminal ring having been replaced or cast back on (Port-Sainte-Foy). Clearly further technological comment would be unwise in the absence of comprehensive scientific analysis of these instruments.

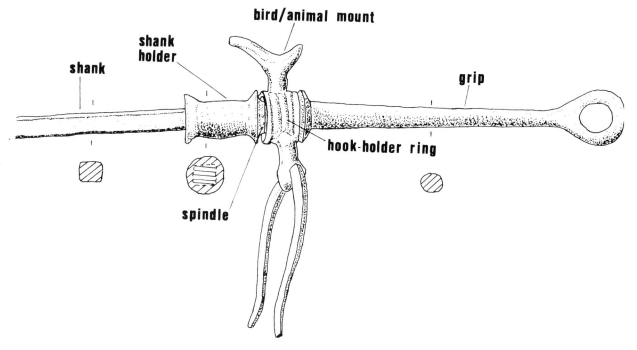

Fig 22:1 Rotary spits: terminology.

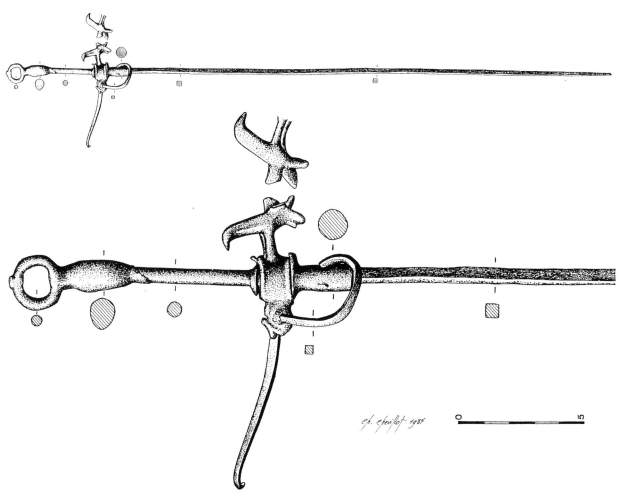

Fig 22:2 Port-Sainte-Foy, no. 12, length 670mm (courtesy of Christian Chevillot).

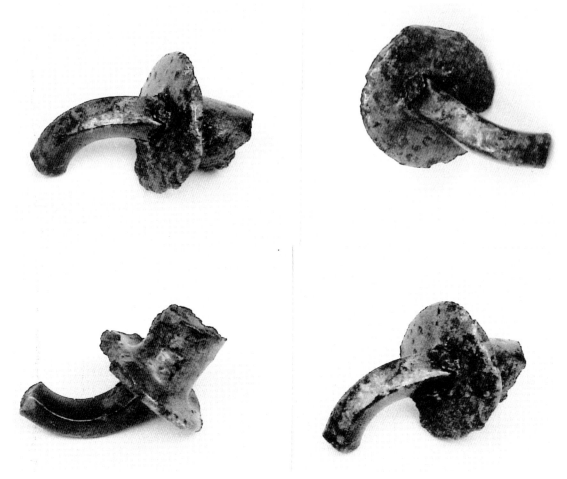

Fig 22:3 Sainte-Marguerite hoard, no. 13; length c. *30mm (courtesy of Muséum d'Histoire Naturelle de Nantes).*

Function

While writers have tended to accept that these rather odd implements are indeed spits, there is no definite indication that this was indeed so, or any clear consensus on how they functioned. If they worked like other spits, on two supports over a fire, it is difficult to see how meat could have been roasted both impaled on the hooks and skewered on the shank at the same time. Furthermore, if the instrument was turned within the hook-holder ring over a fire, the meat held on the hooks would always present the same aspect to the fire, which rather defeats the purpose of a roasting spit. The only other possibility is that meat impaled on the shank turned over the fire, while the hooks held joints either awaiting or finished roasting. What seems clear is that these pieces are too insubstantial to roast more than a meagre, perhaps token joint in this way, or something like a small game bird, and this brings us to Vilaça's comments at the head of our paper. Clearly such complicated, costly instruments were too valuable to be used in everyday life for normal cooking. They can only make sense in some sort of prestigious, ceremonial or ritual context such as Vilaça's *repas sacrés*, when it was more the choice of the cut than

its size that mattered. If, for the moment, since hooks and points could as well serve in some other ritual as in roasting, we continue to call these pieces *rotary spits*, it is purely out of convenience, without any automatic connotation of function.

Distribution and origins

This paper adds examples to previous lists of rotary spits, but removes some, one of which, from Isleham, Cambridgeshire (no. 24), has loomed large in discussions of the chronology of the type (see below). Our catalogue lists twenty-one certain examples and three possibles (Fig 22.4) but there are various other long, rectangular-sectioned shanks, and double hooks of square/rectangular section that could conceivably be from rotary spits. There are also two instruments that seem to be related to rotary spits. Since all but two of these finds are from Atlantic Europe, it is tempting to agree with most other writers that this must have been an Atlantic type. Of the twenty one certain examples (from 16 find-spots) in Part A of our List below, eleven come from north Portugal and the adjoining area of Spanish Extremadura, six from France, one from Jersey, only one from Britain, and one each from Sardinia and Cyprus. Taking the eleven complete or near-complete examples, no less than eight come from north Portugal/Extremadura. If one adds the three possibles in Part B of our List, and the related spit from Monte da Costa Figueira (no. 20), also from this region, it does leave north Portugal/Extremadura as the undoubted focus of rotary spits, and the obvious candidate for their area of origin

This traditional view that rotary spits had Atlantic beginnings has been questioned by Gomez (1991, 370), who pointed out, quite rightly, that an area of maximum concentration need only indicate an area of maximum success, and not necessarily where something was originally developed. Gomez' doubts arose in considering the status of the Amathus spit (no. 8): was it an Atlantic import to Cyprus or a Cypriot prototype of a fashion that subsequently succeeded in the far West? At first glance the possibility of a Cypriot origin might seem to be supported by the presence in south-west Iberia of another form of spit supposedly of east Mediterranean origin, the obeloi (Coffyn 1985, 177–8, carte 28; Júdice Gamito 1988, 41–3, map 10). These are probably too late, however, to have had any bearing on the origin of rotary spits.

Gomez' concerns about the Amathus spit were prompted partly by morphological differences between the Amathus spit and all the Atlantic examples, and partly by contradictory chronological pointers. The Amathus example differs from all the other rotary spits in that it has no clear differentiation between grip, spindle, shank holder and shank. The hook holder, itself notably different from all the other examples, revolves around the main shaft, and is held in place between separate disc-shaped stops, instead of revolving on a spindle between the trumpet-expanded ends of the grip and the shank holder. The hook holder, again unlike all the others, is not a ring. Certainly it is tubular on the interior, otherwise it could not have rotated around the shaft, but on the outside it is U-shaped, as Gomez noted, and instead of a protruding tongue or tab to take the hooks, the latter are in one with the rotating holder. There appears to have been some sort of device or ornament protruding from the other side of the holder, but its end is missing, so that it is impossible to know whether this was an animal or bird like those sported by the western spits.

In addition to these morphological differences, Gomez was also bothered by apparent chronological contradictions. He had to reconcile the date of *c.* 1000 BC for the Amathus example (no. 8), the supposed Isleham example (no. 24) in a Wilburton context (traditionally *c.* 900 BC), and the fact that the majority of associations were with carp's tongue material in France and Sardinia, traditionally around the 8th century BC. In searching for a solution he realised that first he had to raise the absolute dates for the Atlantic Bronze Age to bring them into line with the latest dendro-based chronology for central

Europe. Effectively these pushed all the Atlantic phases earlier by a century or so. Even then he felt it was impossible to decide whether the Amathus spit was different because it was an eastern prototype of a fashion taken up in a much bigger way in the far West, or because it was a provincial copy in the East of a distinctly Atlantic phenomenon. If it was a Cypriot invention, then one has to accept that, like many more recent inventions, it was only developed seriously in lands far away. On the other hand, in favour of a Cypriot source was the fact that the spit or obelos as a culinary/ritual fashion was well established in Cypro-Geometric Cyprus (Karageorghis 1983, 75). To explore these problems further it is necessary to delve deeper into the chronology and nature of the Atlantic Bronze Age. In view of the prominence of the supposed Isleham rotary spit in previous chronological treatments of the type, we begin with the British evidence.

Rotary Spits in England – true or false? – and a new find from the Channel Islands

In his study of the Atlantic Late Bronze Age, our much-lamented colleague André Coffyn (1985, cartes 21, 1–2 and 28, 7–8) included two English finds on his maps of rotary spits, Isleham and Saltwood (nos 24 and 16). These hoards recur on subsequent distributions (Ruiz-Gálvez 1986, mapa 1; Karageorghis and Lo Schiavo 1989, fig. 5; Giardino 1995, fig. 118; Mederos 1996, Tabla 4; Armbruster 2000, 181) and José Gomez uses Isleham in his discussion of the Amathus spit and the absolute chronology of the Atlantic Late Bronze Age (1991). However, Coffyn provides little documentation for the English finds. For Isleham there is only a reference that does not appear in his bibliography – perhaps intended to be to the unpublished thesis of another late and much-lamented friend, David Coombs – and no illustration. No published reference is given for Saltwood, though a drawing by David Coombs is reproduced alongside other rotary spits (Coffyn 1985, fig. 51, 6).

Hayne Wood hoard, Saltwood, Kent (no. 16)

This hoard was found in the parish of Saltwood during construction of the railway branch line from Sandling to

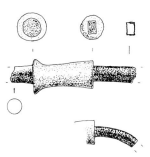

Fig 22:4 Hayne Wood hoard, no. 16, scale 1:2 (courtesy of Hythe Town Council).

Fig 22:5 Isleham hoard, no. 24, scale 1:3 (after O'Connor 1980, fig. 45, 37–8).

Hythe in 1872. The location was about 25m from the summit of a hill known variously as Haines, Haynes, Hayne or, on the current edition of the Ordnance Survey 1:25,000 map Heane, Hill or Wood (National Grid Reference TQ 152366). Recent excavation for the Channel Tunnel Rail Link has revealed possible evidence of Late Bronze Age occupation about 700m away (*Current Archaeology*, no. 168, 462). The hoard is divided between the Museums in Folkestone and Hythe. The piece that concerns us is in Hythe Museum (Identity Number Y 589.6). We are grateful to Hythe Town Council for permission to publish it here and to Mrs Janet Adamson of Kent County Council for facilitating access.

Several notices of the hoard appeared before it was brought to the British Museum in 1938 for recording in the Bronze Age Catalogue and a more extensive note was prepared by A O'N Osborne (1939). This was entitled 'The Hayne Wood Hoard' and we shall retain that name for the hoard. Osborne recognised the hoard as characteristic of the carp's tongue phase of the Late Bronze Age in southern England (Colquhoun and Burgess 1988, 71 no. 295, 77 no. 349, pl. 167D). One unusual piece caught his attention (Osborne 1939, 205–6, fig. 1), which he identified as part of a linch-pin: this is clearly the piece drawn by David Coombs for André Coffyn and identified as part of a rotary spit.

Our fragment (Fig 22.4) is 67mm long, in three parts, and broken at both ends. At one end is a round-section tang, 13mm long and 8mm in diameter, broken at a slight angle. This joins the central section, 31mm long, which is broader and has at this junction a trumpet-shaped terminal, *c*. 16mm in diameter; from the base of this terminal the central section expands again to 13 x 14mm at the other end. At this end of the central section, there is a rectangular tang, 24mm long and 8 x 5mm, which is slightly bent. While the round tang and the central section appear to be the same casting, corrosion and conservation have obscured the junction of the rectangular tang and the central section to visual inspection. The fragment has many corrosion hollows and bears bronze-coloured patina on the original surface, which survives on most of the central section and some of the rectangular tang. 'Slight scratches' noted by Osborne on the round tang are no longer visible.

X-rays confirm that the Hayne Wood fragment is made of two pieces, the rectangular tang fitted tight into a tapering squared hollow. This indicates that the tang is indeed the shank of a rotary spit, preserved with the shank holder and broken spindle.

Isleham hoard, Cambridgeshire (no. 24)

This large hoard from East Anglia belongs to the Wilburton phase of the Late Bronze Age (Colquhoun and Burgess 1988, 42, nos. 164–6, pls 152B-157A). Publication is in preparation by Dr. Peter Northover for Oxford University School of Archaeology.

Coffyn gave no indication which of the thousands of objects from Isleham he identified as belonging to a rotary spit. However, in his discussion of spits, Claudio Giardino (1995, fig. 117, 13) reproduced a drawing by one of the present authors (O'Connor 1980, fig. 45, 37–8) and, like Gomez (1991, 370) and Mederos (1996, tabla 4), we assume this is the identification intended by Coffyn. This fragment (Fig 22.5) is in two joining pieces, 329mm long in total. The longer piece is a circular-section rod, 13mm in diameter, slightly bent towards the junction with the shorter piece and having at the other end a trumpet-shaped terminal 36mm in diameter from which an irregular broken stub projects. The shorter piece is also bent near its junction with the longer; at the other end it has a bulbous terminal, 35mm in maximum diameter, forming a socket out of which a continuation of the same diameter as the rod appears to have been broken.

Although the trumpet-shaped terminal of the Isleham fragment bears a superficial resemblance to a rotary spit, there are significant differences in form and size. This trumpet terminal could hardly represent the junction of shank holder and spindle, since the whole Isleham fragment would have to be a shank holder and it is about ten times longer than these components of rotary spits. To be part of a rotary spit, the Isleham fragment would have to be a grip. However, its bulbous terminal cannot be matched on complete grips, which have ring terminals. In addition, each piece of the Isleham fragment is longer than the complete grip from Notre-Dame-d'Or, about 120mm (Mohen 1977, fig. 1, 1), while the complete grips of the spits from Orellana la Vieja and Alvaiázere appear to be even shorter (Kalb 1980, Abb. 10, 49, 3; Enríquez Navascués 1984, fig. 3). The grip of the Challans spit (Mohen 1977, fig. 1, 4) is narrower than the Isleham fragment.

So although we cannot present a conclusive identification for the fragment from the Isleham hoard, there seems to be no doubt that it is not from a rotary spit of the type we have defined here.

Saint Mary's hoard, Jersey (no. 15)

In 1996 a carp's tongue hoard was found in the parish of Saint Mary in the northwest of the Channel Island of

Jersey; publication is in preparation by one of the writers (BO'C) in collaboration with the Jersey Heritage Trust. Meanwhile, we take the opportunity to publish here part of a rotary spit from this hoard, acknowledging the assistance in particular of Mrs Margaret Finlaison of the Archaeology Section of the Société Jersiaise.

Though this is a small piece (Fig 22.6), only 58mm long, all the distinctive elements of a rotary spit are present. The shank has been broken out of the shank holder, but the stump of the rectangular-section shank remains in place in the end of the socket. The hook-holder ring, with five ribs, rotates freely on the spindle and bears the base of a figure. The stump of the square-section hook remains in the hook holder. The grip is broken just beyond the spindle.

The Saint Mary's spit resembles closely the examples from the Notre-Dame-d'Or hoard and the Forest of Compiègne (Mohen 1977, fig. 1, 1 and 3); the base of its figure appears to expand, like the animal on the former example rather than the bird on the latter.

Conclusion

It follows from this that there is no evidence from Britain to show that rotary spits were known there in the Wilburton/Saint-Brieuc-des-Iffs horizon of the Atlantic Bronze Age (*pace* Gomez 1991, 370). Confirmation of the Hayne Wood fragment as part of a rotary spit, and the new find from Jersey, attest only that these spits were deposited there during the following Ewart Park/carp's tongue phase. We turn next to the evidence from other parts of the Atlantic world.

Chronology: Iberia and the Mediterranean

Vilaça may well be right to put rotary spits into the same Atlantic milieu as flesh-hooks and cauldrons, except that they hardly occur in Britain and never in Ireland. One might have added buckets, socketed sickles, and all manner of novel warrior equipment, comprising especially slashing swords, long and often ornate ("fancy") spear-heads, and armour, including bronze shields, corselets, greaves and helmets. The spits would then become part of that world of feasting, fighting and flamboyance (Almagro Gorbea 1995, 140–44) which characterised Atlantic heroic society in the opening phases of the Late Bronze Age, the last centuries of the Second Millennium BC. Absolute chronology will be considered below, but in relative terms this is LBA 1-BF I in traditional Atlantic terms, Penard-Ballintober in Britain and Ireland, and Rosnoën in western France; and then LBA 2-BF II, Wilburton in Britain and Saint-Brieuc in western France. It all looks so much like Celtic heroic society, but several centuries earlier. This material is largely of central European Early Urnfield origin (Gerloff 1986), but beyond that the ultimate Aegean contribution has always been stressed. Mycenaean influence there undoubtedly

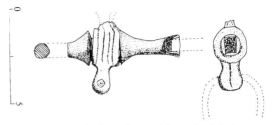

Fig 22:6 St Mary's hoard, no. 15, scale 1:2 (courtesy of Jersey Heritage Trust; after drawing by Ann Spencer of the Archaeology Section, Société Jersiaise).

was, but just how much is something urgently in need of reconsideration. Aegean influence clearly played on central Europe at the turn of the Tumulus and Urnfield periods, and it is hard to deny the spread of technologies from the south such as sheet metalworking. But the beginnings of heroic societies were already there in central and western Europe, with traditions of prestigious weapons, ornaments and equipment going back through the Middle Bronze Age. What is different in the early Urnfield period is the introduction of a range of novelties connected with feasting and fighting: the flesh-hooks and metal vessels on one side and an array of new weapons on the other, both offensive, the swords and spearheads, and defensive, the shields and armour. While the spread of these novel barbarian weapons into the Aegean and east Mediterranean has long been accepted (Catling 1956, 1961; Sandars 1985), the body armour has always been seen as spreading from the Aegean in the other direction (*e.g.* Snodgrass 1971; 1999). This seems odd when the defensive and offensive weapons so clearly go together, and when the armour is so widespread in barbarian Europe, and in comparison so rare in the Aegean. One of us has suggested elsewhere that no matter what the source of the metalworking techniques involved, the corselets, greaves and shields could have spread with the new offensive weapons southwards into the Aegean world (Burgess 2001a); that is, the armour was also invented in barbarian Europe.

Deciding whether the rotary spits also belong to this heroic world is not straightforward if only because one is not dealing with a homogeneous Atlantic phenomenon. Many of the bronze types on this "feasting-fighting" list are concentrated in Ireland and Britain: early, "A", cauldrons, Kurd buckets (Gerloff 1986; Armada 2002), flesh-hooks (Coffyn 1985, 55, carte 21; Gomez and Pautreau 1988; Almagro Gorbea 1995, 143, fig. 51), socketed sickles (Fox 1939; Coffyn 1985, cartes 23, 56), "fancy" spearheads (Burgess 1968, 9, 36, fig. 9; Coffyn 1985, carte 17), and early bronze shields (Needham 1979; Burgess 1991). But some, equally, are mainly French, and are absent or very rare in Britain and Ireland, notably the corselets, greaves and helmets – unless the latter are represented by typical pointed rivets from Flag Fen, Cambridgeshire (Pryor 1991, 115–117; Coombs 2001),

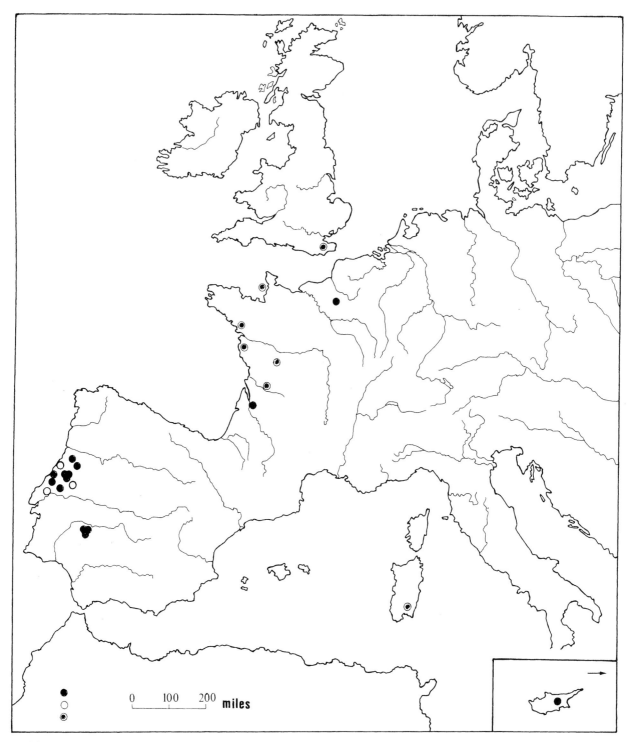

Fig 22:7 Rotary spits: distribution map (solid circles = definite examples; open circles = possible examples; hoards encircled).

and the Nottingham Hill hoard, Gloucestershire (Hall and Gingell 1974). Only the early swords, both the early flanged hilt swords (Cowen 1951; Colquhoun and Burgess 1988) and hilt-tang swords (Rosnoën-Ballintober: Briard 1965, 151–68; Burgess 1968, 3–11; Needham 1982; Gomez 1987; Colquhoun and Burgess 1988, 13–24; Burgess 2001a) are as typical of western France as of Britain and Ireland.

So far western Iberia has not figured in this discussion at all, but it is immediately apparent that the rotary spits do not sit happily with this Irish-British-western French "feasting-fighting" phenomenon, at least in its primary Penard-Rosnoën stage. The distribution map of flesh-hooks and rotary spits is particularly instructive (Fig 22.7; Coffyn 1985, carte 21; Almagro Gorbea 1995, 143). Whereas the flesh-hooks are primarily concentrated in

Ireland and Britain, occurring less commonly in western France and Iberia, the rotary spits reverse this pattern; they focus overwhelmingly in Portugal/Extremadura, secondarily in France, and scarcely touch Britain or Ireland. The point here is that the Atlantic Late Bronze Age of Penard-Rosnoën effectively failed to reach Iberia (Burgess 1991). So rotary spits can hardly be part of this same flowering of Atlantic heroic society, but must be part of some entirely different phenomenon, not necessarily even of the same period.

In following the development of the Atlantic Bronze Age it must be made clear from the start that as a concept this is all about metal, and has nothing to do with settlement, burials, religion and ritual, ceramics or any other aspect of the Bronze Age of the Atlantic fringes. It could be argued that the origins of the Atlantic Bronze Age lay in Chalcolithic connections up and down the Atlantic façade, with the spread of international forms of Beakers and associated metalwork. This included Palmella points, tanged "West European" daggers, thick-butt copper flat axes (Harrison 1977; 1980; Briard 1965, figs 14, 16, 18; Cordier 1969; Monteagudo 1977), halberds (Ó Ríordáin 1937; Harbison 1969), and gold-work such as lunulae (Taylor 1980). But it could also be argued that this Atlantic Copper Age was a flash-in-the-pan, and that this precocious internationalism did not continue smoothly into the Early Bronze Age. Then, any Atlantic Bronze Age was a limited cross-Channel affair linking Britain and Armorica, subsequently extending to northwest France and the Low Countries (Burgess 1996). Throughout the Middle Bronze Age it continued to be a phenomenon largely restricted to the lands on both sides of the North Sea and the Channel (Smith 1959; Butler 1963; O'Connor 1980; Burgess 1996). Bronzes and bronze-working influences from the north seldom reached Iberia, nor conversely did Iberian types often reach even southwestern France. Maps of almost any of the bronze weapon, tool and ornament types shared by Britain, Ireland and northwest France in the Middle Bronze Age make it clear that as far as Iberia is concerned, the so-called Atlantic Bronze Age was still a non-starter. Indeed, in this period metalworking even in France south of the Loire looks very different from that in France north of the Loire. In contrast, goldwork may have circulated up and down the Atlantic fringes, notably the *torques massifs incisés* (Coffyn 1985, fig. 25, carte 15), widespread from Britain, through Atlantic France to southwest Iberia. There has been much controversy about their date, but their decoration is certainly Franco-British and Middle Bronze Age.

It was only at the very end of Penard-Rosnoën that southwest France and Iberia began to receive more than occasional metalwork influences from the north. The evidence comes with examples of the earliest flanged-hilt swords in the Atlantic tradition, characterised by steeply pitched shoulders, and modelled on the Early Urnfield, especially Erbenheim, prototypes. In Britain these would be termed Clewer swords (Colquhoun and Burgess 1988, 31–3). The few Iberian examples are widely scattered but mostly from Atlantic regions: from Guarda in Portugal, and in Spain from Seville, Orense, Cuenca, and an atypical specimen from Badajoz (Meijide Cameselle 1988, IV–VI; Coffyn 1985, pls IX, XI, XII). But there are also some swords best classed with the U-shouldered swords of Britain and France, the British Limehouse type (Colquhoun and Burgess 1988, 33–5). In Britain these should be slightly later than Clewer swords, and immediately precede Wilburton swords. While in Britain Limehouse and Wilburton swords do not mix, and appear chronologically separate, in France their equivalents are much less discrete typologically and chronologically. In fact French swords corresponding to Limehouse, which we can term Essonne swords after the fine example from the Paris basin (Mohen 1977, no. 439), are more common in the hoards of the Saint-Brieuc-des-Iffs group than French equivalents of Wilburton swords. Unfortunately there has never been a comprehensive study of Saint-Brieuc swords, French writers normally treating them altogether under the general heading *epées pistilliformes Atlantiques* (*e.g.* Gaucher and Mohen, 1972). Briard, for example, in his pioneering work on the Saint-Brieuc group, has U-shouldered Essonne swords as the sword symbol on his map of the Saint-Brieuc group (Briard 1965, fig. 65), and this seems to be the only sword type in the eponymous hoard (Briard and Onnée, 1972). Similarly Mohen (1977, 121) does not distinguish the two series in his treatment of Bronze Final II in the Paris Basin. The French equivalents of British Wilburton swords, which for convenience can be termed Brécy swords after the Aisne hoard with a typical hilt (Blanchet 1984, 251, fig. 137), occur seldom in the best-known hoards. It appears that Essonne swords and their variants are more common than Brécy swords, reversing the British situation, where Wilburton swords are much more common than Limehouse swords (Colquhoun and Burgess 1988).

It is with a rich array of material corresponding to Wilburton/St.-Brieuc further north, that Iberia finally, and briefly, was drawn into an Atlantic Bronze Age. As a type hoard for this stage in Spain one of us (Burgess 1991) has suggested the find from Hío in Galicia (Schubart 1961; Coffyn 1985, pls LX–LXI; Armada 2002, 97–8). There is no similarly varied hoard to represent Portugal, where hoards tend to be smaller and more restricted in their contents. Amongst the best-known are those from Arganil and Solveira (Coffyn 1985, pl. XLIII), but just across the Spanish border the hoard from Cabezo de Araya, Badajoz, (Coffyn 1985, pl. XXXIV) shows some of the other products that were available in this phase in western Iberia.

Hío and the Portuguese hoards share much in a long list of Atlantic types which appear to be local equivalents of Wilburton/St.-Brieuc products: swords, tongue chapes, fancy spearheads, including hollow lozenge-sectioned, stepped-blade and lunate-opening types; spear-shaft ferrules, often with expanded foot; heavy palstaves with one and two loops, including the bizarre single-face forms; socketed chisels; socketed sickles; bifid razors; flesh-hooks and cauldrons. From the warrior stelae (Burgess 1991) one can add V-notched shields, but probably normally in leather, and studded helmets like the French examples. Significantly there seem to be very few socketed axes, and these of characteristically slender forms, so that socketed axes in Iberia may have belonged mostly to the phase after Hío-Arganil.

Not surprisingly the Iberian swords of this Hío-Arganil phase resembled those in Western France more than in Britain, owing more to U swords, Limehouse and Essonne, than Wilburton-Brécy swords. There was also an early preference for straighter blades, more rounded centre sections, retention of blade grooves and a fondness for multiple hilt slots. The logical end in this development was similar in France and in Iberia: the development of the swords termed the Saint-Nazaire type in France (Cowen 1956; Briard 1965, 190–2; Colquhoun and Burgess 1988, 53–4), and a type which in Iberia is best represented by the large number in the Huelva find (Almagro Basch 1958).

The Huelva swords have been the biggest source of confusion in Iberian Late Bronze Age studies, since they have so often been confused with carp's tongue swords (*e.g.* Almagro Basch 1958; Briard 1965, 237; Savory 1968, 232; Ruiz-Gálvez 1987, 256; Gomez 1991). The misidentification has been repeated uncritically from one study to another. The problems which result we see, for example, in Gomez' consideration of the Amathus spit, where he aligns the Huelva phase with Ewart Park-carp's tongue, and unfortunately this mis-alignment continues to mislead (*e.g.* Lo Schiavo 1995, 49). But there is nothing in the Huelva find which is either carp's tongue or Ewart Park, and on the contrary, everything can be accom-modated quite happily in Hío-Arganil, and thus related to Wilburton/St.-Brieuc (Needham *et al.* 1997, 92**).** The list includes long and fancy spearheads, notably a lunate-opening example, long ferrules and fragments of studded helmets. It cannot be stressed too often that these Huelva swords are *not* carp's tongue swords, but the confusion in identification results from paying too much attention to the blade and not enough to the hilt. An absolutely vital characteristic of carp's tongue swords is the form of the hilt and ricasso. The sides of the grip curve flowingly into the shoulders, and "the underside of the shoulders are horizontal or nearly so, and overhang a short, vertical ricasso; in effect the line from the shoulder tip to the prominent ricasso notch is a right angle rather than a curve." (Colquhoun and Burgess 1988, 108). These features are more important than the point, for, bizarrely, there are carp's tongue swords which lack the distinctive point (Colquhoun and Burgess 1988, pl. 98), and other sword forms which have tongued points like carp's tongue swords, including Italian swords of types Terni and Vulci

(Bianco Peroni 1970). The connection is not as irrelevant as might seem, since a sword of type Terni, though without the tongued point, was found in Valencia (Coffyn 1985, 158, pl. XV). The problem has not been helped by the fact that Briard in his original treatment of carp's tongue swords included an example that is most definitely not a carp's tongue sword (Briard 1965, fig. 69.1). The Iberian situation has been further confused by the way in which the blades of some Huelva swords have worn to resemble carp's tongue points, but the configuration of the hilt is always the give-away. Having said all this, the similarity of some Huelva swords to carp's tongue swords is undeniable, enough to raise questions about the precise relationship of the two, even to contemplate how Huelva swords could have contributed to the development of the carp's tongue weapons.

Once it is realised that Huelva swords are not carp's tongue but a local equivalent of Saint-Nazaire swords, the Huelva find and much else falls into place. Sword typology places the find at the end of Hío-Arganil, the end of Wilburton/St.-Brieuc metalworking, and as an assemblage it correlates with the Blackmoor group of late Wilburton hoards in Britain, and Saint-Nazaire in France. What came next in Iberia? This brings us to the third quotation at the head of this essay. After this flowering of the Atlantic Late Bronze Age in Iberia, one might have expected an Iberian equivalent of carp's tongue if not Ewart Park. But it is not there! Despite the impression one might get from the literature, the amount of carp's tongue material in Iberia is tiny (Burgess 1991). The number of true carp's tongue swords there is no more than half a dozen, and perhaps ten of variant forms such as Vénat, Monte Sa Idda and Boom (Cowen 1971). We are grateful to Dirk Brandherm (pers. comm.) for con-firming that his current survey of Iberian swords shows these figures to be approximately correct. There is a matching dearth of other carp's tongue types. A few spearheads of Vénat type have been claimed (Coffyn *et al.* 1981, 96, pl. 11, carte 3), but it is important to note that some of the examples mapped there are *not* in fact of the Vénat type as claimed. This is particularly so for the supposed Iberian examples. All these should now be re-examined, for examples in such important finds as Huelva and Porto de Concelho have been misidentified and must be removed from the map (For a more reliable appraisal of the type, see Pautreau *et al.* 1984, 36–43, figs 13–16, nos. 5–10, which makes clear that the widest part of the narrow, rather angular rhomboidal blade must be at about the middle, while the base to the blade is so abrupt as to be slightly barbed, and the point cuts in sharply). Even more noticeable, where are examples of the extensive range of carp's tongue socketed axe and tool types, and, even more significant, of the distinctive range of carp's tongue bric-a-brac?

Some of the clues to what followed Huelva are in Huelva itself, in its eastern imports, especially the Cypriot fibulae, and its pieces of iron. One of us (Burgess 1991,

39) has suggested elsewhere that in view of the difficulty of finding a clearly-defined post-Huelva bronze industry, there may have been a precocious, if partial and patchy, switch to iron, at least in those parts of the Peninsula open to Cypro-Phoenician influence. On the other hand some bronze-working clearly continued, for most Iberian socketed axes appear to belong to the phase after Huelva. There was also continuing production of bronze weapons, for example carp's tongue sword variants though few are widespread, from Obidos in Portugal to El Peñon de la Reina in Almería (Martínez and Botella 1980) and El Bierzo in León (Coffyn 1985, pl. LXII.2). The fact that bronze survives so much better in the soil than iron may have distorted the impression one gets of the relative importance of bronze in settlements of this period. But alongside the bronze there is sometimes iron, if only scrappy bits, from one side of the Peninsula (*e.g.* Baiões, Portugal: da Silva 1986, Est XCI:1) to the other (*e.g.* Aldovesta, Catalunya: Mascort *et al*. 1991). The great difficulty in this phase after Huelva is that the deposition of hoards almost ceased in Iberia and neither are there the stray finds to suggest a full-scale bronze industry. Both these factors may be pointers to the relative importance of iron-working.

Implications

So where do the rotary spits fit in all this, and where did they originate? Gomez (1991), bothered by the ambiguities in the dating evidence, perceptively recognised the need to move the absolute chronology of the Atlantic later Bronze Age back by a century or so, as a logical response to the revision of central European chronology demanded by dendrochronology. Even then he felt unable to decide whether rotary spits were originally eastern or western, but his difficulties were not helped by the red herring of the supposed rotary spit in the Isleham hoard (see above), and also by his misalignment of Huelva with carp's tongue. His revised Atlantic chronology has since been repeated by others, notably Lo Schiavo (1995, 49) in reviewing relations between the Mediterranean and the West, and has now been confirmed by the Oxford programme of accelerator radiocarbon dating of wood directly associated with bronzes (Needham *et al*. 1997). What is important for the present enquiry is that dates for Wilburton/St. Brieuc are now at least a century earlier, while the beginning of Ewart Park-carp's tongue also has to move back to 1000/950 from the long-accepted 900 BC. In Britain this particular boundary has been confused by deciding what makes up early Ewart Park metalworking, in particular whether the Blackmoor hoard is end-of-Wilburton as one of the present writers (CB) believes, or early Ewart Park as Needham prefers. Needham's recent amendments to British Bronze Age chronologies and sequences (Needham 1990; 1996; Needham *et al*. 1997; Rohl and Needham 1998, 98–109, fig. 21) can be considered on another occasion, since the

important matter for present purposes is to recognise the need for earlier Atlantic dates:

LBA 1 – Penard-Rosnën – **1275–1140/1100** (instead of 1200–1000)

LBA 2 – Wilburton (with Blackmoor at its end)/St.-Brieuc/ Hío-Arganil – **1140/1100 – 1000/950** (instead of 1000–900)

LBA 3 – Ewart Park / Carp's Tongue – **950–800** (instead of 900–700)

In parenthesis one has to add that this backwards shift in the West cannot happen in isolation. The logic is that if traditional correlations (Müller-Karpe 1959) through central Europe to the Aegean and Egypt remain valid, then the eastern dates must go back too. But if they stand, then the correlations will have to be re-examined. All of this might not matter except that the Amathus rotary spit brings the East directly face-to-face with the West.

Since the obvious working hypothesis is that rotary spits were first developed in the north Portugal/Extremadura region, this seems the logical area to start the chronological enquiry. Unfortunately here there are two immediate problems. Firstly, there are no certain associations with rotary spits in Portugal and western Spain (except with other rotary spits); and secondly the content and character of metalworking here are largely unknown before and after Hío-Arganil. What was being produced at a time equivalent to Penard-Rosnoën, when the Atlantic feasting-fighting milieu with flesh-hooks, cauldrons and the like, was emerging further north? And what was the metalworking situation at the time of Ewart Park-carp's tongue, which is when most of the rotary spits from France and England found their way into hoards?

One is forced back on the indirect evidence. Crucial to the dating of rotary spits in Portugal is the material from the Baiões castro (Kalb 1978, 1980; da Silva 1986). This includes a complete rotary spit and a shank possibly from a second, though this is of round-section and thus probably from something else. Now there is a lot of Late Bronze Age metalwork from north Portuguese castros (Kalb 1980), and the first crucial point to make is that while none of it positively demands a date later than Hío-Arganil, much of it is patently Hío-Arganil material. The Baiões spit is in a large assemblage of bronzes sometimes taken to be wholly or partly a hoard. Alas, the find circumstances of this extraordinary collection may never be known, apart from the pieces found in the most recent excavations (Kalb 1978; Armada 2002, 96). On the other hand much of the assemblage is remarkably coherent in its affinities. It is entirely representative of Hío-Arganil metalworking, with such characteristic types as cylinder-socket sickles, a stepped-blade spearhead, a ferrule, cauldron fragments, heavy, narrow-blade palstaves (single and twin-looped, and including flat-faced examples), and a magnificent decorated flesh-hook, with unique triple hook. There are some armlets which might belong to an earlier, even Middle Bronze Age, horizon, but there is nothing which demands a date later than Hío-Arganil, never mind with carp's tongue metalworking. There are, though, pieces which are "eastern" in the broadest sense, and decidedly exotic: a fragment of a central Mediterranean fibula; hemispherical bronze bowls probably of Cypriot origin or inspiration, at the Cypro-Geometric stage; and the famous wheeled cauldron, for which both Cypriot and central European affinities have been suggested. Some of the Baiões elements are repeated in another castro nearby, Santa Luzia (Vaz 1987): a cylinder-socket sickle, cauldron fragments, and the fibula, and this site also adds a bifid razor. The fibulae at these two sites are very simple, describing a flattened triangle with spring at the apex, and the best parallels are to be found in the central Mediterranean at the Pantalica II stage, thus Ha A2-B1 in central European terms (Müller-Karpe 1959, 198, Abb. 32, Abb. 64). This brings us back to Wilburton/St.-Brieuc in the West, and thus to Hío-Arganil in Iberia. The wheeled vessel must await much more detailed study before it can contribute to this chronological study, because at the moment it remains *sui generis*.

On this basis what little evidence there is in Iberia could point to rotary spits being made and used in north Portugal and Extremadura in the Hío-Arganil stage, and then spreading northwards into western France. The close similarity of Iberian and French examples suggests that this may have happened quickly, though there are no associations in France or Britain to confirm when rotary spits were in use there, as opposed to when they were being scrapped. The situation is not helped by the paucity of Wilburton/St.-Brieuc hoards in western France south of the Loire. Alas, the one piece of dating evidence that appeared vital to this problem is no longer available, the supposed rotary spit in the hoard from Isleham. This piece has been included in all the recent studies of rotary spits (*e.g.* Coffyn 1985; Karageorghis and Lo Schiavo 1989; Gomez 1991), but the investigation above makes clear that the Isleham fragment cannot be from a rotary spit. This seemed to be the only certain association of a rotary spit as early as Wilburton/St.-Brieuc. Without it we are left only with a number of associations in carp's tongue hoards: several in France, the new Jersey example, and the one English find in yet another at Hayne Wood. What these associations mean depends on how one views carp's tongue hoards. If their deposition took place throughout the phase of Ewart Park-carp's tongue metalworking, the implications may be completely different from what might be indicated by a short episode of deposition (Burgess and Coombs 1979, i–vi). Various scenarios are possible, one of us (Burgess 1979) suggesting, for example, that carp's tongue hoards could represent dumping of bronze stocks over a short span of time as iron was coming in at the end of the Late Bronze Age. Certainly there are carp's tongue hoards in parts of Britain and France where just such a late date of deposition seems likely, but the concept has yet to be explored in sufficient detail to provide a

convincing explanation. But since many carp's tongue hoards contain residual material patently from earlier periods (another aspect which has never been thoroughly explored), technically these associations may provide no more than a *terminus ante quem*, and tell us nothing about the overall period of use of rotary spits.

Travelling eastwards through the Mediterranean, the one Sardinian example, from Monte Sa Idda (Taramelli 1921), is no more helpful, being another fragment in a hoard with carp's tongue material. Alas, the Monte Sa Idda find was made by shepherds in 1914, and the site was disturbed before Taramelli could excavate there. But the hoard was in a built stone structure amongst boulders and rocks, the bronzes contained in one pot inside a larger pot. The scrap nature of the material, and abundant traces of ash and slag in the deposits outside the structure, persuaded Taramelli that this was a founder's hoard, and that there was a metal workshop somewhere in the vicinity. But nothing is necessarily as it seems in nuragic Sardinia (Burgess 2001b), and there are many deposits of ingot metal and scrap in nuragic contexts which have the appearance of classic founders' hoards but which may in fact have been votive or otherwise cultic.

There are two striking points to make about the Monte Sa Idda material. The first is that the bulk of it was of Iberian origin, including, presumably, the fragment of rotary spit. Though it does have a twisted grip, in all other respects it is exactly like all the Atlantic spits, including its animal mount so like those from Cachouça in Portugal (no. 3) and the Notre Dame d'Or hoard in western France (no. 11).

The second point is that more than any carp's tongue hoard, this find was clearly an accumulation of material from various periods, going back to the dawn of metallurgy in the West. The earliest pieces are thick-butt copper flat axes, but there are also later flat axes, and lugged and twin-looped flat axes of the Middle Bronze Age, twin-looped heavy palstaves, ferrules and flat (not socketed) sickles of Hío-Arganil forms, and many twin-looped socketed axes which are later still. These last go with the range of carp's tongue sword variants from this find. There is thus Iberian material here stretching over at least 1500 years. Non-Iberian elements are limited mainly to mounts and fitments of uncertain function, a fragment of a human figurine, and two handle attachments for metal vessels. These are both of the double disc "figure-of-eight" type, ultimately of Cypriot origin and going back at least to Cypro-Geometric 1, when the first examples reached Sardinia (Matthäus 1989). But these two are probably of local manufacture, one sporting bird mounts very much in nuragic style. The Monte Sa Idda find, then, tells us no more than the French hoards about the overall chronology of rotary spits.

Which brings us finally to the Amathus example. Gomez was unhappy about the stratigraphic position of this piece in a multi-period tomb, and whether it needed to be Cypro-Geometric I and "c. 1000 B.C. or soon after" as Karageorghis argued (Karageorghis and Lo Schiavo 1989, 16). Gomez (1991 371–2) thought that certainty was impossible in a tomb disturbed for later burials in Cypro-Geometric II, and that a case could be made for the rotary spit being deposited in this later phase. Karageorghis (pers. comm.) has confirmed his original dating to the writers, but whether it was deposited around 1000 or nearer 850 BC seems immaterial in pursuing the possibility that the Amathus spit was a prototype for the Atlantic series and not an Atlantic import. In view of the revised absolute dating for the Atlantic Bronze Age, and if one accepts that rotary spits were being used in Portugal in the Hío-Arganil phase, then they were current there at a time centring on the 11th century BC, beginning possibly in the late 12th century. This would make them comfortably earlier than the Amathus example, for though spits were quite common in Cyprus in the Cypro-Geometric period, that is at the time of the Amathus burials, they seem unknown earlier, in the Late Bronze Age (Karageorghis 1983, 75; Karageorghis and Lo Schiavo 1989, 17; Karageorghis pers. comm.). This view might be challenged if, for example, the dates for the Cypro-Geometric period themselves prove to be earlier, or if the Amathus spit was an heirloom and old when deposited. Otherwise one has to conclude that it is difficult in the light of present evidence to argue that the Amathus spit was a prototype, which sparked off an Atlantic tradition. Although Mediterranean influences in general, and Cypriot influences in particular, were undoubtedly pervading Iberia, including north Portugal-Extremadura, as early as the Hío-Arganil stage, those simpler – supposedly oriental – spits, the obeloi of south-west Iberia (Júdice Gamito 1988), now seem too late to be relevant to our enquiry. That is not to deny all possibility of a Mediterranean contribution to rotary spits, in particular as a source of the bird and animal mounts. Gomez was troubled by the origin of these, but suggested that an Early Urnfield source was possible. Unfortunately there is very little sign of Early Urnfield influence in north Portugal-Extremadura. If the rotary spits did emerge here, however, there is an alternative source for their mounts. It is from the East, but Sardinia rather than Cyprus. In nuragic Sardinia animal and bird mounts were commonplace, and part of a much wider tradition of human and animal figurines (*e.g.* Lilliu 1966; Lo Schiavo 2000). Iberia and Sardinia were engaged in two-way traffic from at least the beginning of Hío-Arganil onwards, providing nuragic Sardinia with an Atlantic sword tradition for example (Burgess 2001b), so there is no problem in getting Sardinian animals to Portugal/Extremadura.

In the end, while we have to agree with Gomez that no absolute certainty is possible in deciding where rotary spits were invented, earlier Atlantic dates combined with distribution patterns must incline us to Atlantic origins. Furthermore, our reappraisal of the Atlantic Late Bronze Age and of the Iberian Late Bronze Age sequence suggests as a working hypothesis that the type emerged in north Portugal/Extremadura in the Hío-Arganil stage. This would have been an appropriate context in view of the dramatic changes that were transforming the region at this time, under influences both from the North (Atlantic metalworking) and the East. The development of castros was an important aspect of these changes, not least because they make finds of rotary spits and other metalwork susceptible to recovery by excavation.

That rotary spits were quickly carried north of the Pyrenees into St.-Brieuc France is suggested by the uniformity of design of the French and Iberian examples; and Karageorghis's preferred date for the Amathus example *c.* 1000 BC suggests the idea quickly reached Cyprus. The type presumably continued in use into the carp's tongue stage, to judge from the fragments in carp's tongue hoards.

The Amathus rotary spit is thus more likely to have been a provincial copy than a Cypriot prototype, but whether it was imported from the West, copied somewhere en-route or made locally is a problem that might, but only might, eventually yield to metal analysis.

Acknowledgements

Many friends and colleagues helped us in our search for rotary spits and with relevant data. We owe a special debt to Christian Chevillot for showing us the Port-Sainte-Foy spit and allowing us to use his illustration of it. We must also thank Margaret Finlaison of the Archaeology Section of the Société Jersiaise for help with finds in the Channel Islands, and especially the new rotary spit from the St. Mary's hoard; Hythe Town Council and Mrs Janet Adamson of Kent County Council for facilitating access to the Hayne Wood hoard; Serge Regnault of the Muséum d'Histoire Naturelle de Nantes for arranging to have photographs taken of the fragment in the Ste.-Marguerite hoard, and for permission to reproduce them here; and Jacques and Marie-Hélène Santrot of the Musée Dobrée, Nantes, and Michel Le Goffic, for their help in that process. Raquel Vilaça and Lois Armada kindly advised us on our corpus. We owe a great debt to Dirk Brandherm and Sabine Gerloff for discussing with us at length various aspects of the problem, to Anna Grazia Russu for help with the Monte Sa Idda hoard, and to Maria Isabel Martínez Navarrete, Ignacio Montero, Marisa Ruiz-Gálvez and Virgílio Correia for their help with the Iberian sources and material. In England Avril Oswald and Margaret Maddison kindly tracked down sources for us. CB is grateful to his wife, Norma Burgess, for help with translations. We owe a special debt to Sheila Day for undertaking the illustrations at short notice. Finally, we are particularly grateful to Vassos Karageorghis and Fulvia Lo Schiavo for kindly reading versions of our text, and for their helpful suggestions. Any fault in what is written here is of course entirely that of the authors.

List of Rotary Spits, Actual, Possible and Alleged

Included in Part A of this list are only examples the writers have examined or examples where published illustrations leave no doubt of identification as a rotary spit. Other examples are included in Parts B and C as possible or alleged rotary spits.

A. Rotary spits

Portugal

1. Serra de Alvaiázere, Leiria
    Almagro Gorbea 1974, 355–7 no II, table p. 392 nos 2–4, figs 1 and 9, 1–3, lám, 1, 1; Kalb 1980, 30 no. 49, Abb. 10, 2–8; A Idade do Bronze 1995, 32 no. 23; Armbruster 2000, 199, Taf. 10; Three examples.
    Museu Nacional de Arqueologia, Lisboa, 17 448–50
2. Nossa Senhora de Guia, Baiões, Viseu
    Kalb 1980, 30 no. 43, Abb. 9, 21; da Silva 1986, 210 no. 314, Est XCVIII, 7; Armbruster 2000, 180 n. 256, 200, Taf. 23, 4 and 24, 1.
    One complete. Said to be part of the hoard from this castro, but found earlier (Armada 2002, 96).The round-section shank (Kalb 1980, Abb. 9, 27) is presumably not from a rotary spit.
    Universidade Católica Portuguesa, Viseu
3. Cachouça, Castelo Branco
    Vilaça 1990; A Idade do Bronze 1995, 32 no. 24.
    Two fragments, probably making up most of one spit: part of shank; hook-holder ring, spindle and most of grip.
    Instituto de Arqueologia, Universidade de Coimbra
4. Canedotes, Vila Nova de Paiva, Viseu
    Vilaça and da Cruz 1995, 257, fig. 2.
    Fragment: shank holder, spindle and stump of grip.
5. Reguengo do Fetal, Leiria
    Ruivo 1983; Coffyn 1985, 395 no. 275.
    Two examples. One certainly rotary spit, with shank, shank-holder, hook-holder ring and stump of grip; second shank only, but apparently with remains of junction with shank-holder.
    Museu do Seminário de Leiria

Spain

6. Orellana la Vieja, Badajoz
    Enríquez Navascués 1984.
    Three examples
    Museo Arqueológico Provincial de Badajoz (Inv. Geral. 175–7)

Sardinia

7. Monte Sa Idda hoard, Decimoputzu, Cagliari
    Taramelli 1921, fig. 79; Karageorghis and Lo Schiavo 1989, 19–22, fig. 4a; Lo Schiavo 1991, 216, fig. 6.1.
    Shank holder, hook-holder ring and part of grip.
    Museo Archeologico Nazionale di Calgliari

Cyprus

8. Amanthus, Limassol, tomb 523
    Karageorghis and Lo Schiavo 1989, 15–17, fig. 3b, tav III, 1.
    Extreme point missing.

France

9. Challans hoard, Vendée
    Mohen, 1977, 34, figs 1, 4 and 2, lower; Verney, 1990, fig.7:31.
    Stump of shank, shank holder, hook-holder ring and part of grip.
    MAN St-Germain
10. Forêt de Compiègne, Oise
    Mohen 1977, 34, figs 1, 3, 2, upper, and 3, 1; Blanchet, 1984, 316–18, fig. 178.
    Complete, except for broken grip.
    MAN St-Germain, 13 684
11. Notre-Dame-d'Or hoard, Vienne
    Mohen 1977, 43–5, fig. 1, 1; Pautreau, 1979, figs 82, 85.
    Grip, hook-holder ring and part of shank holder.
    Musée de Poitiers
12. River Dordogne at the Gué du Chantier, Port-Sainte-Foy, Dordogne (Fig 22.2)
    Chevillot 1989, 161–2, 232, fig. 32, pl. 324.
    Complete.
    Collection G. Parcelier, Brantôme
13. Sainte-Marguerite hoard, Pornichet, Loire-Atlantique (Fig 22.3)
    Bigoteau 1976, 137, pl. 12, 81; Coffyn *et al.* 1981, 222, no. 10.
    Stumps of shank and shank holder with pronounced discoidal expansion at terminal of shank holder.
    Muséum d'Histoire Naturelle, Nantes
14. Vénat hoard, Charente
    Mohen 1977, 37, fig. 1, 2; Coffyn *et al.* 1981, 174, pl. 50, 27.
    Junction of spindle and grip.
    Collection Triou, Musée de la Société Historique et Archéologique de la Charente

Channel Islands

15. St Mary's hoard, Jersey (Fig 22.6)
    Unpublished.
    Shank holder, hook-holder ring and stump of grip.
    Jersey Museum

England

16. Hayne Wood hoard, Saltwood, Kent (Fig 22.4)
    Osborne 1939, 205–6, fig. 1, pl. XLVIII; Coffyn 1985, 139, Cartes 21, 2 and 28, 8, fig. 51, 6.
    Stump of shank, shank-holder and broken spindle.
    Hythe Museum

B. Possible rotary spits

Portugal

17. Bocas, Santarém
Armbruster 2000, 181, n. 258.
Small fragment, said to be similar to example in Vénat hoard.
Museu Nacional de Arqueologia, Lisboa, 0010

18. Moreirinha, Idhana-a-Nova
Vilaça and da Cruz 1995, 259.

19. Santa Olaia, Figueira da Foz
Vilaça and da Cruz 1995, fig. 3.

C. Alleged rotary spits

Portugal

20. Monte de Costa Figueira, Porto
Almagro Gorbea 1977, 355 no I, table p. 392 no. 1, 'Museo de Guimaraes'; Kalb 1980, 28, Taf. 4, 23; Coffyn 1985, 395 no. 271.
Not a rotary spit according to Armbruster (2000, 181 n. 259, Taf. 64, 8) and an early illustration (Cardozo 1946, fig. 5) shows shows remains of a second 'hook' opposing the surviving 'hook', suggesting this spit was turned over rather than rotated.
Museu de Guimaraes

21. Corôa do Frade, Évora
Arnaud 1979, 63–5, fig. 6, 1; Kalb 1980, 32 no. 68; Coffyn 1985, 395 no. 276.
Shank only, of square/rectangular section, so possibly from a rotary spit, but in this area perhaps more likely from an obelos of the winged stop type, as suggested by Júdice Gamito (1988, 42).

Spain

22. El Berrueco, Salamanca
Coffyn 1985, 395 no. 274, pl. LVIII, 3; Mederos 1996, Tabla 4.
Not a rotary spit according to Armbruster (2000, 181, n. 259).

Sardinia

23. Grotta Pirosu, Santadi
Mederos 1996, Tabla 4; Lo Schiavo 1991, 216; Lo Schiavo and Usai 1995.
Terminal or grip only, like that of the spit from El Berrueco (no. 22), but could be from anything, and not even necessarily from a spit. This site has also produced several points or shanks, of circular section, with stumpy square-sectioned tang fitting into ornate head, but at *c.* 15–20cm. these are much too short to be spits.

England

24. Isleham hoard, Cambridgeshire (Fig 22.5)
See p. 188 above. Not a rotary spit.

Bibliography

A Idade do Bronze 1995 *A Idade do Bronze em Portugal. Discursos de poder*. Catálogo do Museu Nacional de Arqueologia, Lisboa.

Almagro Basch, M. 1958 *Depósito de la Ría de Huelva*. Inventaria Archaeologica, E. 1, Madrid.

Almagro Gorbea, M. 1974 Los asadores de bronce del suroeste peninsular, *Revista de Archivos, Bibliotecas y Museos* **77**, 351–95.

Almagro Gorbea, M. 1995 Ireland and Spain in the Bronze Age. In J. Waddell and E. Shee Twohig, (eds) *Ireland in the Bronze Age*, 136–48. The Stationery Office, Dublin.

Armada Pita, X.–L. 2002 A propósito del Bronce Atlántico y el origen de los calderos de remaches peninsulares, *Saguntum* **34**, 91–103.

Armbruster, B.R. 2000 *Goldschmiedekunst und Bronzetechnik*. Monographies Instrumentum 15, Montagnac.

Arnaud, J.M. 1979 Corôa do Frade, *Madrider Mitteilungen* **20**, 56–100.

Bianco Peroni, V. 1970 *Die Schwerter in Italien/Le spade nell'Italia continentale*. Prähistorische Bronzefunde, IV/1, München.

Bigoteau, M. 1976 Collection d'objets de bronze "Ch. Mercier" déposée au Museum d'Histoire Naturelle de Nantes (Cachette de Sainte Marguerite à Pornichet, Loire-Atlantique), *Etudes Préhistoriques et Protohistoriques des Pays de la Loire* **4**, 125–47.

Blanchet, J.-C. 1984 *Les premiers métallurgistes en Picardie et dans le Nord de la France*. Mémoires de la Société Préhistorique Française 17, Paris.

Briard, J. 1965 *Les dépôts bretons et l'Age du Bronze Atlantique*. Travaux du Laboratoire d'Anthropologie Préhistorique de la Faculté des Sciences de Rennes, Rennes.

Briard, J. and Onnée, Y. 1972 *Le dépôt du Bronze Final de Saint-Brieuc-des-Iffs (I. et V.)*. Travaux du Laboratoire «Anthropologie-Préhistoire-Protohostoire-Quaternaire Armoricains», Université de Rennes, Rennes.

Burgess, C.B. 1968 The later Bronze Age in the British Isles and north-western France, *Archaeological Journal* **125**, 1–45.

Burgess, C.B. 1979 A find from Boyton, Suffolk, and the end of the Bronze Age in Britain and Ireland. In C.B. Burgess and D. Coombs (eds) *Bronze Age Hoards: Some Finds Old and New*, 269–83. British Archaeological Reports 67, Oxford.

Burgess, C.B. 1991 The East and the West: Mediterranean influence in the Atlantic world in the later Bronze Age, *c.* 1500–700 B.C. In C. Chevillot and A. Coffyn (eds) *L'Age du Bronze Atlantique*, 25–45. Actes du 1er Colloque ... de Beynac. Publication de l'Association des Musées du Sarladais, Beynac-et-Cazenac.

Burgess, C.B. 1996 *«Urns»*, Culture du Wessex et la transition Bronze Ancien – Bronze Moyen en Grande-Bretagne. In C. Mordant and O. Gaiffe (eds) *Cultures et sociétes du Bronze Ancien en Europe*, 605–21. Actes du 117e Congrès National des Sociétés Savantes, Clermont-Ferrand, 1992. Éditions du Comité des Travaux historiques et scientifiques, Paris.

Burgess, C.B. 2001a Swords, warfare and Sea Peoples: the end of the Late Bronze Age in the East Mediterranean. In C.-T. Le Roux, (ed.) *Du monde des chasseurs à celui des métallurgistes: hommage ...Jean L'Helgouach et mélanges offerts à Jacques Briard*, 277–87. Revue Archéologique de l'Ouest, Supplément 9, Rennes..

Burgess, C.B. 2001b Problems in the Bronze Age archaeology of Sardinia: seeing the nuragic wood for the trees, in W.H. Metz, B.L. van Beek and H. Steegstra, (eds) *PATINA: Essays Presented to Jay Jordan Butler*, 169–94. The Editors, Groningen and Amsterdam.

Burgess, C.B. and Coombs, D. (eds) 1979 *Bronze Age Hoards: Some Finds Old and New*. British Archaeological Reports 67, Oxford.

Butler, J.J. 1963 Bronze Age connections across the North Sea, *Palaeohistoria* **9**, 1–286.

Cardozo, M. 1946 Carrito votivo de bronce, del Museo de Guimaraes (Portugal), *Archivo Español de Arqueología* **19**, 1–28.

Catling, H.W. 1956 Bronze cut-and-thrust swords in the eastern Mediterranean, *Proceedings of the Prehistoric Society* **22**, 102–25.

Catling, H.W. 1961 A new bronze sword from Cyprus, *Antiquity* **35**, 115–22.

Chevillot, C. 1989 *Sites et cultures de l'Age du Bronze en Périgord.* Archéologies 3, Périgueux.

Chevillot, C. and Coffyn, A. (eds) 1991 *L'Age du Bronze Atlantique.* Actes du 1er Colloque ... de Beynac. Publication de l'Association des Musées du Sarladais, Beynac-et-Cazenac.

Coffyn, A. 1985 *Le Bronze Final Atlantique dans la Péninsule Ibérique.* Publications de la Centre Pierre Paris 11, Paris.

Coffyn, A., Gomez, J. and Mohen, J.-P. 1981 *L'apogée du Bronze Atlantique: le dépôt de Vénat.* L'âge du bronze en France 1, Paris.

Colquhoun, I. and Burgess, C.B. 1988 *The Swords of Britain.* Prähistorische Bronzefunde, IV/5, München.

Coombs, D. 2001 The metalwork, in F. Pryor *The Flag Fen Basin*, 255–98. English Heritage Archaeological Reports, London.

Cordier, G. 1969 Deux hallebardes du Bronze Ancien de la Vallée de la Loire, *Antiquités Nationales* **1**, 47–51.

Cowen, J.D. 1951 The earliest bronze swords in Britain and their origins on the Continent of Europe, *Proceedings of the Prehistoric Society* **17**, 195–213.

Cowen, J.D. 1956 Les origines des épées de bronze du type en langue de carpe. In A. Beltrán (ed) *Congresos Internacionales de Ciencias Prehistóricas y Protohistóricas, Actas de la IV Sesión, Madrid, 1954*, 639–42. Librería General, Zaragoza.

Cowen, J.D. 1971 A striking maritime distribution pattern, *Proceedings of the Prehistoric Society* **37**, 154–66.

Da Silva, A.C.F. 1986 *A cultura castreja no Noroeste de Portugal.* Museu da Citania de Sanfins/Camara Municipal de Paços de Ferreira.

Enríquez Navascués, J.J. 1984 Una nueva estela de guerrero y tres asadores de bronce procedentes de los alrededores de Orellana la Vieja (Badajoz), *Museos* **2**, 9–13.

Fox, C.F. 1939 The socketed bronze sickles of the British Isles, *Proceedings of the Prehistoric Society* **5**, 222–48.

Gaucher, G. and Mohen, J.-P. 1972 *Typologie des objets de l'Age du Bronze en France, I: Épées.* Société Préhistorique Française, Paris.

Gerloff, S. 1986 Bronze Age class A cauldrons: typology, origins and chronology, *Journal of the Royal Society of Antiquaries of Ireland* **116**, 84–115.

Giardino, C. 1995 *Il Mediterraneo Occidentale fra XIV ed VIII secolo a.C.* British Archaeological Reports S612, Oxford.

Gomez, J. 1987 Les épées du Cognaçais (Charente) et la chronologie des épées du type Chelsea-Ballintober en France. In J.-C. Blanchet (ed) *Les relations entre le continent et les Iles Britanniques à l'Age du Bronze*, 125–31. Actes du Colloque du Lille ... 1984, Supplément à la Revue Archéologique de Picardie, Amiens.

Gomez, J. 1991 Le fondeur, le trafiquant et les cuisiners. La broche d'Amathonte de Chypre et la chronologie absolue du Bronze Finale Atlantique. In C. Chevillot and A. Coffyn (eds) *L'Age du Bronze Atlantique*, 369–73. Actes du 1er Colloque ... de Beynac. Publication de l'Association des Musées du Sarladais, Beynac-et-Cazenac.

Gomez, J. and Pautreau, J.-P. 1988 Le crochet protohistorique en bronze de Thorigné à Coulon (Deux-Sèvres), *Archäologisches Korrespondenzblatt* **18**, 31–42.

Hall, M. and Gingell, C. 1974 Nottingham Hill, Gloucestershire, 1972, *Antiquity* **48**, 306–9.

Harbison, P. 1969 *The Daggers and the Halberds of the Early Bronze Age in Ireland.* Prähistorische Bronzefunde, VI/1, München.

Harrison, R.J. 1977 *The Bell Beaker Cultures of Spain and Portugal.* American School of Prehistoric Research, Bulletin 35, Cambridge, Massachusetts.

Harrison, R.J. 1980 *The Beaker Folk.* Thames and Hudson, London.

Júdice Gamito, T. 1988 *Social Complexity in Southwest Iberia, 800–300 BC.* British Archaeological Reports S439, Oxford.

Kalb, P. 1978 Senhora da Guia, Baiões: Die Ausgrabung 1977, *Madrider Mitteilungen* **19**, 112–38.

Kalb, P. 1980 Zur Atlantischen Bronzezeit in Portugal, *Germania* **58**, 25–59.

Karageorghis, V. 1983 *Palaepaphos-Skales. An Iron Age Cemetery in Cyprus.* Ausgrabungen in Alt-Paphos auf Cypern 3, Konstanz.

Karageorghis, V. and Lo Schiavo, F. 1989 A West Mediterranean obelos from Amathus, *Rivista di Studi Fenici* **17**, 15–29.

Lilliu, G. 1966 *Sculture della Sardegna Nuragica.* Mondadori, Verona.

Lo Schiavo, F. 1991 La Sardaigne et ses relations avec le Bronze Final Atlantique. In C. Chevillot and A. Coffyn (eds) *L'Age du Bronze Atlantique*, 213–26. Actes du 1er Colloque ... de Beynac. Publication de l'Association des Musées du Sarladais, Beynac-et-Cazenac.

Lo Schiavo, F. 1995 Cyprus and Sardinia in the Mediterranean trade routes towards the West. In V. Karageorghis and D. Michaelides (eds) *Cyprus and the Sea*, 45–59. Proceedings of the International Symposium, Nicosia, 25–26 September 1993. University of Cyprus, Nicosia.

Lo Schiavo, F. 2000 Sea and Sardinia: nuragic bronze boats. In D. Ridgway *et al.* (eds) *Ancient Italy in its Mediterranean setting: studies in honour of Ellen Macnamara*, 141–58. Accordia Specialist Studies on the Mediterranean 4, London.

Lo Schiavo, F. and Usai, L. 1995 Testimonianze cultuali di età nuragica: La Grotta Pirosu in località su Benatzu di Santadi. In V. Santoni (ed) *Carbonia e il Sulcis: archeologia e territorio*, 147–86. Editrice S'Alvure, Oristano.

Martínez, C. and Botella, M.C. 1980 *El Peñon de la Reina (Alboloduy, Almería).* Excavaciones Arqueológicas en España **112**, Madrid.

Mascort, M.T., Sanmarti, J. and Santacana, J. 1991 *El jaciment protohistòric d'Aldovesta (Benifallet) i el comerç Fenici arcaic a la Catalunya Meridional.* La Diputació de Tarragona, Tarragona.

Matthäus, H. 1989 Cypern und Sardinien im frühen 1. Jahrtausend v. Chr. In E. Peltenburg (ed) *Early society in Cyprus*, 244–55. Edinburgh University Press, Edinburgh.

Mederos Martín, A. 1996 La conexión Levantino-Chipriota. Indicios de comercio Atlántico con el Mediterráneo Oriental durante el Bronce Final (1150–950 AC), *Trabajos de Prehistoria* **53**, 95–115.

Meijide Cameselle, G. 1988 *Las espadas del Bronce Final en la Península Ibérica.* Arqueohistorica 1, Santiago de Compostella.

Mohen, J-P. 1977 Broches à rôtir articulées de l'Âge du Bronze, *Antiquités Nationales* **9**, 34–9.

Monteagudo, L. 1977 *Die Beile auf der Iberischen Halbinsel.* Prähistorische Bronzefunde, IX/6, München.

Müller-Karpe, H. 1959 *Beiträge zur Chronologie der Urnenfelderzeit Nördlich und Südlich der* Alpen. Römisch-Germanische Forschungen 22, Berlin.

Needham, S. 1979 Two recent British shield finds and their continental parallels, *Proceedings of the Prehistoric Society* **45**, 111–34.

Needham, S. 1982 *The Ambleside hoard: a discovery in the Royal Collections.* British Museum Occasional Paper 39, London.

Needham, S. 1990 The Penard-Wilburton succession: new metalwork finds from Croxton (Norfolk) and Thirsk (Yorkshire), *Antiquaries Journal* **70**, 253–70.

Needham, S. 1996 Chronology and periodisation in the British Bronze Age, *Acta Archaeologica* **67**, 121–40.

Needham, S., Bronk Ramsey, C., Coombs, D., Cartwright, C. and

Pettitt, P. 1997 An independent chronology for British Bronze Age metalwork: the results of the Oxford Radiocarbon accelerator programme, *Archaeological Journal* **154**, 55–107.

O'Connor, B. 1980 *Cross-Channel relations in the later Bronze Age*. British Archaeological Reports S91, Oxford.

Ó Ríordáin, S.P. 1937 The halberd in Bronze Age Europe, *Archaeologia* **86**, 195–321.

Osborne, A. O'N. 1939 The Hayne Wood hoard, *Antiquaries Journal* **19**, 202–6.

Pautreau, J.-P. 1979 *Le Chalcolithique et l'Age du Bronze en Poitou*. Centre d'Archéologie et d'Ethnologie Poitevines, Musée Sainte-Croix, Poitiers.

Pautreau, J.-P., Gendron, Ch. and Bourhis, J.R. 1984 *La cachette de Triou*. Musée de Niort, Niort.

Pryor, F. 1991 *Flag Fen: prehistoric Fenland centre*. B.T. Batsford, London.

Rohl, B. and Needham, S. 1998 *The circulation of metal in the British Bronze Age: the application of lead isotope analysis*. British Museum Occasional Paper 102, London.

Ruivo, J.S. 1993 Os espetos articulados de Reguengo do Fetal (Batalha, Leiria), *Estudos Pré-Históricos* **1**, 105–110.

Ruiz-Gálvez Priego, M. 1986 Navegación y comercio entre el Atlántico y el Mediterráneo a fines de la Edad del Bronce, *Trabajos de Prehistoria* **43**, 9–42.

Ruiz-Gálvez Priego, M. 1987 Bronce Atlántico y "cultura" del Bronce Atlántico en en la Península Ibérica, *Trabajos de Prehistoria* **44**, 251–64.

Sandars, N.K. 1985 *The Sea Peoples: warriors of the ancient Mediterranean*. Thames and Hudson, London.

Savory, H.N. 1968 *Spain and Portugal*. Thames and Hudson, London.

Schubart, H. 1961 Atlantische Nietenkessel von der Pyrenäenhalbinsel, *Madrider Mitteilungen* **2**, 35–54.

Snodgrass, A.M. 1971 The first European body armour. In J. Boardman *et al.* (eds) *The European Community in Later Prehistory: Studies in Honour of C.F.C. Hawkes*, 31–50. Routledge and Kegan Paul, London.

Snodgrass, A.M. 1999 *Arms and armor of the Greeks*. John Hopkins University Press, Baltimore.

Taramelli, A. 1921 Ripostiglio di bronzi nuragici di Monte Sa Idda, Decimoputzu, *Monumenti Antichi dei Lincei* **27**, 5–98.

Taylor, J.J. 1980 *Bronze Age goldwork of the British Isles*. Cambridge University Press, Cambridge.

Vaz, J.L.I. 1987 *Roteiro arqueológico do Concelho de Viseu*. Camara Municipal, Viseu.

Verney, A. 1990 Le dépôt de Challans (Vendée'), *Bulletin de la Société Préhistorique Française* **37**, 396–417.

Vilaça, R. 1990 Broche à rôtir articulée de Cachouça (Idanha-a-Nova, Castelo Branco, Portugal), *Bulletin de la Société Préhistorique Française* **87**, 167–9.

Vilaça, R. and da Cruz, D.J. 1990 Canedotes (Vila Nova de Paiva, Viseu). Povoado pré-histórico do Bronze Final, *Estudos Pré-históricos* **3**, 255–61.

23. NIETHOS-Néit: The earliest documented Celtic God (*c.* 575 BC) and the Atlantic relationships between Iberia and Ireland

Martín Almagro-Gorbea

An archaic Greek graffito, NIHΘΩI, *written on a bowl from Miletos found in Huelva, is believed to be the first Celtic god name known. It is well dated by East-Greek pottery between 590–560 BC, probably related to a harbour-sanctuary of the tartessian town of* Onuba *(Huelva).*

Niethos can be related both with Nēton, *a warrior and solar divinity from* Acci *(Guadix, Granada) referred to Macrobius (*Saturnalia *I, 19,5), and with the Irish war-god* Néit. *Its Indo-European root,* *neigh- *ninth-, *means "warrior", "hero", "shining" and "holy" is attested in Celtic, and maybe in the Celtiberian word* neito *and the Iberian* neitin.

This god-name Niethos-Nēton-Néit *should confirm a solar and warrior Celtic God in Tartessos at the beginning of the VI century BC. In addition, it could be the earliest Celtic word known today. Finally, it also brings some light on the deep Atlantic relationships between Iberia and Ireland and the problem of the origin of the Celts in the Atlantic areas.*

Introduction

In the ancient Tartessian port-town of *Onuba*, well known through the Late Atlantic Bronze Age "Ría de Huelva hoard" (Almagro 1958; Ruiz Gálvez 1995), a *graffito* made up of eight archaic Greek letters was discovered in 1983 (Fernández Jurado and Olmos 1985; *SEG* 1989, n° 954; de Hoz 1997, 74; Almagro-Gorbea 2002). It was found in an archaeological excavation in Puerto street n° 9, at the base of the Molino de Viento hill, which rises up over the natural port of *Onuba* next to the ancient banks of the Odiel estuary (Fernández Jurado 1989, 1, fig. 9). This is the oldest Greek *graffito* ever found in Iberia (Figs 23.1 and 23.2) and the most occidental known in the Ancient World. The *graffito* was written on a bowl 25cm in diameter and over 4.5cm tall, although its foot is missing (Fernández Jurado and Olmos 1985, 108; Fernández Jurado 1989, 1: 252, fig. 46). This is believed to have been made in Miletos (Voigl3nder 1982, 85, fig. p. 40, n° 252–257) and has been dated back to *c.* 590 – 570/560 BC (Fernández Jurado 1989, 1: 253). This chronology was accepted by Olmos (1985, 110), who dated the *graffito* somewhere "in the first half of the sixth century BC, at the height of the Greek trade in Tartessos", of which Herodotus (I, 163; IV, 152) gave us some descriptions. The high concentrations of Greek pottery (Ortega 1999: 269, fig. 1C and 3) and other discoveries

Fig 23.1: *Bowl from Miletos, c. 575 BC, found in Huelva with the graffito* Niethoi *(after Fernández Jurado).*

Fig 23.2: *Detail of the graffito* NIHΘΩI *(photo Real Academia de la Historia, Madrid).*

found in this area indicate that this was a Greek port of trade or *emporion*, just like Naucratis in Egypt (Petrie 1886; Johnston 1978; Bresson 1980), Gravisca in Italy (Torelli 1977) and others in Iberia (Almagro-Gorbea and Moneo 2000, 153s.; Moneo 2003, 62 s., 184 s.; *vid. infra*).

The first letters of the inscription have been lost, but the last 'I' can still be discerned broken on the right side (Fig 23.2). Olmos (1985) had no difficulty in reading […] NIHΘΩI, the dative form of the name of the person to whom the offering was made. The letters belong to an archaic Ionian alphabet (Jeffery 1961, 325; Johnston 2000, lam. 1.3), which are consistent with the typology of the Milesian bowl and the context in which it was discovered, and coincides with the peak period of Greek imports in Huelva, in the first half of the sixth century BC.

The inscription was made just under the exterior rim, to make it easier to read (Petrie 1886, lam. 32,162; Gardner 1886; Cook and Woodhead 1952; Williams 1983, 169–178; Johnson 2000, 17 s.). The formula normally used in Greek trading colonies such as Naucratis (Cook and Woodhead 1952; Wachter 2001) or Gravisca (Johnston 2000) is also found here: the verb νέθηκεν used to dedicate offerings to the Gods. The inscription should therefore be interpreted as [ὁ δεινας νέθηκε]ν Νιηθωι (Olmos 1985, 109), in other words, "[...] dedicated to *Niethos*").

The theonym **Niethos** *and its parallels in Iberia and Ireland*

Olmos (1985) interpreted NIHΘΩI to be the dative form of a non-Greek male name, and suggested that it was the Hellenised version of a local name, even though there are no Tartessian equivalents (Untermann 1997, 177 s.). However, given its context, and other similar pieces found in ancient *emporia*, we are led towards the hypothesis that it must be a theonym (god's name), just like the inscriptions found in Naucratis (Gardner 1886; Cook and Woodhead 1952; Johnston 1978), Samos (Kyrieleis 1981, fig. 8), Gravisca (Johnston 2000, 23), *etc*. The formula used should have included the name of the giver (nominative) + ´ανέθηκεν + the name of the God (dative indicated by the final 'I') (Cook and Woodhead 1952; Johnston 2000, 17 s.; Wachter 2001, 214 s.). In Gravisca, forty three vases have been found that were dedicated to Hera, in the dative form, six to Aphrodite, and two to Apollo (Johnston 2000, 17–19, lams. 1–3), dated *c.* 550–525 BC (Torelli 1977); this is a port sanctuary culturally and chronologically contemporary with the *graffito* found in Huelva. Furthermore, in Naucratis, numerous dedications have been found to Apollo, Aphrodite and Hera, along with other deities, all in dative.

Then, if the dative form is *Niethoi*, the nominative form must be *Niethos*. This theonym does not belong to the Greek pantheon. Therefore, it represents a local deity, which we can consider as the first documented Tartesssian God. This deity must have had a sanctuary in the port of

Onuba, and would have been associated with the colonial trade, since the offering seems to have been made by an Ionian (Almagro-Gorbea 2002).

This research into this Tartessian theonym opens up some extremely interesting new lines of investigation. The word *Niethos* does not appear in records of the Tartessian language (Untermann 1997, 181), but it could be linked to the theonyms *Nēton*, documented in *Acci*, a South Iberia pre-roman town, to *Néit* from Ireland, as well as to the Celtiberian word *neito* and the Iberian word *neitin*. All of these possible theonyms appear to come from a Celtic root, which makes this inscription of particular interest:

1. **Nēton,** *radiis ornatum*, was a god from *Acci* (Guadix) whom Macrobius (*Saturnalia* I, 19,5) links to the god *Mars* because of the shared connections with the sun (Mielentz 1936). Epigraphs dedicated to *Nēton* have been discovered in *Conimbriga* (*CIL* II, 365), Trujillo (*CIL* II, 5278) and Guadix (*CIL* II, 3386), although their authenticity has been brought into question owing to the Spanish tradition of falsifying inscriptions to *Nēton*, a deity who was well known to antiquaries from the eighteenth century onwards (Menéndez Pelayo 1911, 8: 279).

2. **neito**. This suggests a possible link between *Niethoi* and the Celtiberian word *neito*, documented in the Celtiberian bronze inscription of Botorrita I (Beltrán and Tovar 1982, 37, fig. VII). Most Celtists links *neito* to the deity *Nēton* from *Acci* because they believe the two words share the same etymology: Lejeune (1973, 644), Eska (1989, 78–79), Eichner (1990, 39), Gorrochategui (1991, 6), Meid (1993, 100), Marco (1994, 338), Orel (1995, 303), Schmidt (1995, 237) and Epstein (1998). However, Fleuriot (1979, 173), Rodríguez Adrados (1976, 40) and Villar (1989) interpret the word to be the imperative form of a verb of movement, while Untermann (1997, 573) and Wodtko (2000, 273–275) waver between both options.

3. **neitin**. This Iberian word was believed to be a personal name (Albertos 1966, 167; Siles 1985, 270, n° 1178–1179; Untermann 1990, 2: 228, n° 89[N]), although the word *neitin*[..., appears on the stele found in Binéfar, Huesca; Beltrán (1969, 521–522) and Marco (1994, 338; 1998, 391, n. 21) link this to Macrobius's *Nēton*. The recorded epigraphs do little to solve this problem (Untermann 2001, 617–619): a possible dedication on a *rython* found in Ullastret, Gerona, from the third century B.C. (Siles 1985, 251–252, n° 1071–1075) begins with the words *neitin-iunstir*, which Untermann (1990, 50–52, n° C.2.8) believed to be part of a compound anthroponym (personal name). An inscription found near Ensérune contains the word *neitiniunstir* (Untermann 2001, 618–619). A lead inscription was found in Granada (Untermann 1998; Untermann 2001, 617–618) with the word *neitin: iunstir* and also *neitiniunstir,* like in the *rython* from Ullastret, separated in one case by

interpunction and in other represented as one whole word. On a lead inscription from *Emporion*, Ampurias, Untermann (2001, 619) reads *nei]tin : iunstir.* Other examples include: the word *atuneitin* found on a lead inscription from Yátova, Valencia, which has been interpreted as **atun-neitin* (Untermann 1990, 1, 122; Untermann 2001, 620); another lead inscription from Ullastret with the word *neitekeŕu*, a morphological variation of *neitin* and *ker.e* (Unterman 1990, C.2.3, 41 s.; Untermann 2001, 620); *neintinke* is also found in an inscription from Guissona, Lérida, which has been interpreted to be "*neintinke*'s funeral stele" (Velaza 2001, 655; Untermann 2001, 620, n. 20) and the anthroponym *M·Licinius·Neitinbeles* in a Latin inscription found in Tarrasa (*CIL* II, n° 6144; Albertos 1966, 167; Untermann 1990, 228, n° 89^{N}3; Abascal 1994, 437).

Untermann (2001, 619–620) believes that *neitin* in the combination *neitin-iunstir* was definitely an anthroponym, as in *Neitinbeles*. However, the inscriptions found in Granada, Ensèrune and possibly even Ampurias show a separation symbol between *neitin* and *iunstir*, and this is found so frequently as to preclude the possibility of a simple anthroponym. Then, the word *neintin* cannot be interpreted with concrete certainty: for Siles (1985, 270, n° 1178–1179), Abascal (1994, 437) and Untermann (1990, 228, n° 89^N; Untermann 2001, 620), it is an anthroponym, whereas Beltrán (1969, 521–522) and Marco (1994, 338; Marco 1998, 391, n. 21) believe that the word refers to a deity linked with *Neto* in the context of the stele found in Binéfar and the *rython* of Ullastret.

Thus, it would appear to be a noun, a title or epithet, which could be related to the root **neit-*, recorded in Celtiberian (*vid. supra*) and attested in the deity from *Acci, Nēton* (Macrobius *Saturnalia* I, 19,5). It could then have been a theonym used in Iberian to form anthroponyms, as among the Celts (*vid. infra*), Phoenicians and Carthaginians (Benz 1972) and Greeks (*Herakles, Apolodoros, Poseidonios, etc.*). Therefore, *neitin* might have been an epithet, according to its Celtic etymology, which could be translated as "The Warrior", "The Hero", "The Guide" or "The Radiant One" (*vid. infra*). The iconography of *Nēton, radiis ornatum* (Macrobius *Saturnalia* I, 16,5), would certainly fit with an interpretation such as "The Radiant One", which was a epithet frequently used in Celtic theonyms such as *Belenus* (Green 1992, 30–31), especially for warrior gods such as *Néit* in Ireland (*vid. infra*), *Lug* (Sergent 1995, 5 s.) and other deities linked with Mars, such as *Belatucadrus* or *Loucetius* (Green 1992, 42, 143). If this were the case, the theonym *Niethos* found in Huelva would be linked to the god of *Acci, Nēton*, and, although the connection is less certain, there is no evidence to preclude a link with the Celtiberian word *neito* and the Iberian word *neitin.*

4. **Néit** or **Néid** is a theonym from Celtic Ireland. Its use and existence have been documented in glossaries and epic poems. The link between this name and *Netos* was first identified many years ago by d'Arbois de Jubainville (1899), Holder (1904, 750), Costa (1917) and Schulten (1945, 27, n. 3), a theory that is still supported by subsequent linguists (*vid. supra*). Now, *Niethos* adds new archaeological and epigraphic documentations to this theory.

    Irish literary references to *Nēit* are few and far between, but extremely interesting. *Néit* appears in the *Sanas Cormaic* glossary, which is attributed to Cormac MacCuilenan (836–908), Bishop and King of Cashel, Munster (O'Donovan 1868; Knight 1999). This glossary is dated around the eleventh century (Stokes 1862, xviii), since it is referred to in the *Book of Leinster* (H.2.18), from the twelfth century, and also in the *Yellow Book of Lecan* (H.2.16), from the late fourteenth century.

Néit was the "God of Battle" worshipped by the Goidelics, and according to the glossaries, the name means "battle", "wound" or the act of "wounding", possibly because of the semantic derivation of its etymological meaning (*vid. infra*). According to the aforementioned texts, *Néit* had a destructive nature, he was fierce, merciless and always ready for battle, all of which is consistent with his links to war.

The pre-Christian *Néit* might have been isolated within the mythological genealogy of Celtic Ireland, although it is difficult to confirm whether the genealogies devised during the Christian period are actually valid, in which he is situated as the son of *Indui*, the father of *Dalbaith* and the grandfather of *Balor*. The wives of *Néit*, whose characteristics help to flesh out the bare bones of information available on this god, are even more interesting. Some genealogies represent *Néit* as having two wives (Meyer 1912, 17; Stokes 1859, 31, 191; Macalister 1941, 130, 188, 194): one is *Bé Néit*, who is identified with *Nemain-Nemon* and with *Badb* ("The Raven"), and the other is *Fea. Bé Néit, Nemhain* and *Badb* form a Celtic ancestral triple goddess of Indo-European origin, which is equivalent to *Morrigan*, the great Irish war goddess, although *Morrigan* is never linked to *Néit* (Le Roux and Guyonvarc'h 1983; Epstein 1998). In Ireland, the ancestral war goddess(es) had at the same time a single and triple personality, and they were often interchangeable. They were the "Goddess-Mother" of sexuality, maternity and fertility, magic and prophecy. They were also the wife of the "supreme god" as well as local deities in their own right. They were goddesses of water and rivers, forests, seasonal festivals and animals (especially cows). In other words, they were the incarnation of all the forces of nature related to fertility and destruction (Ross 1967, 232; Sjoestedt 1982, 112; Carey 1983; Epstein 1998; Green 1992, 154 s.). Hence, they represent the terrifying and destructive goddess of war, who provoked madness, panic, frenzy and even death. Together with *Néit* they formed a malevolent couple who shared the same bellicose personality.

Glossaries state that *Bé Néit* means "wife of *Néit*" or "the wife of battle". Therefore *Néit* means "battle". Medieval Irish texts compare *Bé Néit* to *Enyo* and the Furies since they all incite war. However, *Nemhain* or *Nemon* ("frenzy"), as well as *Bé Néit* are both referred to as *Badb*, "the Raven" or "the Crow", and *Babdh Catha*, whose name denotes "rage, fury and violence", since the goddess would take the form of this scavenger bird to devour the bodies of fallen heroes on the battlefield and take them to the Other World. Then, links have been drawn with the Gallic goddess *Cathubodua*, who is also associated with the raven (Green 1992, 38). The role of the deity as a psychopomp, or leader of souls, is an attribute reminiscent of *Lug* (Sergent 1995). Furthermore, *Bé Néit, Nemhain* and *Badb* are associated with fire and other bright lights linked with war, which brings us back to *Néton, radiis ornatus* (Macrobius *Saturnalia* I, 19,5), a connection that the etymology of *Néit* (*vid. infra*) could well corroborate. Therefore, all these deities share common characteristics that help to define the personality of *Néit*, which in itself is now practically unknown, and they also provide crucial information in the search for knowledge about *Neithos*.

The Celtic etymology of Niethos-Netos-Néit

According to most Celtists, the figure of *Néton* described by Macrobius (*Saturnalia* I, 19,5) and the Irish deity *Néit* share the same Celtic root. Similarly, these Celtists also link the Celtiberian word *neito* with the deity *Néton* of *Acci* and the root **nēt < *neit*, which Pokorny (1959, 760) suggests is a double root. According to d'Arbois de Jubainville (1899), Holder (1904, 738, 750) and Rix (1998, 406), this root may be *nei-, neiə-, nī*, in the sense of "to direct", "to lead", or "to guide". The root can be seen in the following languages: in Old Indian *náyati*, with the participle *nīta-* and in the noun *nayeiti,* meaning "guide"; in Old Irish, *nūth,* or *nītho-* means "leading", **nītu* "combat" or "struggle" and *nīa,* with the genitive form *–níath* or *níad*, means "hero" or "warrior"; in Ogamic *Netta-* exists, with derivations such as *...Nettace* and *Nettasagru*; in Gothic, *neið, nanðjan*; in Germanic, *nīða*; in Old English, *nêdan*; in Old German, *–nindan* forms ethnonyms such as *Nitio-brŏg-es*, meaning "able to fight" or "powerful", as well as toponyms such as *Nitio-genna* (Holder 1904, 750–751). Alternatively, these roots could be linked to the concept of "radiance" or "shine", such as *noi-bho-*, "good" or "holy", whence the Celto-Germanic word *nei-to* could derive, "furore", the Latin verb *nitēo*, meaning "to shine" or "to blaze" and **nei-bho-*, "vitality", "life force", and in Cimmerian the word *nwyd* also means "furore". The Accitan theonym *Neton* and the Irish anthroponym *Nīall*, with the genitive form **neit-s-lo-s > Nēill*, could also be included in this list.

Vendryes (1959, N17) proposes a synthesis of these theories, and states that the root *níth* means "combat", "warrior zeal" or "anger", and is linked to *nia*, whose genitive and dative forms are *niad* and *niaid* respectively (Vendryes 1959, N15), and which means "champion" or "hero". All these forms are closely related to the word *Niethos* from the *graffito* found in *Onuba*. This root appears in Ogamic compound nouns that have *neta-* as a prefix, such as *Netacunas, Nettasagri*. Irish anthroponyms that are derived from these compound nouns include words such as *Neth, Niath* or *Nioth* and also, so it would seem, *Nēid*, the name of the "god of battle" mentioned in Cormac's Irish glossary (Meyer 1912, 82, § 965; *vid. supra*). Vendryes (1956, N17) adds that the word *nia*, whose genitive form is **nei-t-os*, and which derives from the root **nei*, expresses the notion of vigorous force of strength and is present in the Sanskrit word *náyati,* meaning "he leads". It can also be found in the word *níth*, meaning "dazzling light", "shine" and "beauty", and is linked with the Latin *ni-t-ēre* "to shine" and *ni-t-idus* "shining". The form **nei-bh-* contains the idea of divine inspiration, and gives rise to the derivative adjective *noib*, meaning "holy" or "sacred".

This common etymological thread would also tie in with Macrobius's *Néton radiis ornatum* (*Saturnalia* I, 16,5), the Irish god *Néit*, the deity *Niethos* of *Onuba* and possibly, according to most authors (*vid. supra*), with the Celtiberian word *neito* and the Iberian word *neitin*. *Niethos-Néton-Néit* and may also – although here the connection is less certain – *neito* and *neitin* (*vid. infra*), be the same deity documented in Tartessos and later among Celtiberians and Iberians.

The linguistic differences between these theonyms are possibly due to the fact that 1500 years had passed between *Niethos* and *Néit*: *Niethos, c.* 575 BC, *neito, c.* 50–75 BC, *neitin, c.* 300–50 BC. *Néton, c.* 400 AD – although the source of this word, which presumably is Punic, must date back to before Christ – and *Néit, c.* 900 AD. (Fig 23.3), but the relationship of these words confirms the links between Hispanic-Celtic and Goidelic (de Hoz 1988, 207).

The conversion of *ie* to *ei* does not appear to be a spelling mistake nor due to the incorrect transcription of the indigenous word by a Greek, who was not used to hearing the Tartessian language, and who mistook the *ie* of the first syllable for a long *ē*, and althought the slightly fricative intervocalic dental sound he heard was in fact a *th*. The *ie* diphthong found in *Niethoi* is documented in Tartessian inscriptions from the south of Portugal, in words such as *lielao* or *Ki(i)elao* (Untermann 1997, J.23.1, J.18.1), in which Celtic anthroponyms also appear (*ibid.*, 168; Correa 1989, 244 s., 251). Furthermore, the oldest recorded Gaelic name for Ireland, probably from the sixth century BC (*Ora Maritima* 111; Str. 4,5,4), shows the conversion ie>ei, Ἱερνη>*Ériu*>Éire (from **Éueriju*, cf. Holder 1904, 99 s.; Haverfield 1913; Pokorny 1953, 119; Ó hÓgáin 2002, 14). This transformation could be

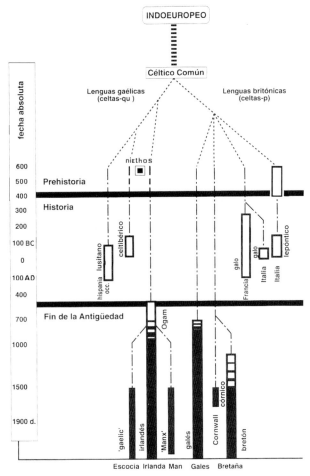

Fig 23.3: Philogenesis of Celtic languages (after Untermann, with modifications).

*arganton-, which seems to be similar to *Niethos > Nēton-Néit.*

The Tartessian deity **Niethos**, *the oldest known Celtic god*

The Celtic theonym *Niethos* appears within a Tartessian cultural context. It must have meant "The Warrior" or "The Shining One" (*vid. supra*), epithets that would have been used to describe a Tartessian deity with these characteristics. In fact, bronze figures of *smiting gods* have been discovered in Tartessos (Almagro 1980; Bisi 1986), whose warring attitude and role could fit in with *Niethos*. These figures are linked to the God of sun and war, and are Phoenician in origin, just like *Reshef, Melkart* or *Baal* (Collon 1972; Negbi 1976; Seeden 1980), whence also stems the iconography of the *Mars Italicus* (Scholz 1979), which is associated with war, fertility and the protection of the fields. Therefore, the iconography, ideology and roles of *Niethos* would have been very similar to those of *Melkart-Herakles* and the orientalizing *smiting gods*, who were also linked to the sun and war, and had become widespread throughout the Mediterranean as deities who protected the king and his subjects (Almagro-Gorbea 1996). *Niethos* might have been the protector god of *Onuba*, a Celtic version of the Phoenician *Melkart-Herakles* or another similar deity. *Niethos* was worshipped in a Greek port of trade or *emporion* in *Onuba*, which was used by Ionian merchants (Garrido and Ortega 1995; Ortega 1999), who may have had the right to seek refuge there, as was often the case with Greek *emporia* sanctuaries. Perhaps a Greek merchant from Ionia, who had made it safely to the Atlantic coast of Iberia, made an offering to this god.

It is also interesting to point out that *Niethos* would be one of the oldest documented Celtic words. *Niethoi* is dated *c*. 580–560 BC, and is therefore contemporary to the first "Lepontic" inscriptions (Lejeune 1971; Prosdocimi 1989; 1991; Solinas 1995), made from the early sixth century BC onwards in the north of Italy (Kruta 2000, 680). The *graffito* found in Huelva is dated a little after the inscription in Sesto Calende from the end of the seventh century BC, "in alfabeto e con ogni probabilità anche in lingua etrusca" (Colonna 1988, fig. 11), although Prosdocimi (1991, 148) believes that "potrebbe essere non etrusca, allora celtica". It would also have been written shortly after the pseudo-inscription at Presualdo (Roca and Binaghi 1999, 439), which dates from the early sixth century BC, since both inscriptions show evidence of the earliest signs of Lepontic writing (Prosdocimi 1990). *Niethoi* would have been contemporary with the Celtic anthroponym *katakina* (De Simone 1978) and other inscriptions, the Celticity of which Prosdocimi questions (1987, 574 s.). *Niethoi* would also have been either contemporary or possibly slightly pre-dated the Lepontic inscription *xosioiso* found at Castelletto Ticino (Gambari and Colonna 1988), dated between 575–550 BC and

comparable to *Niethos>Nētos>Néit*. The *ē* in *Nēton* might be the transformation of the Celtic root **nieth-, *neith-*, meaning "to lead" or "to shine" into a monothong. The evolution of *ie, ei*, and + indicates that *Niethos* is an archaic form that includes the original root **nieth-*, which was subsequently transformed into the monothong *Nēto* and into *Néit*.

Niethoi also contains a fricative, Θ, instead of the unvoiced T. This fricative appears to be original, as in Ἀργανθώνιος, which is the most well known Tartessian anthroponym (Herodotos I, 163–165; Appianos, *Iberica*, VI, 7,267; Strabon, II, 3,14; Suidas, *sub voce* Αγαθώνιος). This hypothesis is confirmed by the *graffito* found in Sindos, ΑΡΓΑΝΘΟΝΙΟΣ, which dates to *c*. 450 BC (Tiverios 1998, 78–79; Blech 2000, 311). Roman authors also wrote *Arganthonios* (Valerius Maximus VIII, 12; Plinius maior, *Naturalis historia* VII, 154 and 156; Silius Italicus III, 396), but the anthroponyms and family names found in Roman inscriptions, such as *Argant(onius), Arganta, Arganto, Argantioq(um)* and *Argantïcaeni* (Palomar 1957, 40 and 145; Albertos 1966, 33; Albertos 1979, 138; *HAE* 1965, 3, nº 1804; Abascal 1994, 285) corroborate a *th>t* evolution in words with the Celtic root considered to be the oldest known Celtic inscription (Colonna 1988, 160; Prosdocimi 1991, 142 s., 149 s.).

Niethos-*Néit and the Atlantic Celts*

If we accept the Celtic etymology proposed for *Niethos*, this theonym is the oldest testimonial of the Celtic language currently on record (Fig 23.3) as well as the oldest Celtic deity known to us, predating Irish references by 1500 years, and references from Caesar (*BG*, VI, 17–18) and Lucanus (*Pharsalia* I, 444–446) by 500 years. The date is of great importance, since it confirms just how early Celts were present in the Atlantic countries. This information is very useful in order to understand the complex ethnogenesis of the Celts and the ethno-cultural evolution and developments in countries that bordered the Atlantic Ocean.

The ostensible relationship between *Niethos, Nēton* and *Nēit,* if it is not pure coincidence, which seems unlikely, could also be explained by something as complex as a linguistic, religious and socio-ideological borrowing. Conversely, this link indicates that the same "God of War" existed in Iberia, Ireland and quite probably in other areas around the Atlantic Ocean, which may have shared the same language and an extremely archaic Celtic pantheon, as well as religious beliefs in the first half of the first millennium B.C., which could therefore have originated in the Bronze Age. Moreover, all of this seems to suggest that links between the Atlantic areas of Iberia and Ireland might have affected religion and language, aspects that have not yet been assessed.

The identification of *Niethos-Nēton* with the Celtic deity *Néit* confirms the existence of Celts in Tartessos. *Niethos* bears out the Celtic nature of the King of Tartessos *Arganthonios* (Herodotos I, 163–165; Appianos, *Iberica* VI, 7,267; Strabon II, 3,14). Its structure, *arg-a-nt-onio-s* (Palomar 1957, 40 and 145; Albertos 1966, 33, 268, 291, 294, 305; Albertos 1977, 35) and its etymology – its link to *arg-ant-*, meaning "white, brilliant, silver" (Albertos 1959, 33) – reveals a Celtic name, which is confirmed by the survival of the anthroponym *Argant(onius)* (*vid. supra*) into the Roman period.

Niethos also confirms the news brought by Herodotus (II, 33,3; IV, 49,3) of Celts beyond the Pillars of Hercules, in the Atlantic area of Tartessos (Fischer 1972). The presence of *Cempsi, Cynetes, Dragani* and *Sefes* in the *Ora Maritima* (180, 195–201, 205, 223, 257, 301) as well as *Ligures* (*Ora Maritima* 196, 284) was not dated accurately (Schulten 1955, 34 s.; Tovar 1976, 193–196; Mangas and Plácido (eds) 1994, 76 s. 85 and 91). However, the *graffito* in Huelva, alongside other possible Celtic anthroponyms (Correa 1989) and Celtic elements identified in Tartessian epigraphs (Untermann 1997, 165 s.), indicate that they were present in areas bordering the Atlantic in the early sixth century BC, long before the *Celtici* in the South West mentioned by Pliny (*Naturalis Historia* III, 13–14; cf. Berrocal 1992, 70 s.).

Therefore, the traditional theory regarding the arrival of the Celts in Hallstatt D and La Tène (Sangmeister 1960, 82 s.; Lenerz–de Wilde 1991, 206, 218; 2001; de Bernardo 2002) is no longer viable, since it confuses the Celts with the culture of La Tène. The 'solutions' of Bosch Gimpera (1942) and Almagro (1952) are similarly unsatisfactory: they trace the origin of the Celts only back to the Urnfield culture, although this hypothesis has recently become fashionable once more (de Hoz 1992; Arenas 1999; Ruiz-Zapatero and Lorrio 1999). Yet these theories do not explain how the Celts came to arrive in the west of Iberia from Central Europe so early in the Late Bronze Age, but also do not solve the question of the archaic Celtic characteristics of the deities worshipped in western areas of Iberia (Olivares 2002, 257 s.), regardless of whether the Lusitan language is considered Celtic (Untermann 1987) or not (Gorrochategui 1985).

Bearing in mind Hawkes' theory (1973) vis-à-vis *Cumulative Celticity*, the best solution would be to link the origin of Celts (Celtic ethnogenesis) to a wide, polymorphous and fluid proto-Celtic culture that inhabited from Central Europe to the Atlantic areas during the Bronze Age (Almagro-Gorbea 1994; 1995; Waddell 1995), probably with roots in the Beaker period. This hypothesis would be the best explanation to the link between *Niethos-Nēton* in Iberia and *Néit* in Ireland, where the theonym survived right into the Middle Ages, along with so many other features of Celtic culture. It would also clarify the affinity between the Hispanic Celtic language and Goidelic (Fig 23.3). This explanation adds a rich cultural dimension to the links between Atlantic areas, especially between Iberia and Ireland, which were previously thought to be based solely on material culture and commercial exchange (Ruiz-Gálvez 1998; Cunliffe 2001, 255 s.).

Niethos and *Néit* would seem to suggest that the Atlantic world was not only linked by the material culture uncovered by archaeology, but also by fundamental sub-systems such as ideology, religion and language. Such affinities only seem to be possible if there was a polymorphous *Celtic ethnos*, which would explain the deep bonds that existed between the Atlantic regions in spite of all their differences. This ethnic affinity could be explained by an extremely ancient ethno-culture that existed in the Atlantic regions, whose roots can be traced back further than the Bronze Age, probably as far back as the Beaker Culture (Gallay 2001). The ethnogenesis of the Celtic peoples developed progressively in this region through a process of interaction with Western Central Europe (Almagro-Gorbea 1995; Kruta 2000, 123 s.).

The complex Celtic ethnogenesis, more than from a "cumulative Celticity" model from Central Europe to the Atlantic, would be explained by a "fluid polymorph" model with different and interactioned centres between the Atlantic and Central Europe. This "fluid polymorph" model could be comparable in some ways to the ethnogenesis of some other Indo-European peoples, such as

Iranio-Scythians and related peoples in the Eurasian steppes. Therefore, suggesting that the Celts arrived in Iberia and at the Atlantic as a people with a Central European culture (Sangmeister 1960; Lenerz–de Wilde 1991; *etc.*) or ignoring or denying all other evidences of the existence of the Celts (Chapman 1992; Collis 1997; James 1999), is just trying to impose simplistic and anachronistic solutions on such a complex and attractive problem. Indeed, such 'solutions' could indicate some underlying historiographical and ideological prejudices.

Conclusions

The *graffito NIHΘΩI* found in Huelva, dated *c.* 590–570/ 560 BC, is the oldest Greek inscription in Iberia and is the most western of the Greek colonial world. It refers to a god, *Niethos,* which could be the first Tartessian theonym known to us.

Niethos appears to have links to the god of *Acci, Nēton* (Macrobius, *Saturnalia* I, 19,5), to the Irish god *Néit,* and perhaps also to the Celtiberian word *neito* and the Iberian word *neitin,* since all they are derived from the Indo-European root **neith-,* meaning "warrior", "shine" or "holy", which is well recorded in the Celtic language.

Niethos may be the oldest Celtic theonym known so far, and one of the first records of the Celtic language together with the Lepontic inscriptions.

Niethos confirms the disputed presence of Celts in Tartessos, beyond the Pillars of Hercules, from the beginning of the first millennium BC, as intimated in the *Ora Maritima* and Herodotus.

The close link between *Niethos* and *Néit* is a new and important piece of evidence for the Atlantic relationship between Iberia and Ireland. *Niethos* proves that this relationship extended to their ideological and religious system. It also helps to clarify the proto-Celtic culture that existed within the Atlantic peoples, which dated at least as far back as the Bronze Age.

***

These ideas, the inspiration for which are taken from the Tartessian god *Niethos* and the Irish god *Néit,* are merely intended to add another snippet of information to this attractive enigma. In-depth interdisciplinary research and analysis are certainly required into this area as it stretches further than the field of Archaeology alone.

However, these theories are also and overall a sincere tribute to Professor George Eogan, who has shown such an interest in the prehistoric relationship between Ireland and Iberia and who senses the mutual attraction between these two lands at opposite ends of the Atlantic world.

Bibliography

Abascal, J.M. 1994 *Los nombres personales en las inscripciones latinas de Hispania.* Murcia.

Albertos, Mª.L. 1966 *La onomástica personal primitiva de Hispania: Tarraconense y Bética.* Acta Salmanticensia **13**, Salamanca.

Albertos, Mª.L. 1977 Correciones a los trabajos sobre onomástica personal indígena de M. Palomar Lapesa y Mª Lourdes Albertos Firmat, *Emerita* **45**, 33–54.

Albertos, Mª.L. 1979 La onomástica de la Celtiberia, *II Coloquio de Lenguas y Culturas Prerromanas, Tübingen* 1976, 131–167, Salamanca.

Almagro, M. 1952 La invasión céltica en España. In R. Menéndez Pidal *Historia de España* I, 2, 1–278, Madrid.

Almagro, M. 1958 *Depósito de la Ría de Huelva. Inventaria Archaeologica Hispana I.* Madrid.

Almagro, M. 1980 Un tipo de exvoto ibérico de origen orientalizante, *Trabajos de Prehistoria* **37**, 247–308.

Almagro-Gorbea, M. 1994 Proto-celtes et Celtes dans la Péninsule Ibérique. *XVIéme. Colloque International pour l'Étude de L'Age du Fer. Agen, 1992, Aquitania* **14**, 283–296.

Almagro-Gorbea, M. 1995 Ireland and Spain in the Bronze Age. In J. Waddell and E. Shee Twohig (eds) *Ireland in the Bronze Age,* 136–148. Stationery Office, Dublin.

Almagro-Gorbea, M. 1992: *Ideología y poder en Tartessos y el mundo ibérico.* Madrid.

Almagro-Gorbea, M. 2002 Una probable divinidad tartésica identificada: *Niethos/Netos, Palaeohispanica* **2**, 37–70.

Almagro-Gorbea, M. and Moneo, T. 2000 *Santuarios urbanos en el mundo ibérico,* Bibliotheca Arqueologica Hispana **4**. Madrid.

d'Arbois de Jubainville, H. 1899 *La Civilisation des Celts et celle de l'épopée homérique* Cours de littérature Celtique **6**. Paris.

Arenas, J.A. 1999 El inicio de la Edad del Hierro en el sector central del Sistema Ibérico. In J.A. Arenas and Mª.V. Palacios (eds) *El origen del mundo celtibérico,* 191–211. Molina de Aragón.

Beltrán, A. 1969 La inscripción ibérica de Binéfar en el Museo de Huesca, *XI Congreso Nacional de Arqueología. Mérida, 1968,* 518–522. Zaragoza.

Beltrán, A. and Tovar, A. 1982 *Contrebia Belaisca (Botorrita, Zaragoza) I. El bronce con alfabeto "ibérico" de Botorrita.* Zaragoza.

Benz, F.L. 1972 *Personal Names in the Phoenician and Punic Inscriptions: A Catalogue, Grammatical Study and Glossary of Elements.* Roma.

Bernaldo Stempel, P. de 2002 Centro y áreas culturales: la formación del Celtibérico sobre el fondo del Celta peninsular hispano, *Palaeohipanica* **2**, 89–132.

Berrocal, L. 1992 *Los pueblos célticos del Suroeste de la Península Ibérica,* Complutum Extra 2. Madrid.

Bisi, A.M. 1986 Le «Smiting-God» dans les milieux phéniciens d'Occident, *Studia Phoenicia* **4**, 169–187.

Blech, M. 2000 Tartessos. In T. Ulbert (ed.) *Hispania Antiqua. Denkmäler der Frühzeit,* 305–348. Mainz.

Bosch Gimpera, P. 1942 *Two Celtic Waves in Spain,* Proceeding of the British Academy XXV. London.

Bresson, A. 1980 Rhodes, l'Hellenion et le statut de Naucratis, *Dialogues d'Histoire Ancienne* **6**, 291–349.

Carey, J. 1983 Notes on the Irish War-goddess, *Éigse* **19**, 263–75.

Chapmann, M. 1992 *The Celts: The construction of a Myth.* London.

Collis, J. 1997 Celtic myths, *Antiquity* **71**, 195–201.

Collon, D. 1972 The Smiting God, *Levant* **4**, 111–134.

Colonna, G. 1988 L'iscrizione (p. 130–159). In F.M. Gambari and G. Colonna, Il bicchiere con iscrizione arcaica da Castelletto Ticino e l'adozione della scrittura nell'Italia nord-occidentale, 119–164, *Studi Etrusci* **54**.

Cook, R.M. and Woodhead, A.G. 1952 Painted Inscriptons on Chiot Pottery, *Annnual of the British School at Athens* **47**, 159–170.

Correa, J.A. 1989 Posibles antropónimos en las inscripciones en escritura del SO. (o tartesia), *Veleia* **6**, 243–251.

Costa, J. 1917 *La religión de los celtíberos y su organización política y civil.* Madrid.

Cunliffe, B. 2001 *Facing the Ocean. The Atlantic and its Peoples 8000 BC–AD 1500.* Oxford.

De Simone, C. 1978 Un nuovo gentilizio etrusco di Orvieto (katakina) e la cronologia della penetrazione celtica (gallica) in Italia, *La Parola del Passato,* 370–395.

Eichner, H. 1990 Damals und heute. Probleme der Erschliessung des Altkeltischen zu Zeussens Zeit und in der Gegenwart. *Erlangen Gedenkfeier für Johann Kaspar Zeuss,* 9–56. Erlangen.

Epstein, A.G. 1998 *War Goddess: The Morr'gan and her Germano-Celtic Counterparts* (Ph. Dr., University of California, Los Angeles; University Microfilms International UMI n° 9906152).

Eska, J.F. 1989 *Towards a Interpretation of the Hispano-Celtic Inscription of Botorrita* Innsbrucker Beiträge zur Sprachwissenschaft 59. Innsbruck.

Fernández Jurado, J. 1989 *Tartessos y Huelva (Huelva Arqueológica X–XI,1–3).* Huelva.

Fernández Jurado, J. and Olmos, R. 1985 Una inscripción jonia arcaica en Huelva, *Lucentum* 4, 107–113.

Fischer, F. 1972 Die Kelten bei Herodot, *Madrider Mitteilungen* 13, 109–124.

Fleuriot, L. 1979 La grande inscription Celtibère de Botorrita. État actuel du déchiffrement, *Actas del II Coloquio sobre Lenguas y Culturas Prerromanas de la Peninsula Ibérica, Tübingen 1976,* 169–184. Salamanca.

Gallay, A. 2001 L'enigme campaniforme. In F. Nicolis (ed.) *Bell Beakers today I,* 41–57. Trento.

Gambari, F.M. and Colonna, G. 1988 Il bicchiere con iscrizione arcaica da Castelletto Ticino e l'adozione della scrittura nell'Italia nord-occidentale, *Studi Etrusci* 54, 119–159.

Gardner, E. 1886 The Inscriptions, in W.M.F. Petrie *Excavations at Naucratis,* 54–63, I. London.

Garrido, J.P. and Ortega, J. 1995 A propósito de unos recientes hallazgos cerámicos griegos arcaicos y orientalizantes en Huelva, *Huelva Arqueológica 13–1,* 51–66.

Gori, B. and Pierini, T. 2001 *La ceramica comune II. Ceramica comune di argila figulina (Gravisca. Scavi nel santuario greco, 12, 2).* Bari.

Gorrochategui, J. 1991 Descripción y posición lingüística del Celtibérico, *L. Mitxelena magistri sacrum,* 3–32. San Sebastián.

Green, M.J. 1992 *Dictionary of Celtic Mythology and Legend.* London.

HAE 1965: Hispania Antiqua Epigraphica 12–16 (1961–1965). Madrid.

Havenfield, F. 1913 Hibernia, *Real-Encyclopädie der Classischen Artertumswissenschaft* 8, 1388–1392. Stuttgart.

Hawkes, C. 1973 'Cumulative Celticity' in Pre-Roman Britain, *Études Celtiques* 13, 2, 607–628.

Holder, A. 1904 *Alt-Celtischer Sprachschatz.* Leipzig.

Hoz, J. de 1988 Hispano-Celtic and Celtiberian, *First North American Congress of Celtic Studies,* 191–207. Ottawa.

Hoz, J. de 1992 The Celts of the Iberian Peninsula, *Zeitschrift für celtische Philologie* 45, 1–37.

Hoz, Mª.P. de 1997 Epigrafía griega en Hispania, *Epigraphica* 69, 29–96.

James, S. 1999 *The Atlantic Celts. Ancient People or Modern Invention?* London.

Jeffery, L.H. 1961 *The Local Scripts of Archaic Greece.* Oxford (1990, 2nd ed.).

Johnston, A. 1978 *Pottery from Naucratis.* London.

Johnston, A. 2000 Greek and Latin Inscriptions. In A. Johnston, and M. Pandolfini, *Le iscrizioni (Gravisca. Scavi nel santuario greco, 15),* 11–66. Bari.

Knight, K. (ed.) 1999 Cormac MacCuilenam, *Catholic Encyclopaedia (1905).* Online Edition Copyright © 1999 Kevin Knight.

Kruta, V. 2000 *Les celtes. Histoire et dictionaire.* Paris.

Kyrieleis, H. 1981 *Führer durch das Heraion vom Samos.* Athens.

Lejeune, M. 1971 *Lepontica.* Paris.

Lejeune, M. 1973 La grande inscription celtibère de Botorrita (Saragosse), *Comptes Rendues des séances de l'Académie des inscriptions et belles-lettres,* 622–647.

Lenerz–de Wilde, M. 1991 *Iberia Celtica.* Stuttgart.

Lenerz–de Wilde, M. 2001 Los Celtas en Celtiberia, *Zephyrus* 53–54, 323–351.

Le Roux, F. and Guyonvarc'h, Chr.-J. 1983 *Mórrígan-Bodb-Macha, la souveraineté guerrière de l'Irelande.* Celticum 25. Rennes.

Macalister, R.A.S. 1941 *Lebor Gabḟla frenn: The Book of the Taking of Ireland,* 4. London.

Mangas, J. and Plácido, D. (eds) 1994 *Avieno. Testimonia Hispaniae Antiquae I.* Madrid.

Marco, F. 1994 La religión indígena en la Hispania indoeuropea, *Historia de las religiones de la Europa antigua,* 313–400. Madrid.

Marco, F. 1998 Texto e imagen, ethos y creencias en la Hispania indoeuropea de época republicana. In J. Mangas (ed.) *Italia Hispania en la crisis de la república Romana,* 387–402. Madrid.

Meid, W. 1993 *Die erste Botorrita-Inschrift. Interpretation eines keltiberischen Sprachdenkmals* Innsbrucker Beiträge zur Sprachwissenschaft 76. Innsbruck.

Menéndez Pelayo, M. 1911 *Historia de los heterodoxos españoles²,* I. Madrid (1880).

Meyer, K. 1912 *Anecdota from Irish Manuscripts,* IV. Halle-Dublin.

Mielentz, F. 1936 s. v. Netos (Neton), *Real-Encyclopädie der Classischen Altertumwissenschaft* 17, 1, 146–147. Stuttgart.

Moneo, T. 2003 *Religio Iberica (Bibliotheca Praehistorica Hispana 20).* Madrid.

Negbi, O. 1976 *Cannanite Gods in Metal.* Tel Aviv.

O'Donovan, J. 1868 *Sanas Chormaic: Cormac's Glossary* (Translation edited by W. Stokes). Calcutta.

Ó hÓgáin, D. 2002 *The Celts. A History.* Woodbridge.

Olivares, J.C. 2002 *Los dioses de la Hispania Céltica,* Bibliotheca Archaeologica Hispana 15. Madrid.

Olmos, R. 1985 Lectura e interpretación de la inscripción, *Lucentum* 4, 109–112.

Orel, V. 1995 Notes on the inscription of Botorrita, *Studia Celtica* 29, 301–304.

Ortega, J. 1999 Poblamiento y población en la *Onuba* prerromana, *Complutum* 10, 267–277.

Palomar, M. 1957 *La onomástica personal pre-latina de la antigua Lusitania.* Salamanca.

Petrie, W.M.F. 1886 *Excavations at Naucratis,* I. London.

Pokorny, J. 1953 *Keltologie.* Bern.

Pokorny, J. 1959: *Indogermanisches etymologisches Wörterbuch,* Bern-München.

Prosdocimi, A.L. 1987 Celti in Italia prima e dopo il V secolo a.C., *Celti e etrusci ell' Italia cento-settentrionale dal V secolo a.C. alla romanizzazione,* 561–581. Bologna.

Prosdocimi, A.L. 1990 Insegnamento e apprendimento della scrittura nell'Italia antica. In M. Pandolfini, and A.L. Prosdocimi (eds) *Alfabetari e insegnamento della scrittura in Etruria e nell'Italia antica,* 9–56. Firenze.

Prosdocimi, A.L. 1991 Note sul celtico in Italia, *Studi etrusci* 57, 139–177.

Rix, H. (ed.) 1998 *Lexikon der indogermanischen Verben. Die Wurzeln und ihre Primärstammbildungen.* Wiesbaden.

Roca, G. and Binaghi, M.A. 1999 Sesto Cálende (VA), Loc. Presualdo, *Studi etrusci* 63, 437–447.

Rodríguez Adrados, F. 1976 Aportaciones a la interpretación del bronce de Botorrita, *Actas del I Coloquio sobre Lenguas y Culturas Prerromanas de la Peninsula Ibérica, Salamanca 1974,* 25–47. Salamanca.

Ross, A. 1967 *Pagan Celtic Britain: Studies in Iconography and Tradition.* London.

Ruiz-Gálvez, M. 1995 *Ritos de paso y puntos de paso. La Ría de Huelva en el mundo del Bronce Final Europeo (Complutum Extra 5).* Madrid.

Ruiz-Gálvez, M. 1998 *La Europa Atlántica de la Edad del Bronce.* Barcelona.

Ruiz-Zapatero, G. and Lorrio, A. 1999 Las raices prehistóricas del mundo celtibérico. In J.A. Arenas and Mª.V. Palacios (eds) *El origen del mundo celtibérico*, 191–211. Molina de Aragón.

Sangmeister, E. 1960 Die Kelten in Spanien, *Madrider Mitteilungen* **1**, 75–100.

Schmidt, K.H. 1995 Zur historisch-sprachvergleichenden Analyse des keltiberischen/hispanokeltischen Lexikons, *Veleia* 12, 235–241.

Scholz, U.W. 1979 *Studien zum altitalischen und altrömischen Marskult und Marsmythos.* Heidelberg.

Schulten, A. 1945 *Tartessos*². Madrid.

Schulten, A. 1955 *Avieno, Ora Maritima*². Barcelona.

Seeden, H. 1980 *The Standing Armed Figurines in the Levant.* Munich.

SEG 1989 *Supplementum epigraphicum Graecum* XXXVI–1986. Amsterdam.

Sergent, B. 1995 *Lug et Apollon.* Bruxelles.

Siles, J. 1985 *Léxico de inscripciones ibéricas.* Madrid.

Sjoestedt, M.-L. 1982 *Gods and Heroes of the Celts.* Berkeley.

Solinas, P. 1995 Il celtico in Italia, *Studi Etrusci* **60**, 311–408.

Stokes, W. (ed.) 1859 Irish Glosses, edited by a Member of the Council, from a Manuscript in the Library of Trinity College, Dublin, *Transactions of the Philological Society* 1859, 168–215.

Stokes, W. (ed.) 1862 *Three Irish Glossaries.* London.

Tiverios, M.A. 1998 Hallazgos tartésicos en el Hereo de Samos, *Los Griegos en España. Tras las huellas de Heracles*, 66–84. Madrid.

Torelli, M. 1977 Il santuario greco di Gravisca, *La Parola del Passato* 1977, 398–458.

Tovar, A. 1976 *Iberische Landeskunde* II, 2. Baden-Baden.

Untermann, J. 1987 Lusitanisch, Keltiberisch, Keltisch, *IV Coloquio sobre Lenguas y Culturas Preromanas.* 57–76. Vitoria.

Untermann, J. 1990 *Die iberischen Inschriften aus Spanien, 1 and 2*, Monumenta Linguarum Hispanicarum III. Wiesbaden.

Untermann, J. 1997 *Die tartessischen, keltiberischen und lusitanischen Inschriften.* Monumenta Linguarum Hispanicarum IV. Wiesbaden.

Untermann, J. 1998 Comentario sobre una lámina de plomo con inscripción ibérica de la colección D. Ricardo Marsal, Madrid, *Habis* **29**, 7–22.

Untermann, J. 2001 Algunas novedades sobre la lengua de los plomos ibéricos, *VIII Coloquio Internacional de Lenguas y Culturas Prerromanas, Salamanca 1999*, 613–627. Salamanca.

Velaza, J. 2001 Chronica Epigraphica Iberica II: Novedades y revisiones de Epigrafía Ibérica (1995–1999), *Actas VIII Coloquio Internacional de Lenguas y Culturas Prerromanas, Salamanca 1999*, 639–662. Salamanca.

Vendryes, J. 1959 *Lexique étymologique de l'Irlandais ancien*, I–II. Dublin-Paris.

Villar, F. 1989 Tratamiento de -o- en sílaba final. Algunas posibles formas de imperativo en] celtibérico, *Veleia* **6**, 199–205.

Voigländer, W. 1982 Funde aus der Insula westlich des Buleuterion in Milet, *Istambuler Mitteilungen* **32**, 30–173.

Wachter, R. 2001 *Non-Attic Greek Vase Inscriptions.* Oxford.

Waddell, J. 1995 Celts, Ceticisation and the Bronze Age. In J. Waddell and E. Shee Twohig (eds) *Ireland in the Bronze Age*, 158–169. Stationery Office, Dublin.

Williams, D. 1983 Aegina. Aphaia-Tempel, V. The Pottery from Chios, *Archäologischer Anzeiger*, 155–186.

Wodtko, D.S. 2000 *Wörterbuch der keltiberischen Inschriften*, Monumenta Linguarum Hispanicarum V, 1. Wiesbaden.

24. Venus arising

Barry Cunliffe

Where better to begin this brief tribute to George Eogan than at Brugh na Bóinne where, for the last four decades, he has been patiently dissecting the remarkable mound of Knowth and presenting to us the story of the monument as part of the *longue durée* of Irish history. As George has so often reminded us, Knowth is only one element in a rich and complex landscape – a single location in a

great theatre that has staged five thousand years of drama – and to begin to appreciate the full story we must embrace the whole landscape. He will not mind therefore if I begin this little side action, not at Knowth itself but at its near neighbour New Grange, and if we come in quite late on in the action.

Long after the origins and purpose of New Grange had

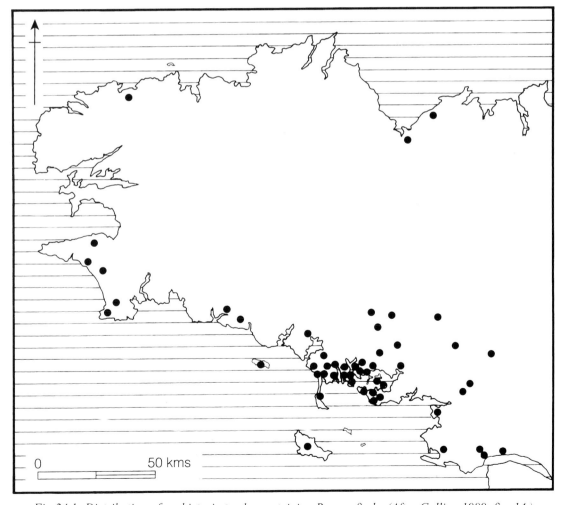

Fig 24.1: Distribution of prehistoric tombs containing Roman finds. (After Galliou 1989, fig. 14.)

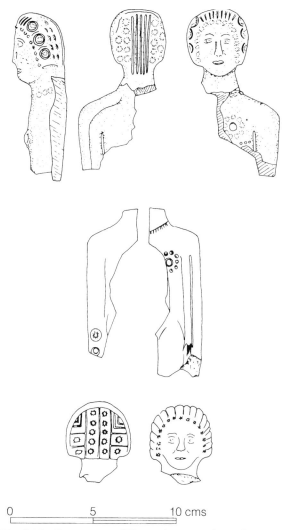

0   5   10 cms

Fig 24.2: Fragments of Venus figurines from the passage grave of Le Petit Mont, Arzon, Morbihan. (After Lecornec 1994, figs 63 and 66.)

of which 25 can be listed (Carson and O'Kelly 1967). Taken together the collection spans the period from the first to fifth centuries AD but this does not, of course, mean that deposition was necessarily as extended since votive deposits may include heirlooms. The processes by which these items found their way to New Grange are beyond recovery but that such an unusual collection should be found in close proximity to the monument is a sign of the very special part it must have played in the belief systems of the time – it was clearly a place of exceptional sanctity and the British origin of so much of the material offered to the gods might argue that it was a focus of pilgrimage for devotees from across the sea. These are fascinating issues but to go further would be to enter the realms of speculation.

The broad theme of the continuing sanctity of Neolithic monuments and their reincorporation into the belief systems of succeeding generations has often been addressed in the past, most recently, with regard to Britain and Brittany, by Ken Dark (Dark 1993) and Richard Bradley (Bradley 2000). Both writers have stressed that there is ample evidence for the reuse of megalithic monuments for ritual purposes in the Roman period. It is this theme that I would like to explore in a little more detail in the context of one of the other great megalithic landscapes of Europe – the Morbihan.

The issue is most vividly focused by a map, showing the distribution of prehistoric tombs containing Roman small finds, published by Patrick Galliou (Galliou 1989, fig. 14) and reproduced here as Fig 24.1. The concentration of this practice on the Morbihan is self-evident, and while it might be argued that the distribution may be skewed by the large number of megalithic monuments occurring in the area, even so the percentage of the tombs containing Roman material is remarkable. This must reflect a strong but very localized belief system centring on the Morbihan – a belief which regarded the ancient tombs as places of particular veneration. As Galliou remarked, "On peut penser que la taille de ces monuments, l'obscurité et le mystère de leurs entrailles, suffisaient à créer une atmosphère propice aux pratiques magiques ou funéraires" (Galliou 1989, 31). Yes, but why particularly in this very circumscribed region? We will return to this intriguing question later.

Much of the evidence for the reuse of monuments in the Roman period comes from old excavations and is not particularly well published but the recent thorough presentation of the results of excavation and restoration of the passage grave of Le Petit Mont, Arzon, Morbihan (Lecornec 1994) provides a well-documented example of reuse. Le Petit Mont occupies a commanding position on a promontory of gneiss overlooking the narrow approach from the open sea, the Baie de Quiberon, to an enclosed sea, the Mor-Bihan: it is a location visible for miles around. Excavations over the years have produced a considerable quantity of Late Iron Age and Roman material from the passage graves set within the mound,

been forgotten it acquired an honourable trail of names, accreting to it as successive generations attempted to explain its history and meaning in terms of a lively mythology deeply embedded in a distant and ill-remembered past. It was *Brug Oengusa*, the house of Oengus, son of the great god Dagda, or *Brug maic ind Óc*, the house of the 'youthful hero' (another name for Oengus). To some it was known as *Síd in Broga* reflecting its liminal function as a portal to the frightening underworld. Whatever name was used connotations of great sanctity and of the chthonic realms hovered around, ever present. It was no wonder then, that in the early centuries of the first millennium AD, New Grange seems to have become a focus of pilgrimage. For such must be the explanation of the remarkable collection of Roman objects found distributed around the outside of the tomb – items of gold including rings, bracelets and a chain, trinkets including beads, brooches and torc fragments, and a scatter of coins, mostly of the third and fourth centuries,

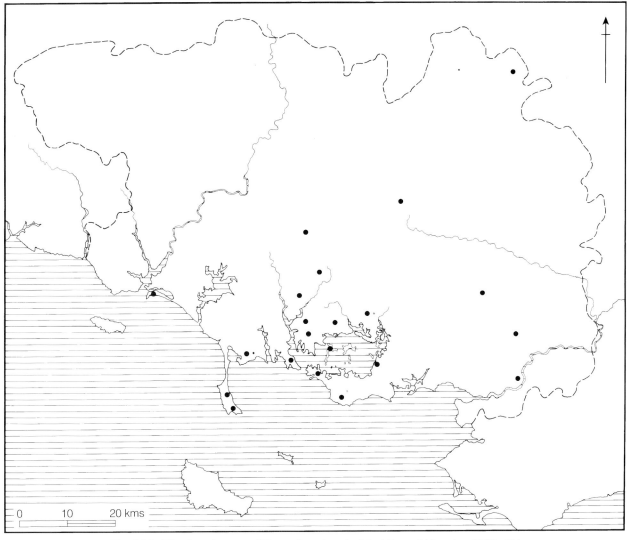

Fig 24.3: The distribution of Venus figurines in Morbihan. (After Ars 1997, 45.)

and from the immediate vicinity. Pre-conquest finds include pottery, Gaulish coins and glass beads while the Roman period is represented by pottery, coins, a large number of pipe-clay Venus figurines and an inscribed altar. The altar is not particularly informative, since the inscription is very weathered, but it records that the unknown suppliant, "son of Quintus Sabinus, willingly and deservedly fulfilled his vow". To which deity the vow was made is not recorded but the Venus figurines are an eloquent indication that the native deity was likely to be a chthonic goddess whose attributes may have approximated to those of the Roman goddess. Between 62 and 66 individual *ex votos* were represented in the collection recovered in the recent work (Fig 24.2).

Venus figurines are surprisingly common in the southern part of the Département of Morbihan centring in a tight cluster around Mor-Bihan where some 28 separate findspots have been identified (Ars 1997, 45) (Fig 24.3). The most frequent locations are in megalithic monuments but some were found in caves and natural crevices and a

few come from settlement sites. One large collection, of some 144 examples, was also recovered from a marsh at Kerloquet, Carnac. Clearly, the depositions were mostly made at locations, natural or manmade, that could be considered to provide access to the underworld. If this were the attraction of these sites then it is easy to see why the inhabitants of the region, in the Gallo-Roman period, were particularly drawn to megalithic monuments. Redolent of the past, and no doubt enmeshed in myths and legends, these prominent old monuments might present themselves as gateways to the underworld. They would have occupied the same position in local popular belief as did the Síd mounds in the folklore of the Irish countryside.

Surveys of the reuse of megalithic monuments in the Gallo-Roman period (André 1961; Lecornec 2001) list some 10 megalithic tombs producing Roman material in the southern part of Morbihan alone:

Petit Mont, Arzon
Toulvern, Baden

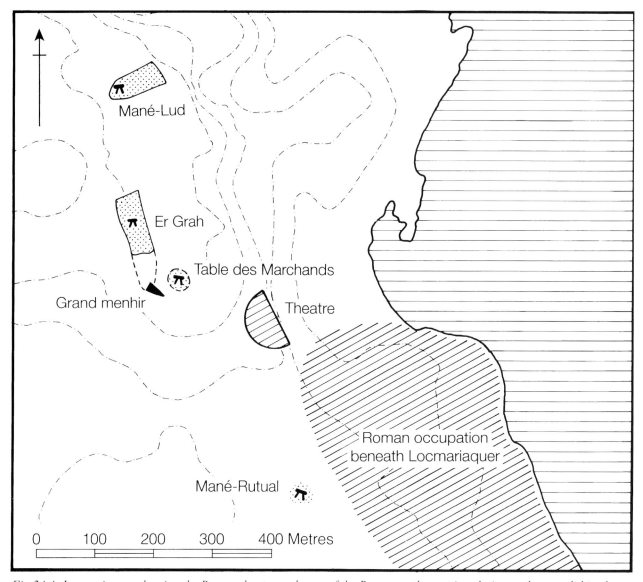

Fig 24.4: Locmariaquer showing the Roman theatre and area of the Roman settlement in relation to the megalithic cluster of famous megalithic monuments.

Lanester, Baden
Mané Ritual, Locmariaquer
Mané Hröeck, Locmariaquer
Table des Marchands, Locmariaquer
Le Net, Saint Gildas de Rhuys
Clos er Bé, Saint Gildas de Rhys
Er Roch, Le Trinite sur Mer
Crucuny, Carnac.

Seven produced Venus figurines. Of the other three, Er Roch yielded only a coin while Mané Hröeck and Table des Marchands produced Roman material including roof tiles but apparently from the body of the mounds.

Thus, not only does Roman reuse of megaliths concentrate in southern Morbihan but so too does the distribution of Venus figurines *and* the occurrence of these *ex votos* within reused tombs. These coincidences need explanation. Could it be that the Mor-Bihan or some

particular location around its shores was believed to be endowed with particular sanctity? At the very least it would seem that the region was one where the chthonic deities were believed to be particularly accessible through liminal places represented by megalithic passages, caves and marshes.

The search for a possible religious focus in the Roman period need go no further than the famous cluster of great megalithic monuments at Locmariaquer – Mané Lud, Er Grah, Le Grand menhir, Table des Marchands and Mané Rutual – for in the very centre of the cluster the Romans had built a monumental theatre. The theatre, with a façade of some 80m, was set back into the flank of the ridge upon which the main megalithic monuments lay and faced northeast to a small embayment 50m or so away (Fig 24.4). It was partly excavated at the end of the nineteenth century (de Closmadeuc 1893) but is now largely occu-

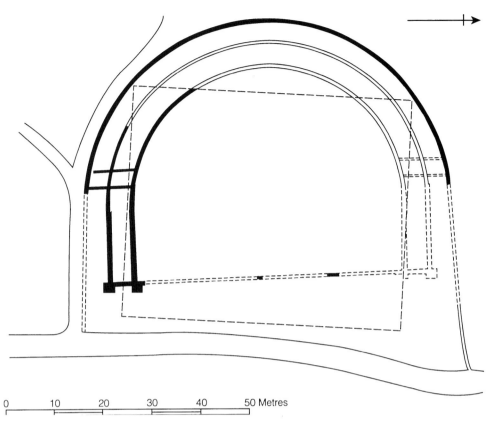

Fig 24.5: The Roman theatre at Locmariaquer based on the plan of de Closmadeuc 1893. The rectangle in broken line is the boundary of the cemetery.

pied by a municipal cemetery (Fig 24.5). Other Roman remains recorded from time to time, now largely beneath the village of Locmariaquer immediately to the southeast of the theatre, include a temple near the chapel of Saint-Michel and possibly another temple with ionic columns not far away. There are also records of a substantial bathing establishment and of other buildings (Merlat 1951; Marsille 1972; Galliou 1983, 82–3; Langouët 2002, 92–3, fig. 8). It is also likely that the Roman aqueduct that crosses the river Auray between the promontory of Kerisper and Rosnarho, about 7km to the north, was designed to serve the baths at Locmariaquer (André and Bougis 1992).

The exact nature of the Roman settlement at Locmariaquer is difficult to define with any degree of certainty in the absence of adequate publication of the early discoveries. It has generally been regarded to be a small town yet the imposing theatre, the temples and baths are highly reminiscent of a major rural sanctuary and one of sufficient status to attract pilgrims. The location of such an establishment in the midst of a cluster of megalithic monuments and immediately next to the unique Grand menhir brisé which, when intact, might have stood to a height of 20m, is hardly likely to have been an accident. Here, surely, we are seeing a resurgence of new religious interest in the heart of a sacred landscape. Monu-

mentalized for the first time in the Neolithic period, four thousand years later it was fitted out again in a manner appropriate to allow those who were drawn to the same landscape to worship the deities of the place though now in a more contrived architectural setting.

But were the Gallo-Roman suppliants *continuing* a tradition of religious observance or *reinventing* one in an ancient landscape setting? What of those millennia in between? Can they be bridged? It is certainly the case that Iron Age stelae, particularly the low hemispherical variety, cluster densely in the coastal region around Mor-Bihan, and the estuaries of the Auray and Etel (Tanguy 1997; Lecornec 1999) but then there are clusters of similar densities in other parts of Brittany especially in western Finistère. Nor need there be any direct relationship between the kind of belief system of which the stelae are a part and the chthonic beliefs which lie behind the reuse of megaliths and caves.

Another approach would be to see how far back in time the reuse of megalithic tombs can be traced in the region. Here again Le Petit Mont provides some useful evidence. Among the finds recovered are Gallic coins, glass beads and a glass bracelet fragment, and sherds of pottery all belonging to the first century BC and probably of pre-conquest origin. At the very least these items suggest Late Iron Age interest in the site and the significant number of coins (more than eight) would be consistent with ritual observance. The site has also produced a few sherds of Late Bronze Age date implying periodic if not continuous activity in the more distant past. On this evidence it is reasonable to suppose that ritual reuse of at least some of the megaliths in southern Morbihan was under way by *c.* 100 BC and the beliefs involved were not, therefore, a Roman introduction. Of ritual use before this there is no convincing trace.

How the native deity or deities were envisaged it is impossible to say except that the context of the ritual activity suggests that they were chthonic and the Venus figurines that they were perceived to be female. While there is no reason to suppose that the indigenous deities shared the attributes of the strictly Classical Venus, the issue is worth exploring.

In Classical mythology Venus is presented in many guises and in early inscriptions often appears conflated with other deities. In such cases the other deity is the dominant power with the name of Venus being used in the context of the one who facilitates the favour or indulgence of the other. One of these conflations, Venus Kerria, is of particular interest for she embodies Ceres, the goddess who presides over the growing corn and ensures its fertility and abundance. Ceres is also to be identified with the Greek goddess Demeter about whom there is a rich mythology deeply embedded in Indo-European tradition. One central part of the Demeter myth provides an explanation to embrace the seasons and the fertility of the crops. In summary, Demeter's daughter Persephone is lured down into the underworld by Pluton, ruler of the dead, but, as the result of a cleverly negotiated deal, is allowed to return to our world each year when the fields are ploughed and to remain until the crops are sown after which she has to return to the underworld. It was a simple but powerful story designed to explain the seasons – while the crops were in a liminal state, growing in the soil, Persephone was also in the chthonic realms. To ensure Persephone's annual return and the well-being of the cycle it was necessary to make propitiatory offerings.

In some such belief system may lie the reason why Venus *ex votos* and other items were placed in the passage graves and caves of the Morbihan, for those were the places where access to the underworld was to be gained. If these speculations are correct the Roman sanctuary at Locmariaquer may have been the centre of an agrarian fertility cult. One day, perhaps, inscriptions or statuary may be found to throw some light on the issue.

But to return to the question left unanswered – continuity or reinvention? The honest answer is, of course, we cannot tell. There is no need to suppose that some

continuous thread of belief directly linked the ancestral monuments of the Neolithic period with the fertility practices of the Gallo-Roman world. It is possible – but equally it could have been that later generations were simply intent to harness the mystery and power they perceived these ancient structures to have in pursuit of their new imperative.

Similar questions also surround that other monumentalized landscape with which we began – the Brugh na Bóinne. What was it that drew the pilgrims to New Grange and what belief encouraged the local élite to establish themselves on Knowth? Folk memory of sanctity and the legitimizing power of place no doubt played a part – but how much more there is to learn of this intriguing place. Clearly, it is to the broader theatre of the landscape that research must now turn.

Bibliography

André, J. 1961 Les dolmens morbihannais remployés à l'epoque romaine, *Ogam* **74–75**, 248–54.

André, P. and Bougis, F. 1992 Le pont-aqueduc romain de Kerisper-Rosnarho (Morbihan), *Bulletin de la Société Polymathique du Morbihan* **118**, 143–55.

Ars, E. 1997 Les figurines gallo-romains en terre cuite du Morbihan, *Bulletin de la Société Polymathique du Morbihan* **123**, 41–54.

Bradley, R. 2000 Vera Collum and the excavation of a 'Roman' megalithic tomb, *Antiquity* **74**, 39–43.

Carson, R.A.G. and O'Kelly, C. 1967 A catalogue of the Roman coins from Newgrange, Co. Meath and notes on the coins and related finds, *Proceedings of the Royal Irish Academy* **77**C, 35–55.

Dark, K.R. 1993 Roman-period activity at prehistoric ritual monuments in Britain and in the Armorican Peninsula. In E. Scott (ed.) *Theoretical Roman Archaeology: First Conference Proceedings*, 133–46. Aldershot.

De Closmadeuc, G. 1893 Théâtre romain de Locmariaquer, *Bulletin de la Société Polymathique du Morbihan,* For 1893, 181–92.

Galliou, P. 1983 *L'Armorique romaine*. Braspars.

Galliou, P. 1989 *Les tombes romaines d'Armorique*. Documents d'Archéologie Française 17, Paris.

Langouët, L. 2002 Principaux sites portuaires de l'Armorique gallo-romaine, *Les Dossiers du Ce. R.A.A.* **30**, 87–111.

Lecornec, J. 1994 *Le Petit Mont, Arzon, Morbihan*. Dossiers archéologique de l'Ouest, R.A.O., Rennes.

Lecornec, J. 1999 *Les steles de l'Age du Fer dans Le Morbihan. L'arrondissement de Vannes*. Rennes.

Lecornec, J. 2001 Réutilisation des monuments mégalithique a l'époque gallo-romaine. In Le Roux, C.-T. (ed.) *Du monde de chasseurs a celui des metallurgists*, 289–94. Revue Archéologique de l'Ouest, Supplément **9**, Rennes.

Marsille, L. 1972 *Répertoire archéologique du sites Morbihan gallo-romain. Société Polymathique du Morbihan*.Vannes.

Merlat, P. 1951 Cronique, *Gallia* **9**, 85–6.

Tanguy, D. 1997 *Les steles de l'Age du Fer dans Le Morbihan. Les arrondissements de Lorient et Pontivy*. Rennes.

25. International weight units and the coming of the Age of Iron in Europe

Jan Bouzek

The identity of weight units of the Bronze Age period in large parts of Europe has been widely studied in recent years, and their existence can hardly be doubted any longer. New finds and the identification of oxhide ingots have extended the area of distribution of this type, and the progress of study of ancient religions has made it even more probable than supposed earlier that the mythological and religious connotations of metals and their melting shared common traits in many parts of the world.

Metallurgy

Our perception of Copper and Bronze Age metallurgy in southeast Europe has changed extensively during the last thirty years, as has the picture of a similar development in Turkey and in Mesopotamia.

Native copper started to be used in southeast Turkey and in Mesopotamia in the 7th millennium BC and casting was developed there in the early 6th millennium BC. But some copper is known from the Early Neolithic in southeast Turkey, and its technology probably spread westwards from there. The first copper objects in southeast Europe date from the late 6th millennium BC, while the copper mining known from Rudna Glava and Ajbunar dates from the 2nd quarter of the 5th millennium BC.

The dispersal of tin-bronze technology from the southeast, where it had already started in early 4th millennium BC, over Anatolia and the Aegean (late 4th millennium), the southeast Balkans (25th century BC), to Central Europe (20th century BC), was rather slow. In the British Isles tin-bronze was also known roughly at the same time as in southeast Europe, probably due to the occurrence of tin ores there (cf. Pare 2000, 1–8; Nikolova, 2000). The basic conclusion is that the slow dispersal of copper and bronze technologies can be understood in the context of diffusion from its first Near Eastern centres.

Alloys other than tin were less deliberate. Arsenic, antimon and lead were sometimes used in the Near East in the 4th millennium, while a collapse of production at the end of the 4th millennium BC was marked by a return to arsenical bronze in the southeast; Central Europe was only slightly affected by the latter process.

It is no longer necessary to stress the "autonomy of the Balkan Copper Age" in the same way as C. Renfrew did in the sixties. This is a fate similar to his study of Wessex without Mycenae (Renfrew 1969, 1968). The basic chronological framework is now safe, and we are able to return to a more balanced system, which makes better sense in the context of mutual relations between the various regions (Bouzek 1995). This, however, does not mean that the Balkan peoples were less able to produce sophisticated copper and bronze objects: the opposite is true. They certainly possessed enough ideas of their own in these respects, and also enough resources to produce many elegant items. First, as could be expected, the technique was transmitted without the specific vocabulary. Only later the vocabulary became common to larger areas, as known already noted by Deshayes (1960; cf. Bouzek 1985, 21–27).

Already in the third and early 2nd millennia BC it is possible to recognise a general *koine* of bronze objects of the so-called circumpontic production centre as defined by Chernych (1977), and large parts of Europe show phenomena inspired by Aegean bronze and gold working. Similarly, close interrelationships are known in the early 2nd millennium: the shapes of bronze objects, the vehicles with spoked wheels (with which the Hyksos people and the Mycenaeans celebrated their military successes), were well-known at the same time as far as Arkaim in western Siberia.

Oxhide ingots and other shapes, weights

New finds of bronze ingots, shaped like oxhides, from northeast Bulgaria (two now exhibited in the Varna museum, a third in a private collection in the area) confirm the trade links between the Black Sea and the Mediterranean. A fragment of another oxhide ingot has been identified in a hoard found at Oberwilflingen in Suebia (Primas - Pernicka 1998; add all to the distribution maps of Gale 1991 and Bouzek 1985). Their number is

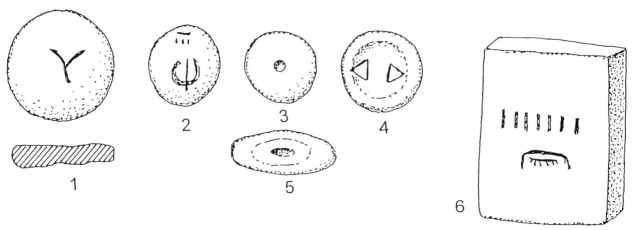

Fig 25.1: Aegean and Near Eastern weights 1 Akrotiri, 2 and 5 Knosos, 3–4 Kea, 6 Egypt. XIIth dynasty. 1–2 and 6 after Michailidou 2001a, 3–5 after Petruso 1992. Drawing A. Waldhauserová.

significantly increased in Sardinia, with 26 new sites, distributed all over the island. It seems that all of them came from one specific mining area in Cyprus (Lo Schiavo 2001, 139–141), while other centres in Sardinia and Europe preferred other shapes of ingots: mainly the round and rectangular 'cakes'.

In Sardinia, the copper plano-convex ingots are of local Sardinian copper (Lo Schiavo 2001, 140). There are also other standard shapes of cast bronze objects known from many parts of Europe: this shows that the "trade" in metals had some general rules that were accepted over large territories.

A detailed survey of the metals in the Aegean and in the Near East has recently been carried out by A. Michailidou (2001a; 2001b) and in the conference volume edited by Pare (2001). In all these areas, metal was costly and was measured and weighed carefully. This involved all metals known during the Bronze Age – bronze, gold and silver. Large amounts of metal were generally in state or public possession (royalty, temples, holders of higher administrative positions) but less valuable amounts possessed by private individuals (and sometimes larger quantities owned by tradesmen) were also the subject of inheritance, of sale and of other transformations of ownership. Generally, there is a close resemblance between the situation in the Near East and in the Aegean in the distribution system of metals (cf. also Gillis *et al.* 1996). In prehistoric Europe, the system also worked as a kind of exchange-redistribution pattern, accepted in large territories and enabling access to metal even by small village units in all Bronze Age European 'cultures'.

Weights were of bronze, lead or stone. They were of various shapes and also of different materials in different parts of the Mediterranean and of temperate Europe (Figs 1–2, cf. especially the series from the Uluburun shipwreck [Pulak 2000], and those from Kea, [Petruso 1992, Pare 1999, Ruiz Galvez 2001], and with the Italian weights [Cardarelii *et al.* 2001; Peroni 2001; Bossi 2001; Cattani 2001; Maggiani 2001]). Small balances are known not

only from the Eastern Mediterranean, but from several parts of central Europe as well (especially Pare 1999, with examples illustrated). Shapes of weights were not identical, even in the Near East and in the Aegean, and they were of different materials (Fig 25.1). A group of stone weights is known from Bronze Age Italy (Fig 25.2), while most of the weights known from Central and Western Europe are of bronze (Fig 25.3). Balances of the type referred to here are known from all parts of the world, and scale-beams even from prehistoric Europe (Fig 25.4). While the ideas behind weighing and weight units were common property, the shapes of weights show local varieties.

Weight units

The Aegean weight units have been studied for many years and are generally well known (cf. especially Michailidou 2001; Ruiz Gálvez 2000). For small weight units in the Aegean there are two main calculations. Petruso (1978) came to 61.5g and Parise to 65.27g (Ruiz Gálvez 2000). The main Aegean sub-unit was probably 6.7g, (between 6.5 and 6.8g); the system was binary.

J. Eiwanger (1989, 449) in his analysis came to two possible weights for the talent in prehistoric Europe. One was calculated from the hoard of Féregyháza in Hungary (31,439.7g), and another from the Eberswalde hoard (31,437.3g). Both are reasonably similar to the Aegean talent, and the differences between these two are very small. The standard measures are especially typical for gold hoards. He takes the small unit, known from many parts of Europe, as 55.21g. For the bronze objects he sees the standard unit *c.* 12 and 17g (*op cit.*, 462). The calculations of Bronze Age weight units in large parts of Europe show that these areas used the Mycenaean weight units for weighing metals. Malmer (1983) had also 26.6g as a quarter unit, 107.07 as the basic unit. Pare (1999) calculates with 12.2g, that is 1/5 of the Mycenaean unit

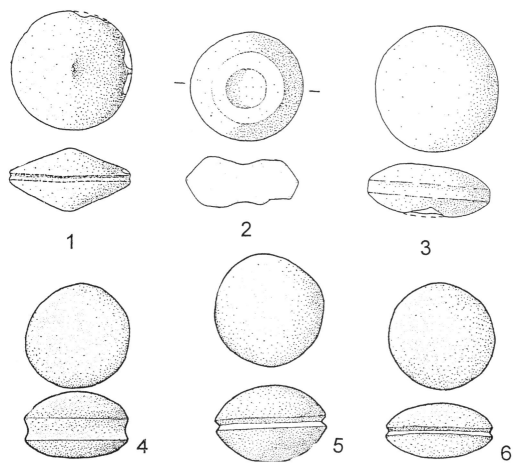

Fig 25.2: Italic stone weight types. 1–3 Frattesina, 4 Scandiano, 5 Gazzado, 6 Montale, after Cardarelli et al. 2001. Drawing A. Waldhauserová. Scale 1:2.

of 61g. 24.4g is 1/20 of 4,888g. For Bronze Age D the usual units were 6.9g and 31g, and for the final Bronze Age the unit as far as known was *c.* 27g. Peroni (2001) calculates the main weight unit as *c.* 26g, a second as 62–63g; multiplications and fractions of these values also existed. Even if there are small differences in present calculations (ancient people did not measure as exactly as our modern machines), there is an apparent relationship between the Bronze Age Aegean, Italic and European systems. Cardarelli *et al.* (2001) came to a unit of *c.* 52–53g, suitably comparable with the 26g unit.

The collapse of the Mycenaean civilization around 1200 BC brought changes into the generally accepted system, and the shekel (7.9g) became the main international weight unit (Ruiz Gálvez 2000). Multiple units known are: 36–37g = 5 shekels; 79g = 10 shekels; 160g = 20 shekels; 296g = 35 shekels; 320g = 40 shekels.

Other units, and their possible relations to measuring units in Bronze Age Europe

The units of length of the ancient Near East are known from various sources. A good example is the stick of Maya, the finance minister of Tutenkhamon, in the Louvre. Its total length of 52.3cm is divided into 28 digits, each measuring 1.86cm, and further into half digits of 9.3mm and in 1/16 digits of 1.16mm. With my colleague D. Koutecký we tried to calculate the contents of some large vessels and of the storage pits (silos). The latter had apparently some relation to the size of the field for which grain destined for the sewage was stored, but also to the hollow measures for dry substances in the Mycenaean world. Many studies examined the objects also in view of their metal weight value (for example Eogan 1984 is this 1983??).

Trade partners

A two volume work published by the Römisch-Germanisches Zentralmuseum at Mainz in 1999 – *Die Eliten in der Bronzezeit* – discussed parallel developments in the elite systems of the Aegean Bronze Age and in temperate Europe. This colloquium helped to remind us of many resemblances in the systems of Bronze Age societies in these two parts of the ancient world. All areas with comparable *élites* apparently had some compatible systems of administration, of diplomatic interrelations, of distribution and redistribution of metals, even if, on a

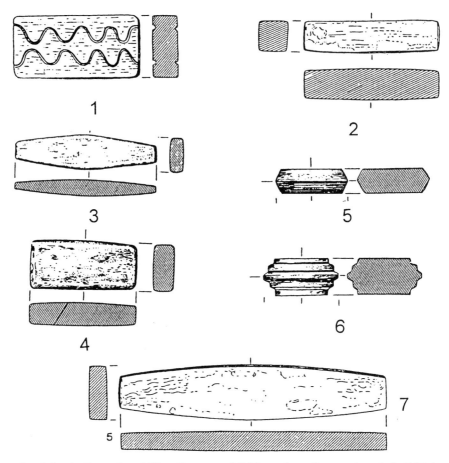

Fig 25.3: Examples of weights in Central and West European Middle to Late Bronze Age. 1–2, 7 Richemont . Pépeville, Dépt. Moselle; 3–6 Steinfurth, Wetteraukreis. After Pare 1999. Drawing A. Waldhauserová. Scale 1:1.

more primitive level in temperate Europe, the general traits of the Central European *élites* 'administration' resembled that of the Minoan and Mycenaean palace economy.

These social systems and the general way of life of these *élites* (kings-priests and their sub-leaders, priests *etc.*) were to a certain degree compatible with each other, being understandable in their basic traits by the political and economic partners even in distant areas. The common system of values in social life facilitated a large-scale 'trade' in metals, the most important raw materials for any part of the Bronze Age world (cf. Eogan 1990; 1997).

Common traits in spiritual life. Astrology and the religious significance of metals

Not only metallurgy itself, but other elements of civilisation traits also spread with metallurgy. One of these was apparently a kind of astrology, connected with observatories and calendars that established a regular rhythm to annual feasts and agricultural activities. The second was a form of artistic symbolic expression, preferring abstraction to the former Neolithic "naturalism". The latter probably also had geometric connotations

as applied in various domains: construction of houses, measurement of fields, ploughing. None of these innovations could have been introduced without some practical geometry, similar to that used for ziggurats in Mesopotamia and for pyramids in Egypt.

It is also very probable that this spread of a system of ideas and beliefs included a connection between metals, planets and their divinities: copper was connected with Astarte and Aphrodite – Venus, tin with the predecessors of Zeus – Jupiter in the ancient world. All literary sources of the ancient Near East and Egypt document that the religious and secular domains were not separated. Smelting metals was connected with some rituals and sacrifices, and the spread of metallurgy should thus be connected with a sophisticated system of thoughts and beliefs which formed the mind –set of ancient Europeans as well of their Near Eastern relatives (cf. also Hansen 1999).

The hoards were probably reused in times of necessity, but their deposition was the final phase and confirmation of a ritual, involving sacrifices to deities. Müller-Karpe (1998) has shown that Jasper's system of the structural and chronological development of civilisations can also be applied to prehistory, and many cultural elements were

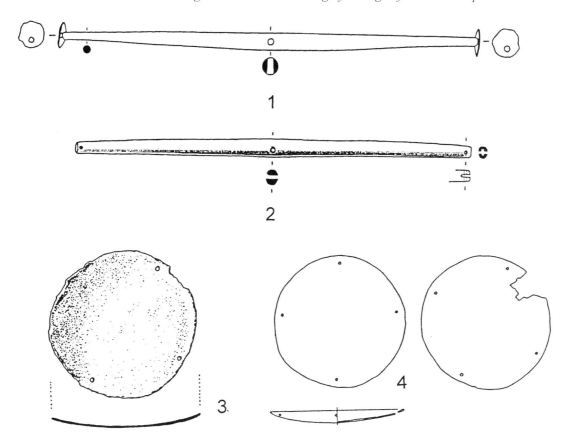

Fig 25.4: Examples of beams and dishes of balances. 1 Maolles-sur-Seine, Dépt. Seine et Marne, 2 Bordjoš, Banat (bone), 3 Susa, 4 Cyprus. After Pare 1999. Drawing A. Waldhauserová.

common to many areas. This could not be achieved without some kind of communications – perhaps prospectors, pilgrims, *etc.* Long-distance pilgrimages are described in the stories of Gilgamesh, of Abraham and Sara, *etc.*, and were apparently not unusual.

The transition from Bronze to the Early Iron Age

The process was slow, but the changes substantial. The new community turned from the king-priests to strong individuals. In the language of Hesiod, the Age of the Heroes was a transitional period between the Copper and Iron Ages. The new communities were divided into small units: the small *oikoi* of the important persons were more independent of larger communities, the Dionysiac separation of the individuals from the community brought the system of *Gefolgschaft*, arranged according to personal relationships between the leader and his followers, or relations inside his *druzhina*.

This formed a new society, the new Iron Age mind, preparing the rise of philosophy, first as a ruse of Odysseus and David. The trade and exchange network also changed substantially. By this time, the units of weight are no longer pan-European, there are substantial local differences (Maggiani 2001; Cattani 2001; Neri 20001;

Peroni 2001), but weighing systems of metals and other commodities were also indispensable, as they also were in other parts of the world (Bosi 2001).

Conclusions

A series of phenomena shows that Europe was not fully isolated from the Eastern Mediterranean and from the Near East. The units of weight of the European Middle and Late Bronze Age were common to the two areas, the astrology and the mythological teaching about metals was international, as were the shapes of the majority of metal objects, the technology of casting, of architecture and so on. There must have been some basic common understanding also in establishing long-distance relations and an attempt to understand them more properly is one of the challenges of our time.

The system of distribution of metals during the Bronze Age probably resembled more the state-directed system of the Eastern Mediterranean than the 'privatised' trade of the Early Iron Age, as was the case with Phoenicians and Greeks. The temperate zone of Europe probably underwent similar changes in the redistribution pattern in the early 1st millennium BC, as did the Mediterranean (cf. Bouzek 1997; Sherrat 1997).

Note
The preparation of the paper was supported by the grant of the Ministry of Education of the Czech Republic J13/98: 1122100004.

Bibliography

Bonfante, L. and Karageorghis, V. (eds) 2001 *Italy and Cyprus in Antiquity, 1500–1400 BC.* Proceedings of an international symposium held at the Italian Academy for Advanced Studies in America at Columbia University, November 16–18, 2000. Leventis Foundation, Nicosia.

Bosi, F. 2001 Rinvenimenti di elementi ponderali nelle culture delle steppe dell'Europa orientale. In C. Corti and N. Giordani (eds) *Pondera, Pesi i misure nell'Antichitá*, 29–32. Museo della Bilancia, Prov. Modena.

Bouzek, J. 1985 *The Aegean, Anatolia and Europe: Cultural Interrelations in the 2nd Millennium BC.* Åström, Lund – Academy of Science, Prague.

Bouzek, J. 1995 Greece and the Aegean area and its relationship with continental Europe. In *Absolute Chronology, Archaeological Europe 2500–500 B.C.*, *Acta Archaeologica Kobenhavn*, Supplementary volume I, 1996 (1997), 175–182.

Briard, J. 1987 Systèmes prémonetaires en Europe protohistorique: fiction ou réalité, in. G. Depyrot *et al.* (eds) *Rhythmes de la production monétaire d'antiquité à nos heures*, 731–743. La Neuve, Louvain.

Cardarelli, A., Pacciarelli, M. and Pallante, P. 2001 Pesi i bilance dell'etá del bronzo italiana. In C. Corti and N. Giordani (eds) *Pondera, Pesi i misure nell'Antichitá*, 33–58. Museo della Bilancia, Prov. Modena.

Cattani, M. 2001 I pesi in pietra in Etruria padana. In C. Corti and N. Giordani (eds) *Pondera, Pesi i misure nell'Antichitá*, 89–94. Museo della Bilancia, Prov. Modena.

Chernykh, E.N. 1977 Ob evropejskoj zone circumpontijskoj metalurgicheskoj provincii, *Acta Archaeologica Carpathica* 17, 29–53.

Corti, C. and Giordani, N. (eds) 2001 *Pondera, Pesi i misure nell'Antichitá.* Museo della Bilancia, Prov. Modena.

Cour-Marty, M.-A. 1990 Les poids égyptiens, de précieux jalons archéologiques, *Sociétés urbaines en Egypte et aus Sudan* (Cahiers de recherches de l'Institut de papyrologie et d'egyptologie de Lille 12), 17–55. Presses de l'Université, Lille.

Courtois, J.-C. 1983 Le trésor de poids de Kalavassos – Aghios Dimitrios 1982. In R. Gyselen (ed.) *Prix, saleries, poids et mesures,* 119–127. Res Orentales II, Paris.

Courtois, J.-C. 1990 Poids, prix, taxes et salaries à Ougarit (Syrie) au IIe millénaire. In R. Gyselen (ed.) *Prix, saleries, poids et mesures,* 119–127. Res Orentales II, Paris.

Deshayes, J. 1960 *Les outils de bronze de l'Indus au Danube*, Librairie orientale, Paul Geuthner, Paris.

Dialismas, A. 2001a Metal artefacts as recorded in the Linear B tablets. In A. Michailidou (ed.) *Manufacture and Measurement, Counting, Measuring and Recording: Craft Items from Early Aegean Societies*, 121–143. Research Centre of Greek and Roman Antiquity, National Hellenic Research Foundation, Meletemata 33, Athens.

Dialismas, A. 2001b The databases on the quantities recorded in Linear B tablets. In A. Michailidou (ed.) *Manufacture and Measurement, Counting, Measuring and Recording: Craft Items from Early Aegean Societies*, 337–349. Research Centre of Greek and Roman Antiquity, National Hellenic Research Foundation, Meletemata 33, Athens.

Eiwanger J. 1989 Talanton, Ein bz. Goldstandard zwischen Ägäis und Mitteleuropa, *Germania* 67, 443–62.

Eogan, G. 1983 *The Hoards of the Irish Later Bronze Age.* University College, Dublin.

Eogan, G. 1990 Possible connection between Britain and Ireland and the East Mediterranean region during the Bronze Age. In *Orientalisch-Ägäische Einflüsse in der Europäischen Bronzezeit*, Bonn, Römisch-Germanischen Zentralmuseums Monographien 15. Mainz.

Eogan, G. 1997 Hair-rings and European Late Bronze Age society, *Antiquity* 71, 308–320.

Gale, N. 1991 Copper Oxhide ingots, their origin and their place in the Bronze Age metal trade in the Mediterranean, in N. Gale (ed.) *Bronze Age Trade in the Mediterranean*, 197–239. SIMA 90, Jonsered.

Gillis, C., Risberg, Ch. and Sjöberg, B. (eds) 1996 *Trade and Production in Pre-monetary Greece: Acquisition and Distribution of Raw Materials and Finished Products.*Proceedings of the 6th International Workshop 1996, Jonsered (SIMA pocket-book 154).

Hänsel, B. (ed.) 1995 *Tausch und Verkehr in bronze- und früheisenzeitlicher Südosteuropa*, Prähistorische Archäologie in Südosteuropa 11. Marie Leidorf GMBH, München.

Hansen, S. 1999 Migration und Kommunikation während der späten Bronzezeit. Die Depotfunde als Quelle für ihren Nachweis, *Dacia* 40–42, 1996–98, 5–28.

Harding, A. F. 2000 *European Societies in the Bronze Age.* Cambridge University Press, Cambridge.

Lassen, H. 2000 Introduction to weight systems in the Bronze Age East Mediterranean, the case of Kalavasos – Aghios Dhimitrios. In C.F.E. Pare (ed.) *Metals Make the World Go Round. The Supply and Circulation of Metals in Bronze Age Europe*, 233–246. Oxbow, Oxford.

Lo Schiavo, F. 2001 Late Cypriot bronzework and bronzeworkers in Sardinia, Italy and elsewhere in the west. In L. Bonfante and V. Karageorghis (eds) *Italy and Cyprus in Antiquity, 1500–1400 B,* 131–152. Proceedings of an international symposium held at the Italian Academy for Advanced Studies in America at Columbia University, November 16–18, 2000. Leventis Foundation, Nicosia.

Maggiani, A. 2001 Pesi i balance in Etruria. In C. Corti and N. Giordani (eds) *Pondera, Pesi i misure nell'Antichitá*, 67–74. Museo della Bilancia, Prov. Modena.

Malmer, M. 1992 Weight systems of the Scandinavian Bronze Age, *Antiquity* 66, 377–388.

Marazzi, M., Tusa, S. and Vagnetti, L. (eds) 1986 *Traffici micenei nel Mediterraneo.* Taranto.

Michailidou, A. (ed.) 2001 *Manufacture and Measurement, Counting, Measuring and Recording: Craft Items from Early Aegean Societies.* Research Centre of Greek and Roman Antiquity, National Hellenic Research Foundation, Meletemata 33, Athens.

Michailidou, A. 2001a Script and metrology: practical processes of cognitive inventions. In A. Michailidou (ed.) *Manufacture and Measurement, Counting, Measuring and Recording: Craft Items from Early Aegean Societies*, 43–82. Research Centre of Greek and Roman Antiquity, National Hellenic Research Foundation, Meletemata 33, Athens.

Michailidou, A. 2001b Recording quantities of metal in Bronze Age societies in the Aegean and the Near East. In A. Michailidou (ed.) *Manufacture and Measurement, Counting, Measuring and Recording: Craft Items from Early Aegean Societies*, 85–119. Research Centre of Greek and Roman Antiquity, National Hellenic Research Foundation, Meletemata 33, Athens.

Müller-Karpe, H. 1998 *Grundzüge früher Menschheitsgeschichte. vol. I.* 1. Von den Anfängen bis zum 3. Jahrtausend v. Chr.; vol. 2. 2: 2. Jahrtausend v. Chr.. Darmstadt – Stuttgart.

Neri, D. 2001 I ripostigli di metallo nell'Etruria padana. In C. Corti and N. Giordani (eds) *Pondera, Pesi i misure nell'Antichitá*, 95–102. Museo della Bilancia, Prov. Modena.

Nikolova, L. (ed.) 2000 *Technology, Style and Society: contributions to the innovations between the Alps and the Black Sea in prehistory*. British Archaeological Reports International Series **409**, Oxford.

Orientalisch-ägäische Einflüsse in der europäischen Bronzezeit, conference Mainz – Bonn 1990. Römisch-Geramnisches Zentralmuseum, Mainz.

Pare, C.F.E. 1999 Weights and weighing in Bronze Age Central Europe. In *Die Eliten in der Bronzezeit,* 421–514. Römisch-Germanischen Zentralmuseums Monographien **43/2**, Mainz.

Pare, C.F.E. 2000 Bronze and the Bronze Age. In C.F.E. Pare (ed.) 2000 *Metals Make the World Go Round. The Supply and Circulation of Metals in Bronze Age Europe,* 1–38. Oxbow, Oxford.

Pare, C.F.E. (ed.) 2000 *Metals Make the World Go Round. The Supply and Circulation of Metals in Bronze Age Europe.* Oxbow, Oxford.

Parise, N.F. 1986 Unitá ponderali egee. In M. Marazzi, S. Tusa and L. Vagnetti (eds) *Traffici micenei nel Mediterraneo,* 303–314. Taranto.

Peroni, R. 2001 Sistemi ponderali nella circolazione dei metalli dell'età del bronzo europea. In C. Corti and N. Giordan (eds) *Pondera, Pesi i misure nell'Antichitá,* 21–28. Museo della Bilancia, Prov. Modena.

Petrruso, K.M. 1978a *Systems of Weights in the Bronze Age.* Univ. Microfilms, Ann Arbor.

Petrruso, K.M. 1978b Marks on some Minoan balance weights, *Kadmos* **17**, 26–42.

Petrruso, K.M. 1992 Aia Irini, The Balance Weights, *Keos VIII, Mayence, Zabern 1992* 00–00, Mainz.

Primas, M. and Pernicka, E. 1998 Der Depotfund von Ober-wilflingen. Neue Ergebnise zur Zirkulation von Metallbarren, *Germania* **76**, 25–65.

Pulak, C. 2000 The balance weights from the LBA shipwreck at Uluburum. In C.F.E. Pare (ed.) 2000 *Metals Make the World Go Round. The Supply and Circulation of Metals in Bronze Age Europe,* 247–266. Oxbow, Oxford.

Renfrew, C. 1968 Wessex without Mycenae, *Annual of the British School in Athens* **63**, 277–285.

Renfrew, C. 1969 The Autonomy of the East European Copper Age, *Proceedings of the Prehistoric Society* **35**, 12–47.

Ruiz Gálvez, M. 2000 Weight system and exchange networks in BA Europe. In C.F.E. Pare (ed.) 2000 *Metals Make the World Go Round. The Supply and Circulation of Metals in Bronze Age Europe,* 267–79. Oxbow, Oxford.

Sherrat, A. 1993 What would a Bronze Age world system look like; Relations between temperate Europe and the Mediterranean in Later Prehistory, *Journal of European Archaeology* **1**(2), 59–72.

Stoss-Gale, S. 2000 Trade in metals in the Bronze Age Mediterranean: an overview. In C.F.E. Pare (ed.) *Metals Make the World Go Round. The Supply and Circulation of Metals in Bronze Age Europe,* 56–69. Oxbow, Oxford.

26. An Enduring Tradition: Incised Rock Art in Ireland

Elizabeth Shee Twohig

Over the past forty years George Eogan's excavations at Knowth have uncovered literally hundreds of examples of megalithic art. Most of the carvings were produced by "picking" (marking the surface of the stone by a series of individual "pickmarks"), but a considerable number of "incised" carvings from the site have also been recorded and discussed (*e.g.* Eogan 1997; 1998; 1999). This paper investigates the largely neglected topic of incised art that is not part of passage tomb art (though it may be found in them) and examines carvings from a wide variety of contexts throughout Ireland. I will show that within this large and miscellaneous body of incised carvings, it is possible to identify a group of carvings that is distinct in style from both the passage tomb and cup and ring/rock art style of carvings. The acronym COMBS carvings is proposed for these incised carvings, the name being taken from the types of site in which they occur – **C**aves, **O**utcrops, **M**egaliths and **B**oulder-**S**helters. I will also discuss other examples of incised carvings that do not fit into the COMBS group.

The term incised carving is used here to describe a technique of marking stone (or other material) by a cutting action. The terms scoring or engraving have also been used for this type of carving. The marks can vary from very fine, shallow lines to ones that are quite deep. Finely incised lines are obviously more vulnerable to weathering, and are likely to survive only in protected locations, for example at the boulder-shelter of Cooleenlemane. Details of each site are given in Table 26.1. Many of the carvings on exposed rock outcrops have become obscured by lichen growth (*e.g.* Tinure (Tempest 1939) and Ballydorragh), and growths have developed also over the carvings in the cave sites (*e.g.* Knockmore Lettered Cave).

Incised carvings of the COMBS type have been recorded in Ireland from the mid nineteenth century onwards, for example by Jones (1846). Such sites were generally discussed by men who were also studying cup and ring art and/or passage tomb art, for example Eugene Conwell (1864–66), George Du Noyer (1864–5; 1866) and William Wakeman (1874–75), and the essential differences between the three types of carvings were

recognised from an early stage. W.C. Borlase (1897) brought together reports of incised carvings on megalithic tombs, using work compiled by earlier writers. Breuil included several of these carvings in a group that he believed to be the "...oldest extremely simple decorations on the Irish dolmens, menhirs or natural rocks" (Breuil 1934, 290–91). During the twentieth century, discoveries of individual examples of incised carvings were published from time to time. Finola Finlay's (1973) useful list of sites remains unpublished, and in 1981 I discussed a number of examples of incised designs associated with megalithic tombs (Shee Twohig 1981, 234–5).

The COMBS type of incised carving is always abstract and geometric, averaging 10–15cm in maximum dimensions, and comprises principally the following designs (Fig 26.1):
- single straight lines
- groups of parallel lines
- grids
- lines crossed by one or more lines, usually at right angles
- radials, some with one line elongated to form a "windmill"
- squares, rectangles or lozenges with the diagonals joined
  (aka framed crosses)
- three-line arrows
- circles/arcs (rare)
- dots

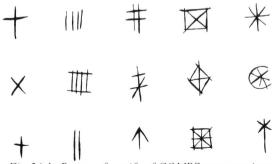

Fig 26.1: Range of motifs of COMBS type carvings

County	Site	Type	Details	Reference
Cavan N626815	Ballydorragh (Ryefield)	outcrop	lines, crosses, + in lozenge	Du Noyer (1864-65)
Cork V984592	Cooleenlemane (Bealick)	boulder-shelter	lines, crosses, crosses + arms joined, radials, cro	UCC topographic files
Cork V978562	Kealanine	outcrop	lines, radials, arc, dots	UCC topographic files
Cork W313789	Scrahanard	wedge tomb	lines, grids, crosses	Borlase (1897)
Fermanagh H109434	Aughaglack	outcrop	lines, grids, crosses,	Wakeman (1874-75)
Fermanagh H090490	Knockmore (Gillie's Hole)	cave	x elaboratd in interlace, row of lines, lines	Wakeman (1866-69c)
Fermanagh H089506	Knockmore (Lettered Cave)	cave	+ in lozenge, lines, x in square, interlace	Wakeman (1866-69a)
Fermanagh H061462	Loughnacloyduff	cave	crosses, offsets, + in lozenge, x in square, radial	Wakeman (1866-69b)
Kerry V829575	Glenrastel	boulder-shelter	blocks of vertical lines, some horizontals	unpublished
Kerry V537695	Sallahig	outcrop	lines, crosses, three line point	O'Sullivan and Sheehan (1996)
Longford N145852	Clernaugh	outcrop	x in square, grids, radials, three line point	Jones (1845-47)
Louth O554835	Tinure	outcrop	lines, radials, crosses	Du Noyer (1866); Tempest (1939)
Meath O024738	Dowth	passage tomb	lines, + in lozenge, circles	O'Kelly and O'Kelly (1983)
Meath N572773	Loughcrew	passage tomb	lines, triangles,	Shee Twohig (1981)
Meath N888798	Rathkenny	"dolmen" capstone	groups of lines, grids,	Conwell (1864-66)

Table 26.1: List of sites with COMBS type carvings.

The carvings occur at the following types of locations:
1. Rock outcrops (throughout the country)
2. Boulder-shelters (in the south west)
3. Caves (Co. Fermanagh)
4. Megalithic tombs (various locations)

(For details of these sites, see Table 1 and distribution map Fig 26.2).

Outcrop sites

Aughaglack, Co. Fermanagh; Ballydorragh Co. Cavan (Fig 26.3B); Tinure, Co. Louth; Cleanaugh, Co. Longford; Kealanine, Co. Cork (Fig 26.3A); Sallahig Co. Kerry. The carvings on the outcrop sites are all on horizontal or gently sloping surfaces, as in cup and ring art, except at Tinure where the carvings are on a vertical surface. All the sites have examples of several of the motif types listed above. Two of the south western outcrop sites occur near old route ways: carvings can be seen on a number of adjacent outcrops at Kealanine and I was told by a local man that the rocks are adjacent to the "Butter Road", which connected west Cork with the Butter Market in Cork city. At Sallahig the carvings occur "at the summit of the old roadway that traverses the Coomduff ridge". At Aughaglack the incised carvings occur in association with picked cup and ring art.

Six lightly incised circles have also been noted recently on an outcrop with conventional cup and ring art at Carhoomeegar East, Co. Kerry (Coyne 2001). All have a diameter of 17cm and are accurately incised around a central (compass point?) mark. These are very different from COMBS group of carvings.

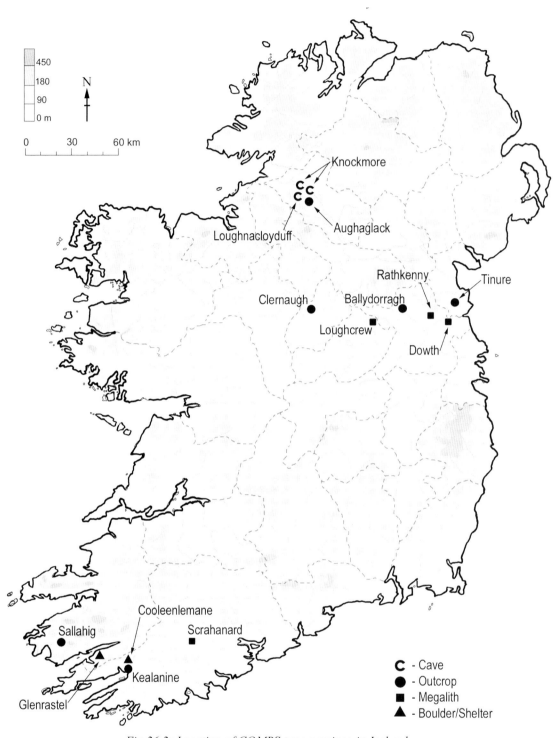

Fig 26.2: Location of COMBS type carvings in Ireland

Boulder-shelters

Two of the most intriguing sites, Glenrastel and Cooleenlemane, Co. Kerry, occur in the south western peninsular valleys, in what I propose to call boulder-shelters sites, and neither of these has been published other than in brief journalistic notes. Glenrastel (Fig 26.4) consists of a large boulder (*c.*12m x 4m x 3m high), with a large slab (*c.* 8m x 5m x 1m thick) leaning against it, forming a sheltered space. Locally known as Pluais na Scríobh (Cave of the Inscribings), this is situated on the rough hill pasture slopes of Cummeenbaun Mountain at about 350m OD, on the north side of the Glenrastel river valley. The carvings are located on the almost vertical face of the boulder that is sheltered by the leaning slab; this surface is relatively smooth, though crossed by horizontal cracks, and the carvings extend over an area of c. 5.8m x 1.9m. They consist mainly of short straight vertical lines of varying depths, set generally in groups and sometimes with horizontal lines crossing or delimiting the verticals. I am grateful to Mr. Connie Murphy of the Co. Kerry Archaeological Survey for the details of location and the measurements of the stone.

Cooleenlemane has carvings in two adjacent boulder-shelters, which are like Glenrastel but somewhat smaller. They are situated at 160–170m OD in the north-south valley of the Cooleenlemane River, which is bounded by Cobduff Mountain to the west and the Coomhoola Mountain to the east. The boulder-shelters are situated in rough pasture, just to the north of old field walls. The markings occur on the vertical eastern faces of the rock supporting the boulder in each shelter. The easternmost shelter has a more extensive range of carvings, which includes vertical and horizontal lines, some radials, and a large number of crosses, most of which have their arms joined to form lozenges. The lines vary in depth, and it is sometimes difficult to distinguish the finer carvings from the natural fissures that cross the stone horizontally. The western shelter has just a few well-preserved carvings. A number of initials and names are also carved on these surfaces. People lived in this valley within living memory, at least on a seasonal basis, and the well known travellers, Mr. and Mrs S. C. Hall, described their surprise at finding a "mass of huge rocks" occupied by a couple and their three children. The site was illustrated with a drawing by A. Nicholl, and shows a boulder-shelter very like the Cooleenlemane ones. The woman said that the family lived in the shelter for the summer months but moved to "some neighbouring town" for the winter (Hall and Hall 1841–43, 149). Here the Halls also encountered a man on a pony engaged in conveying butter along the route from Kerry to the Cork Butter Market (Hall and Hall 1841–43, 150).

Caves

Incised carvings were recorded during the 1860s by W.F. Wakeman, in three limestone caves in Co. Fermanagh (Wakeman 1866–69 a, b and c). These were the two caves at Knockmore, "The Lettered Cave" and "Gillie's Hole" and a cave at Loughnacloyduff in the townland of Clogherbog. All have a range of COMBS type incised carvings, including crosses, boxed Xs and radials. The Knockmore caves in addition have interlaced knots, crosses and small rectangular panels filled with angular interlace. The carvings are now covered in a growth of algae and it is not possible to see if there is any super-imposition of carvings.

Megalithic tombs

Cairns L and F, Loughcrew, Co. Meath; Dowth, Co. Meath; Scrahanard, Co. Cork; Rathkenny "dolmen", Co. Meath (Fig 26.3C). A small number of megalithic tombs appear to have incised carvings of the COMBS group. These carvings are in accessible positions, and are more

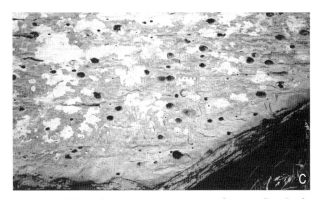

Fig 26.3: COMBS type carvings . A. Kealanine, Co. Cork; B. Ballydorragh, Co Cavan; C. Rathkenny, Co. Meath

deeply incised than those in definitely primary positions in passage tombs (see below for discussion of the latter). The motifs incised near the base of orthostat C12 in Dowth South are very similar to the COMBS group, though C. O'Kelly states that "...they are overrun by the pick-dressing which also tends to demonstrate that they are original" (O'Kelly and O'Kelly 1983, 178). If this is so, then we have to accept that these incised carvings are early, or consider the possibility that pick-dressing is a late feature of the Boyne valley sites. Indeed C. O'Kelly suggested that a small incised panel on C8 Dowth North might not be ancient (O'Kelly and O'Kelly 1983, 170). Other possible examples of such markings occur at the Loughcrew passage tombs, on two stones in Loughcrew

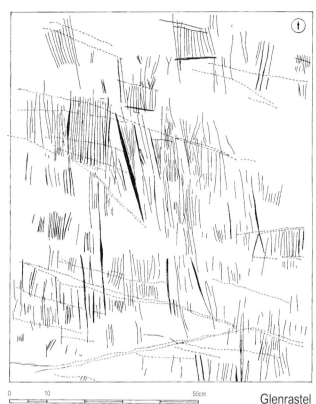

Glenrastel

Fig 26.4: Glenrastel Co. Kerry. Boulder shelter with incised carvings.

Cairn L (C16, C19 west) and in Cairn F (R4) (Shee Twohig 1981, figs. 226, 229 and 213).

On the basis of artefacts found in these tombs it is clear that Loughcrew L was used in the Iron Age and Dowth was used in the early medieval period. In fact it is possible that they were accessible continuously from the time of their original construction and so the carvings could have been added at any time up to the mid nineteenth century when they were first recorded. It should not be forgotten that the big eastern (cruciform) tomb at Knowth seems to have been accessible, and that Irish names in Irish were incised there in the early historic period.

Similarly accessible from the time of its construction, the capstone of the small megalithic tomb at Rathkenny, Co. Meath, has a range of short lines and other COMBS motifs (Fig 26.3C). A number of circles are picked on the underside of the capstone and on one of the supporting orthostats, where there is also a small, clearly picked triskele motif; an adjacent ring barrow may also indicate Iron Age activity in the area.

Scrahanard, Co. Cork, wedge tomb has COMBS type carvings on at least three of its orthostats, and W. C. Borlase (1897, 20) noted that at the time of his visit in 1895 several "little scorings in the shape of crosses... had been quite recently made, just as pilgrims still scratch on pieces of slate or on venerated rocks".

Other types of Incised art

Other types of incised art in Ireland may be grouped as follows: (a) as part of passage tomb and related art; (b) primary (?) on other megalithic tombs; (c) simple undated incised art on or at megalithic monuments; (d) incised Christian symbols.

(a) Passage tomb and related art

As noted above, the practice of incising angular geometric motifs/symbols on stone is known from the fourth millennium BC onwards in Ireland, notably at passage tombs, where finely incised lines are often preserved by the protected environments in which they occur. This can be seen best at Fourknocks (Hartnett 1957), Newgrange (O'Kelly 1983) and Knowth, and seems to be present at an early stage in the megalithic art of these sites (Shee Twohig 2000; Eogan 1997; 1998; 1999). Some of the incised work functioned as guidelines for the picked carvings and some looks almost like graffiti. Late Neolithic incised carvings occur at Millen Bay, Co. Down (Collins and Waterman 1955). In the Orkney Islands, passage tombs of Maes Howe type have all been found to have a range of very lightly incised lines, which have been suggested as being marking-out guidelines for painting (Bradley *et al.* 2001, 54). Examples of more deeply incised carvings are also known from the Orkney Neolithic, at the settlement of Skara Brae (Shee Twohig 1981).

The incised designs on the stone in the kerb of the Bronze Age cairn at Lyles Hill, Co Antrim (Evans 1953), have affinities on the one hand with certain aspects of Skara Brae art (Shepherd 2000, 149) but may also be compared with patterns on earlier Bronze age artefacts such as gold lunulae, bronze axes, and ceramics. Likewise, the stone with parallel incised lines from the cist at Knocknashee, Co Sligo, which was found within the cairn of a probable passage tomb (Shee Twohig 1981, fig. 280) could belong either to the passage tomb repertoire or to the Bronze age.

(b) Primary (?) on other megalithic tombs

Examples of incised lines at the megalithic tombs of Baurnadomeeny, Co. Tipperary, and Clontygora Large, Co. Armagh, have been argued as belonging to the Bronze Age. The carvings on one of the orthostats in the portico of the wedge tomb of Baurnadomeeny, Co. Tipperary, comprise an extensive series of mostly vertical and sloping lines and grooves of varying depths, but seem to lack the distinctive features of the COMBS group. In the excavation report O'Kelly (1960, 92) notes that the lines stopped exactly along the line of the old ground level and were partially covered by a layer of packing boulders along the north side of the cist in the portico. O'Kelly argued that the lines must have been carved after the deposition of burial 1 (in the cist) but before the insertion of burials 2, 3 and 4 in the portico. Since the burials almost certainly date to the Bronze Age, the carvings too are likely to be of the same period.

Some long horizontal and vertical lines on one of the orthostats of the gallery of the court tomb of Clontygora Large, Co. Armagh, may also have been carved in the Bronze age. The excavators argued that since the carvings stopped at the line of a yellow brown layer, they were contemporary with the deposition of late Bronze age pottery in the gallery (Davies and Paterson 1936–7).

(c) Simple undated incised art at megalithic monuments

Incised carvings of very simple form have been recorded at a number of megalithic monuments. These could have been added at any time and there are probably many more examples to be found. The portal tombs of Lennan, Co. Monaghan, and Churchtown, Co. Tyrone (both Ferguson 1872–3), and possibly Drumhawnagh, C. Cavan (Meehan 1909), all have short straight lines, as has the boulder burial at Uragh, Co. Kerry (Twohig 1987), and possibly the boulder burial at Gaggan, Co. Cork (Ó Ríordáin 1931). At Ballymarlagh, Co. Antrim, court tomb a panel of lightly incised lines was recorded on a stone in the gallery, and some simpler lines were noted on an adjacent stone (Davies 1949). At Cregg, Co. Meath, incised lines were recorded across the arris of a small stone (Corlett 1999). Other examples of very simple lines on stones were listed by R.A.S. Macalister (Royal Irish Academy, MSS 3B58) with notes on some stones recorded in G.V. Du Noyer's sketchbooks (Vols I, 17–18, also in the Royal Irish Academy). These include carvings on stones at Monsaher, Co. Wexford, and Currabeha, Co. Cork, but it is not clear if these are picked or incised. A loose stone found near a wedge tomb at Drombohilly, Co. Kerry, has deeply cut lines/grooves, which I have argued as being tool-sharpening marks (Twohig 1986).

(d) Incised Christian symbols

Christian style crosses on rock outcrops have been discussed recently by M.A.M. van Hoek (1993a) in the context of documenting the incised and picked crosses at Clehagh, Co Donegal. At that site, several different forms of crosses were carved on both outcrops and boulders, and some of these also had cupmarks. Van Hoek (1993a) noted that such crosses rarely occur on outcrops with cupmarks, but that Boheh, Co Mayo, has a single incised cross in addition to its elaborate cup and ring markings (Van Hoek 1993b). Incised crosses are known on a stone from a probable passage tomb site at Tournant, Co Wicklow, and a picked cross can be seen on the basin stone in the Baltinglass, Co. Wicklow, passage tomb (Shee Twohig 1981, figs. 256 and 250 respectively).

As noted above, W. F. Wakeman recorded an unusual range of incised Christian carvings at the Knockmore caves, Co. Fermanagh. The crosses and related motifs are elaborated into interlace and knot patterns and are associated with designs of the COMBS type.

Non-abstract incised carvings occur occasionally; as for example the quadruped that accompanies the roughly cut circles in the earth cut souterrain at the stone fort of Leacanabuaile (Kilmego Townland) Co. Kerry (O'Sullivan and Sheehan 1996, 184, fig. 123a). At the earliest these could be of early medieval date, and they may well be much more recent.

Discussion

There is a tendency in Ireland to regard all rock carvings as Neolithic or Bronze Age, and while this is true of passage tomb art and cup and ring art, in other parts of the world it is clear that the practice of carving on rocks goes on for much longer. Costas Goberna and Pericot García (1998) describe a range of picked carvings attributable to historic periods in the Galician region of Spain and argue that "..such carvings merit the same attention and respect as those of the prehistoric period" (p. 168, my translation). These include christianisation symbols, markers of pilgrimages and boundary markers, many of which have the *phi* shapes known here from the outcrop at Clonfinlough, Co. Offaly (Graves 1864–66). Likewise, in the French Pyrenees, many carvings were made by shepherds on rock outcrops or on megalithic tombs within living memory (Abelanet 1966) and there seems to be a long continuity of marks as property markers, animal brands and "monograms of illiterates" in this area (Bahn n.d.).

Incised straight lines and other angular geometric motifs somewhat like the COMBS designs occur all over the world and in all periods, on both rocks and other media. For example, in Australia Rosenfeld and Smith (2002, 115) have recently shown that incised marks post-date picked markings at the Cleland Hills rock shelter site in Central Australia. Closer to home, rock outcrops at Traprain Law, East Lothian in Scotland, had several series of deeply incised marks, mostly parallel lines, but with some circles incised around picked cupmarks (Edwards 1934–35). Similar sets of straight line incisions (and other carvings) are well known on limestone rocks in the Fontainbleu area south of Paris (Tassé 1982; Bahn 1998, 223).

Straight line markings of significance to the makers are known in medieval times in the form of masons' marks. Hourihane (2000) has shown that thirteenth century marks in Ireland are generally incised angular geometric marks (in fact many are like the COMBS marks). In the fifteenth century masons' marks become more elaborate, with examples of knots and interlace and Hourihane sees these and related carvings in churches as evidence a revival of Gaelic art after an absence of several hundred years (Hourihane 2000, 11–12; 2003, fig. 8). The interlace designs in the Knockmore caves are very like those illustrated by Hourihane from fifteenth century contexts. Alternatively, they could belong to the nineteenth century Gaelic revival art or they might be early medieval.

Markings like the COMBS type occur on other media, such as on the wooden lid of an Iron Age bog butter container from Rosmoylan, Co. Roscommon (Earwood 1997, 28, fig. 3).

Conclusions

None of the COMBS type carvings can be dated with certainty and those that occur in megalithic tombs could have been added at virtually any time. The sharpness of some of the motifs in the boulder-shelters and the likelihood that these places were used during shepherding or even as simple habitations, and the proximity of some sites to route ways used in the 19th century, leads to the conclusion that some at least of these markings are of relatively recent period.

Basically these incised marks are emblems or signs, and the groups of lines in particular may be regarded as artificial memory systems or AMSs, *i.e.* "physical devices specifically conceived to store and recover coded inform-ation" (d'Errico 1998, 20). The codes may have been known to only a select group of people, and knowledge of the codes may have been related to status and power.

The apparent similarity of form and a certain similarity in the locations where the COMBS carvings occur suggests that their meaning may have been understood throughout the country, and that their execution was not random or casual, but significant for those who executed the carvings and for some or all of those who saw them. The fact that these carvings are not datable does not make them less interesting, but may explain why they have been largely ignored in the archaeological literature.

Acknowledgements

My thanks to those who helped on fieldwork at the boulder-shelters, to Hugh Kavanagh for sorting out the table and figures at short notice and to Colum Hourihane for a preview of his book on *Gothic Art* and for in-advertently supplying part of the title for this paper.

Bibliography

Abelanet, J. 1966 Les gravures rupestres schématiques des Pyrénées Orientales, *Bullétin de la Societé Préhistorique Française*, 293–7.

Bahn, P.G. n.d. (*c.* 1993–4) *Pyrenean Prehistory*. Aris and Phillips, Warminster.

Bahn, P. 1998 *The Cambridge illustrated history of prehistoric art*. Cambridge University Press, Cambridge.

Borlase, W.C. 1897 *The Dolmens of Ireland*. Chapman and Hall, London.

Bradley, R., Phillips, T., Richards, C. and Webb, M. 2001 Decorating the Houses of the Dead: Incised and Painted motifs in Orkney Chambered Tombs, *Cambridge Archaeological Journal* **11**, 45–67.

Breuil, H. 1934 Presidential address for 1934, *Proceedings of the Prehistoric Society of East Anglia* **7**(3), 289–322.

Collins, A.E.P. and Waterman, D.M. 1955 *Millin Bay: a late Neolithic cairn in Co. Down.* Her Majesty's Stationery Office, Belfast.

Conwell, E.A. 1864–66 On an inscribed cromleac near Rathkenny, Co. Meath, *Proceedings of the Royal Irish Academy* **9**, 541–45.

Corlett, C. 1999 Primitive incised markings on a stone from Cregg near Nobber, Co. Meath, *Riocht na Midhe* **9**, 27–29.

Costas Goberna, F.J. and Pericot García, E. 1998 Los grabados rupestres en épocas historícas. In F.J. Costas Goberna (ed.) *Reflexiones Sobre el arte rupestre prehistórico de Galicia*, 129–173. Museo Municipal, Leon.

Coyne, F. 2001 Ever-increasing circles – a newly discovered piece of rock art near Kenmare, Co. Kerry, *Archaeology Ireland* **63**, 16–19.

Davies, O. 1949 Excavations at the horned cairn of Ballymarlagh, Co. Antrim, *Ulster Journal of Archaeology* **12**, 26–42.

Davies, O. and Paterson, T.G.F. 1936–7 Excavations at Clontygora Large cairn, Co. Armagh. *Proceeding of the Belfast Natural History and Philosophical Society* **1936–37**, 20–42.

d'Errico, F. 1998 Palaeolithic origins of artificial memory systems. In C. Renfrew and C. Scarre (eds) *Cognition and material culture: the archaeology of symbolic storage.* Chapter 3, McDonald Institute, Cambridge.

Du Noyer, G.V. 1864–5 Remarks on a carved rock at Ryefield, County of Cavan. *Journal of the Kilkenny and South East Ireland Archaeological Society* **5**, 379–385.

Du Noyer, G.V. 1866 Remarks on a Kistvaen, and on some carvings on an 'Earth-fast' rock, in the county of Louth, *Journal of the Kilkenny and South East Ireland Archaeological Society* **5**, 497–501.

Earwood, C. 1997 Bog-Butter: a two-thousand year history, *Journal of Irish Archaeology* **8**, 25–42.

Edwards, A.J.H. 1934–35 Rock sculpturings on Traprain Law, East

Lothian, *Proceeding of the Society of Antiquaries of Scotland* **49**, 122–137.

Eogan, G. 1997 Overlays and Underlays: aspects of megalithic art succession at Brugh na Bóinne, Ireland, III Colloquio Internacional de Arte Megalítico, *Brigantium* **10**, 217–34.

Eogan, G. 1998 Knowth before Knowth, *Antiquity* **72**, 162–72.

Eogan, G. 1999 Megalithic Art and Society. *Proceedings of the Prehistoric Society* **65**, 415–446.

Evans, E. 1953 *Lyles Hill.* Her Majesty's Stationery Office, Belfast.

Finlay, F. 1973 *The rock art of Cork and Kerry.* Unpublished MA thesis, National University of Ireland (Cork).

Ferguson, S. 1872–3 Proceedings, 15 October 1873, *Journal of the Royal Historical and Archaeological Association of Ireland,* 4th ser. II, 523–31.

Graves, J. 1849. Proceedings, 11 June 1849, *Proceedings of the Royal Irish Academy* 4, 368–9.

Graves, J. 1864–66 On a boulder with presumed pagan carvings at Clonfinlough, King's County, *Journal of the Kilkenny and South East Ireland Archaeological Society* **5**, 354–62.

Hall, S.C. and Hall, A. 1841–43 *Ireland, Its Scenery, Character, etc.* London.

Hartnett, P. 1957 Excavation of a passage grave at Fourknocks, Co. Meath. *Proceedings of the Royal Irish Academy* **58**C, 197–277.

Hourihane, C. 2000 *The mason and his mark.* British Archaeological Reports 294. Oxford.

Hourihane, C. 2003 *Gothic art in Ireland 1169–1550: enduring vitality.* Yale, New Haven and London.

Jones, H.D 1846 Proceedings, 29 November 1845, *Proceedings of the Royal Irish Academy* **3**, 147–8.

Meehan, J. 1909 The Loughduff Cromlech, Co. Cavan, *Journal of the Royal Society of Antiquaries of Ireland* **39**, 88–91.

O'Kelly, M.J. 1960 A wedge shaped gallery grave at Baurnadomeeny, Co. Tipperary, *Journal of the Cork Historical and Archaeological Society* **65**, 85–115.

O'Kelly, M.J. 1983. *Newgrange: archaeology, art and legend.* Thames and Hudson, London.

O'Kelly, M.J. and O'Kelly, C. 1983 The tumulus of Dowth, County Meath. *Proceedings of the Royal Irish Academy* **83**C, 135–190.

Ó Ríordáin, S.P. 1931 The place names and antiquities of Kinalmeaky Barony, Co. Cork, *Journal of the Cork Historical and Archaeological Society* **36**, 1–8.

O'Sullivan, A. and Sheehan, J. 1996 *The Iveragh Peninsula: an archaeological survey of South Kerry.* Cork University Press, Cork.

Rosenfeld, A. and Smith, M.A. 2002 Rock art and the history of Puritjanna rock shelter, Cleland Hills, Central Australia, *Proceedings of the Prehistoric Society* **68**, 103–124.

Shee Twohig, E. 1981 *The Megalithic Art of Western Europe.* Oxford University Press, Oxford.

Shee Twohig, E. 2000 Frameworks for the megalithic art of the Boyne Valley. In A. Desmond, G. Johnson, M. McCarthy, J. Sheehan and E. Shee Twohig (eds) *New agendas in Irish prehistory: papers in commemoration of Liz Anderson.* 89–105. Wordwell, Bray.

Shepherd, A. 2000 Skara Brae: expressing identity in a Neolithic community. In A. Ritchie (ed.) *Neolithic Orkney in its European context,* 139–58. McDonald Institute, Cambridge.

Tassé, G. 1982 *Pétroglyphes du Bassin Parisien. 16 Supplément à Gallia Préhistoire,* CNRS, Paris.

Tempest, H.G. 1939 A pre-historic scribed rock in Tinure Td., *County Louth Archaeological Journal* **9**(3), 248–261.

Twohig, E. 1986 A wedge tomb and other antiquities at Drombohilly Upper, *Journal of the Kerry Archaeological and Historical Society* **19**, 143–151.

Twohig, E. 1987 Two stone circles at Uragh, Kenmare, *Journal of the Kerry Archaeological and Historical Society* **20**, 111–118.

Van Hoek, M.A.M. 1993a Early Christian rock art at Clehagh, Co. Donegal, *Ulster Journal of Archaeology* **56**, 139–147.

Van Hoek, M.A.M. 1993b The Prehistoric Rock Art at the Boheh Stone, Co. Mayo, *Journal of the Westport Historical Society* **13**, 1–15.

Wakeman, W.F. 1866–69a The cave on Knockmore, near Derrygonelly, County of Fermanagh; with remarks on the character of the primitive scorings and early Christian symbols inscribed upon its sides, *Proceedings of the Royal Irish Academy* **10** (ser.1), 229–232.

Wakeman, W.F. 1866–69b On the incised cavern at Lough Nacloyduff, Parish of Bohoe, County of Fermanagh, *Proceedings of the Royal Irish Academy* **10** (ser.1), 327–329.

Wakeman, W.F. 1866–69c On a cavern called "Gillie's Hole" at Knockmore, Co. Fermanagh, *Proceedings of the Royal Irish Academy* **10** (ser.1), 395–397.

Wakeman, W.F. 1874–75 On certain markings on rocks, pillarstones and other monuments, observed chiefly in the County Fermanagh, *Journal of the Royal Historical and Archaeological Association of Ireland* **3**, 445–474.

27. A note on the building history of Ardmore Cathedral

Conleth Manning

Ardmore Cathedral is best known today for the remarkable Romanesque figure sculpture on the west end of this relatively small ruined church. All recent writers on the building are agreed that the figure sculpture, arranged within two large lunettes and an arcade of thirteen smaller arches, now set above the lunettes, has been rearranged at some time in the past. However, there are many conundrums in the structure including the chancel-arch capitals, which appear to be of two phases. In general the sequence and dating of the different building phases are difficult to disentangle. No two writers to date agree fully on a solution to these problems.

Before discussing the different theories it may be worth summarising the relevant historical information on the short-lived diocese of Ardmore and on the building of the church. Attached to the list of bishoprics approved at the synod of Kells in 1152, there is a note stating that Ardmore and Mungret claimed episcopal status but that their claim was held to be doubtful. A bishop of Ardmore submitted to Henry II in 1172, and Eugenius, bishop of Ardmore, witnessed a charter between 1172 and 1179. The diocese was listed in a papal confirmation of 1210 but disappears from the record after this date (Gwynn and Hadcock 1970, 53, 62). The *Annals of Inisfallen* record that "Mael Étain Ua Duib Rátha, noble priest of Ard Mór, died having finished the building of the church (tempall) of Ard Mór" (Mac Airt 1951, 333).

In an interesting and seminal article on Ardmore Cathedral, J.T. Smith (1972) worked out a seemingly logical building history for the structure and in particular produced cogent arguments that the figure-carved and arcaded panels in the present west wall were designed to fit around a doorway in the original west wall of the building, which was situated some seven metres to the east. He suggested that the doorway survived, having been reused as the present north doorway, and that its outer arch is the same size as the two largest panels or lunettes, which must have flanked it originally, forming an arcade of three similar arches. The arcade of smaller arches could have been set above these. He cited parallels in France for such a western entrance facade. Smith was of the opinion that the western extension of the nave and rearrangement of the figure sculpture could have happened before 1203 (Smith 1972, 10).

A subsequent article (McNab 1987) concentrated mainly on a thorough analysis of the sculpture and the placing of these stones within the frames, and corrected some errors in Smith's article especially as regards the mouldings around the windows of the nave. She would associate Mael Étain with the building of the nave and the commissioning of the original figure sculpture and saw the western extension of the nave as post-dating 1203. An article by Tadhg O'Keeffe (1992) was the next to be published and this is discussed further below. This was followed by Peter Harbison's article (1995), in which he concentrated on identifying some of the panels and made the new suggestion that some of them were originally part of a scene representing the Building of Solomon's Temple. He accepted Smith's three main phases of construction, made no reference to O'Keeffe's new theory on the building history of the cathedral and argued that the original Romanesque nave probably dated to the 1170s, with the western extension of the nave being Mael Étain's work of shortly before 1203 (Harbison 1995, 100–1).

O'Keeffe's 1992 article is a comprehensively illustrated account of the building, which included internal and external elevations and discussion and illustration of parallels in France. In this a new theory on the building history was put forward, that the present long nave was part of the original design of the Romanesque phase. The arguments used to back up this theory were: 1) that the nave approximates in proportion to two rectangles of 1: square root of 2 and that this must have been planned from the start, and 2) that the anomalies in the panels in their present location and the lack of a string course externally and arcading internally on the west end of the side walls was due to extensive rebuilding of the west end of the church on the original foundations. Some differences in the masonry towards the base of the west wall externally are used to argue for this very extensive rebuilding.

Fig 27.1: Part of the inner face of the north wall of the nave. Note break of joint a short distance to the right of the doorway where the exact line of the original inner north-west corner can be seen in the lower half of the wall, with almost every second stone projecting west of the line to be bonded into the original west wall.

In the present writer's opinion these arguments have no basis. It is dangerous to argue that a building is or is not original because it either does or does not conform to proportions that we have deduced were important to medieval builders. In fact a great variety of proportions seem to have been used and a lot more work needs to be done on this subject before definite conclusions can be drawn. The supposed evidence for rebuilding of the west wall in its present position simply does not exist and certainly not on the scale necessary to remove all traces of the string courses from the west ends of the north and south walls. There is a variation in the masonry below the lunettes but this does not constitute an argument that the wall was rebuilt. One might also ask why should the greater part of a wall be rebuilt while leaving the lower part in place. A wall might be rebuilt if its foundations failed or if it began to lean dangerously but this would involve the entire wall including the foundations.

The published internal and external elevations of the north and south walls (O'Keeffe 1992, figs. 4.2, 4.3) constitute a strong argument that Smith's analysis of the building sequence is correct, because externally the string course stops just east of the north and south doorways and likewise internally. Also the string course takes a step down at this point and changes from a hollow chamfer to a plain chamfer exactly as it does approaching the north-east corner on the north side. At the southeast corner the evidence has been removed and the wall repaired. Smith

(1972, 5) pointed to "clear breaks of joint a little way east of the north and south doorways". These breaks can still be seen (Fig 27.1) and are clear evidence for an original west wall at this point. Further conclusive evidence for an earlier west wall, not previously noted in print, is the survival of two quoin stones of the original corner on the north side (Fig 27.2).

Smith gives the internal dimensions of the original nave as 48 x 26 feet. This would give a proportion of 1: $\sqrt{2}$ + ($\sqrt{2}$-1), which would be very easily worked out on the ground by making a square, extending out its diagonal to form the $\sqrt{2}$, and adding the difference between the side of the square and the $\sqrt{2}$. The extended nave is apparently in the proportion of 1:2 x $\sqrt{2}$, as deduced by O'Keeffe.

All of the parallels in France mentioned and illustrated by O'Keeffe (1992, fig. 4.13) have a west doorway and his conclusion that Ardmore's facade did not originally have a doorway made it exceptional. O'Keeffe's theory has to be rejected on the basis of factual evidence visible in the walls of the building. What the original west wall looked like is a matter for conjecture but the most certain point about it is that it had a central doorway and that the present south doorway is the most likely candidate to have been in that position. The lunettes would suit to flank its arch but how the remainder of the figure sculpture was displayed is debatable and having some of it beneath the lunettes at each side of the doorway might solve some of the anomalies in the present upper arcade. The present

Fig 27.2: Part of the exterior of the south wall of the nave with two large dark corner stones surviving in situ *in the upper courses of the wall. They are above the east jamb of the blocked-up doorway. A little to the right the step-down of the string course can be seen.*

west window with its very fine internal mouldings, capitals and former pillars looks out of place in a west wall in Romanesque/transitional architecture in Ireland. One wonders might it have been the original Romanesque east window of a shorter chancel, which may have become available for reuse, if the chancel was extended at the same time as the nave. Certainly the chancel extension appears to be of twelfth/thirteenth-century date, as indicated by Smith rather than the seventeenth-century date suggested by O'Keeffe (1992, fig. 4.1).

Ardmore Cathedral needs to be studied in greater detail in conjunction with detailed stone-by-stone drawings of the walls, stone and mortar analysis, limited archaeo-logical excavation and further study of related architecture in Ireland and France. Only then might we be in a position to understand the chancel arch, with its two-period capitals, the original west facade and what phase is attributable to Mael Étain in the years before his death in 1203. There is a possibility that there was an earlier Romanesque phase of the church, which may have been contemporary with or earlier than the round tower, but of

which no standing masonry survives, as was suggested by O'Keeffe (1992, 84). Some of the figure sculpture might even have belonged to such a phase. In the meantime the one thing we can be certain about is that the original west facade of the present nave stood immediately east of the north and south doorways and had a central doorway with sculpture somehow arranged about it.

Bibliography

Gwynn, A. and Hadcock, R.N. 1970 *Medieval religious houses Ireland*. London.

Harbison, P. 1995 Architectural sculpture from the twelfth century at Ardmore, *Irish Arts Review* **11**, 96–102.

Mac Airt, S. (ed.) 1951 *The Annals of Inisfallen*. Dublin.

McNab, S.L. 1987 The Romanesque sculptures of Ardmore Cathedral, Co. Waterford, *Journal of the Royal Society of Antiquaries of Ireland* **117**, 50–68.

O'Keeffe, T. 1992 Romanesque architecture and sculpture at Ardmore. In W. Nolan and T.P. Power (eds) *Waterford history and society*, 73–104. Dublin.

Smith, J.T. 1972 Ardmore Cathedral, *Journal of the Royal Society of Antiquaries of Ireland* **102**, 1–13.

28. Excavation of the High Cross in the Medieval Market Place of Kells

Heather A. King

Introduction

The 'Market' Cross of Kells[1] was located on the north-east corner of Cross Street at an extremely busy junction where traffic from Market Street, Castle Street, John Street and Cross Street converge (Fig 28.1) The danger posed to the cross by the ever increasing amount of traffic in the town had given rise to much debate during the 1970s and early 80s and an incident in March 1985 when a lorry ran into the monument increased people's concerns.[2] In December 1996 a decision on the future of the monument became a matter of urgency when a school bus collided with the plinth. That the cross remained unharmed at that time despite the plinth being severely damaged was little short of a miracle (Fig 28.2). The level of debate became quite heated after this event between those who thought that the cross should be moved to a more secure environment and those who felt that Cross Street should be pedestrianised and the cross left *in situ*. Leo Swan favoured the latter arguing that the cross was most likely a Termon cross situated on the eastern side of the monastic site adjacent to a monastic gateway in the outer enclosure where a medieval market developed (1998, 49–55). He compared the situation in Kells with that of Armagh and with the location of crosses in the Book of Mulling and concluded that the cross was almost certainly in its original position and "to have it removed would break a tradition already over 1,000 years old". While the discussions continued an agreement was made in early January 1997 between Kells Urban District Council and the National Monuments and Historic Properties Service that the cross should be moved to the National Monuments depot in Trim for safe-keeping and conservation while an assessment of the damage to the plinth and archaeological excavation were undertaken.

The Market Cross is one of a group of Irish High Crosses known as Scriptural crosses because they are decorated with scenes from the Old and New Testament. The iconography of this cross has been expertly and comprehensively documented by Helen M. Roe (1975, 26–43) and Peter Harbison (1992, 103–108). The purpose of this paper is not to comment further on the iconography but rather to look at the construction of the cross and discuss the siting of the monument in light of the excavation results.

It is offered to this Festschrift for George in recognition of his boundless enthusiasm for the archaeology of Meath[3] and in grateful appreciation for giving me the opportunity to work at Knowth over several very happy and productive Summers in the 1970s, and for his support and interest when I undertook a Master's degree on the later medieval crosses of Meath while he was Professor of Archaeology at University College Dublin.

Removal of cross and excavation.

The cross consists of three elements, a pyramidal shaped base, a ringed cross shaft and evidence in the form of a mortise for a long missing upper shaft. Structurally the monument is not in good condition; the edge mouldings and part of the panels on the lower edge of the shaft have been smashed away and there is additional damage to the base and the upper section of the ring into which the cross head would have been tenoned. The inaccurate orientation of the cross, as it was situated in Cross Street, with the crucifixion facing north rather than west has been noted by both Roe (1975, 28) and Harbison (1992, 103). Removal of the cross from its site involved freeing the cross from it's base by loosening the mortar which held the cross and cross base in position and wrapping and protecting both sections with timber planking and hessian (Fig 28.3). This work allowed for a close examination of the constructional aspects of the cross prior to conservation work. The actual transfer of the cross and base to the National Monuments regional depot in Trim was carried out early on the morning of 15th January 1997 with assistance from the National Monuments staff in the Athenry depot (Fig 28.4).

The surviving height of the cross is 275cm with a width across the arms of 165cm while the height of the shaft between the base and the ring is 161cm and it is 54cm by 38cm in width (Harbison 1992, Vol. 1, 103). The mortise for the missing upper shaft is 9cm in depth and 17cm

Fig 28.1: Centre of Kells. Reproduced from the Irish Historic Towns Atlas, No. 4 Kells, by kind permission of the Royal Irish Academy. Below and National Library of Ireland: Detail of town centre and cross plinth by Gerry Woods.

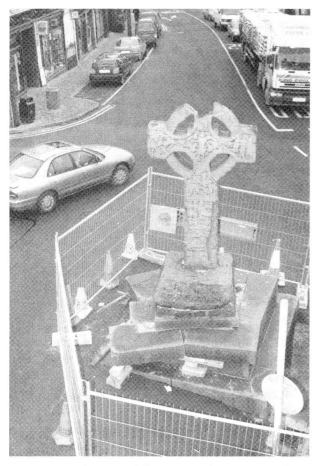

Fig 28.2: Market cross following accident in 1996. Photo: Matt Kavanagh. The Irish Times Dec. 18th 1996.

Fig 28.4: Removal of cross. Photo: W. Cumming.

Fig 28.3: Preparation of cross for removal. Photo: W. Cumming.

Fig 28.5: View of the mortise in the cross head. Photo: W. Cumming.

Fig 28.6: Tenon showing spalling. Photo: Heather A. King.

Fig 28.7: View of mortise in base. Photo: Heather A. King.

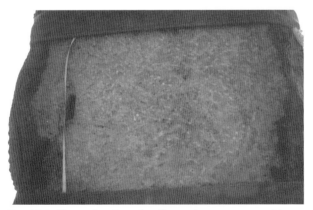

Fig 28.8: View of underside of base showing recess. Photo: Heather A. King.

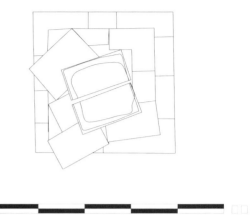

Fig 28.9: Plan of the plinth following the December accident. Gerry Woods.

NO.	HEIGHT	WIDTH	LENGTH
Upper step			
1	17.5	69	138
1a	17.5	69	138
Middle step (upper level)			
2	26	91	98
3	26	91	57
4	26	73.5	114
5	26.5	116	71
6	26	66	74
7	26	91	129
Middle step (lower level)			
8	29	36	110
9	30	149	28
10	29.5	135	46
11a	30	94	72
11b	29	120	33
12	28	119	38
Lower step			
13	28	62	149
14	31	70	49
15	35	77	44
16	40	95	120
17	43	61	47
18	45	54	122.5
19	39	83	51
20	40	93	47
21	33	155	74

Table 28.1 Measurement of the stones in the plinth.

square (Fig 28.5). The tenon narrows slightly to 51cm by 34cm and is 32cm in height (Fig 28.6). There is a substantial chamfer, the result of a natural spall, on the north face of the tenon approximately 13cm in width and 10cm in height above the bottom of the tenon. There were also a number of small chips or spalls removed from the west and south faces of the tenon that resulted in the broad faces of the tenon being reduced to 37cm in width.

The cross base measures 134cm by 126cm at ground level, 116cm by 112cm at the top and is 60cm in height. The mortise is 53.5cm by 41cm at the opening and slopes inwards to an approximate depth of 25cm (Fig 28.7). The dimensions at this point were 37cm by 29cm as a residue of mortar adhering to the sides and the bottom of the mortise obscured the original depth and width.[4] The underside of the base also had a number of spalls removed and was very roughly finished but had one significant feature in the northwest corner (Fig 28.8). Approximately

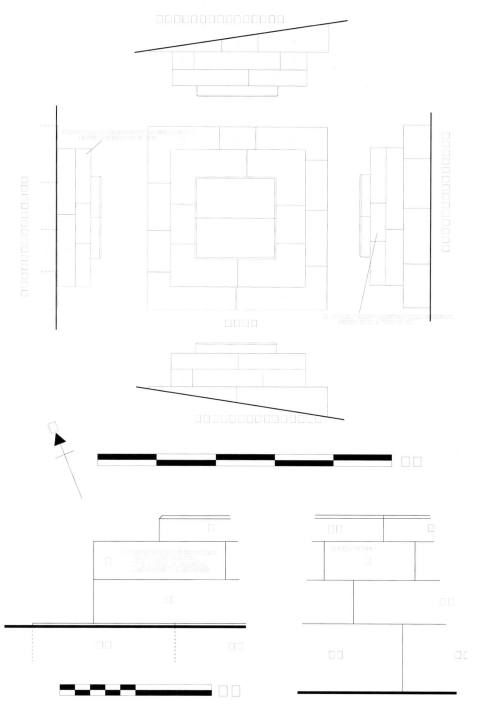

Fig 28.10: Reconstruction plan and section of plinth prior to accident. Gerry Woods.

22cm from the north face and 56cm from the west face a small rectangular recess had been cut into the stone. This had its long axis east-west, was well-finished internally and measured 10cm by 3cm with a depth of 7cm.

In March a survey of the damaged three-stepped plinth was made before it was taken down and stored in the yard of the Urban District Council at John Street (Fig 28.9). It stood on ground that sloped both from west to east and from south to north and consisted of twenty-three large dressed limestone blocks with a rubble core (Fig 28.10). The stones varied greatly in width and length, from 28cm

to 149cm, and most of the inner faces of the stones were undressed (Table 28.1). The upper step consisted of two stones with a chamfered upper edge and measured 138cm east-west by 69cm north-south and was 17.5cm in height. The second step, 29cm in height, consisted of 13 stones on two levels and measured 229 by 229cm. The basal step was 305 by 305cm and consisted of nine stones varying between 44cm to 155cm in width. The heights of the stones in this step varied between 28cm and 45cm and were clearly cut to allow for the difference in ground levels. Resurfacing of the street meant that the west side of the plinth was buried below street level to a depth of 26–33cm with 2–7cm protruding above the surface while the pavement, or east side of the plinth, was buried to a depth of 10–14cm but stood to a height of 23–31cm above ground.

The plinth carries two inscriptions; the principal one relating to its erection in 1893, and is as follows, 'THE BASE OF THIS CROSS/ WAS ERECTED BY / JAMES O'FERRALL ESQ / OF KELLS A.D. 1893.' This was incised in Roman lettering on the north end of the west side (Stone No.7) of the upper level of the second step. The name T. DILLON is incised in Roman lettering on the central stone (No. 3) on the same level of the east side.[5] There is quite an amount of graffiti incised onto the upper surface including the names Farrelly and a repeat of T. Dillon.

Excavation of the area was undertaken in late April 1997 under licence number 97E290. Directly below the plinth *c.* 20cm of a yellow gritty mortaring gravel, containing pieces of concrete, stones and partly decayed wedges of timber was removed. This material had clearly been used as a foundation for the lower step of the plinth. It was laid on a concrete and stone base that was extremely solid and could only be removed with a jackhammer. This sub-base varied in depth between 68cm and 72cm and contained a few pieces of brick. It was completely removed and overlay subsoil. A section of the cutting was then dug to a maximum depth of 100cm as archaeological black soils had been noted some 12m east of the cross site in John Street at a depth of *c.* 70cm below present street level. There was no trace of this material visible in the sections after excavation and no stratified deposits were uncovered although a French drain was noted in the north baulk below street level during subsequent engineering works. This drain was functioning and had been observed running along the south side of Market Street and continuing down John Street in other works connected with cable-laying.

Discussion

It is only in recent years that archaeologists have had the opportunity to begin to redress the lack of knowledge about some of the locational and constructional aspects of High Crosses. A number of factors including deteriorating climatic conditions and cross sites under threat, such as the traffic problem in Kells, have resulted in the removal of a number of crosses from what has been perceived to have been their traditional sites allowing for an examination of the crosses and excavation to take place. Excavations at the sites of the High Crosses in Clonmacnoise were particularly informative in producing evidence of settlement, earlier wooden monuments and confirmation that the crosses were in their original positions (King 1994, 66; 1995, 74). The excavator at Cashel concluded that the cross was not in its primary position but examination of the monument revealed an unusual rectangular depression in the underside of the

base which it was thought could have covered a relic or some other object of a dedicatory nature (Lynch 1983, 9–18). These crosses were moved indoors and replaced on site with replicas while the crosses at Moone and Carndonagh were also found not to be in their original positions and have now been placed in new protected outdoor locations (Clyne 2000, 109; King and Crumlish 2000, 27–8).

The results of the excavation at Kells do not unfortunately shed any additional light on the siting of the cross. It is clear that, in preparation for the new plinth commissioned in 1893 by James O'Ferrall, the ground was dug to a depth of *c.* 1m into subsoil thereby removing any previous occupation material that may have existed. Historically it appears clear that the cross has been re-erected at least three times between 1688 and the late 19th century (Roe 1975, 26). The earliest reference to intervention at the cross site is recorded on the original west face of the monument itself:

> THIS CROSS
> (W)AS ERECTED
> (A)T THE CHAR
> (G)E OF ROBERT
> (BA)LFE OF GALL
> (I)RSTOWNE E(SQ)
> (BE)ING SOVERAI
> (GN)E OF THE CORP
> (O)RATION OF KEL
> LS. ANNO DOM
> 1688

Clearly the cross had been compromised by 1688 and Roe has suggested that it may have been the result of "iconoclastic fury of the religious factions of the 17th century" (1975, 26). While religious emblems were undoubtedly destroyed during this period over one-third of the town had also been reduced to a 'heap of rubbish' by 1654 as a result of the confederate wars and the houses immediately adjacent to the cross on John Street are shown in ruins in 1663 (Simms and Simms 1990, 3, fig. 2). The castle, probably built by the De-Lacys in the late twelfth or thirteenth century (Simms and Simms 1990, 2, 9, figs. 1 and 2), depicted at the south end of Castle Street directly opposite the cross is apparently in good condition at that time but there is no account of the cross. One can only assume that the cross must have fallen or been damaged pre-1688 to cause Robert Balfe to re-erect it. What we do not know is how badly the cross was damaged nor precisely where he re-erected it.

In any event not all of the damage visible today on the edge mouldings and lower panels of the cross can be ascribed to the pre-1688 period as Balfe himself, despite his good deed in re-erecting the cross, is responsible for some of the damage to the bottom panel of the west face. He clearly had the lower section of the shaft cut back and dressed to create a surface for his own testamentary. One can reasonably speculate that he may have obliterated the

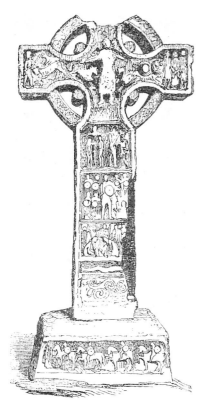

Fig 28.11: Illustration of east face of cross 1849. From Wilde's Beauties and Antiquities of the Boyne.

Fig 28.12: Illustration of west face of cross 1887. The National Monuments Photographic Unit.

remains of an Early Medieval inscription as Roe was of the opinion that the 'pictorial scheme' on the west face was 'fully coherent' and that no obvious scriptural panel was missing (1975, 27).[6] In support of that opinion there are good parallels for inscriptions on the lower west or crucifixion faces of crosses, *e.g.* the Cross of the Scriptures at Clonmacnoise, and examples at Kinnity, Durrow, Killamery and Monasterboice (Harbison 1992, Ills. 139, 97, 254, 411, 482). Balfe may also have oriented the monument so that his inscription on the crucifixion side faced north toward the castle and the main market area of the town. His re-erection of the cross probably seemed an entirely appropriate act of civic pride in celebration of the 1688 charter granted to Kells by King James II providing for a free borough with a sovereign and burgesses and his own appointment as first sovereign[7] of the new corporation[8] (Simms and Simms 1990, 4).

The cross appears to have been on the ground again within forty to fifty years as there is a strong tradition, firstly recorded by O'Donovan in 1836 that the cross had "lain prostrate in the street for a long time" (1928, 51) and that it was raised from this position by Dean Swift[9] in the early part of the 18th century (Lewis 1837, Vol. 2, 37). Balfe's own inscription was certainly damaged sometime before *c.* 1749 when Isaac Butler made a visit to the town on his Journey to Lough Derg and, in noting the cross located opposite the castle, recorded some letters missing along the left side of the inscription (1892, 129

note 2). Otherwise he described the cross as being "one entire stone erect, adorned with several Figures in Bass relief with Irish Inscriptions altogether unintelligible, of great Antiquity."[10] This would suggest that the cross was relatively intact. Further damage could have occurred when the cross was apparently used as a gallows in 1789 and "a regiment of soldiers sharpened their lances on the pedestal"[11] (Cogan 1862, I, 205, Note *) but it is still shown as having an upper shaft in a view of the town and castle *c.* 1800 (Simms and Simms 1990, 1. view 1). The Headfort Estate Maps locate the monument on the northeast end of Cross Street in 1817 (Simms and Simms 1990, figs 5a–c). References during the 19th century are contradictory; the condition of the cross is described as "a beautiful stone cross, elaborately enriched with sculptured figures and devices" by Lewis in his Topographical Dictionary of 1837 while Cogan (1862, I, 201) refers to "the great cross of Kells, so often alluded to and eulogized by every antiquarian and tourist", standing in the Market Place. One would have thought that some or all of these commentators would have noted that the cross was compromised if the head had been lost prior to 1688 or even pre-1749. However it certainly was missing by the middle of the century when Wilde (1849, 148) illustrated the east face of the cross in his book on the *Beauties and Antiquities of the Boyne* (Fig 28.11). Further damage occurs to the south edge of the east face of the shaft between Wilde's depiction in 1849 and 1887 when

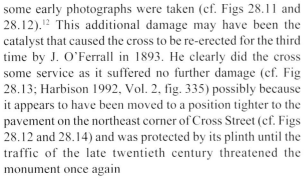

Fig 28.13: Illustration of east face of cross pre-1893. The Welsh Collection Ref. No. W29/01/10 courtesy of the Ulster Museum.

Fig 28.14: West face of cross c. 1958. The National Monuments Photographic Unit.

some early photographs were taken (cf. Figs 28.11 and 28.12).[12] This additional damage may have been the catalyst that caused the cross to be re-erected for the third time by J. O'Ferrall in 1893. He clearly did the cross some service as it suffered no further damage (cf. Fig 28.13; Harbison 1992, Vol. 2, fig. 335) possibly because it appears to have been moved to a position tighter to the pavement on the northeast corner of Cross Street (cf. Figs 28.12 and 28.14) and was protected by its plinth until the traffic of the late twentieth century threatened the monument once again

The foregoing saga of the damage suffered by the cross, the inaccurate orientation of the crucifixion and the interventions by Balfe, Swift and Farrelly mitigate against the idea that the cross could possibly be precisely in its original position. Bradley (1985, 440) suggested that the cross might have been moved into the Market place by Balfe in 1688 (1985, 440) but the Kells Valuation indicates the existence of Cross Street in 1663 (Simington 1960, 267–8) and a Crown Grant of 1669 places the cross in Cross Street some twenty years before the Balfe re-erection (Simms and Simms 1990, 8). The 1st edition of the O.S. map 1837 appears to indicate that the cross was in the centre of the junction where the four principal streets converge and Healy's map of 1830 shows the cross at the south end of Castle Street. The view of Kells from the east *c.* 1800 (Simms and Simms 1990, 1, view 1) and the illustration of the cross pre-1893 (Fig 28.13) appears to

show the cross some distance further north than the north east corner of Cross Street while comparison of the cross before and after the plinth was built (cf. Figs 28.12 and 28.14) would suggest that the cross was moved at least 60cm to the east. The only conclusion that one can come to is that the cross has been moved around the central junction of the town particularly in the area of Cross Street and John Street on at least three if not four occasions and the critical question then is whether one believes that the cross was located in this area of the town from the time it was first carved.

Compelling arguments in the context of the layout of Early Medieval monastic sites have been made for a Market and a 'Market' cross *in situ* on the eastern side of the monastic site of Kells by possibly as early as the 10th century (Doherty 1980, 83; 1985, 60, 67; Swan 1985, 84–6; 1998, 49–55; Simms and Simms 1990, 1–2; Swift 1998, 116–7). Without rehearsing those arguments again there is certainly a market in operation by 1106 (Mac Niocaill 1961, no. iv; Herbert 1996, 105) and a reference in 1156 to a cross "at the door of the airdam (portico) to Siofaic,"[13] would appear to place a cross close to the gateway of the outer enclosure and in the area where markets were held continuously from pre-Norman times until the early nineteenth century (Hamlin 1987, 138; Simms and Simms 1990, 1–2, 10). Whether the cross was called a Market or a Termon cross by the early inhabitants of Kells we may never know but the use of the term

Fig 28.15: Photo of cross as re-erected in front of the Heritage Centre. Photo: David Sleator. The Irish Times.

'Market', absent from the medieval literature, may justifiably have been re-attributed to it by Healy in 1930.

As pointed out above (see Note 4) full analysis of the morphology of the cross was not undertaken but the existence of the previously unknown recess in the underside of the base is worth noting. Its function is unclear; it appears to be too small and far too neatly carved for use as a keying feature. It was not connected with the 19th century plinth and the early photographs show that the base was sitting directly on the ground. Nothing similar was noted at Clonmacnoise or Moone and the only Irish comparable feature is the recess in the cross base at Cashel which the excavator regarded as being large enough (79cm long, 67cm wide and 23cm deep) to have covered relics (Lynch 1983). The Kells recess could only have held something *c.* 2cm in width and perhaps 8cm by 5cm in length and so we are left with a new intriguing challenge.

The original cross was unveiled in its new position to the west of the Heritage Centre on Saturday 28th April 2001 (Fig 28.15) and a replica was placed on display in the centre. While the entire monument is now protected from the elements by a steel framed glass covered shelter and its orientation is once again correct with the cruci-fixion facing west it is a pity that the 1893 plinth was not reconstituted as it had been in Cross Street. Many of the original stones have been re-used but in a different order

and at a lower height while the O'Ferrall inscription now faces east. The conclusion, however, that the monument was almost certainly not in its original position will hopefully allay the concerns of those who wished to retain the monument in Cross Street.

Acknowledgements

I am most grateful to Willie Cumming, Senior Architect, Michael Moore, and Gerry Woods of the National Monuments Service, Con Brogan, John Scarry and Tony Roche in the National Monuments Photographic Unit, David Little (Stone Mason; National Monuments, Athenry), Peter Harbison, K.M. Davies, Robert Heslip of the Ulster Museum whose comments, opinions, illustrations and photographs have contributed hugely to this paper. I would also like to thank D. McLoughlin (assistant County Manager in 1997), Jim Butler, Michael Killeen, John Farrelly and more recently Pat McCabe for assistance on site and Catherine O'Reilly of the Urban District Council for information on the initial accident in 1985.

Notes
1   The term 'Market' cross appears to be first used by John Healy in 1930.
2   Information from a report dated 20/09/93 in UDC, Kells.
3   It seemed appropriate to offer this paper to George's

Festschrift as he has also contributed to the discussion on High Crosses in Meath. See Eogan 2001.

4   It was intended to complete scale drawings of the tenon, mortise of base, bottom of the base with recess and carry out petrological analysis but unfortunately the cross was re-erected without the opportunity being provided.

5   James O'Ferrall was one of the commissioners of Kells in 1893 (Thom's Directory, 1243). T. Dillon may have been the builder of the plinth.

6   Roe (1975, 7) and Porter (1931, 22, 24) suggest that the 'Market' cross was connected with Gormlaith, daughter of King Flann Sinna who erected the Cross of the Scriptures in 909 AD at Clonmacnoise. This is an interesting hypothesis as the iconographical repertoire is comparable and the location of a possible early inscription on the 'Market' cross would have found a parallel on her father's cross. However the date of the Kells cross could well be argued (Harbison 1992, Vol. 1, 48-53). The suggestion that she was buried underneath the cross seems entirely improbable.

7   While Simms and Simms (1990, 4) suggest that a member of the Taylor family was always the sovereign of the corporation the cross names Robert Balfe as sovereign in 1688.

8   1688 was a period when Catholicism in Ireland was undergoing a revival under James II and public figures and wealthy patrons were not averse to proclaiming their allegiance to the faith. Two other Early Medieval crosses, Ballymore Eustace and Dysert O'Dea were re-erected (Manning 1998, 112; King forthcoming; Harbison 1992, 83-4), and a number of Late Medieval crosses were newly carved by landed families (King 1985, 13-33).

9   Dean Swift died 1745.

10   Butler must have been capable of reading the Balfe inscription. Is it possible that there were Irish inscriptions on the base of the cross? The upper sections of the base are very worn and appear to have been damaged at the end of the 18th century. See Note 13 and Fig 27.13.

11   The upper surface of the base has evidence for having been used for sharpening knives and possibly lances or swords (see Harbison 1992, Vol. 2, fig. 342).

12   A well is mentioned in 1669 as being next to the Market Cross but 'unlocated' in Simms and Simms (1990, 10). This photograph includes a water pump directly to the southeast of the cross and must indicate the site of the late seventeenth century well.

13   The Annals of the Four Masters record the burning of Kells "from the cross at the door of the airdam (portico) to Siofoic" and Simms and Simms (1990, 1) suggest that present day Suffolk Street preserves this ancient name.

Bibliograpahy

Bradley, J. 1985 Planned Anglo-Norman Towns in Ireland. In H.B. Clarke and A. Simms (eds) *The Comparative History of Urban Origins in Non-Roman Europe: Ireland, Wales, Denmark, Germany. Poland and Russia from the Ninth to the Thirteenth century.* British Archaeological Reports International Series **255**(i), 411–467.

Butler, I. 1892 A Journey to Lough Derg, *Journal of the Royal Society of Antiquaries of Ireland* **22**, 126–36.

Clyne, M. 2000 Moone Abbey, Moone. In I. Bennett (ed.) *Excavations 1998, Summary Accounts of Archaeological Excavations in Ireland*, 108–9. Wordwell, Bray.

Cogan, Rev. A. 1862 *The Diocese of Meath Ancient and Modern.* Vol. 1, Dublin.

Doherty, C. 1980 Exchange and Trade in early Medieval Ireland, *Journal of the Royal Society of Antiquaries of Ireland* **110**, 67–91.

Doherty, C. 1985 The Monastic Town in early Medieval Ireland. In

H.B. Clarke and A. Simms, (eds) *The Comparative History of Urban Origins in Non-Roman* Europe: Ireland, Wales, Denmark, Germany. Poland and Russia from the Ninth to *the Thirteenth century*, 45–75. British Archaeological Reports International Series **255**(i), Oxford.

Eogan, G. 2001 High crosses in Brega, *Ríocht na Midhe* **12**, 17–24.

Hamlin, A. 1987 Crosses in Early Ireland: The evidence from Written Sources. In M. Ryan (ed.) *Ireland and Insular Art A.D. 500–1200*, 138–40. Dublin.

Harbison, P. 1992 *The High Crosses of Ireland An Iconographical and Photographic Survey.* 3 Vols. Dr. Rudolph Habelt GMBH, Bonn.

Healy, J. 1930 *Historical Guide to Kells (Ceanannus Mór), Co. Meath.* Dublin.

Herbert, M. 1996 (edition) *Iona, Kells and Derry The History and Hagiography of the Monastic Familia of Columba.* Four Courts Press, Blackrock.

King. H.A. 1985 Irish wayside and churchyard crosses 1600–1700, *Post-Medieval Archaeology* **19**, 13–33.

King. H.A. 1994 Clonmacnoise High Crosses. In I. Bennett (ed.) *Excavations 1993*, 66. Wordwell, Bray.

King. H.A. 1995 Clonmacnoise High Crosses. In I. Bennett (ed.) *Excavations 1994*, 74. Wordwell, Bray.

King, H.A. and Crumlish, R. 2000 Churchland Quarters, Carndonagh. In I. Bennett (ed.) *Excavations 2000*, 27–8. Wordwell, Bray.

King, H.A. 2004 Excavation at the North Cross, Ballymore Eustace, Co. Kildare. In C. Hourihane (ed.) *Irish Art Historical studies in Honour of Peter Harbison*, 165–74. Index of Christian Art, Department of Art and Achaeology. Princeton University, in association with Four Courts Press, Dublin.

Lewis, S. 1837 *Topographical Dictionary of Ireland.* Vol. 2, London.

Lynch, A. 1983 Excavations at the Base of St. Patrick's Cross, Cashel, *North Munster Antiquarian Journal* **25**, 9–18.

Mac Niocaill, G. (ed.) 1961 *Notitiae as Leabhar Cheanannais, 1033–1161.* Cló Móráin. Dublin.

Manning, C. 1998 Miscellanea. The Inscription on the North Cross at Ballymore Eustace, County Kildare, *Journal of the Royal Society of Antiquaries of Ireland* **28**, 112.

O'Donovan, J. 1928 *Letters containing information relative to the Antiquities of the County of Meath collected during the progress of the Ordnance Survey in 1836.* Bray, Co. Dublin.

Porter, A.K. 1931 *The Crosses and Culture of Ireland.* Arno Press, New York.

Roe, H. 1975 *The High Crosses of Kells.* Meath Archaeological and Historical Society. Dublin.

Simington, R.C. 1960 Valuation of Kells (1663) with note on Map of Kells *c.* 1655, *Analecta Hibernica* **22**, 231–68

Simms, A. and Simms, K. 1990 No. 4 Kells. In J.H. Andrews and A. Simms (eds) *Irish Historic Towns Atlas*. Royal Irish Academy, Dublin

Swan, L. 1985 Monastic Proto-Towns in Early Medieval Ireland: The Evidence of Aerial Photography, Plan Analysis and Survey. In H.B. Clarke and A. Simms (eds) *The Comparative History of Urban Origins in Non-Roman Europe: Ireland,* Wales, Denmark, Germany, Poland and Russia from the Ninth to the Thirteenth *Century*, 77–102. British Archaeological Reports International Series **255**(i), Oxford.

Swan, L. 1998 The Market Cross, Kells, Co. Meath, *Ríocht na Midhe* 9, 49–55.

Swift, C. 1998 Forts and Fields: a study of Monastic Towns in Seventh and Eight century Ireland, *Journal of Irish Archaeology* **9**, 105–125.

Thom's Official Directory of the United Kingdom of Great Britain and Ireland. 1893. Dublin.

Wilde, W.R. 1978 (edition) *The Beauties of the Boyne and its Tributary the Blackwater.* Tower Books, Cork.

29. Explicit data and tacit knowledge, exploring the dimensions of archaeological knowledge

Charles Mount

Introduction

Throughout his career George Eogan has been concerned not only with discovering new knowledge about the past but through his teaching was intimately involved in making his knowledge available to generations of archaeologists. I was one of those students who was privileged to be taught by George Eogan, and later assist him in his research. It was through his example that I learned that archaeology is a discipline not just concerned with generating data, but with creating, organising and diffusing knowledge about the past. I have used the opportunity presented by this *festschrift* to look at the nature of archaeological knowledge and emphasise the importance of tacit knowledge and the limitations of data.

The dimensions of archaeological knowledge

The objective of archaeology is to increase knowledge of the past through the study of material remains. As archaeologists we know things in many ways, as individuals, as groups, and both consciously and unconsciously. Knowledge can be divided into two primary types: explicit knowledge and tacit knowledge. Explicit knowledge is learning that is available to consciousness and can be expressed unambiguously in signs, words or numbers. Explicit knowledge, because it can be codified and stored (in books, computer records and archives), can be handed on without direct interpersonal communication and can be communicated and shared across space and time.

The concept of tacit knowledge was defined by Polanyi (1966) as learning that is not available to consciousness, that is experiential and difficult or impossible to communicate through language or other coded processes. Tacit knowledge is often person and context specific, consisting of insights and intuitions as well as technical abilities. It is difficult to successfully communicate across space and time. Tacit knowledge can be held by an individual, where it is manifested as complex skills. For example, an individual may be able to ride a bicycle but may have no explicit idea of how they do this; they are unable to explain the process. Most skills that require

comprehension of information which is too complex to be verbalised, such as overtaking on a motorway, recognising subtle archaeological features, or the ability to see and explain patterns in raw data, rely on unconscious tacit thinking.

Many innovative theories have sprung into the conscious minds of thinkers from the subconscious fully formed, and empirical proofs added later. Frederich Kekulé is said to have apprehended the circular structure of Benzene in a dream (Cohen and Stewart 1995, 41). Edward Szilard imagined the mechanism of a nuclear chain reaction while waiting for a traffic light to change on a London street (Rhodes 1986, 28). Trigger (1980) has suggested that Gordon Childe's synthesis in *The Dawn of European Civilisation* relied heavily on intuition and "was conditioned more by his assumptions about human behaviour than by the archaeological data at his disposal". Hawkes (1982, 148) refers to Mortimer Wheeler's "famous archaeological intuition". A number of groundbreaking theories have been developed by individuals who were relatively unfamiliar with the data. For example, Alfred Wegener (1966) was a meteorologist who had never worked in the area of geology when he proposed the theory of continental drift in 1912. This indicates that large quantities of data may not be necessary for the development of theory.

Cook and Brown (1999) note that tacit knowledge is also held collectively by a group in what they describe as a 'genre'. An individual may know part of a language, but the whole language is only known by a group. Similarly a group may hold a common view of the world based on unconscious tacit assumptions. Kuhn (1996) has described these world views as paradigms. Professional groups, like archaeologists, that hold a body of knowledge in this way are also called communities of practice. These are informal social networks with a shared repertoire of concepts, actions, tools, stories, artefacts and discourse (Wenger 1997). Cook and Brown suggest that there is a distinction between possessing knowledge and the active process of using and generating knowledge in the course of practice, which they call knowing. Taking a pluralist

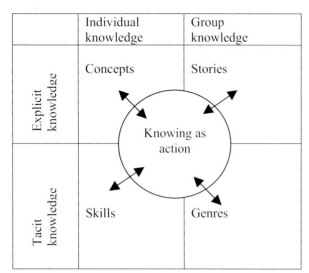

Fig 29.1: Cook and Brown's four forms of knowledge and the bridge formed by knowing as action.

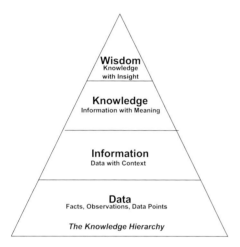

Fig 29.2: The Knowledge hierarchy.

view, they argue that the four types of knowledge (tacit individual and group and explicit individual and group) are involved in a reciprocal interplay or bridged in purposeful activity (Fig 29.1).

Types of knowledge

Taking an empirical view, archaeological knowledge is a hierarchical process commencing with raw data, which can consist of artefacts, observations or numbers, words, or even sounds and images (Fig 29.2, and Davenport and Prusak 1998). Data by itself has no inherent meaning, only when it is given meaning, by being arranged and processed into patterns, placed in context, categorised, calculated mathematically or statistically, corrected or summarised, does it become information. Ironically, too much data makes it difficult to identify and make sense of the information that matters. Only once this information is put to some use, is given meaning or is transformed

through comparison with other information, its implications established, its connections to other information assessed or is discussed with others, does it become knowledge. To take another scientific example, the planet Uranus was observed on seventeen different occasions between 1690 and 1781 before Lexell realised that it was a planet (Kuhn 1996, 115). The observations (data acquisition) alone were not enough to identify it, it had to be placed in the context of contemporary astronomical discourse. We generally tend to find data in records, and information in messages, but we obtain knowledge from individuals or groups, or embedded in organisational and cultural routines (see below).

Taking a more human-centred approach, knowledge can be viewed as a typology, such as the know-that to know-why scheme that divides it into six types (Skyrme and Amidon 1997). Know-that is the basic sense of knowing, having cognitive knowledge, facts, experience and access to learning. This is characteristic of a new graduate. Know-that is most useful when joined by Know-how, which is advanced skills, and knowing how to get things done. Much Know-how is tacit knowledge and requires skill and practice gained over time, so it is characteristic of experienced workers.

Other types of knowledge include Know-who, a knowledge of the capabilities of others, which also relies on experienced judgement. For example, the ability to put together a research team with the appropriate mix of knowledge, skills and abilities. Know-when is a sense of timing, knowing when to do something like apply for a research grant. Know-where is a spatial sense, knowing where things are best done, such as the ability to identify the best location to excavate. Finally, Know-why is a strategic sense, requiring a sense of context and vision, understanding systems and how, for example, a research project will contribute to a whole system of knowledge.

The cost and value of knowledge

All knowledge, in whatever socio-economic system, has associated costs and value. The primary cost of archaeological knowledge is associated with specifying it in the form of a research proposal or project brief. Locating it, whether in an existing archive or in the field has costs, as does accessing or capturing it in some sort of a recording system. There are also costs associated with evaluating its significance, transferring it through various forms (paper to database to report), assimilating it into the body of existing knowledge and curating it in an archive.

Data may have great cost but is not knowledge and has little value without further work. The value of knowledge is not always self-evident or universal, its value varies between individuals or groups (see Carver 1986 for an extended discussion of archaeological value). However, the value of knowledge is not diminished by copying and is usually enhanced by sharing. Knowledge is a collective good and can still be used by the originator after it has been communicated to others. Presenting a paper at a conference, for example, encourages reciprocity and feedback that can increase the value of the knowledge. Increasing the amount of similar data does not make knowledge more valuable (although it does drive up the costs of knowledge), the value of knowledge is increased by adding different data. Too much data or information can swamp the ability of the recipient to assimilate and use it and may divert attention from what is important (Simon 1978). Information is only useful if the recipient can understand and apply it, and this requires an existing level of knowledge to allow the assimilation of the new information. Other costs include classifying the nature of the information and relating it to the knowledge base. This can be made difficult (and more costly) if it is disorganised, lacks a summary, a list of contents, categories, *etc*.

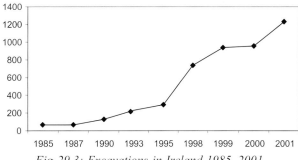

Fig 29.3: Excavations in Ireland 1985–2001.

Knowledge capture

Another issue is how knowledge is captured and stored. In general it can be embrained, embodied, encultured, embedded and encoded (Blackler 1995). Individual knowledge can be embrained in the form of conceptual skills and cognitive abilities (this is similar to know-that). It can also be embodied, acquired by doing and problem-solving and rooted in a particular context. Collective knowledge can be encultured in a group or community. This is achieved through shared understandings, socialisation and shared language. Knowledge can also be embedded in systemic routines, technology and structures. Material culture embeds knowledge (much of the information obtained from an excavation will be embedded in the artefacts), as do organisational and social structures. Finally, knowledge can be encoded, it can be externalised and conveyed by signs and symbols and made available to anyone who understands the code.

Discussion

In the search for objectivity and the focus on data collection the importance of tacit knowledge can be overlooked. Tacit knowledge or know-how can never be truly expressed in a book, report or a database, yet it provides the ability to accomplish all archaeological activities. Because it has such a large tacit component Know-how can only be passed from the experienced to the inexperienced in an interactive process in the course of practice. This emphasises the importance of experienced archaeologists who possess know-how, and the processes by which this knowledge is passed to others.

The concept of the knowledge hierarchy is an important reminder that data is not the same as knowledge. Data may have been produced at great cost but it must still be developed through a series of stages before it becomes knowledge. Today more archaeological data is being collected than ever before, in the form of artefacts, bones,

descriptions, measurements, *etc*. This data acquisition is being driven in an attempt to preserve monuments by record that would otherwise be removed in the course of development (DAHGI 1999, 25). However, most of this is remaining as data (Fig 29.3, Mount 2002). The data is situated within and has value related to the community of practice that created it. It may have little or no relevance or value in other contexts. We have noted that the value of data does not relate to its quantity (indeed too much data can reduce its value) but to its perceived relevance to individuals and groups. It is by no means certain that raw data collected today, even if carefully archived, will continue to have meaning or value to archaeological communities of practice in the future. Also, without careful checking, the validity of the data may come into question (see Lambrick and Doyle 2000, 22–5, for questions which have already arisen regarding the reliability of archaeological data). Therefore two questions arise, is it wise to collect more data than can be successfully assimilated without incurring overload? Is it worthwhile archiving excessive data quantities that may have no relevance in the future?

A final issue is the opportunity costs of investing scarce resources in data that may have no future relevance. Could the resources be more usefully invested in some other activity that would have a more tangible or immediate benefit? The risk that data collected today might have limited relevance in the future suggests that investment in other activities might be wiser. The alternative is to collect data, not in an attempt to preserve archaeology by record for some future community of practice, but to answer questions related to a matrix of theoretical frameworks which develop questions about periods and themes of relevance to archaeology in the present. This approach would aim to make the creation of knowledge the primary aim of archaeology rather than the collection of data.

Bibliography

Blackler, F. 1995 Knowledge, knowledge work and organizations: an overview and interpretation, *Organization Studies* **16**, No. 6, 1021–46.
Carver, M. 1996 On archaeological value, *Antiquity* **70**, 45–56.
Cohen, J. and Stewart, I. 1995 *The collapse of chaos*. Penguin Books, London.

Cook, S.D.N. and Brown, J.S. 1999 Bridging epistemologies: the generative dance between organizational knowledge and organizational knowing. *Organizational Science.* Institute for Operations Research and Management Sciences.

DAHGI 1999 *Framework and principles for the protection of the archaeological heritage.* The Stationery Office, Dublin

Davenport, T.H. and Prusak, L. 1998 *Working knowledge,* Harvard Business School Press, Boston.

Hawkes, J. 1982 *Mortimer Wheeler.* Weidenfeld and Nicolson, London.

Lambrick, G. and Doyle, I.W. 2002 *Review of archaeological assessment and monitoring procedures in Ireland.* The Heritage Council, Kilkenny.

Kuhn, T.S. 1996 *The structure of scientific revolutions.* 3rd ed. The University of Chicago Press, London.

Mount, C. 2002 The Irish Heritage Council, *Antiquity* **76**, 485–92.

Polanyi, M. 1966. *The tacit dimension.* Routledge and Keegan Paul, London.

Rhodes, R. 1986 *The making of the Atomic Bomb.* Penguin Books, London.

Simon, H. 1978 Rationality as a process and product of thought, *American Economic Review* **68**, No. 2, 1–16.

Skyrme, D.J. and Amidon, D.M. 1997 *Creating the knowledge-based business,* Business Intelligence Ltd., Wimbledon.

Trigger, B.G. 1980 *Gordon Childe.* Thames and Hudson, London.

Wegener, A. 1966 *The origin of continents and oceans.* John Biram, translator. Dover Publications New York.

Wenger, E. 1997 *Communities of practice: learning meaning and identity.* Cambridge University Press, Cambridge.

30. Three Midland Megaliths as drawn and described in 1786 by J. Brownrigg, Surveyor

Peter Harbison

A man with a 'laudable passion for Irish antiquities' was how Joseph C. Walker (1788, 120 and Nevin 1996) characterised John Brownrigg, the original artist of the three midland megalith drawings reproduced here for the first time, and the same description could easily be applied to you, George, in whose honour they are presented in these pages. Archaeologist, professorial teacher, senator, European traveller, author, excavator and (with your good wife, Fiona) a genial host, you are a man of many parts. Our careers have touched in varying ways – your un-mistakeable italic script graced index cards when I joined Bord Fáilte in 1966 after the death of the gentle Paddy Hartnett, whose assistant you had been, and three years later I wrote an article about your discoveries at Knowth in that organisation's magazine, *Ireland of the Welcomes*, which I was later to edit. We both specialised in Bronze Age studies, each compiling a corpus of hoards in our respective periods, and contributing to *Prähistorische Bronzefunde Europas* thirty years apart. I would take my hat off to you (if I wore one) for keeping up such a wonderfully steady flow of publications into your seventies – and, fortunately, there is no end of them in sight! Even more do I pay homage to you for your pertinacity in continuing to excavate at Knowth for four decades, which must surely be something of a record – at least in these islands, if not beyond – and, as I am sure we all do, I congratulate you on the spectacular discoveries you have made there, some of which I assisted in producing in printed form through your *Knowth (2)* volume. In saluting you as a master of megalithic studies, too, I hope that you will find this small contribution to be of value and interest.

It is, anyway, about time that you and Brownrigg met. Unknown to one another, you narrowly avoided doing so some twenty years ago, because – according to the same Walker (1788, 120 with Plate XIII, fig. 2) – Brownrigg was the owner of a "brass [bronze] Spear-head, of an elegant form, which was found with five more, in the year 1774, very near the surface of the earth under a carne, in the Kings county" – and the illustration of this (Fig 30.1) I offer you here as a small addition to your Late Bronze Age hoard corpus. So, George, now let me introduce you

Fig 30.1: This bronze spearhead from Plate XIII, Fig. 2 of Joseph C. Walker's Dress of the ancient and modern Irish (1788), was once owned by John Brownrigg, and was found in Co. Offaly along with five others in the year 1744. It is offered here as a small addition to George's Hoards of the Irish Later Bronze Age.

at last to John Brownrigg of Dublin – "a gentleman" (again in Walker's partially repeated words) "who unites with excellent abilities in his profession of a surveyor, a laudable passion for Irish antiquities".

Brownrigg (*c.* 1748–1838) had an extensive practice surveying and mapping many city properties and country estates in the eighteenth and early nineteenth centuries, being considered by John Andrews (1967, 287–8) as a product of the 'French School' of land surveyors in Ireland, as represented by John Rocque and Bernard Scalé. He was the latter's pupil and, between 1774 and 1778, his partner, later joining up in another separate but brief partnership with Thomas Sherrard (also a Scalé alumnus) before setting up on his own in Dublin's Grafton Street around 1779 (Andrews 1985, 279; 1991, 25). From the 1780s onwards, he was heavily involved with canals – the Grand and the Royal – and he was also assistant engineer to the Boyne navigation in your own native county of Meath. As his very recent biographer, Ron Cox (2002, 89–90), pointed out, he was appointed around 1803 as engineer to the Directors General of Inland Navigation, and remained in the job until they were transformed into the Board of Works in 1831. Some of the maps which he produced in the course of his surveying career have managed to survive, particularly among the Longfield Collection in the National Library (Andrews 1991), and it was probably while occupied in furnishing such maps in the midlands that he must have sufficiently indulged his passion for antiquities to make drawings of the three megaliths which form the focus of this paper.

These are preserved for us in a small copy-book entitled *Famous Irish Cromliacs* that is now preserved in Box 1 of Acc. 4841 in the National Library. They were part of a collection assembled by the antiquary Austin Cooper (1759–1830), which included drawings that he had acquired from the portfolio assembled by William Burton Conyngham of Slane Castle (Trench 1985), who died in 1796. We know that Burton Conyngham had amassed a considerable number of antiquarian drawings from a variety of sources, and it is probable that he obtained Brownrigg's megalithic sketches in the later 1780s, possibly from Brownrigg himself. All three of the pen-and-wash pictures in the National Library illustrated here (Figs 30.2–30.5) state that they were 'drawn by J. Brownrigg 1786' – one caption describing him as a surveyor, and another giving a precise date of September 4th. We might have expected Brownrigg to have simply signed his name on each sheet, instead of which the formula we find used is 'drawn by', which would raise initial doubts as to whether these are Brownrigg's own originals. This suspicion is raised to a certainty by the fact that the paper of the Aghnacliff sketch (Fig 30.3) has a watermark (Fig 30.4) bearing the year 1794, and the tops of letters forming the name J. Whatman, a well-known paper manufacturer of the period. That same year saw the extended family of the antiquary Austin Cooper making copies of drawings in the Burton Conyngham collection (Harbison 2000, 14; 2002) and, though unproven, the likelihood is that it is to the artistic activity of Cooper's circle in 1794 or later that we owe these copies of Brownrigg's original views of 1786 which would probably once have been in Burton Conyngham's collection, but which are now lost – showing us how much we are in the debt of the Cooper family for having preserved these images for us. It is probable that the three drawings reproduced here originally formed a sheaf of loose sheets but, in March of 1891, Cooper the antiquary's grandson, Austin Damer Cooper, J.P. (1831–1900), of Drumnigh, Baldoyle, Co. Dublin, pasted them into the copy-book referred to above, which bears the following inscription on the title-page:

> A Descriptive Account, with Illustrations
> of Three remarkable Cromliacs – from
> the unpublished Antiquarian Collection of the
> late Austin Cooper F.S.A., M.R.I.A.
> now furnished by his grandson
> Austin Damer Cooper, Member of
> the Royal Antiquarian Society of Ireland
> (1891), also of County of Kildare
> Archaeological Society.

The drawing of one of the three – that at Cleenragh (Fig 30.5) – must have been slightly larger than the others, as Austin Damer Cooper seems to have cropped it so that it would fit into the copy-book, thereby removing the upper horizontal line of the frame.

The three 'cromliacs' (an eighteenth-century term usually applied to dolmens or 'portal tombs', and which

Damer Cooper takes to be derived from two words meaning 'sloping stone') will be taken in turn as they appear in the copy-book, with its accompanying texts written in Austin Damer Cooper's hand but doubtless copying Brownrigg's lost original texts, as each bears the date 1786.

Ballyhattan, Co. Westmeath (Fig 30.2)

The first of these three megaliths was at Ballyhattan, Co. Westmeath – a townland about a mile north of the village of Horseleap. Between them is the large motte-and-bailey of Ardnurcher, erected probably by a de Lacy around 1192, though this was disputed by Brownrigg (1788), who wrote an article about it in the 1788 volume of the *Transactions of the Royal Irish Academy* – probably his only scientific article in print and, as John Andrews (1986, 45) pointed out, the only contribution from a land surveyor to be published in the 'Antiquities' section of the *Transactions* of the Academy – a body of which you, George, have been a member for more than thirty years. It is probably reasonable to presume that the occasion that brought Brownrigg to do his survey and view of Ardnurcher also gave him the opportunity of drawing the 'cromliac' which was located only two townlands away, and to pen the following description of it, as found in the copy-book:

"Ballyhatton" (1786)

> This small Cromliac stands in the *County of West-meath*, on the lands of Ballyhatton, opposite the Green of Donore Geoghegan from which it is seperated by a river, and lying within 20 yards of the highway, at a village called the four wrocks and on the Estate of a Mr. Aughmuty – It is obscured by a ditch or bank built with it, which I have purposely left out of the view and I apprehend is considerably filled up with clay and rubbish, the little chamber not being more than four feet high, and the upper point of the covering stone only eight feet above ground. It stands on the brow of an eminence and was surrounded by a circle of rude stones 24 yards in diameter, a sufficient number of them are still standing to describe the circle, though many of them have been demolished in the memory of the present neighbouring inhabitants. There appears to have been a double row of stones like an avenue from the circle to the Cromliac, and not leading to the chamber or opening but to the covered or back part of it, as in the margin [note: nothing is shown in the margin!]. The people have no kind of traditions concerning it, except an aged blacksmith who told me he often heard old people say that in ancient times a Judge used sit on top of it. Close to the Cromliac a few years since was found the remains of a place of Christian worship, now entirely defaced.
>
> Skeletons and detached human bones are often dug up near it, and very lately a skeleton was found erect

Fig 30.2: Megalith in Ballyhattan, Co. Westmeath, as drawn by J. Brownrigg in 1786, but preserved in a later copy in the National Library of Ireland. Photo: National Library of Ireland.

in the ground, with a pavement formed round the neck of it from which it is conjectured to be the bones of a great criminal buried alive, with his head above ground as a public example. And from this and the tradition mentioned by the Blacksmith I think there is reason to imagine the Druids were not only Priests having the mysteries and religious ceremonies entirely in their hands but were Judges at the head of the Law, with its power of life and death entrusted to them. As the country this Cromliac stands in, is a rough stony district of high hills, shrubs and rocks known by the name of "the woods", and the last part of Meath that submitted to the English, being without the Pale for some centuries, I have a strong inclination to believe many more monuments of antiquity would be found there was it properly examined by a person of leisure round the hill of Knockasta, the hills of Clane, Bishopstown Ballymore etc., and the very ancient town of Kildare.

The demolition of the stones described by Brownrigg must have continued unabated, so that nothing is now known to survive of the monument. There is no sign of it on the first edition of the Ordnance Survey map of 1838. Nor is it mentioned in the *Megalithic Survey*, which lists only one megalith in the County – a wedge-tomb at Lickbla, a considerable distance away, some three miles north of Castlepollard (deValera and Ó Nualláin 1972, 91).

Was Ballyhattan (or Ballyhatton, as Brownrigg spells it) a second wedge-tomb in the County? This seems improbable, to judge by the description – *surrounded by a circle of stones, 24 yards in diameter.* This circular setting and the fact that it stood *on the brow of an eminence* would argue for it to have been a megalith more in the Passage Grave tradition, perhaps akin to those at Carrowmore, Co. Sligo, though the *double row of stones like an avenue from the circle to the cromliac...... leading to the back part of it* is not easy to parallel. Perhaps the tomb's classification is best left to the realm of specu-lation, as it is no longer with us. However, we can but be thankful to Brownrigg for having gone to the trouble of drawing it, as otherwise knowledge of its former existence would have been entirely lost to us. I have searched for a Brownrigg survey of the area which might help us to pinpoint a precise location, but – even with the kind assistance of Paul Ferguson of Trinity College's map department, and John Andrews, the College's professor emeritus of geography – I have been unable to find one, so that the townland will probably remain the closest we can get to saying where it once stood.

Aghnacliff, Co. Longford (Fig 30.3)

Our problems of classification and location are con-siderably eased when we cross the border into County

Fig 30.3: The dolmen at Aghnacliff, Co. Longford, that J. Brownrigg drew on September 4th, 1786, as preserved in a copy on paper watermarked with the year 1794 and now in the National Library of Ireland. Photo: National Library of Ireland.

Longford, and journey northwards to near the western shores of Lough Gowna, where the other two megaliths still survive near the village of Aghnacliff (spelled Aughnecliffe by Brownrigg). About a quarter of a mile to the northeast there is what the *Megalithic Survey* (de Valera and Ó Nualláin 1972, 88; see also Cody *c.* 2002a) defines as a 'portal-tomb', which stands in a field at the bottom of quite a steep slope, not far from a small stream. This is surely one of the least known of the more impressive dolmens in Ireland (now, at last, dignified as a National Monument), with not one but two capstones standing precariously on top of one another and resting on a single recumbent boulder beneath them, as Brownrigg clearly shows in his drawing (Fig 30.3). His description of it is as follows:

"Aughnecliffe" (1786)

This Cromliach is on the lands of Aughnacliffe near

Dunbiggan in the Barony and County of Longford, either the estate of Lord Belmore, or Counciller Maconchy, 5 miles from Granard. The top stone is 4f 6 thick – 7 feet broad at one end; 6 feet at the other, 9 feet long on each side, and the upper surface 10 feet from the ground. It is extremely curious, being sustained at one end on the point of a single stone. I am informed that some few years since it was moveable by touch, but from frequent experiments I apprehend the nice point on which it moved at the other and is worn down, as it is permanent at present. It is an easy matter to pass under it from side to side yet at one end of it, between the two lower stones there is an open with a flagged bottom or floor, wide & high enough for a man to creep into. This open is at the south end, in which situation I observe the opening of every cromliac I have seen is placed. I could not perceive any circle of stones round the Cromliac, as it stands at the foot of a stony hill incumbered with shrubs. But at the south end at the

Fig 30.4: The year 1794 and the name J. Whatman appear upside-down on the copy of the Brownrigg drawing of the dolmen at Aghnacliff, Co. Longford, that is now preserved in the National Library of Ireland. Photo: National Library of Ireland.

distance of 10 yards is a heap of larger stones and bushes, under which I was shewn the entrance of a small passage or sewer now nearly filled up, but which not long since was open some spaces inwards, from the appearance of this heap I really cannot help thinking it was an altar for burnt offerings, some persons have thought the Cromliacs were altars, but from the inclined position of the upper stone of most of them, I think they would not well answer that purpose. I am rather inclined to think they were the visible objects of worship in which the spirit of the Deity was supposed to preside, and that the little chamber underneath was either the seat of the Chief Priest, or a sacred place for the purification or absolution of the religious penitent. It is probable that a circle of Stones formerly existed round this Cromliac also.

The *heap of larger stones and bushes* under which was the entrance to a small passage (souterrain?) is probably that shown on the right of the illustration (Fig 30.3), which is stated to have been 'drawn by J. Brownrigg 4th Sep. 1786'.

Cleenrah, Co. Longford (Fig 30.5)

The third drawing (Fig 30.5) also shows what the *Megalithic Survey* (deValera and Ó Nualláin 1972, 88; see also Cody *c.* 2002b) describes as a portal-tomb, this time on land which – to use an old-fashioned phrase – margins on to boggy terrain to east and west. It stands in a field just under a mile north-northeast of the village of Aghnacliff, and thus not far away from that just described, though less impressive than it – and also less known. Brownrigg's description of it is as follows:

"Cleanragh" (1786)

This Crom-liac called by the country people Clough Diarmuidh Grania, is on the lands of Clenragh, the Estate of Lord Belmore near Dunbiggan in the Barony and County of Longford, within 40 yards of the high road from Killyshandra to Granard. The great top stone is 4 feet thick – 6 feet wide at one end – 7 feet 6 inches at the other, and 9 feet long – The upper surface 10 feet from the ground. The entrance of the recess or chamber is 5 feet high and the Chamber well enclosed

Fig 30.5: The dolmen at Cleenrah, Co. Longford, copied after a lost drawing by John Brownrigg in a drawing now preserved in the National Library of Ireland. Photo: National Library of Ireland.

on all sides except the entrance. The ground on which this Cromliac stands is rough and rocky and at first view does not show any circle to have been round it, though I don't doubt but a careful excavation might trace it out if time would permit. This and the last mentioned Cromliac stand about half a mile asunder, and a third one stood at nearly the same distance from each of them, the three forming a triangle. This last one stood on the declivity of the hill of Dunbiggan near the chapel, and within 60 yards of the high road above mentioned. The circle of such stones round it is very distinct, notwithstanding a potato garden on the lower side has encroached very near to the centre of it – some rough stones are scattered through the area at present, but it appears to me that it had once been entirely cleared of them. Unfortunately some years since a presentment had been obtained to build a trifling bridge over the little river of Dunbiggan and the masons that undertook the work considered the

Cromliac near them as so many good stones already quarried to their hands and actually blasted the top stone and used its sacred fragments in their building. Two of the upright stones and a part of a third still remain in their places, and point out to the traveller what they once had been.

This description is valuable not only in adding substance to Brownrigg's fine drawing (Fig 30.5) of the dolmen – which makes it seem taller and more dramatic than it is in reality – but also because of its allusion to the former existence of yet a third example of the type in the same locality, of which no trace is visible, not even on the earliest Ordnance Survey map of 1837.

As an Eastmeath man, George, I hope that you will have gained a measure of pleasure – and enlightenment – from the foregoing paragraphs which help to swell the sparse number of megaliths in the midlands by showing the former existence of one megalith in Westmeath and another probable dolmen in Longford – in the same way that you have uncovered many more hitherto unknown megaliths around Knowth, but have also added to our knowledge of megaliths in Ireland and in other parts of Europe as well.

Acknowledgements

The copy-book and its drawings of the three midland megaliths presented here are the property of the National Library of Ireland and have been reproduced with the permission of the Council of Trustees of the National Library of Ireland, as granted through Dr. Noel Kissane, Keeper of Manuscripts. I am grateful to Elizabeth Kirwan, Assistant Keeper of Manuscripts, and Tom Desmond, for arranging to have the illustrations photographed, and to Eugene Hogan's photographic section for providing the photos. My thanks also to John Andrews, Paul Ferguson, Ron Cox and Edward McParland for furthering my knowledge about Brownrigg and his maps.

Bibliography

Andrews, J.H. 1967 The French school of Dublin land surveying, *Irish Geography* **5**, 275–92.

Andrews, J.H. 1985 *Plantation Acres. An historical study of the Irish land surveyor and his maps.* Ulster Historical Foundation, Belfast.

Andrews, J.H. 1986 Mapping the past in the past: cartographer as antiquarian in pre-Ordnance Survey Ireland. In C. Thomas (ed.) *Rural landscapes and communities. Essays presented to Desmond McCourt*, 31–63. Irish Academic Press, Dublin.

Andrews, J.H. 1991 The Longfield maps in the National Library: An agenda for research, *Irish Geography* **24**(1), 24–34.

Brownrigg, J. 1788 A descriptive account of the fort of Ardnorcher or Horseleap, near Kilbeggan, in the County of Westmeath, Ireland; with conjectures concerning its use, and the time of its erection. In a letter to Joseph C. Walker, Esq., Secretary to the Committee of Antiquities, *Transactions of the Royal Irish Academy* **2**, 43–5.

Cody, E. *c.* 2002a. Aghnacliff Portal Tomb. *Antiquities of the Granard Area*, 16. Granard Area Action Group, Granard.

Cody, E. *c.* 2002b. Cleenrah Portal Tomb. *Antiquities of the Granard Area*, 14–15. Granard Area Action Group, Granard.

Cox, R. 2002 Brownrigg, John. In A.W. Skempton et al. (eds) *A biographical dictionary of civil engineers in Great Britain and Ireland. Volume 1: 1500–1830*, 89–90. Thomas Telford and the Institution of Civil Engineers, London.

DeValera, R. and Ó Nualláin, S. 1972 *Survey of the megalithic tombs of Ireland. Vol. III* –Counties Galway, Roscommon, Leitrim, Longford, Westmeath, Laoighis, Offaly, Kildare, Cavan. The Stationery Office, Dublin.

Harbison, P. 2000 *Cooper's Ireland. Drawings and notes of an eighteenth-century gentleman.* The O'Brien Press, Dublin.

Harbison, P. 2002 *'Our treasure of antiquities'. Beranger and Bigari's antiquarian sketching tour of Connacht in 1779.* Wordwell, Bray.

Nevin, M. 1996 Joseph Cooper Walker, 1761–1810 *Journal of the Royal Society of Antiquaries of Ireland* **126**, 152–66.

Trench, C.E.F. 1985 William Burton Conyngham (1733–1796), *Journal of the Royal Society of Antiquaries of Ireland* **115**, 40–63.

Walker, Joseph C. 1788 *An historical essay on the dress of the ancient and modern Irish.* Dublin.

31. Adolf Mahr and the making of Seán P. Ó Ríordáin

Patrick F. Wallace

Introduction

Two figures seem to me to tower above all others in the development of Irish archaeology over the last seventy years. They flourished at and shortly after the real commencement of the subject, and, it is proposed here, one profoundly influenced the other. Yet both had comparatively short careers in Irish archaeology: Adolf Mahr (1887–1951) was 40 years old when he came to the National Museum of Ireland (NMI) in August 1927 and Seán P. Ó Ríordáin (1905–1957) had been a teacher before being appointed to a museum assistantship in 1931. Mahr, who was appointed Director of the Museum in July 1934, was to spend barely twelve years in Ireland before, as it turned out, he returned to Germany for the last time in September 1939 and Ó Ríordáin was to die aged fifty two in 1957 while in his prime having completed his campaign at Lough Gur and barely a couple of seasons into work at Tara.

Adolf Mahr's impact at the National Museum

Mahr came from the Natural History and Prehistoric Museum in Vienna in succession to Walther Bremen, another energetic German who had come to the museum in 1926 barely lasting a year before dying of a fever. The new man was an Iron Age specialist with a lot of museum experience and a wide network of contacts. He was to be centrally involved in bringing to Ireland the Harvard Archaeological mission with its modern excavation techniques and legacy of scientific reports as well as in the introduction of the new National Monuments Act of 1930 and the compilation of the album (Vol. 1 of *Christian Art in Ancient Ireland*) of Christian antiquities which was produced for the Eucharistic Congress of 1932. He was later to be president of the Prehistoric Society for whose 1937 *Proceedings* he produced his magisterial survey of Irish prehistory (Mahr 1937). He developed new exhibitions at the museum and planned a loan exhibition to Utrecht. He addressed the importance of folk life and its natural link with archaeology and posed the possibility of having a folk museum. He discussed this subject on our

fledgling radio station with Åke Campbell of Uppsala in 1937 and from an early stage encouraged other broadcasts from and about the museum. He acquired the Bender collection of oriental tapestries and was involved in a prolific correspondence with colleagues around Europe as well as with people from many different walks of life in Ireland. The latter included a 1916 committee from whom an idea of a permanent War of Independence gallery at the museum originated. And, of course, he performed all the other administrative and social demands of the job of Director of the National Museum, not least among these entertaining the great Austrian painter Oskar Kokothska during his visit to Dublin in July 1928.

Mahr's most enduring legacy relates to none of these sketchily summarised activities as Keeper and Director (to which I will return elsewhere) but to the way he set about introducing the concept of trained staff to his Irish antiquities division. He managed to convince the parent Department of Education to have recruits exposed to the best modern museum practices and excavation techniques while at the same time using them to catalogue holdings of Irish material in foreign museums. Thus Mahr laid the foundations of museum practice but he also had a formative role in developing university training in archaeology in Ireland. He guided and supervised Seán P. Ó Ríordáin and Michael Heaney (Mícheál Ó hÉanaigh) on their respective fifteen month stints around foreign museums and their collections. He also influenced the training of Joseph Raftery, William O Sullivan and G. A. Hayes McCoy who were appointed in his time while both Kevin Danaher and H. E. Kilbride Jones were employed as draughtsmen at the museum. Ó Ríordáin was to leave the museum to take up, successively, the chairs of archaeology at Cork (1936–1943) and Dublin (1943–1957). Michael Duignan, the first real professor of archaeology in Galway, was also a Mahr protégé who served as an assistant at the museum after a spell at the National Library of Ireland.

The concentration of the present paper is mainly on Seán P. Ó Ríordáin's training, the degree to which Mahr originated, guided and supervised it, and how it contrasts in some ways with that of Ó Ríordáin's contemporary at the museum, Heaney. The evidence is based on correspondence between Mahr and his assistants including Ó Ríordáin, which have been preserved at the director's office at the National Museum. While the original correspondence was two way in nature, Mahr's letters to his assistants were mainly handwritten and only the reports and letters of the assistants survive in the museum's archives, apart, that is, from the few occasions when Mahr had his letters typed by his secretary, Miss Crook.

Because I believe our present laureate produced in his 1964 later Bronze Age (Eogan 1964) paper a work of the calibre and import of Mahr's 1937 presidential address and of Ó Ríordáin's 1937 work on the halberds I trust the present offering to him is appropriate. It is offered in gratitude for his courageous stand on the Wood Quay issue in the High Court. Given G. F. Mitchell's connections with George Eogan's life and work it is of some relevance to Eogan that it was Mahr and Ó Ríordáin's network that brought Knud Jessen to Ireland thereby inaugurating Mitchell's involvement with Irish archaeology and quaternary studies. Although Eogan was not a student of Ó Ríordáin (unlike A. T. Lucas and A. B. Ó Ríordáin, two more recent directors of the National Museum), he will at least be interested to learn from the letters that Mahr guided Ó Ríordáin to Ernst Sprockhoff and was in correspondence with J. D. Cowen as early as November 1933.

First contact

The earliest letter from Ó Ríordáin dates from August 1931 when he writes to 'Dr. Mahr' whom he obviously already knows and whom he clearly trusts. Ó Ríordáin was concerned that the Civil Service Commission required him to pay back the cost of his two year's training as a national teacher on his recently taking up the assistantship. On a different matter, he tells Mahr that he was "working away on the Studentship course" but was finding it difficult to get the Department of Education to grant extra study leave saying "it's a pity they won't do something practical, even a little thing such as this, to help archaeology". A memo from Michael Quane for the Secretary of the Department of Education on 21st December 1931 informed Mahr that Ó Ríordáin had been told to report at 9.30 a.m. on the 1st January 1932 "for duty as Assistant in your division", there being no director since J. J. Buckley retired in 1929. Two years later the deputy Secretary wrote on 5th January 1934 to get "a Probationary Report on the prescribed Form E. Gen 4" in respect of Ó Ríordáin.

We learn from a letter to Heaney on 5th October 1932 that Mahr's two reasons for supporting his and Seán P. Ó Ríordáin's extended study tours were to expose them to top class practices and, while abroad, to get them to form a *corpus* of Irish archaeological specimens in the holdings of the various museums in which they were being trained.

"I want you as well as Mr. O'Riordan to share two purposes at the same time; to do your own work and to learn…. And to card-index the Irish stuff in the individual institutions so that sooner or later we will have at least something to guide us in the question of how the Irish stuff is scattered". More than anything Mahr himself was an inveterate card-indexer and compulsive cuttings hoarder. Nothing it seemed was irrelevant to the many compartments of his myriad interests within the broad culture – archaeology – museology spectrum. Even in the period before his early death in 1951 when he was preparing for a position in a mining history museum he had already embarked on building up categorised cuttings and references to his breakdown of the subject matter.

Seán P. Ó Ríordáin's museum travels: England, Scotland and Wales

Training abroad started for Ó Ríordáin before the end of his first month at work for, according to a typed *résumé* of his various reports, by the last week of January 1932 he was already in London at the British Museum "under the guidance of the officers of the Department of British and Medieval Antiquities". There, he worked "on prehistoric archaeology with special attention to their Irish Bronze Age collections". During his stay in London "I was enabled on your introductions" to examine collections in several other museums as well while "Dr. Mortimer Wheeler of the London Museum very kindly allowed me to attend his weekly lectures on pre-history". In April he attended the Easter school at the Pitt-Rivers Museum, in Farnham, Dorset. The lecturers included several well-known authorities and there were visits to local museums and field monuments in the afternoons. He spent some days at Bristol and went on to Cardiff for a few days where Cyril Fox, the Director, and E. Nash-Williams, the Keeper, and their assistants showed him the exhibitions and the reserve material as well as "the temporarily withdrawn Folk Collection". The relevance of folk material to archaeology was a tenet of Mahr's faith and one to which we will return. Its recognition by Ó Ríordáin would have pleased Mahr.

After Cardiff Ó Ríordáin went to Oxford stopping on the way at G. C. Dunning's excavation at Gloucester. He found Henry Belfour most helpful in showing him the ethnographical material and he spent most of his time in Oxford at the Ashmolean where "Mr. E. T. Leeds gave me complete freedom for work and I was fortunate in being able to get card indexed most of the Evans collection of Irish bronze implements". Leeds also allowed Ó Ríordáin to join in the "excavation of an Iron-Age dwelling site near Oxford". His return to London saw him getting information "on the Tibetan silk paintings presented to this museum and of which you sent me photographs". This is a reference, presumably, to the Bender collection that Mahr procured for the Museum.

That Mahr's interest in Ó Ríordáin was for the long

term good of his career is evident in his letter of 30th April 1932 telling him to go to Vere Gordon Childe in Edinburgh: "I should strongly advise you to join him, even if it be only for a few days… I have reason to believe that afterwards you will be glad to have done it." So in early May Ó Ríordáin left for Edinburgh on the advice of Mahr who arranged that he work with Childe on a hillfort excavation in Scotland. "This work continued until May 30th after which I was able to spend some days in the National Museum of Scotland and to visit the Royal Scottish Museum". The fact that he did not excavate on some Saturday afternoons "permitted me to visit some of the more interesting monuments in the Edinburgh district". On 17th May Ó Ríordáin wrote to Mahr saying that up to then he had had only "one wet afternoon, when he could not dig" in Edinburgh museum and how "Edwards introduced me to Callander and they both went around with me". His comment that "Callander I found a rather gloomy person" shows the relative maturity of his friendship with "Dr. Mahr".

Before resuming duty in Dublin on Saturday morning 4th June, Ó Ríordáin found time to visit Glasgow Museum and the Hunterian at the University! Mahr had singled out Childe who is the only one to write to him as 'My Dear Adolf' (*deingetreuer*, *vgc*) as he did after Ó Ríordáin's visit. 'I must congratulate you on your new assistant and thank you for putting him in touch with me. He struck me as remarkably intelligent and well in-formed…moreover, he is a pleasant companion on a dig'. The Mahr – Childe friendship and its human side is clear from a message in a letter of 30th May "Childe sends his love and says to tell you he has done the worst ausgrabung ever seen" but clearly not wishing to be guilty of making a judgement on the work of a senior colleague's friend Ó Ríordáin quickly adds – "this of course you need not believe" because "it was a tangled subject to excavate but I think he managed to clear up the problems well".

Ó Ríordáin's letters from his various stops show that Mahr was not only in regular correspondence with him but was also in contact with the people whom he was meeting. Part of his purpose was to ensure that Ó Ríordáin was accommodated free of charge because he does not appear to have been paid expenses. W. J. Hemp of the Welsh Royal Commission wrote (20th April 1932) of meeting "your Mr. O'Reardon" and asking "would you like him to have a round with "the staff" when they are doing the ordinary routine work of measuring up churches, houses, etc?" T. D. Kenrick's letter to Mahr on 7th September 1932 refers to "the labels Riorden (have forgotten the spelling!) did for our Irish Bronze Age case" and to Heaney's work on the new arrangement of the gold…"so you can say we have made some use of your assistants". Ó Ríordáin's official progress report written from the Central Hotel, Cardiff, on 26th April praises Fox and Nash-Williams who "were very nice to me here" and of how both "invited me out to the house". He had stopped at Gloucester because "Wheeler advised me

strongly to have a look at the work as he says Dunning's technique is very good". He would make up his mind about taking in Cambridge "after discussing things with Hemp". "I am glad to have Hemp's offer to allow me work with him, as several people including Wheeler have told me that Hemp is the best excavator in the country and you will be interested to hear that Wheeler (who seems to have taken an interest in my archaeology) has also invited me to join him on his dig at Verullamium…. (of course Wheeler's dig is Roman but he says he may, if finds permit, begin on the pre-historic part of the site and also he says that the technique is really a constant not affected by the subject dug)." The same letter asks for instructions in regard to the Tibetan silk material and finishes by mentioning his hurried card-index of the Irish "stuff" at the Pitt-Rivers Museum "and of how Stephens at Salisbury has a fine collection of Irish material also, and has a fairly good slip catalogue of it. Some time we might get the slips on loan from him and add it to the lists". It seems to have been Museum practice to type up Ó Ríordáin's larger written reports and to place both the original manuscript and a copy of the typescript on file. The original typescript would have been sent to the Department as a note in Mahr's hand on the copy of Ó Ríordáin's report of 29th November 1932 says "sent to Dept. 2.12.32".

Further afield: northern Europe, Germany, Switzerland and France

This earliest British experience was but an introduction to what archeologically inspired travel had in store for Seán P. Ó Ríordáin in 1932. His travels resumed on 21st September when he went to Bristol where he made a card-index of the Irish material at the museum. Under the guidance of Mrs Dobson (who is referred to as a nice old lady by Mahr in a letter to Heaney) of Bristol he visited the excavations at Mere Lake Village and the Wells and Glastonbury museums. The same experience was repeated at Salisbury where a card-index of "the very large collections of Irish Stone and Bronze Age material" was undertaken. He took photographs of the gold ornaments in the Irish collection at the Pitt-Rivers Museum, Farnham, and was in London by 8th October. He journeyed to Sid-cup, Kent, to see the Hassé collection of antiquities because of the National Museum's interest in acquiring these.

The period 12th to 31st October was spent at Gron-ingen in the Netherlands where, under the direction of A. E. Van Giffen, he took part in the excavation of a terp at Exinge. Ó Ríordáin also examined the museum collections at Assen and Groningen and investigated the Biologisch – Archaeologisch Instituut and saw several monuments in the vicinity of Groningen. After this in early November he visited the National collection of the Netherlands at Leiden where he saw the reserve and exhibited collections as well as the material in the great Ethnographical museum.

Moving to Germany for the first time, Ó Ríordáin

called on Dr. F. B. von Richthofen and Dr. Hansen, the former showing him his own and other museums and explaining how the museum system worked. After this at Kiel from 10th to 21st November he examined the collections and attended Professor Dr. G. Schwantes' lectures. He visited a "ring-wall" excavation as well as the Hedeby (Haithabu) site that was then being excavated by Schwantes and Herbert Jankuhn. He got to Berlin by 21st November and began training under Professor Dr. W. Unverzagt. He got home to Monkstown, Co Cork, for Christmas and was on his travels again on 25th January returning to Hamburg where he was contactable care of Professor Dr. Mülhausen. After that it was back to Berlin and on to Halle and later to Mainz, Switzerland and Paris. Ó Ríordáin broke his tour and returned to Ireland in the late Spring/early Summer as he had the year before but was back in Kiel by 22nd October 1933 after which he went to Stettin (Szezetin) and Copenhagen. He was to return to northern Europe and Paris at the end of 1934.

Going back to the end of November 1932 we learn (in a letter of 23rd) that the weather "during the whole of my stay" was "very bad". However, "van Giffen was embarrassing with kindness and hospitality". At Kiel he found Schwantes kind and although somewhat elusive he did introduce Ó Ríordáin to the 'ring-wall' excavation and 'the Haithabu site, Danework and barrows etc... (the Haithabu excavation was, of course, over but the invitation stands)". He travelled to the Statlisches Museum for Vorgeschichte in Prinz Albrecht Strasse, Berlin, with Dr. Jankuhn "who is going on a study tour". Jankuhn introduced him to Dr. von Jenny. There seems to have been some confusion about the extent of his involvement at the Berlin museum. "I have found that there is a nice (not very large) collection of Irish (mostly bronze) stuff here and I have begun with a card-index of that. (I did the same with the little they have in Hamburg)....." He found Hamburg "very good and Richthofen has certainly got fine organisation and management there...he and Hansen (were) very very good to me. They and Schwantes, van Griffen etc all send you kind regards." He continued to find it difficult to meet Unverzagt but did manage to get him after a Saturday lecture when he "seems a kindly person when one manages to get at him". In the same note (28th November) Ó Ríordáin managed to say that the farmer at Old Castle, Coachford, Co. Cork, with whom he was dealing was willing not to remove the cairn on his land if the museum excavated it instead! In a rushed note the following day Ó Ríordáin said he was going to visit Unverzagt's excavation at Zantock and that his Berlin mentor was "giving instructions that I am to see all the technical processes in the museum, and at the same time I can continue to study the collections".

The next we hear of our overworked traveller is from Monkstown, Co. Cork, on 14th January 1933 when he suggests he get on with cataloguing the College Museum collection in Cork in lieu of filling in the time (a week) between the end of his leave and the departure of the Cobh-Hamburg liner on the 25th January. He also promised to send on the indexes (sic) "from the stuff in Hamburg, Berlin and Cork before I leave." A further note (24th January 1933) from Cork before he embarked shows that the file of the Curraghbinny excavations (Co. Cork, Ó Ríordáin 1933a) accompanied the "card-indexes". His attention to the record is evident in a post-script in which he tells Mahr that two photos in the Curraghbinny file which "got in by mistake" should instead be with the Ballyconnel cairn (Killarah townland, Co. Cavan, published by Ó Ríordáin (1933b) in December). Ó Ríordáin took them out and added another of Curraghbinny from his own negatives. He also changed the relevant registration numbers. The consistency of the archive was paramount; he was learning well!

At Hamburg his address was care of Prof. Dr. Mülhausen. He went from there to Hanover visiting the Luneburg Museum en route, which he noted, on a NMI post card from Hanover on 1st February. In a later letter from Halle Ó Ríordáin describes this as "a nicely displayed museum." Earlier, in a letter of 14th February he acknowledged Mahr's recent letters. He asks whether a note on the Co. Cavan cairn burial and its bones might be suitable for the *Irish Naturalists Journal* and, if so, whether Mahr might send on the relevant file. He also mentions a bronze sword he brought back from Castletownbeare on his first museum trip and a nearby souterrain though he thought the cairn "our first choice" for publication. In the same letter (14th February 1933) he reports he had met Schultz at Halle "and found him very nice" observing that "there's a great social spirit in Halle" where, apparently, they had dug grave stones carved with lines representing "spear-heads". He seeks Mahr's reassurance: "We haven't anything of this type in Ireland, have we?" He is becoming more confident with his boss!

By the time of his letter of February 23rd Ó Ríordáin has received a letter and the Killarah photos from Mahr. He describers the acquisition of the Castletownbeare sword from a man called O'Sullivan who among other things was a local correspondent for the Cork and Dublin papers – "like most local correspondents he has imagination rather than a facility of exactness". For the first time Ó Ríordáin seems to lose his patience with Mahr who mistakenly, in his view, has asked him in Germany for details about the find places of the leaf-shaped sword and the souterrain which could be checked by O'Connor in the files in Dublin "in less than five minutes". He then resumes normal transmission by saying he "was at Kickebush's museum on Wednesday. He was all enquiries for you". He finishes the letter by saying "I don't propose to leave Berlin for some weeks. My halberd material is growing still" and adds a postscript to explain a cutting regarding Castletownbeare and an offprint from Lindenschmitt which assigns the Lisnacroghera sword-sheath to Northumberland adding, presumably tongue in cheek, "I suppose it is a mistake". Cuttings and references of this type were grist to Mahr's mill all his life.

That Ó Ríordáin remained under Mahr's rigorous scrutiny is evident from his next letter from Halle; in this he answers questions that show that Mahr had carefully combed through his Cork card-index. He explains that the bronze horns from Cork "were not included because they are locked away in a separate case and I could not get anyone to open it the evening I was finishing up". He says a card could be made up from a pair of publications to which he refers, and that he was very busy on his index and did not have time to include the stone implements. This may indicate what I perceive to be a slight impatience with his mentor that grew from confidence, and matured with wider contacts and travel. We get a hint of this in his February 14th letter in which he seeks Mahr's assurance on a matter of detail. On 23rd of the same month Ó Ríordáin is slightly more impatient about a provenance that ought better to be dealt with in Dublin. And now Ó Ríordáin is defending with a hint of testiness his not having indexed the Cork horns.

To be fair, in the same letter Ó Ríordáin reveals pride in the NMI postcard series, a set of which he asks Mahr to send to Hansen in Hamburg adding "if they cannot be sent officially I'll pay for them". It appears he was gradually becoming his own man, confident enough to comment on others' museums and their approaches and to pass on complements and greetings in a decliningly cloying manner. "Hansen and Richthofen have always been very kind to me at Hamburg... they all send you greetings from Hanover. They were most decent to me – gave me special permission re: working late etc. Schroller was especially good". Luneburg, as we have noted, Ó Ríordáin found to be "a nicely-displayed museum". Hanover "is the best museum I've seen, I think, as fine as Cardiff".

Although he found Brunswick museum closed, he found Madgeburg had "a nice collection – particularly their Neolithic stuff" though "the museum was unheated and the cold was pretty bad". He went to a lecture by Bogen, the Director, whom he met: "He is not, I think, primarily a prehistorian but was very nice and presented me with a Festschrift of the museum."

By early March at the Prehistoric Museum in Berlin Ó Ríordáin is back to musing about whether he should publish the Castletownbeare stone circle from which the sword came. However, he had not had time to survey it and did not trust the locals to do a proper job. He thought he could write up the Castletownbeare souterrain but needed the file, which he was asking O'Connor to send on to him, a practice that would now be frowned upon but this is seventy years ago. He felt an article on German museums somewhat too general for the *Irish Naturalists Journal* but appropriate to a less specialised journal. The idea for the general article obviously came from Mahr who cannot but have noticed the tiny Germanisms which were slowly and almost imperceptibly slipping into Ó Ríordáin's written English: "leaving to an excavation of Unverzagt's and Götze's". He considered going to Vienna ("I think Menghin ought to be back...who else would be

useful to me there?). Pokorny says that if I go he can arrange it that I lodge with Prof Much and family)" and making "a short trip to Buda-Pest". He finishes his letter of 7th March by mentioning new acquisitions and saying his sister had sent him a cutting about the graves at Islandbridge. This was from the *Irish Independent* while another, presumably gleaned from the relevant annual report of the Museum, from the *Irish Press* informed him about the Museum's activities for 1932.

A longer letter of 27th March 1933 from Berlin shows that Ó Ríordáin is mixing with distinguished scholars. In Berlin it was he who introduced Pokorny to Childe with both of whom he "had a most pleasant evening" where he learnt "Childe is rewriting his Ancient east". He received a letter from van Giffen forwarded from Dublin in which he asked Ó Ríordáin to give his regards to the Mahr family. He is very much following the advice of Mahr as to where he went and to whom he had introductions. It suited him better to be Mahr's man rather than his own. Mahr put him off Vienna and Budapest which he wanted to see because of the Danubian copper period "(and also their parallels to our souterrains)". In going to Dresden, and then to Frankfurt he was advised by Unverzagt to use his name to Gerhart Bersu at Frankfurt who would then advise him. Later in Mainz he had Mahr's introductions to Zeis and Spockhoff. His aim now was to get back to Dublin early in June as in the year before and leave in the autumn for Schwantes's excavation at Haithabu from which he would go to Copenhagen.

Meanwhile Mahr in a letter of 28th March thinks Ó Ríordáin should take advantage of his intended Mainz location to attend the Swiss course of prehistory; Mahr arranged a reduced fee for him and wrote on his behalf to the relevant personnel including the secretary of the Swiss Prehistoric Society, Dr. K. Keller-Tarnuzzer: "I attach very much importance that you should participate and perhaps Dr. Jenny, who knows Switzerland well, can give you still some useful hints (I think they have special cheap tickets on the Swiss Railways)." Mahr applied to the Royal Irish Academy to get some additional money (£5.00) for Ó Ríordáin to cover this additional travel.

In a letter of 11th April he tells Mahr that he would next be care of Sprockhoff at Mainz because Bersu informed him the guest room at the Kommission was in the course of construction and, anyway, he could go to Frankfort for a few days any time. As usual, he enclosed a letter from Unverzagt, the Director of the Berlin Museum, outlining what he had been up to most recently and "although I was there when he dictated it I forgot to get him to mention that I had also attended his lectures". Inevitably, he did get to Zürich according to a postcard from Mainz on 20th April where we learn that Keller-Tarnuzzer fixed everything for him and that although Sprockhoff was in Groningen he did manage to meet Behrens and Bersu.

Ó Ríordáin next wrote to Mahr from the Romish-Germanischs Zentral Museum in Mainz saying he found the Swiss trip "on the whole very useful and very pleasant also". He had spent a day at the National Museum in Zürich and joined Keller-Tarnuzzer on the Insel Werd excavation on Lake Constance. The latter colleague he found "most decent…being a guest of his on a visit to Frankenfeld" and during the few days on the excavation. Keller-Tarnuzzer was also very good at notifying curators of Ó Ríordáin's upcoming visits to their respective institutions.

He met P. Vouga who wondered, having met Mahr in London, whether Mahr had been able to get his 'La Tène' book at the author's price? Otherwise, Vouga offered to rectify the situation. Ó Ríordáin 'fobbed off' a man in Basel Museum's prehistoric department on the subject of exchanges – "I didn't believe they have anything we want or that we can give them anything they'd be likely to require, but for politeness sake I told him to write to you" – the classic deference to the director from the polite staff member who should have used his own initiative! He also warned Mahr that he had encouraged Keller-Tarnuzzer to have the 1935 excursion of his *Gesselschaft* in Ireland. On a personal note he concludes by hoping Mahr is "very well – a breakdown would do no good so why not ease up in time" which testifies to Mahr's legendary work-rate and commitment and probably also to a complaint about his workload which Mahr must have made in the, sadly, now inevitably missing letter, to which Ó Ríordáin is replying.

Ó Ríordáin makes some interesting references to the Swiss museums he visited. Apart from Zürich and the excavation he visited, he went to the museum at Schaffhausen and two museums at St. Gallen as well as the library that houses the Irish manuscripts. Keller-Tarnuzzer showed him "his collection". Vouga accompanied him to Neuchatel and he met Dr. Ischor ("a very nice fellow") at Bern which "has some Irish bronze material but I only saw it just before leaving and there was no use in trying to do it as Prof. Tschumi had the catalogue locked up and he is in Italy for his health at present". After Neuchâtel Ó Ríordáin left for Biel "where they have some Irish stuff that I got done – but no localities". Basel he considered had a "poor prehistoric but good folklife collection". On the return journey to Mainz he stopped long enough for Wahle to show him "his stuff" at Heidelberg and at Manheim from where Prof. Gropengissen sent his regards to Mahr. Further testimony to Mahr's widely flung museum contacts is a reference in the following letter to "Kutsch of Wiesbaden" whom Ó Ríordáin met on an outing and sent his greetings to the director in Dublin. A few days later Ó Ríordáin was off to Frankfurt and asking whether he could go on to Bonn, which he heard "has a very good collection". He hoped to be able to visit Paris on his way home from Frankfurt because "I am particularly anxious to see if there are not some halberds there" and "I can't understand the absence of such in France". He also asks Mahr for a name in France "to show me the collections". He suggested that "it must be someone who speaks either English or German".

Mahr's advice about France and who to meet there wasn't long in forthcoming for on the 18th May 1933 he wrote to "Mr O Reardon". He had the letter typed (which is why a copy survives on file in contrast to most of his communications which were handwritten) so that copies could reach Ó Ríordáin at both Frankfort and Mainz in order to avoid delay because "you have little time to spend". Before giving advice on France he suggested a visit to Professor Oelmann, Director of the Provincial Museum at Bonn (he gives Ó Ríordáin Oelmann's private address), saying that if he gave him Mahr's best greetings "he will look after you". While in Bonn Mahr felt Ó Ríordáin should also visit Dr. Thurneysen who loved visits from "travelling Irish scholars" and "speaks wonderful English and may be of any amount of use to you".

The main contact in Paris was to be Professor R. Lantier, Keeper at the Musée des Antiquities Nationales at St. Germain-en-Laye. He speaks "English quite well and German still better". Mahr had separately written to "Miss Henry" (Françoise Henry) "to write a letter to him so that she knows of your impending visit". In a rare political revelation in this correspondence Mahr warns, "be careful with Lantier and do not speak about political developments in Germany because he is a great friend of Bersu, Unverzagt, and there is no use in your being mixed up with inter-continental quarrels". Bersu was later to contribute to the barring of Mahr's return to Ireland.

Showing how aware he was of the politics of archaeology even outside Germany Mahr also advised Ó Ríordáin to pay a visit to M. R. Vanfrey of the Institute de Paléonthologie Humaine. He was the editor of *L'Anthropologie*, spoke "excellent English and is a very enterprising man" but was "on very bad terms with the museum people". Mahr felt he "had better be careful not to speak on matters of scientific policy where some delicate developments might enter the discussion. Otherwise you are quite free to discuss with him everything which is neither French not (sic) German". Mahr also advised Ó Ríordáin to visit the Louvre, the Trocadero and the Musée de Cluny of which the Keeper was J. J. Marquet de Vasselot "with whom we had some correspondence quite recently". He also promised to write separately to a Mr. Ó Clérigh's address in Paris so Ó Ríordáin would have a suitable introductory letter to Lantier and advised him to contact Ó Clérigh and Miss (Ada) Longfield who were both in Paris at the time. They were possibly on parallel learning trips on behalf of the Art and Industrial division where the latter was to work before her marriage to H. G. Leask of the National Monuments branch of the OPW. Leask while cooperative with Mahr before the war was apparently less supportive in its aftermath.

Britain and Scandinavia, France and Germany again

In a letter of 4th December 1933 Ó Ríordáin made a general report of the next period of his training abroad –

from 1st October to the beginning of December. His first task on this stint was to spend a week on Mortimer and Mrs. Wheeler's excavation of Roman Verulamium and "its prehistoric forerunner Prae Wood" near St Albans. This was followed by a study of the collection at the Cambridge Museum of Ethnology and Archaeology in the company of E. W. Phillips who brought him to see some of the monuments near Cambridge, which he was then surveying. Then, after a few days at the Royal Archaeological Institute in London, he left for the Haithabu excavation in Schleswig-Holstein under the direction of Schwantes and Jankuhn. He spent ten days on the site and visited the museums of Kiel, Schleswig and Flensbourg. He refers to Haithabu as "Prof Schwantes' excavation", Jankuhn, apparently, being the junior partner. Next at Copenhagen he was allowed to study the reserve collections at the National Museum which was then being rebuilt and also managed to visit the collections at Lyngby, the Folkmuseum and the Kunstindustrie Museum and after them Lund where the Historiska and Folk Museums were studied. From Lund he went to the Historiska Museum at Göthenborg and from there to Oslo where he saw the collections in the National Museum as well as at the Folk Museum and the Viking ship museum at Bygdø. Dr. J. Bøe facilitated his study of the Irish Viking material at Bergen while, next, at Stockholm he concentrated on the rich Bronze Age material and its Irish connections as well as inevitably (especially in Scandinavia) taking in the "museums of folk lore-material and their organisation" at Nordiska Museet and the open-air museum at Skansen, outside Stockholm. Upsala and Gamla Upsala were also visited, as were the monuments in their regions.

Ó Ríordáin crossed to Stettin (Szezetin) from Stockholm and while the Stettin museum was being extensively renovated "every facility and all freedom were given for the study of the collections". Following this, he again visited the museum für Vorgeschichte at Berlin to tie up some loose ends and, inevitably, also visited the Volkskunde museum before going on to Hanover where a one day stop was used to look at the Early Bronze Age collection and visit the Folk Museum, the director of which, Dr. Pessler "is most interested in Irish material and was pleased at an opportunity to further reciprocal museum relationships". Next at Nijmwegen museum Ó Ríordáin managed to see originals of some of the casts of prehistoric material he had seen at the Romisch-Germanisch Zentral Museum at Mainz. From Brussels, where with Dr. Bruer's "kind permission and help" he managed to see the reserve collection of the material from the famous Siret excavations, Ó Ríordáin made his way to Paris and Professor R. Lantier at St. Germain-en-Laye and promised to see the ethnographical exhibition at the Trocadero. We learn that this and other museums were visited from a typed report of 4th January 1934 and that in Paris Ó Ríordáin worked in particular on material from the Breton megalithic monuments as well as on the Bronze

Age collection. "M. Vanfey and M. l'Abbé Breuil were both most kind in making me acquainted with the collections of Palaeolithic material housed at the Institute de Palaeothologie Humaine and M. l'Abbé Breiul added to this kindness by discussing at length some questions of Irish prehistory."

Returning to the individual letters from the various stops mentioned in this report we find in the first from October 1933 that Ó Ríordáin was back in northern Europe en route to Schwantes (and Jankuhn) at Haithabu. He came via Esbjerg in Jutland and went south via Hamburg, which he also visited. He later took in Kiel and its museum and went to the "Haithabu museum" at Schleswig. After that, he went to Copenhagen (although he heard that J. Brøndsted was ill) and after a week there on to "Norway, Sweden and Stockholm and the principal museums there – Lund, Göthenburg, Oslo, Bergen and Stockholm". He had accumulated a list of names and had written to J. Delargy of the Irish Folklore Commission for others. He planned to come back to Paris via Stettin from Stockholm, his contact at Stettin being care of Dr. O. Kunkel at the Provincial Museum when he would pick up his correspondence. In his letter of 22nd October from Kiel he wondered whether Mahr had heard of Richthofen's appointment as professor at Königsberg (Kaliningrad) adding "I am pleased – he is a very nice fellow and I should say deserves his luck".

Bergen, which he reached from Oslo, Ó Ríordáin found "the prettiest place I've seen yet". In a pencilled message (as opposed to his usual fountain pen) on a post-card of 3rd November he reported that Bøe had "come along specially to show me the museum". He found him "very nice and the best of the Scandinavians I've met so far". From Bergen Ó Ríordáin went to Stockholm. He is in Berlin en route to Paris when we next hear from him on 17th November. By then, he informs Mahr, he had picked up his mail in Stettin and had "got on well in Scandinavia and met most of the people I wanted". He would break his journey to Paris in Berlin, Hanover and Brussels.

Ó Ríordáin met Dr. Knud Jessen in Copenhagan where they talked "for a good while". Jesssen "is most anxious that some Irish botanist or quaternary geologist should come to Copenhagen and Stockholm to do pollen–analysis". Ó Ríordáin promised to discuss this further on his return to Dublin. This is where, presumably, G. F. Mitchell is about to come into the story! Although Brøgger was the obvious target of Mahr's and Ó Ríordáin's attentions in Oslo and Ó Ríordáin had written to him, he did not meet him at the Oslo Museum because Dr. Grieg who showed him around did not introduce him to Brøgger whom he was sorry to have missed. H. Shetelig was also away. He found Bøe to be "the nicest of the lot", not least because he was "very free with his knowledge and most helpful". He specifically asked Mahr to thank Bøe for all his help. In Stockholm he met "most of the Statens Historiska people and some of those at the Nordiska Museum." He also passes on the good wishes of Schich and Arne who "were asking for" Mahr who, incidentally, had, evidently, passed on a message from J. M. de Navarro. Dr. Martin, the bone annalist had also written to Ó Ríordáin asking for a skeleton, presumably for a reference collection, but he deferred to the Director on this matter.

Ó Ríordáin only had three weeks in Paris and was "making a desperate attempt to learn French". "Classes and tuitions are taking nearly all my time" and "candidly I am giving more energy to French than to St. Germain" (museum) where he went in afternoons "but spent the rest of the day "at language work". He tells Mahr of this in a personal letter appended to his written report of 4th December 1933, adding "of course, I did not say this in the official report which I send herewith". He mentions Dr. Pessler of Hanover, "a very pleasant old gentleman…most delighted at meeting someone from Ireland", a folklife man anxious to get photographs, books or offprints ("which don't exist!") on his subject. He had met Pessler on the recommendation of Dr. Hahm of Berlin. By December 20th he was on the point of leaving Paris for London en route home for Christmas. He adds that Breuil and Vanfey send Mahr their greetings and Vanfey an offprint that he would give him on his return.

Domestic concerns

Ó Ríordáin had more on his mind than his homecoming for Christmas however. Cork archaeology and university politics feature in his concerns, particularly, it would appear, a lack of support for him from Power (presumably, Canon Power, the professor of archaeology (1915–32) at UCC). He "has a feeling for some time that Power would not be much use to me in the matter (of a job in UCC?) though what is really in his mind I cannot quite understand". "I can make guesses but may be quite wrong," adding "although I always managed to pull along all right with him, he is a very difficult man" and "one never knows when he is suffering from an overdose of conscience or when he is merely playing with some peculiar idea of his own. And sometimes his ideas are inspired by others – there are some people in Cork who are willing to decide all about policy in archaeology without knowing anything about it". Ó Ríordáin finished by promising to discuss the matter fully with Mahr whom he asked to "please accept my best thanks for your interest in the question".

The final references to Seán P. Ó Ríordáin that I have been able to find in the present correspondence date to a year later, December 1934. At that time Ó Ríordáin was abroad again in Edinburgh and on a presumably short study trip to Paris where he tried to extend his paid study leave with the strong support of Mahr but was refused by the Department of Finance. Mahr tried to persuade the Education official Michael Quane who, ironically, was to be put in charge of the museum as Administrator before the appointment of A. T. Lucas as Director in 1954. Refusal of Ó Ríordáin's application for special leave was

conveyed to Mahr by Ó Dubhthaigh, Deputy Secretary of Education, who informed the Director that the Minister for Finance could not agree to sanction the proposal "to enable him to make a study in France of the problem of the connection by the Continental souterrains with those of this country". To be fair to Ó Dubhthaigh in his letter to the Secretary of Finance of 4th December 1934, which he copied to Mahr, he supported Ó Ríordáin's application explaining that "his proposed visit to France is expected to be of much assistance in the solution of certain important archaeological questions arising out of this discovery, made recently by Ó Ríordáin at Temair Erann (Cush, Co. Limerick, which Ó Ríordáin (1940) began excavating in August 1934), indicating that souterrains were in existence in Ireland in the Bronze Age". He added that it was not intended to make any payment to Mr. Ó Ríordáin in respect of travelling and subsistence, that all that was required was the sanction of special leave and that "the Minister for Education desires to urge" the Minister for Finance to agree to that. Whether the powers-that-be felt they had already been generous enough, as they appear to have been to Ó Ríordáin, is not indicated. Given present knowledge of such matters and the, to present day archaeologists, outlandish nature of the thesis maybe Finance can, in retrospect, be forgiven for discouraging this line of research, that is, if they didn't have some sixth sense about its wisdom which seems most unlikely! Mahr accepted the thesis and outlined it in his letter to the Secretary of Education on 29th November 1934. Incidentally, in Mahr's report also of 29th November to Ó Ríordáin, care of T. D. Kendrick at the British Museum, he also puts on his Civil Service hat. "But you must understand that your proposed cuts right across all the accounting principles of our administration (a principle which holds good also for leave and similar matters) viz the principle that nothing can be carried over from one year to another, except economy on the Grant-in-Aid". In Ó Ríordáin's reply from the Hotel de l'Europe, Paris, he mentions that he met Stephens at Salisbury and that "he had some suggestions to make regarding his Irish bronzes going to Dublin." Ó Ríordáin had a slightly more *laisez-faire* attitude than Mahr to the Civil Service and its rules as his letter of 5th December implies. On Mahr 7th December explained the Department of Finance mindset to his junior. Ó Ríordáin was already en route to Southampton from Le Havre on 11th December. Mahr's letter of 8th December, which Ó Ríordáin probably never received, explained how Mahr, in order to mollify the sticklers in Education, used the excuse to Quane that Ó Ríordáin had gone to France before his leave expired. He returned a letter from Miss L. Chitty with the same note. A final irony, perhaps, in relation to Ó Ríordáin's familiarisation with the Civil Service is implicit in Quane's letter of New Year's Eve 1934 which permitted Ó Ríordáin to "display a selection of Museum objects in connection with his forthcoming lecture to Cumann Gaolah na Stát-Sheirbhíse, on the assumption that adequate precautions will be taken for the safety of the objects". Although it had been very good to him in many ways Ó Ríordáin was probably glad in the end to leave the Museum to take up the professorship of archaeology at UCC in 1936. Incidentally, Mahr was seriously ill at the time of Ó Ríordáin's application and was unable to furnish a testimonial on behalf of his protégé.

Adolf Mahr's role of mentor and guide in the practical training of museum staff

A letter to Heaney, the other newly appointed Assistant in Irish Antiquities, on 17th June 1931 from the Secretary of the Department of Education informed him that on taking up his appointment not more than fifteen months of his first two years probationary period would be spent abroad. A condition of accepting the appointment was that the candidate "be prepared for training, at such British or Continental Museums as may be selected by the Department of Education for the purpose". It was understood that no travel or subsistence expenses would be paid which shows how central the role of Mahr with his knowledge of British and Continental museums was in terms of the "selections" of institutions considered appropriate for the training by the Department of Education. Even more important Mahr's network of colleagues and friends were expected to accommodate the trainees in gastzimmers where they existed or otherwise at the homes of friends. The life of the trainee would also be made more tolerable by the hospitality of the various scholars and curators to whom Mahr could write letters of introduction.

The concentration of Heaney's training seems to have been on British rather than Continental museums, not least probably because Heaney called to the Department of Education in September 1931 to tell them he was unemployed since he had given up a teaching post and because of "the recent drop in the value of British currency" causing O Dubhthagh of the Department to say in a memo to Mahr on 25th September that "it may make it difficult for us to start immediately with our plan for training Mr. Heaney at Continental museums". He commenced work at the Museum on October 1st 1931, three months before Ó Ríordáin, which was a worry to Mahr who clearly from the outset considered the Corkman the better prospect.

In his reply to the Secretary of the Department of Education on 28th September, 1931, Adolf Mahr as Keeper of Irish Antiquities in his definition of the duties to be carried out by Heaney shows the extent to which he considered training necessary for the new assistants. Mahr also indicates the extent to which he was central to a new approach to training archaeological recruits and underlines his own emphasis for the way the museum (particularly his division) should be run, as well as the directions archaeology should take and of the interests it should embrace. He had satisfied himself that prehistoric archaeology and Irish Folk-civilisation should be Heaney's main interests adding that a further development of folklife "is the very thing which the country wants".

Mahr felt that "whilst a prehistorian need not necessarily go to Scandinavia for additional training a man who is expected to carry out good work in European ethnography cannot but get his main training in Stockholm" adding that "the reasons which led the Department four years ago to select Dr. Lithberg as foreign expert for the Committee of Enquiries into the National Museum hold good also for the present case and I beg to suggest that Mr. Heaney goes first for 6 months to Stockholm. Here he can learn the ethnographical parish-research method and any amount of useful things which equally well apply to Ireland..." He further proposed that Heaney could join an excavation in the spring and "such will be the best transitional step to the next stage which I propose to be 3 months say in the big provincial museum in Breslau (Germany)." (Breslau is now Wrocław, Poland). His reason here was that "this museum has to work for the big province of Silesia in exactly the same manner as the national depository for archaeological finds as we have to work in Dublin". He pointed out that Breslau had "a splendid tradition" in excavation, surveying and "in museum technique" and the Breslau museum hadn't suffered "from such a heavy reduction of public grants as many other German museums". After that, Mahr suggested Heaney go for three months to Bonn and then to Wales for another three months. Bonn, he felt, should be sacrificed if there was any reduction in the amount of time allowed to the trainee. He didn't think Heaney should go to Stockholm until the 1st December for "a month or so, to get a bit of an introduction to museum work (so that his first impressions he makes in Stockholm will be favourable) and to learn, in the evenings, some German and Swedish".

Showing perhaps that he already had decided between Heaney and Ó Ríordáin as to whom he considered most likely to succeed, Mahr queried the Secretary about seniority and entitlement as to promotion down the road. He worried that if Heaney started before Ó Ríordáin they might "be ranked by seniority". Without naming Ó Ríordáin (whom he refers to as "another assistant") he enquires: "should in far-off years the Keepership become vacant, the difference (of only a few months) should not, in my opinion" provide the first to report for duty with "a stronger claim for a higher position". Mahr even went so far as to suggest the Department consider insisting "a aliena into the appointment minute that seniority comes from the time of definite appointment" presumably to give himself a chance to access more fully his new charges and to time recommending the finalisation of their respective probations in order to give Ó Ríordáin an equal chance in a competition. As it happened the Keepership was filled long after Mahr's time by Joseph Raftery who, in turn, was replaced respectively by A. B. Ó Ríordáin, M. F. Ryan and E. P. Kelly, all without competitions.

Seosamh Ó Néill, (a Galwayman and novelist of among other works *The Wind from the North*, a story about the Dublin Vikings) wrote to Mahr on 6th October 1931 agreeing his proposals regarding training and authorising him to inform other museum Directors about the proposed training programme as well as agreeing that his other suggestion would "be kept in mind" when the assistants were being informed of their permanent appointment.

Conclusions

Ó Ríordáin's letters to Mahr show the richness of the network of contacts Mahr commanded in Britain and Europe and the high degree to which he was esteemed by the enduring names of European archaeology – Brønsted, Childe, Hawkes and Kendrick among them. The young traveller's enthusiasm for Europe, its museums, their collections and their systems of organisation seem to underline the need Mahr perceived in Ireland for such contacts, for the modernisation of the subject and for the very training of new recruits for which he had argued in the Department of Education. By the same token, in Ó Ríordáin's case, but less obviously with Heaney because he was not as committed, the need for such training and his zeal when exposed to it demonstrates how inadequate and out of touch the degree courses in archaeology offered by R. A. S. Macalister in Dublin and the Canons, Power and Hynes, at Cork and Galway respectively must have been. Mahr was the catalyst that enabled Ó Ríordáin to return to Ireland a changed and inspired man from the exciting and productive world of contemporary European archaeology to a country, apparently up to then out of touch with such developments.

The letters also tell us something of Mahr's shrewdness in picking his man and in Ó Ríordáin's ability, diplomacy and skill at taking advantage of such an undreamed of opportunity, one which none of the other recipients would capitalise upon with the same effectiveness.

Mahr, apparently, encouraged his trainees to stay aloof from the political developments of the day, particularly on the Continent. He warned Ó Ríordáin not to engage in political discussions with Bersu, and in this he was prophetically correct because it seems that after the war Bersu campaigned to prevent his return to Ireland. He also urged caution with one or two others especially in France. However, it was probably also the case that Mahr did not welcome over familiarity preferring relationships with his trainees to remain on a formal basis. Ó Ríordáin appears to have read this properly by hardly ever becoming familiar enough even to wish the Director the Season's Greetings, never writing salutations in languages (including Irish) that Mahr didn't understand and by

always speaking well of the more senior foreign colleagues he met through the Director's introductions. Heaney was more political and in his letters to Mahr showed his anti-Cosgrave /pro deValera views with which he may not have been as ingratiating as he hoped. His Irish salutations might have hurt Mahr by making him feel inadequate about his inability to use the first official language while with his use of Danish, Swedish and German he was fooling nobody, least of all his Director who, clearly, would have preferred if his reporting energies had gone more into archaeology, collections and museums and less into generalisations, excuses, platitudes and familiarities.

In some ways the lack of social historical detail in Ó Ríordáin's letters is a disappointment and may even betray a somewhat obsessed focus. There are no mentions of the technological wonders he must have witnessed nor of contemporary culture including the cinema and entertainment and no eyewitness accounts of the tumultuous political and military events that were then consuming Germany. It seems that in his letters to Mahr Ó Ríordáin stuck rigidly to reporting on the task in hand, his training and the encounters associated with his archaeological development. He possibly wrote of less official matters to others, including his sister with whom in one letter to Mahr he says he was in correspondence. His relationship with Mahr appears to have been concentrated on the museum and archaeology and that would appear to have suited them both.

What the correspondence does provide is a relatively detailed snapshot of the archaeological and museum scene in Britain, the northwest Continent and Scandinavia in the early 1930s through the eyes of an enthusiastic trainee on whom the whole experience was to have the profoundest impact, an impact so great that it still reverberates positively in Ireland seventy years later.

Bibliography

Eogan, G. 1964 The Later Bronze Age in Ireland in the light of recent research, *Proceedings of the Prehistoric Society* **14**, 268–350.

Mahr, A. 1937 New Aspects and Problems in Irish Prehistory, *Proceedings of the Prehistoric Society* **3**, 262–436.

Ó Ríordáin, S.P. 1933a Excavation of cairn in Townland of Curraghbiny, Co. Cork, *Journal of the Cork Historical and Archaeological Society* **38**, 80–84.

Ó Ríordáin, S.P. 1933b Discovery of an ancient burial in a cairn near Ballyconnell, Co. Cavan, *Journal of the Royal Society of Antiquaries of Ireland* **63**, 167–171.

Ó Ríordáin, S.P. 1937 The halberd in Bronze Age Europe: a study in prehistoric origins, evolution, distribution and chronology, *Archaeologia* **86**, 195–321.

Ó Ríordáin, S.P. 1940 Excavations at Cush, Co. Limerick, *Proceedings of the Royal Irish Academy* **45C**, 83–181.